AF520740

The Mughal State and Culture 1556-1598

Selected Letters and Documents from *Munshaat-i-Namakin*

The Mughal State and Culture 1556-1598

Selected Letters and Documents from *Munshaat-i-Namakin*

Edited by

ISHTIYAQ AHMAD ZILLI

CENTRE OF ADVANCED STUDY
Department of History
Aligarh Muslim University

MANOHAR
2007

First English edition 2007

ISBN 81-7304-738-3

Published by
Ajay Kumar Jain for
Manohar Publishers & Distributors
4753/23 Ansari Road, Daryaganj
New Delhi 110 002

Printed at
Lordson Publishers Pvt Ltd
Delhi 110 007

Contents

Preface

Insha collections compiled in India during the medieval period constitute an important source of information for the history of medieval state and society. But scholars working in the area are severely handicapped in using this potential source due to the fact that properly edited texts of the majority of these collections are not available. A number of them were, no doubt, published by Nawal Kishore and other publishers but these are out of print for many decades now and hard to procure. Moreover, *insha* collections published by Nawal Kishore and others were invariably based on only one of many surviving manuscripts and hence don't include all the documents and variants of the texts available in different manuscripts of the book. It is, however, heartening to note that in the recent years historians have started paying greater attention to *insha* literature as a source of historical evidence. This has inevitably stimulated interest in textual studies of *insha* collections. As a result, critical editions of a number of such collections have come out in the recent past. These include *Insha-i Mahru, Riyaz ul Insha* and *Ruq'at-i Hakim Abul Fath Gilani* edited by Shaikh Abd ur Rashid, Shaikh Chand and Muhammad Bashir Husain respectively. It was against this background of growing interest in *insha* literature as a source of historical evidence that this critical edition of the *Munshaat-i Namakin* was taken up.

Insha was a popular branch of literature during the medieval period. Besides those who were interested in it as a matter of taste, it was needed by those who aspired to enter government service. *Insha* collections which contained specimen documents and drafts for various occasions served as guides for acquiring necessary skill in the art of drafting, which was an important requirement for government servants. This is the reason why so many *insha* collections have come down from the medieval period. *Munshaat-i Namakin* is one such *insha* collection that was compiled during the last years of Akbar's reign. Its compiler, Abul Qasim Namakin was a nobleman of some eminence and served under Akbar and Jahangir.

Munshaat-i Namakin is, however, different in many ways from traditional *insha* collections. Its contents include entries and items which would not qualify as a part of an *insha* collection in the light of available definition of this branch of literature. For example, the entire discussion in the concluding part (*khatimah*) relates to subjects which did not conventionally come under the purview of *insha*. It deals with matters of religious interest in the day-to-day life of the faithful. It also contains few prescriptions for some of the more common diseases. There is also a section on humour. Obviously, these items would not come under the definition of *insha* by any stretch of imagination. Possible reasons for the compiler's decision to include this section in his collection have been discussed elsewhere.

Munshaat-i Namakin is a very large collection. In fact, it is one of the largest *insha* collections coming down from the Mughal period. The documents put together in the Munshaat belong to a very wide range. Some of these are altogether missing from other *insha* collections surviving from the Mughal period. This imparts unique significance to the collection as a source of history as well as a book of great literary interest as it provides the only available specimens of a number of categories of documents.

Structurally the collection is divided into a brief introduction, eight chapters (*bab*) and a rather long concluding section (*khatimah*). A list of the chapters is given below:

Chapter I	:	The Origin of the Art of Writing
Chapter II	:	The Drafting of Imperial *Farmans*
Chapter III	:	The Drafting of Letters
Chapter IV	:	The Drafting of Petitions
Chapter V	:	The Drafting of Letters Exchanged Among Spiritual Preceptors and their Disciples, Parents, Teachers, Brothers, Sisters and Children
Chapter VI	:	The Drafting of Letters of Congratulation and Condolence
Chapter VII	:	The Drafting of Legal Documents

The concluding section (*khatimah*) constitutes almost a separate chapter. Each of the eight chapters (*bab*) and the *khatimah* are further divided into several sections (*fasl*), each comprising a number of documents belonging to a particular category. For example, Chapter II which relates to the drafting of imperial *manshurs*, is divided into 15 sections as detailed below:

Section I	:	Imperial *Manshurs* Issued to the Great Nobles
Section II	:	The Conciliatory *Manshurs* Addressed to the Nobles
Section III	:	The *Manshurs* Issued after the Receipt of Petitions
Section IV	:	The *Fathnamas* (Letters of Victory)
Section V	:	The *Manshurs* Assigning Administrative Charges to the Nobles
Section VI	:	The *Manshurs* Conferring the Posts of *Wikalat* and *Wizarat*
Section VII	:	The *Farmans* Conferring Post of *Sadarat*
Section VIII	:	The *Farmans* Conferring the Post of *Ishraf-i diwan*
Section IX	:	The *Manshurs* Conferring the Posts of *Istifa* and *Bakhshi-i 'asakir*
Section X	:	The *Manshurs* Conferring the Posts of *Risalt* and *Insha*
Section XI	:	The *Farmans* Conferring the Post of *Faujdari* and *Mir-i 'adl*
Section XII	:	The *Manshurs* Conferring the Post of *qazi*
Section XIII	:	The *Manshurs* Conferring the Posts of *Naqib, Shaik ul Islam* and *Mudarris*
Section XIV	:	The *Manshurs* Conferring the Posts of *Shaikhi, Sajjadanashini* and *Tauliyat* (trusteeship)
Section XV	:	The *Manshurs* of Appointment to the Posts of *Mir-i bahr, Mir-i barr* and others.

Other chapters are also similarly divided into a number of sections (*fasls*). Many of these sections contain quite a large number of documents. Sometimes scores of specimen and model documents have been given under one head. This would give some idea about the richness, variety and volume of the documents included in this collection. It may, however, be noted that all the documents included in the *Munshaat* do not belong to Akbar's reign or even to Hindustan. A considerable number of these documents come from Timurid chancelleries of Central Asia and Khorasan. The compiler belonged to a distinguished family of Khorasan under the Timurids. This may explain the strong presence of documents belonging to Central Asia and Khorasan in the collection. These documents may provide useful material for a comparative study of some of the Timurid institutions with those evolving under the Mughals. Documents belonging to this category have not been included in this selection as they don't come within its scope.

The present volume consists of selected documents and letters from the *Munshaat-i Namakin*. The very large number of documents put together in this collection made it necessary to select only those documents that had a direct bearing on the history of Akbar's reign during which period it was compiled. A volume containing all the different kinds of material included in the collection would have made it unwieldy and unduly bulky. Moreover dozens of specimens of the same document could not be expected to enhance its utility as a source of historical evidence. For example, majority of the entries in the concluding chapter would be totally out of place in such a volume. Moreover, a large number of the letters collected under various heads are in many cases simply duplications with minor variations in style, diction and presentation. For a book of *insha* that was intended to serve as a guide for those who were interested in the art of drafting, this would have been a great boon as it provided a variety of models and hence greater choice of documents for various occasions. But for a volume primarily meant to serve as a source of information for the history of the period, these kinds of documents would not be of much help. The main criterion, therefore, for selecting a document for the volume has been its utility as a source of history. All those documents, letters and other material that could be expected to be of any help in the task of reconstructing the history of medieval India have been included in this volume. Moreover, all those documents, which appeared in the light of internal evidence to be copies of genuine documents, have been included and these have not been subjected to any kind of selection. It was because of this reason that almost all the documents relating to appointments to various posts have been included.

As far as the letters are concerned the basic criterion again was their utility as a source of history. All the letters that shed some light on any aspect of state or society have been included. As internal scrutiny would reveal, an overwhelming majority of these letters are copies of genuine letters exchanged among the people belonging to the educated upper strata of society. The specimen letters, which were apparently drafted by the compiler as models and included in the collection, are also not entirely without historical utility. They reflect and enshrine general norms and rules that governed the composition of such documents during those days and hence provide an insight into the intellectual and social dynamics of the period and help us understand the level of the discourse among higher echelons of the society. It was due to this reason that some such letters have also been included.

A selection of legal documents has also been included in the present volume. Besides shedding light on legal processes and procedures during the period under discussion, it enables us to have an idea about the kind of legal problems that the people faced and for which they were obliged to go to the courts for redressal. As the problems were multifaceted, the legal documents are also diverse in nature and cover many different aspects of human life as would appear from their perusal. Similarly, a judicious selection of the entries of the concluding section has also been given. As noticed above, this section deals with religious matters. The reasons that lay behind the compiler's decision to append this section to his collection are important enough to persuade us to include a selection of this part as well. Besides showing the religious leanings of the compiler and his jurisprudential affiliation, it provides significant insights into the religious practices, beliefs and even superstitions prevalent in the society. It also sheds light on the kind of stresses, strains and tensions that people underwent and which they sought to ward off with the help of invocations and even charms.

All the documents included in this selection relate to Akbar's reign. Though the compiler lived and served Jahangir also for a few years, he does not seem to have updated the book after he revised it in 1599. It therefore does not contain any document of that period. The only document that does not belong to Akbar's reign and that has been included in this selection is the copy of a *farman* of Ulugh Beg addressed to the last Saiyid ruler, Ala ud din Alam Shah. This document belonging to the Delhi Sultanate has been included as an appendix due to its great importance for understanding the nature of Saiyid rule in India.

Only three manuscripts of the *Munshaat* have been located so far. The India Office Library manuscript is the earliest and most complete. It was transcribed four years after the compilation of the book during the life of the compiler and was collated from his personal copy. It has been therefore used as the basic text. The two other manuscripts have been used for the purposes of comparison. Editor's additions have been put in brackets.

It was on the suggestion of my late teacher, Professor S. Nurul Hasan, that I undertook to edit *Munshaat-i Namakin* for my Ph.D. Degree in History. He very kindly allowed me to use his personal transcript of the Aligarh MS of the book. I will remain beholden to him for this kindness and the encouragement that I always received from him. It is with a deep sense of respect and gratitude that I remember him today.

The publication of this collection was taken up by the University Press in early 1990s on the initiative of Professor Zamir ud din Siddiqui, the then chairman of the Department of History. The spadework for it was done by my late friend, Professor Jamal Muhammad Siddiqi. Unfortunately both of them left us before the collection could see the light of the day. I can imagine how happy they would have been had they been alive today. It is with a deep sense of gratitude that I recall many pleasant memories associated with them. May their souls rest in peace.

By the time the University Press finished its printing, the portions printed earlier had turned pale and become unfit for publication. For some time its fate hung in balance till the Centre agreed to put it in its publication programme. I am grateful to Professor Mansura Haidar who took the initiative in this regard. It was through her efforts that the Centre accepted it for publication. But she retired before the book could be sent to the press and it had to wait till Professor Shahabuddin Iraqi took over as chairman and coordinator. I am grateful to him for taking personal interest in the matter and ensuring its publication.

I would like to take this opportunity to thank Professor Iqtidar Alam Khan for the many acts of kindness during the period I worked for my Ph.D. under his supervision. I am also grateful to Professor Irfan Habib for helping me in the analysis of some of the documents included in this collection. Professor Iqtidar Husain Siddiqui took the trouble of going through the Introduction and made useful suggestions for its improvement. I would like to place on record my sincere thanks to him. To Professors Muzaffar Alam, Afzal Husain, Iqbal Husain and Kirti Kumar Trivedi I would remain ever grateful for their unstinted help and support during the long drawn process of the publication of the book. I am also grateful to Qaiser Zaman for the support that I always received from him and to Professor B.L. Bhadani for his deep interest in the publication of the book. Thanks are due to Muhammad Idris and Bahauddin for computer processing the Persian text and the English introduction respectively. Thanks are also due to the librarians and staff of Salarjung Museum, Maulana Azad Library and the Library of the Centre for their help. My maternal uncle Janab Maqbool Ahmad Khan Sahib has always been a source of inspiration for me. I owe so much to his love and affection that I would never be able to thank him adequately for all that he has done for me. I would like to place on record my deep appreciation of the love of my brothers, Ashfaq, Imtiyaz and Javed that has been a source of strength for me throughout my life. My debt to Farhat and Mohsin and now also Uzma cannot be expressed in words.

INTRODUCTION

Section I: Biographical Sketch of Abu'l Qasim Namakin

Saiyid Abu'l Qasim Namakin, the compiler of *Munshaat-i-Namakin*, was the son of Mulla Mir Subzwari of Bijak, presumably a village near Sabzwar.[1] Mulla Mir, himself a Husaini Saiyid, is reported to have been *mutawalli* (trustee) of the shrine of Imam Ali Riza at Mashhad.[2] As the head of the greatest Shia shrine in Persia and keeper of a very considerable estate, he must have enjoyed a high position in Khorasan. It is, however, not known when and under what circumstances Mulla Mir was appointed as *mutawalli* at the shrine of Mashhad. No details are available about his life. The contemporary and near contemporary sources have totally failed to notice him. The only reference to him is found in *Tuhfat-ul Kiram*, a history of Sind compiled in the seventeenth century. As the family had settled in Sind, it is possible that its author received this information from family sources. The Uzbek invasion of the region in 1507 under Shaibani Khan forced Mulla Mir to leave Mashhad and migrate to Qandahar.[3] Nothing is, however, known about his life in Qandahar.

---

[1] Cf. Mir Ali Sher Qani' Tnattavi, *Tuhfat-ul Kiram*, vol. III, Matba Nasiri, Delhi, H. 1304, p. 127. Bijak could not be identified as no other reference to the place is found. Sabzwar was also known as Asfuzar. See G. Le Strange, *The Lands of the Eastern Caliphate*, Cambridge: Cambridge University Press, 1930, p. 412.

[2] *Tuhfat-ul Kiram*, vol. III, p. 127. For the vast resources of the shrine at Mashhad and the position of the *mutawalli* see Imad al din Isfahani, *Zindagani-i Hazrat Imam Ali bin Musa Riza*, Tehran, 1925, pp. 422-5; M. Streek, *Encyclopaedia of Islam*, Leiden and London: Luzac & E.J. Brill, 1936, vol. III, p. 471.

[3] *Tuhfat-ul Kiram*, vol. III, p. 127. For Uzbek invasion of Khorasan under Shaibani Khan see Zaheer-ud Din Babur, *Babur Nama*, trans. A.S. Beveridge, vol. I, London, 1922, pp. 326, 327, 328 n. 2; Khawandmir, *Habib-us Siyar*, vol. III, Part III, Bombay, 1857, pp. 356-9.

Abu'l Qasim's date of birth is not recorded but it is known that he died in 1018/1609-10.[4] His eldest son, Abu'l Baqa Amir Khan, who died in 1057/1647-8, is said to have lived for more than one hundred years.[5] It would be reasonable to assume that at the time of latter's birth Abu'l Qasim would have been around twenty years old. It would be, therefore, safe to infer that Abu'l Qasim was born some time in the late 1920s or early 1930s of the sixteenth century at Qandahar, where his father had settled after his migration from Khorasan. Qandahar was held at that time by Mirza Kamran.

Nothing is known about Abu'l Qasim's early life at Qandahar. It is, however, evident from his administrative and literary achievements that he had acquired particular proficiency in Persian *insha*. This enabled him to distinguish himself not only as an administrator but also as an excellent prose-writer. From the epilogue of the *Munshaat*, which contains a long discourse on a variety of religious issues, it is evident that Abu'l Qasim had also received good instruction in religious subjects.[6]

Abu'l Qasim's family seems to have moved to Kabul in the wake of Qandahar's capture by the Persians in 1558.[7] At Kabul Abu'l Qasim joined the service of Mirza Muhammad Hakim but no details are available. Most probably he entered Mirza Hakim's service some time after Munim Khan's departure from Kabul in 1560—as Bayazid Bayat's list of the nobles present at Kabul during this period does not contain his name—and before 1567 when he appears to have joined Akbar's service.[8] Throughout this period Kabul was in a disturbed and unsettled

---

[4] Yusuf Mirak, *Mazhar-i Shah Jahani*, ed. Saiyid Husam-ud Din Rashidi, Sindhi Adabi Board, Karachi, 1962, Introduction, p. 13. For the epitaph inscribed on the grave of Abu'l Qasim see p. 294. It contains a number of chronograms yielding the same date. Also see Cousins, *The Antiquities of Sind*, Calcutta, 1929, p. 156.

[5] Fareed Bhakkari, *Zakhirat-ul Khwanin*, ed. Saiyid Moin-ul Haq, vol. I, Pakistan Historical Society, Karachi, 1961, p. 200.

[6] *Selected Letters and Documents from Munshaat-i Namakin*, text, pp. 381-97.

[7] Abu'l Fazl, *Akbar Nama*, eds. Agha Ahmad Ali and Abdur Rahim, Bibliotheca Indica, vol. II, p. 78.

[8] *Zakhirat-ul-Khawanin*, vol. I, p. 198; Shah Nawaz Khan, *Maasir-ul-Umara*, ed. Mirza Ashraf Ali, Asiatic Society, Calcutta, 1894, vol. III, p. 74. Also see Abu'l Fazl, *Ain-i Akbari*, trans. Blochmann, Bibliotheca Indica, vol. I, p. 525. According to *Tuhfat-ul Kiram* (vol. III, p. 12) Abu'l Qasim presented himself before Akbar

condition. Mirza Muhammad Hakim was a minor and those around him conspired against each other to gain upper hand in the administration. Besides their intrigues, the ruler of Badakhshan also tried to take advantage of the disturbed conditions of Kabul.

In such a situation there was hardly any chance for a new entrant in service like Abu'l Qasim to improve his position unless he had considerable support of one of the Turani factions fighting for supermacy. One could visualize the difficulties that Abu'l Qasim might have experienced during his stay at Kabul. It is also possible that the hostility and resentment that was growing among the Turani nobles in Hindustan against the Khorasanis might have influenced the mood of officers at Kabul as well. On the other hand, rapid promotion of comparatively junior and low-ranking Khorasani officers between 1560-6 must have offered a strong temptation to a person of Abu'l Qasim's background to go over to Hindustan.[9]

Earliest reference to Abu'l Qasim occurs in Abu'l Fazl's account of Akbar's first expedition to Gujarat. It may therefore be assumed that he came to India and joined imperial service some time before July 1572.[10] *Tuhfat-ul Kiram* mentions that Abu'l Qasim presented himself before Akbar when he was encamping at Lahore.[11] As it is known that between 1560 and 1572 Akbar was at Lahore only in January 1567,[12]

---

while he was camping at Lahore. From *Akbar Nama* (vol. III, p. 6) it is known that Abu'l Qasim was already in Akbar's service in 1573. During the period 1560-73 Akbar visited Lahore only once in 1567 (*Akbar Nama*, vol. II, p. 277). Therefore 1567 may be accepted as the year of Abu'l Qasim's coming to Hindustan and joining Akbar's service. For Bayazid Bayat's list of nobles present at Kabul at the time of Munim Khan's departure for India see *Tazkirah-i Humayun wa Akbar*, ed. Mohammad Hidayat Hosain, Bibliotheca Indica, 1941, pp. 224-5.

[9] The period 1560-7 witnessed a steady increase in the number of Persian nobles in the higher cadres of nobility. On the other hand, this was the period of systematic decline of the Turani nobility. This situation naturally led to mutual suspicion, bitterness and resentment among these two groups. For example see *Tazkirah-i Humayun wa Akbar*, pp. 287, 375. Also see Iqtidar Alam Khan, 'The Nobility under Akbar and Development of His Religious Policy 1560-80', *Journal of Royal Asiatic Society*, 1968, pp. 30-1.

[10] *Akbar Nama*, vol. III, p. 6. Akbar set out to invade Gujarat on 4 July 1572 (*Akbar Nama* vol. II, p. 370).

[11] *Tuhfat-ul Kiram*, vol. III, p. 127.

[12] *Akbar Nama*, vol. II, p. 277.

this date may be accepted as the timing of Abu'l Qasim's joining imperial service.

Abu'l Qasim's first posting was in Bhira and Khoshab in the Salt Range and he was also given *jagir* in the same region. While serving in the region, he presented to Akbar cups made of salt rock and in consequence earned the moniker Namakin.[13] It is interesting to note that Abu'l Fazl uses it with his name in the very first reference to him in the account of Gujarat expedition of 1572.[14] Apparently, Abu'l Qasim had already received this nickname by that time.

It seems that some time before July 1572 he was recalled to the court, most probably as a part of mobilization for the Gujarat expedition. Subsequently, he accompanied Akbar to Gujarat where he was entrusted with important assignments during the operations against Muzaffar Shah.[15]

We next hear about him in the account of Bengal expedition where he is reported to have been very active.[16] At the battle of Tukarai he was posted in the left wing along with Ashraf Khan, Raja Todar Mal and others.[17] The fact that his name is mentioned in the list containing the names of first rank officers[18] would obviously imply significant improvement in his position. It, however, seems that Abu'l Qasim was party to the unruly and selfish behaviour of some Mughal officers in Bengal following Munim Khan's death in October 1575. It is reported that a golden elephant chain was found in his possession.[19] It was apparently included among the items which were taken away from the official stores. It is, however, not very clear how it came in his possession. Fareed Bhakkari who has reported the recovery of the item from Abu'l Qasim's possession, does not clearly say that it was a case of

[13] *Zakhirat-ul Khawanin*, vol. I, p. 198; Shah Nawaz Khan, *Maasir-ul Umara*, vol. III, p. 74; Abu'l Fazl, *Ain-i Akbari*, English trans. by H. Blochmann, Bibliotheca Indica Series, vol. I, p. 525.

[14] *Akbar Nama*, vol. III, p. 6.

[15] Ibid.

[16] For his activities in Bengal before the battle of Tukarai see *Akbar Nama*, vol. III, pp. 119-21.

[17] Ibid., pp. 122-7.

[18] Ibid., p. 123.

[19] *Zakhirat-ul Khawanin*, vol. I, p. 198; *Maasir-ul Umara*, vol. III, p. 75.

proven theft. Still it was a serious matter and for the next five years we do not hear about him. This would clearly indicate a temporary eclipse in his position owing to his disgrace for this misconduct. By 1581 he seems to have been rehabilitated to his earlier position as we find him accompanying Akbar to the Punjab where the Emperor had gone to put down Mirza Hakim's rebellion.[20] Subsequently he remained stationed in one capacity or other in the Punjab for quite some time. From this time onward whenever an expedition was sent against refractory tribes of the north-west, Abu'l Qasim was invariably serving in it.[21] This would strongly suggest that in all probability his *jagir* and charge were located in the same region. It would further indicate that his ability as a commander and administrator was by now widely recognized. Some time in the 32nd regnal year (March 1587–March 1588) he was appointed as *Karori* and *Faujdar* of Sawat, Bajur and Tirah region inhabited by the Yusufzai Afghans.[22] In the expeditions which were frequently undertaken against the refractory Afghan tribes Abu'l Qasim rendered notable service.[23]

It appears from the account of *Akbar Nama* that some time during or before 39th regnal year (March 1594–March 1595) Abu'l Qasim was given Bhakkar as *jagir* and was stationed there.[24] According to Yusuf Mirak it was the *jagir* vacated by Abdur Rahim Khan-i Khanan at Bhakkar that was assigned to Abu'l Qasim at this occasion.[25] Apparently, as the commander and *jagirdar* of Bhakkar, Abu'l Qasim's military charge extended to the whole of the territory previously administered by Abdur Rahim Khan-i Khanan whom he had replaced as the *jagirdar* of Bhakkar.[26] In other words the command that was now given to Abu'l

---

[20] *Akbar Nama*, vol. III, pp. 336, 353.

[21] For example, he accompanied Ismail Quli Khan in the campaigns of 1586 and 1587 against the Baluchis. For details of this and some other campaigns in the region see *Akbar Nama*, vol. III, pp. 475, 492, 495, 511, 525-6.

[22] *Maasir-ul Umara*, vol. III, p. 75.

[23] *Akbar Nama*, vol. III, pp. 532, 559.

[24] Ibid., p. 666. Farid Bhakkari, however, specifically gives 1004 AH (16 September 1595–24 August 1596) as the year of Abu'l Qasim's posting to that place. See *Zakhirat ul Khawarin*, vol. I, p. 198.

[25] *Mazhar-i Shah Jahani*; p. 28.

[26] Abu'l Qasim has reproduced the *farman* appointing him as the *jagirdar* of Bhakkar. See Document No.34, pp. 91-2. From this *farman* it is clear that only

Qasim was almost as significant as that of a *subedar*. Moreover, if it is also kept in view that Abu'l Qasim was appointed to Bhakkar on the eve of the occupation of Qandahar by the Mughals,[27] the significance of the appointment would be further emphasized. It would seem that one of the major tasks entrusted to him was to pacify the region through which the routes connecting Qandahar with Multan and Sind passed. Obviously, reduction of Sivi was a part of this scheme.[28] Abu'l Qasim accomplished this task with credit.[29] During 1595-6, he was promoted to the rank (*mansab*) of 700, apparently in recognition of his success at Sivi.[30] Later, he was sent on official duty to Kashmir, though the nature of duty is not clear. He was, however, allowed to retain his *jagir* at Bhakkar for which he seems to have developed special liking. Abu'l Qasim returned from Kashmir in 1598.[31] His *jagir* was soon transferred to Bihar Sharif, which was placed under his military charge.[32] It would appear that he was not satisfied with this assignment and manipulated to get it transferred to Sindh once again. Consequently, his *jagir* was transferred to Bhakkar within a few months of his coming to Bihar.[33] Some time around AD 1600 he was transferred to Sehwan.[34]

Abu'l Qasim was in Sehwan when Mirza Jani Beg, the Turkhan prince who had entered Akbar's service after the Mughal annexation of Sind and who was holding Thatta in *jagir*, died in February 1601. His son, Mirza Ghazi Beg, tried to assume an independent attitude which

---

some *mahals* of *Sarkar* Bhakkar were given in his *jagir* but for military purposes the whole of *Sarkar* Bhakkar was placed under his charge.

[27] *Akbar Nama*, vol. III, p. 669. Qandahar was occupied by the Mughals in April 1595.

[28] *Mazhar-i Shah Jahani*, p. 28.

[29] *Akbar Nama*, vol. III, p. 666; *Mazhar-i Shah Jahani*, pp. 28-9. According to Yusuf Mirak over-all command of the expedition against Sivi was in the hands of Abu'l Qasim. After its annexation, Sivi was made a part of fiscal administration of Bhakkar.

[30] *Maasir ul Umara*, vol. III, p. 75; *Ain-i Akbari*, vol. I, p. 525.

[31] *Akbar Nama*, vol. III, p. 746.

[32] Ibid., pp. 746, 748.

[33] *Maasir ul Umara*, vol. III, p. 75; *Mazhar-i Shah Jahani*, p. 108.

[34] *Mazhar-i Shah Jahani*, p. 108. For the peculiar problems of the region and the way Abu'l Qasim tackled them see *Mazhar-i Shah Jahani*, pp. 63, 65-8, 72, 73, 75-77, 85-111.

was noted with concern at the court.[35] Saeed Khan Chaghtai was assigned the *jagir* of Bhakkar and was directed to bring Mirza Ghazi Beg to the court. Abu'l Qasim was instructed to collaborate with Saeed Khan.[36] They successfully accomplished their mission and escorted Mirza Ghazi Beg to Agra reaching there a few days before Akbar's death.

Apparently, at the time of Abu'l Qasim's arrival Akbar was already bed-ridden. Abu'l Qasim seems to have found favour with the dominant group of the nobles which was manoeuvring to exclude Salim from succession. He was appointed as the *subedar* of Qandahar and certain *mahals* in Bhakkar, Sivi and Sehwan were given to him in *jagir*.[37] It would appear that his success in restoring law and order in Sehwan against considerable odds was appreciated at the court and he was rewarded for it by such a high appointment. But before he could proceed to take charge of his new office, Akbar died and after the accession of Jahangir this appointment was cancelled. Abu'l Qasim was, however, compensated by raising his *mansab* to 1500 and assignment of a *jagir* in *pargana* Gujarat in the Punjab.[38]

At Gujarat Abu'l Qasim distinguished himself by capturing Khusrau while he was trying to cross the Chenab after his escape from Agra in April 1606.[39] As a reward, Abu'l Qasim's *mansab* was raised to 3,000 and he was reappointed to Bhakkar.[40] As mentioned earlier, he seems to have developed a special liking for the region. One gets the impression that on this occasion he went to Bhakkar with his family. Farid Bhakkari who had been a disciple of Abu'l Qasim supports this assumption.[41] Subsequently, the family settled at Bhakkar and was absorbed by the local Muslim gentry, which mostly consisted of Saiyids,[42] a class to

---

35 *Akbar Nama*, vol. III, p. 816; *Mazhar-i Shah Jahani*, p. 109.

36 *Akbar Nama*, vol. III, pp. 816-39.

37 *Mazhar-i Shah Jahani*, pp. 112-13.

38 Syed Ahmad Khan (ed.), *Tuzuk-i Jahangiri*, Aligarh, 1864, p. 13; *Maasir-ul Umara*, vol. III, p. 76.

39 *Tuzuk-i Jahangiri*, pp. 31-2; *Zakhirat-ul Khawanin*, vol. I, p. 134; *Maasir ul Umara*, vol. III, p. 77.

40 *Zakhirat-ul Khawanin*, vol. I, p. 199; *Maasir-ul Umara*, vol. III, p. 76.

41 Ibid.

42 There was huge concentration of Saiyid families in and around Bhakkar. *Antiquities of Sind* (p. 155) mentions that as many as 1700 Saiyid families were living in Bhakkar at the time of Mughal occupation. Certain references in *Ma-*

which Abu'l Qasim also belonged. It is possible that part of the *jagir* given to him at Bhakkar on this occasion was in the form of *altamgha* grant which enabled him to settle there.

Soon after the restoration of *jagir* at Bhakkar, Abu'l Qasim was sent to Jalalabad but in the same year he was appointed *thanadar* of Bajaur.[43] Shortly afterwards, around March 1608, he was again posted to Sehwan for the second time.[44] While he was at Sehwan, Mirza Ghazi Beg was appointed the *subedar* of Qandahar. Abu'l Qasim was directed to assist him in the discharge of this responsibility.[45] Mirza Ghazi Beg seems to have had great faith in Abu'l Qasim's administrative ability and wisdom. Abu'l Qasim appointed his eldest son, Abu'l Baqa, as his deputy in Sehwan and proceeded to Qandahar in the company of Mirza Ghazi Beg.[46]

Abu'l Qasim stayed at Qandahar for about one year. No specific details are available about his role during his stay at Qandahar. It can, however, be guessed that his presence at Qandahar might have been necessitated by the Persian threat to the region during that time. Persia had already made an abortive attempt upon Qandahar in 1606.[47] Mirza Ghazi Beg's appointment as the Governor of Qandahar and that of Abu'l Qasim as his deputy, viewed from this angle, would appear to be very significant. Apparently, Jahangir hoped to consolidate the Mughal hold over Qandahar by placing it under the charge of an Arghun prince whose family had for long ruled over the region as autonomous kings. With a view to further ensure Mirza's success, services of an old and experienced officer like Abu'l Qasim, who, because of his family background, must have been well acquainted with the region, were placed at his disposal.

---

zhar-i Shah Jahani would suggest that besides general concentration of Saiyids in Bhakkar, there was also a considerably large number of Abu'l Qasim's own connections, for whom Yusuf Mirak uses the terms '*Qabila*' (tribe). See *Mazhar-i Shah Jahani*, pp. 3, 122, introduction, p. 62. Also see Abdul Baqi Nahawandi, *Maasir-i Rahimi*, ed. Mohammad Hedayat Hossain, Asiatic Society of Bengal, Calcutta, 1924, vol. II, p. 340.

[43] *Tuzuk-i Jahangiri*, p. 114.

[44] *Mazhar-i Shah Jahani*, p. 114.

[45] Ibid., pp. 115-17.

[46] Ibid.

[47] *Tuzuk-i Jahangiri*, pp. 33-4.

After a stay of one year at Qandahar, Abu'l Qasim set out for Sehwan. On the way he fell ill and died. His body was brought to Bhakkar—the town that had become the permanent abode of the family—and buried in *Suffa-i Safa*, a mausoleum which he had built for himself on the hill of Rohri overlooking the fort of Bhakkar and which is reported to be a structure of exceptional beauty.[48]

The two terms of Abu'l Qasim's command of Sehwan, taken together, extended about six years (1009-13, 1016-18).[49] But during the second term he could not stay in his charge for more than a year as he had to proceed to Qandahar with Mirza Ghazi Beg. By and large his administration of Sehwan was a success. He succeeded in giving the region peace and stability by containing tribal turbulence. In view of the prevelant conditions it was indeed a great achievement.

Abu'l Qasim's relations with the religious elite of Sind were very cordial. He showed much deference and consideration for them. Yusuf Mirak reports that the credit for introducing in Sehwan the practice of giving land to the deserving people as *madad-i mash* goes to Abu'l Qasim.[50] He made special efforts to secure grants from the central *sadarat* for as large a number of people in Sehwan as possible. According to Yusuf Mirak he took deserving people to Agra at his own expense and pleaded with the central authorities for the grant of *madad-i mash* land to them.[51] This concern for the welfare of the religious classes must have considerably added to his popularity in the region.

Abu'l Qasim had numerous children. According to Jahangir 'There are few men such as he for abundance of children; he has thirty sons, and if his daughters don't number so many, they must be half of that number.'[52] But history has preserved account of only two of his sons; Abu'l Baqa Amir Khan and Yusuf Mirak. Abu'l Baqa Amir Khan served under Jahangir and Shah Jahan and rose to the *mansab* of 3,000/2,000

---

[48] *Mazhar-i Shah Jahani*, pp. 120, 123, 293-4; *Zakhirat-ul Khawanin*, vol. I, 199; *Maasir-ul Umara*, vol. III, p. 77. Also see *Antiquities of Sind*, p. 156.

[49] *Mazhar-i Shah Jahani*, pp. 114 ni, 117 ni; *Akbar Nama*, vol. III, p. 839; *Tuzuk-i Jahangiri*, p. 72.

[50] *Mazhar-i Shah Jahan*, pp. 216-17.

[51] Ibid., p. 121.

[52] *Tuzuk-i Jahangiri*, p. 13.

and twice served as the *subedar* of Thatta.[53] Following his appointment to Thatta a branch of the family settled there and came to be known as Sadat-i Amir Khani. The other branch that remained at Bhakkar was called Sadat-i Qasim Khani.[54]

Several of Amir Khan's sons rose to prominence. His eldest son Abdur Razzaq received a *mansab* of 900 under Shah Jahan. His other son, Zia-ud Din Yusuf, held the *mansab* of 1,000/500 at the close of Shah Jahan's reign.[55] A third one, Mir Abu'l Makarim Shuhud, was a man of mystic bent of mind. He was also a poet of some eminence and the collection of his poems entitled *Pari Khana-i Sulaimaní* is extant. He died before the completion of his second poetical collection *Qissa-i Badi'-ul Jamal wa Saif ul Muluk*.[56] Most famous among the sons of Amir Khan was Abu'l Karim Amir Khan who was closely associated with Aurangzeb and was allowed to inherit the title of his father. At various points of time he received the titles of Multafat Khan, Khanzad Khan and Mir Khanzad Khan. Under Bahadur Shah he held the *mansab* of 3,500 and was appointed as *Sadr-us Sudur*.[57]

A number of grandsons of Abu'l Baqa Amir Khan achieved distinction in various fields. One of them was Nawab Amin-ud Din Khan, son of Abu'l Makarim Shuhad who was appointed to the *subedari* of Thatta in 1702-3 but his main interest was literature. He has left behind two books: *Rashhat-ul Funun* and *Ma'lumat-ul Afaq*.[58] Among other descendants of Abu'l Baqa Amir Khan who achieved distinction in the field of literature were Mir Razi-ud Din Fida, Moin-ud Din Hasan, Mir Hafiz-ud din and Mir Haider-ud-Din Abu Turab Kamil.[59]

The other son of Abu'l Qasim who made a notable literary contribution was Yusuf Mirak, the author of *Mazhar-i Shah Jahani*, an administrative history of Sind. It is surprising that none of the contemporary records has mentioned his name. He is known to us only because of his

[53] Abdul Hamid Lahori, *Badshah Nama*, ed. Kabirud Din and Abdur Rahim, Biliotheca Indica, vol. I, p. 287.

[54] *Tuhfatul Kiram*, vol. III. pp. 208-9.

[55] *Maasir ul Umara*, vol. I, p. 106.

[56] *Tuhfat ul Kiram*, vol. III, p. 208.

[57] *Maasir-ul Umara*, vol. I, pp. 303-10.

[58] *Tuhfat ul Kiram*, vol. III, pp. 98-9, 208.

[59] Ibid., vol. III, p. 209.

book. But *Mazhar-i Shah Jahani* contains little information about his life and activities. It would appear that during Abu'l Qasim's lifetime he was holding some *mansab* but after the former's death he renounced the service and lived on a *madad-i mash* grant located in Sehwan. He passed the rest of his life in retirement keeping himself busy in the acquisition of knowledge.[60] It would, however, seem that even after his retirement he continued to take interest in the political and administrative affairs of the region. It was concern for his adopted home that prompted him to write *Mazhar-i Shah Jahani,* which was originally planned to be presented to Shah Jahan to bring to his notice the malpractices of the officers posted there and its ruinous effects on the region. The book is in two parts. The first part contains general comments on the art of governance after the model of Nizam-ul Mulk's *Siyasat Nama,* while the second part deals exclusively with the administration of the region. It is doubtful that it ever reached the hands of Shah Jahan.

It is thus clear that Abul Qasim's family continued to play an active role in the political, social and cultural life of Sind even after his death.

---

[60] *Mazhar-i Shah Jahani* , p. 122.

Section II: *Munshaat-i-Namakin* as a Source of History

The Arabic word *insha* means 'creation' or 'construction'.[1] In the classical Arabic literature it has been used in this meaning.[2] With the passage of time it came to denote the prose composition of letters, documents and state papers. Still later, it was used as synonym of *munshaat*, the documents composed in accordance with certain norms that would distinguish the diction and style of such pieces from ordinary prose. Gradually, the term *insha* came to represent a distinct form of literature in Arabic and later in Persian language as well.[3] In the classical Arabic and Persian writings also *insha* has been defined as a branch of learning that enables one to discern the merits and defects of the prose composition of letters and documents as distinct from regular and continuous treatises and books.[4]

The term *Ilm-i-insha* is sometimes loosely used for refined prose writings in general,[5] but in strictly technical sense it is applied only to the different forms of letters and documents and does not cover other forms of prose writings. Some literary historians have pointedly made

---

[1] For example, see Ibn Manzur, *Lisan-ul Arab*, Beirut, 1955, vol. I, pp. 170-3.

[2] For the use of the word in classical Arabic see Quran, 6/133, 141, 11/61, 18/42, 23/78, 53/32, 56/72, 67/3, etc. For the use of the word *Munshaat* in the Quran, see 55/24.

[3] Compare H.R. Roemer, *Encyclopaedia of Islam* (New Edition), Leiden and London, 1971, vol. III, pp. 1241-2. It is, however, not clear as to when the word *insha* began to be used for this branch of literature. It was already in use around AD 900 as it appears in Qudama's *Kitabul Kharaj wa Sana'atul Kitabat*.

[4] Cf. Khwaja Jahan Mahmud Gawan, *Manazir-ul Insha*, Aligarh Ms., Sulaiman Collection, 276/9 *Insha-i Farsi*, ff. 9 a-b, 11b, 13a, 15b; Bhupat Rai, *Dastur-i Shigarf*, Aligarh Ms., Aftab Collection, 78/1 *Farsiya* 3 *Nasr*, ff. 2b-3b.

[5] Cf. Momin Mohiuddin, 'The Mughal Chancellery and Persian Epistolography', *Indo-Iranica*, September, 1964, vol. XVII, no. 3, p. 16.

out this distinction. According to them *insha* is mainly concerned with the expression of one's inner feelings as against the exposition of learned sciences. This, according to them, is the main reason why *insha* style has been more prone to change and development than any other branch of literature.[6]

In the classical Persian literature most representative forms of *insha* are identified as *rasail* (literally, letters).[7] According to available definition there are two broad categories of *rasail:* (a) *tauqi'at* and (b) *muhawarat. Tauqi'at* consist of *ahkam* and *misals* (orders and directives) of the rulers and officials. *Muhawarat* consist of *maktubat* and *mufawazat* (letters and correspondence).[8] *Rasail* can be further classified according to the nature of relationship between the writer and the addressee.[9] If the addressee is superior in status than the writer, the communication will be designated as *murafa'a*, but in case the addressee is inferior in status, it will be designated as *ruq'a*. If both the writer and the addressee are of equal status, the document will be known as *murasala*.[10]

Mahmud Gawan suggests still further categorization of the documents covered under *insha*. According to him if the writer of a document is higher in status than the addressee, he would either be a ruler or an ordinary person. If he is a ruler, the letter issuing from him will be designated as *manshur, farman* or *fathnama* depending upon the nature of its contents. In case the sender is higher in status but he is not a ruler, the letter emanating from him will be termed as *misal*, such as the letters of the *wazirs*. If both the sender and addressee are equals, their correspondence would be known as *maktub*. In case the sender is inferior to the addressee, his communication would be termed as *'ariza*. *Ruqa'a*, as noted above, is normally addressed to the

---

[6] See Jurji Zaidan, *Tarikh-u Adabil Lughatil Arabiyyah*, Darul Hilal, vol. III, p. 308. For a detailed discussion on the development of *Insha* see I.A. Zilli, 'Development of *Insha* Literature till the End of Akbar's Reign', in Muzaffar Alam, Nalini Delvoye, Marc Gaborieau (eds), *The Making of Indo-Persian Culture*, Manohar, New Delhi, 2000, pp. 309-49.

[7] See *Manazir-ul Insha*, ff. 9a-b; *Dastur-i Shigarf*, f.3a.

[8] Muhammad Yusuf Yusufi, *Badai-ul Insha*, Aligarh Ms., Aftab Collection, No. 22/1, *Farsi Insha*, f.2a.

[9] Ibid.

[10] *Manazir*, ff. 149b-150b.

inferiors but the rules permit the use of this term for a communication addressed to an equal or even a superior. Similarly, the communications termed as *'ahdnama* (covenant), *ta'ziatnama* (letter of condolence) and *tahniatnama* (letters of congratulation) also belong to the category of documents exchanged between people belonging to different strata of the society.[11] For all these different kinds of documents elaborate rules were set down and these were composed strictly in accordance with those rules.[12]

Medieval India has a very rich tradition of *insha* literature. Those who led the way include some of the finest intellects this country has produced. Amir Khusrau, Khwaja-i Jahan Mahmud Gawan and Abul Fazl set a model that was followed by generations of writers. From the Sultanate period, however, *insha* collections of only Amir Khusrau, Mahmud Gawan and Ain-ul Mulk Mahru have come down to us. But during the Mughal period there was a virtual explosion of such writings and a large number of *insha* collections have survived and are available to scholars in printed and manuscript forms. *Munshaat-i Namakin* is one of the *insha* collections that has come down to us from early Mughal period.

Munshaat-i-Namakin is among the largest known collections of *insha* writings surviving from early Mughal period. The documents put to-

[11] Ibid.

[12] Mahmud Gawan has discussed these rules at great length in his book *Manazir-ul Insha*. For example, a *manshur* is to consist of seven clauses: (i) praise of God, (ii) encomium on the Prophet, (iii) the cause of the issue of the *manshur*, (iv) praise of the person to whom the *manshur* is addressed, (v) the gist of the order of the king sanctioning an appointment or assigning command, etc., to the person to whom the *manshur* is addressed, (vi) exhortation that the assignment be taken care of in a commendable manner, and (vii) instructions to the *diwans* and other officials of the state to abide by the imperial order and a general warning against any deviation from it. (See *Manazir*, ff. 154b-155a). Besides these, there are four further requirements to be fulfilled while drafting a *manshur*: (i) the praise of God and encomium on the Prophet should be couched in such words and phrases that may be in harmony with the subject matter, (ii) if for the sake of brevity the detailed statement of the praise of God and encomium on the Prophet is to be dispensed with, care should be taken that the *manshur* begins with the name of God, (iii) the diction and the general tenor of the *manshur* should be in keeping with the dignity and status of the ruler, and (iv) the titles used for the addressee should be in conformity with his status. See *Manazir*, ff. 187a-b.

gether in this collection provide extremely interesting, sometimes even unique information on a wide range of subjects relating to the political, institutional, cultural, legal and even religious aspects of Akbar's reign. On the point of sheer volume and variety of documents contained in it, *Munshaat-i-Namakin* stands almost unsurpassed by any of the other collections surviving from the entire Mughal period. Contrary to the general practice of the period, *Munshaat-i-Namakin* does not contain compositions of a single person like *Insha-i Abul Fazl, Lalifa-i Faiyyazi* or *Ruq'at-i Hakim Abul Fath Gilani*. Abu'l Qasim Namakin, the compiler, has clearly stated in his preface that the documents included in this collection fall under three different categories: (a) compositions of the compiler himself; (b) letters and other communications received by him; and (c) a selection of the writings of other masters of the style.[13] A considerably large number of official documents included in the collection probably belong to the last two categories. Many of the documents were apparently received by the author in his capacity as the commandant and assignment holder of different places particularly in the Punjab and Sind. Between 1581-1618 he was stationed for considerable durations in places like Tirah, Sawat, Bajaur, Gujarat (Punjab), Jalalabad, Bhakkar, Sehwan and Qandahar in the north-western part of the Mughal Empire. A considerably large number of documents belong to the Timurid chancelleries of Central Asia and Khorasan. This is obviously due to the family background of the compiler. It, however, does not come under the purview of this work.

It would also seem that Abu'l Qasim had access to documents preserved in the central *Diwan-i-Risalat* at Agra. Copies of documents like Shah Tahmasp's letter to Akbar and his mother Hamida Bano Begum, Abdullah Khan Uzbek's letter to Akbar and Akbar's letter to Shah Tahmasp,[14] and a number of other such documents of this nature included in the *Munshaat* could be obtained by him only from there. This greatly enhances the value of the *Munshaat* as a unique source of historical information. It contains scores of appointment orders relating to different branches of administration and providing specific information about the duties and functions of the state officials at vari-

---

[13] Introduction, p. 2.

[14] Documents No. 58-62, pp. 131-47.

ous levels from *Wakil-i-Mutlaq*[15] to *Qaush Begi*[16] and from *Sadr*[17] to the *Mutawalli* of a *dargah.*[18] It also contains copies of diplomatic communications like Akbar's letter to Shah Tahmasp[19] and letters of Shah Tahmasp[20] and Abdullah Khan Uzbek to Akbar.[21] Some of this unique historical evidence is not found even in *Akbar Nama* and *Ain-i-Akbari*. For example, the letter of Shah Tahmasp addressed to Hamida Bano Begum and Akbar's letter to Shah Tahmasp have not been noticed so far by any scholar writing on Mughal-Iranian relations. Riazul Islam had noticed Shah Tahmasp's letter addressed to Akbar and had given a gist of it in his book *A Calendar of Documents on Indo-Persian Relations (1500-1750)* on the authority of a manuscript preserved in the British Museum[22] but its full text has not been provided. Until this collection was tapped for historical evidence, our understanding of the administrative and political set-up was based, at least in some cases, on the selective evidence preserved by Abul Fazl and others.

The value of this collection as a source of historical evidence can be judged from yet another angle. For the later years of Akbar's reign there is no dearth of records of different kinds. But there is a marked paucity of records and documents for the early years of his reign. *Munshaat-i-Namakin* is probably the only collection, which contains a considerably large number of important documents coming from the early period of Akbar's reign. Some of the more significant documents of this nature reproduced by Abu'l Qasim Namakin are mentioned below. Here these documents are simply being listed to illustrate the point. Brief comments on some of these will follow later.

---

[15] Document No 6, pp 29-32

[16] Document No. 17, pp. 55-6.

[17] Documents No. 9-10, pp. 38-42.

[18] Document No. 22, pp. 66-9.

[19] Document No. 59, pp. 134-8.

[20] Document No. 60, pp. 139-44.

[21] Document No. 58, pp. 131-4.

[22] Cf. Riazul Islam, *A Calendar of Documents on Indo-Persian Relations (1500-1750)*, Iranian Culture Foundation, Tehran, and Institute of Central and West Asian Studies, Karachi, 1979, vol. I, no. 418, p. 97.

(i) Two *fathnamas* (letters of victory) issued on the occasion of the surrender of Mankot and Shergarh by Sikandar Sur in 1557.[23]

(ii) Akbar's *farman* to the officers of Punjab on the occasion of Bairam Khan's revolt in 1560.[24]

(iii) Appointment order to the post of *Wikalat*.[25]

(iv) Akbar's *farman* appointing Muzaffar Khan as *Wazir-i Kul* issued some time between August 1563–March 1564.[26]

(v) Akbar's letter to Mirza Muhammad Hakim on the occasion of Shah Abul Maali's flight to Kabul in 1564.[27]

(vi) Shah Tahmasp's letter to Hamida Bano Begum, 1564.[28]

(vii) Akbar's letter to Shah Tahmasp sent some time in 1565 rejecting his suggestion to confer the titles of *Khan-i-Khanan* and *Sipah Salar* upon Sultan Mahmud Bhakkari.[29]

(viii) Shah Tahmasp's letter to Akbar making amends for having made an odd request in an earlier letter that the titles of *Khan-i-Khanan* and *Sipah Salar* be conferred upon Sultan Mahmud Bhakkari.[30]

(ix) *Fathnama* issued in 1567 after the defeat of *Khan-i-Zaman* Ali Quli Khan.[31]

(x) *Fathnama* issued in 1568 after the conquest of Chittor.[32]

In the following pages an attempt would be made to study some of the historical evidence gleaned from the documents included in the *Munshaat* to illustrate the point that regarding many problems these provide significant information not to be found even in the contemporary chronicles, or corroborate and add to the information furnished

---

[23] Documents No. 3-4, pp. 20-3.
[24] Document No. 53, pp. 119-22.
[25] Document No. 6, pp. 29-32.
[26] Document No. 8, pp. 34-7.
[27] Document No. 62, pp. 147-9.
[28] Document No. 61, pp. 144-6.
[29] Document No. 59, pp. 134-8.
[30] Document No. 60, pp. 139-44.
[31] Document No. 2, pp. 19-20.
[32] Document No. 1, pp. 7-18.

by these chronicles. Comments are not arranged in chronological order. The attempt, therefore, is to present these illustrations in the order of their significance highlighting the unique and corroborative nature of the evidence contained in the individual documents.

But before doing so, it is necessary to point out to a serious drawback from which this collection suffers as a source of historical evidence. In most of the documents included in the *Munshaat* names and dates have been omitted. It is difficult to explain why the compiler decided to do so. It may be due to the fact that he visualized his compilation not as a collection of documents of historical significance but simply as a volume containing illustrations of different kinds of *insha* writings for the instruction and use of those interested in learning the art of *insha* composition. This was obviously the purpose behind the compilation of most of *insha* collections, but other collections generally retained these details. However, Abu'l Qasim due to some unknown reason decided to omit these details in the majority of the documents and letters included in his collection. This drawback has naturally affected the utility of the collection as a source of history. It may, however, be useful to remember that there are still some documents like the *Fathnama-i-Chittor* which contain dates. There are many more which contain names of persons and places or some other indication. It is, therefore, quite possible in the case of many other documents to establish the identity of the persons involved as well as dates and circumstances in which they were issued by comparing their contents with the evidence contained in the contemporary sources as would emerge from the following study.

WIZARAT-I KUL

Munshaat contains a copy of a *farman* appointing some person to a position in the central government that carries the rather unusual designation of *mansab-i-Wizarat-i Kul Sarkar-i Humayun*.[33] When the contents of this *farman* are compared with Abul Fazl's description of the powers and functions assigned to Muzaffar Khan after his

[33] Document No. 8, pp. 34-7.

appointment to *Wizarat-i-Diwan-i Kul* in August 1563,[34] it becomes clear that this document pertains to the same position. Moreover, as the office of *Wizarat-i-Kul* or *Wizar-i-Diwan-i-Kul* has been mentioned by the chronicles only once in connection with Muzaffar Khan's promotion in 1563, it would appear that this was a special arrangement which continued only for a short time.[35] Abul Fazl has given a summary of this order while reporting Muzaffar Khan's elevation to this unique position in the central administration in 1563. The text reproduced by Abu'l Qasim enables us to considerably improve our understanding of the real nature of the change that was brought about by Akbar in the structure of his central government at this point of time. It is only on the basis of the full text of this order that Muzaffar Khan's simultaneous rise to *wikalat* replacing Munim Khan has come to light.[36]

CHAKLA AS AN ADMINISTRATIVE UNIT

The general impression of modern historians that *chakla* as an administrative unit was not known before Shah Jahan needs to be revised in the light of the mention of this territorial unit in a document contained in the *Munshaat*.[37] This document is undated but reference to *suba* in it makes it possible to determine its date. As is well-known *subas* were constituted in the 24th regnal year, i.e. AD 1580, and therefore the document definitely belongs to some date after 1580.

This document also sets at rest an old controversy between Moreland and Saran about the nature of *sarkars*. Moreland maintained that '*Sarkars* and their subdivisions represented only fiscal divisions while the administrative divisions were different from them.'[38] On the

---

[34] Cf. Abul Fazl, *Akbar Nama*, eds. Agha Ahmad Ali and Abdur Rahim, Bibliotheca Indica series, vol. II, p. 197. Abul Fazl refers to the post as *Wizarat-i-Diwan-i Kul*. For a detailed discussion see Iqtidar Alam Khan, *The Political Biography of a Mughal Noble: Munim Khan-i-Khanan, 1497-1575*. Orient Longman, 1973, pp. 72-3.

[35] *The Political Biography of a Mughal Noble*, p. 72, n. 7.

[36] Ibid., p. 73, n. I. For English translation of the operative part of the appointment order see p. 72.

[37] Document No. 31, pp. 85-8.

[38] Cf. Moreland, *Journal of Indian History*, 1927, vol. VI, part 11, quoted from Saran, *The Provincial Government of the Mughals*, p. 78.

other hand, Saran arrived at the conclusion that 'the contemporary chronicles furnish quite clear evidence of *Sarkar* and *pargana* being all administrative and not only fiscal divisions.'[39] The *sarkars* constituted an administrative area under the *faujdar's* jurisdiction. On this point the document under discussion provides conclusive evidence. It shows that in addition to the *sarkar* there existed even its subdivision *chakla* which was an administrative unit.[40] This is very clearly spelled by the *farman*. It states

> although in every *suba* we have appointed one of the high nobles who by his nature and training is fully familiar with the good and bad and is aware of the causes of prosperity and decline, and has the capacity to dispense justice, so that he may be able to implement the regulations of the imperial court. However, not deeming it sufficient and as a measure of further precaution we put each of the *Sarkars* of every *suba*, in some case even dividing the *Sarkar* into subdivisions, we have entrusted each of these divisions to one of those servants whose integrity is beyond reproach. We have specified each of these divisions which are commonly known as *chakla*.[41]

Clearly, this is the earliest reference to the use of this term. Earlier it was believed that this administrative unit was introduced in the reign of Shah Jahan by Sa'dullah Khan, as a statement in the *Khulast us Siyaq* would indicate.[42] From the contents of this document, however, it is firmly established that this territorial division was in fact introduced during the reign of Akbar.

DAH SALA SETTLEMENT

A document contained in this collection for the first time brings to light the actual procedure that was adopted for collecting necessary data for the introduction of *Ain-i Dah Sala*.[43] This document also does not

---

[39] Saran, pp. 78, 207-8.

[40] For a more detailed discussion on the subject see I.A. Zilli, 'Two Administrative Documents of Akbar's Reign', *Proceedings of Indian History Congress*, 1970, pp. 367-73.

[41] Document No. 31, p. 85. For English translation of the document see *Two Administrative Documents of Akbar's Reign*, pp. 369-70.

[42] *Khulast us Siyaq*, British Museum, London, MS. Add 6588, f.17a.

[43] Document No. 33, pp. 89-91.

contain any date but reference to the *Sarkar-i Punjab* in the text, instead of the expected *Suba-i Punjab*, would suggest that it was issued some time before 1580 in which year *subas* were constituted. This document is actually an appointment order for the post of *diwan* of the *Sarkar-i Punjab*. Apparently, it was issued when preparations for the introduction of *Ain-i Dah Sala* were afoot. It highlights the elaborate arrangements and measures which were employed for collecting necessary information for the introduction of the new system. Obviously, great care was taken in this regard and an entire system was put in place for the purpose. *Qanungos* were summoned from every *pargana* to the court to secure relevant information about every region. They were required to stay for one year at the court furnishing detailed information about local assessment, revenue, crop rates and the like. After the conclusion of one year they were to be replaced by others.[44]

Ain-i Dah Sala also states that the necessary information in this regard was gathered from the *qanungos*. It states 'when this great office devolved on Muzaffar Khan and Raja Todar Mal, in the 15th year of the reign, a redistribution of the imperial assessment was made through *qanungos* and estimating the produce of the lands, they made a fresh settlement. Ten *qanungos* were appointed who collected the accounts from the provincial *qanungos* and lodged them in the imperial exchequer.'[45] The *Ain*, however, does not provide details about the procedure that was adopted for this purpose. It is provided only by this document.

Besides appointment orders for the more important and well-known administrative posts such as those of *Wakil*,[46] *Wazir*,[47] *Diwan*,[48] *Sadr*,[49]

---

[44] For full translation of the document see 'Two Administrative Documents of Akbar's Reign', *Proceedings of Indian History Congress, 1970*, pp. 371-2.

[45] Abul Fazl, *Ain-i Akbari*, English translation by H.S. Jarret, Oriental Book Reprint Corporation, Delhi, 1978, vol. II, p. 94.

[46] Document No. 6, pp. 29-32.

[47] Documents No. 6-7, pp. 33-7.

[48] Document 32, pp. 88-91.

[49] Document No. 9, 10, pp. 29-32.

Bakhshi,[50] *Mustaufi,*[51] *Qazi,*[52] *Faujdar,*[53] *Mir-i Insha,*[54] *Shaikh ul Islam,*[55] the *Munshaat* contains a number of appointment orders for posts which are not quite well known and are rarely mentioned in the chronicles. In fact, some of the posts are not even mentioned in the contemporary chronicles. These include posts of *Mi'mar,*[56] *Mir-i Barr,*[57] *Naqib*[58] and so on. These documents have great historical significance and provide useful information about little known or even hitherto unknown aspects of administration as well as society.

MIR-i BAHR

Mir-i Bahr was an important officer at the centre. At the time of the constitution of the provinces, along with *Sipah Salar, Diwan, Bakhshi, Mir-i 'Adl, Kotawal, Sadr* and *Waqa'i' Navis*, a *Mir-i Bahr* was also appointed in every *suba.*[59] This would clearly indicate that it was an important administrative post that existed both at provincial as well as central levels. But sources provide little information about this post and besides this solitary evidence contained in the *Akbar Nama*, not much information is available about its existence particularly at the provincial level. While Saran has referred to the post of *Mir-i Bahr* as in-charge of river transport, ferries, port duties, customs, and boat and ferry taxes, he has failed to cite any evidence in support of his contention.[60] According to Qureshi the Mughals did not have sea-faring navy worth the name but they did have a department for the purpose. It was headed by *Mir-i Bahr* who 'had double duty of maintaining fleet for fighting purposes

[50] Document No. 12, pp. 45-6.
[51] Document No. 11, pp. 42-5.
[52] Documents No. 23, 24, pp. 69-74.
[53] Document No. 30, pp. 81-5.
[54] Document No. 13, pp. 46-9.
[55] Document No. 21, pp. 63-5.
[56] Document No. 19, pp. 59-61.
[57] Document No. 15, pp. 51-3.
[58] Document No. 28, pp. 79-81.
[59] *Akbar Nama*, vol. III, p. 282.
[60] The *Provincial Government of the Mughals*, p. 328.

and for policing main inland waterways'.[61] Moreover, according to him building of boat bridges was also included among the *Mir-i-Bahr*'s duties.[62] The provincial *Mir-i Bahr*, Qureshi holds, was 'responsible for the maintenance of river and sea ports within his jurisdiction in good condition, to guard and supervise river communication and keep the *nawwara* in good order'.[63] But for most of these assertions he does not cite any evidence.

Munshaat contains an appointment order for the post of *Mir-i Bahr*.[64] According to it, the duties of the *Mir-i-Bahr* included keeping watch on rivers and fords, and maintaining boats, sailors and boatmen. His jurisdiction extended over sailors, boatmen and those who guarded fords and crossings of rivers.[65] The *Munshaat* thus only partly supports the conclusions drawn by Qureshi. As far as the assertions of Saran are concerned, it is absolutely silent about them.

It is, however, interesting to note that the only incumbent of this office whose name has come down to us from Akbar's reign is not referred to in the sources as performing any of these responsibilities. Muhammad Qasim Khan who held the post of *Mir-i Bahr* during Akbar's reign and whose name is mentioned as *Mir-i Bahr*[66] is rather known as a 'military engineer' and a 'builder'.[67] He was involved in many important building projects of both military and civil nature including the construction

---

[61] I.H. Qureshi, *The Administration of the Mughal Empire*, N.V. Publications, Patna, p. 87.

[62] Ibid., p. 139.

[63] Ibid., pp. 230-1.

[64] Document No. 14, pp. 49-51.

[65] Document No. 14, pp. 49-51. Also see A.J. Qaiser, *Building Construction in Mughal India—The Evidence from Paintings*, Oxford University Press, Delhi, 1988, p. 7. However, development of agriculture and gardening were not included in the responsibilities of *Mir-i Bahr*, as A.J. Qaiser would seem to think. In fact, it was included among the responsibilities of *Mir-i Barr*. See Document No. 15, pp. 52-3.

[66] Document No. 1, p. 13. Abul Fazl, however, mentions him as *Mir-i Barr wa Bahr*. See *Akbar Nama*, vol. II, p. 270. Other sources including *Munshaat-i Namakin* refer to him only as *Mir-i Bahr*. Also see *Building Construction in Mughal India*, p. 7.

[67] *Building Construction in Mughal India*, p. 7.

of the Agra Fort. The sources are almost totally silent regarding his activities relating to his position as *Mir-i Bahr.*

MIR-i BARR

As far as the post of *Mir-i Barr* is concerned, there is absolutely no reference to it in the sources except the solitary and casual reference in the *Akbar Nama* where Muhammad Qasim Khan is referred to as *Mir-i Barr wa Bahr.*[68] *Munshaat,* however, contains an appointment order for this post.[69] According to it, the responsibilities attached to this office included maintenance of old and new gardens and agricultural lands, rehabilitation and extension of cultivation in the *mahals* included in the *khalsa sharifah* of both *zara'at-i khassa* and *zara'at-i ra'iyati.*[70] The subjects, both free and slaves, peasants, gardeners and others associated with *khalsa* lands are directed to abide by the *Mir-i Barr's* directives, consider him as independent *Mir-i Barr* and render every possible help to him.[71]

MI'MAR—OFFICER FOR BUILDING CONSTRUCTION

The Mughals were great builders. Akbar's reign was particularly marked by extensive building activity. But the available evidence does not provide any clue about the officer who was responsible for supervising the overall building enterprises of the empire. It would appear that during the late Sultanate period an officer with the designation of *Mir-i Imarat* used to head the building department.[72] But this term does not figure in the chronicles of Akbar's reign.[73] Even the *Ain-i Akbari* fails to mention this office in its section on buildings.[74] As noticed earlier, some of the most important construction projects of the reign were executed under

---

[68] *Akbar Nama,* vol. II, p. 247.

[69] Document No. 15, pp. 51-3.

[70] Document No. 15, p. 52.

[71] Document No. 15, pp. 52-3.

[72] I.H. Qureshi, *The Administration of the Sultanate of Delhi,* Shaikh Muhammad Ashraf, Lahore, 1944, p. 188.

[73] See *Building Construction in Mughal India,* p. 6.

[74] *Ain* 85 on buildings, *Ain-i Akbari,* vol. I, p. 232.

the supervision of Muhammad Qasim Khan, *Mir-i Bahr*, who was an accomplished engineer,[75] but this responsibility was not included among the duties of the *Mir-i Bahr*. *Munshaat*, however, contains an appointment order to the post of *m'imari* of a particular region. Among the qualifications for the post, besides expertise in the art of construction, the incumbent is required to have a very good knowledge of mathematics and geometry.[76] According to the order, he was assigned independent charge of the office of *m'imari* of the region under question and was charged with the responsibility of preparing layouts and carrying out construction of the imperial as well as ordinary buildings (*tarrahi wa sakhtan-i imarat-i khassa wa ghair-i an*). Men belonging to professions associated with building activity such as clay workers (*gilkaran*), brick makers (*khisht malan*), stone cutters (*sang trashan*), wood sellers (*chaub fraushan*), wood cutters (*chaub trashan*), carpenters (*durodgaran*), brick burners (*khisht pazan*) and lime burners (*ahak pazan*) were placed under his charge.[77] In the light of this document it would not be far-fetched to assume that like the regional *m'imar* there would certainly have been a central *m'imar* as well even though the contemporary sources have failed to record it.

OFFICER IN CHARGE OF *NAQQAR KHANA*

There is a very interesting *manshur* appointing Ustad Muhammad Shams ud din and Mihtar Imam ud Din Mahmud as joint supervisors of *Naqqar Khana*. It is dated Safar 3, 999 H./December 1591. It is one of the few documents included in the *Munshaat* in which names and dates are not omitted.[78] The words of *Kilantar* and *Muqaddam* have been used to specify their designation. According to this order various categories of musicians attached to the imperial *Naqqar Khana*, such as beaters of kettledrums (*naqqachian*), buglers (*surnaian*), trumpeters (*nafirchian*) and other such professionals were placed under the *Kilantar's* and *Muqaddam's* supervision. But the interesting part of the document is that a number of other professions, which apparently don't seem to have

[75] *Building Construction in Mughal India*, p. 7.
[76] Document No. 19, p. 60.
[77] Ibid., p. 61.
[78] Document No. 18, pp. 56-8.

had any particular association or link with *Naqqar Khana*, were also placed under their supervision. The professional groups placed under their overall charge were very diverse in nature. These included children of prostitutes (*Gharib-zadgan*), storytellers (*qawwalan*), hawkers (*tawwafan*), bath attendees (*hammamian*), hairdressers (*sar trashana*), bath waiters (*dallakan*), wine servers (*bada banan*), millers (*asyaban*), sieve makers (*ghirbalbafan*), prostitutes (*luliyan*), weavers (*jaulàhan*) and all others who had any relationship with such professions. People attached to these various professions were advised to consider the above-mentioned as their head and chief (*kalantar wa paishawa*).[79]

SAJJADANASHIN OF THE *DARGAH* OF SHAIKH BAHA UD DIN ZAKARIA MULTANI

A *manshur* appointing Shaikh Kabir as the *sajjadanashin* of the *dargah* of Shaikh Baha ud Din Zakaria Multani and Shaikh Rukn ud din Multani[80] would go to suggest the extent of imperial interference in the affairs of institutions earlier considered to be outside the domain of the state power. Till that time the position of *mutawallis* and *sajjadianshins* of the *dargahs* of Sufi saints were by and large hereditary, virtually reducing monasticism to a profession. Succession to these positions was regulated by the government to the extent that any dispute about it would come within the purview of the Qazi's court. But this *farman* gives an entirely different picture from Akbar's reign. Shaikh Kabir was appointed as *sajjadanashin* of the *dargah*. The document maintains that he was appointed due to his qualifications as well as his hereditary rights. But another person from the family challenged this appointment, putting forward his own claims for the office. Eventually he succeeded in replacing Shaikh Kabir as the *sajjadanashin* of the *dargah*. But as he proved to be incompetent, Shaikh Kabir was resorted to his earlier position. This would clearly suggest that during Akbar's reign the ruler had emerged as the final arbiter in the affairs of the religious establishments like the Sufi monasteries and its administration came to be regarded as a concern of imperial authority. This naturally invested

79 Ibid., p. 58.

80 Document No. 22, pp. 66-9.

it with enormous control over groups living on the income of such establishments.

MIR-i 'ADL

Mir-i 'Adl was an important judicial officer under the Mughals. Saran thinks that this office was peculiar to India and no officer of this name was found in Muslim caliphate outside India or in India during the Delhi Sultanate. 'The idea of *mir 'adal's* post and functions was thus purely a creation of the Mughals.'[81] But Qureshi correctly points out that it existed under the Delhi Sultans and the officer holding this office was known as *dadbek* or *amir-i dad* and occupied a high position in the administrative hierarchy.[82] Ibn Hasan would seem to suggest that *mir-i 'Adl* was also appointed along with the *qazi* in all the important cities and towns and their duties were accordingly defined. According to him, 'In all big cities and towns they existed side by side.'[83] Saran, however, believes that *mir-i 'Adls* were very rarely appointed.[84] Abul Fazl discussing the duties of the *qazi* says, 'If capacity and vigour are not to be found united, he should appoint two persons, one to investigate whom they call a *Qazi*, the other the *Mir-i 'Adl* to carry out his findings.'[85] This would seem to be fully corroborated by the contents of an appointment order contained in the *Munshaat*.[86] The officer is referred as responsible for providing solace to the seekers of justice and the oppressed. It is clear from the text that he was charged with the responsibility of carrying out important decisions which sometimes required the use of force on a big scale. The nature of his court and those who attended his office to assist him is indeed formidable. Those who were required to attend his office included a member of the royal family, a *sadr*, a *qazi*, a *bakhshi* besides forty *yasawals* and footmen.[87] It was obviously intended to invest

[81] *The Provincial Government of the Mughals*, p. 327.

[82] I.H. Qureshi, *The Administration of the Sultanate of Delhi*, pp. 10-11, 161-2; idem, *Administration of the Mughal Empire*, p. 190.

[83] *Ibn Hasan*, p. 315.

[84] Saran, pp. 327-9.

[85] *Aiṇ-i Akbari*, vol. II, p. 43. Also see Qureshi, p. 190.

[86] Document No. 26., pp. 74-7.

[87] Ibid., p. 76.

prestige and authority to his office and provide him necessary means to carry out his task effectively. This would clearly indicate that his responsibilities included implementation of judgements, which could sometimes involve powerful people.

MIR-i ATISH

Mir-i Atish (commander of the artillery) was an important officer at the centre. Saran says that *kotawals* were appointed on his recommendation,[88] but he has not cited any evidence in support of this contention. Rafat Bilgrami also thinks that *kotawalls* were appointed on the recommendation and under the seal of *Mir-i Atish*.[89] For this she has relied on Waheed Husain's *Administration of Justice During Muslim Rule in India*.[90] Apparently Waheed Husain has also not cited any evidence in support of his contention.

Munshaat contains an appointment order for the post of *Mir-i Atish*.[91] The post is referred to in the document as *Munsab-i mir atishi-i Sarkar-i Humayun*. The duties of the incumbent are defined as management and maintenance of *topkhana* and related affairs.[92] By no stretch of imagination appointment of *kotawals* could be included in the matters allied to the management of *topkhana*. There is no hint at all that his duties extended beyond the domain of *topkhana*.

---

[88] He writes 'The *Kotawal* was appointed from the headquarter, that is, by the imperial government, on the recommendation and by a *sanad* bearing the seal of the imperial commander of the artillery (*Mir-i Atash*)'. See *The Provincial Government of the Mughals*, p. 214.

[89] See Rafat M. Bilgrami, *Religious and Quasi-Religious Departments of the Mughal Period (1556-1707)*, Munshiram Manoharlal, Delhi, p. 186.

[90] *Waheed Husain, Administration of Justice During Muslim Rule in India*, Allahabad, 1954, p. 173.

[91] Document No. 16, pp. 53-5.

[92] Ibid., p. 54.

SHAIKH UL ISLAM

During the Delhi Sultanate the term *Shaikh ul Islam* was normally used as an honorific that was bestowed by the Sultans upon eminent religious personages. Sultans Shams ud din Iltutmish conferred this title on Shaikh Baha ud din Zakaria Multani.[93] The same ruler had also appointed Saiyid Nur ud Din Mubarak Ghaznavi as *Shaikh ul Islam* of Delhi.[94] Shaikh Najm ud din Sughra, who had entered into an unseemly controversy with the eminent Suharwardi saint, Shaikh Jalal ud din Tabrizi, was also *Shaikh ul Islam* of Delhi.[95] In some of these cases the title is purely honorary which carried with it some privileges. But in other cases, like that of Shaikh Najm ud din Sughra, it clearly had official connotation and carried with it some official responsibilities. In *Fawaid ul Fuad*, however, the term is used simply as a mark of respect.[96]

As far as the position of *Shaikh ul Islam* under the Mughals is concerned, Ibn Hasan is of the opinion that it was synonymous with the *Sadr*.[97] Rafat Bilgrami also thinks that *Sadr us Sudur* was also known as *Shaikh ul Islam*. 'The post of the *sadr* or the *Shaikh ul Islam* was established to keep the Sultan informed of the affairs of the subjects and to keep the people on the path of rectitude and to make them perform the functions enjoined by the *Shari'at*.[98] Both the scholars have relied on the evidence of *Suluk ul Muluk* of Fazl bin Rozebahan (1455-1521) to arrive at this conclusion. As is well known he wrote the book at the request of Ubaidullah Khan as a guide for him. Its main quality lies in the fact that it makes a very intelligent attempt to reconcile the norms of the *Shari'at* with the realities of a tribal set-up whose body politic was nomadic. Moreover, like Al Mawardi's *Al Ahkam us Sultaniyyah*,

---

[93] Jamali, *Siyar ul Arfin*, Matba Rizvi, Delhi, 1311, p. 169; Shaikh Abdul Haq Muhaddis Dehlavi, *Akhbar ul Akhyar*, Kutub Khana-i Rahimiyyah, Deoband, 1332, p. 32. Also see K.A. Nizami, *Salatin-i Dehli ke Mazhabi Rujhanat*, Nadwat ul Musannifin, Delhi, 1981, p. 115.

[94] *Akhbar ul Akhyar*, p. 34.

[95] Hasan Sizji, *Fawaid ul Fuad*, ed. Muhammad Latif Malik, Lahore, 1996, p. 245.

[96] For example at one place it is used for Shaikh Qutb ud din Bakhtiyar Kaki (p. 185) while Shaikh Farid ud din is invariably referred as *Shaikh ul Islam*.

[97] *The Central Structure of the Mughal Empire*, p. 256.

[98] *Religious and Quasi Religious Departments*, p. 2.

this book also puts forward the ideals of governance as it ought to be. The functioning of various administrative institutions discussed there in a different time and in a different country and that too in a theoretical framework would not be necessarily applicable to the situation obtaining in India under the Mughals or for that matter to any other government.

In this context the contents of an appointment order to the post of *Shaikh ul Islam* reproduced in the *Munshaat-i Namakin*[99] assume significance and help in deciding the actual nature, duties and functions of the post. It is an appointment order to the post of *Shaikh ul Islam* of some region. This would indicate that this post also existed at the regional level. In fact, the text of the document states it as a matter of policy that well qualified scholars should be appointed as *Shaikh ul Islam* in every region of the empire to ensure the implementation of the rules and regulations of the religion as well as to look after the needs of the religious classes.[100] The incumbent was expected to guide the people to the right path and strengthen the *Shari'at* of the Prophet. The *muhtasibs, imams, muazzins* and *mutawallis* of the *waqfs* were directed to settle all religious matters in his presence and all the legal documents were to be affixed with his seal without which they would not be considered legal.[101] This would clearly indicate that the post of the *Shaikh ul Islam* was not synonymous with that of the *sadr* and their duties and responsibilities did not match with each other.[102]

QAZI

A number of appointment orders for the post of *qazi* have been reproduced in the *Munshaat.*[103] Two of them are dated.[104] One of the

---

[99] Document No. 21, pp. 63-5.

[100] Ibid., p. 64.

[101] Ibid., p. 65.

[102] For the duties of the *sadr* see Document No. 9, pp. 38-42, Also see *Religious and Quasi Religious Departments*, pp. 5-8.

[103] Documents No. 23, 24 and 25, pp. 69-74.

[104] Appointment order for the post of the *Qazi* of Ajmer is dated 1 Rabi-I, 979 (p. 70). The other document is an appointment order for the post of the *Qazi* of some town and it bears the date of 29 *Ramazan*, 987 (p. 72).

documents sheds fresh light on the jurisdiction of the *qazi* of a town. According to it the *qazi* is authorized to administer justice in the town along with its dependencies in an area extending over twenty *karoh* into twenty *karoh* independently as was the case earlier.[105] This might have been the limit of the jurisdiction of a *qazi* during those days.

Some other interesting aspects also emerge regarding the functions and duties of the *qazi* from these documents. Among the duties of the *qazi* it enumerates certain functions, which were normally considered to be associated with the office of *Muhtasib*. For example, destruction of wine and other intoxicants, suppression of unlawful and forbidden activities and ensuring the observation of religious duties and obligations are clearly included among the traditional responsibilities of the *muhtasib*.[106] But here these are included among the responsibilities of the *qazi*.[107]

NAQIB

Saiyids have always been held in great esteem among the Muslims. Medieval Muslim governments also showed great deference to them. As a result, they constituted a highly privileged class. This tempted many non-Saiyids to falsely claim to be Saiyids to become entitled for the privileges reserved for this class. It also provided an easy route to rapid social mobility. For the purpose they even invented fake genealogies to trace their lineage to some important Saiyid personality. This was considered a very serious offence not only on moral grounds but also because it constituted an attempt at defrauding the people and the government. Steps were therefore taken by the government to rectify this situation. The *Munshaat* contains an appointment order to the post of *naqabat*.[108] A distinguished member of the Saiyid fraternity was given the responsibility to carry out thorough investigation into the authenticity of the lineage of all those who put

---

[105] Document No. 24, p. 71.

[106] For the duties of the *muhtasib* see *The Administration of the Mughal Empire*, pp. 200-02; *Religious and Quasi Religious Departments*, pp. 175-6. Also see Text, p. 78.

[107] Document No. 24, p. 72.

[108] Document No. 28, pp. 79-81.

forward a claim to be Saiyid and issue certificates of genealogy to those whose claims were found to be true. But those whose genealogy could not be established and whose claims were found to be fake were to be severely punished so that it could serve as a deterrent to those fraudulent and impudent people who pretend to be Saiyids without entitlement.[109] It would seem that outside India, there was a tradition of some eminent Saiyid being appointed as *Naqib us Sadat* to take care of the welfare of Saiyids. Moreover, the word *naqib* also means an expert genealogist.[110] In the case of this office both the functions seem to have been united.

PERQUISITES OF VARIOUS POSTS

Some of the documents provide very interesting sidelights about the perquisites of some of the officers of the state both at the central as well as provincial levels. Some of this could not be corroborated by contemporary sources and would seem to be quite improbable. But it has been very clearly set forth in the documents reproduced in the *Munshaat* and there does not seem to be any particular reason for the compiler to manipulate the text and interpolate into it incorrect information. For example the appointment order for the post of *Mir-i Bakhshi* contains the additional information that as a special imperial favour the incumbent was assigned as *in'am* a sum of one rupee per year from every single trooper. *Fotadars* of the *Sarkar-i Khassa* and the *fotadars* of the *parganas* as well as *jagirdars* are directed to hand it over to his agents (*gumashta*). It has been referred as *muqarrar-i mir-i bakhshi*.[111] Similarly, an appointment order to the post of *sadr* speaks of *rasm-i sadarat* (perquisite of *sadarat*) in accordance with the old law and established rule (*muwafiq-i qanun-i qadim wa qa'ida-i istimarar*.[112] The appointment order for the *Mir-i Insha* stipulates that besides the stipend as detailed in the *zimn* (endorsement), the incumbent is further entitled to an *in'am* which has been termed as *sad dui* for those *farmans* that

[109] Ibid., pp. 80-1.

[110] Dahkhuda, *Lughat Nama*, Tehran, 1346 Hijri Shamsi, Serial No. 134, pp. 716-17.

[111] Document No. 12, p. 46.

[112] Document No. 9, p. 40.

he would himself draft.[113] He is further entitled to another perquisite that has been termed as *sad wa nim*. This has been named as *haqq ul insha*.[114] In the same way an appointment order to the post of *faujdar* speaks of an unspecified *rusum-i faujdari* to which a *faujdar* is entitled. It also speaks about a special cess of one *dam* from every cultivated *bigha* of land. This will be realized from those who need *faujdar's* help in the collection of revenue. Those who do not require any help in this regard, need not pay it. This cess is specifically meant for the maintenance of musketeers (*banduqchi*).[115]

DIPLOMATIC CORRESPONDENCE

The diplomatic correspondence reproduced in the *Munshaat-i Namakin* is extremely important. It sheds new light, particularly on India's relations with Iran during Akbar's reign. It contains some letters which were exchanged between the ruling houses of Iran and India and which have not been noticed so far by scholars working in the area. It includes two hitherto unpublished letters of Shah Tahmasp to Akbar[116] and Hamida Bano Begum,[117] Akbar's letter to Shah Tahmasp[118] and Abdullah Khan Uzbek's letter to Akbar.[119] The significance of this evidence lies in the fact that the letter of Shah Tahmasp to Hamida Bano Begum and Akbar's letter to Shah Tahmasp have not been noticed so far by scholars writing on Mughal-Iranian relations. Riazul Islam has noticed Shah Tahmasp's letter to Akbar but has provided only a gist of it.[120] Shah Tahmasp's letter to Hamida Bano Begum is unique

---

[113] Document No. 13, p. 49.

[114] Ibid.

[115] Document No. 31, pp. 87-8.

[116] Document No. 60, pp. 139-44.

[117] Document No. 61, pp. 144-7.

[118] Document No. 59, pp. 134-8.

[119] Document No. 58, pp. 131-4.

[120] Riazul Islam has noticed Shah Tahmasp's letter to Akbar on the authority of a British Museum manuscript (B.M. Add. 7654 ff. 176-78a). He had used *Munshaat-i Namakin* but seems to have missed this letter as also the two other letters being introduced here. This is clear from his observation that 'Neither the letter under reply, nor the Shah's previous letter referred here, are available.' Cf. Riazul Islam, *A Calendar of Documents on Indo-Persian Relations (1500-1750)*,

for more than one reason. Firstly, this letter has not been referred to by any contemporary or later chronicler. Secondly, it is the only known document of its nature from the early Mughal period. One does not come across any other instance of a Mughal lady receiving a letter from the ruler of another country.

In the available text of this letter, the name of the addressee is not given. In fact, in most cases, as noticed earlier, the compiler has omitted names and dates, as he did not visualize his collection as a source of history. However, the contents of the letter leave little doubt regarding the identity of the addressee. From the fact that there is great similarity in the contents as well as the language of this letter and that of the other letter of Shah Tahmasp addressed to Akbar sent in 969/1562 and reproduced in the *Akbar Nama*[121] one may conclude that perhaps both the letters were brought to India by the same envoy, Saiyid Beg Safavi. This letter could not be considered as a 'draft prepared by the way of literary exercise in which there is an attempt to paraphrase Shah Tahmasp's letter to Akbar' as suggested by some scholars.[122] It is true that *insha* collections were primarily meant to provide samples and illustrations of various kinds of documents for the use and instruction of those interested in learning the art of *insha* writing. But obviously no one interested in the art of *insha* would have needed specimen of a letter supposedly written on behalf of a reigning sovereign of a neighbouring country to the mother of a great ruler like Akbar. No compiler of an *insha* collection could have dared to

---

Iranian Culture Foundation, Tehran, and Institute of Central and West Asian Studies, Karachi, 1979, vol. 1, Calendar No. A.18, p. 97.

[121] *A.N.*, vol. II, pp. 170-3. Also see Riazul Islam, *Indo-Persian Relations,* Iranian Culture Foundation, Tehran, 1970, pp. 49-50. The ambassador who brought the letter was Saiyid Beg Safavi, son of Masum Beg Safavi. Besides the royal descent, Masum Beg Safavi was host of Humayun during his stay in Iran at Ardbil.

[122] Cf. Iqtidar Alam Khan, 'The Mughal Empire and the Iranian Diaspora of the Sixteen Century', in Irfan Habib (ed.), *A Shared Heritage: The Growth of Civilization in India and Iran,* Aligarh Historians Society, Tulika, New Delhi, 2002, pp. 112-13 n. 17 Iqtidar Alam Khan thinks that this letter was a 'draft prepared by the way of literary exercise in which there is an attempt to paraphrase Shah Tahmasp's letter to Akbar' and hence holds it to be 'spurious'. According to him it is because of this reason that Riazul Islam did not include it in his Calendar.

take this kind of liberty, particularly when he intended to dedicate his work to Akbar as Abu'l Qasim actually did. No collection of *insha* is known to contain a specimen of this kind. In fact, specimens of only those documents were provided which were needed in the practical life. To make the Queen Mother an object of literary exercise would require a degree of impertinence of which an intelligent person of the taste and refinement of Abu'l Qasim could hardly be capable. If Riazul Islam did not include this letter 'because of its spurious nature' then why has Akbar's letter to Shah Tahmasp also not been included in his *Calendar*, as its genuineness is beyond doubt in the light of an earlier letter of the Shah on the same subject referred to by Abul Fazl.[123] If the history of Shah Tahmasp's special relationship with Humayun is kept in mind, it would appear quite natural that he would have wished to enlist the help of Hamida Bano for the normalization of the relations between the two empires which had come under considerable strain following Persian capture of Qandahar. The choice of the ambassador on this occasion was also a calculated one to emphasize the close relations of the two houses. As is well known, Saiyid Beg Safavi was not only a member of the royal family of Iran but also the son of Masum Beg Safavi who was Humayun's host during his stay at Ardbil. Hamida Bano Begum could therefore be naturally expected to have grateful memories of those days when she along with Humayun had taken shelter in Iran and were extended every help and hospitality by its ruling house. By sending Saiyid Beg as ambassador, the Shah was very discretely trying to play on those sentiments and remind her of those distressful days when Iran had stood solidly by their side. Moreover, a thorough scrutiny would reveal that all such letters included in the *Munshaat-i Namakin* are in fact copies of genuine letters and not drafts of literary exercise.

The general tenor of Shah Tahmasp's letter to Hamida Bano Begum is courteous and friendly. He makes special mention of the strong bond of friendship that had existed between him and Humayun, emphasizing his own contribution to the restoration of Mughal rule in India. Significantly enough, in both these letters he does not make any mention of Qandahar which had been occupied by him in 965/1558 after expelling

[123] *A.N.*, vol. II, pp. 170-3.

the Mughal officer from there.[124] While acknowledging a letter that was sent to the Shah by Bairam Khan[125] in his capacity as the Regent, he does not make any reference to the embarrassing circumstances of his dismissal and subsequent assassination. It is difficult to believe that even after the passage of one and half years, Shah Tahmasp 'did not know of it when he despatched the embassy' as has been suggested by Riazul Islam.[126]

Apparently, Shah Tahmasp's embassy to Akbar in 1562 was aimed at restoring the friendly ties between the two courts that had snapped following the Persian occupation of Qandahar in 1558.[127] It is significant that on this occasion the Shah thought it fit to write a separate letter to Hamida Bano Begum. This would suggest that at the time his envoy set out for India, he was perhaps under the impression that Hamida Bano was playing an important role in framing state policies and he hoped that he would be able to enlist her support for the restoration of friendly ties between the two courts. It may be recalled that Hamida Bano had accompanied Humayun to Iran when he had sought refuge there with the Shah and this presumably led the Shah to claim a special relationship with her. There is some evidence to suggest that a special relationship did indeed exist, at least between the ladies of the two royal families Decades later when in 1605 Mir Masum Bhakkari returned from his embassy to the court of Shah Abbas I, besides the Shah's letter for Akbar, he also brought a letter from the Shah's aunt addressed to Maryam Makani (Hamida Bano Begum). But she had died before the arrival of the embassy.[128] It would, however, seem that the Shah's objective could not be achieved on this occasion. As is well known, by 1562 Akbar had already succeeded in containing *harem's* influence over his administration. By

---

[124] Ibid., pp. 78-9.

[125] *Indo-Persian Relations,* p. 49.

[126] *Indo-Persian Relations,* p. 49, n. 6.

[127] Cf. Khafi Khan, *Muntakhab ul Lubab,* Bibliotheca Indica, vol. I, p. 161.

[128] *A.N.*, vol. III, p. 836. It may be recalled that according to Gulbadan during Humayun's stay in Iran, Shah Tahmasp's sister gave a big party in the honour of Hamida Bano Begum in which about 1,000 guests were invited. Aparently, it was the same sister of the Shah and hence the aunt of Shah Abbas I, who later sent the letter. See Gulbadan Begum, *Humayun Nama,* English tr. by A.S. Beveridge, London, 1902, p. 170. Also see *Indo-Persian Relations,* pp. 37 n. 10, 67.

the time Shah Tahmasp's letter reached India, Hamida Bano no longer had much political power left.[129]

Shah Tahmasp wrote the second letter[130] sometime in 1565 offering apologies to Akbar for having made a rather odd request in a letter sent in 1564. A summary of that earlier letter and Akbar's reply is given by Abul Fazl in the *Akbar Nama*.[131] From that summary one comes to know that in 1564 the Shah had recommended that the titles of *Khan-i Khanan* and *Sipahsalar*, then held by the senior-most Chaghtai noble of the realm, Munim Khan, be conferred on Sultan Mahmud Khan Bhakkari.[132] To this letter Akbar had sent a courteous reply but had declined to accede to the Shah's request.

The letter that the Shah wrote to Akbar explaining his position in the matter is an interesting piece of diplomatic correspondence. In this letter, on the one hand, the Shah appears to be anxious to make up for any offence that might have been caused to Akbar as a result of his earlier request, but on the other hand, he seems to regard it below his dignity to openly express regret. He tries to avoid this embarrassment by attributing to Akbar the statement that not only Humayun had high regard for Munim Khan but also in fact it was he who had given him the title in question. An interesting statement is added, repeating one

---

[129] *A.N.*, vol. II, pp. 149-50, 173. Ataka Khan's appointment in November 1561 as *Wakil* marks the end of petticoat influence. Also see Iqtidar Alam Khan, *The Political Biography of a Mughal Noble, Munim Khan Khan-i Khanan*, Aligarh, 1973, pp. 63-8.

[130] Document No. 60, pp. 139-44.

[131] *A.N.*, vol. II, p. 237. For the text of Akbar's reply see Document No. 59, pp. 134-8.

[132] For a detailed account of the episode see Mir Masum Bhakkari, *Tarikh-i Masumi*, ed. U.M. Daudpota, Bombay, 1938, pp. 23-5, 235. Also see *A Calendar of Documents*, vol. I, p. 97. For details about Mahmud Khan see *A.N.*, vol. II, pp. 237, 278, 362-3; *Tarikh-i Masumi*, pp. 223, 225, 235-6; *Maasir ul Umara*, vol. III, pp. 240-5. Also see *Indo-Persian Relations*, p. 50, n. 1. According to Masumi (p. 22) Gauhar Taj Begum, daughter of Shah Tardi Beg, a relative of Bairam Khan, was married to him. Apparently, his relations with the Mughal court did not remain cordial after Bairam Khan's fall. Abul Fazl does not mention the title of I'tibar Khan having been conferred on him. According to him at this time the Shah was financially hard pressed and had taken large sums from Mahmud Khan to recommend his name to Akbar for the title of *Khan-i Khanan*. Akbar refers to Munim Khan as *Khan Babaam*.

made in the Akbar's own letter, that one title could not be given to two persons in India. He expressly accepts these arguments, developed by himself, as good enough reason why Akbar could not accede to his earlier recommendation. Obviously, he wishes the matter to be closed.

Besides the correspondence that was carried out between the Mughals and the Safavids, the *Munshaat* also contains a letter that was written by Abdullah Khan Uzbek to Akbar and was sent through Mir Quraish.[133] The full text of the letter has been reproduced by Abul Qasim. The only other known copy of the text is available in *Majma' ul Insha*.[134] It was written after the expulsion of Shah Rukh Mirza from Badakhshan.[135] Abdullah Khan refers to friendly relations with the Mughal ruler and goes to say that the delay in sending an envoy to the Mughal court was due to his own problems and not on account of any lack of regard for Akbar. Then he goes on to justify his occupation of Badakhshan. He maintains that such a course had become necessary as Shah Rukh Mirza was acting in an irresponsible manner by extending shelter to the rebels and interfering in the affairs of Balkh. He expresses the hope that the situation will be appreciated in its true perspective by the unblemished mind of Akbar, which is the repository of the invisible world. At the end, the letter refers to the dispatch of some pigeons from Farghana along with a pigeon fancier (*kabutarbaz*).[136]

This section also contains the copy of a letter written by Akbar to Mirza Muhammad Hakim. This is perhaps the only surviving letter of Akbar addressed to Mirza Hakim. It was written at the time of Shah Abul Maali's revolt and flight to Kabul. After enumerating some of the misdeeds of Shah Abul Maali, it goes on to say that the expectation was that the latter would be suitably dealt with. But it was a matter of great surprise and anguish that contrary to the expectations, Abul Maali was well received in Kabul. While troops were being dispatched for his suppression, it was brought to Akbar's knowledge that Abul

---

[133] Document No. 58, pp. 131-4.

[134] Cf. *Majma'ul Insha*, B.M.M.S. or 1702; Cf. 199b quoted from Abdur Rahim, Mughal Relations with Persia and Central Asia, *Islamic Culture*, vol. X, p. 86.

[135] Abdur Rahim, p. 73.

[136] Document No. 58, p. 134.

Maali had met his nemesis. At the end the latter promises every help to the addressee whenever needed.[137]

FATHNAMA-I CHITTOR

Mention should be made of a whole category of documents identified as *fathnama* (letter of victory). *Fathnama* is defined as official announcement of victory.[138] This definition would exclude *fathnamas* written by private persons such as *Fathnama-i Lakhnauti* written by Amir Khusrau. It was a long-standing tradition among the Muslim governments to issue *fathnamas* when important victories were achieved. Technically the term *fathnama* would apply only to the communication sent by a ruler to convey the news of victory. If the commander of the army sends news of victory to the court, it would be designated as *ariza* and not *fathnama*.[139] But in actual practice the application of the term was often extended to include communications from the commanders of the army that had won the battle.[140] *Fathnamas* were sent to various regions within the dominion of the ruler as well as outside it to inform the people about the victory. When the commanders sent *fathnama* from the site of the conquest, it occasioned great rejoicing and celebration, and it was even read from the pulpits of the mosques.[141] In Persia there was a tradition of issuing letter of defeat (*shikashtnama*) to explain the reasons for the defeat and provide solace and consolation to the people.[142] From Medieval India, however, there is no instance of a *shikashtnama* having been ever issued.

Accomplished scholars and eminent writers were engaged by the rulers to compose *fathnamas*. Zia ud Din Barani respectfully refers to

---

[137] Document No. 62, pp. 147-9.

[138] See G.L. Lewis, *Fathnama, Encyclopedia of Islam* (New Edition), Leiden and London, 1964, vol. II, p. 839.

[139] Khwaja-i Jahan Mahmud Gawan, *Manazir ul Insha*, Sulaiman Collection, Maulana Azad Library, Aligarh Muslim University, MS No. 276/9, *Insha-i Farsi*, ff. 149b-150b.

[140] Barani (p. 326) refers to the communication of victory sent by Malik Kafur from Deogir as *fathnama*. Similarly, he also refers (p. 330) to the letter of victory sent by the same commander after the conquest of Arangal as *fathnama*.

[141] *Tarikh-i Firoz Shahi*, pp. 326, 330.

[142] Dehkhuda, *Lughat Nama* Tehran, 1341 Hijri Shamsi, Serial No. 79, p. 55.

Kabir ud din, son of Taj ud din Iraqi, who drafted *fathnamas* for Sultan Ala ud din Khalji announcing many victories of his reign. In fact, he is said to have composed volumes of these *fathnamas*.[143] From the Sultanate period, however, only two *fathnamas*—*fathnama-i Lakhnauti*[144] and *fathnama-i Jajnagar* [145]—have survived. But as noted earlier, *fathnama-i Lakhnauti* would not qualify to be designated as a formal *fathnama*. It is also interesting to note that besides the *fathnamas* contained in the *Munshaat-i Namakin*, only two other *fathnamas* have come down to us from the early Mughal period. One of these is the famous *fathnama* written by Shaikh Zain after the battle of Kanwa, which was reproduced by Babur in *Babur Nama*.[146] The other is *fathnama-i Gujarat*.[147]

Munshaat-i Namakin contains a number of *fathnamas*, issued by Akbar after important victories. These include the *fathnamas*, issued after the defeat of Ali Quli Khan[148] and capture of the forts of Shergarh[149] and Mankot.[150] These documents not only convey the news of victory but also provide important and useful details about the actual conduct of the siege or the military campaign leading to that particular victory. But by far the most important *fathnama* included in this collection is *Fathnama-i Chittor* issued by Akbar after the conquest of Chittor.[151] No other copy of this *fathnama* is known to exist. It was issued from Ajmer where Akbar has stayed for few days en route to Agra after the conquest of Chittor. It bears the date of Ramazan 10, 975 H./9 March

[143] *Tarikh-i Firoz Shahi*, pp. 14, 361.

[144] Amir Khusrau, *I'jaz-i Khusravi*, Nawal Kishore, Lucknow, 1876, vol. V, pp. 5-14.

[145] Ain ul Mulk Mahru, *Inshai-i Mahru*, ed. Shaikh Abd ur Rashid, Idarah Tahqiqat-i Pakistan, Punjab University, Lahore, 1965, pp. 28-34.

[146] *Babur Nama*, tr. A.S. Beveridge, Low Price Publications, Delhi, 1989, pp. 559-74.

[147] A copy of this *fathnama* is preserved at the Maulana Azad Library, Aligarh Muslim University, Aligarh, under the title *Naql-i Farman-i Fathnama-i Gujarat*, University Collection, Persian, Akhbar, No. 171. For an extended translation and a discussion on the nature of the document see *The Political Biography of a Mughal Noble*, pp. 125-30.

[148] Document No. 2, pp. 19-20.

[149] Document No. 3, pp. 20-2.

[150] Document No. 4, pp. 22-3.

[151] Document No. 1, pp. 7-18.

1568 and is addressed to the officials of Punjab among whom Mir Muhammad Khan and Qutb ud din Muhammad Khan[152] are specifically mentioned. The sentiments expressed in the *fathnama* as well as its very strong and aggressive phraseology has led Iqtidar Alam Khan to conclude that around 1567 when Akbar carried out his attack against Chittor, his religious policy had suffered a certain degree of regression from the liberal postures of the early 1560s as reflected by such measures as abolition of pilgrimage tax and *jizya*.[153]

The *fathnamas* could be used as an important source of information for the details of the battles in question as they contain short and on occasions very precise history of the events. But scholars working on the Ottoman *fathnamas* have even questioned this utility of these documents as they found that they tended to suppress unpleasant aspects of the proceedings of the battles. For example, it is pointed out that the most important aspect of the conquest of the fortress of Eger in 1596 during the reign of Sultan Muhammad III was the massacre of the entire garrison after they surrendered on the promise of safe conduct. But the *fathnama* issued on the occasion does not mention it at all.[154] Similarly, contents of the *fathnamas* sent to different destinations about the same victory considerably differ from each other in the matter of detail and emphasis.[155] His study of Ottoman *fathnamas* has led B.L. Lewis to conclude that 'The primary function of the *fathnama* was propaganda.'[156] It seeks to project the persona of that particular state and the kind of image that the ruler issuing the *fathnama* wanted to be regarded by those to whom it was addressed.[157] It is mainly because of this that its tone and tenor differs in accordance with the difference in the nature of the audience.

---

[152] Brothers of Shams ud din Ataka Khan who were posted at the time in the Punjab along with other members of the Ataka Khail.

[153] Cf. Iqtidar Alam Khan, 'The Nobility under Akbar and the Development of His Religious Policy 1560-80', *Journal of Royal Asiatic Society*, 1968, p. 32.

[154] See G.L. Lewis, 'The Utility of Ottoman Fathnamas', in Bernard Lewis and P.M. Holt (eds.), *Historians of the Middle East*, Oxford University Press, London, p. 192.

[155] Ibid., pp. 193-6.

[156] Ibid., p. 193.

[157] Compare *The Utility of Ottoman Fathnamas*, p. 193.

But unlike the *fathname of Eger*, the *Fathnama-i Chittor* is very useful as a reliable source of history for the siege and subsequent conquest of the fort. It provides a concise and accurate account of the progress of the siege under the personal supervision of the Emperor and the valiant resistance of the defenders of the fort. Like Eger, here also the entire garrison was put to sword when the fort fell but this gruesome fact has not been concealed and the *fathnama* clearly mentions it. The description of the siege is quite detailed and in complete conformity with the accounts of the chronicles. It provides minute details about the actual execution of the siege and also gives the names of the important people involved in the struggle on both sides. Therefore as a source of history for the battle that ended in the Mughal capture of the fort of Chittor, its utility and importance cannot be over emphasized.

One would, however, be building on 'shaky foundations' if one were basing on the sentiments expressed in the *fathnama* for assessing the actual policies of Akbar. From this point of view it is nothing more than sheer propaganda and a shrewd attempt at building a particular image among a section of his kingdom's population. This is not the occasion to go into the details of Akbar's Rajput policy. This much may, however, be said that control of Rajputana was one of the essential components of Akbar's vision of his empire. This end he wanted to achieve through peaceful means and his efforts in this direction were rewarded with some success. But defiance of the Rana was proving to be a stumbling block in his way and majority of the Rajput states were yet to accept this friendly offer. Akbar's patronage of the Kachwahas had already set an example for those who wished to join him in the enterprise of empire building. He felt that for success in Rajputana another example also needed to be set for those who continued to defy him. Chittor expedition was, therefore, undertaken solely to achieve this objective and it was successful as most of the Rajput states accepted his suzerainty after this event.[158] It was absolutely political in nature and religious considerations were not involved at all. Even Badauni does not allude to any such motive. He describes the expedition as a normal military campaign.[159] Abul

---

[158] *The Nobility under Akbar and the Development of his Religious Policy*, p. 32, n. 19.

[159] See Abd ul Qadir Badauni, *Muntakhab ut Twarikh*, ed. Ahmad Ali and Kabir ud din, College Press Calcutta, 1865, vol. II, pp. 102-4. Issuing of *Fathnama* is mentioned by him (p. 104) but Abul Fazl does not mention it.

Fazl, on the other hand, would like us to believe that this expedition was undertaken on the spur of the moment and it was not pre-planned. According to him this expedition was originally undertaken to quell the rebellion of the sons of Muhammad Sultan Mirza in Malwa and in fact it was brought about by foolish behaviour of Sakat Singh, son of Rana Udai Singh, who misunderstood a pleasantry of Akbar said in a jocular mood and fled from the royal camp. 'When the news of his flight reached the royal hearing, the Shahinshah's wrath was stirred up, and jest became earnest. And His Majesty's world-conquering genius decided to chastise him.'[160]

It would seem that Akbar's liberal religious policy was already causing uneasiness in some Muslim circles. The conquest of Chittor and ruthless massacre of the inhabitants and defenders of the fort provided him with an opportunity to project his image among the Muslims as a staunch and orthodox Muslim ruler and he decided to take advantage of it. This is the only instance in Akbar's entire career as a ruler when he went to such extremes. It was a calculated move to impress upon the Rajputs that for securing Rajputana he could go to any extent. As far as Akbar's liberal policy was concerned, its progress was not affected by this development in any way and it continued to evolve uninterrupted till it found its ultimate expression in the policy of *Sulh-i Kul* as Afzal Husain has convincingly proved.[161]

As noted earlier, *fathnamas* issued on the occasion of important victories were sent to different destinations within the dominion of the ruler and even outside it. However, *fathnamas* coming down from medieval India are very scarce and different versions of the same *fathnama* are not available. However, copies of the same Ottoman *fathnama* sent to various destinations are available. From their study it would clearly emerge that there is much difference in emphasis, content and details, which are sometimes quite substantial. Even the basic message that is sought to be conveyed through the medium of the letter of victory vastly differs from each other. Apparently, it is the nature of the audience to which a particular *fathnama* was addressed that determined the content

---

[160] *Akbar Nama*, vol. II, pp. 441-3.

[161] Afzal Husain, *Akbar's Religious Policy (1560-1579)—A Re-examination*, presented at the seminar 'Culture, Economy and Social Change in Medieval India (12th-18th Century)', CAS, Department of History, Aligarh Muslim University, Aligarh, January, 2002.

and tenor of its text. The *fathnamas* issued after the Ottoman victory at Chaldiran, for example, are preserved in *Mejmua'a-i Munshe 'at-i Selatin.*[162] Among the addressees are included people of vastly different backgrounds such as Selim's son, Suleyman, Khan of Crimea, *begs* of eastern lands, the *amirs* of the Kurds, chiefs of the tribes, notables of Tabriz and Rustem, the ruler of Luristan. These widely differ from each other in content, tenor and emphasis.[163] Clearly, difference in nature of the audience was responsible for this divergence in the content.

It would be only natural to presume that after significant victories like the conquest of Chittor, *fathnamas* would have been sent to many other regions and persons besides the nobles posted in the Punjab to whom this *fathnama* is addressed. But unfortunately no other copy of the *fathnama* has survived. Had other versions of this *fathnama* come down to us particularly those addressed to Rajput nobles, it would have been possible to conclude with some degree of confidence whether some change had really taken place in Akbar's religious policy around this time and whether this expedition was motivated in any degree by religious considerations.

The problem posed by the phraseology and tenor of the *Fathnama-i Chittor* could also be considered from yet another angle. Till the appearance of Abul Fazl on the Mughal literary scene, the tradition of Indo-Persian historiography as well as *fathnama* writing was familiar with only religious idiom. As no alternative interpretation of historical developments was available, history was written and understood in religious terms and it used to be profusely saturated with religious terminology. The struggle between the central authority headed by Muslim rulers and the regional powers represented by local chiefs was almost invariably presented as a struggle between Islam and infidelity. Moreover, in the area of the composition of *fathnamas* the only prototype that was available to the scribes at the court was the *fathnama* of Shaikh Zain, which in all likelihood served as the model for those who composed the *Fathnama-i Chittor.* A comparative study of these two *fathnamas* would go to reveal that in the composition of *Fathnama-i*

---

[162] Feridun Bey, *Mejmu'a-i Munshe'at-i Selatin,* Istanbul, 1265, vol. I, pp. 386-96, quoted from G.L. Lewis, p. 193.

[163] For discussion on this point see Lewis, pp. 193-4.

Chittor Shaikh Zain's *fathnama* has been very closely followed; even the opening lines are the same. Therefore even if Akbar had not wanted to use the occasion to bolster his image as *Badshah-i Islam*, since no alternative prototype was available to those who were charged with the responsibility of composing it, it is more likely that they would have pursued the same line of argument that they eventually did. It was only after the appearance of Abul Fazl on the scene that an attempt was made to break with the established prototypes and craft new literary traditions to suit the new philosophy and vision of the empire. Until then it was only a vision in the mind of Akbar and it was yet to be invested with the contents of a rational political philosophy that could serve as an alternative to the age-old ideas and practices. The credit for doing so goes entirely to Abul Fazl. He emphasized the Indian context in the writing of history and created an altogether new idiom that was non-religious and non-partisan. For this purpose he fashioned a new vocabulary. Time-honoured expressions, which had come to enjoy almost a degree of sanctity, were replaced by entirely non-religious terms. For example the term *ghazian-i Islam* that was in fact one of the key terms in the religious idiom, was changed with words like *ghazian-i daulat* and *ghazian-i Iqbal*. This provided an entirely new perspective to the Indian History writings and created space for an alternative interpretation of history. But before Abul Fazl it would not have been even conceivable. Therefore for all that we know, *Fathnama-i Chittor* might have acquired this particular character simply due to the fact that those who composed it did not have any other prototype to take recourse to. More cautious approach, therefore, needs to be adopted while using documents like the *Fathnama-i Chittor* for assessing Akbar's religious policy.

PETITIONS TO THE KING

There are a number of petitions addressed to the Emperor. Some of these were written in response of imperial *farmans*. Besides providing specimens for such petitions, they also throw light on the issues that formed the subject matter of this kind of correspondence between the Emperor and members of the nobility. History of Mughal relations with the kingdom of Khandesh is too well known. It began when Miran Mubarak married his daughter to Akbar in 1564 and reached its climax with the submission of Raja Ali Khan. In the light of available evidence on the subject, it would appear that during the reign of Muhammad Khan, Khandesh did not have any contact with the Mughals. But a petition included in the *Munshaat* would indicate that it was not the case. It would appear that at some point during his brief reign (1566-76) there was a move to annex the kingdom to the Mughal Empire. It would seem that Muhammad Khan succeeded in securing the good offices of some important Mughal noble who wrote a petition to the Emperor in this regard. This petition is preserved in the *Munshaat*.[164] It speaks about the receipt of successive letters from Muhammad Khan Farooqi expressing sincerity and sentiments of loyalty. It pleads for forgiveness for him and sparing his territories. One of the petitions dewells on the intense desire of the writer for going on Hajj pilgrimage but the impediments in the way, more particularly the dangers of the sea travel, had rendered it impossible. Without naming the Portuguese, it indirectly refers to their menace by quoting a verse of the Qur'an to convey this sense: 'There was a king who would confiscate the boats.'[165] Another petition speaks of the receipt of the *farman* directing the addressee to procure Circassian male and female slaves; jewels and other fine items for the imperial court and expresses regret for his inability to do so in spite of his best efforts.[166] Another petition seeks to draw the imperial attention to the depredations and devastation caused by the Uzbeks near Qallat.[167] One petition is in response of a *farman* directing the petitioner to make preparations for the conquest of the fort of Siwi.[168]

PETITIONS TO THE ROYAL LADIES

Munshaat-i Namakin also contains a number of petitions (*ariza*) addressed to the ladies of imperial household, including letters to a royal

[164] Document No. 67, pp. 161-2.

[165] Document No. 71, p. 168. This refers to the story of Prophet Musa and Khizr in the Qur'an (18/79).

[166] Document No. 72, pp. 169-71.

[167] Document No. 76, p. 174.

[168] Document No. 83, p. 182.

lady who is addressed as Bilqis Makani.[169] Apparently, it refers to Mother Queen Maryam Zamani. This is a unique feature of the *Munshaat*. Other *insha* collections generally don't contain letters addressed to the royal ladies. The petitioners include both male and female suppliants.[170] While some of the petitions would seem to have been included in the collection to serve as models for composing petitions to the ladies of the imperial household, others are clearly genuine letters, which refer and respond to specific situations and instructions. This could not be the case if the drafts were composed as models. It emerges from the contents of the petitions that communications were exchanged between the royal ladies and the members of the nobility on regular basis. The inclusion of model drafts would also indicate that this was the case otherwise there would not have been any need for it. It would also appear that the royal ladies took keen interest in the administrative affairs of the empire and they were approached by the members of the nobility to secure favours such as transfer of their postings, etc.

The first petition seeks to clarify the misunderstanding that some interested persons have sought to create in the mind of the addressee about the writer obviously as a part of palace intrigues.[171] One petition is in response of a communication received from a royal lady. The writer was asked to submit a report about general conditions obtaining in the region of his posting. In response he reports back that the people of the region are leading a life of peace and prosperity under the shadow of royal benevolence and justice.[172] Another petition is also in response of the instructions of a royal lady. The writer was directed to gather and send information about a certain person who has been referred as *besa'adat* (wretch). The writer informs the addressee that he had complied with the orders and instructions have been issued to the *shiqdars* and *amils* of the *parganas* to trace him out and assures her that as soon as any information is received in this regard it would be immediately communicated.[173] Another petition is also in response of a communica-

[169] Text, pp. 183-94. It would appear that the title of Bilqis Makani also refers to Maryam Zamani.

[170] For female petitioners, for example, see pp. 185, 186 and 189-90.

[171] Document No. 85, p. 183.

[172] Document No. 86, p. 184.

[173] Document No. 87, pp. 184-5.

tion from a royal lady. After expressing her grateful thanks for the favour, she goes to say that her directive has been carried out. She was asked to console a certain dignitary who was apparently bereaved about that time.[174] But by far the most interesting petition is addressed to Bilqis Makani and it has been sent from Sind where the writer was posted at that time. The petitioner says that he has been serving in the region for the last two years, some of which has been spent in Bhakkar and the rest in Siwistan and Thatta. Earlier he had served in places such as Kabul and Kashmir. As a result, he has remained separated from his family for the last twelve years. As humans are granted but short life, he pleads with the queen for the grant of leave to join his family.[175] All this would go to suggest that royal ladies played significant role in matters of administration.

LETTERS

The *Munshaat* contains a large section of letters, which are addressed to the highest officers of the government, friends, poets, physicians, parents, teachers, brothers, sisters, sons and so on. Besides providing examples of the kind of letters that were exchanged between the people belonging to the various strata of the society, they also provide useful insights about contemporary society and give an idea about the issues that formed the subject matter of this kind of correspondence.

A letter addressed to the *wazir* and sent from Sind throws interesting light on the relations of the Tarkhans and the Mughals.[176] It was written in response of a letter of the *wazir* and besides seeking to remove a number of misunderstandings and misconceptions about Sind and its ruling family ostensibly expressed in the letter of the *wazir*, it provides a wealth of information about the conditions obtaining in Sind, its material resources and the nature of its agricultural products. It sheds interesting light on the relations of the Tarkhans with the Portuguese. In this connection it goes to say that in the last 78 years when the Tarkhans left their hearth and home in Qandahar and came and settled in Sind,

[174] Document No. 88, pp. 185-6.
[175] Document No. 94, pp. 190-1.
[176] Document No. 112, pp. 218-22.

the Portuguese simultaneously extended their authority over most of the islands of the region, but maintained cordial relations with the Tarkhans. In fact, it had been a tradition for the Portuguese captain to come every year to Sind with tribute (*rasm-i khidmat*), offerings (*pesh-kash*) and gifts (*tuhaf*).[177] It states that in general Sind produced only rice and fish. The best districts of Sind were Bhakkar, Sivi, Gunjaba and Fathpur. But agricultural production there too was also confined to barley, wheat, gram and *juwar*.[178] According to it the ruling family of Sind had very cordial relations with the Qizlibash whose territory lay at a distance of 16 days journey and envoys were regularly exchanged between them but since the Tarkhans entered into a relationship with the Mughals these ties had been totally snapped.[179] The letter contains many other titbits of information about Sind.

Another letter addressed to the *wazir* speaks about a siege that is not making satisfactory progress as the enemy is entrenched in a near-invincible fort. It requests for some *tufang* to be sent so that the sky-high fort could be reduced to rubble.[180]

A letter addressed to *sadr* speaks about the outbreak of plague in the region in which majority of the weaver community perished and the few who were left were in a very bad condition. It would appear that the region was known for producing quality clothes and the writer was asked to send some of it to the addressee. He apologises for his inability to do so due to this reason.[181] A letter to a Saiyid talks about the sale of red gems (*aqiq*) which it would seem, he was commissioned to sell on behalf of the addressee. Now he wants to know whether it should be bought again.[182] A letter acknowledges the receipt of two Arabian dogs sent by the addressee.[183] Another letter to a Saiyid speaks about some unspecified disaster that had destroyed both the winter and spring crops and enough water was not available for summer sowing. In spite of this pitiable condition the revenue officers were extremely

---

177 Document No. 112, p. 219.

178 Ibid., p. 221.

179 Ibid., pp. 219-20.

180 Document No. 106, p. 207.

181 Document No. 118, pp. 230-1.

182 Document No. 124, p. 238.

183 Document No. 123, p. 237.

active in their demand.[184] One of the letters addressed to a scholar informs the addressee about the completion of commentary on *Tuhfa-i Shahi*. It also informs that at present the writer is busy in the study of *Sahih Bukhari*[185] in the company of a gentleman who is a disciple of Ibn Hajar.[186] Besides he is also engaged in the study of the *Commentary of Baizawi*[187] on the Holy Qur'an. The writer also seems to have compiled another commentary on some book that he does not name.[188] A letter addressed to a *qazi* requests the addressee to buy selected books from the collection of a late *qazi* if these are put on sale.[189] A letter to a physician speaks with great satisfaction about the pleasant and prosperous conditions in which the writer finds himself and that he is using this opportunity in the acquisition of the knowledge of Arabic language and *tafsir* (exegesis of the Qur'an). He also adds that most of the time he is busy in the study of various branches of knowledge particularly *Sharh* of *Isharat, Muhakamat, Shifa* and *Mijasti* (the *almagest*) with great attention. He further informs the addressee that he had also finished writing a commentary on *Tuhfa-i Shahi* and had sent it for the perusal of his teacher along with a treatise in the refutation of the theory of *Huyula* (matter). He makes a fervent request for correcting any errors that might have found way into the text.[190] In yet another letter, also to a physician, the author says that during his studies of *Isharat* and its commentary *Muhakamat* he had some doubts about the expositions

---

[184] Document No. 125, pp. 240-1.

[185] The most authentic collection of *Hadith* compiled by Imam Muhammad bin Ismail Bukhari (810-70). For a brief biographical account see J. Robeson, *Encyclopedia of Islam* (New Edition), Leiden and London, 1960, vol. I, pp. 1296-7.

[186] Ibn Hajar 'Asqalani (1372-1449) was one of the most renowned scholars of *Hadith* and compiler of the most authoritative commentary of Bukhari, *Fath al Bari*. His work in the field of *Hadith* is considered to constitute the final summation of the science of *Hadith*. For a brief life sketch see F. Rosenthal, *Encyclopedia of Islam*, Leiden and London, 1971, vol. III, pp. 776-8.

[187] Abdullah bin 'Umar al-Baizawi (d.1286) was a scholar and exegete. He is best known for his exegesis of the Qur'an entitled *Anwar-ut Tanzil wa Asrar ut Tawil* popularly known as *Tafsir-i Baizawi*. See Khair ud din al-Zarkali, *Al A'lam*, Berut, 1984, vol. 4, p. 110.

[188] Document No. 135, p. 254.

[189] Document No. 137, pp. 256-7.

[190] Document No. 140, pp. 259-60.

of the author of *Muhakamat* and wrote down his objections but not being sure of his own abilities, he decided to send it for the perusal of the addressee for his expert opinion so that its actual worth could be ascertained.[191] All this would go to show the popularity of philosophy among the educated and the literati of the period. A letter to a Shaikh acknowledges the receipt of a ring with *Ayat al Kursi*[192] inscribed on a red gem set in it and a *khil'at* of brocade embroidered with gold.[193]

A letter to a poet most probably located in the capital speaks about the unusual assemblage of poets and literati of rare excellence, both of Indian extraction and those who have risen in foreign lands, leading to extraordinary literary activity there. The writer frets for not being a part of this august company.[194] A letter to a spiritual preceptor (*murshid*) states that the writer had the honour of belonging to the *Qadiri Silsilah* and therefore he interested in the *Tafsir-i Qadiri* and other writings related to the *silsilah*. He has therefore requested a certain person to take the trouble of travelling to different regions to procure that book for him.[195]

This section also contains letters to parents, brothers and sisters. A letter to father states that the writer is languishing for the last one year in prison (*bandi khana*) and sees little hope for getting out of it. He requests his father to intercede and bring an end to his misfortune.[196] In another letter the writer seeks forgiveness of his father for his inability to send fruits of a certain place, which were apparently liked by the father. The son writes that he took the trouble of travelling to that place, but found that excessive heat had destroyed the crop that year and the precious little that was left was unworthy of being sent.[197]

A number of letters are addressed to teachers. One of them contains recommendation for a certain person whose name has been omitted, in accordance with the general policy of the compiler. The person is said to have achieved great excellence in poetry and other branches of

---

[191] Document No. 141, pp. 260-3.

[192] The celebrated verse of the Qur'an (2/255).

[193] Document No. 133, p. 249.

[194] Document No. 143, pp. 264-6.

[195] Document No. 145, pp. 268-9.

[196] Document No. 149, pp. 272-3.

[197] Document No. 150, pp. 273-4.

learning. As he is heading for the capital, where presumably the teacher is located, and he is very keen to join imperial service, the addressee is requested to extend every possible help to him and introduce him to the court at an opportune time.[198] Another letter of recommendation also addressed to a teacher talks about a certain Mir Iraqi who is said to have been in the service of Shah Abbas and had achieved distinction in poetry, history and recitation of the *Shah Nama*. He had left his hearth and home to join the imperial court. When he reached this region he was obliged to stay here as it was rainy season and it was excessively hot. It is requested that he may be kindly received and introduced at the court at an appropriate time.[199] There is another very interesting letter to a teacher. First it recommends a particular young man to the care of the addressee. Then it talks about dispatch of supplies to Qandahar, which appears from the context to have been recently brought under the imperial control. Consequently the inhabitants are enjoying a very blissful life so much so that the price of grain is cheaper there in comparison to this place. It states that the writer had sent his son with a petition to the court and it is hoped that he would kindly see to it that the latter receives some good job there.[200] In both the cases addressees are apparently important people who are in a position to introduce others to the court.

There are also some letters addressed to brothers. The addressee of one of the letters would seem to be holding some important position at the court. The letter cautions him against intoxication of the proximity of the king as the world and its charms are transient and ephemeral and reliance on them only leads to disgrace both in this world as well as the world to come. Besides giving numerous advices, it also exhorts him to say the truth in which in fact lies the good of the king and the subjects.[201] There are also a large number of letters of congratulations for various occasions as well as letters of condolence.[202]

---

198 Document No. 154, pp. 277-8.
199 Document No. 155, pp. 278-9.
200 Document No. 156, p. 280.
201 Document No. 157, pp. 281-2.
202 Text, pp. 292-328.

NIKAH AND ITS CONDITIONS

Munshaat-i Namakin contains a large number of legal and contractual documents which throw considerable light not only on legal procedures that were followed during those days but also inevitably reflect the conditions obtaining in the contemporary society.[203] Besides documents relating to buying and purchasing and other such normal activities of day-to-day life, there are some very important documents included in this section, which are not found in any other *insha* collection of the period. For example there are two documents relating to *nikah* (marriage contract),[204] which throw very interesting light on the institution of marriage as it existed among the aristocracy and apparently these are the only documents relating to *nikah* coming down to us from the early Mughal period. It would seem that during the early Mughal times, the Muslim women had rights and powers, which remain a distant dream for their sisters even at the beginning of twenty-first century. Besides a very high marriage settlement (*mahr*), four very significant conditions were contained in the marriage contract and all these were clearly in favour of women. These conditions are referred in the documents as the four conditions of *Shari'at,* which are well known among the Muslims. This would mean that these were the usual terms of marriage contract during those days at least among the well-to-do Muslims. First, the man would not enter into marriage contract with any other woman. Secondly, the man would not stay away from the woman for one complete year in a manner that her maintenance would not reach her and in case this happens, the women would be entitled to terminate the marriage with one final *talaq* (*talaq-i bain*). Thirdly, unless warranted by some serious offence or perfidy committed by the woman, the man would not beat her in such a manner that leaves its impression on any part of her body. In case of the materialization of any of these conditions, the woman would be at liberty to dissolve the marriage with one final *talaq* (*talaq-i bain*) from the man who is guilty of a religious crime (*mujrim-i shara'i*) whenever and wherever she desires and the settlement amount would be payable to her. The fourth condition is that the man would not bring a concubine of any description upon her, be it Indian, Armenian or

[203] Text, pp. 331-70.

[204] Documents No. 205-6, pp. 333-5.

of any other description. In case he brings a concubine upon her, she would be free to sell the same at the prevalent price and keep the price as part of her marriage settlement.[205] It was only with these stringent conditions that a marriage was solemnized. It may also be useful to note in this regard that violation of these conditions has been termed a religious offence. Moreover, in both the cases the amount of settlement is also quite substantial. The first document stipulates a settlement of four thousand *dinars,* one *dinar* weighing one *misqal* and half *dang* of pure silver. The other document sets it at forty *mann* of dried fine saffron-coloured silk weighed with the silk of Herat, half of which is to be handed over immediately and the other half would have to be paid in the case of the dissolution of the marriage for any reason. In addition to it, two thousand rupees also had to be paid, half of it immediately and half to be differed till the termination of the marriage.[206]

SLAVERY

A number of documents in this category belong to various aspects of slavery including the marriage of the slaves that would suggest wide prevalence of the institution of slavery during the period under discussion.[207]

WAQF

Other legal documents included in the collection are of very diverse nature such as giving the power of attorney, *hiba, wadi'at* (keeping something in trust) and *'ariyat* (borrowing).[208] There are also some documents relating to *waqf,* which are again not found in other collections of *insha* coming down from early Mughal period. In fact, there are three documents relating to *waqf.*[209] First relates to a *waqf* on a *madrasah,* the second on self and offspring and the third on a mosque. After giving complete details about the property to be bequeathed

[205] Document No. 206, pp. 333-5.
[206] Ibid., p. 335.
[207] Text, pp. 335-40, also see pp. 365, 366-8.
[208] Documents No. 214-19, pp. 340-3.
[209] Documents No. 220-22, pp. 344-8.

and its surroundings, the document prescribes the conditions set by the donor (*waqif*). The first condition is that the donor will be the custodian (*mutawalli*) during his own life with full liberty to manage the endowment according to his judgement. After him the one who is most competent and learned among his male offspring would be custodian of the endowment generation after generation. In case all of them are equally competent and learned, the one who is senior in age would take the charge. If none remains in the male line, then someone from the female line of his offspring would be the custodian. In case no one remains from among his descendants to look after the property, the teacher of the *madrasah* would be the custodian. If the custodian were from among the descendants of the donor, he would take one-tenth of the income of the property as his fee for looking after it. Others would take their fee according to their work.[210]

IJARA, RIHN AND TRADE

The other legal documents included in this collection relate to *ijara* of *sarai* and *ijara* of land,[211] hiring a maid for feeding milk to the child,[212] hiring beast of load,[213] confession for having taken loan,[214] document for entering into arrangement for *rihn* (pawn),[215] and *rihn* of slaves and maids.[216] This would suggest that even slaves and maids were used as objects for *rihn*. There are also some documents that relate to various aspects of trade particularly various conditions of partnership in which one party provides the capital and the other carries on the trade, and profits are shared.[217] There are two documents concerning handing over the land to somebody to carry on agriculture (*muzara'at*) on the condition of paying a fixed portion of the produce. The owner of the land would hand over the land to the farmer (*bazrgar*) along with the

[210] Document No. 220, pp. 344-7.
[211] Documents No. 223-24, pp. 348-50.
[212] Document No. 225, pp. 350-1.
[213] Document No. 226, p. 351.
[214] Document No. 227, pp. 351-3.
[215] Document No. 228, p. 353.
[216] Document No. 229, pp. 353-4.
[217] Document No. 234-36, pp. 356-7.

necessary quantity of seeds. The other inputs would be arranged by the farmer. The produce would be shared between them equally or one-third would go to the owner of the land and two-thirds to the farmer.[218] The other document stipulates that one-fourteenth of the produce would go to the owner of the land. But in this case the farmer would be responsible for the payment of revenue as well as cost of the seeds.[219]

WASIYAT (WILL)

Islamic law spells out the rules of inheritance very clearly leaving no scope for any kind of ambiguity. But at the same time, it gives permission to make a will for one-third of the property if one wishes to do so. It should, however, be kept in mind that those who are entitled by law to a share in the inheritance could not be beneficiary of the will. The will could be made for charitable purposes or in favour of those who have no share in the inheritance. Due to this reason there has been a general tendency among the rich and wealthy to make a will and thereby allocate one-third or a portion thereof in favour of some person or some institution. It would be useful to remember that the will has full legal sanctity. It would, therefore, not be far-fetched to assume that in medieval India many people would have made wills but unfortunately we don't have any model of a will in the traditional *insha* collections. *Munshaat-i Namakin* is perhaps the only *insha* collection coming down from early Mughal period that contains one model of *wasiyat* (will).[220] It also speaks about the appointment of an executor of the will and payment of debts outstanding against the name of the testator.

BATAI (CROP SHARING) AND *IJARA*

There is a document containing an agreement for *batai* (crop sharing). It is also probably the only document of its nature coming down from the early Mughal period. It is in the form of agreement of the *muqaddams* of two villages. As is usually the case with the documents contained in

218. Document No. 237, p. 358.
219 Document No. 238, p. 358.
220 Document No. 239, pp. 359-60.

this collection names of the *muqaddams*, villages and *pargana* as well the date are omitted. The basic thrust of the document is that this arrangement was arrived at on the request of the *muqaddams* as they considered it more beneficial to their interests and more conducive to their prosperity and well-being. According to this arrangement the produce would be equally shared after deducting the expenses. The authorities acceded to this request. In return, the *muqaddams* agreed to exert themselves to the best of their ability to protect the grain from pilferage. They also undertook to increase the revenue by substantially extending the cultivation.[221]

Another document relates to the *ijara* of land. This arrangement has also been made at the request of the *muqaddams*. They approached the concerned authorities with the request that the wasteland of a particular village be assigned to them with effect from the beginning of the *kharif* harvest and agreed to pay the revenue (*mal-i wajibi*) according to the terms of *ijara*. Their request was acceded and the land in question was assigned to them on the terms of *ijara*. While a portion of the money payable according to *ijara* was remitted in favour of the *muqaddams*, they undertook to pay the rest.[222] Both in this document as well in the earlier one relating to *batai*, the concerned authority has been named as *nawab-i namdar* and *nawab-i namdari* respectively, which obviously refers to the *jagirdar* of the region. Similarly, in both the documents it is mentioned in the end that the purpose of this writing is that it could be used whenever there is a need for it.[223]

DIRECTIVES AND UNDERTAKINGS

A document directs the shop owners, merchants, *sarrafs* and the rest of the inhabitants of the city of Bhakkar to make transactions with the government employees only in cash and not on credit. The troopers as well as other employees of the state either get their salary through *jagir* or in cash from the treasury on a monthly basis. In spite of this, they make their purchasing on credit and don't pay for it easily. The

[221] Document No. 245, p. 368.
[222] Document No. 246, p. 369.
[223] Documents No. 245, 246, pp. 368-9.

inhabitants of the city are, therefore, directed that during the tenure of *nawab namdar* all transactions should be made only in cash. Anybody found violating this rule would be taken to task.[224]

Besides referring to the *jagirdar* as *nawab-i namadar* in this document the name of the place has also been retained. This makes it possible for us to identify the person who has been referred to in these documents as *nawab-i namdar.* Obviously, it refers to Saiyid Abu'l Qasim himself. Bhakkar was assigned in his *jagir* in the 39th regnal year (March 1594–March 1595).[225] According to Yusuf Mirak, it was the *jagir* vacated by Abdur Rahim Khani-i Khanan at Bhakkar that was assigned to Abu'l Qasim.[226] Abu'l Qasim has reproduced the *farman* appointing him as the *jagirdar* of Bhakkar.[227] Again Bhakkar was assigned to him in 1007/August 1598–July 1599.[228] Most probably these documents belong to the period when Abdu'l Qasim was holding the charge of Bhakkar. Some of the documents that follow also seem to belong to that period.[229] These include undertakings and agreements, which are termed as *katabah* and *'adhnama* respectively. First *katabah* is a commitment of the members of the Saiyids of a city to acknowledge two members of their own community as their chief (*naqibs*) and accept their authority to settle their affairs in accordance with the *Shari'at.*[230] Another pledge is by some people who had committed theft and were duly punished for that crime. Later, their punishment was remitted and an undertaking was taken from them not to commit theft or any other heinous crime in future and not to give quarter to thieves. In case of violation they would be liable for punishment appropriate to their offence.[231] In another such document Bomia *zamindars* undertake to provide help

---

[224] Document No. 247, pp. 369-70.

[225] *Akbar Nama,* vol. III, p. 666.

[226] *Mazhar-i Shah Jahani,* p. 28.

[227] Documents No. 34, 36, pp. 91-2, 95-6.

[228] *Maathir ul Umaro,* vol. III, p. 75. Also see Document No. 36, pp. 95-7.

[229] See Documents No. 248-53, pp. 370-5.

[230] Document No. 248, pp. 370-71. For the office of *naqib* see Document No. 28, pp. 79-81.

[231] Document No. 249, p. 371.

to the royal army whenever needed.[232] This section also contains three *'ahdnamas* (pledges) affirming loyalty to the royal authority.[233]

HUMOUR

Obviously, *Munshaat-i Namakin* is an *insha* collection with a difference. It contains many items and categories of documents which are not found in other contemporary or even later collections of *insha*. Some of these would not be even considered by many to come within the purview of *insha*. Some of these categories have been noticed above. One such category is a section containing a number of entries relating to humour. Apparently, humour could not be included within the ambit of *insha* by any definition of the term. But Abu'l Qasim seems to have believed that humour, being part and parcel of a balanced life, could not be excluded from the scheme of instruction of the cultured and the refined. He prefaces the section with the general remark that humour and wit are well received by the people as they serve as means of refreshing the soul and providing entertainment to the mind. However, excessive humour and hilariousness leads to forgetfulness and negligence and causes dullness of heart. Constant seriousness saddens the heart while too much joviality and jesting affects the religious sensibility.[234] This preface is followed by some extremely humorous pieces. The first is a description of a miser whom the author and his friends supposedly met while they were on a delightful pleasure trip. The description of the miser is so vivid and humorous that it would require not only great command over the language and its usages but also very sharp and witty imagination. Though it is well nigh impossible to attempt a rendering of its various shades and nuances, an attempt is being made to provide an idea of Abu'l Qasim's sense of humour tinged with very subtle satire and his competence to very effectively communicate it to the readers. The way Quranic verses have been used to heighten the effect would go to show his wide knowledge of the Holy Book. Some idea of these things can be formed from the following snippets.

---

[232] Document No. 250, p. 372.

[233] Document Nos. 251, 252, 253, pp. 372-6.

[234] Document No. 254, pp. 376-7.

A party of friends undertakes a pleasure trip in the delightful season of spring. They were having wonderful time until they bumped into a miser, which dealt a severe jolt to their blissful state. They had knocked at his door with the hope of hospitality but they were in for a shock. 'In the meanwhile the eye fell on his kitchen which presented the spectacle of "the valley without cultivation," '[235] the plates were lying in prostration as if before the Lord and the spoons were left with eyes wide open as if 'his eyes had turned white with sorrow',[236] the table had obviously taken leave from holding any kind of burden and on the bread, that was already withering, was written that none has ever been able to see your face though there are so many in race for this privilege. His cook intonated that

Your bread is more inviolable than your wife
Neither strangers nor relatives could ever hope to see its face.
Better keep your bread in place of your wife,
And turn the wretch out of the place.

The butler raised his hand in supplication 'Our Lord, send from heaven a table (laden with viands)'.[237] On the corners of the goblets was written, 'Those who drink from it do not belong to me'[238] and at the borders of the dishes was inscribed, 'Those who don't taste it belong to me.'[239] Both slaves and free men who are in his service chant this song with the weeping eyes and burning heart;

The miser whose niggardliness is such
If his filthy hands were to be severed
It would not be possible that even one or two drops of blood
Would get out of his luckless hand.[240]

---

[235] Qur'an, 14/37.
[236] Qur'an, 12/84.
[237] Qur'an, 5/114.
[238] Qur'an, 2/249.
[239] Qur'an, 2/249.
[240] Document No. 255, pp. 377-9.

The other humorous piece consists of a hilarious letter addressed to a comedian who was considered to be unrivalled in his profession and it makes an extremely interesting reading.[241]

THE BASIC PRECEPTS OF ISLAM

Structurally *Munshaat-i Namakin* is divided into an introduction, eight chapters and a rather longish *Khatimah* (conclusion). The concluding remarks almost constitute a full-fledged chapter. Apparently, this entire section falls out of the scope of *insha* literature. *Insha* has not been defined by any scholar working in the area to include religious precepts and practices. It would appear that Abu'l Qasim was also perhaps conscious of this anomaly and hence felt it necessary to offer some explanation for it. He says in his introduction that the concluding remarks (*Khatimah*) contain things which would apparently seem to fall outside the scope of *insha*. But he insists that on deeper consideration this would appear not to be altogether irrelevant either.[242] This explanation, however, does not solve the problem and the question remains why the author felt it necessary to include a chapter on the precepts and practices of Islam in a book of *insha* and what he actually means by deeper consideration. For finding an answer to these vexed questions one has perhaps to take into consideration the unusual conditions obtaining at the time of its compilation, which are most likely to have influenced his decision to append a chapter on religion at the end of his collection. Obviously, unusual conditions would necessitate unusual responses.

Munshaat was compiled towards the end of Akbar's reign in 1599 when the emperor's power and glory were at their zenith. It also constitutes the last phase of his religious experimentation culminating in the policy of *sulh-i kul*. This was responsible for triggering a chain of events, which generated considerable disquiet and tension among the Muslim religious circles. What Rizvi terms as 'new trends of Islam in India'[243] which required those who subscribed to them to abjure what was termed as traditional and metaphorical Islam (*Din-i taqlidi wa*

[241] Document No. 256, pp. 380-1.

[242] Introduction, p. 3.

[243] S.A.A. Rizvi, *Religious and Intellectual History of Muslims in Akbar's Reign with Special Reference to Abul Fazl*, Munshiram Manoharlal, Delhi, 1976, p. 44.

majazi)[244] were perceived by Muslims with much apprehension and foreboding as it tended to weaken the grip of the religion and create indifference towards religious prescriptions. As it was backed by the power of the state and the proponents of the new policy at the court were going all out to impress upon the people that the traditional religion was no more relevant and it had outlived its utility. This was increasingly affecting the people at large. The religious classes, therefore, felt it necessary to do something to resist, reform and reverse this trend. It was the realization of this need that led Badauni to write *Najat ur Rashid* in the beginning of the last decade of the sixteenth century.[245] Apparently, the same concerns prompted Abu'l Qasim to append a section on basic practices of religion in a collection of *insha* where it did not obviously belong. Both the works might have emanated from the same concerns but their approach is widely different from each other. *Najat ur Rashid* is basically concerned with don'ts; the things religion prohibits and wants to be shunned and avoided. These are the small and big sins, offences and misdemeanours some of which would not even seem to many to be part of religion. But in fact these transgressions not only militate against the spiritual well-being of the individuals but also tend to generate tension in the society. Hence they assume great importance and need to be avoided to safeguard the society against these dangers.

The *Munshaat-i Namakin* is concerned more with the positive aspect of the religion; what the faithful need to do to remain within the confines of the religion. It deals with those basic aspects of Islam which a Muslim needs to know and act upon to remain a Muslim. As a literary form *insha* was very much in vogue in those days because it helped in cultivating a refined and sophisticated taste for communicating with others as well as opening up possibilities for government employment by providing necessary training in dealing with various kinds of government papers. A work of *insha*, therefore, could be expected to have wide circulation among the educated classes and within easy reach of the elite, which

---

[244] Abdul Qadir Badauni, *Muntakhab ut Tawarikh*, vol. II, p. 304.

[245] Badauni wrote *Najat ur Rashid* in 1591. It has been edited by Saiyid Moinul Haq and published by Idarah Tahqiqat-i Pakistan, Lahore in 1972. For an analysis of the work see I.A. Zilli, Badauni Revisited: An Analytical Study of *Najat ur Rashid* in Iqtidar Husain Siddiqui (ed.), *Medieval India—Essays in Intellectual Thought and Culture*, Manohar, Delhi, 2003, pp. 143-68.

were in the forefront of the new dispensation. This would have been perhaps the most unobtrusive way to bring the basic teachings of the religion to the notice of those who, according to the perception of the author, would have been in greatest need for it, but without appearing to be taking recourse to preaching and thereby causing offence to their sensibilities and arousing suspicion. This would seem to be the reason behind Abu'l Qasim's decision to append a full-fledged section under the misleading caption of *khatimah* at the end of his collection.

The *khatimah* thus deals with the essentials of the Islamic faith. It is divided into nine sections. It is to be noted that the pronouncements set in the section are in accordance with the Hanafi School of Jurisprudence. A brief description of the various sections of this chapter would give us some idea about its contents.

Section I	Basic articles of Islamic faith.
Section II	Preconditions of *Salat* (prayer).
Section III	How to perform *Salat*.
Section IV	Relates to the *Salat* of *Id* and the *Khutba* of *Id* and *Juma'*.
Section V	Relates to the *Salat* for rain (*istisqa*) and that of eclipses (*kusuf* and *Khusuf*).
Section VI	Relates to *'Aqiqa*.
Section VII	Relates to prayers and invocations (*du'a*).
Section VIII	Some more prayers. The prayers and invocations noted in this section are those which are resorted to in contingencies like epidemics, other natural calamities and difficult situations. It gives formulae for preparing amulets (*t'awiz*) for various situations. The number of invocations included here is very large and these cover almost all the common diseases and other such difficult situations, which are bound to occur in the day-to-day life of an ordinary man.
Section IX	Relates to last rites.

However only very select portions of this section have been included in this selection, to give an idea about aspects of religious life during those days.

KHUTBA OF *JUMA'* AND *IDS*

Besides their religious significance, *khutbas* of Friday congregations (*Juma*) and *Ids* occupy great political importance. During the medieval times *khutba* and *sikka* were considered to be the main instruments of the declaration of authority of a ruler. Inclusion of the name of the ruler in the *khutba* signified the acknowledgement of his authority by the concerned people. This was, however, not the main function of the *khutba*. During the early period of Islamic history, the *khutba* in fact provided to the rulers a platform to discuss issues that concerned the community and share views with them. But as time passed it assumed the position of a ritual with a set pattern. Instead of delivering a speech on the current issues, it became a recitation with a set phraseology. Some verses of the Qur'an and some Prophetic traditions were put together along with invoking blessings for the first four Pious Caliphs as well as members of the Prophet's family. The *khutbas* of *Id ul Fitr* and *Id ul Azha* also contain some traditions specifically relating to these occasions. The *khutba* also contains general exhortation to the Muslims to lead a virtuous life in accordance with the prescriptions of the religion.

The *Munshaat* contains a number of *khutbas* for Friday congregations (*Juma*) as well as *Id ul Fitr* and *Id ul Azha*.[246] Most of them seem to have been given as illustrations and only two appear to be reproductions of actual *khutbas* used for the purposes of recitation in mosques as only these two contain the names of Akbar and his ancestors.[247] In both the cases the ancestry of Akbar is traced up to Amir Timur. An analysis of the contents of *khutbas* would reveal that these are strictly in line with the traditional *khutbas* without any apparent deviation from the traditional framework that was used for them. Except on one instance when Akbar had recited some verses of Faizi,[248] while delivering the Friday *khutba* in the mosque of Fathpur Sikri, he did not seem to have made any attempt to alter the content, format and phraseology of *khutba* read in his realm.

---

[246] See Documents No. 257-62, pp. 381-8.

[247] Documents No. 259 and 262, pp. 381-5, 387-8.

[248] *Muntakhab ut Tawarikh*, vol. II, p. 248.

DU'A (INVOCATIONS)

There is a section on invocations (*du'a*).[249] In the beginning the preconditions of the *du'a* have been discussed,[250] followed by a very large number of invocations for every possible contingency. But only a few have been included in the present selection. These would give an idea about the concerns and anxieties of the people, the common ailments from which they suffered and the problems which they faced in their day-to-day life. A number of invocations deal with the problems relating to the kings such as protection from the tyranny of rulers,[251] invocations for going to the presence of the rulers and[252] invocations for warding of evil from the kings.[253] There are some other invocations which are also concerned with the rulers though indirectly. For example, there is an invocation which is to be read when one fears evil from someone.[254] Another invocation is for deliverance from the mischief of oppressors.[255] This would give an indication of the risks an individual had to face in his daily life. Some of the other invocations relate to relief from ailments,[256] invocation for the recovery of run-away slaves,[257] invocation for lost property[258] and for the protection of merchandise.[259] There are a number of invocations as well as *naqsh* (charm) relating to horses,[260] suggesting the importance of the animal during the period. Among the invocations is a prescription for curbing turbulent behaviour of a horse. Incidentally, the same prescription is recommended for curing impudence of wayward boys and girls.[261] There are also some invocations and *naqsh* (charm) for curing the evil influence of demons

---

[249] Documents No. 263-79, pp. 389-98.
[250] Document No. 263, pp. 389-91.
[251] Document No. 264, p. 392.
[252] Document No. 268, p. 394.
[253] Document No. 271, p. 395.
[254] Document No. 269, p. 395.
[255] Document No. 271, p. 395.
[256] Document Nos. 273, 274, p. 396.
[257] Document No. 275, p. 397.
[258] Document No. 276, p. 397.
[259] Document No. 277, p. 397.
[260] Document Nos. 278, 282, pp. 397-9.
[261] Document No. 281, p. 399.

and evil spirits.[262] Inclusion of these invocations in a book like this and in a chapter that was meant to give some idea about the basic precepts of Islam would go to suggest that belief in demons and such other superstitions must have been very strong in the society. There is also an invocation for the rupture of the navel.[263] This may be taken to indicate that perhaps this ailment was common in those days.

MEDICINES AND SPELLS FOR SOME AILMENTS

The *khatimah* also contains a small section on what the author calls 'The Medicine for the Poor.' (*Dawa' ul Masakin*)[264] Prominence in this section has been given to the treatment of small pox (*judari*), which the author also refers to as *sitla* in Hindi. The treatment of this dreaded disease includes a detailed prescription consisting of items which could be available even to the poor. It also prescribes the diet that should be given to the patient during the period of treatment.[265] An amulet has also been prescribed for curing small pox, which should be put under the pillow of the patient.[266] The most interesting part of this section consists of two spells for scorpion bite, which have been termed by the author as *afsun*.[267] These are not in Persian but in Hindi, nevertheless the author has chosen to include them in his work. It is indeed surprising to find this entry in a section that in itself is out of place in the book. The inclusion of this section can be justified only by the strong desire of the author to introduce to the readers the most essential teachings of Islam at a time when the grip of religion was perceived to be weakening. But these two spells clearly contravene the basic Islamic belief in monotheism as they make appeal, among other things, to Mahadev, and contain references Luna Chamari and Dhanwanter Ved. While the first is entirely composed of non-Islamic ideas and concepts,[268] the second contains some words and concepts from Muslim cultural

[262] Documents Nos. 279, 280, p. 398.
[263] Document No. 274, p. 396.
[264] Document No. 283, pp. 400-2.
[265] Document No. 283, p. 400.
[266] Document No. 284, p. 401.
[267] Document Nos. 285-6, pp. 401-2.
[268] Document No. 285, pp. 401-2.

tradition such as *takht-i Sulaiman* and *pak pani* (pure water).[269] The first consists of only Hindi vocabulary while the second contains a number of Persian words such a *takht, pak, zamin* and *asman* though the main thrust remains the same as in the first. This tends to make the language more akin to Urdu and most clearly demonstrates that the exchange of ideas was freely taking place on both sides.

Coming as it does from a man of Abu'l Qasim's background, these references acquire added significance. It is evident from the contents of the book that Abdu'l Qasim was a deeply religious person. He hailed from a strong religious background. His father was trustee of the mausoleum of Imam Ali Riza at Mashhad.[270] He was born in Qandahar and hence was a first generation immigrant. Most probably he did not have much opportunity to mix and interact with the non-Muslim population of the country as most of his postings were in Sind and frontier regions. Still he was not only familiar with these spells but also did not have any reservation about including them in his collection. Obviously, origins of this highly eclectic approach rooted in open-minded appreciation for the cultural norms of other segments of the society and respect for local traditions cannot be traced to the religious policies of Akbar. Such developments do not happen overnight; they evolve over a long period of time. In fact, it was part and parcel of the new cultural ethos that had come into being as a result of the coming together of the two communities and mutual appreciation for each other's religion and culture. This process of assimilation was facilitated and made possible by the very sensible policies of the majority of the Delhi Sultans as well as the Sufi and Bhakti movements. These factors combined to create necessary conditions in which ideas could be freely exchanged between the two cultural traditions. Akbar's policies were not the beginning of the process; rather they were culmination of a long drawn process that had taken centuries to mature and reach this point. There could not be a better proof of this new ethos than the mixed vocabulary of the spells and their inclusion in this collection in a section

---

[269] Document No. 286, p. 402.

[270] See Mir Ali Sher Qani Thattavi, *Tuhfat ul Kiram*, Matba Nasiri, Delhi, 1304 II, vol. III, p. 127.

devoted to religion. The process of give and take had begun in earnest and the policies of a ruler like Akbar had given it a great boost.

SAIYID RULERS OF INDIA AND TIMURIDS OF CENTRAL ASIA

At the end of this selection has been given a document as an appendix. It is copy of the *farman* issued by Ulugh Beg (1447-9) and addressed to the last Saiyid ruler, Ala ud din Alam Shah (1445-51).[271] It is the only document included in the *Munshaat* that comes from the Delhi Sultanate period. It greatly adds to our understanding of the nature of the Sultanate under the Saiyid rulers (1414-51) and their relationship with the Timurids of Central Asia. *Munshaat* contains a considerably large number of documents of various categories relating to Central Asia. This very strong presence of the documents of Central Asian origin could be explained by Abu'l Qasim's family background. This is also indicative of the eminence the family would seem to have enjoyed in its ancestral land.

It is common knowledge that Saiyid rulers owed their rise to power to Timur. Khizr Khan, the founder of the dynasty, had joined the entourage of Timur during his march to Delhi. Before his departure from India, Timur assigned the territories of Multan, Depalpur and Delhi to Khizr Khan.[272] It is generally acknowledged that Khizr Khan continued to recognize Timur and his successor, Shah Rukh, as his overlords.[273] During his entire tenure extending over seven years he

---

[271] Document No. 287, pp. 403-5.

[272] There is much difference of opinion among the chroniclers regarding the territories Timur assigned to Khizr Khan. For details see Sharf ud din Ali Yezdi, *Zafar Nama*, Bib. Indica, vol. II, p. 75; Bihamad Khani, *Tarikh-i Muhammadi*, British Museum Manuscript, OR 137, f. 306b; Yahya Sirhindi, *Tarikh-i Mubarak Shahi*, pp. 166, 167. Peter Jackson (*A Political and Military History of Delhi Sultanate*, Cambridge University Press, Cambridge, 1999, pp. 318-19) considers Sirhindi's claim regarding asignment of Delhi to Khizr Khan as 'apocryphal' and thinks it was an attempt to bolster the legitimacy of the Saiyid dynasty.

[273] For example see R.P. Tripathi, *Some Aspects of Muslim Adminsitration*, Allahabad, Central Book Depot, 1978, pp. 78-80; K.S. Lal, *Twilight of the Sultanate*, New Delhi, 1963, pp. 71-2; Aziz Ahmad, *Studies in the Islamic Culture in the Indian Environment*, Oxford, Clarendon Press, 1964, pp. 10, 19. Basing himself

did not assume any title of royalty and continued to style his court as *Rayat-i A'la* (Sublime Standard).[274] It is, however, not very clear whether he accepted any other obligations relating to *khutba* and *sikka* as well. Similarly, the nature of relationship of the successors of Khizr Khan and the Timurids is not clear. Some modern historians hold the view that the 'fiction' of allegiance to the Timurids was brought to an end by Mubarak Shah, son and successor of Khizr Khan.[275] It would appear from the evidence gleaned from contemporary and near contemporary sources, particularly *Tarikh-i Muhammadi* of Bihamad Khani and *Mtla'-i Sa'dain* of Abdur Razzaq Samarqandi that the Saiyid rulers continued to fulfil the obligations towards the Timurids which were accepted by Khizr Khan at the time of the assignment of these territories to him. These obligations included not only allegiance to the Timurids but also entailed payment of annual tribute to them as well as recitation of *khutba* and coining of money in their name. *Tarikh-i Muhammadi*, which was compiled by Bihamad Khani in 1438 at Kalpi, contains evidence that conclusively proves this point. It clearly shows that at least till the time of the compilation of *Tarikh-i Muhammadi* in 1438 the *khutba* was recited in the name of Shah Rukh at Delhi, coins were struck in his name and regular tribute was sent to his court. Moreover, the Saiyid rulers received from the Timurids almost all those favours and insignia, such as robes of honour, throne and *chatr*, which are normally bestowed by the sovereigns upon their subordinates.[276]

---

on the evidence of Bihamad Khani, Peter Jackson maintains (p. 322), that Khizr Khan acknowledged the overlordship of Timur and paid tribute to Shah Rukh and the family continued to receive orders from the Timurids.

[274] *Tarikh-i Mubarak Shahi*, p. 181. Abul Fazl says that 'Khizr Khan in gratitude (to Timur) did not assume the regal title but styled his court 'the Sublime Standards'. See *Ain-i Akbari*, English tr. H.S. Jarret, Orient Book Reprint Centre, New Delhi, 1978, vol. II, p. 312.

[275] Tripathi, p. 7; Aziz Ahmad, p. 10.

[276] For a detailed study of this problem see I.A. Zilli, 'Relations of Saiyid Sultans of Delhi with the Timurids—A Reappraisal' in Nazir Ahmad, Asloob Ahmad Ansari (eds.), *Fakhruddin Ali Ahmad Memorial Volume*, Ghalib Institute, New Delhi, 1994, pp. 221-8; idem, 'Saiyid Sultans of Delhi and the issue of Coins in the name of Timurids—Fact or Fiction' in Amiteshwar Jha (ed.), *Medieval Indian Coinage: A Historical and Economic Perspective*, Indian Institute of Research in Numismatic Studies, Nasik, 2001, pp. 97-104.

The *farman* of Ulugh Beg reproduced by Abul Qasim not only conclusively proves this contention but also adds a new dimension to India's relations with Timurids during the first half of the fifteenth century.[277] It goes beyond other contemporary and near contemporary sources in reaffirming the subordinate position of the Saiyid Sultans of Delhi *vis-à-vis* the Timurids. It shows that not only Khizr Khan, the founder of the dynasty, owed his rise to power to Timur but his successors were also confirmed in their position by the contemporary Timurid rulers till the very end of their rule. In spite of the fact that some of these rulers did not apparently relish this relationship and seem to have strong reservations about it, they nevertheless felt obliged by the harsh ground realities to continue to abide by it. The contents of this *farman*, therefore, more than prove the contention of the author of *Tarikh-i Muhammadi* and the evidence contained in other contemporary sources.

As usual, the text of the *farman* included in the *Munshaat* does not contain the name of the issuing authority as also that of the person to whom it is addressed and who is being thereby assigned the government of Delhi and its dependencies. However, since the *farman* contains obvious references to Timur and Shah Rukh as the predecessors of the ruler issuing the *farman* and mentions the names of Khizr Khan, Mubarak Khan and Muhammad Khan as the forerunners of the recipient, it would not perhaps be far-fetched to assume that this is a formal *farman* granted by Ulugh Beg to the last Saiyid ruler, Ala ud din Alam Shah, after the latter's accession to the throne of Delhi in 1445. A close analysis of the internal evidence, the setting of the *farman* and the language and the terms used would clearly indicate that it is a copy of a genuine and authentic document. There could not have been any motive for the compiler to fabricate such a document. Moreover, the contents of the *farman* are fully corroborated by contemporary and near contemporary sources.

A closer scrutiny of the *farman* brings out some very interesting points. First, it is noteworthy that the *farman* describes the confirmation of Ala ud din Alam Shah on the throne of Delhi as the conferment of a

[277] For an annotated translation of the *farman*, see I.A. Zilli, 'New Light on Timurid Relations with Saiyid Sultans of Delhi' in Mansura Haidar (ed.), *Sufis, Sultans and Feudal Orders—Professor Nurul Hasan Commemoration Volume*, Manohar, Delhi, 2004, pp. 117-24.

suyurghal consisting of Delhi and its dependencies, which would imply that the Timurids considered Hindustan as a part of their dominion and regarded the Saiyid rulers of Delhi as their subordinates. They sought to reinforce this position by constantly sending robes of honour, throne and *chatr* and ensuring that the obligations accepted by the Saiyids were scrupulously discharged. In case of any default, prompt action was taken to force them to continue to adhere to these obligations. Secondly, it suggests that not only Khizr Khan owed his kingship to the Timurids but his successors, Mubarak Khan and Muhammad Khan, were also confirmed in their succession by Shah Rukh. It may be noted that the *farman* does not use any title for Khizr Khan and his successors higher than *malik, malik zada* and *khan*. This is clearly to remind them about their obligations towards the Timurids. It need not be emphasized that the words used in a formal *farman* are very carefully chosen. Lastly, confirming Ala ud din Alam Shah in the government of Delhi (*ayalat wa sultanat*) and its dependencies, the nobles and *maliks* are directed to consider those territories as the *suyurghal* of the above-mentione great *Malik* and to consider him as an independent ruler (*hakim wa farmanrawa alal itlaq*) and rightful *wali* and *badshah*. They are further directed to remit *mal-i wajibi* and *huquq-i diwani* to him season by season, year after year. If words like the *wali* and *badshah* are not taken very seriously, and the contents of this *farman* are compared with the Mughal *farman* of land grants, not much difference will be noticed. This does not leave much scope for speculation about the nature of the relationship that existed between the Saiyid rulers of Delhi and the Timurids of Central Asia.

Section III
Manuscripts of the Book

So far only three manuscripts of *Munshaat-i-Namakin* have been noticed. These are preserved at the India Office Library, London; Maulana Azad Library, Aligarh Muslim University, Aligarh; and Salarjung Museum, Hyderabad. *Munshaat-i-Namakin* has not been mentioned in any of the known *Insha* collections or other literary and historical works surviving from the Mughal period. This would suggest that the book had a very limited circulation. In view of the nature and contents of the book it is rather surprising. The India Office Library MS is the earliest and most complete. It has been used therefore as the basic text. The other two manuscripts have been used for the purpose of comparison and collation. A brief description of the manuscripts follows:

INDIA OFFICE LIBRARY MS

The earliest known MS of the *Munshaat* is preserved at the India Office Library, London.[1] It was transcribed by Ibn-i Muriya. According to a noting in the MS, he completed the transcription on 14th Jumada I, 1012 AH/20 October 1603. This would indicate that this copy was transcribed only four years after the compilation of the original work.[2] Parts of this manuscript were collated with the author's personal copy.[3] However, Ethe's assertion that the entire book was collated with the original is not borne out by the notings. It would appear from the notings that the work of collation was carried out on different occasions.

[1] Cf. Catalogue India Office Library, No.2064, pp. 1141-2.

[2] According to the Colophon, the book was completed in the forty-fourth year of Akbar's reign on 23 Shaban 1007 AH/21 March 1599. Ethe has incorrectly read the year as 1006 AH.

[3] The word *asl* has been used. See f. 413a.

The first collation would seem to have been carried out by Qazi Jafar and Maulana Ismail Mufti within a month of the completion of the transcription. One of them used to read out the original text, the other checked the transcription. On this occasion in all twenty items[4] were collated, five at the end and fifteen from different places in the book which have been left unspecified. Subsequently, twenty-two items were collated by Qazi Husain and Muttalib, twelve from the beginning and ten from the middle. Another four items were compared by Nasrullah and Nimatullah. It would, therefore, appear that instead of collating the entire book, these teams carried out only sample checking with a view to verify the authenticity of the manuscript. Apparently, on finding the transcription accurate, the collation of entire text was not considered necessary. Absence of over writings and notings between the lines and on the margins would clearly indicate that in the process of checking many errors of transcription were not discovered.

The India Office Library copy seems to have been transcribed for the use of one of Abu'l Qasim's sons. A note on the title page states that it was owned by Salah ud Din bin Abu'l Qasim Namakin al-Husaini, may God preserve him.[5] The last portion would further suggests that it was written at a time when the author was still alive. Incidentally this is the only reference to indicate that Abu'l Qasim had a son with this name.

The manuscript bears six impressions of seals and four notings. This may give some idea about the identity of persons who owned it from time to time. Four of the seals are on the title page and two at the end. Out of these one is blurred and cannot be read. Four of the seals belong to Salah ud Din and one to his son, Abdul Khaliq Husaini. The first seal which is placed on the left side of the lower half of the page, reads بندہ کمترین صلاح الدین (Salah ud Din, the most humble). The other seal located a little lower to the right side of the first seal is a *saja'* مرید شہنشہ (Salah ud Din, the disciple of the emperor). The third seal located below the second reads عبدالخالق بن سید صلاح الدین (Abdul Khaliq, the son of Saiyid Salah ud Din). The fourth and the damaged one on the

[4] The word *Ajza'* has been used. *Ajza'* is plural of *juz'* meaning part, division or section. It is not clear as to what is meant by *ajza'* here, a document, a *fasl* or something else.

[5] The actual words are

من متملکات ذرہ احقر کمترین عباد اللہ صلاح الدین بن ابو القاسم خان نمکین الحسینی سلمہ اللہ

left lower margin has a note above it which is also partially damaged. It reads: الله اکبر بتاریخ ۱۲ شهر ربیع الاول سنه ۴۵ واصل کتابخانه ـ ـ ـ ـ شد (God is great. The book was entered in the library of . . . on 12 Rabi I, 45th regnal year). Here the name of the library has got blurred to such an extent that it cannot be deciphered. This could have provided crucial information about the history of the manuscript. The two seals at the end of the MS read respectively بنده کمترین صلاح الدین (Salah ud Din, the most humble) and صلاح صلاح الدین دوست دار چهار یار گزین (well-being of Salah ud Din who is a well-wisher of the four noble friends, i.e. the first four caliphs) which is again a *saja'*. All the seals are round and beautiful. There is also a note on the top of the title page which reads:

سرکار نواب صاحب، مبارز الدوله، مفتخر الملک، حسام جنگ مسٹر رچارڈ جانسن صاحب بهادر دام اقباله

(Nawab, Mubariz ud Daulah, Muftakhar ul Mulk, Husam Jang, Mr Richard Johnson Sahib Bahadur, may his authority be perpetuated.)

Most probably the manuscript reached India Office Library through this Mr Richard Johnson.

This manuscript is written in beautiful *naskh* in very small hand. It contains 412 folios each measuring 85"/8 × 47"/8. There are 23 lines on every side of the folio and each line approximately contains 20 words. Compared to the Aligarh manuscript, this earlier transcription carries fewer orthographical problems, though there are a number of words which are spelt incorrectly. For example the words مخلص، مهذب، ایادی، تجمل، عزیمت، سمت، صورت are spelt as مخلص، محذب، عیادی، عظیمت، سمط، سورت. As it is known that a considerable portion of this manuscript was collated with the author's copy prepared only four years earlier, the possibility of these errors being present in the original copy as well cannot be entirely ruled out.

This MS contains some documents that are missing from the Aligarh MS. This would indicate that the Aligarh MS is a copy of an earlier draft and the author's copy from which this MS was transcribed was in fact the final version. This impression is reinforced by the difference in the dates of compilation given by this MS on the one hand, and Aligarh and Hyderabad MSS on the other.[6]

[6] For a discussion on the date of compilation see below.

THE ALIGARH MS

The Aligarh MS[7] is written in bold *nast'aliq* and contains 612 folios of the size 33½"×21. Each side of the folio contains 16 lines and each line carries approximately 12 words. However, ff. 292 a-385b are written in comparatively smaller hand with the result that in this section each side of a folio contains 19 lines and each line carries approximately 20 words. Portions of the MS have been damaged by dampness and worms. At places these holes run through scores of folios. In spite of the fact that it has been thoroughly repaired, at places words or even sentences have been so badly affected that it is not possible to retrieve them.

The year of transcription given at the end is 1131/1718-19 but the name of the transcriber is not mentioned. There is a note on the title page to the effect that the owner bought it from Abdul Barr, a book seller of Agra presently residing in Delhi for 120 rupees during the 13th regnal year of Muhammad Shah. The MS is stated to have originally belonged to the library of Bairam Khan Akbar Shahi. This is obviously a forgery; a book compiled in 1598 and transcribed in 1718-19 could not have belonged to the library of Bairam Khan who died in 1561.

The date of the compilation of the book given in this MS as well as in the Hyderabad MS is Ormuzd, the first day of the divine month Farwardin, 39th regnal year of Akbar's reign. The corresponding *Hijra* date has been given as Sunday, 23 *Sha'ban*, 1002/14 May 1594. This would suggest that Abul Qasim Namakin had already completed compilation of the book about four years earlier than the date given in the India Office MS. Both these MSS end with the chronogram *Munshaat-i ma Namakin* which also yields 1002/1594. It may also be noticed that in the case of these two dates details like day, date, month of *Ilahi* as well as *Hijra* calendars are identical. Besides it, all the three manuscripts give the day as Ormuzd or Sunday, the date as first of the divine month of *Farwardin* or 23rd of *Sha'ban*. But there is a difference of four years in the *Hijra* and *Ilahi* years in the two sets of dates. It cannot be attributed to the transcribers' mistake as in both the manuscripts the years of *Ilahi* as well as *Hijra* calendars are given in words. It is quite likely that the first version of the book was compiled in 1002 H/

---

[7] University No. 26, 27, Farsiya 3, Nasr.

AD 1594 which went into circulation. Four years later a revised version was prepared with the addition of a considerable number of new documents. Apparently, the Aligarh and Hyderabad MSS are copies of an earlier version, while the India Office Library MS was transcribed from the later version. This may be the reason why the India Office Library MS contains a number of additional documents that are not found in the Aligarh and Hyderabad MSS. It is also worth noting that the India Office Library MS that gives the year of compilation as 1007 H, does not contain the chronogram *Munshaat-i ma Namakin* yielding 1002 H. It would indicate that while giving the date of the compilation of the revised version, Abu'l Qasim took care to drop this chronogram as it was no longer relevant. Obviously, other specifications such as Ormuzd, the first day of the divine month *Farwardin* or Sunday, 23 *Sha'ban* would also no longer be relevant for the 44th regnal year or 1007 H. The retention of these specifications in the revised version was apparently a slip on the part of the author himself.

There are many more orthographical mistakes in this MS than in the India Office Library MS. Possibly this MS was not transcribed from author's copy and most probably the transcriber did not care to collate it with the original. As a result, it abounds in mistakes like

حدس (حدث)، امزاء (امضاء)، منظمن (متضمن)، الطفات (التفات)، صریر (سریر)، موضف (موظف)، نضام (نظام)، مناج
(مناهج)، تزاهم (تزاحم)، شرائط (شرافت)، صامی (سامی)

SALARJUNG MS

The third known MS of the *Munshaat* is preserved at the Salarjung Museum.[8] It is written in good *nast'aliq*. From the numbering of the folios, it would appear that originally it contained 486 folios. However, ff. 3-231 are missing from the present volume. The actual number of folios, therefore, is reduced to 257. Each side of the folio contains 21 lines and each line carries about 15 words. Many folios contain stains caused by dampness as well as worm-holes, still the contents remain fairly readable. A sort of rubrification is present almost throughout

[8] Cf. *Catalogue of Persian Manuscripts*, Salarjung Library, vol. III, pp. 77-8, No. 790.

the book. As noticed earlier, the date of the compilation given in the colophon of this manuscript is the same as that of the Aligarh MS.[9] It also contains the chronogram *Munshaat-i ma Namakin*. The name of the transcriber is Muhammad Hashim Sistani and the year of transcription is 1102/1690-1. There is no evidence to support the assertion of the compiler of the *Catalogue of Persian Manuscripts*, Salarjung Museum, that the noting containing the date is a later fabrication and the MS is in fact an autograph copy.[10]

[9] Ormuzd, the first day of the divine month of Farwardin, 39th regnal year corresponding to Sunday, 23 Sha'ban 1002 H.

[10] See *Catalogue of Persian Manuscripts*, Salarjung Museum, p. 78.

منشآت نمکین

نامه ها و اسناد برگزیده

تالیف

سید ابوالقاسم نمکین حسینی
(متوفی ۱۰۱۸ھ)

ترتیب و تصحیح

اشتیاق احمد ظلی

بخش تاریخ، دانشگاه اسلامی، علی گڑھ
۲۰۰۷ء

فهرست

نامه ها:

عرائض:

مراسلات وصحائف:

متفرقات:

ضمیمه:

بسم الله الرحمن الرحيم

مقدمه مولف

زیبا ترین نگاری که منشیان فصاحت انتماء خال چهره صحیفه سخن گردانند وخوب ترین نقشی که مترسلان بلاغت انتساب زیب رخسار مجموعه انشاء کنند، سپاس وستائش متکلمی است که هر آیه از کلام او سفینه ایست مملوبه زوارف عوارف و گنجینه ایست مشحون از زواهر جواهر۔ فله الحمد علی زوارف عوارفه والشکر علی زواهر جواهره۔ درود نامحدود برناطقی که بوصف[1] "وما ینطق عن الهویٰ"[2] منصوب[3] وبتشریف "أنا أفصح العرب والعجم" مخصوص گشته، فصلی الله علیه وعلی آله واصحابه واتباعه اجمعین - وبعد براخلای پاك سریرت وبر اجلای طیب طینت مخفی نیست که حضرت بیچون، عم نعمائه، راهیچ نعمتی بر افراد بشری، که بدائع ودائع مخلوقات او اند، بعد موهبت صحت وعطیه ایمان مثل نعمت بیان نیست۔ چه تبلیغ اوامر ونواهی حضرت الهی به عباد، که در انتماء بآن سعادت کونین وانفراد بآن فلاح دارین حاصل تواند بود، بسخن است۔ ومشارکت آدمی، که مدنی الطبع است، با بنی نوع موقوف بران، چه تا هر احدی ما یحتاج خودرا بغیری نگوید، حاجتش بکفایت نرسد وفوائد مشارکت بحصول نه انجامد. ولهذا حضرت واجب، جل ذکره وعم بره، تعلیم بیان را با خلقت انسان مقرون فرمود حیث قال فی الکلام المتعال "خلق الانسان علمه البیان"[4] تا اشعار شود برآن که تمامت

۱۔ ع، س: بنض

۲۔ قرآن مجید: ۳/۵۳

۳۔ ع، س: منصوص

۴۔ قرآن مجید: ٤/۵۵

خلقت آدمی، که نسخه جامع بین الوجوب والا کمال وخلیفه فی ارض الرحمان آمده، وابسته برنعمت بیان است۔ واز جمله فوائد شریفه وعوائد لطیفه این نعمت آن که بر مر اعصار و کر ادوار از متقدم ومتاخر یادگاری جز او نیست، وظهور احوال اسافل واعالی ووضوح منوال اقاصی وادانی بی اونه۔ واگر این عطیه جلیله وبخشش جزیله به حسن ادا از تلفیق عبارات وتنمیق استعارات مقرون شود در افاده ادخل گردد۔ ازین جهت بعضی از بلغاء در نظم او کوشیده وبرخی از فصحاء در لباس نثر در آورده وجمعی جامع بین الطرفین[۱] گشته در محاورات ومکاتبات نیز این طریقه را مرعی داشته اند. چه کلام حسن بمقتضی "إن من البیان لسحرا[۲] وإن من الشعر لحکمة[۳]" سحر آئین تاثیر در صرف قلوب دارد۔

بناءً علی ذالك بنده کمترین ابو القاسم الحسینی النمکین، رزقه الله حلاوة التحقیق ومنه بالتوفیق، اگر بدوستی رقعه ای یا به مخلصی کتابتی رقم زده کلك اخلاص می نمود حتی الامکان در ربط آن سعی نموده پاره از فیض طبیعت وبرخی از منشآت اکابر بر او می افزود ومسوده آن بر بیاض بنهاد۔ چه هر گاه صاحب فطرتی عروس سخن را در منصه عرض اکابر جلوه دهد، مقتضاء فطرت سلیم ومرتضاء عقل مستقیم آنست که حسب المقدور در تصفیه کسوت ودر تحلیه لباس آن کوشش نماید تا ناقدان اهل بصیرت را به مقدار مشاهده آن سرور حاصل آید وسعی مشاطه قلم مشکور گردد۔ واگر از احباء کتابتی باو می رسید نقل آن نیز ثبت می نمود تا آن که بر بقیة من الاوان منقولات وافره ومسودات کثیره مجتمع شد، وبعضی از مخلصان استدعاء نمودند که اگر این اجزاء را ترتیب داده مجموعه سازد سبب استفاده مردم

۱۔ ع، س : الطریقتین

۲۔ صحیح بخاری، کتاب النکاح

۳۔ صحیح بخاری، کتاب الادب

وموجب بقاء اثر که:

إن آثارنا تدلّ علينا
فانظروا بعد نا الی الآثار

دال بر آنست، گردد۔ اگرچه ایں قلیل البضاعت، عدیم الاستطاعت را قابلیت ایں منصب عالی قدر وقدرت ایں موقف عظیم الخطر نه بود، امابر مقتضاء "مالا يدرك كله لا يترك كله" واداءً لمسئولهم وتحصيلاً لمامولهم ترتیب آں مسودات منثور را با بعضی مناشیر[۱] ومراسلات ومکاتباتی که از کتب انشاء معتبر انتخاب کرده بود، به نظم جمعیت وترتیب احسن منظوم گردانیده مبوب بهشت باب ساخت[۲] هرباب مفصل بچند فصل، مختوم بخاتمه دربیان چیزهای که نظربه شآیب وجه داخل ایں صفت نه بود لیکن بسبب مناسباتی که بامعان نظر مبصرذوی البصائر می شد، خارج هم نمی نمود، کرد۔ وآں را 'منشآت نمکین' نام نهاده جهت حصول تبرك وتیمن تحفة عاکفان پایه سریر خلافت مصیر، حضرت قطب الا قطاب، المرشد المكمل، بندگان نواب خلافت پناهی، شاهنشاهی، قبله گاهی، صاحب قِران[۳] فیض رسان سکنه کون ومکان، درة التاج دریای عرفان، محمود خواقین نامدار، مسجود سلاطین عالی مقدار، مظهر انوار، السلطان العادل، حبیب الله، تاج بخش تخت نشینان ممالك سلطنت وتخت ستان تاج بخشان سرادق ابهت، صاحب السلاطين الا عظم، مالك رقاب الامم مولی ملوك الترك والهند والعرب والعجم، الذی عدل ساعة منه بعمل الثقلين يوازی، ابو المظفر جلال الدين محمد اكبر بادشاه غازی، اللهم كما جعلته فی بسيط الارض مويداً فاجعل ظلال خلافته علی العالمين موبداً۔ الهی تا انقراض عالم عرصه جهان بنفحات عنایات بادشاهانه

۱۔ ع، س: مناشیر، ندارند
۲۔ ع: ساخت، ندارد
۳۔ س: صاحب قرانی

معطر واكناف گیتی به لمعات انظار خسروانه مزین ومنور باد وظلال دولت وسلطنت باهره بر مفارق عالم وعالمیان ممد د و موّبد وبساط خلافت قاهره برتارك جهان وجهانیان مبسوط ومخلد باد، بحق الحق وعارفه!

مسئول از کرم عمیم باریك (بین)، خورده شناس آن که چون بر زلتی وهفوتی اطلاع یابند، به قلم عاطفت رقم اصلاح فرمایند ویا بذیل اغماض مستتر نمایند که 'لکل جواد کبوة ولکل صارم نبوة ولکل عالم هفوة، هذا ابان الشروع فی المقصود والتوفیق من الله المعبود وانه ولی التوفیق۔

فتح نامہا

(۱)
فتح نامه
(بمناسبت فتح چتور صادر شد)☆

الحمد لله الذی صدق وعده ونصر عبده واعز جنده وهزم الاحزاب وحده ولا شی بعده.[۱] فوائح حمد وسپاس وقرائح شکربی قیاس حضرت فتاحی را سزد که مفاتیح ابواب قلعه گیری و کشور کشائی سلاطین باداد ودین در قبضه ارادت واختیار اوست، ومناشیر اوضاع خلافت وفرمان روائی خواقین نصرت آئین موشح بتوقیع عنایت واختیار او، کریمی که دست قدرت کامله اش بمحض رحمت شامله لوای نصرت انتماء اهل ایمان را بطراز اعزاز "وکان حقاً علینا نصر المومنین[۲]" برافراخت، جباری که انهدام بنیان حیات اشرار کفار را بضرب شمشیر صاعقه کردار مجاهدان حق گذار بحکم "قاتلوهم یعذبهم الله بایدیکم ویخزهم وینصر کم علیهم[۳]" متعلق است.

مثنوی[٤]:

یکی را بسر بر نهد تاج بخت　　یکی را زپا اندر آرد زتخت
کلاه سعادت یکی برسرش　　گلیم شقاوت یکی دربرش
گلستان کند آتشی بر خلیل　　گروهی بآتش برد زآب نیل
گر آنست منشور احسان اوست　　دریں است توقیع فرمان اوست

تعالی شانه عما یقولون علوا کبیراً وتعاظم سلطانه من ان یکون

☆ بمناسبت فتح چتور در مارس ۱۵۶۸ بامراء پنجاب صادر شده
۱ـ کلمات افتتاحی خطبه پیغمبر علیه السلام هنگام فتح مکه، رجوع کنید صحیح بخاری، کتاب الجهاد، باب التکبیر بعد الحرب،
۲ـ قرآن مجید: ۴۷/۳
۳ـ قرآن مجید: ۱۴/۹
٤ـ ع: مثنوی، ندارد

له فی الملك ولیا ونصیراً۔ وترادف تحیات مبارکات ولطائف صلوات طیبات برسید کائنات وخلاصه موجودات که چون فرمان واجب الاذعان "یا ایها النبی جاهد الکفار والمنافقین واغلظ علیهم[۱]" نازل گشت، از برای اعلاء اعلام دین وملت وتعظیم مطیعان طوائف امت، عنان توجه عالی همت به تسخیر قلاع فلك ارتفاع خیبر ومدن واما کن دیگر معطوف داشته، بهر ناحیه وقبیله که تشریف قدوم میمنت لزوم ارزانی فرموده بامداد جنود نصرت الهی که بمقتضاء فحواء "وانزل جنوداً لم تروها[۲]" پیشواء عزیمت او بود، باسهل وجوه فتح فرمود۔ هر دولت مندی که پیش توفیق ازلی وحسن تائید لم یزلی بصدق نیت وخلوص عقیدت زبان بکلمه طیبه "لا اله الا الله، محمد رسول الله" کشاد بسعادت دارین مشرف گشت۔ وهر زاغ صفت بی عاقبت که بواسطه حطام دنیوی چشم از نعیم اخروی پوشیده قدم درمضیق جهالت ودائره ضلالت نهاد، ناوك عقوبت جحیم وعذاب الیم را هدف گشت۔

قطعه:

رسولی که بی دعوی تخت وتاج　　زشاهان بشمیشر بستد خراج
غلط گفتم آن شاه سدره سریر　　که هم تاج ده بود وهم تخت گیر
تنش محرم تخت افلاك بود　　سرش صاحب تاج لولاك بود

وبرزمره آل واصحاب نامی وفرقه جنود احباب گرامی او که پیشوایان صفوف ارباب دین وراه نمایان اصحاب صدق ویقین اند، صلوات الله وسلامه علیهم ورضوان الله علیهم اجمعین الی یوم الدین۔ وبعد:

چون مالك ملك، جل جلاله وعم نواله، سلطنت ممالك هندوستان راکه سواد اعظم اقالیم جهان است، بحکم "انی جاعلك للناس اماماً[۳]" بجانب ما مفوض فرموده ومنشی دیوان خانه کرامت

۱۔ قرآن مجید: ۸۳/۹
۲۔ قرآن مجید: ۲۶/۹　　۳۔ قرآن مجید: ۱۲۴/۲

وفرماندهی منشور خلافت وشاهنشاهی مارا به پروانچه "انا مکنا له فی الارض[۱]" بزیور طغراء "وذالك فضل الله یوتیه من یشاء[۲]" مزین ومحلی نموده والحق کافه خلائق، که بدائع ودائع حضرت خالق اند، در کنف حمایت وحریم مکرمت ورعایت از مکاره زمان وشدائد دوران در ضمان امان درآمده بفر اقبال بوظائف طاعت وعبادت حضرت ذوالجلال اشتغال دارند، همواره شکر گذاری این نعمت عظمی وسپاس داری این موهبت کبری برذمت همت والا نهمت واجب ومتحتم شناخته ایم۔ چون بروفق "توجه حیث شئت فانك منصور" روی توجه بهر جانب که می آریم، دولت واقبال بعزم استقبال تلقی می نمایند وعنان عزیمت بهر طرف که معطوف می گردانیم فتح ونصرت به طریق استعجال پیش می آیند "هذا من فضل ربی لیبلونی اشکر ام اکفر[۳]" برحسب اشارت فرخنده بشارت "وجاهدوا فی سبیله لعلکم تفلحون[٤]" اوقات بابرکات را بقدر وسع وامکان بغزوات[۵] وجهاد مصروف سازیم، وبعون عنایت قادر بیچون که مقوی دولت روز افرون ما است، اماکن وقلاع ومساکن وبلادی که به تصرف اشرار کفار، خذلهم الله ودمرهم اجمعین، است بحیطه تسخیر درآورده اعلام سعادت فرجام اسلام در ساحت هر ولایت ومقام بر افرازیم، وبصیقل حسام خون آشام مبارزان بهر ام انتقام وپرواز سهام شهب التئام قدر اندازان قضا پیغام ظلام شرك وآثارم عدوان از صحائف صفحات خواطر بت پر ستان محو گردانیده، بنیان معابد اصنام را از آنجا واطراف ممالك هند براندازیم، "والحمد لله الذی هدانا لهذا وما کنا لنهتدی لو لا ان هدانا الله[٦]"۔

۱۔ قرآن مجید: ۸٤/۱۸
۲۔ قرآن مجید: ٤/٦۲
۳۔ قرآن مجید: ٤۰/۲۷
٤۔ قرآن مجید: ۳۵/۵
۵۔ ع: بغزوات، ندارد
٦۔ قرآن مجید: ٤۳/۷

مصداق این مقال آن که درین ایام فیروزی انجام که بعد از قتل علی قلی وجماعت نمك حرام بدار الخلافة آگره بصفت 'کرام بررة' نزول اجلال فرمودیم وجهت ازدیاد مواد تفریح خاطر فیض مآثر بعزم شکار فیل حدود سوی سوبر[١] وککراون[٢] را که از مضافات ولایت چتوراست، مخیم سرادقات عز واقبال نمودیم۔ مقارن این حال بمسامع قدسی جوامع رسید که رانا اودی سنگه، دمر الله، بخلاف آن که متصور بود که به تهنیت موکب ظفر قرین ملازمت وعبودیت مسلوك داشته متوجه عتبه بوسی شود یا ولد خود رامع خراج وپیشکش بدر گاه عالم پناه فرستد، از کمال غرور وپندار در مقام عناد واستکبار در آمده، در قلعه چتور، که مامن وموطن موروثی اوست و از جمیع قلاع[٣] هند بزیادتی استحکام وارتفاع ممتاز است، آذوقه درمی آورد که متحصن شود۔ چون غره اندیشه غزا وجهاد همه وقت در مرآت ضمیر منیر عکس می انداخت، نایره حمیت دین الهی وآتش غضب بادشاهی ملتهب ومشتعل گشته، با آن که اکثری از عساکر فیروزی مآثر بعد از ظهور فتح سابق بجاگیر های خود رفته بودند، در حین توجه شکار از حاضران دار الخلافت چند فوجی بملازمت رکاب سعادت انتساب حاضر شدند، بعزیمت قلع وقمع آن کافر عنان توجه معطوف فرمودیم۔ او خود از خبر توجه رایات عالیات متوهم گشته سامیداس[٤] عم خود وچتمل[٥] واودیبان

١۔ سردی سوپر۔ رجوع کنید ابو الفضل، اکبر نامه، تصحح عبد الرحیم، ١٨٧٧، طبع کلکته، جلد٢، ص ٢٠٢؛ عبدالقادر بدایونی، منتخب التواریخ، تصحیح احمد علی، طبع کلکته، ١٨٦٨، جلد ٢، ص١٠٢

٢۔ گاگرون۔ رجوع کیند امپیریل گزیٹیر، جلد ١٢، ص٢٢۔ ١٢١

٣۔ ع: قلعه

٤۔ راوت سائیس داس۔ رجوع کنید مهتا نام سی ری کهیات، جلد اول، ص ١٦۔١٥؛ ٹاڈ نامش ساهید اس می دهد Annals and Antiquities of Rajasthan, Oxford Press, 1920, vol.1, P. 260)

٥۔ جیمل۔ مآخذ مثل اکبر نامه (٢/ ٣٢٠)؛ عارف قندهاری (تاریخ اکبری ص ١١٠)؛ طبقات اکبری (ص ٣٠٢)؛ بدایونی (٢/ ١٠٢) متفق اند که رانا(☆)

رتبا[۱] را که درمیان اشرار کفار، خذلهم الله کما اوصلهم دار البوار، بسمت دلاوری اشتهار داشته، هریك را درشان[۲] تهور ومردانگی مقابل هزار سوار می انگاشته اند، با پنج هزار راجپوت، که یك بیك بدعوی برخاسته اند، وده هزار مرد ویك هزار سائر لشکریان خود بحراست قلعه گذاشته وخود مع سپاهی به اودیپور وکنبلمیر که درمیان کوهها وجنگلها مضوط است، شتافته۔ چون در قصبه رام پور که از قصبات متعلقه مشهور چتور است، این معنی بوضوح پیوست که آن کافر مدبر این چنین خیالی کرده، رای کشور کشای بدین قرار یافت که اولاً بامداد جنودِ رعایت ربانی فتح قلعه را فرموده بعد ازان انچه مصلحت باشد بعمل آوریم۔ بدین جهت عزم محاصره قلعه جزم کرده روز پنجشنبه ۲۰ شهر ربیع الثانی بساعت سعد وطالع مسعود در ظاهر قلعه چتور نزول اجلال فرمودیم۔ قلعه مشاهده افتاد که کوه البرز بعظمتی وسطوتی که دارد در دامنش کمتر از سنگی نماید وطور وهنلو کش بطور یکه نشان می دهند در فصیلش راست دیواری نماید۔ رفعت بروجش بمرتبه فلك اطلس سر کشیده، آفتاب عالم گرد گردون نیز هر چند گرد گردید[۳] جز بمنطقه البروجش (بروجش) نرسید۔ مهندسان روز گار در تعین درجات ارتفاعش متفکر وحیران، ومقوّمان دهور واعصار از چگونگی خاك ریزش انگشت حیرت بدندان۔ مسافت طول وعرضش قریب بسه فرسنگ واز احصاء کنگرهایش پی محاسب اندیشه لنگ۔

مثنوی:[٤]

مهندس که این قلعه بنیاد کرد　　　اساس وی ازسنگ بیداد کرد

(☆) هنگام مراجعت خود از قلعه جیمل را سردار نامزد کرده بود۔ نیز رجوع کنید ٹاڈ، ۲٦۱/۱

۱۔ ادی بهان پٹه (ٹاڈ، ۲٦۱/۱)

۲۔ ع: میدان

۳۔ ع: گرد برگرد گردید

٤۔ ع: مثنوی، ندارد

فلك همچو سنگی بپایش نهاد　　چوسد سکندر بنایش نهاد
وزان کوته اندیشهای کمند　　ز اندیشه اهل دانش بلند
فصیلش رسیده باوج فلك　　ره سیر بسته بفوج ملك

هر چند مدبر عقل محاصره آن قلعه را از قبیل ممتنعات شمرد، مثنوی[1]

چون بشمول کرم ذو الجلال　　وز مدد باطن اهل کمال
روبهر سوی که در آورده ایم　　یافته ایم انچه طلب کرده ایم

همان روز اطراف وجوانب قلعه را بنظر فراست ودیده بصارت ملاحظه نموده، هر محلی را به یکی از خوانین شجاعت آئین وسلاطین باتمکین وامرای نصرت اقتران وباقی ملازمان درگاه رفیع المکان که در ملازمت بودند نامزد فرمودیم. اگرچه مبارزان کوه نورد ودلاوران معرکه حرب ونبرد، که بجان ودل طالب غزا وجهاد اند وشهادت را سرمایه دنیا وآخرت می دانند، رخصت می خواستند که قدم توکل پیش نهاده بعون عنایت ربانی که مقوی دولت خاقانی است، به حمله های شیر انه پلنگ وار خود را بسر برج وباره رسانند وبقوت پنجه زور آوری قلعه را از روی دست برد بحیطه تسخیر وتصرف در آورند. چون آن قوم کثیر اللوم اسباب قلعه داری از دیگ وضرب زن وتوپ وتفنگ ومنجنیق وجر ثقیل ونفط وناوك بحدی که اگر سی سال لا یزال بکار بردی وفا می کرد، درین مدت سامان کرده بودند، بر آنها وبر رفعت برج وبازو (باره) وقوت بازوی خود اعتماد تمام داشتند، بملاحظه حفظ اعمال[2] اهل اسلام، حفظهم الله تعالیٰ الی یوم القیام، که بعضی بیباکانه کشته شوند، نگذاشتیم که جنگ کنند وبطلب رعدهای اژدها نما، دیگها قرا بغرا وسائر اسباب توپخانه که در دار الخلافه مانده بود، فرمان فرستادیم ودر اردوی ظفر قرین نیز بساختن توپها ودیگهای کوه

۱ـ ع: مثنوی، ندارد
۲ـ ع: احوال

شگاف امر نموده مقرر فرمودیم که در چند محل نقب زنند وبر آوردن ساباط وسر کوب اقدام نمایند. ویك فوج از برانغار به تاخت وقتل واسیر بلده ادیپور ولشکریان ومردم رعنا (رانا) که آنجا بودند وخود به ده کروهی نشسته بود، تعین نموده، فوج دیگر از لشکر بتاخت وتاراج وقتل رام پور فرستادیم که در هر جابسیاری را از کفار نابکار متوجه دار البوار گردانیده، اسباب وغنایم بی شمار آوردند. بعد از رسیدن اسباب توپخانه وبرآمدن ساباط وآتش زدن نقبها وبهوا رفتن وفروختن برجها وباروها، حکم فرمودیم که مجموع سپاه نصرت دستگاه از اطراف وجوانب پیشتر رفته[۱] بربالای خاك ریز جا ومقام ساخته، قلعه را مرکز وار درمیان گرفته.

آن فرقه جهنمی دریں مرتبه برقوت وقدرت لشکر اسلام وغلظ نخوت دیندار خود اطلاع یافته از روی عجز وابتهال زبان استشفاع واستمهال کشودند وبعضی از کلاں تران بیرون آمده. چوں از روی کوته اندیشی با وجود آں که جمعی از خواص وعوام اهل اسلام را دریں ایام محاصره بضرب تفنگ وسنگ متوالیه ومنجنیق بشهادت رسانیده بودند، التماس چند می نمودند که بشرف اجابت مقرون نه بود، آنها را رخصت معاودت نمودیم. روز دیگر به نفس نفیس به ساباط محمد قاسم خاں میر بحر که نزدیك تر بقلعه بود، تشریف برده بجنگ سلطانی امر فرمودیم. از بیرون جنود مقترن بسعود اسلام دست اعتقاد بعروة وثقی "حسبنا الله ونعم الوکیل"[۲] استوار کرده، پای ثبات ووقار از کمال تهور واقتدار بمدارج معارج حرب وکارزار نهاده، واز اندرون وفود کفار یهودی کردار آتش جنگ وپیکار بر افروخته منجنیقهای آتش بار وتوپهای صاعقه آثار از پی یك دیگر کشاده می دادند، وشیران بیشه شجاعت وپلنگان قله[۳] جلادت که از وفور مردانگی دست طمع

۱ـ ع: رفته، ندارد
۲ـ قرآن مجید، ۱۷۳/۳
۳ـ ع: قلعه

بکمربند جوزاء کنند واز کمال جلدی تاج اکلیل از فرق بهرام خون آشام بردارند۔

قطعه:

همه شرط مردی بجا آورند　　سر دشمنان زیر پا آورند
ربایند از بزم جم جام را　　ستانند اکلیل بهرام را
خروشند زان گونه روز مصاف　　کزان پیچد آواز در کوه قاف
به دشمن که چون کوه افشرده پا　　کنند انچه باکه کند کهربا

بموجب حکم جهان مطاع "واعدوا لهم ما استطعتم من قوة"[1] فوج فوج بریك دیگر مسابقت می نمودند وسردر کشیده خود را به برجها، که بضرب توپها شگاف[2] در برج ودیوار آن حصار رفیع الاطراف شده بود، می رسانیدند۔ وازان گروه انبوه جماعه جماعه مانند خوکان تیر خورده بدر دویده بطعن نیزه وضرب شمشیر راه دخول بر مبارزان مسدود می گردانیدند۔ توپ اندازان نیز از هر کنار سنگ تفرقه در سلك جماعت گریزان انداخته، آتش مجادله ومحاربه[3] بر می افروختند واز صداء وحشت افزای رعدهای پی در پی زلزله تسخیر در خیل اعداء افگنده خرمن حیات ایشان را بصاعقه قهر قهرمانی می سوختند۔

گرفت آتش کین یمین ویسار　　زمین پر غبار آسمان پرشرار
ازان خیل اعداء مشوش همه　　چون اهل جهنم در آتش همه
ز دود وشرار تفنگهای جنگ　　کمانها چون قوس قزح رنگ رنگ

تا سه شبان روز بدین منوال گذشت که فریقین لحظه از جنگ وجدال نیا سودند وبدانچه آن روبه صفتان بسر انگشت حیله وتزویر می بستند شیران بیشه دلاوری بقوت پنجه بهادری می کشودند۔ بالآخر شب

۱۔ قرآن مجید : ۸/۶۰
۲۔ ع؛ کوه شگاف
۳۔ ع: محاربه، ندارد

(سه شنبه) بست وپنجم شهر شعبان المعظم (٩٧٥هـ) که بمقتضاء فحواء "لایکفون عن وجوههم النار ولا عن ظهورهم ولاهم ینصرون"[١] ترامی سنگهای آتشین وتعاقب توپهای آهنین دفعه دفعه بروجهی روی نمود که برطبق مراد "بل تاتیهم بغتة فتبهتهم فلا یستطیعون ردها ولاهم ینصرون"[٢] کرده مخذول العاقبت را تاب دفع[٣] وطاقت آن نبود. درین حالت ساعت بساعت منادی غیبی نداء "إن تنصروا الله ینصرکم ویثبت اقدامکم"[٤] بمسامع علیه رسانید ولحظه به لحظه ملهم آسمانی بشارت فرخنده اشارت "الا إن نصر الله قریب"[٥] مسموع می گردانید. مبارزان کینه شعار ودلاوران خنجر گذار، که کمر بخون اعداء بسته از غایت خوں ریزی تاکمر در خون نشسته بودند، به یکبار حمله نمودند. تختهای که آن بدبختان سد رخنها کرده بزور بازوی دلاوری در ربودند. از مشاهده آن حال چتمل، که درمعرکه جنگ وپیکار ومیدان نبرد وکارزار ازاں سه سردار درپیش بود وباعث نگاه داشت قلعه از اول تا آخر هموں بود، باجمعی قدم پیش نهاد[٦] که سد رخنها نماید. مقارن ایں حال از جانب آن فرقه شقاوت مآل چند توپ بردار بقصد مبارزان از پی یك دیگر آتش زده بنوعی افروختند که چتمل وجمعی که همراه او بودند معانیه نمودار شدند. چوں دریں سه شبان روز آنجا تشریف داشتیم، به نیت غزا[٦] اکثر اوقات تیر وتفنگی می انداختیم. وهمانا که سرنوشت چتمل بوده که بدست حق پرست ما بدرك اسفل شتابد، دریں حالت که نمایاں شد بحکم "اذا اراد الله شیئا هیأ اسبابه" تفنگی که بدست داشتیم چاق ومهیا بود. بمجرد دیدن وکشاد دادن به پیشانی

١ـ قرآن مجید : ٣٩/٢١
٢ـ قرآن مجید : ١٢/٤٠
٣ـ ع: رفع، ندارد
٤ـ قرآن مجید : ٤٧/٧
٥ـ قرآن مجید : ٢/٢١٤
٦ـ ع: نهاده

ظلمانی آن کافر نابکار رسیده وصدای "اینما تکونوا یدرککم الموت ولو کنتم فی بروج مشیدة"[1] شنیده متوجه دار البوار گردیده۔ وبدان جهت تزلزل تمام درمیان خورد و کلان آن فرقه کالانعام افتاد۔ هر چند سرداران دیگر جنگ وجدال کردند نتوانستند که دلاوران را از پس رخنها باز گردانند، تابوقت طلوع سحر کما نداران قدر انداز که در شب تاریك قضا کردار چشم مور می کشایند ونیزه بازان سحر ساز که بطعن نیزه شهامت آثار گرد آن[2] را از روی زمین در می ربایند، فیلان کوه نورد وصف شگاف را از پیش روان ساخته بار دیگر براعداء زور آورده به نیروی جلادت ومرادنگی بقلعه درآمده بسیار نیزه بازی وتیر اندازی[3] کردند۔

مثنوی:

زابروی خوبان کمان یادکرد　　زهر گوشه فتنه بنیاد کرد
روان ناوك فتنه از هر کنار　　بتاراج جانها چون مژگان یار
سپرها لبالب بخون متصل　　چو دامان عشاق پرخون دل
کمرهای زرین بخون لاله گون　　یلان تاکمر غرق دریای خون
زخون چشمهای زره قطره بار　　چون باران که ریزد زابربهار

چون دست قضا دیده پندار آن شرذمه ضلال واستکبار را به غشاوه ادبار "وحسبوا الا تکون فتنة فعموا وصموا"[4] پوشانیده بموجب فرموده "فما استطاعوا مضیاً ولایرجعون"[5] راه نجاح ونجات برایشان مسدود گردانیده۔ واز اهل اسلام بدعاء "ربنا افرغ علینا صبراً وثبت اقدامنا وانصرنا علی القوم الکافرین"[6] رطب اللسان بودند۔ واز عالم بالا

١۔ قرآن مجید : ٧٨/٤
٢۔ ع: نان
٣۔ ع: تیرباری
٤۔ قرآن : ٧١/٥
٥۔ قرآن مجید : ٦٧/٣٦
٦۔ قرآن مجید : ١٣/٦١

نـدای فـرح افزاء "نصر من الله وفتح قریب وبشر المومنین"[١] بگوش هوش مـی شنودند، بر اشرار کفار که جوق درجوق پیش آمده از برای گرفتن رخنها سینه سپر می کردند، غالب آمدند واکثری را بر بالائی یك دیگر بـضـرب حسـام خون آشام وپرواز سهام شهب التئام انداخته واز کشتها هرجا پشتها ساختند وبقیة السیفی را که "کانهم حمر مستنفرة فرت من قسورة"[٢] گـریـختـه بهـر سوی می دویدند ودرپیش انداخته به سنان جان ستـان بـدرك اسـفـل مـی رسانیدند. وچون کوکب فتح واقبال از مطلع فـضـل وافـضـال حضرت ملك متعال، جلت آلائه وعمت نعمائه، از افق کـرامت "وما النصر إلا من عند الله العزیز الحکیم"[٣] طلوع نموده، جمیع عسـاکر فیروزی مآثر به قلعه درآمدند. برحسب فرمان واجب الاذعان "اقتـلـوا المشرکین کافة"[٤] تـمـامـی مـردان آن متمردان را که در هرجا دویست نفر وسی[٥] صـدنـفـر جمع شده جنگ می کردند بقتل رسانیده، زنان وفرزندان ایشان را اسیر کردند وبموجب وعده "وعدکم الله مغانم کثیرة تاخذونها"[٦] امـوال وغنائم بی شمار از نقد وجنس بدست درآودند "فقطع دابر الذین ظلموا والحمد لله رب العالمین"[٧]۔

مـی بـایـد که شرافت مآب، عمدة الملك، رکن السلطنة القاهرة عـضـد الـدولة الـباهـرة، موتمن الخلافة الزاهرة، قدوة اماجد الخوانین فی الـزمان، عارج معارج الایالة والرفعة بین الاقران، مخلص جان سپار، نیك اندیش، فارس پردل، شجاعت کیش، صف آرای معرکه جلادت وتهور، مبـارز الـدین میر محمد خان بهادر، وشرافت مآب، عمدة الملك، رکن

١۔ قرآن مجید : ١٣/٦١
٢۔ قرآن مجید : ٧٤/ ٥٠
٣۔ قرآن مجید : ١٢٦/٧
٤۔ آیت کریمه غلط نقل شده، صحیح "قاتلوا المشرکین کافة کما یقاتلونکم کافة" است. رجوع کیند قرآن مجید : ٣٦/٩
٥۔ ع: سه
٦۔ قرآن مجید :٢٠/٤٨
٧۔ قرآن مجید : ٤٥/٦

السلطنة القاهرة، عضد الدولة الباهرة، زبدة المخلصين فی الدوران، لائق الاعتبار والاحسان، فارس میدان مبارزت وتهور، قطب الدین محمد خاں بهادر وباقی خوانین عظام وسلاطین کرام مع زمره سادات صاحب سعادت وعلماء افادت آیات ومشائخ کبار وقضات شریعت دثار وسائر اصول واعیان وعموم مقیمان ومتوطنان وچودریان وقانون گویان ورعایا ومزارعان سر کار پنجاب علی تفاوت درجاتهم وتباین طبقاتهم بدین بشارت فرخنده اشارت این فتح نامه که مقدمه فتوحات گرامی است، مبتهج ومسرور گشة، سجدات شکر نامحصور از سرحضور بجا آورند ودر اوقات طیبات، که مظان اجابت دعوات است، بدعای بقاء ذات خجسته آیات وثبات دولت فرخنده سعادت ومزید توفیق ما باداء مراسم جهاد وغزا وجمیع طاعات وعبادات ووظائف خیرات ومبرات اشتغال نموده مترصد باشند که یوماً فیوماً ابواب فتح وفیروزی ونصرت وبهروزی بچهره دولت وجبهه حشمت ما مفتوح ومکشوف گردد۔ وچون بعد از انتظام مهام ولایت چتور عنان عزیمت بجانب دار الخلافة آگره معطوف فرموده ایم:

مطلع:

اسپ زیرران چتر ظفر برسر فتح ونصرت پیش ویس عون الهی رهبر

انشاء الله دریں چند روز بمقر خلافت نزول اجلال می فرمائیم۔ آن رکن السلطنة خاطر اشرف متوجه انتظام احوال ستوده مآل خود وحصول امانی وآمال تمامی دولت خواهان دانسته، چگونگی حالات وواقعات راپیوسته عرض داشت[1] می نموده باشد ومدعای که بوده باشد معروض گرداند که بشرف اجابت وقبول مقرون وموصول خواهد گشت ۔ کتب بالامر العالی خلد نفاذه ولازال مطاعاً فی مقام اجمیر عاشر شهر رمضان المبارك ۹۷۵ھ۔

۱۔ ع: عرضه داشت

(۲)
فتح نامه
(بمناسبت شکشت وقتل علی قلی خاں صادر شد)

سادات عظام ومشائخ کرام وقضات کرام وخوانین نامدار وبیگچها وملازمان درگاه خلائق پناه وعموم ساکنان ومقیمان ممالك محروسه[۱] وچودریان وقانون گویان ومقدمان ورعایا ومزارعان سرکار آگره علی تفاوت مراتبهم بدانند که دریں ولا بامداد جنود حضرت الهی بالشکر فیروزی مآل از نواحی لکهنو بعزیمت رفع ودفع علی قلی وبهادر متوجه شدیم۔ چوں به قصبه رای برولی[۲] رسیدیم خبر رسید که مشار الیهما در موضع سکرور از توابع مانکپور نشستهٔ داعیه پل بستن دارند که از سرآب گنگ بگذرند۔ شب یکشنبه از قصبه مذکور عبور نموده۔ آنها بمجرد خبر توجه رایات نصرت آیات از پل گذشته خود را بجوسی پیاگ کشیدند۔ چوں خوانین عظام سرکار آگره ومانکپور راکه زعقب آں دونمك حرام آمده بودند، حکم جهاں مطاع بنفاذ پیوست که بسرعت متوجه آنها شده خود نیز بنفس نفیس بابعضی از خوانین وسلاطین وسائر جاں سپاران که درملازمت بودند بطریق استعجال عزیمت قلع وقمع آں دونمك حرام وسائر اهل ضلال فرمودیم۔ صباح روز دوشنبه خوانین عظام مانکپور بآنها رسیدند وبنیاد جدال وقتال نمودند[۳] وتا نیمروز یك دیگر از خوانین حمله های مردانه وکوشش های دلیرانه نموده، دقیقه از دقائق جد واجتهاد ودلاوری نامرعی نگذاشته، آخر باغیه غلبه نموده خوانین را از جای برداشته بوده که دریں حالت بدولت ونصرت واقبال بافوجی از جاں سپاران مبارز کیش که

۱۔ وملازمان درگاه خلائق پناه وعموم ساکنان ومقیمان ممالك محروسه، ندارد
۲۔ رای بریلی۔ رجوع کنید اکبر نامه، جلد دوم، ص ۲۹۰
۳۔ ع: نموده

درملازمت بودند بآن گروه انبوه مقابله شده، بعون عنایت بیغایت ملك متعال که شامل حال دولت بادشاهی است، آنها را از پیش برداشتیم ودلاوران صف شکن بسیاری را به تیغ بیدریغ بقتل رسانیده، علی قلی را در مغلوبه جنگ به سزا رسانیده، بهادر را زنده گرفته بملازمت آوردند. وباقی اشرار متفرق وپریشان وپیاده بجنگلها گریزان پنهان شدند وتایك صد زنجیر فیل بدست آمد وغنائم بی شمار به تصرف عساکر نصرت مآثر درآمد. الحمد لله علی تکاثر نعمائه وتواتر آلائه.

می باید که به شنیدن خبر این فتح مبین مبتهج ومسرور گشته وظائف شکر توالی فتوحات نامیات ما را از حضرت واهب العطایا مستدعی شده بلوازم دعا گوئی اشتغال نمایند وخاطر اشرف متوجه حصول امانی وآمال خود دانسته درین باب قد غن لازم دانند. تحریراً بالامر العالی خلد نفاذه ولازال مطاعاً.

(۳)
فتح نامه
(بمناسبت فتح قلعه شیر گڑھ)

سادات رفیع الدرجات وعلماء افاضت آیات ومشائخ کرامت شعار وقضات شریعت دثار وموالی واهالی واعیان وحکام ودارو غکان وکلانتران وعموم ساکنان وجمهور متوطنان سرکار پنجاب بدانند که چون بامداد توفیقات الهی سپاه نصرت دستگاه اطراف وجوانب قلعه مانکوٹ را بنوعی محاصره کردند[۱] که راه بدر شدن سکندر و سائر مخالفان افغان بالکلیه مسدود گشة وذخیره که داشة اند بآخر رسید[۲] وقبل

---

۱ - ع: کرده اند
۲ - ع: رسیده

ازیں بچند روز اهل قلعه از جلیل وحقیر و کبیر وصغیر فریاد الامان برده وزبان استغفار بمضمون "واعف عنا واغفر لنا وارحمنا أنت مولانا"[۱] کشوده اند[۲] وسکندر از روی عجز غازی خاں و کیل خود را بدرگاه معلی فرستاده درمقام اطاعت وفرماں برداری بوده، بعضی ملتمسات اورا اجابت فرمودیم. بعد از آں چناں ظاهر شد که برقول خود ثابت نیست ودرپی مکر وتزویر اند وبآنچه قرار یافته بود عمل نمی نمایند وطریق بغی وفساد پیش می گیرند. بنابراں حکم فرمودیم که لشکریان نصرت اقتران از هر طرف پیش رفته گرد بر گرد قلعه را از آنچه بود تنگ تر گرفتند. وبعضی از امراء ویکه جوانان ومردم سکندر که ایں معنی رامشاهده نمودند ویقین ایشاں شده بود که سکندر وبعضی امراء او خیال محال بخاطر گذرانیده اند ومآل کار ایشاں بخساره می انجامد، جماعه جماعه خود را از قلعه انداخته بدرگاه معلی آمدند تا در عرصه سه چهار روز قریب هزار کس بدولت عتبه بوسی مشرف گشته ازاں ورطه خلاص شدند. چوں سکندر وبعضی مخالفاں ملاحظه ایں حال نمودند ودانستند که عساکر نصرت مآثر بنوعی احاطه وغلبه کرده اند که قلعه را می گیرند وایشاں را مجال[۳] محافظت همه قلعچها نیست، خود را بقلعه های دیگر کشیده کلید قلعه شیر گڑه را بدرگاه فرستادند وبتاریخ فلاں شهر فلاں نماز شام شب شبنه سنه فلاں ناصر الملك مولانا پیر محمد خاں باقریب دو هزار کس بقلعه در آمدند الحمد لله علی ذالك.

اکنوں احوال آنها بریں منوال است که اکثر از امراء وسرداراں[٤] ومردم سکندر که مانده اند بعد تاتار خاں و مردمی سه چار دیگر هر کس که

۱ـ قرآن مجید، ۲/۲۸٦

۲ـ ع: کشوده آمد

۳ـ ع: مجال، ندارد

٤ـ ع: سوداگراں

هست عرائض بدرگاه معلی فرستاده التجا بآستان عالی شان دارند۔ وجماعه خود را از قلعه انداخته می آیند۔ وقد غن فرموداه ایم که محافظت اطراف وجوانب بیشتر از پیشتر اهتمام نموده فروگذاشت نکنند۔ امید بدرگاه الهی چناں است که درین پنج شش روز بلکه زودتر قلاع دیگر فتح شود وخاطر از ممر شرارت سکندر ومخالفان که هستند بالکلیه جمع گردد، انشاء الله تعالی۔ می باید که بنوید ایں فتح نامه مسرور وشاداں گشته وظائف شکر وسپاس الهی بتقدیم رسانند واز حضرت فتاح بی منت تواتر فتوحات مارا مسألت می نموده مترصد اجابت باشند وخاطر اشرف متوجه انتظام احوال وحصول[1] امانی وآمال خود دانند۔

(٤)

فتح نامة

(هنگام محاصره قلعه مانکوٹ صادر شد)

سادات رفیع الدرجات وعلماء افاضت آیات ومشائخ کرامت شعار وقضات شریعت دثار، موالی واهالی واعیان وحکام وداروغکان وعمال ومباشران وعموم ساکنان وجمهور متوطنان دار السلطنت لاهور، صینت عن آفات الاعوام والشهور، بدانند که مجمل فتوحاتی که بمواهب حضرت واهب العطیات روی نموده ومی نماید ایں است که چوں سکندر وسپاه او از صدمات عساکر فیروزی مآثر از نواحی فلاں گریزاں شده بقلاع فلك ارتفاع مانکوٹ که، در رفعت واستحکام درمیاں قلاع وجبل آفاق طاق است، متحصن گشته اند بمصلحت وصوابدید اعتضاد السلطنة القاهرة شجاع الدین بیرم خاں بهادر بابام[2] ایدالله بنصرته، که الحق مدار ایں دولت پائدار است، بعزیمت محاصره آں قلاع متعاقب متوجه شدیم۔ وآں اعتماد السلطنة جهت تحقیق

۱۔ ع : حصول، ندارد

۲۔ ع: بابام بهادر

وتفحص اطراف وجوانب آن قلاع افاضل پناه، افادت شعار، مستعد الرعایة والاعتبار، کامل الاعتقاد، پاك ضمیر صاحب السیف والتدبیر، ناصر الملك ، ناظم الدولة، لازم العز[۱] واجب التوقیر، خادم دولت خواه جانی، معز الدین مولانا پیر محمد شیروانی را فرستادند که حقیقت درهاء قلعها[۲] وقلعچها وجاهای را که مرچال نو[۳] باید ساخت بواقعی معلوم نموده کیفیت بدرگاه معلی خاطر نشان سازد۔ بنا بران روز دیگر اطراف وجوانب راخان بابام مرچل[٤] بخش کرده، اطراف وجوانب قلعه تعین نمودند۔ مبار زان حق گذار ودلاوران شجاعت شعار از هر جانب بنیاد کارزار نموده، هر گاه از مخالفان جمعی بداعیه شوخی بیرون می آیند، اکثری از آنها بقتل می رسانند۔ وقحط وتنگی درمیان ایشان پدید آمده، وشب وروز جماعه جماعه دفعه دفعه خود را از قلعه انداخته بدرگاه معلی می آیند۔ امید بدرگاه حضرت الهی چنان است که درهمیں چند روز فتح قلعه روی نماید ودولت خواهان بر اعداء مظفر ومنصور ومخالفان از غلبه احباء مغلوب ومقهور گردند۔ دریں باب قدغن لازم دانند۔ تحریراً فی تاریخ۔

(٥)
فتح نامه
(بمناسبت کامرانی درمهمات گرم سیر وزمین داور)

عمدة الملك، رکن السلطنة القاهرة، لائق الاعتبار والاحسان نظام الدین فلان بعنایت بیغایت بادشاهی عز امتیاز وشرف افتخار یافته بداند که

۱ـ ع: العزة
۲ـ ع: قلعها، ندارد
۳ـ ع: باید، ندارد
٤ـ ع : پورچل
٥ـ ع : قریب، ندارد

کیفیت احوال این محال بدین منوال است که قبل ازین فلان، که از جمله اقوام قریب[1] عبد الله خان است، باجمعی کثیر از اوزبکیه شومیه ظل نکبت بر ساحت مملکت فلان برانداخته قلعه خلنج که عمده محال آنجا است، باچند قلعه دیگر باغواء واضلال که شیوه ایشان است، بتحت تصرف خود در می آوردند، وسکنه[2] آن نیز از طریق صواب انحراف جسته بتصورات باطل اطاعت ومطابعت (متابعت) آن جماعت بی بضاعت می نمایند۔ ومعتمد الملك فلان در قلعه بست که دونیم فرسخی قلعه مذکور[3] است نشسته از مدافعه ومحاربه ایشان عاجز شده، غازی خان وکیل خودرا بملازمت فرستاده التماس استغاثه امداد واعانت از درگاه معلی نموده۔ وبا آنکه خاطر اقدس اشرف بواسطه اعمال شنیعی که قبل ازین بظهور رسیده بود، بغایت مکدر بود، قلم اغماض ونسیان برصفحه تقصیرات وزلات ماسبق او کشیده موازی چهار[4] هزار سوار، که هریك در روزگار ثانی رستم واسفندیار بمدد وکومك او فرستادیم۔ بمجرد رسیدن عساکر ظفر مآثر معتمد الملك مومی الیه از آب عبور نموده برسرآن جماعت می رود وفیما بین جنگ وجدال عظیم دست داده، آنجماعه نابکار برگشته[5] روزگار را شکست داده قریب بدویست نفر از آنجماعه بی استطاعت بقتل می رسانند ودوست محمد اغلن را دستگیر کرده بملازمت عالی فرستادند۔ والحال مشارالیه را باجمعی دیگر که درین مدت بدفعات گرفتار شده اند درقید وحبس داریم۔ وبعد از فتح آن قلاع غازی خان وکیل مومی الیه آمده حالت عجز واضطراب[6] او مرتفع گردانید، حسب التماس

١۔ قریب، ندارد
٢۔ ع: ورعایا وکدخدایان آنجا
٣۔ ع: خلنج
٤۔ ع: چهار ده
٥۔ ع: برگشته، ندارد
٦۔ اضطرار

مشار الیه هزار نفر را مقرر داشتیم که بالکاء گرم سیر وزمین داور رفته بمحافظت ومحارست آن مملکت اشتغال نمایند. فاما چون معتمد الملك بغایت از آنجماعه ترسیده ومتوهم بود، ترك الكاء گرم سیر وزمین داور داده متوجه الكاء ترین گردید. از رفتن مشار الیه مخالفین دلیر شده ملا قرابهادر ومحمد یار مرزا، که دو سردار عمده اند، جمعی کثیر از مخالفان تبه روزگار را برداشته بقصد آن که دران ملك بر مسند حکومت متمکن گردند، درتاریخ شهر فلان بالکاء مذکور آمده قلعه زمین داور را باچند قلعه دیگر محاصره نمودند. وچون این خبر بسمع اقدس رسید، دران روز عمدة الملك، لائق الاحسان سلطان قلی سلطان با دو هزار سوار شجاعت نشان مقرر فرمودیم. چون عساکر ظفر مآثر بکنار هرمند می رسند، دوچار لشکر مخالف شده بین الفریقین مجادله ومقاتله عظیم دست می دهد. جوانان نصرت شعار ومردمان معارك کارزار اعلام مردی ومردانگی برافراشته، بیمن تائید حضرت آفریدگار، جل شانه وعظم سلطانه، ومیامن توفیقات پروردگار آنجماعه نابکار وآن طبقه برگشته روزگار را شکشت داده هفتاد وهشتاد نفر را بقتل می رسانند و باقی خود را در آب هرمند انداخته غریق بحر هلاکت می گردانند.

الحمد لله والمنه که مهمات اینجا بروفق اراده اولیاء دولت قاهرة است، ومخالفان منکوب ومخذول وموافقان مبتهج ومسرور اند وازهیچ ممر امری که موجب نقص این دولت بی زوال باشد، حادث وواقع نیست. دغدغه وتفرقه بخاطر راه ندهد واز اخباری که بافواه مذکور می شده باشد اندیشه ننماید که مهمات الکاء گرم سیر وزمین داور را انجام داده، بعد از شکست مخالفان هزار سوار دیگر را مقرر داشته ایم که بمحافظت آنجا اشتغال نمایند. وخاطر اشرف متوجه انتظام احوال وحصول امانی وآمال خود دانسته، روز بروز حقیقت اراده ومدعیات خود را معروض می گردانیده باشد که انجام پذیر است. درین قدغن لازم داند.

مناشیر

(٦)

منشور در تفویض منصب وکالت سرکار همایون

چون از هبوب نسائم فضل منان ذوی الاحسان حدائق خلافت واقبال که "جنة عرضها السموٰت والارض"[۱] صفت سعت اوست، طراوت ونظارت گرفته واز تقاطر غمام لطف دیّان واهب البروالا متنان ریاض[۲] دولت سلطنت واجلال، که "جنة عرضها کعرض السماء"[۳] بیان فسحت[٤] اوست، خضارت ونزاهت پذیرفته، چتر والا اساس بادشاهی ما، که غیرت شادروان سپهر معلی است، سایه الطاف واعطاف برمرافق ساکنان جهان انداخته لواء زیبا لباس، که رشك سپهر مینا است، کافه متوطنان دوران را از تاثیر حرارت حوادث ونوائب مصئون ومامون ساخته[٥]؛

قطعه:

انچه اسباب جهان داری وکار خسرویست
دولت ما را بحمد الله مهیا کرده اند
وانچه از بهر جهانگیری وکار سروریست
در ازل ما را ندا انا فتحنا کرده اند

مانیز بر حسب مشیت لازم التمشیت "بالشکر تدوم النعم" جوامع نیت خورشید ارتقاء وبواعث نهمت کیوان اعتلاء مصروف ومعطوف بران داریم که جمعی از مقتبسان آفتاب دولت ارجمند وبرخی از مستفیضان

۱ـ قرآن مجید : ۱۳۳/٤
۲ـ ع: دولت، زیاده دارد
۳ـ قرآن مجید : ۲۹/۱۹
٤ـ ع: فصحت
٥ـ ع: ساختند

آثار کوکب حشمت بی گزند از مفتح "من کان فی المهد صبیا"[۱] تا مختم "مادمت حیا"[۲] شمع امانی وآمال وچراغ اوضاع واحوال را از سراج وهاج ایں دودمان عالی شان که منطوق "یکاد زیتها یضئی ولو لم تمسسه نار"[۳] مبین انوار برکات است، روشن ونورانی دارند - واز خلوص عقیدت فطری وخصوص طویت جبلی آناء الیل واطراف النهار دریں آستان آسمان مقدار باشاعت آثار دولت خواهی وخیر اندیشی واطاعت اطوار جان سپاری ووفا کیشی حتی الامکان اجتهاد واهتمام گمارند تا باصناف رعایات متعالی وآلاف هدایت (هدایات) متوالی که فراخور همت والا نهمت بادشاهی ولائق حالت وقابلیت سالکان مسالك دولت خواهی توانند بود، از نظائر واشباه امتیاز واختصاص یابند وبدستیاری فضل بیغایت وپائمردی لطف بی نهایت فراز مدارج[٤] مرادات ومدعیات شتابند -

وازاں فرقه اخلاص آثار وزمره اختصاص کردار، ناظم السلطنة والخلافة، صاعد مصاعد الوکالة والامارة، مخلص ثابت الاعتقاد ولائق التقریب والاعتماد وموتمن الملك والحال، معتمد الحضرة العلیة بجلائل الخصائل مبارز الدین فلاں بایں خصائل امتیاز یافته وپرتو انوار "التوفیق شی عزیز ولا یعطی الا لعبد عزیز" وقوع ایں حالات وظهور ایں مقالات برساحت احوال او تافته، چه از مطلع مهد رضاع تا ارتفاع اختر دولت بیضاء شعاع چوں بخت معاون دمساز ومانند طالع مساعد رفیق وهمراز بوده، یوماً فیوماً بوسیله ظهور خدمات شائسته وواسطه وفور عبودیات بائسته باعلی مدارج واسنی معارج عارج وصاعد می نمود - ودراں زمان حدوث حوادث ونزول نوازل که مصدوقه "ظلمات بعضها فوق بعض"[۵] ظاهر می شد، رای آفتاب قرین وفکر رزیں نیز از

۱- قرآن مجید : ۲۹/۱۹
۲- قرآن مجید : ۳۱/۱۹
۳- قرآن مجید : ۳۵/۱٤
٤- ع: معارج
۵- قرآن مجید : ٤۰/۲٤

میامن تعلیم وتلقین "نور علی نور یهدی الله لنوره من یشاء"[۱] بمامن خلاص ونجات راه نما بود وآثار شجاعت ومردانگی وانوار مبارزت وفرزانگی او درزمان صدمات جنگ وجدال واوان اشتعال نائره قتال بایادی اهتمام واجتهاد ابواب فتح ونصرت برچهره احوال همگنان می کشود، وبنیان سلطنت وجهان بانی را بقوائم مساعی جمیله مشید می ساخت، ودر تمهید دعائم اساس خلافت وکامرانی رایت مساعی جلیله[۲] می افراخت ـ فلاجرم باقتضاء ایں مقال دریں ولا نسائم عنایات وافیات از مهب لطف خاقانی (به) نضارت ریاض فرخنده حال او وزیده وغنچه مقاصدش از مصب شبنم فضل سلطانی شگفته گردیده، منصب جلیل القدر، عظیم الوقع وکالت سرکار همایون را من حیث الانفراد والاستقلال دون المساهمه والاشتراك بآن ناظم السلطنة مفوض داشتیم وزمام حل وعقد وقبض وبسط ورتق وفتق ایں امر رفیع الشان را بید شهامت وحراست او گذاشتیم که چنانچه از وفور فطانت ودراست ودرایت وفراست او متصور است، بلوازم ایں امر قیام واقدام[۳] نموده مضمون "التعظیم لامرالله والشفقة علی خلق الله" را نقش تیقظ وانتباه دارد، ودر تعظیم واحترام وتوقیر واکرام طوائف انام از سادات لازم الاجلال وعلماء دانش خصال ومشائخ کرامت مقال وقضات شریعت دثار وموالی واهالی وافر الافضال وامراء ووزراء ومحمبوع سپاهیان وغیر ذالك از وضیع وشریف واقاصی وادانی علی تفاوت طبقاتهم وتباین درجاتهم دقیقه از دقائق نامرعی نگذارد، وچنان نماید که همه طوائف راضی وشاکر بوده، شجره معاش وسلوك او از باب شهرت ونیك نامی باشد وآثار ستوده مرضیه اوتا انقراض زمان دستور العمل اصحاب حکم

۱ـ قرآن مجید : ۲۵/۲۴
۲ـ ع: جلیله ندارد
۳ـ ع: اقتدام

وفرمان گردد- وبرظهر فرامین واحکام مقدم برهمه ارباب دخل مهر زند- سبیل برادران سلیمان مکان وفرزندان سکندر نشان وخوانین ظفر لواء وسلاطین حشمت انتماء وامراء تهمتن تن وصدور موتمن ووزراء آصف صفوت وعمال کفایت مرتبت وناظمان اعمال دیوانی ووافقان اشغال سلطانی وباقی ملازمان عتبه علیه[۱] نامداری وسائر خدمه سده سنیه کامگاری وزمره انام از طبقه خواص وقاطبه عموم، صان[۲] الله تعالیٰ ارکان بنائهم من الانهدام، که عظام الدولة مشارالیه را وکیل مطلق العنان[۳] دانسته اوامر ونواهی اورا مطیع ومنقاد باشند وجمیع امور ملکی ومالی را برای وررویت او مفوض ومرجوع شناسند، وهمه فرامین واحکام را بمهر او رسانیده بی مهر او منظور ومعمول ندانند- ومیربخشی تعین علوفات را درحضور او کند ودیوانیان تن جاگیر مردم را بوقوف واستصواب او مشخص سازند- وجزوی وکلی را باستحضار او فیصل دهند- ومبلغ فلان از محل مذکوره فی الضمن در وجه علوفه آن موتمن الدوله مقرر شناخته واصل گردانند، وچیزی قاصر ومنکسر نسازند- عمدة الملك مومی الیه نیز باید که ملاحظه فرق برایا فراخور احوال ایشان منظور دارد ودرجمیع اوقات نظر برعواقب امور انداخته درهمه حالات امعان نظر گمارد وچنان سازد که صادرات افعال وواردات اعمال او بطریقه صواب وبنهج اولو الالباب بوده، نتائج آن بر روزگار او عائد ولاحق گردد- از جوانب برین جمله بروند وچون بتوقیع وقیع منیع مطاع، لازال نافذاً فی الاقطار والارباع، موشح وموضح ومزیّن ومحلی ومجلی گردد اعتماد نمایند-

---

۱- ع: علیه، ندارد
۲- ع: صانها
۳- ع: العنان، ندارد

(۷)

منشور در تفویض منصب وزارت

امراء نامدار ونصرت شعار ووزراء کفایت آثار وارکان دولت قاهره واعیان حشمت باهره ونواب بارگاه واصحاب درگاه وعمال ومباشران مهمات ومعاملات وارباب وکلان تران وکدخدایان ومتوطنان ومقیمان واحشام وصحر انشینان وجمهور انام از فرقه خواص وقاطبه عوام صانها (صانهم) اللّٰه تعالی عن الآفات والبلیات بدانند که لایزال همت صافی نیت ونیت شافی رویت مصروف ومعطوف بر آنست که دولت خواهان صادق الاخلاص وجان سپاران کامل الاختصاص که خلوص ارادت وحق گذاری وخصوص عقیدت وخدمت گاری ایشان بظاهر وباطن درجمیع مواقع ومواطن مرة بعد اولی وکرة بعد اخری بوضوح پیوسته شد، باصناف الطاف خسروانه مخصوص ومفتخر گردندتا سائر بندگان آستان اقبال آشیان بعنایت بادشاهانه امیدوار بوده دردولت خواهی ویك رنگی پدرود نمایند[۱]۔ وچون عمدة الملك، کامل العقیدة، صادق الاعتقاد، اعتماد الدولة العلیة، رئیس جلیس مجالس خاص، نظام الدین فلان را مدتی است که شیوه خدمت گذاری ویك جهتی را دثار خود ساخته، قدم از جاده عبودیت بیرون نه نهاده وانواع خدمات شائسته ازو بظهور رسیده، وقامت بااستقامتش لائق خلعت رعایت وتربیت است۔ بنابران درین ولا بموجب "اذا اراد الله بملك خیراً جعل له وزیراً صالحاً" وزارت دودمان رفیع المکان، که از اعاظم کارگاه سلطنت وخلافت است، بعمدة الملك مشارالیه مفوض فرمودیم که چنانچه از حسن اهتمام وفراست او سزد باتمام وانجام این

۱۔ ع: بمانند

عارفه قیام واقدام نماید وبمعنی "اذا حکمتم بین الناس ان تحکموا بالعدل"[١] عمل نموده، نوعی نماید که یوماً فیوماً مورد تزاید الطاف گردد۔ می باید که عمدة الملك مشارالیه را وزیر من حیث الاستقلال این دودمان عالی شان دانسته از سخن وصلاح او که هر آئینه موافق قانون سلطنت بوده باشد، بیرون نروند ورسوم این عارفه را مخصوص او شمرده مخلد الدوام دانند وحسب الفرمان قضاجریان، سعادت توأمان درنگذرند۔ وچون بتوقیع وقیع رفیع منیع اشرف اعلی موشح وموضح ومحلی ومزین گردد اعتماد نمایند۔ کتب بالا مرالعالی خلد نقاذه ولا زال مطاعاً۔

(٨)

منشور در تفویض منصب وزارت کل سرکار همایون

فهرست فرامین کامگاری، عنوان مناشیر نامداری، سپاس وستائش بادشاهی را سزاوار است که در دیوان کثیر الفیضان "نحن قسمنا بینهم"[٢] منشور وافر السرور خواقین داد گستر را بطغراء غراء "ثم جعلنا کم خلائف فی الارض"[٣] وتوقیع وقیع "مایفتح الله للناس من رحمة فلا ممسك لها"[٤] مزین ومحلی گردانیده، وانتظام امور جاه وجلال والتیام مهام حشمت واقبال این زمره خلافت مرتبه را بمساعی جلیلة ناهجان مناهج دولت خواهی وسواعی جزیله سالکان مسالك خبرت وآگاهی روَاج ورونق (داده) کافه رعایا وعامه برایا را از یمن عدالت وفرط نصفت ایشان از توزع بال وفرسودگی نجات داده، برضاء

١ـ قرآن مجید : ٥٨/٤
٢ـ قرآن مجید : ٣٢/٤٣
٣ـ قرآن مجید : ١٤/١٠
٤ـ قرآن مجید : ٢/٣٥

(برفاه) حال وآسودگی رسانیده۔

قطعه:

ای لطف تو سردفتر اصناف حکم — بخشد کرمت ملك باشراف امم
از مدح تو عاجز است مداح زمان — وز وصف توقاصر است وصاف قلم

وطغراء صحائف کامرانی وسر ورق دفاتر جهان بانی نعت ودرود دین پناهی است که چون تارك مبارکش رابا تاج باابتهاج "کنت نبیا وآدم بین الماء والطین" محلی ساختند، دست حق پرستش به نگین "ولکن رسول الله وخاتم النبین"[۱] مزین گرد انیدند وپروانچه "إن الدین عند الله الاسلام"[۲] وفرمان واجب الا ذعان "ومن یبتغ غیر الا سلام دیناً فلن یقبل منه"[۳] به شش جهت هفت اقلیم ارسال داشتند وقامت بااستقامتش بتشریف شریف "وما ارسلناك إلا رحمة للعالمین"[٤] مقرر ساختند ورایت عظمت "بعثت الی الاسود والاحمر" درشش رکن گیتی وچارسو برافراشت۔

مثنوی:[۵]

ای نام توسر دفتر ارباب وجود — شد آدم وعالم به طفیلت موجود
از نور دلت صبح هدایت روشن — وز صبح رخت شام ضلالت نابود

بر دفاتر روزگار ثبت یافته ومی یابد، وپرتو انوار رافت وامتنان بواسطه قلم زرین رقم راقمان نوادر آثار آناء الیل واطراف النهار بر عرصه احوال سکنه هر بلاد ودیار تافته ومی تابد۔ وازان زمره عقیدت پیشه وفرقه کفایت اندیشه عمدة الملك، رکن الدولة العلیة، موتمن المملکة البهیة، ناظم مناظم الامور، کافل مصالح الجمهور، عالی رای، عالم آرای،[٦]

۱۔ قرآن مجید : ۴۰/۳۳
۲۔ قرآن مجید : ۱۹/۳
۳۔ قرآن مجید : ۸۵/۳
٤۔ قرآن مجید : ۱۰۷/۲۱
۵۔ ع: قطعه
٦۔ ع: عالم رای

کارفرمای، مشکل کشای خواجه فلان است، که ازبدایت حال تا اکنون که قریب قرنی می شود باوجود سبقت خدمت گاری آباء واجداد طریق خدمت گاری مانند قدم بفرق راه حق گذاری پیمود، در بصر بصیرتش غیر از مآثر فرمان برداری وخدمت گاری ملحوظی ومنظوری ننموده، رای صواب نمایش در تدابیر امور ملك ومال مرآت غیب نما است وفکر ظلمت زدایش در رفع تیرگی حوادث ونوائب آفتاب جهان آراست، نظام احوال رعیت وسپاهی را باناملِ کثیر الفواضلش سببی است مقرون بخیر وصواب وانتظام آمال تمامی سالکان مسالك دولت خواهی (را) ایادی عظیم الفوائدش مفتاحی است فاتح مغلقات ابواب ـ بالجمله ذات فائض البرکاتش مستحق اصناف رعایات بادشاهی است وعنصر موفور السعادتش مستعد آلاف هدایت نامتناهی ـ بناءً علی ذالك درین ولا رایت مقاصدش را در ساحت اعتبار افراشته وآیت مطالبش را بر صفحه اختیار نگاشته، منصب وزارت کل سرکار همایون را، که از جلائل امور شهر یاری وعظائم مهام کامگاری است، من حیث[1] الانفراد والاستقلال بدو تفویض فرموده ارزانی داشتیم، وزمام حل وعقد وقبض وبسط وفتق ورتق (این) شغل رفیع القدر بکف کفایت او گذاشتیم که چنانچه از فرط وقوف ودانائی وکمال شعور وبینائی او متصور است، بلوازم این امر عظیم الوقع دقیقه از دقائق اجتهاد واحتیاط فرو گذاشت نکند ودر توفیر اموال دیوانی وتنظیم اعمال سلطانی وتکثیر زراعت وعمارت وترفیه احوال سپاهی ورعیت وایجاب مسئولات واسعاف مامولات فرق انام شرائط سعی واهتمام مرعی دارد ودرهمه حال شیوه امانت ودیانت را حتی الامکان رعایت نموده، دفتر اعمال خود را بارقام رعیت پروری ونصفت گستری[2] وچنان

۱ـ ع: حیث، ندارد
۲ـ ع: پذیر سازد، زیاده دار

نماید که آثار آن یوماً فیوماً بعرض رسیده موجب افزونی مواد مرحمت ومکرمت درباره او گردد.

می باید که خواقین بلند مقدار وسلاطین باوقار وامراء تهمتن تن[۱] وصدور موتمن ووزراء آصف نژاد ونواب باصدق وصداد (سداد) ومقربان درگاه خلافت پناه وابچکیان بارگاه سپهر اشتباه ومباشران اعمال دیوانی ومتصدیان اشغال سلطانی وارباب وکلان تران ورعایا ومزارعان واحشام وصحرا نشینان وعموم سکنه وجمهور متوطنه ممالك محروسه صینت عن الآفات والبلیات، عمدة الملك مومی الیه را وکیل کل صاحب اختیار ووزیر باتدبیر وافراقتدار دانسته، دست تعهد اورا در اعتناق[۲] این امر قوی دارند، امداد واعانت وتمشیت او بجای آورند ودرتعین علوفات ومرسومات ووظائف وسیور غالات واکرامات وهرچه از جهت متعلق به دیوان باشد بدو رجوع نموده، تعلیقه ومهر اورا کافی ومعتبر دانند وبی مهر او جاری ومعمول ندانند. وجمیع مناشیر و پروانجات ویورات رابمهر او رسانیده بی مهر او ممضی ومجری ندانند وانچه مفوض بدیوان بوده باشد بدو رجوع نموده از جزوی وکلی برای ورویت او مرجوع ومنحصر دانند وبهیچ کس غیر ازو رجوع ننمایند. ومبلغ فلان از محال مذکوره فی الضمن در وجه علوفه او مقرر دانسته بدو رسانند ودر ایصال این اهتمام بلیغ مبذول دارند. وآن ناظم الامور نیز باید که مضمون "التعظیم لامر الله والشفقة علی خلق اللّٰه" را نقش خاتم تیقظ وانتباء دارد وبرظهر مناشیر واحکام در محلی که جای وزارت است مهر زند ودر جمیع امور نوعی سازد که مزیدی بران متصور نباشد. ودر عهده دانند. چون بتوقیع وقیع منیع مزین ومعنون ومحلی ومجلی گردد اعتماد نمایند.

۱ـ ع: تن، ندارد

۲ـ ع: اسعاف

(۹)

منشور در تفویض منصب صدارت علیا

صدور صحائف احوال سلاطین لازم الاجلال وبدور خواقین[1] خجسته فال، فرخنده فر، نور گستر وقتی تواند بود که مزین باشد بحمد وثناء بادشاهی که منشور فائض النور "أفمن شرح الله صدره للاسلام فهو علی نور من ربه"[2] بر کمال عنایت بی زوال او دلیلی قاطع است، وفرمان واجب الاذعان "یعلم خائنة الأعین وماتخفی الصدور"[3] برغایت علم لا یزال او برهانی ساطع، جل شانه وظهر برهانه۔ وحصول جرائد اوقات بادشاهان تاجور وشمول مراتب ساعات شهنشاهان داد گستر مصحح ومنقح وقتی تواندنمود که معنون باشد بنعت ودرود دین پناهی که صدر مجلس نبوت برطبق حدیث صحیح "کنت نبیاً وآدم بین الماء والطین"۔[4] بتقدیم ذات فائض البر کاتش اعتراف دارند وواقفان مواقف رسالت بر وفق منطوق صحیح "اللهم اجعلنی من امة محمد"[5] اطاعت دین قویم ومتابعت ملت مستقیمش را موجب مباهات ومفاخرت می شمارند، صلی الله علیه وآله واصحابه واحبابه۔

اما بعد، بر ضمائر غیبی سرائر صدر نشینان مجامع دین ودولت وخواطر انجم نظائر خورده بینان محافل ملك وملت در نقاب واحتجاب

۱۔ ع: خواقین، ندارد

۲۔ قرآن مجید : ۲۱/۳۹۵

۳۔ قرآن مجید : ۱۹/۴۰

۴۔ ایں حدیث بایں الفاظ در کتب حدیث یافته نمی شود البته باختلاف الفاظ وارد شده۔ رجوع کنید کتاب الطیب من الخبیث فیما یدور علی السنة الناس من الحدیث، تالیف الشیخ الامام عبد الرحمن بن محمد، دار الکتاب العربی، بیروت، ۱۹۸۵ء، ص۱۲۶

۵۔ درصحاح یافته نمی شور

مستور نماند که چون دبیران کارخانه الهی نشان خلافت واقبال ما را بتوقیع "وإذا حکمتم بین الناس أن تحکموا بالعدل"[۱] پرداخته، در ازاء این موهبت عظمی وحذاء این مکرمت کبری رعایت جانب واجابت مطالب[۲] (و) مآرب سادات وعلماء ومشائخ وصلحاء وتکثیر موقوفات وتوفیر مستغلات وترویج بقاع الخیر وتنسیق ابواب البر ومایتعلق بها برذمه همت والا نهمت واجب ولازم ولابد ومتحتم داشته ایم۔ وحصول این مامول وشمول این مسئول را صدر الکتاب صحائف نامداری وفخر الخطاب صفائح کامگاری می دانیم۔ وبنا بر آن که انتظام والتیام این امر بوسیله صدری بلند قدری، که زبان حالش بفحواء "رب اشرح لی صدری ویسّرلی امری واحلل عقدة من لسانی یفقهوا قولی"[۳] جاری شده، میسر نیست۔ لاجرم منصب علیة المرتبت صدارت علیا را، که از جلائل مهام وشرائف امور لازم الاحترام است، بامجد العلماء الکرام واقدم الفضلاء فی الانام فلان که قامت قابلیتش بتشریف جمعیت فضائل وکمالات آراسته است وتارك فطرتش بحلیه استحقاق سعادات وجلالات پیراسته، تقویض فرمودیم تا چنانچه از وفور دین داری وشریعت پروری او متصور است در تحقیق احوال سادات وعلماء ومشائخ وصلحاء وغیر آن از انچه انکشاف احوال ایشان تعلق بصدر می دارد اتمام نموده، دقیقه فرو گذاشت نکند، وآن طائفه را در پایه تخت عالی بخت نیابت نموده، احوال هر کسی را کما ینبغی معروض گرداند، ودر تحقیق اوقاف و کثرت حاصل آن مساعی جمیله مبذول داشته متولیان امین متدین تعین نماید که حاصلات آن را موافق شروط واقفان بمصارف وجوب وارباب استحقاق رسانند۔ ودر جمیع لوازم این منصب بروجهی

۱۔ قرآن مجید : ٥٨/٤

۲۔ ع: مطالب : ندارد

۳۔ قرآن مجید : ۲۰/۲٥۔۲۸

اهتمام نمايد كه آثار آن بعرض رسيده يوماً فيوماً موجب تزايد مواد ومراتب درجات او گردد، ورسم الصدارت موافق قانون قديم وقاعده استمرار گيرد.

مي بايد كه برادران كيوان رفعت، بيضاء علم وفرزندان گردون حشمت، انجم حشم، وخواقين كشور گير وسلاطين باتدبير وامراء رستم تهور وصدور فضائل تفاخر ووزراء آصف صفوت وسائر منشيان عتبه دولت ومباشران اشغال ديواني ومتعهدان اعمال سلطاني وزمره انام از طبقه خواص وقاطبه انام[1] عوام، احسن الله احوالهم وانجح بالخير والسعادة آمالهم، صدارت مآب مومي اليه را صدر بلند قدر تصور نموده، دست تقلد او را در اعتناق اين شغل قوي دارند واعانت وتقويت وتمشيت بجا آورند، در مهمات كه تعلق بصدور دارد رجوع بدو نمايند وبي وقوف وشعور او هيچ امري از امور صدارت را نسازند ونپر دا زند، وفرامين احكام ارباب شريعت را بمهر او رسانند، بي مهر او منظور ومعمول ندانند[2] وجميع سيورغال داران ووظيفه خواران درمهام خود رجوع بدان عمدة الصدور نمايند وارباب مناصب شريفه واصحاب امور دينيه نيز برين موجب عمل نمايند وبنيابت او بشرف ملازمت وجلوس در مجلس جنت مرتبت مشرف گردند ومناشير خود را بتمام بمهر او رسانند. عمدة الصدور مومي اليه نيز بايد كه ملاحظه احوال طبقات انام را كما ينبغي منظور نظر دارد ودرين امور كه مذكور شد دقيقه نامرعي نگذارد وچنان سازد كه عند الخالق والخلائق مرضي ومستحسن بوده آثار سلوك پسنديده او بر همگنان واضح ولائح گردد. از جوانب برين جمله روند وچون بتوقيع وقيع رسد اعتماد نمايند.

١ـ ع: قاطبه، ندارد

٢ـ ع: ندارند

(١٠)

منشور در تفویض منصب صدارت

صدر الکتاب صحیفه کامگاری وفصل الخطاب منشور بختیاری محمدت وستائش بادشاهی تواند بود که خاصان درگاه بحکم "آتینا آل ابراهیم الکتاب والحکمة"[1] بانواع اصطناع ممتاز وسرفراز ساخته، جل شانه وعظم سلطانه، ورایت خجسته آیت صدر رسل، خواجه دنیا ودین ابو القاسم محمد الامین[2] را بذروه فلك عزت برافراخته، صلی الله علیه وآله الی یوم الدین۔ بعده بر صدور صدر نشین پیش گاه علم وعمل وبدور فلك نشان بارگاه خالی از شوائب خلل مختفی ومحجوب نماند که مقاله استبقاء ذکر جمیل واستیفاء اجر جزیل بملاحظه احوال ومراقبه امانی وآمالی معتبر شریف سادات عظاماً وعلماء اعلام وطبقه وقیع مشائخ اسلام موشح ومشحون است۔ ونیز انتظام ایں امر خطیر بی تطرق وجود خجسته ورود صدور عظیم القدر منشرح الصدر که لامحاله مستدعی احیاء مراسم بقاع الخیر ومستتبع ترویج مناهج مرافق البر تواند بود، ازحیّز قوت بدرجه فعل نمی آید۔ بناءً علی ذالك کفایت این شغل خطیر بحسن اهتمام زبده اصول، صاحب هدایت ونقاوه فروع، دوحه صدارت وکیاست، قدوة الاشراف بشرائف[3] مواجب ربه الکریم خواجه فلان، شرح الله صدره، که من المبدا الی الغایة اباً عن جد در خانواده خلافت روزافزوں متعهد ضبط وربط آں مهمات همایوں بوده اند وهمه وقت درخدمات شائسته اسلاف نامدار وسلاطین خاندان بزرگوار ما قیام نموده اند، لامحاله همواره اثر امانت

١۔ قرآن مجید : ٨٤/٤
٢۔ ع: امین
٣۔ ع: شریف

وکار گذاری برصفحات مجاری حالات او واضح ولائح است، برحسب پروانچه 'انزل الدار بانیها' مفوّض وموکول گشت تابمیامن تولیت الهی بر وجهی که از خصائل رضیه وشمائل مرضیه سزد بشرف لوازم ایں امر مشرف گشته، اصناف اشراف را درمراتب مناسب متمکن دارد (و) بانشراح صدر وانکشاف ضمیر در تعمیر مساجد ومدارس وخوانق ومعابد ومزارات ومشاهد ورباطات وسائر بقاع خیر وتکثیر محصولات وقف وضبط امور بیت المال وایتام (و) غیّب دقیقه فرونگذارد وتحقیق رقبات موقوفات از کلیات وجزئیات واجب دانسته، دست اختیار متغلبه را از تصرف در وجوه جهات آں قاصر ومنکسر گرداند، ودرا استحکام مبانی خیرات ومبرات کوشیده، ازسر استظهار هرچه تمام تر بلوازم آں اشتغال نماید وتفویض مناصب شرعیه باربابِ استحقاق منظور نظر اعتبار داشته غیر مستعد ومستحق را درمقام تقلد وتکفل ندارد ودر ملاحظه حال فقراء و مستحقان از میل ومحابا محترز ومجتنب باشد۔

(۱۱)

منشور در تفویض منصب استیفاء

بعد از طرح دفاتر حمد وثناء بادشاهی که مستوفیان وهم سریع الخیال میزان گوشواره مجملی از آوارجه آلاء والای اونتو اندند نمود، وپس از ترتیب اوراق نعت ودرود دین پناهی که محاسبان خیال جهان پیما بحرف نه توحید مفرده از جمع نعماء بی انتهاء او لب نتواندند کشود، بازنموده می شود که چون[۱] خانه تدبیر "وهو علی کل شئی قدیر"[۲] صحائف سلطنت وجهان بانی مارا بقلم خجسته رقم ثبات وبقا

۱۔ ع: سرکار

۲۔ قرآن مجید : ۵/۱۲۰

تحریر وتسطیر نموده ومشیر نگار خانه تصویر صفائح خلافت کامرانی مارا بخامه مشکین شمامه خلود ودوام تصویر وتنقیش فرموده، روز نامه جات اوقات فرخنده سمات مارا بسیاق حشمت واستقلال مرتب ومکمل ساخته، برضلع هر فردی از افراد ساعات بابرکات بارقام مجدد اقبال وتاریخ عظمت واجلال پربار پرداخته، واز مجمل ومفصل لطف واحسان آن مقدار که از قیاس وتخمین فاضل تواند بود ارزانی داشته، واز مراحم بی غایت ومکارم بی نهایت دقیقه باقی نگذاشته، هاتف غیب مضمون موزون این مقال بگوش هوش دبیران آستان عز واقبال می رساند۔

قطعه:

ای کلك ترا رقوم ارقام صواب　　به آواز فلك بنام خصمت ابواب
سال ومه روزت از حساب افزون باد　　تا سال ومه وروز شب آید بحساب

ما نیز در ازاء این عواطف جلیله وجمیله وجزاء این عواطف علیه جزیله منظور نظر فرخنده آن داریم که آوارجه جمع وخرج اوان میمنت نشان ودولت بی علت ماکه آحاد آن بعشرات[1] وعشرات آن بمآت ومآت آن بالوف وهلم جراً الی مالایتناهی مقرون باد، بتوجهی منتظم وملتئم[2] که بجائزه "یحاسب حساباً یسیراً"[3] مصحح ومنقح گردد، ودر مدارج "والباقیات الصالحات خیر عند ربك ثواباً وخیر املاً"[4] از عروض عوارض وحدوث حوادث مصئون ومامون ماند۔ وحصول این مامول وقتی میسر تواند بود که یکی از قلم زنان کاردان ومحاسبان معامله گذاران (به) منصب رفیع القدر استیفاء تعین یابد که جمیع مهمات دیوانی وتمامی معاملات سلطانی را بقانون حساب ومیزان صواب فیصل

۱ـ　ع: بعشره
۲ـ　ع: مهتم
۳ـ　قرآن مجید : ۸/۸٤
٤ـ　قرآن مجید : ٤٦/۱۸

داده، دفتر اعمالش فرد فرد بارقام دیانت وراستی مزین واوراق افعالش حرف حرف عنوان امانت وکوتاه دستی معنون بود۔ والحق این حالات در ذات درایت سمات، کفایت صفات، ناظم امور الدولة السلطانية، کافل مهام السلطنة السلیمانية[١]، قدوة ارباب السیاق فی الآفاق، زبده اصحاب العلم بوفور والاستحقاق، خواجه فلان موجوداست وامارات وقوف وکاردانی وعلامات شعور ومعامله گذاری او از صادرات اعمال وواردات افعالش مشهور۔ بناءً علیه فرمان واجب الا ذعان شرف نفاذ یافت که مومی الیه مستوفی کل سرکار همایون بوده کما ینبغی بلوازم ومراسم این شغل اشتغال نماید ودر ترتیب دفاتر وتزئین مفاخر وتنقیح محاسبات اعمال از ارباب التحاویل وابواب المال جهد موفور مبذول شمرده، فاضل و باقی ایشان را مشخص سازد، واسناد وخطوط وقبوض که حسابی بوده باشد مجری داشته انچه بی حساب بوده رد کند۔ چنان نماید که چون[٢] سال آخر رسد چیزی نامشخص ونامضبوط نماند۔ وجمیع لوازم این منصب کماحقه ساخته وپرداخته شده، ذکر مآثر ایام دخل او دستور العمل مستوفیان ماهر الادوار ومحاسبه (محاسبان) باهر الاعصار گردد۔ ومبلغ فلان از محل مذکور فی الضمن در وجه علوفه خود ومحرران دفتر استیفاء بازیافت نموده متصرف شود۔

می باید که ارکان دولت قاهره واعیان حضرت باهره از خوانین کامگار وسلاطین نامدار وامراء رستم صفت وصدور صاحب شریعت ووزراء وافر کفایت وعمال متکاثر درایت ومباشران اشغال دیوانی ومتکفلان اعمال سلطانی وباقی ملازمان عتبه گردون مدار وسائر خادمان سده سپهر آثار وزمره انام از خواص وعوام مومی الیه را مستوفی بااستقلال دانسته دست تقلد او را قوی دانند وامداد واعانت وتقویت

١۔ ع: السلطانية

٢۔ ع: چون، ندارد

وتمشیت او بواجبی بجا آرند وجمیع فرامین را که مبلغ و مقدار دران بوده باشد بدفتر اور رسانیده بثبت او رسانند۔ تحویل داران وتحصیل داران ومشرفان وقابضان ومستاجران وغیر آن از انچه محاسبه ایشان وابسته بمستوفی است محاسبات خود را نزد او و کارکنان او مفروع (مرفوع) سازند وهر قبض وستدی که طلبد بلاعذر حاضر سازند(و) اوامر ونواهی او را مطیع ومنقاد باشند۔ داروغکان دفتر خانه وعمله که در اداء محاسبات اهمال ورزند اول به نصیحت بدفتر خانه حاضر سازند وهرچه مومی الیه در تنقیح محاسبات گوید بعمل آورند۔ از جوانب برین جمله روند وچون بتوقیع وقیع مزین ومعنون ومحلی ومعلی وموضح وموشح گردد اعتماد نمایند واز فرموده در نگذرند وتخلف ننمایند۔

(۱۲)

منشور در تفویض منصب میر بخشی

چون همگی نیت خاطر قدردان مصروف ومعطوف بر آنست که کسانیکه بحلیه استعداد وحسن کیاست وزمره که بزینت قابلیت وفرط کفایت محلی ومزین بوده، ناصیه حال وحالت خود را بزیور قدمت خدمت وسبقت معرفت آراسته باشند، از سائر اکفاء وسائر اشباه وجمله اقران[۱] وامثال سمت[۲] امتیاز یافته بمراتب بلند ومناصب ارجمند فائز گردند۔ لهذا شمه از حسن شفقت وفرط عاطفت شامل حال رفعت مآب، کفایت شعار، عمدة الملك خواجه فلاں نموده مشارالیه را منصب میر بخشی، که از عظائم[۳] مناصب کار ومهام خانه بزرگی ودولت است، سرفراز فرمودیم که دیانت و کفایت خود را از اقران برسر

۱ ۔ ع: جماعت اعوان وجمله امثال
۲ ۔ ع: سمت، ندارد
۳ ۔ ع: عظام

آورده ومورد روز افزون توجه وعنایت گردیده، برمعارج مناصب ارجمند ترقی نموده، همچنین بدستور ایں اندازه را منظور نظر حق شناس خود ساخته بنوعی که از حقیقت قابلیت واستعداد وشعور ووقوف ودل سوزی ودیانت او سزد در امر مذکور ولوازم آں قیام واقدام نماید تا روز بروز منظور نظر عاطفت وعنایت بوده فنون احسان خود را درباره او تمام بجا آوریم۔ واز روی وفور شفقت ومرحمت هر ساله از روی آحاد سپاهیان وملازمان کائناً من کان از کل واحد یك روپیه[۱] در وجه انعام او مقرر فرمودیم که هر ساله از هریك از سپاهیان وملازمان مبلغ مذکور را بازیافت نماید۔ می باید که فوطه داران سرکار خاصه از فوطه داران حضور وپرگنات وجاگیرداران حسب الحکم العالی (عمل) نموده مقرری میر بخشی مشارالیه را مقرر دانسته واصل گماشته مومی الیه نمایند، وحصه جاگیرداران را انچه متعلق بسرکار خاصه بوده باشد تحصیل دار تعین نمایند که تحصیل نموده بخزانه واصل نماید،[۲] وانچه حصه مشارالیه بوده باشد بگماشتهای[۳] او واصل سازند۔ سبیل سپاهیان وملازمان وخدمت گاران وعمال ودیوانیان وغیرهم آں که مومی الیه را میر بخشی مستقل دانسته در تعظیم اکرام وتوفیر احترام او دقیقه فرو گذاشت ننموده، از سخن وصوابدید او که هر آئینه موافق اخلاص ودولت خواهی است، عدول وانحراف نجویند۔ دریں ابواب قدغن عظیم دانسته تخلف را مجال ندهند وچوں بتوقیع وقیع[٤] رفیع منیع ارتسام یابد اعتماد نمایند۔

(۱۳)

منشور در تفویض منصب میر انشاء سرکار همایوں

سپاس عظمت اساس که منشیان عرصه انشاء از مطلع دیباچه

۱۔ ع: عدد، زیاده دارد
۲۔ ع: نمایند
۳۔ ع: ب،ندارد
٤۔ ع:وقیع، ندارد

'الحمد لله علی ماانعم' اقتباس نمایند وشکر سعادت لباس که مترسلان نسخه املاء در محفل تعلیم "علم الانسان مالم یعلم"[۱] زبان باداء آن کشایند نثار درگاه بادشاهی شاید که قلم وزبان ناهجان مناهج سخن وری در تفصح کمال سلطنت واستقلالش بعجز وفتور اعتراف می نمایند وزبان قلم سالکان مسالك نکته پروری در تلویح غایت عنایت واجلالش ابواب قصور وناتوانی می کشایند،[۲] جل شانه وعظم سلطانه۔ ودرود خجسته ورود[۳] که نقاشان نگار خانه آفرینش بتلقین ملقن غیبی بر صحائف ظهور نگارند وصلوة نامحدود که کاتبان کارخانه دانش وبینش بالهام ملهم لاریبی بر صفائح بروز آرند، ایثار مشهد معطر ونثار مرقدمنور دین پناهی لائق نماید که غواصان بحار فضل ودانائی لآلی حقائق دین وبینش را باحسن عبارات وایمن استعارات در سلك حصول منظم ساخته، زیور افسر عالم وعالمیان می سازند، ونقادان مخازن فهم وبینائی جواهر زواهر[٤] دقائق ملت مستقیمش،[٥] بابلغ اشارات وافصح بشارات درسلك رشته وجود ملتئم[٦] ساخته وبوسیلة آن رایت مباهات ومفاخرت بایوان کیوان می افرازند، صلی الله علیه وسلم۔

امابعد، برضمائر اصحاب سرائر که مکنون خزائن خواطر ایشان مضمون مآثر "ن والقلم ومایسطرون"[۷] است بازنموده می شود که چون منشی مناشیر دیوان "قل اللهم مالك الملك توتی الملك من تشاء"[۸] منشور منصور خلافت واقبال ما را بتوقیع وقیع "انی جاعل فی الارض خلیفة"[۹] مزین ومحلی ساخته وکاتب خوش نویس اسرار "وآتاه الله

۱۔ قرآن مجید : ٥/٩٨٦

۲۔ ع : نمی کشایند

۳۔ ع: خجسته ورود، ندارد

٤۔ ع: زوایر، ندارد

٥۔ ع: مستقیمش، ندراد

٦۔ ع: ملتئم، ندارد

۷۔ قرآن مجید : ١/٦٨

۸۔ قرآن مجید : ٢٦/٣

۹۔ قرآن مجید : ٣٠/٢

الملك والحكمة وعلّمه مما یشاء»[1] مثال بی مثال عظمت واجلال مارا بنشان عظیم الشان «وإذا حکمتم بین الناس ان تحکموا بالعدل»[2] موشح ومحلی ساخته، همواره مطمح خاطر خطیر، که مطرح اشعات بارقات مهر منیر است، بر آن داریم که انشاء فرامین سرکار بادشاهی واملاء مناشیر روزگار شاهنشاهی بفاضلی فصیح وکاملی بلیغ باید که خامه مشکین شمامه اش بتحریر کلمات بلاغت آیات رقم نسخ بر توقیع خوش نویسان اقطار جهان کشیده باشد، وعبارات خجسته اشعارش از غایت فصاحت منشآت منشیان بدیع بیان را برطاق نسیان منسوخ ومندرس گردانیده، از شمائم قلم عنبرین رفمش مشام جان متنفسان ریاض فضل وکمال تعطر یافته، از نواء نامه کافوری شمیمش پرتو انوار صفا وضیاء برساحت احوال طالبان مطالب بلاغت و افضال تافته ـ والحق این خصائل در ذات فضیلت سمات، عمدهٔ اعاظم ارکان الدولة القاهرة، قدوه اکارم بنیان السلطنة الباهره، منشی مناشیر دولت وفرمان روائی، منشی السلطنة، گیتی آرای فصیح الدین فلان موجود است واین خوالص درصفات با برکاتش مشهور، لاجرم منظور انظار مرحمت آثار داشته ولواء استظهار اورا درساحت گیتی افراشته منصب میر انشاء سرکار همایون را من حیث الاستقلال والانفراد بر او مفوض داشتیم وزمام ضبط وربط این امر شریف را بید کفایت او گذاشتیم که بواجبی بدین شغل پرداخته، دقیقه فروگذاشت نکند وفرامین که عمده باشد وانچه مشافهه فرمائیم[3] بقلم بلاغت رقم خود تحریر وتسطیر نماید، وانچه منشیان جزوی نویسند نظر فطانت اثر برکلی انداخته اگر سهوی یا غلطی بوده باشد اصلاح نماید، ومجموع فرامین برظهر میان مرکز توقیع کند ودر جمیع لوازم این امر چنان اهتمام نماید که مزیدی بران

۱ـ قرآن مجید : ۲۵۱/۲

۲ـ قرآن مجید : ۵۸/٤

۳ـ ع : کفایت او گذاشتیم که بواجبی بدین شغل پرداخته دقیقه فرو گذاشت نکند وفرامین که عمده باشد وآنچه مشافهه فرمائیم، ندارد

متصور نباشد۔ وآثار آن بر صفحات صحائف روزگار ابد الدهر والاعصار مثبت ومرقوم ماند۔ ومبلغ فلاں از محال مذکوره فی الضمن هر ساله در وجه علوفه متصرف شود وفرامین که خود نویسد صددوئی بروجه انعام بر دوام خود گیرد۔

باید که فرزندان شبیه البدر وخواقین بلند قدر وسلاطین ستوده سیر وامراء رستم اثر وصدور شریعت طراز وناظم (ناظمان) مناظم اعمال وواقفان مواقف اشغال وزمره انام از خواص وعوام مومی الیه را میر انشاء مستقل دانسته تعظیم واحترام او بجای آورند ودست تعهد اورا در اعتناق ایں شغل قوی دارند ودانند، وتمامی فرامین را بتوقیع او رسانیده بی توقیع او منظور ومعمول ندانند، ومبلغی که تنخواه علوفه اوشده صدونیم حق الانشاء بلا انکسار بدو رسانند وچیزی درمعرض فتور وقصور نگذارند۔ ومنشیان جزوی متابعت او کما ینبغی بظهور آورند وخود را بعزل ونصب او منصوب ومعزول دانند۔ از جوانب بریں جمله روند۔ وچوں بتوقیع وقیع رفیع منیع اشرف اقدس اعلی مزین ومحلی ومعلی ومعنون گردد اعتماد نمایند۔ درین باب قد غن عظیم لازم دانند وتخلف نورزند۔

(١٤)

منشور در تفویض منصب میر بحر

غواصان بحار خلافت وجهانبانی ونقّادان مخازن سلطنت وکامرانی از فرزندان دریا کف واخوان موفور الشرف وامراء رستم سیر وصدور شریعت مخبر ووزراء آصف صفت ونواب جلیل المراتب وناظمان اعمال دیوانی و واقفان اشغال سلطانی وسائر خدم عتبه علیه نامداری وباقی ملازمان سده سنیه کامگاری وزمره انام از طبقه خواص وقاطبه عوام بدانند که چوں ملاح عنایت قادر متعال باسعاد ریاح وافر

الارتیاح عاطفت بی زوال سفینه دولت واقبال مارا بر حسب "وجرین بهم بریح طیبة"[1] درلجه امانی وآمال جاری ساخته بر طبق "ألم تر أن الفلك تجری فی البحر بنعمة الله"[2] دست توفیق بوسیله بادبان تحقیق رخت عافیت ورفاهیت خدام ذوی الاحتشام مارا بساحل مراد ومقصود انداخته، مانیز بشکرانه ایں موهبت عظمی وعطیه کبری توجه خاطر دریا مقاطر مصروف ومعطوف بران داریم که جمعی از مخلصان عقیدت پیشه وبرخی از متخصصان خبرت اندیشه که سباحان[3] بحار خدمت گاری وسیاحان[4] امصار جان سپاری اند، مزرع احوال خود را[5] از ترشح جوئبار معدلت واحسان ماسرسبز وسیراب یابند وبدستیاری فضل بیکران وپایمردی بر وامتنان فراز مدارج مرادات ومدعیات شتابند. والحق ایں خصائص در ذات اخلاص سمات، عمدة الخواص، موفور الاختصاص، لائق المرحمة والعنایة[6] بین النظائر والاقران فلان موجود بود ودر ظهور ایں حالات وشمول ایں مقالات برا کفاء و امثال فائق نمود، لاجرم اورا بمزید مرتبت وعواطف نواخته بافزونی شفقت ومکرمت سر افراز ساخته، منصب میر بحری ممالك محروسه را من حیث الاستقلال والانفراد بدو ارزانی داشته تفویض فرمودیم که بواجبی بلوازم ومراسم ایں امر پرداخته دقیقه از[7] دقائق اجتهاد واهتمام فروگذاشت نکند ودرتحقیق اوضاع بحار ومعابر ومسالك وتفحص احوال سفائن و کشتی بانان وما یتعلق بها چنان اهتمام نماید که مزیدی بران متصور نباشد، ولوازم ومراسم ایں منصب را موافق قانون قدیم

١ـ قرآن مجید : ٢٢/١٠

٢ـ قرآن مجید : ٣١/٣١

٣ـ ع: سبان

٤ـ ع: بحار خدمتگار وسباحان، ندارد

٥ـ ع: را، ندار

٦ـ لائق عنایت

٧ـ ع: از، ندارد

وقاعده استمرار بازیافت نموده متصرف شود- می باید که مومی الیه را میر بحر منفرد ومستقل دانسته امداد واعانت وتقویت وتمشیت او[١] بواجی بجا آورند وغیری را بدو شریك وسهیم ندارند وندانند- وملاحان و کشتی بانان و گذربانان وغیر ذالك اوامر ونواهی او و گماشتگان او را مطیع ومنقاد باشند وازسخن وصواب دید او و کسان او بیرون نروند، ورسوم متعلقه را مخصوص او دانند- دریں باب قد غن لازم دانند-

(١٥)

منشور در تفویض منصب میر بر[٢]

دو حات ریاض خلافت واقبال وثمرات شجرات سلطنت واجلال از فرزندان برخوردار وامراء بهرام انتصار وصدور شریعت طراز ووزراء کفایت آغاز وارکان دین ودولت واعیان ملك وملت ومتصدیان اشغال دیوانی ومتعهدان اشغال سلطانی وسائر طائفان درگاه وباقی عاکفان بارگاه ومالکان و کلان تران ورعایا ومزارعان وعموم سکنه وجمهور متوطنه ولایت فلاں بدانند که چوں ریاض دولت بی علت ماکه "جنات تجری من تحتها الانهار"[٣] صفت ولطف هواء جان فزای اوست، به نهال عقیدت مخلصان وافی طویت زیب وزینت گرفته، وحدائق فرخنده حقائق حشمت بی علت ماکه "إرم ذات العماد التی لم یخلق مثلها فی البلاد"[٤] شرح صفاء فضاء دلکشاء اوست، از مآثر اظهار فائض الانوار متخصصان راسخ العبودیت رونق وبها پذیرفته، جوامع همت بلند اساس وبواعث نیت خورشید اقتباس مقصود ومحصور بوده واست که جمعی از مقتبسان انوار دولت بی زوال وبرخی از مستفیضان آثار

١ـ ع: او، ندارد
٢ـ درنسخه خطی دانشگاه علی گڑه ایں فرمان یافته نمی شود
٣ـ قرآن مجید: ١٥/٣
٤ـ قرآن مجید: ٨٩/٧ـ٨

حشمت بی انتقال که همواره در اراضی قلب اخلاص قالب خود تخم عبودیت "من کان یرید حرث الآخرة نزد له فی حرثه"[۱] کاشته اند واز رشحات سحاب لطف واحسان وبرکات آفتاب بر وامتنان "کمثل جنة أنبتت سبع سنابل فی کل سنبلة مأة حبة"[۲] برداشته اند، برعایات لائق وهدایات مناسب از بنی نوع امتیاز یابند، وبه پایمردی عنایت فراز مدارج مرادات ومدعیات شتابند- وازان زمره اعتقاد پیشه وفرقهٔ اخلاص اندیشه مخلص اخلاص نشان، مزین بساتین الرحمان، مروج حدائق دوران، لائق لطف وقابل احسان فلان بدین موهبت امتیاز یافته، وپرتو انوار توفیق وتائید بر وجنات احوالش تافته، حدائق ممالك محروسه از ترشح ینابیع وقوف و کاردانی اش مانند روضه رضوان از ترشح سلسبیل ناضر ونامی است، وبساتین بلاد مانوسه از پرتو انوار هنروری ومهارت گستری اش بسان ریاحین بهاری از پرتو لمعات مهر خاوری خاضر و گرامی، باغات فرخنده وروضات خجسته، که در زمان دولت حضرت والد جم حشمت آفریدون صولت ما، ایجاد نموده وتعمیر فرموده اند، اوراق مآثر خورنق وسدیر را برطاق نسیان نهاده ومزرع مرغوب وقریات مطلوب که بوسائل حفر انهار وقنوان دریا آثار احداث کرده، از مزرع فلك دهر غدار ملك یاد داده- بالجمله بدائع آثار وصنائع کردار که ازو بظهور آمده زیب مفاخر ابناء روز گار است وزینت مآثر اشباه وانظار- لاجرم بوسیله این حالات مستعد فنون نوازشات خسروانه ومستحق صنوف تفقدات بادشاهانه گردیده، منصب میربری بلاد محروسه را من حیث الاستقلال والانفراد بدو ارزانی داشته تفویض فرمودیم که بواجبی بلوازم ومراسم این امر پرداخته در تعمیر مزارع و باغات از قدیم وجدید وافزونی ومعموری محال که

۱- قرآن مجید : ۲۰/۴۲

۲- قرآن مجید : ۲۶۱/۲

بخالصه شریفه منصوب است، از زراعت رعیتی وزراعت خاصه وغیره از انچه اهتمام آن تعلق به میربر دارد حتی الامکان اهتمام نموده به هیچ وجه فروگذاشتی نکند ـ ودر جمیع امور متعلقه چنان سعی کند که مزیدی بران متصور نباشد وآثار آن یوماً فیوماً بظهور رسد ـ می باید که مومیٰ الیه را میربر باستقلال دانسته دست تعهد اور را قوی دانند وامداد واعانت وتمشیت او کما ینبعی بجا آورند ـ وسر کارداران خالصات از عبید واحرار ورعایا ومزارعان وباغبانان از سخن ومصلحت او بیرون نروند، واوامر ونواهی اورا مطیع ومنقاد باشند ـ از جانب جوانب برین جمله روند ـ وچون بتوقیع وقیع رسد اعتماد نمایند ـ کتب بالامر العالی خلد نفاذه ولا زال مطاعاً ـ

(١٦)
منشور در تفویض منصب میر آتش

چون اقتباس انوار مشاغل فتح ونصرت بآتش تیغ برق آثار مجاهدان حق گذار منوط[١] است واندراس اساس ثبات ووقار مخالفان دین ودولت بسنگ صاعقه کردار رعد اند ازان نادره کار مربوط، وعمده در تهیه اسباب خلافت وکامگاری بمقتضاء مواد "أو کصیب من السماء فیه ظلمات ورعد وبرق یجعلون اصابعهم فی آذانهم من الصواعق حذر الموت"[٢] خرمن[٣] عمر دشمنان خاکسار بآتش[٤] باد رفتار توان سوخت ودیده حیات معاندان غدار را از ضرب تیر آتش بار توان دوخت، آلات جنگ وادوات توپ[٥] وتفنگ است ـ لاجرم در حصول این

١ ـ ع : منوط، ندارد
٢ ـ قرآن مجید : ١٩/٢ ـ
٣ ـ ع : دمن
٤ ـ ع : آتش، ندارد
٥ ـ ع : توپ، ندارد

مامول از رعایت احوال جمعی از استادان ماهر الآثار، که انهدام بنیان زندگانی اعداء وابسته به منجنیق فکر وخیال ایشان است، چاره نیست۔ و در وصول بدین مسئول از مراقبت[١] آمال برخی از کاملان نادر الاعصار، که اختلال قصر عمر اضداد موقوف بآمد وشد تیر مرگ ایشان است، گریزی نه۔ والحق عمدة الخواص، ماهر الزمان، نادر الدوران فلاں درفن آتشبازی ورعد اندازی از اکفاء واقران قصب السبق ربوده، در هنگام رزم از ظهور آثار عجائب ودقائق این[٢] امر ید بیضاء بهمگنان نموده[٣] ودر معرکه وغا از[٤] انداختن قدرهاء عظیم القدر، که سنگهای آسمان شگافش باکره زمین هم سنگ است وآواز ضربش فرسنگ در فرسنگ حصار ابدان معاندان این خاندان را منهدم ساخته، ودر روز هیجا از تواتر تفنگ های رعد آهنگ وسائر ادوات توپخانه بافرهنگ در معارك جدل وجنگ لواء استیلاء واقتدار برافراخته۔ بناءً علیه اورا مشمول[٥] نظر عاطفت سمات داشته، منصب میر آتشی سرکار همایون من حیث الاستقلال والانفراد بدو ارزانی داشتیم وزمام اختیار این امر را بید شهامت وحراست او گذاشتیم که بواجبی بلوازم ومراسم این امر[٦] قیام واقدام[٧] نموده دقیقه فرو گذاشت نکند، ودر سامان وسرانجام توپ خانه وما یتعلق بها چنان اهتمام نماید که مزید بران متصور نباشد وآثار آن یوماً فیوماً بعرض رسیده موجب افزونی عنایت ورعایت درباره او گردد۔

می باید که خوانین صاحب احتشام وسلاطین رفعت مقام وامراء اسفندیار وصدور شریعت دثار ووزراء عطا رد طراز وعمال کفایت پرداز ونواب آستان سپهر مرتبت وسائر منتسبان سده فلك رفعت مومی الیه را میر آتش مستقل دانسته امداد واعانت اورا من

١۔ ع: مراقب
٢۔ ع: این، ندارد
٣۔ ع: نمود
٤۔ ع: از، ندارد
٥۔ ع: مشول
٦۔ ع: این امر، ندارد
٧۔ ع: اقتدام

جمیع[۱] الـوجـوه پیش نهاد همت دارند ومبلغ فلان از محال[۲] فلان دروجه علوفه او مقرر دانسته واصل گردانند ودر ایصال آن اهتمام نموده چیزی منکسر نگردانند. وجماعه توپچی متابعت اورا از همه وجوه به تقدیم در آورده اوامر[۳] ونواهی اورا مطیع ومنقاد باشند واز سخن صلاح او در نگزرند. وچون بتوقیع وقیع رفیع منیع مزین ومحلی ومجلی ومعنون گردد اعتماد نمایند.

(۱۷)
منشور در تفویض منصب قوش بیگی

تاهماء قدسی هواء همت بلند[۴] وباز بلند پرواز دولت ارجمند فراز پنجه قدرت وبهله عزت نشیمن دارد وتدور خوش خرام سپهر مرغ زرین جناح مهر صید سر پنجه شاهین دولت ما است وهر لحظه شنقار گردون شکار بخت فیروز ما را، که دست آموز عنایت "یا ایهاالناس علمنا منطق الطیر واوتینا من کل شئی[۵] است، از صداء بال ملك وصفیر مرغ فلك بگوش تیز هوش چنین می رسد:-

بازیست همت تو که پرواز می کند
زیر پرش فلك چو بزیر فلك کلنگ

وچون اسلاف عظام واجداد فلك احتشام مارا عادت خسروانه چنان بوده که بعد از ترتیب اسباب دین ودولت وتمهید قواعد ملك وملت ساعتی بقصد تنزیهه خواطر دریا مآثر بحری تیز طبع را بصید وشکار مشغول می داشته اند، ما نیز اقتداء بدین سیرت[۶] پادشاهانه نموده،

۱- ع: جمیع، ندارد
۲- ع: محل
۳- ع: اوامر، ندارد
۴- ع: خجسته
۵- قرآن مجید: ۱۶/۲۷
۶- ع: امر

بعد از اشغال خلافت گردون پناه واشغال سپاه ظفر دستگاه که "وحشر لسلیمان جنوده من الجن والانس والطیر"[١] نمونه آنست، خود را بانعام عام "قل احل لکم الطیبات وما علمتم من الجوارح"[٢] سرفراز دانسته گاه گاه طائر همت بلند را که از عالم ملکوت مخاطب برین خطاب است:-

زهره ابریشم دهد از چنگ تا دوزد سهیل[٣]
باز داران ترا بر بهله بلغار کل

وهواء صید وشکار در سردولت افسر می باشد- وچون درین امر از هم عنانی لائق، که بحلیه مهارت ووجه بصارت از همگنان قصب السبق ربوده، بزوائد اخلاص وعوائد اختصاص امتیاز داشته باشد،[٤] ناگزیر بود، بنا بران قدوة الامراء فی الزمان، عمدة الملك فلان که حقوق خدمات[٥] پسندیده وصنوف دولت خواهی وحسن عقیدت او اباً عن جدٍ به نسبت دولت این دودمان وحسشمت این خاندان بر اهل جهان ظاهر وباهراست، واز دیوان عنایت ما بشرف پیشوائی امراء درگاه ومنشیان بارگاه جهان پناه مستثنی است، حکم فرمودیم که متعهد ومتکفل قوشخانه همایون بوده حل وعقد وقبض وبسط آن بید اهتمام وقبضه انتظام مشار الیه متعلق باشد وبشرکت معتمد الخواص جلال الدین فلان برلاس بسر انجام امور مذکور قیام نماید-

(١٨)
منشور در تفویض کلانتری نقارخانه

چون کوس دولت وکامگاری ما بتائید حضرت قادر لم یزل

١- قرآن مجید : ١٧/٢٧
٢- قرآن مجید : ٤/٥
٣- ع: فلك
٤- ع: باشد، ندارد
٥- ع: خدمت

ونفیر نوبت عظمت وشهر یاری ما بتوفیق دستیاری ملت احمد مرسل صداء دل کشاء "إذا جاء نصر الله والفتح"[۱] را در دور حیز گردون ونداء ملك آراء "انا فتحنا لك فتحا مبینا"[۲] را فراز نقارخانه استوار سپهر نیلگون تا نفخ صور وصبح نشور بلند آوازه گردانیده ارکان شان این دولت چون[۳] جرم ثقیل کوه متمکن وپائدار وبنیان خلافت این حشمت (بصفت) مضطرب وبیقرار است، پس شکرانه این عطیه سنیه یزدانی وعنایت بی نهایت ربانی که احسن القول[۴] فقرات کامگاری وبیت الغزل نقرات شهر یاریست بر ذمه همت حسن عمل که پیش روعاقبت روزگار ونقش پرداز صحیفه خاتم کار است، واجب ولازم گشته که منتهاء نیت وقصاری امنیت برقطع وقمع اعداء شرع ودین ودفع ومنع ارباب ظلم وکین مقصور ومحصور بوده، لواء عرش فرسای امت احمد وطبل زرین حبل شریعت محمدی بتقویت دست قدرت[۵] واستیلاء ما سرفراز وبلند باشد۔ وتمشیت وتقویت این موهبت جز بترویج وتجدید اسباب مقابله ومدافعه وآلات مقاتله ومحاربه، که در صف هیجا ومیدان وغا باعث پردلی مردان ومورث جلادت پردلا ن روز نبرد است، میسّر نی۔ واز جمله داعیه دولت چنان است که نقارخانه میمون، که صیت پائدار وصداء نوبت سلطنت واقتدار ما را بمسامع سکان[۶] عالم جبروت وقطان مجامع ملکوت رسانیده ومی رساند، بر اطراف نشیمن خاك واقطار بسائط افلاك موافق باشد وبحکم کریمه "إن الله یامر أن تودوا الأمانات الی اهلها"[۷] زمام ریاست وعنان کفایت این امر بدست جمعی باشد که از اقران واکفاء بفنون شهامت وهنروری وصنوف کفایت ومهتری ممتاز ومستثنیٰ باشند۔ ازان جمله استاد هنر پیشه، نیکو

۱۔ قرآن مجید : ۱/۱۱۰

۲۔ قرآن مجید : ۱/۴۸

۳۔ ع: چون، ندارد

۴۔ ع: است، زیان دارد

۵۔ ع: قدرت، ندارد

۶۔ ع: مکان

۷۔ قرآن مجید : ۵۸/۴

اندیشه، مظهر العجائب بیده الاحد الامجد استاد شمس الدین محمد را که انواع هنر مقرر وباصناف چابك دستی از امثال بر سر آمده بود، ودریں وقت بعز بساط بوسی صحبت فلك رتبت مستسعد گشته، از دور شاهی جرعه نوشیده وبشادیانه آں ظرائف هنر وناز کی ولطائف لعب وچابکی را لباس ادا پوشانیده، منظور انظار عنایات گشته وخلعت شاهانه پوشیده، مقرر فرمودیم که در نقار خانه همایون بمشارکت مهتر عماد الدین محمود مقدم وکلانتر نوبتیان درگاه سپهر اشتباه است، براه ورسم مهتری مقرر بوده از انچه ازیں مهم بایشان متعلق است ربع کامل بدو تفویض باشد۔ سبیل مهتران مشار الیهم آنکه اورا شریك وسهیم خود دانسته موافقت ومرافقت اورا در جمیع ابواب مهمات نقار خانه واجب ولازم شمرند۔ وسائر نقارچیان وسرنائیان[۱] ونفیرچیان وشحبتان (سحبتان) ومنتسبان ایں مهم آں که مشار الیه را کلاں تر وپیشوای خود دانسته سخن او را دریں ابواب معتبر شناسند واز مشورت ومصلحت او تجاوز نه نمایند۔ وجماعه غریب زادگان وعنالان وقوالان وقَرَش[۲] مالان وطوافان وحمامیان وسرتراشان ودلاکان واسیابان وحجامان وترك طبیبان وباده بانان وغربال بافان ولولیان ونکارشکتان وسفیده(سپیده) بیزان وجولاهان وسائر جماعت که بدیں طائفه[۳] انتساب داشته باشند، استاد مشار الیه را کلانتر وپیشواء خود دانند وانچه حصه دستوری نباشد نپرسند ومدخل نکنند۔ دریں ابواب قدغن عظیم دانسته از مضمون صدر تخلف نورزند وچوں بتوقیع وقیع اشرف اعلی موشح ومزین ومحلی گردد اعتماد نمایند تحریراً فی تاریخ ۳ شهر صفر ۹۹۹هـ۔

۱۔ ع: سائبان

۲۔ ع: مسرت

۳۔ ع : گله بانان

(١٩)
منشور در تفویض منصب معماری

چون حضرت واحد احد وقادر صمد "الذی رفع السموات بغیر عمد"[١] که بقدرت کامله رفع قواعد شدید المعاقد ایجاد وتکوین می فرمود "انا زینا السماء الدنیا بزینة الکواکب"[٢] چندین هزار خشت سیم وزردر قالب سپهر دوّار ریخته طاق نه رواق فلك اطلس وسپهر مقرنس را زینت فزود، بنوعی که در مدارج ارتقاء شرفات عرفاتش مقیاس مهندسان کامل نظر احصاء یابد ونه درمبانی مراتب اعتلاء قصور بی قصورش معمار وهم وخیال بقدم اهتمام شتابد، "ما خلقت هذا باطلاً سبحانك"[٣] او در هنگام خلقت خلیفه اعظم که منطوق لازم الوثوق[٤] "خلقت العالم لاجلك وخلقتك لا جلی" مبین آنست که گل وجود اورا در فضاء فضل وافضال وعرصه کمال واکمال بهر دو دست قدرت که یکی عبارت از مآثر جلالی ودیگری کنایت از مفاخر جمالی است، تخمیر نموده، پیکر باخرد وهیئت باهیبت اورا در احسن وجود برحسب "لقد خلقنا الانسان فی احسن تقویم"[٥] بپرداخت ونقش "خمرت طینة آدم بیدی اربعین صباحاً" برصفحه در ودیوار جهان وفراز ونشیب عالم امکان بنگاشت، "فتبارك الله احسن الخالقین"[٦] ونواب همایون مارا حسب قضیه مرضیه "الاصل یسری فی الفروع" از میراث آن در گران مایه وجوهر بلند پایه نصیب اوفی وبهره مستوفی ممتاز وسرفراز ساخته، وخلقت باٰبهجت "ولقد کرمنا بنی آدم"[٧] را بقامت با استقامت ما پرداخته۔ ما نیز در ازاء سپاس داری نعم حضرت قادر بیچون وحق

١۔ قرآن مجید : ٢/١٣
٢۔ قرآن مجید : ٦/٣٧
٣۔ قرآن مجید : ١٩١/٣
٤۔ ع: اعظم که منطوق لازم الوثوق، ندارد
٥۔ قرآن مجید : ٤/٩٥
٦۔ قرآن مجید : ١٤/٢٣
٧۔ قرآن مجید : ٧٠/١٧

گذاری کرم صانع "کن فیکون"[١] تعمیر امصار وبلاد وترفیه احوال کافه عباد را منظور نظر مرحمت اثر داشته می خواهیم که بنیان احوال طبقات انسان از مساعی معمار فضل واحسان ما ممهد ومستحکم ورياض آمال اصناف آدمیان از اجراء انهار لطف بی کران ما سرسبز وخرم باشد وبی شائبه تکلف زینت بلدان وزیب مدائن جهان درضمن احداث عمارات عالی وقصور متعالی که در مناظر با چرخ بلند نهاد "ارم ذأت العماد التی لم يخلق مثلها فی البلاد"[٢] دم همسری تواند زد، سمت تحصیل[٣] می گیرد ومبنای منازل رفیع وطاقهاء بدیع، که باساس هرمان وسدیر دعوی برابری تواندنمود، صورت تیسیر می پذیرد. وبر همگنان محقق است که وصول بدیں ماموں وقتی میسر است که جمعی از استادان چابك دست نادره کار وبرخی از طراحان بدیع الاختراع، ماهر الآثار[٤] که از طراحی[٥] اشکال بدیع تمثال ایشان مجسطی در اضطراب واز تصور صور غرائب منظر ایشان اقلیدس در پیچ وتاب باشد، ملحوظ مرحمت اثر درایم ودر ظهور عواطف کامل ومعاطف شامل درباره ایشان بذل مجهود مبذول شماریم. والحق مصداق این مقال استاد نادر، هنرمند، عدیم المثال فی الآفاق، نادر العصر بالوفاق والاتفاق، مهندس طرفه کار، استاد فلاں معمار است، که این ابیات نادره آیات نظیر احوال اوست:

برسم هندسی کار آزمائی — قوانین رصد را راهنمائی
زتفتیش[٦] مجسطی سخت آسان — زتشکیك وی اقلیدس هراسان
مجسطی بردرو بر طاق اطلس — بر ایوان زحل بندد مقرنس
چو سوء تیشه آرد دستش آهنگ — زخشت خام گردد نرم ترسنگ
عمارات جهان بی سر وبی[٧] بن — نماید جمله دریك روی ناخن

١ـ قرآن مجید : ١١٧/٢
٢ـ قرآن مجید : ٨/٨٩
٣ـ ع : تحصیل، ندارد
٤ـ ع : بدیع آثار
٥ـ ع: طراحی، ندارد
٦ـ ع : زتشکیکش
٧ـ ع: بی، ندارد

بناءً علیه اورا مشمول مواهب خسروانه داشته، منصب معماری ولایت فلان را من حیث الانفراد والاستقلال بدو تفویض فرمودیم که بواجبی بلوازم ومراسم این امر اشتغال نموده دقیقه فرو گذاشت ننماید ودر طراحی وساختن عمارات خاصه وغیر آن از هرچه تعلق به معمار دارد چنان اهتمام نماید که مزیدی بران متصور نباشد وآثار آن بظهور رسد۔ سبیل همگنان آن که مومی الیه را معمار با اختیار دانسته امداد[1] واعانت وتقویت او بجای آورند۔ وگل کاران وخشت مالان وسنگ تراشان وچوب فروشان وچوب تراشان ودرود گران وخشت پزان وگچ پزان[2] وآهك پزان وهرچه ازین قبیل است اورا معمار وپیشواء خود دانسته، از سخن وصواب دید او بیرون نروند واوامر ونواهی اورا مطیع ومنقاد باشند ودر بر آورد کارهای ایشان هرچه ازین پیشه گوید قول وفعل اورا معتبر دارند، ودر جمیع امور از متابعت او سرنه پیچند، ولوازم این امر را موافق قانون قدیم وقاعده استمرار مخصوص او شناخته واصل گردانند۔

(۲۰)

منشور در تفویض منصب میر بکاولی

چون بناء عمارت دار الملك خلافت وجهانبانی وطرح اساس روضة الخلد سلطنت وکشورستانی بزیب وزینت افاضه خیر وامتنان متسق است وارکان مدارس اسلام وبنیان خوانق ملت حضرت سید الانام باشاعت شفقت واحسان منتظم۔ وحصول آن مامول را بهترین وسیله ونفیس ترین واسطه طریقه مرضیه اطعام نوال و گستردن سفره

۱۔ ع: دارد چنان اهتمام نماید که مزید می بران متصور نباشد وآثار آن بظهور رسد، سبیل همگنان آن که مومی الیه را معمار با اختیار داسته امداد، ندارد

۲۔ ع : گچ پزان، ندارد

نعمت حضرت ذو الجلال است که کریمه "لن تنالوا البر حتی تنفقوا مما تحبون"[1] اقامت دلیل بران می فرماید۔ لاجرم به شکرانه آن موهبت ودر مقابله آن مکرمت برحسب امر عالی "واما بنعمة ربك فحدث"[2] امداد وتائید واسعاد توفیق رفیق حال خجسة فال وقرین احوال فرخنده مآل همایون گشته باحداث مدرسه عرش رفعت وخانقاه کرسی منزلت بموجب "إن المبانی تحکی همة البانی" اوج فلك را زیر دست وذروه فلك را در شکشت دارد، توفیق یافته ایم وبوادی رضاء حضرت بیچون شتافته، مقرر فرمودیم که برطبق "یطعمون الطعام علی حبه مسکینا ویتیما واسیراً"[3] زمره انام وقاطبه خواص وعوام را از فوائد عام بهره مند گردانند تا مثوبات آن بروزگار خجسته آثار همایون لاحق وعائد گردد۔ ورابطه خلوص اعتقاد ونیکو بندگی معتمد خاص ومحرم حریم اختصاص نظام الدین فلان بکاول، که مدت مدید است که در سراپرده خلود وشهریاری علاقه خصوصیت ثابت دارد وسابقه محرمیت او دردرگاه خلائق پناه در غایت ظهور است۔ بنا بران منصب بکاؤلی وخدمت گاری مطبخ مدرسه شریفه وخانقاه مسافر خانه بدو مفوض شد که بوظائف آن خدمت قیام نماید۔ ومادام که مشار الیه درقید حیات باشد من حیث الاستقلال والانفراد به شغل مذکور اشتغال ورزد، وهرگاه بر حسب وعده "کل نفس ذائقة الموت"[4] شربت فنا از دست ساقی اجل چشد، یکی از اولاد او واولاد اولاد او بطنا بعد بطنٍ قرناً اثر قرنٍ که قابلیت امر مذکور داشته باشد، متصدی آن باشد۔ وچون بواجبی بدین امر مذکور قیام نماید وظیفه دستوری گیرد وبرو رسانند۔

سبیل فرزندان کامگار وامراء عالی مقدار وصدور عظام ووزراء

۱۔ قرآن مجید : ۹۲/۳

۲۔ قرآن مجید : ۱۱/۹۳

۳۔ قرآن مجید : ۸/۷۶

٤۔ قرآن مجید : ۱۸۵/۳

ذوی الاحترام وباقی متصدیان امور از متولیان ومباشران امور اوقاف سلطانی آن که در تمشیت امر مذکور وتقویت معتمد مشارالیه قاعده اهتمام بجای آورند واو را واولاد او را بشرحی که در صدر مذبور ست بدین امر جلیل القدر منصوب ومعین دانسته بموجب شرط واقف وظیفه دهند۔ از جوانب برین جمله روند۔ درین باب قدغن عظیم دانند۔

(۲۱)

منشور در تفویض منصب شیخ الاسلامی

اغصان سدره خلافت وجهان بانی واوراق شجره سلطنت وکشورستانی از برادران جلیل الشان[1] رفیع القدر وفرزندان عدیل الشمس، شبیه البدر وخوانین جم قدر وظفر لواء وسلاطین ذی شوکت نصرت انتماء وامراء اسفندیار صولت، تهمتن تن[2] وصدور زحل مرتبت، موتمن، و وزراء عطارد[3] خاصیت، کفایت مرتبت وعمال بادرایت، صاحب خبرت، ونواب آستان آسمان مقدار وحجاب بارگاه سپهر اقتدار وناظمان اعمال سلطانی و واقفان اشغال دیوانی وزمره انام از خواص وعوام بدانند که نضارت ریاض مملکت بی آبیاری چشمه سار شریعت غراء صورت نمی پذیرد وسرسبزی گلزار خلافت بیرون از اشعه آفتاب ملت بیضاء تمشی نمی گیرد[4]، فنعم ما قال الفضلاء، قطعه:

سرسبزی نهال خلافت بباغ ملک　　بی چشمه سار شرع مطهر طمع مدار
لیکن زلال چشمه دین کی شود روان　　بی صلمت[5] سیاست شاهان کامگار

ولهذا قال سید الانبیاء علیه من الصلوة افضلها ومن التحیات اکملها

۱۔ ع : جلیل الشان، ندارد
۲۔ ع : تن، ندارد
۳۔ ع : عظام
٤۔ ع : نگیرد
٥۔ ع : سایه

"الملك والدین توامان" تا ارباب بصیرت واصحاب سریرت بچشم عقل وزبان فضل دانند وخوانند که دین وملك توام اند ودولت وملت متلازمان۔

بناء علیه از منشاء طلوع صبح دولت بی زوال ومبداء شروق آفتاب حشمت بی انتقال الی یومنا هذا، که مهر فرخنده چهر خلافت وسروری بر وسط سماء رتبه اعتلاء وارتقاء یافته وپرتو انوار فرخنده آثارش برمفارق عالمیان تافته، تمهید وتشئید[١] اساس شریعت طاهره راپیش نهاد همت والا نهمت داریم ودر تاسیس وترصیص مبانی ملت زاهره توجه خاطر فیض مآثر بدرجه اعلی ومرتبه قصوی می گماریم، ومی خواهیم که درهر[٢] ولایت وناحیت یکی از ارباب حسب[٣] و اصحاب نسب که اجراء امور دین اسلام وتنفیذ اوامر ونواهی ملت حضرت سید الانام[٤] علیه الصلوة والسلام، را نصب العین ضمیر داشته باشد، ودر ایجاب مامولات واسعاف مسؤلات سادات وعلماء وقضات وعرفاء ومشائخ وفضلاء وتمامی ارباب عمائم، علی تفاوت درجاتهم وتباین طبقاتهم، توجه تمام گماشته، تعین فرمائیم۔[٥] وبدین جهت ابواب فراغ بال ورفاء حال برجبهۀ آمال طبقات عالی درجات کشائیم تابنوید فیروزی "الشاکر یستحق المزید بالشکر" مستظهر توانیم بود ودر مواد وثوق ورجاء توانیم فزود۔ وچون این خصائص حمیده در ذات[٦] نجابت سمات، شرافت مآب، معالی قباب، افاضت شعار، موهبت آثار، نتیجه ارباب هدایت وعرفان، بقیه اصحاب کرامت وایقان، معدن العلوم والکمالات، منبع السعادات والجلالات[٧] فلان موجود ودر ظهور این

١۔ ع : تشهد
٢۔ ع : هر، ندارد
٣۔ ع : حسب، ندارد
٤۔ ع : سید انام
٥۔ ع : فرمائم
٦۔ ع : حمیده در ذات، ندارد
٧۔ منبع السعادات والجلالات، ندراد

مقالات مستعد می نمود،[1] دریں ولا قامت با استقامت اورا (به) تشریف الطاف واکرام مزین ساخته، رایت اعظام واحترام اورا درساحت روزگار افراخته،[2] منصب گرامی شیخ الاسلامی ولایت فلاں را بامضافات ومنسوبات وضمائم وملحقات ازیں تاریخ که مطابق او دایل است، بدو ارزانی فرمودیم که بدستور آباء واجداد رفعت نژاد خود بدین (امر) اشتغال نموده، دقیقه از دقائق فرو گذاشت نکند ودرهدایت وارشاد عباد وتقویت واسعاد شریعت حضرت سید الانبیاء مراسم سعی واجتهاد مبذول دارد و چنان نماید که لوازم امر شریف بواجبی فیصل یافته در روز جزاء جواب او مطابق سوال افتد۔

می باید که آں فضائل پناه را بدیں منصب شریف منصوب دانسته امداد واعانت وتقویت وتمشیت بظهور آورند وسادات وعلماء ومشائخ وفضلاء وموالی واهالی واشراف واعالی واعیان ورعایا ومزارعان وعموم سکنه وجمهور متوطنه ولایت فلاں مومی الیه را شیخ الاسلام صاحب اختیار دانسته از سخن مصلحت وی عدول وانحراف نورزند۔ ومحتسبان وامامان وموذنان ومتولیان اوقاف وغیره بریں موجب عمل نمایند وجمیع امور شرعیه را بحضور شریف آں معالی دستگاه صورت داده همگی صکوك وسجلات وقبالات وتمامی خطوط را بمهر او رسانند وبی مهر وتصدیق او منظور ومعمول ندانند۔ وآں رفعت پناه را مرجع خود دانسته متابعت بجای آورند وچناں نمایند که آثار آں بظهور رسد۔ ومبلغ فلان در وجه وظیفه ومعاش آں جامع الکمالات مقرر دانند ودر ایصال آں اهتمام بلیغ مبذول دارند۔ وچوں بتوقیع وقیع رفیع منیع رسد اعتماد نمایند ودر عهده دانند۔

۱۔ ع : موجود ودر ظهور ایں مقالات مستعدمی نمود، ندارد

۲۔ ع : ورایت اعظام واحترام اورا درساحت روزگار افراخته، ندارد

(٢٢)
منشور در تفویض منصب سجاده نشینی
وتولیت آستان شیخ بهاء الدین زکریا ملتانیؒ

چون تائید ازلی وتوفیق لم یزلی باطن مارا مطرح اشعه انوار ارادت وعقیدت ومهبط شعشعه آثار مودت ومحبت ارباب هدایت گردانیده، صورت ومعنی[١] از سر صفاء نیت وخلوص طویت روی دل متوجه اعتقاد واستعداد از همت و ارادت طبقه رفیعه اقطاب واوتاد داشته ومی داریم وروابط موالات ونیا زمندی ایشان را واسطه اسباب سعادت وسربلندی دنیا وآخرت دانسته بدقیقه نامرعی نمی گذاریم۔ والحق دریں نیت صفاء رویت انجاح مقاصد ومآرب دینی ودنیوی ما بمیامن توفیق الهی در سلك نظام وسمط انتظام منخرط[٢] ومندرج است وهمواره خاطر فیض مآثر داعی وساعی آں بوده ومی باشد که در تنسیق مهمات مزارات متبرکه ومشاهد مقدسه اولیاء وعرفاء طریق حق ویقین، قدس الله تعالیٰ ارواحهم اجمعین، مهما یمکن مساعی جمیله به تقدیم رسانیم ومنصب سجاده نشینی وتولیت موقوفات امکنه شریفه را بعهده جمعی، که آثار رشاد وانوار قابلیت واستعداد از وجنات حالات ایشاں واضح ولائح باشد، باز گذاریم تاهر عملی از اعمال بقدر اندازه واستحقاق قرار گرفته[٣] لایزال روضه حسنات تازه وفیض برکات بی اندازه باشد۔ "الحمد لله الذی هدانا لهذا"[٤]۔

مقصود از ایراد ایں[٥] مقدمه آں که چوں قبل ازیں منصب رفیعه

١۔ ع : همواره
٢۔ ع : منخرط، ندارد
٣۔ ع : یافته
٤۔ قرآن مجید : ٤٣/٧
٥۔ ع : ایں، ندارد

المناصب، جليلة المراتب سجاده نشینی وتولیت موقوفات ونسق صادرات آستان مطهره حضرت عالی مرتبت، متعالی منزلت، قطب اصحاب الالهامات الربانية، قدوة ارباب المكاشفات السبحانيه، مالك ممالك العلم والعرفان، صاعد مصاعد المعرفة والایقان، محی مراسم حضرت سید المرسلین، علیه صلوات رب العالمین، حجة الله علی العارفین، بیت:

راه روی کز سر صدق وصفا

رفته قدم بر قدم مصطفیٰ

المتوجه الی الله والمعرض عما سواه، شیخ بهاء الحق والحقیقة والشریعة والدین زکریا وخلف صدق آن حضرت، زبدة العارفین، قدوة المحقین، اسوه اهل الحق والیقین، قطب فلك الهدایة والولایة والانتباه، شیخ رکن الدین ابو الفتح فیض الله، قدس الله سرهما العزیز، بحسب ارث واستحقاق بارشد اولاد امجاد ایشان، عالی جناب، عرفان مآب، حقیقت ایاب، شریعت شعار، طریقت دثار، موهبت آثار، مجمع الفضائل والکمالات الانسیه، طالب المیامن والسعادات القدسیه، ذوی الخصائل الرضیه والشمائل المرضیه، المستفیض من مواهب الملك الخبیر، نظام الملته والدین شیخ کبیر مفوض ومتعلق بوده۔ درخلال آن احوال بعضی از معارف اولاد آن حضرت که ادعاء این شغل شریف می نمود[۱]، برسبیل مشارکت فرمان عالی شان بنام خود حاصل نموده بود[۲]۔ دریں ولا بموقف عرض رسید که ترتیب اسباب نظام وانتظام شرائط وروابط امور متعلقه آن کما ینبغی از حیز قوت بدرجه فعل نمی آید۔ بعد از تامل نظر اشرف، که مشرف ممالك غیب است، در مرآت ضمیر منیر، عدالت تاثیر چنان انکشاف یافت که بحکم "إن الله یامرکم أن تو دوا الامانات الی ا هلها"[۳] منصب مذکور بدستور سابق من حیث الانفراد والاستقلال

۱۔ ع : نموده اند
۲۔ ع : بود، ندارد
۳۔ ع : قرآن مجید : ۳۵/٤

دون المساهمة والاشتراك، بعالی جناب، عرفان مآب، مومی الیه، که ارشد واصلح اخلاف آن خانواده کریم الاطراف است، تفویض یابد۔ فلهذا فرمان جهان مطاع، لازال نافذاً فی الاقطار والاربا ع، شرف صدور وعز ورود یافت که منصب شیخی وسجاده نشینی وتولیت موقوفات آن دودمان فیض آیات بمقتضی "رجع الحق الی مکانه" ازین تاریخ بی شرکت غیری بآن سلاله خاندان ولایت وهدایت مفوض ومتعلق باشد وبنوعی که از وفور صیانت وحسن معیشت وکاردانی او متصوراست بقواعد وضوابط امر[1] مزبور اشتغال نموده، هیچ گونه تهاون وفروگذاشتی جائز ندارد۔ واز جمله موازی فلان ومواضع فلان ویرانه، که از موقوفات آن دو مقام فرخنده سمات (اند) بموجب فرمان سعادت نشان در وجه مدد معاش فلان مقرر شده بود از ابتداء فلان بمشار الیه مسلم ومفوض داشته به تصرف گذارند۔ وباقی مواضع واراضی وباغات وجائهای موقوفه که از اعمال سرکار ملتان از سواد بلده وغیرها از قدیم وجدید بموجب فرامین مطاعه[2] واسناد معتبره[3] قبل ازین در تصرف او وبرادران اوبود، تمامی آنها حسب الضمن موازی فلان بدستور سابق متصرف شود، ودرباب زیادتی آبادانی ومعموری آن محال سعی موفور[4] وجهد نامحصور بظهور رسانیده مال واجبی آن را، بعد[5] انچه بحصه برادران وخادمان وتوابع قسمت یافته، تمام وکمال سال به سال متصرف گشته صرف مصارف وجوب آن دو منزل جنت مماثل از فرش وروشنائی وعمارت ضروریه واعراس واطعام فقراء والمساکین من المقیمین والمسافرین ومواجب عمال ووظائف خدام نماید، ورسم تولیت بطریقی، که قبل ازین موافق شرط وقف (است) می گرفته باشد

۱۔ ع : امر، ندارد
۲۔ ع : مطالعه
۳۔ ع : معتبره، ندارد
٤۔ ع : موفور، ندارد
۵۔ ع : معه

ودر تنسیق وترویج آن آستان ملائك نشان حتی الامکان کوشیده رعایت احوال اقارب وخویشان بنوعی نماید که آثار شکر گذاری آن بظهور رشد۔

می باید که برادران ارجمند نامدار و فرزندان سعادت مند برخوردار وخوانین نصرت آئین وسلاطین صاحب التمکین[۱] وامراء ملك آرای وصدور صاحب رای ونواب سراپرده عظمت سلطانی ومباشران اشغال دیوانی عموماً وحکام کرام ودیوانیان وعمال ومتصدیان وارباب وکلان تران سر کار ملتان وغیره خصوصاً عرفان مآب مومی الیه را شیخ وسجاده نشین آن دو مقام خلد آئین دانسته، دیگری را شریك وسهیم ندانند، ودر اعزاز واکرام وتبجیل واحترام او دقیقه نامرعی نگذارند تا از سر فراغت خاطر به تنسیق امورارباب طاعات وتنظیم مصالح عبادات مطمئن البال قیام تواندنمود۔ وعرفان مآب مومی لیه نیز در رواج ورونق آن بارگاه ملائك پناه حسب المقدور کوشیده از تقویت وتمشیت این مهام ناتمام نگذارد۔ درین باب قدغن لازم دانند۔

(۲۳)
منشور در تفویض منصب قضاء اجمیر وتوابع

چون رای شریعت آرای بترویج امور شریعت غراء وتنسیق مهام ملت بیضاء متوجه ومصروف است وآثار دیانت ودانش وری وانوار فضیلت وشریعت گستری از وجنات حالات ومقالات فضائل مآب، کمالات اکتساب، فقاهت ایاب، زبدة العلماء والمدرسین، قدوة الصلحاء والمتورعین نظام الدین فلان واضح ولائح وهویدا است، بنابران[۲]

۱۔ ع : صاحب تمکین
۲۔ ع : بنا بران، ندارد

فرمان عالی شان شرف نفاذ یافت که ازیں تاریخ بامر قضاء بلده فاخره اجمیر وتوابع آن اقدام نموده، بلوازم ومراسم این امر چون کتابت صکوك وسجلات وقطع وفصل دعاوی وخصومات وقسمت مواریث ومتروکات وعقود انکحه مع الولی وبلاولی وتحقیق اموال غیب وایتام ومجانین وسفهاء وتعین قوام[۱] واوصیاء ومایتعلق بها غایت سعی ونهایت اعتناء بتقدیم رسانند۔ ودر تزکیه وتعدیل شهود بذل مجهود وجهد[۲] محمود بجا آورده، بین المتخاصمین هرچند تفاوت نه بیند وبحکم "إذ اختصم لدیك خصمان فسو بینهما فی اللفظ واللحظ" طریق مساوات مرعی دارد، واز میل ومداهنه بکلی احتراز واجتناب واجب ولازم دانسته، ایں منهاج قویم وصراط مستقیم بطریقی سپرد که عند الخالق والخلائق[۳] مستحسن ومشکور باشد۔ ومی باید که حکام کرام باسادات عظام وعلماء ومشائخ وصلحاء واهالی واعیان وکافه مسلمانان از مقیمان ومتوطنان و واردان وعامه چو دریان وقانون گویان ومقدمان ورعایا ومزارعان بلده مذکور وتوابع فضائل مآب مشار الیه را قاضی نافذ الامر آن جا دانسته، دست تصدی او را در تقلید ایں امر قوی مطلق[٤] دانند واعزاز واحترام او کما ینبغی بجا آورده دقیقه نامرعی نگزارند و د ر جمیع مهمات شرعیه رجوع باو نموده از سخن او که موافق احکام شریعت غراء خواهد بود درنگذرند۔ از جوانب بریں عمل نموده از مضمون ومدلول صدر عدول وانحراف نجویند۔ و چوں بتوقیع وقیع رفیع اشرف امجد مزین وموشح وموضح ومحلی ومجلی گردد اعتماد نمایند ۔ کتب بالامر المطاع العالی وخلد نفاذه فی اشهر ربیع الاول، ۹۷۹هجـ۔

۱۔ ع : قواسم
۲۔ ع : مهد
۳۔ ع : الخلائق، ندارد
٤۔ ع : مطلق، ندارد

(٢٤)
منشور در تفویض قضاء بلده

چون حضرت قاضی الحاجات بقواعد حجج وشاهد بینات در دار القضاء "والله یقضی بالحق وهو خیر الفاصلین"[١] بر ثبوت قضیه خلافت ما بشهادت شاهدان عدل والاحسان حکم فرموده ومحضر ادعاء ایالت ومعدلت ما را بشهود عدول "أولئك هم العادلون"[٢] موشح ساخته، پس شکرانه گذاری آں موهبت عظمی وسپاس داری آں[٣] عطیه کبری رای ملك آرای متقاضی آں است که دین ودولت را نظامی واسباب ملك وملت را انتظامی حاصل آمده ترویج شرع متین وتنسیق ملت مبین روز بروز در تزاید باشد۔ وبی شبه ثبوت آں معامله جز بنیابت نصفت[٤] وشهود عدالت قضات اسلام وعلماء اعلام، که حافظان ممالك ملت وحارسان ممالك شریعت اند، انجام نمی باید۔ وچوں آں فضائل ستوده در ذات جناب شریعت مآب، فضیلت آیات، فقاهت انتساب، کمالات اکتساب، تقوی شعار، تورع دثار، امانت آثار، کمال الدین قاضی فلاں موجود بود وصورت راستی ودیانت او بوضوح رسیده۔ بنابراں امر جلیل القدر قضاء بلده فلاں مع توابع ولواحق بیست کروه در بیست کروه بلا مشارکت قاضی دیگر بدستور سابق بشریعت مآب مشار الیه مفوض فرمودیم۔

می باید که سادات عظام ومشائخ کرام وعلماء اعلام وحکام وعمال وجاگیرداران ومتصدیان مهمات حال واستقبال وچودهریان

١۔ ایں آیت غلط نقل شده، صحیح، إن الحکم الاالله، یقصّ الحق وهو خیر الفاصلین، است۔ رجوع کنید سورة الأنعام/ ٥٧۔ آیت دیگر که دراں 'والله یقضی بالحق' وارد شده ایں طوراست "والله یقضی بالحق والذین یدعون من دونه لا یقضون بشی"۔ (قرآن مجید : ٢٠/٤٠)

٢۔ ایں آیت، قرآن نیست

٣۔ ع : ع : آں، ندارد

٤۔ ع : نصفت، ندارد

وقانون گویان ومقدمان[1] ورعایا ومزارعان ومتوطنان سرکار مذکور شریعت مآب مومی الیه را قاضی نافذ الامر دانسته، دست تصدی اورا درباب عقود انکحه مع الولی وبلاولی وقسمت ترکات وکتابت صکوك وسجلات ومحافظت اموال ایتام وغیب ونصب وتعین اوصیاء واراقه خمور ومسکرات وازاله فجور ومنهیات واقامت فرائض وواجبات قوی مطلق دانند وشرائط تعظیم وتبجیل اورا بجا آورده، از سخن وصواب دید او که موافق شریعت مطهره باشد، عدول وانحراف نورزند۔ اورا نیز باید که سلوك چنان نماید که یوم یقوم الحساب از عهده جواب تواند برآمد۔ فی تاریخ ۲۹، شهر رمضان المبارك ۹۸۷هجـ۔

(۲۵)

منشور در تفویض منصب قضاء لشکر

چون انهزام جیوش نفس وعصیان از استعداد عساکر فیروزی مآثر شریعت غراء تیسر می پزیرد وانکسار جنود ضلالت وطغیان (از) استعانت سپاه نصرت دستگاه ملت بیضاء تحصیل می گیرد، لاجرم از فرصتی که سجل خلافت واقبال ما در محکمه علیه "آتیناه حکماً وعلماً"[2] بشهادت شاهد "إن الله یامر بالعدل والاحسان"[3] مسجل گردیده، ومحضر دعوی سلطنت وافضال ما در دار القضاء وسیع الفناء "أفمن اسس بنیانه علی تقویٰ من الله"[4] بصورت فتوی "والله یقضی بالحق"[5] بمرتبه تکمیل رسیده، جوامع همت شریعت طراز وبواعث نیت طریقت آغاز مصروف ومعطوف بران بوده وهست که پیوسته مبانی

۱۔ ع: متقدمان
۲۔ قرآن مجید: ۲۲/۱۲
۳۔ قرآن مجید: ۹۰/۱۶
٤۔ قرآن مجید: ۱۰۹/۹
٥۔ قرآن مجید: ۲۰/٤۰

دین قویم بمساعی جمیله ما مشید ومعلی ومشارع شرع مستقیم از مراسم سواعی جزیله ما از شوائب شبهه وریا پاك ومصفی باشد۔ وحصول این مامول وقتی یقین فرمائیم که ریاض دین مبین را بریاحین دانش وری وشرع گستری مزین وآراسته وحدائق ملت متین را از خار بدعت وضلالت پیراسته دارد وبمفتاح لازم الافتتاح تفقه ودانائی قفل جهالت ونادانی را از دلهای سالکان مسالك مسلمانی کشوده، بغایت قصوی در ترویج وتنسیق شرع اقدس لوازم جد واجتهاد مبذول شمرد۔ والحق مصداق این مقال احوال ستوده مآل، فضائل مآب افادت قباب، شریعت شعار، فقاهت آثار، موهبت دثار، عمدة الفضلاء بین الانام، جامع الشرائع والاحکام، قدوة الحفاظ والقراء باستحضار اسالیب القراءة لكلام الملك العلام، قاضی فلان، دامت میامن فضائله وشمائله است که مختصر ومطول فضائل وکمالات از آیات سور حالات ومقالات او بروشن تر تفسیری بر همگنان سمت توضیح وتلویج یافته ومی باید، وموجز ومفصل انوار خصائل وسعادات او از مطلع تحریرات ناشی الاضاء تش بر صفحات امانی وآمال عالمیان تافته ومی تابد۔ بناءً علی تلك المقدمات، درین اوقات بابرکات آن شریعت مآب را منظور انظار الطاف واعطاف داشته، منصب جلیل الاقتضاء قضاء لشکر همایون من حیث الانفراد والاستقلال بدو ارزانی داشتیم که بدین امر عظیم القدر پرداخته دقیقه از دقائق فرو گذاشت نکند، وطریق متابعت شریعت طاهره ومنهاج ملت زاهره را باقدام فراست وکیاست پیموده، سراً وعلانیةً از شوائب میل وریا اجتناب واحتراز لازم داند۔ ودر استماع کلام متخاصمین ملاحظه مساوات طرفین نماید۔ ودرتزکیه وتعدیل شهود وبینات وهرچه لازمه این منصب جلیل القدر است، بنوعی اهتمام کند که مزیدی بران متصور نباشد۔ وچنان که "یوم یقوم الروح والملائکة صفاً لا یتکلمون الا من أذن له الرحمن وقال صواباً"[1]

۱۔ قرآن مجید : ۳۸/۷۸

جواب او مطابق سوال افتد۔

سبیل همگنان علی طریق التعمیم آن که مومی الیه را قاضی عسکر نافذ الامر دانسته، لوازم ایں امر شریف را چوں قطع وفصل مخاصمات وتمادی وقسمت متروکات وارث وضبط اموال ایتام ومجانین وغیب واجراء تعزیرات وحدود وعقود انکحه مع الولی وبلاولی وزجر ومنع فاسقان وفاجران وباطلان وما یتعلق بها مخصوص باو دانسته، مرافعات جمیع ملازمان ومنتسبان درگاه عالم پناه را بید اهتمام او متعلق ومربوط دانند۔ وچوں بتوقیع وقیع رفیع منیع مزین ومحلی گردد اعتماد نمایند۔

(٢٦)

منشور در تفویض منصب میر عدل

زمره خاندان سلطنت وفرقه دودمان خلافت واصول شجره کیانی وفروع دوحه خسروانی از برادران اجله سعادت مند وفرزندان اعزه ارجمند وامراء ظفر قرین نصرت مآل وارکان دولت ابدی الاتصال وصدور صدر نشین ووزراء کفایت آیئن وارباب مراتب ودرجات واصحاب احشامات[١] وتومانات با اعلام مسالك واشراف ممالك از جماهیر نقباء ومشائخ وعلماء[٢] وسکنه مساکن ومتوطنه مواطن وعامه رعایا وکافه برایا سرکار فلاں بدانند که چوں سعی مشکور خسروانه باصغاء مسئول درماندگان صرف نمودن وجهد مستطاع بادشاهانه در انجاح مامول درماندگان تقدم فرمودن از موجبات دوام دولت ومقتضیات ازدیاد مواد رفعت دنیا وآخرت است، قال النبی صلی الله علیه وسلم "من اعطاه الله تعالی مملکة علی عباده ثم عدل علیهم مد الله عمره واذا

١۔ ع : احتشامات
٢۔ ع : علاّم

انصف ضعیفهم من قویهم قواه[۱] الله سبحانه"۔

بیت:

بر نکردند زهم تا باید عدل ودوام　　بر دوام تو دلیل است قوی عدل توزانکه

لا جرم رعایت مقتضاء عدل وداد در باب غوررسی منتظمان (متظلمان) وداد خواهان واجب ولازم دانسته، همگی همت همایون سعت[۲] متعلق بآنست[۳] که پیوسته قواعد معلومات تفحص اوضاع مظلومان واستکشاف احوال مستضعفان[۴] ومحتاجان ممهد گردد ودر همه وقت راه داد خواه کشوده، استماع سخن وهم (ستم) یافتگان وقطع وفصل کلیات وجزئیات ایشان بی مداهنه ومراعات جانبین بظهور انجامد۔ بناءً علی ذالك عمدة الملك الخاقانیة، امین الدولة السلطانیة، خواجه فلاں که سابقاً شرف امتیاز او از بنی نوع گرامی وارباب حقوق نسب عالی وفنون حسب متعالی از السنه وافواه مشاهیر وقت بمسامع جلال پیوسته بود۔ ومبنی بر صحت وثبوت آں که از مبادی دولت ابدپیوند مناظم امور ملك وملت ومصالح ضروریات دین ودولت بر وجهی که ملاحظه مصلحت مسلمانان واسلام کما هی احوال زیر دستاں تواند بود، می سازد ومی پردازد چناں که الیوم درموقف همایون سلطانی در تقلد مقالید حل وعقد امور سلطنت بواسطه کمال کفایت وکاردانی از مرتبه وزارت که مستتبع اشراف دیوان است بدرجه رفیع امارت متصاعد گشته، مرجع تمامت امور وکارساز طبقات جمهور است۔ مع ذالك در خلال ایں اوقات مقرر شد که متعهد پرسش داد خواهان وفریاد رسی محتاجان ومظلومان بود وقطع وفصل ایشاں را بعزم ثاقب ورای صائب از ذخائر مثوبات اخروی وجلائل فتوحات دنیوی داند۔ وازاں جمله هر

۱۔　ع: قوی

۲۔　ع: سعت، ندارد

۳۔　ع: بآں متعلق است

۴۔　ع: متضعفان

صورت که عرض آن واجب شناسد حیثما یقتضیه[۱] الوقت بذروه عرض رساند. ومعتمد الدوله مشار الیه بملاحظه مزید احتیاط واستحکام که از لوازم احوال خجسته مآل اوست، در ضبط وربط آن مهمات خیر انجام، که هر آئینه مستدعی قوام عالم ونظام امور بنی آدم تواندبود، استدعاء حضور افاضت اثر یکی از شاهزادگان نامدار وجمعی از امناء صاحب خبرت که در سر انجام معظمات آن[۲] شغل خطیر[۳] سزاوار این کار باشند، واجب دانسته بر حسب التماس او حکم محکم قضا امضاء سلطانی برین وجه نفاذ پیوست که سلطنت مآب، ابوت انتساب، اعتضاد الدوله، غیاث الدین فلان که براستی در جمیع امور نیتی ارجمند وسعادتی بر دوام روز بروز دران[٤] مجلس خیر شرف قدوم ارزانی داشته مشکل کشائی خود کفایت مهات عجزه ومستضعفان[٥] از وفور اهتمام بظهور رساند، ویوماً فیوماً درتضاعف این احوال دران مجلس رفیع الدرجات[٦] یکی از صدور منشرح الصدور وقضات شریعت سمات ومنشیان وبخشیان باهر وماهر واقف وحاضر باشند، واز یساولان وپیاده روان درگاه ممالك پناه چهل نفر دیگر جهت تردد وکارگذاری طریق ازدحام وجمعیت مسلوك دارند تا قطع مهمات وکفایت ضروریات هیچ یك از دادخواهان جهان وبیداد وستم رسیدگان عالم کون وفساد در عقده اهمال وامهال نماند.

سبیل همگنان، وفقهم الله سبحانه لاشاعة مآثر الخیر والبر، آن که برحسب فرموده، که درقضیه نفاذ حکم قضا دارد، مقرر دانسته قدم از دائره امتثال وفرمان برداری بیرون ننهند[۷] تا غبار حیف وتعدی از صفحات صحائف ایام ستوده گردد. ومقرر است که عمدة الملك مشار الیه در نجات ورستگاری گرفتاران وترحم وغوررسی دادخواهان

۱ـ ع : تقتضیه
۲ـ ع : از
۳ـ ع : خطر، ندارد
٤ـ ع :درین
٥ـ ع: متضعفان
٦ـ ع : درجات
۷ـ نه نهد

صورت مراقبت ونیکوکاری بنوعی منظور اعتبار خواهد داشت که هریك از ایشان دست قدرت واعتماد در دامن شرذمه ظالم نهاد زده از روی استظهار وامیدواری بفحواء این نظم عذب البیان که: بداد خواه زدست تومیروم سوء دیوان[۱] رطب اللسان گردند ومن الله الاعانة والتائید.

(۲۷)
منشور در تفویض منصب احتساب

چون آمر اوامر[۲] "إن الله یامر بالعدل والاحسان"[۳] ذات متعالی صفات ما را بمتابعت شریعت غراء آراسته وناهی[۴] نواهی "ینهی عن الفحشاء والمنکر والبغی"[۵] عنصر فرخنده صفات مارا از مطاوعت بدعت پیراسته، افسر خجسته اثر ترویج دین قویم را زینت تارك مبارك ما ساخته، وخلعت[۶] نفاست مرتبت تنسیق ملت مستقیم را بقامت با استقامت ما پرداخته، ما نیز در ازاء این موهبت شامله وحذاء این مکرمت کامله نصب العین ضمیر شریعت پرور ومطمح خاطر حقیقت گستر آن داریم که جمعی از مقتبسان مشکوة انوار "ومن یتق الله یجعل له مخرجاً ویرزقه من حیث لا یحتسب"[۷] ومستفیضان آثار "الآمرون بالمعروف والناهون عن المنکر والحافظون لحدود الله"[۸] که طیلسان عالی شان امر معروف ونهی منکر را بر کتف همت انداخته باشند ومتابعت سنت سنیه فاروقی "لواء الاسلام قوی بدرة عمر" درساحت گیتی مرتفع ساخته باشند، بمنصب مناسب احتساب امتیاز واختصاص یابند وبامداد دولت بلند وامداد حشمت ارجمند ما در اشاعت انوار شریعت ونصفت وازاله

۱ـ ع : زدست جو راست سوء دیوان
۲ـ ع : امر
۳ـ قرآن مجید : ۹۰/۱۶
۴ـ ع :نامی، ندارد
۵ـ قرآن مجید : ۹۰/۱۶
۶ـ ع : نقابت، زیاده دارد
۷ـ قرآن مجید : ۳/۶۵
۸ـ قرآن مجید : ۱۱۲/۹

آثار ظلمت وبدعت حتی الامکان کوشیده، بوسیله آن بمدارج حسنات ومعارج برکات شتابند. نابر[1] علی تلك المقدمات دریں ولا منصب جلیل الحساب احتساب ولایت فلاں را من حیث الانفراد والاستقلال بشریعت مآب، فقاهت مناب، تقوی شعار، دیانت دثار، مروج دین الاسلام[2]، مزیل البدع والآثام، ناصب الویة الشریعة بین الانام، مولانا فلاں تفویض فرمودیم که بواجبی بدیں امر شریف پرداخته، دقیقه از دقائق اهتمام واجتهاد نامرعی نگذارد و در انتظام والتیام امور شرع شریف وانهدام واندراس مبانی فسق وفجور وبدعت بمرتبه پردازد که مزیدی براں متصور نباشد. واز میل ومداهنه و کذب وریا دور وبی قصور بوده در جمیع لوازم ایں امر جلیل[3] المراسم چناں وچنداں پردازد که روز سوال از عهده جواب بیروں تواندآمد.

باید که ارکان دولت بی زوال واعیان حشمت بی انتقال وناهجان مناهج ملك ومال وصاعدان مصاعد[4] ابدی الاتصال وعموم خدمت گاران درگاه خلائق پناه، عرش اشتباه وجمهور ملازمان سده سدره مثال وتمامی سکنه ومتوطنان ولایت مذکور شریعت مآب مشار الیه را محتسب مستقل دانسته، لوازم ایں منصب شریف را چوں اجراء حدود وتعزیرات، واراقه خمور ومسکرات وتعیین زراع ومکیال واوزان، وتادیب وزجر شاربان خمور وتارکان صلوة، وترغیب وتحریص مردم باداء صلوة واحضار درجمعه وجماعت، وتعمیر وترویج مساجد ومعابد وبقاع خیر، وتفتیش احوال امامان وموذنان ودفع ورفع فسقه وفجره وابطال رسوم مبتدعه و کسر آلات نغمه چوں طنابیر ومزامیر ومنع کبوتر بازان ومحولهو ولعب[5] وبرانداختن رسوم باطله واباطیل ومایکون من هذا

۱- ع : بناءً
۲- ع : اسلام
۳- ع : جمیع
٤- ع : حشمت
٥- ع: لهب

القبیل مخصوص او شمرند ودست تعهد اورا در اعتناق این شغل قوی مطلق دانسته، امداد واعانت وتقویت وتمشیت او کما ینبغی بجا آورند. وموسی الیه نیز باید که تارکان صلوة وشاربان خمر ومرتکبان[۱] سائر منهیات را تادیب وتنبیه بلیغ نموده بصلوة وصیام باعث وراغب، ودرباب امر احستاب بنوعی قیام واقدام[۲] نماید که مزیدی بران متصور نباشد. ووظیفه احتساب را بلا قصور وانکسار و اهمال باو رسانند. سبیل همگنان آن که اطاعت اوامر ونواهی اورا لازم شناسند وچنان سازند که در جمیع امور آثار اهتمام مومی الیه ومتابعت ایشان بوضوح رسد. وچون بتوقیع وقیع منیع رفیع اشرف اقدس اعلی مزین ومحلی گردد اعتماد نمایند.

(۲۸)
منشور در تفویض منصب نقابت

فرزندان سکندر تبار وبرادران نامدار وصدور شریعت دثار ووزراء آصف صفوت وعمال کفایت[۳] مرتبت وسائر سکنهٔ[۴] کرپاس لازم الاجلال وباقی متوطنه درگاه سپهر مثال واصول واعیان ووضیع وشریف واعالی وادانی دیار وخواص وعوام فی الممالک[۵] المحروسة بدانند که ساحت بوستان سلطنت اجلال خواقین همایون فال از ترشح تواتر تقاطر غمام اخلاص ومحبت منتسبان دودمان نبوت ورسالت طراوت ونضارت می گیرد وفضاء گلستان خلافت واقبال سلاطین فرخنده خصال از تلمع آفتاب اعتقاد و مودت[۶] مقتبسان انوار خاندان جلالت خضارت[۷] ونزاهت می پذیرد. بنابرین قاعده ارجمند ونیت دل پسند

۱ـ ع : مرتکبان، ندارد
۲ـ ع : انتظام
۳ـ ع : و، ندارد
۴ـ ع : کفایت، ندارد
۵ـ ع : سکنه، ندارد
۶ـ ع : فی الملك
۷ـ ع : نضارت

اسلاف معالی[۱] اتصال همواره اقتباس انوار سعادت دینی ودنیوی که از مشکوة خواطر مهر مآثر بدور آسمان "قل لا أسالكم عليه اجرا إلا المودة فی القربی"[۲] می نمود واجداد عالی نژاد ما پیوسته التماس اسرار هدایت صوری ومعنوی از پیش گاه ضمائر غیبی سرائر صدور ایوان "ليذهب عنكم الرجس اهل البيت ويطهر كم تطهيراً"[۳] کرده، بوسیله آن ابواب مباهات ومفاخرت بر آمال خود می کشوده اند[۴] ما نیز اطاعت سنن[۵] سنیه خواقین صدر تمکین[۶] را برطبق "إنا وجدنا آباءنا على أمة"[۷] لازم دانسته در انتظام آن ضابطه سعی موفور مبذول می داریم ومتابعت سیر مرضیه سلاطین سپهر تمکین را بر وفق "وإنا على آثارهم مهتدون"[۸] متحتم شناخته در التیام ایں رابطه جهد نامحصور مصروف می شماریم. وچوں موجب فرموده "لعن الله الداخل فيها بغير نسب والخارج عنها بغير سبب" تحقیق وتصحیح انساب ایں طائفه عالی جناب الیق وانسب است، دریں وقت فرمان جهان مطاع مهر ارتفاع شرف صدور یافت که عالی جناب، سیادت پناه، نجابت دستگاه، مرتضی ممالك اسلام، جامع اصول الحسب والنسب بین الانام امیر فلان، صاحب منصب وافر منقبت نقابت بوده، پرتو اهتمام واعتلاء به تصحیح نسب که باسم سیادت معروف ومشهور بوده اند (اندازد) .صحت نسب هریك که (به ثبوت) پیوندد نسب نامه بوی داده کیفیت را معروض گرداند تا باصناف تعظیم واحترام وانواع اکرام وانعام امتیاز واختصاص یابد. وهر کدام مجهول النسب بوده[۹] وبطلان دعوی او[۱۰] محقق گردد ادبی بلیغ نماید تا دیگر کسی را مجال آن نماند که بغیر

۱ـ ع : معالی، ندارد، انصاف، زیاده دارد

۲ـ قرآن مجید : ۲۳/۴۲

۳ـ قرآن مجید : ۳۳/۳۳

۴ـ ع : کشودند

۵ـ ع : سنت

۶ـ ع : سدره نگین

۷ـ قرآن مجید : ۲۲/۴۳

۸ـ قرآن مجید : ۲۲/۴۳

۹ـ ع : بوده، ندارد

۱۰ـ ع : او، ندارد

استحقاق منسوب بایں طریقه شریفه گردد۔ وجید را از زیف وسید را از متسید چنان جدا سازد که مزیدی بران متصور نباشد۔

می باید که سیادت مآب موسی الیه را متصدی منصب نقابت دانسته، انچه لوازم این امر شریف است مخصوص (باو) شناسند وغیری را بدان جناب شریك وسهیم ندانند۔ وانچه کمال تعظیم و احترام توانند نسبت بدان جناب نقابت دستگاه مرعی داشته در ترویج وتنسیق این امر رفیع القدر امداد واعانت وتقویت و تمشیت وی را از لوازم دانند وتجویز او فروگذاشتی نکنند، وآں جناب را در تحقیق[1] انساب معتبر شمارند۔ وشکر وشکایت آں معالی دستگاه را در غایت تاثیر دانند۔ سادات رفیع الدرجات در حضور آں مرتضوی سمات تصحیح انساب خود نمایند واز فرموده اش سر نه پیچند۔ مقرر است که رفعت مناب کمال اهتمام دریں باب بظهور آورده ازمیل ومداهنت دور وبی قصور باشد وچنان سازد که مساعی جمیله او عند الخالق والخلائق مرضی ومستحسن بوده، آثار آں برهمگناں واضح گردد۔ از جوانب بریں جمله روند وچوں بتوقیع وقیع رفیع منیع اشرف اعلی رسد اعتماد نمایند۔

(۲۹)
منشور در تفویض سرداری لشکر وفوجداری سرکار

چوں ارتفاع کوکب دولت واقبال واتساع عرصه جاه وجلال ارباب دولت واعتبار واصحاب عزت واقتدار بوجود اعوان وانصار از ابطال رجال ومردم اصیل وعاقل، کاردان، کار گزار، فطانت وکیاست شعار، وفا وحقیقت دثار وابسته است، وچمن دولت وجلالت وگلشن

۱۔ ع : تحقیق، ندارد

رفعت وایالت بانوار صائب آراء وثواقب افکار[1] آن زمره عظیم القدر، جلیل الشان از خس وخار بی سر انجامی و بی نظامی ونقصان پیراسته- بناءً علی هذا دریں ایام خجسته آغاز فرخنده انجام مجدداً سرداری لشکر وفوجداری سرکار فلان ومضافات وملحقات آن از ابتداء فلان من حیث الاستقلال بعمدة الملك، سلالة الامراء العظام، نتیجة الکبراء فی الانام، مفهوم حقیقت مردی ومردانگی، مدلول مطالبه دلیری وفرزانگی، قدوه مخلصان وفاکیش، خلاصه دولت خواهان وحشمت طلبان مصلحت اندیش، واصل صوری ومعنوی، مستعد ترقیات دینی ودنیوی، چابك سوار مضمار منصوری ومسعودی، نظام الدین فلان، که بجودت طبع وحدت فهم واصابت رای وحسن تدبیر ورزانت عقل ونجابت ذات وخوبی صفات وکمال پردلی وشجاعت ونهایت تهور وجلادت وغایت شرم وناموس متصف وآراسته است، واز آغاز تباشیر صبح دولت وعنفوان طلوع نیر اقبال وحشمت نصرت صفت واقبال آساسراً وجهراً درشدت ورخاء جلیس محافل بزمی وانیس معارك رزمی بوده، در کلیات امور ومعظمات مهمات از انتظام مهام ملکی ومالی وتنقیح معاملات سیفی وقلمی غائبانه وحاضرانه وکیل مطلق العنان ونائب مناب ماست، تفویض فرمودیم که بمقتضاء رای رزین وعقل دوربین خود بلوازم ومراسم آن امر خطیر وخطیب وکبیر بنوعی که باید وشاید، واز کمال کاردانی ومعامله فهمی ورعیت پروری ونصفت گستری او سزد وآید کما یجب، وینبغی قیام واقدام[2] نماید، ودقیقه از دقائق امر سرداری لشکر وفوجداری ولایت ومایتعلق بها نامرعی نگذارد، ودر افزونی معموری وآبادانی ولایت ودارائی سپاهی ورعیت سعی موفور بظهور آورده، دست تعدی وتطاول ظلمه ومتغلبه را از

۱- ع : آن کار
۲- ع : اقدام

عجزه وزیر دستان کوتاه و کشیده دارد، ودر برانداختن ومستاصل ساختن اهل فتنه وفساد و کینه وقهر ارباب طغیان وعناد وامنیت راهها وجمعیت خواطر مترددین اهتمام تمام لازم ومتحتم داند.

باید که اصحاب مناصب وجاگیرداران ومتصدیان مهمات ومباشران[۱] امور واشغال وعمال حال واستقبال پرگنات خالصه نصف رسوم فوجداری را درسنه مذکور بانعام آن نتیجة الامراء مقرر دانسته واصل گماشتهای او سازند ونصف دیگر بخالصه ضبط نمایند. واز ابتداء فلان مرسوم فوجداری بتمام و کمال بانعام مشار الیه مفوض ومسلم شناخته فصل بفصل وسال بسال می رسانیده باشند وهر ساله دریں باب فرمان مجدد نطلبند. وزمین داران وچودهریان وقانون گویان ومقدمان ورعایا ومزارعان وجمهور ساکنان وعموم متوطنان سرکار و محال مذکوره حسب الفرمان جهان مطاع، آفتاب شعاع مقرر دانسته از مضمون صدر عدول وانحراف نور زند، وحاضر شده کمال متابعت واطاعت بجای آورند واحداثی که واقع شود باو وبگماشتهاء او رفع نمایند، ومرفه الحال وآسوده[۲] وفارغ البال بوده بدعاء دوام دولت روز افزون وخلافت ابد مقرون ما اشتغال نمایند، وبکمال شفقت وعنایت واحسان بادشاهی امیدوار بوده وشادمان بوده در تکثیر زراعت وعمارت سعی بلیغ بتقدیم رسانند، وصومی الیه را در امور مرجوعه و رفاهیت رعایا وبرانداختن ومستاصل ساختن اهل فتنه وفساد وامنیت وجمعیت خواطر مترددین چنان سعی نماید که یوماً فیوماً آثار نیك نامی او بظهور می رسیده باشد. وچون بتوقیع وقیع رفیع[۳] اشرف اعلی مزین ومحلی گردد اعتماد نمایند در عهده دانسته از مضمون صدر درنگذرند.

۱ـ ع : آن، زیاده دارد
۲ـ ع : آسوده، ندارد
۳ـ ع : رفیع، ندارد

(٣٠)
منشور در تفویض منصب فوجداری وحراست سر کار آگره

چون همگی خاطر قدردان متوجه رعایت احوال ومراقبت آمال جماعتی بوده وهست که باوجود وفور حسن عقیدت وخلوص نیت وشائستگی ولیاقت رعایت وتربیت وحصول نسبت وقدمت خدمت وسبقت ملازمت در هر وقتی مصدر خدمات شائسته وجان سپاریهای[١] بایسته شده اند، لهذا شمه از مکنونات ضمیر حق شناس بعالم ظهور اورده، فوجداری وحراست سر کار آگره را من ابتداء فلان بعمدة الملك، رکن السلطنة القاهرة، عضد الدولة الباهره، لائق العناية والرعاية والتربية[٢] فلان مفوض ومرجوع فرمودیم که چنانچه از حسن رای ورویت ووفور دانش وفطانت متصور است بلوازم امر مذکور کما ینبغی پرداخته در دارائی سپاهی و رفاهیت رعیت وتکثیر زراعت وعمارت وافزونی آبادانی و کفایت مال ومعاملات ومعموری پرگنات وضبط وربط مهمات وقلع وقمع اهل فتنه وفساد ودفع ورفع ارباب تمرد وعناد وغوررسی مظلومان وستم رسیدگان وتادیب وتنبیه فتنه انگیزان وسرکشان وتحقیق وپیروی اعمال عمال از روی جد واهتمام اشتغال نموده، دقیقه از دقائق کاردانی واحتیاط نامرعی نگذارد، وبجزوی وکلی مهمات پرگنات واحوال سپاهی ورعیت می رسیده باشد۔

متصدیان مهمات وجاگیرداران حال واستقبال سر کار مذکور مشارالیه را فوجدار من حیث الاستقلال والانفراد دانسته، از مقتضیات رای ورویت او، که هر آئینه موافق حساب و کفایت مال دیوان است، بیرون نروند، و۔۔حاضر شده تجاوز ننمایند۔ چودهریان وقانون گویان

١۔ ع: جان سپاری
٢۔ التربية، ندارد

ومقدمان ورعایا وعموم متوطنه آنجا مشار الیه را حارس وفوجدار خود دانسته نهایت متابعت[١] بجای آورند و ــ حاضر شده، دست تصدی اورا دریں امر قوی مطلق دانند وبموجب فرمان جهان مطاع عمل نموده تخلف نورزند۔

(٣١)
منشور در تفویض منصب امیر چکله

ازانجا که همگی همت معدلت اقتباس وجملگی نمهت حق اساس مصروف بر آنست که کافه انام وعموم طبقات مردم در ضمان آسائش وآسودگی حال بوده، در عبادات ایزدی سر گرم باشند، اهل تعلق در رونق هنگامه معاملات وآرائش مدارج صورت همت بسته، سعادت نشأتین را دراں شمرند وارباب تجرد از میامن امنیت ظاهر در نکوهش نفس وتهذیب اخلاق کوشیده نیك بختی دوجهاں منحصر دراں دانند، تجدید نظر دوربیں حقیقت گزین در رفاهیت حال عالمیاں فرمودیم۔ وهر چند در هر[٢] صوبه یکی از امراء بزرگ که بفنون عواطف[٣] وتربیت رموزدان غوامض اسرار سود وزیان ودانای اسباب آبادانی وویرانی وشناسای اندازهای نیك کرداری و بدکاری وتوانای اجراء احکام عدالت باشد، تعین فرمودیم تا در شناخت کردار قوانین بارگاه خلافت قواعد عبادت بجا آرند[٤] لیکن از راه احتیاط بآں اکتفا نفرموده هر سرکاری از سرکارهای هر صوبه را وبعضی جا سرکار را چند قطعه ساخته وهر قطعه را بیکی از بندگان نزدیك، طرزدان که راستی وبی طمعی آں بیقین ما مظنون است، او بامراتب لطف وقهر شاهنشاهی که

---

١ ـ ع : مطابعت
٢ ـ ع : باب، زیاده دارد
٣ ـ ع : عاطفت
٤ ـ ع : آرد

دوبـازوی دولـت مـنـدی و دو بـال طـائـر اقبـال توان دانست، آشنا شده درجـمیع اطـوار واوضـا ع عنان گرفته راه دیده می رود، حواله کـردیم۔ وحـدود پـر کدام را که بزبان وقت چکله نامند معین گردانیده در ضمن مـنـظـور مـنـشـور مـطـا ع نـگاشته تا بی مداخلت رشوت وسائر اغراض بشری نخستین پاسبانی نیکان[1] وخیر اندیشان مرز نماید۔ دوم در اصلاح بـد کـار ان تـمـرد گـزیـن وراه زنـان دزد وامثـال آن همت گمارد۔ اگر بسـخـن پـنـد کـار سـاختـه نـگردد، بـه زدن وبستن وبند کردن وآواره گردانیدن سعی نماید[2] واگر لیاقت آن داشته باشد که علاقه روحانی او گسته گردد، اورا مقید ساخته حقیقت را عرض داشت نماید۔ ودر دور کـردن جـنـگـل وقـلا ع وخندقهاء این گروه کوشش بحا آورد ومواضع متمرد نشین را متصرف ساخته چند جا آبادان گرداند۔ سوم در تحصیل مـال واجبی عـامـلان خـالـصه و جاگیرداران اگر محتاج باشند یاوری نـمـایـد۔ چهارم آن که از سپاهی آن حدود نیز بواقعی خبردار باشد که هـر کدام از عمال وجاگیردار وعمال خالصه چه قدر سوار وپیاده همراه دارنـد۔ پـنـجـم در دفـع زکوة وتمغا ورواج مهر وروپیه (و) سائر احکام خـلافت که در قانون شهنشاهی مندرج است (و) پیشتر نقل آن بجمیع اکـنـاف ممالك مملکت شرف نفاذ یافته واکنون نیز بتجدید آن ضابطه مقدس را بهر یکی از بندگان کار گذار سپرده ایم، آن را نیك فرا گرفته پـاسبـانی نماید تا عوام خلائق امتثال آن نموده اکتساب مراتب سعادت نـمـایند۔ وچنان قرار یافته که هر ستمی ودزدی وراه زنی وسائر آنچه از بارگاه اقبال ممتنع شده، در حدود هر کدام واقع شود او جواب گوید۔

بـنـابـران چـکـلـه فـلان بتـفـصـیل ضـمن بعمدة الملك، ثابت الاخـلاص فـلان مـفـوض شد۔ سبیل عمال خالصه وعاملان جاگیردار

۱۔ ع : نیك نامی

۲۔ ع : دوم در اصلاح بد کاران تمرد گزین وراه زنان دزد وامثال آن همت گمارد، اگر بسخن پند کار ساخته نگردد، بزدن وبستن وبند کردن وآواره گردانیدن سعی نماید، ندارد

وعوام سکنه آں دیار از وضیع وشریف آں که در تقویت موسی الیه واعانت او بوده، از صلاح وصواب دید او درنگذرند۔ وهیچ کدام حمایت دزد و گناه گار او ننمایند۔ وایں چنیں کس نزد هر کدام التجا آورد یا برو دست داشته باشد، مقید ساخته بمشار الیه سپارد۔ واز صمیم قلب ونیروی جوارح در رواج احکام خلافت کوشیده کوشد۔ وهمچناں امراء چکلهای دیگر اولاً وپس ازاں سائر ناظمان قربت مورد احکام مذکور در معاضدت یك دیگر چناں یك جهتی ویك دلی بظهور آورند که بر دور ونزدیك معلوم شود وباعث مزید عاطفت گردد۔ ومتصدیان یك دیگر را حمایت[1] بنموده سرمایه رونق کار یك[2] دیگر شوند واگر احیاناً یکی را احتیاج بفراهم آوردن لشکرها باشد، باستعداد[3] او پیوسته درپاس احکام سلطنت ورواج ورونق آں سعی مشکور نمایند، وماه بماه حقیقت حال بتفصیل سوانح آں حدود ببارگاه اقبال عرض دارند وتاریخ آں را نویسند[4] چناں چه در هر قطعه ملك جواسیس متجسس تعین است۔ واقعه نویس[5] نیز تعین یافته۔ اگر معلوم شود که یکی از عمال پرگنات یا مقدم وچودری وسائر سکنه آں دیار بامراء چکلهای دیگر مساهله نماید ودر لوازم کارسستی رود ویا متمردان یك دیگر را پناه شوند، هر آئینه بقهر پادشاهی که نمونه غضب الهی است، گرفتار خواهدشد۔ نخستیں[6] تغیر جاگیر او و اخراج از وطن خواهیم فرمود۔ وهر کس بقدر توانائی ورسائی ممدو معاون خواهد بود باندازه آں بفنون عواطف روز افزوں شاهنشاهی شرف اختصاص خواهدیافت۔ عمال خالصه شریفه وجاگیرداران از صلاح وصواب دید مومی الیه جدا وبیروں نباشند وهر کدام از سربیگه مزروع یك دام بجهت نگاه داشت بندوقچی جواب گوید۔ واگر در[7] تحصیل

۱۔ ع : حمایت ندارد

۲۔ ع : یك، ندارد

۳۔ ع : استمداد

۴۔ ع : نوشته

۵۔ ع : واقعه نگار

۶۔ ع : نخستیں، ندارد

۷۔ ع : در، ندارد

مال واجبی محتاج بامداد فوجدار نباشند دریں صورت نوشته بمهر خود سپرده یك دام باو ندهند- ودرسائر از موافقت و کومك شدن وحمایت ناکردن حذر نمایند و مقرر است هرکه بموجب حکم عمل نه نماید فراخوربه تقصر تادیب خواهد یافت-

(۳۲)

منشور در تفویض منصب دیوان سرکار

چون آثار رشد و کاردانی[۱] ووقوف وراستی وامانت ودیانت از صورت حال وحقیقت احوال عمدة الخواص، صادق العقیدة والاخلاص کفایت شعاری، تحاسب آثاری، خواجه فلان بسمع اشرف اقدس واضح ولائح است، بناءً علیه من ابتداء خریف پارس ئیل منصب دیوان سرکار فلان بمشار الیه عنایت فرمودیم که بنوعی که از وفور کاردانی و کیاست وامانت ودیانت مشارالیه آید کما ینبغی بلوازم امر مذکور قیام واقدام نموده، دقیقه از دقائق دولت خواهی ونیکو خدمتی فرو گذاشتی نکند ودرتکثیر زراعت وتوفیر عمارت ومعموری سرکار مذکور وضبط وربط ولایت (و) دلاسای رعایا وتنقیح محاسب نهایت سعی وغایت اهتمام بجای آورده به تقصیر از خود راضی نشود، ونگذارد که از قوی بر ضعیف حیف وتعدی وبی حسابی واقع شود، وروز بروز آثار حسن کفایت خود ظاهر ساخته بواسطه نیکوئی خدمات خود را لائق رعایت وعنایت واحسان[۲] بادشاهی گرداند- چودریان[۳] وقانون گویان ومقدمان ورعایا ومزارعان وجمهور سکنه وعموم متوطنه سرکار مذکوره مشارالیه را دیوان من حیث الاستقلال

۱- ع : کامرانی
۲- ع : احباب
۳- ع : جوهریان

خود دانسته، اراضی خود را بتمام و کمال بنظر وقلم او و گماشتهای او درآورده، چیزی پوشیده وپنهان ندارند، واز سخن وصلاح او که هر آئینه موافق حق وحساب و کفایت مال دیوان است بیرون نروند، وبجار موسی الیه حاضر شده هر قضیه از[۱] قضایا که درمیان ایشان واقع شود رفع نمایند۔ درعهده دانسته از مضمون فرمان جهان مطاع درنگذرند۔ وچون بتوقیع وقیع رفیع منیع اشرف اعلی مزین ومحلی ومجلی گردد اعتماد نمایند۔ کتب بالامر العالی خلد نفاذه ولازال مطاعاً۔

(۳۳)
منشور در تفویض منصب دیوانی سر کار پنجاب

جاگیرداران و کروریان وزمینداران سر کار پنجاب بدانند که ازانجا که عاطفت شاهنشاهی شامل حال طبقات انام وعموم رعایا است، دیوانی برای معموری هر صوبه وخبر رسانی سوانح آن یکی از رمز دانان بساط عزت را، که از کاردانی ودیانت مندی ومهر گزینی وفراخ حوصله بهره فراوان داشت، نام زد فرمودیم تا از نقیر[۲] وقطمیر واندك وبسیار آن دیار آگاه شده برلوازم آن منصب والا رتبت، چنانکه[۳] مشکل پسندان هوشیار ومقربان بارگاه حضور تحسین نمایند، تگاپو کند ودر رفاهیت کافه برایا مساعی جمیله بظهور رساند۔ ازان جمله[٤] برای دیوانی آن صوبه معتمد الملك، کامل الاعتقاد، لائق العنایة والاحسان خواجه فلان را مقرر فرمودیم که از عهده اصول مناظم سلطنت وفروع مصالح مملکت تقصی نموده درتمشیت این مهم خطیر آثار مساعی مشکوره بظهور رسانیده، وظائف تیقظ واحتیاط مرعی

۱۔ ع : از
۲۔ ع : نقر
۳۔ ع : چنانچه
٤۔ ع : ازانچه

دارد[۱]

باید که چون بر مضمون فرمان جهان مطاع، قضاتمثال شرف اطلاع حاصل نمایند حقائق هر شهر وقصبه وپر گنه که از ریع وآبادانی[۲] وآسودگی رعایا وفرخ اشیاء ومعمول شدن دستور العمل احکام، که از بارگاه مقدس خلافت ظهور یافته[۳] (و) تفصیل آن را بدیوان مذکور سپارند که نقلهای که بمهر رسد معلوم خواهدشد. وسائر ابواب معدلت وغیر آن هفته بهفته واگر نتوانند ماه بماه وگرنه فصل بفصل[۴] نوشته باو فرستند تا انچه لائق عرض مقدس باشد معروض دارد وانچه مناسب دیوان کل داند باو خاطر نشان کنند (کند). عجالة الوقت بمجرد رسیدن منشور اقبال هر کدام از شهر وقصبه وپر گنه خود بموجب ضمن یکی از قانون گویان را که حقیقت ریع وحاصل آن پر گنه می دانسته باشد بمحصوب (بمصحوب) کس مشارالیه بدرگاه معلی روانه سازند که آمده حال مذکور خاطر نشان همایون سازد وتایك سال در ملازمت بوده از نیك وبد آن حدود معروض داشته باشد که چون یك سال سپری شود، دیگری از برادران[۵] وفرزندان وخویشان اورا که شائسته این کار باشند، روانه سازند که چون او بملازمت[۶] افتخار یابد آن شخص اول رخصت یافته بخانه ومسکن خود شتابد وفراخور خدمت ودولت خواهی بعلوفه وانعام شرف اختصاص خواهد یافت. وازانجا که رافت عظمی بحال جمیع بندگان ابدقرین محیط است، حکم اشرف نافذ شد که از پنج هزاری تا یوز باشی وسائر زمین داران درخور حال خود یك سوار را زهمراهان وتابینان[۷] خود برسم وکالت بدفتر خانه اقدس، که مطاف بزرگان هفت اقلیم است، گذارد،

۱ـ ع : دارند
۲ـ ع : ریع واراضی
۳ـ ع : یافته، ندارد
۴ـ تفصل، ندارند
۵ـ و، ندارد
۶ـ ع: به، ندارد
۷ـ ع : تابان

واز صدی تا پایان یك نفر پیاده هوشیاری، که سرمایه آبروی اوست، مقرر گرداند که همواره دردرگاه معلی باشد- باید که از قهر بادشاهی اندیشند[1] وبلطف عمیم ما امیدوار بوده از فرموده درنگذرند وبزودی قانون گویان را بدرگاه حاضر گردانند- هر کس که تساهل نماید ودیرتر[2] فرستد بغضب وعتاب گرفتار حواهدشد- وهر که مسارعت نموده امتثال حکم جهان آرا کند بعواطف روز افزون مخصوص حواهد گشت- دریں باب قدغن لازم دانند-

(۳٤)

منشور در تفویض حکومت وحراست قلعه بهکر ومحال مفصله ضمن من اعمال بهکر

همگی همت بلند وتمامی[3] نیت ارجمند متوجه ومصروف بر آنست که عامه خلائق، که بدائع ودائع حضرت خالق اند، آسوده حال ومرفه الحال[4] بوده دریں ایام خلافت ابد مقرون دست وزور هیچ ظالمی[5] بگریبان هیچ دلفگاری نرسد وغبار آزار هیچ ستمگاری بر چهره احوال هیچ مظلومی نه نشیند- الحمد لله والمنة که روز بروز صورت این معنی از مکامن قوت بمواطن فعل برحسب دلخواه ظهور نموده، همیشه امراء وافر الاخلاص در اطراف واقطار ممالك محروسه غوررسی مظلومان وعجزه نموده بمیامن خدمات پسندیده بمراتب عالیه ارتقاء می نمایند- وچون سبقت عبودیت وخدمتگاری ونسبت دولت خواهی وجان سپاری سیادت مآب، کمالات اکتساب، معتمد الملك، صادق

۱- ع :اندیشه
۲- ع : تر، ندارد
۳- ع: تمامی، ندارد
٤- ع : الاحوال
۵- ع : ظالمی، ندارد

الاخلاص، کامل الاعتقاد، لائق العنایات والاحسان میر ابوالقاسم خان[۱] نمکین از بدایت ملازمت تا غایت هر خدمتی که بدو رجوع شده بنوعی که مرضی خاطر اشرف بوده بتقدیم رسانیده بعنایات ممتاز است وایں معنی بغایت واضح[۲] و(لائح) است۔ دریں ولا حکم جهان مطاع شرف نفاذ وعز صدور یافت[۳] که محال مفصله ضمن من اعمال سرکار بهکر بمبلغ فلاں از ابتداء خریف۔۔ در وجه جاگیر او وتابینان مقرر ومعین باشد وحکومت وحراست قلعه بهکر وآں محال من حیث الاستقلال باو داشته باشد که[٤] در نگاه داشت ومحافظت وتعمیر قلعه وآبادانی ومعموری آں محال وتکثیر زراعت وقلع وقمع متمردان، سیادت (صیانت) وتائید مظلومان وتنبیه ظالمان مساعی جمیله بظهور آورد۔ واگر احیاناً بواسطه دفع متمردان سیادت مآب مشارالیه بکومك ومدد احتیاج شود جاگیرداران آں حدود ونواحی بامداد و کومك او حاضر شوند۔ می باید که چودریان وقانون گویان ورعایا ومزارعان وجمهور سکنه وعموم متوطنه محال مذکور معتمد الملك مشارالیه را[۵] حاکم وجاگیردار خود دانسته مال واجبی و حقوق دیوانی خود فصل به فصل وسال به سال موافق دستور العمل معمول باو جواب گویند واز سخن وصلاح او، که موافق حساب ومطابق حکم جهان مطاع باشد، عدول وانحراف نورزند۔ وچوں بتوقیع وقیع بدیع اشرف اقدس اعلی مزین گردد اعتماد نمایند۔

۱۔ ع : خان، ندارد

۲۔ ع : وایں معنی بغایت واضح، ندارد

۳۔ ع : نافذ وصادر فرمودیم

٤۔ ع : حکومت وحراست قلعه بهکر وآں محال من حیث الاستقلال تعلق باو داشته باشد، ندارد

۵۔ ع : بکومك ومدد احتیاج شود جاگیر داران آں حدود ونواحی بامداد و کومك او حاضر شوند، می باید که چوِ دریان وقانون گویان ورعایا ومزارعان وجمهور سکنه وعموم متوطنه محال مذکور معتمد الملك مشار الیه را، ندارد

(۳۵)
منشور در تفویض حکومت وحراست ولایت تته

حضرت وهاب ذو الجلال، بادشاه لم یزل ولا یزال بیمن عاطفت بی غایت تخت سلطنت ما را مضی بنور خلافت وجهانبانی باطغرای غراء دولت "إنی جاعلك للناس اماما"[۱] موشح ومحلی گردانیده،لوای عالم آرای کشورستانی ما بطراز اعزاز "وینصرك الله نصراً عزیزاً"[۲] مطرز ساخته، پیوسته بچشم عقل ودیده بصیرت نظرفرموده مصالح هر ولایت ومهمات هر ناحیت را بید اختیار وقبضه اقتدار یکی از خوانین رفیع المقدار وامراء ذوی الاعتبار که خلوص عقیدت وجان سپاری وخصوص ارادت وحق گذاری ایشان در مواقع ومواطن مرةً بعد اولی وکرةً بعد اخری سمت وضوح ودرجه ظهور یافته باشد باز گذاریم۔ چون ازان فرقه اخلاص پیشه وزمره فراست اندیشه عمدة الملك، رکن السلطنة القاهرة، عضد الدولة الباهرة، قدوه دولت خواهان صادق الاخلاص وزبده مخلصان لائق الاختصاص مبارز الدین فلان اباً عن جدٍ حقوق خدمات شائسته وعبودیات پسندیده درباب آستان خلافت مکان ثابت دارد، چنانچه آباء واجداد او بوسیله خدمتهای لائقه در ملازمت حضرت خاقانی، سلیمان مکانی، ظل سبحانی، صاحب قرانی در امراء ذوی الاعتبار شرف انتظام یافته از وفور نوازش وعواطف بیدریغ باسم ترخانی که دررفع حوادث حرزیمانی تواند بود، موسوم وسرفراز گشته بودند، واگرآن عمدة الملك بواسطه مواقع (موانع) ضروریه بعز ملازمت آن آستان رفیع المکان مستسعد وسرفراز نشده بود لیکن ازانجا که کمال اخلاص وجان سپاری وصدق عقیدت وحق گذاری غائبانه حلقه عبودیت وبندگی این درگاه

۱۔ قرآن مجید : ۱۲۴/۲
۲۔ قرآن مجید : ۳/۴۸

در گوش وغاشیه خدمت گاری آن آستان بردوش کشیده، انچه امکان دولت خواهی ویك رنگی است ظهور رسانیده ومی رساند. بناءً علی ذلك عنایت بی غایت بادشاهی وشفقت بی نهایت شاهنشاهی درباره او بشرف اظهار رسانیده بدستوری که آباء واجداد او بموجب فرمان قضا جریان حضرت صاحب قرانی وحضرت خاقان مغفور المستریح فی روضة الجنان، الجالس علی مسند الرحمة والغفران شاهرخ سلطان معاف وترخان بوده، ما نیز اسم ترخانی بدان رکن السلطنة واولاد واقرباء او اطلاق فرمودیم وحکومت وحراست ولایت تته وما بتعلق بها وتوابع را بدستوری که حضرت صاحب قرانی بدان رکن السطنة ارزانی داشته بودند ما نیز تفویض فرمودیم که بهر وجهی که از حسن فراست وکیاست او متصور است در اعلاء اعلام شریعت غرا ونسق مهام ملت بیضا واعزاز واکرام سادات وعلماء وتوقیر واکرام مشائخ وصلحاء واشاعت آثار عدل وانصاف وازاله زنگ جور واعتناف ورفاهیت احوال عموم ساکنان ومتوطنان وفراغت حال جمهور رعایا ومزارعان ودفع ورفع متمردان ومفسدان وقلع وقمع ناپاکان وتادیب وتنبیه هرفریق از فسقه وفجره وقطاع الطریق وامنیت ره گزرها وزاویه جهات ومایتعلق بها غایت اجتهاد بتقدیم رساند، وعامه خلائق راکه بدائع صنائع حضرت خالق اند، از حدوث حوادث ونزول نوازل حصن حصین باشد وسعی امر نموده[1] بهیچ احدی حیف جائز ندارد وبنوعی سلوك نماید که آثار شکر گذاری او از السنه وافواه بظهور می رسانیده باشد.[2] ومال حقوق دیوانی آن ولایت را فصل بفصل وسال بسال بسیورغال ابدی خود متصرف گردد.

می باید که سادات عظام وعلماء اعلام ومشائخ کرام وقضات اسلام واهالی آن ولایت عموماً وارباب وکلانتران و مقدمان ورعایا

١ـ ع : وسعی امور در تذهیب نموده
٢ـ ع : می رسیده باشد

ومزارعان واحشام وصحرانشینان آن ولایت خصوصاً عمدة الملك مومی الیه را حاکم وحارس خود دانسته از سخن ومصلحت او، که مطابق وموافق حساب خواهد بود، درنگذرند و ایشان حاضر آمده متابعت بجا آورند، واحداثی که واقع شود بدیشان رفع نمایند تاموافق قانون عدالت ونصفت صورت ـ وموال وحقوق دیوانی خود را هر سال بسیورغال[۱] او جواب گویند وآن عارفه را از تغیر وتبدیل مصون ومحروس داشته فرمان مجدد نه طلبند ـ وچون بتوقیع وفیع رفیع منیع اشرف اعلی مزین ومحلی وموشح گردد اعتماد نمایند کتب بالامر العالی وخلد نفاذه ولازال مطاعاً ـ

(۳۶)

منشور در تفویض حکومت وحراست سرکار بهکر وتوابع ولواحق ومضافات وملحقات

چون رعایت حال ملازمان جان سپار ومراقبت احوال مخلصان وفادار که نسبت قدم خدمت را باکمال حقیقت وفاداری، ووفور صفائی اعتقاد را با نهایت اخلاص وخدمت جمع نموده باشند، ودر شدت ورخا وخوف ورجا همراه بوده بر مکاره وشدائد روز گار صبر نموده، بدستیاری توفیق معاقد معارك جنگ وجدال را بسر انگشت وقوف وفرزانگی کشوده، در مهالك زور آزمائی[۲] رزم وپیکار ودر مواقف خوفناك وخطرمند قتال و کارزار از سرجان برخواسته، ودل بر قضاء آسمانی نهاده بقوت سرپنجه شجاعت ودلاوری ونیروی جلادت وبهادری چون شیر خشمناك پرخاش جوی بمعرکه درآمده، وچون زر

۱ـ ع :سورغال
۲ـ ع : مرد آزمائی

کامل عیار از بوته امتحان پاك وسالم در آمده؛ بواسط این حسن خدمت بارها قابل انواع توجه ومرحمت ومکرراً مستعد اصناف شفقت وعاطفت شده، برذمه همت حق شناسان مروت کیش وقدردانان وفا اندیش بابلغ وجوه واجب ولازم ومتحتم است- وشجاعت شعار، جلادت آثار، قدیم الخدمت، کثیر الاخلاص، لائق العنایات، واثق الاختصاص، زبده ارباب وفاداری وحقیقت، وخلاصه اصحاب نیکو خدمتی وفتوت[١] فلاں بهادر[٢] که از مبادی حال الی الآن از خدمت گاری معتمد وموتمن این سلسله بوده، ودر بند گی وخدمت گاری معتمد حضرت مغفرت پناهی جنت آشیانی، رضوان مکانی (بوده) در ترددات وجاں سپاری مساعی جمیله وآثار مشکوره بظهور آورده، بواسطه حسن خدمات بمحل اعتقاد ومقام اعتبار رسیده[٣] وتا نقطه آخر نقد جان از روی اخلاص بر کف داشته ودقیقه از دقائق حق خدمت فرونگذاشته وجاں سپاری های شائسته وترددات بائسته او بدرجه ظهور وحد وضوح رسیده- بنا برین حکومت وحراست سر کار بکرو[٤] توابع ولواحق ومضافات وملحقات آں من حیث الاستقلال والانفراد باو مفوض شد که چنانچه از کمال کیاست وکار گذاری ونهایت فراست ووقوف ومعامله فهمی است، در حفظ وحراست قلعه وسر کار مذکوره، سامان ضروریات آں وآبادانی ولایت ورعایت حال ساکنان ومتوطنان آنجا از سپاهی ورعیت وفیصل[٥] قضایای حکمی از جزوی وکلی قیام واقدام داشته نوعی نماید که ولایت معمور ورعایا مرفه الحال ومسرور باشند، واز اقویا بر عجزه وزیردستان حیف وتعدی واقع نشود،

١- ع: فتوحات

٢- ع: بهادر، ندارد

٣- ع: رسید

٤- ع: فلاں

٥- ع: فصل

ومعاملات موافق حق وحساب وحکم جهان مطاع به فیصل رسد۔ سادات وقضات وائمه وعموم سکنه وجمهور متوطنه وچودریان وقانون گویان ورعایا ومزارعان آن جا مشارالیه را حاکم وحارس خود دانسته از سخن وصلاح او، که موافق حق وحساب ومطابق حکم خواهد بود، بیرون نروند ومال واجبی وحقوق دیوانی خود را بلا قصور وانکسار بمومی[1] الیه جواب گویند و او حاضر آمده، لوازم اطاعت وانقیاد بتقدیم رسانند۔ در عهده دانسته از فرموده تخلف نورزند وقدغن عظیم دانند۔

(۳۷)
منشور در تفویض حکومت وحراست سر کار

چون همگی نیت صافی طویت وقصاری همت علیا نهمت مصروف ومعطوف بران است که کسانیکه بحلیه قدامت خدمت وسداد وسبقت نسبت وحسن استعداد وارتکاب شدائد ومهالك والتزام مخاوف ومهالك مزین ومحلی بوده، نقد اخلاص خود از بوته امتحان ندرت در فنون لوازم جان سپاری ومراسم مردانگی کامل عیار برآورده برسکه قبول کل این‌طائفه جلیل الشان، منیع المکان رسانیده باشند، بنابر مصدوقه "السابقون السابقون اولئك المقربون"[2] پایه قدر ومنزلت آن را بر رتبه سائر اکفاء واقران برتری داده، بمر اسم اعتبار واعتماد واختصاص وامتیاز نموده آیند۔ وچون رفعت مآب، عزت ایاب، شجاعت شعار، شهامت آثار، قدوه مخلصان صادق الولاء وعمده متخصصان راسخ الوفاء با صدق وصفا، وحقیقت ومظهر اخلاص وصدق نیت فلان بهادر خلاصه عمر ونقاوه حیات خود را من المصبی

۱۔ ع: موفی
۲۔ قرآن مجید: ۱۰/۵۶

(الصبا) الی یومنا هذا، که سنین عمر او بر حدود ستین مشرف گردید، صرف خدمت این دودمان خجسته نشان نموده بتکرار در معارك هائله مردآزار سر متاع حیات، که سرمایه مطالب کائنات است، و در ملازمت بندگان حضرت غفران پناه، رضوان جائگاه، افاض الله علیه سحاب الرحمة والرضوان، برخاسته دادشمشیر ومردانگی داده، در صفوف مبارزان تنها تاخته و کارهای نمایان که ، وقت گنجائش تفصیل آن ندارد، کرده زخمهای منکر برداشته است[1] وهم چنین بتکرار در یورش بنگاله از امثال واقران بل سائر مبارزان گوی مسابقت ربوده بتجدید مراتب عدید احیاء مراسم نیکو خدمتی ودولت خواهی نموده، چه در تاختن آن بی جیبه ویراق بآن همه توپ وتفنگ ومبارزان شیر جنگ رقم نسخ بر صفحه دلاوری و مردانگی (کشیده) وجان بازی خود را در نظر ترك وتازیك، دور ونزدیك جلوه داده، شمشیر وفرزانگی مشارالیه در همه جا صاف وبی جرم وبی غش آمده محسود[2] همگنان گردیده، ودولت خواهیهای دیگر ودلسوزیها و کار گزاریهای او بوضوح هرچه کامل تر داشت. بنا برین مقدمات شمه از شفقت وعطوفت شامل حال مشارالیه نموده حکومت وحراست سر کار فلان بتمامها از قلعه وقصبات وسائر پر گنات برفعت مآب مشارالیه عنایت فرمودیم که چنانچه از رشد و کاردانی او سزد در حکومت وحراست سر کار مذکور قیام واقدام نموده بنوعی در محافظت قلعه وشهر ورعیت وتعمیر وآبادانی ولایت وتکثیر زراعت وعمارات وتعظیم واحترام سادات وعلماء وقضات وائمه وصلحاء وفقراء و ارباب و کدخدایان وسائر رعایا که ودائع حضرت خالق البرایا اند، خوضی نماید که عند الخالق مرضی ومستحسن باشد. سبیل مشارالیهم وعمال حال واستقبال سر کار

۱ـ ع :است، ندارد
۲ـ ع : محسوس

مذکور آن که شجاعت شعار مومی الیه را حاکم وحارس آنجا دانسته از سخن صوابدید وصلاح او که، هر آئینه موافق حق وحساب ومطابق حکم جهان مطاع باشد، بیرون نروند و او حاضر آمده بهیچ وجه من الوجوه از امر و گفته او عدول وانحراف وتمرد نورزیده تجاوز ننمایند، ومال واجبی خود را موافق معمول جواب گفته قاصر ومنکسر نسازند۔ دریں ابواب قدغن عظیم دانسته تخلف نورزند۔ وچون بتوقیع وقیع منیع رفیع اشرف اعلی مزین ومحلی گردد اعتماد نمایند۔ کتب بالامر العالی وخلد نفاذه ولازال مطاعاً فی شهر صفر ختم بالخیر والظفر سنه۔

(۳۸)
منشور در تفویض منصب امامت وخطابت مسجد جامع

چون خطیب لبیب ادیب حکمت حضرت مهیمن بیچون برفراز منبر عالی منظر نه پایه گردون خطبه بلیغ "إنی جاعلك للناس إماما"[۱] بنام همایون ما ارتسام می خواند وامام مقصوره معموره "و هو قائم یصلی فی المحراب"[۲] آیة ماثوره "إنی اصطفیتك علی الناس"[۳] بگوش هوش صفوف[۴] مقتدیان سلطنت ما می رساند، واجب چنان می[۵] نماید که در اعلاء مراتب ودرجات منابر اسلام واحیاء مراسم فرائض الهی وسنت نبوی علیه السلام غایت سعی واهتمام مبذول گردد۔ چنانچه رواتب ووظائف طاعات وعبادات وقواعد[۶] جمعه وجماعات واصول وقوانین واجبات ومستحبات رونق ورواج هرچه تمام تر بحصول پیوندند۔ وتیسرایں

۱۔ قرآن مجید : ۲/۱۲٤
۲۔ قرآن مجید : ۳/۳۹
۳۔ قرآن مجید : ۷/۱٤٤
٤۔ ع : صفوت
۵۔ ع : می، ندارد
٦۔ ع : عوائد

مطلوب وتحصیل این مقصود موقوف بر آنست که هرامری از امور دین وهر منصبی از مناصب شرع سید المرسلین بیکی[1] از فضلاء وعلماء متدین، که بکمال فصاحت وبلاغت وجمال تقوی و ورع ودیانت وعز فضائل وطیب شمائل ووفور علم وادب وصنوف مکارم موروثی ومکتسبی آراسته باشد، مفوض گردد که در تقویت وتمشیت واعلام معالم وارساء مراسم این مهم اهتمام موفور وسعی مشکور بظهور[2] رساند۔

بنابران درین وقت امامت وخطابت مسجد جامع بلده فلان را من حیث الاستقلال بمولانا افصح اعظم، جامع فنون الحکم مولانا فلان، که باوصاف[3] سنیه متحلی است واخلاق ردیة[4] متخلی، تفویض فرمودیم تا بروجهی که از صدق اعتقاد وحسن اجتهاد وکمال اعتماد او متصور است در نظم ونسق ورواج ورونق این مهم سعی مالا کلام مبذول دارد وهیچ دقیقة از دقائق مواظبت وممارست نامرعی نگذارد۔

سبیل سادات عظام وقضات اسلام ومشائخ کرام وطوائف انام از خواص وعوام آن که مولانا مشارالیه را من حیث الاستقلال بلا مشارکت ومساهمت غیر (ی) متصدی ومتعهد این امور خیر دانسته، شرائط اعزاز واکرام ووظائف اجلال واعظام واحترام او حسب المقدور بظهور آورده، مراسم تقویت وتمشیت بتقدیم[5] رسانند وماذون باستخلاف دانسته، وظیفه که جهت منصب تعین یافته باشد حسب الاستمرار بدو مسلم ومقرر دانند وتغیر وتبدیل ندهند۔ وچون بتوقیع وقیع منیع اشرف اعلی موشح ومحلی گردد، اعتماد نمایند۔

۱۔ ع : به یکجا
۲۔ ع : بظهور، ندارد
۳۔ ع : اوصاف
٤۔ ع : ذمیمه
۵۔ ع : تقویم

(۳۹)
منشور در تفویض منصب تدریس

چون از وهبت[۱] نعماء والاء علیم علی الاطلاق ومکارم آلاء بی انتهاء حکیم با استحقاق، جلت آلاء[۲]ه وعمت نعماء[۳]ه، صحیفه خاطر خبرت مفاخر ما از مآثر معانی شدید المبانی "وعلم الانسان مالم یعلم"[۴] بانبعاث شمسیة البارقات علم ودانش مزین ومنور گردیده، باطاعت فرمان واجب الاذعان "اکرموا العلماء فانهم عند الله کراماً (کرام)" تعظیم واحترام ناهجان مناهج علم وفنون وتوقیر واکرام واقفان مواقف "هل یستوی الذین یعلمون" بر صحیفه رای عالم آرای ما بدرجه توضیح وتلویح رسیده، ومیامن انفاس مسالك "علماء امتی کانبیاء بنی اسرائیل"[۵] ضمیر منیر مارا مورد فیوضات ابدی ومطرح سعادات سرمدی ساخته ولمعات شارقات تحصیل علوم ومعارف از مشارق بواطن فرخنده میامن مقتبسان انوار "اولو العلم قائماً بالقسط"[۶] برساحت احوال خجسته مآل پرتو انداخته، مانیز بشکرانه ایں موهبت عظیم ومرحمت جسیم پیش نهاد همت والا نهمت ومطمح نیت صافی طویت آں داریم که پیوسته ریاض مقاصد ومرادات اصحاب اصول وفروع، که کشاف کنوز معقول ومشروع اند، از ترشح ینابیع بر ونوال مانضارت وطراوت تمام گیرد وهمواره حدائق مطالب ومراعات ارباب فضائل وعلوم، که مصباح رموز محسوس ومفهوم اند، از تقاطر غمام احسان وافضال ما خضارت ونزاهت بلا انجام پذیرد۔ بناءً علی هذه المقدمة دریں ولا منصب نامی گرامی تدریس مدرسه فلاں بجناب افادت مآب، افاضت

۱۔ ع : مواهب
۲۔ ع : آیاته
۳۔ ع : النعمائه
۴۔ قرآن مجید : ۵/۹۶
۵۔ اصلی ندارد، رجوع کنید محمد طاهر پٹنی، تذکرة الموضوعات، بیروت، ۱۳۹۹هـ، ص ۲۰
۶۔ قرآن مجید : ۱۸/۳

ایاب، کشاف المعضلات(بهدایته) الکافیه، حلال المشکلات (بدرایته) الشافیة، نظام عقود جواهر علم ودانش، قسام نقود زواهر فضل وبینش مولانا فلان، زید مفاخره ومعالیه، که اکثر عمر عزیز را بنحو تحصیل علوم دینیه وجهت تکمیل فنون معارف یقینه صرف کرده، بمنطق صحیح وحدیث فصیح وحکمت صریح غوامض مقدمات ومخفیات مقالات علمی وعملی را بایراد دلائل وبراهین ساطعه خالی از شوائب شکوك واوهام متعلقه بروشن ترتفسیری درمعرض بیان (درآورده) مفوض داشتیم وبرطبق "إن الله یامر کم أن تودوا الا مانات إلی اهلها"[1] افاده وافاضه ایں امر شریف را بفرط افادت وافاضت آں جناب گذاشتیم که بواجبی بدیں امر عظیم القدر پرداخته، درمحافل افاده طالبان علوم را از برکات دانش وری وفضل گستری خود محظوظ وبهره ور گرداند ونهال استفاده واستفاضه ایشاں را از اجراء انهار استعداد وضوء آفتاب استحقاق خود بمدارج نشو ونما رسانیده چناں نماید که بی[2] عذر شرعی تعطیل نشود وباوقات تحصیل مواظبت نموده یوماً فیوماً آثار رشد وترقی در احوال طلبه بظهور آید۔ سبیل همگناں آں که جناب مولانا مشارالیه را بریں امرشریف منسوب دانسته، لوازم مداومت وملازمت درس بجا آورند وتعطیل جائز ندارند۔ وچوں بتوقیع رفیع مزین ومحلی گردد اعتماد نمایند۔

(٤٠)

منشور در تفویض منصب مصدری حفاظ

بعد از تصدیر صحائف محمدت وثناء بنام بادشاهی که مصدران جوامع جهاں بمواظبت تلاوت آیات بینات کلام معجز نظام اورا در

۱۔ قرآن مجید : ٥٨/٤

۲۔ ع : بی، ندارد

صبح ومساء ورد زبان دارند، وپس از تحریر تحیت ودعا بروح پر فتوح دین پناهی که معتکفان مجامع عالم امکان بمداومت صلوات نامیات اورا در غدا وعشاء حرز[۱] جان می شمارند، بر رای صواب نمای ارباب خبرت وانتباه در نقاب ارتیاب مستور نخواهد بود که بروفق منطوق لازم الوثوق "اهل القرآن اهل الله خاصة" رعایت حال عندلیبان چمن تجوید نزد مالکان ملك بختیاری قاعده متحتم۔ لاسیما قاری که بمقتضاء موداء "ألذین آتیناهم الکتاب یتلونه حق تلاوته[۲]" بجودت قرأت وصحت تلاوت سوامع مقیمان صوامع جهان را مورد اصناف فیوضات وبرکات گرداند، وباقتضاء فحواء "ورتل القرآن ترتیلاً[۳]" بفصاحت لهجه ولطافت بلاغت وطلاقت لسان قلوب وصدور عالمیان را بانواع سعادات وهدایات رسانیده مجال قال خود[۴] را بحلیه جلیه "زینوا القرآن باصواتکم[۵]" مزین ومحلی ساخته وگوش هوش مستمعان قران مجید وفرقان حمید را بابلاغ معجز بلاغ "وإذا قری القران فاستمعوا له وأنصتوا لعلکم (ترحمون)[۶]" نواخته۔ الحق حاوی ایں اوصاف در ذات[۷] فائض البرکات قدوة الحفاظ والقراء، صحیح اللهجه، فصیح الاداء، الفائق علی ارباب التجوید بتوفیق الله[۸] المنان کمال الدین حافظ فلاں است، که آیات سور کمالاتش در عین تجوید ادا می یابد و پرتو انوار غایت استظهار در اسالیب قرأت وقوانین تلاوت از صوت[۹] غم زادی وقول فرح افزای او برساحت احوال همگنان می تابد۔ لاجرم دریں ولا اورا منظور نظر اعزاز واکرام داشته منصب مصدری حفاظ فلاں ولایت را بدو تفویض فرمودیم که باستقلال بدیں امر پرداخته دقیقه از دقائق

۱۔ ع : مرز
۲۔ قرآن مجید : ۲/۱۲۱
۳۔ قرآن مجید : ۷۳/۴
۴۔ ع : مخایل حال خود
۵۔ بخاری، کتاب التوحید
۶۔ قرآن مجید : ۷/۲۰۴
۷۔ ع : ذات، ندارد
۸۔ ع : الملك
۹۔ ع : صورت

اهتمام واجتهاد نامرعی نگذارد ودر اوقات معینه در جوامع مشخصه بتلاوت وقراءت پرداخته بی عذر شرعی تعطیل جائز ندارد وچناں سازد که آثار سعی او روز بروز بوضوح پیوسته موجب تزاید رعایت وعنایت درباره او گردد۔

سبیل همگنان آں که مومی الیه را مصدر مقرر دانسته، اعانت وتقویت او لازم شمرند وغیری را شریك وسهیم ندارند، وجماعه حفاظ او را مقدم وپیشواء خود دانسته از سخن وصواب دید او، که هر آئینهٔ مستلزم رواج ورونق مهم مذکور خواهد بود، عدول وانحراف نورزند واوامر ونواهی اورا مطیع ومنقاد باشند۔ متصدیان اوقاف جوامع وظیفه اورا سال به سال بلا اهمال رسانند۔ از جوانب برین جمله روند وچوں بتوقیع وقیع رسد اعتماد نمایند۔

(٤١)
منشور در منع زکوة وتمغا

عمدة الملك، رکن السطنة القاهرة، عضد الدولة الباهرة، زبدة المخلصین فی الدوران، لائق الاعتبار والاحسان، مبارز الدین فلاں بالطاف بادشاهی عز اختصاص وشرف امتیاز یافته بداند که چوں طائفه تجار باعث معموری بلاد وامصار اند، وبامید منافع "خیر الناس من ینفع الناس" نفائس امتعه واجناس از هر ولایت وناحیت به هر شهر ومملکت نقل وتحویل ومعاوضه وتبدیل می نمایند، وعامه خلائق از معامله ایشاں متمتع ومحظوظ گشته به مقاصد ومطالب خود فائز[1] می گردند، رعایت احوال ومراقبت امانی وآمال ایشاں رابر ذمت همت والا نهمت واجب ولازم شناخته، ایشاں را از تمامی حوالات ومطالبات تمغا وزکوة در جمیع بلاد وولایات معاف ومسلم[2] وترخاں ومرفوع القلم فرموده ایم۔

١۔ ع : قابض
٢۔ ع : مسلم، ندارد

وچند سال است که این طائفه در ممالك محروسه بفراغ بال آمدورفت می نمایند وبانواع فوائد ومنافع متمتع وبهره ور می گردند. وآن که بآن[١] عمدة الملك درباب منع تمغا فرمان واجب الا ذعان نه فرستاده ایم، جهت همین است که چون ولایت سند خصوصا بهکر سرحد است، وآن رکن السطنة را اخراجات روی می نمایند که گرفتن تمغا من وجه ضرورت می شود. حالا بعضی از سود اگر ان که از ولایت او می آیند چنیں بعرض می رسانند که آن عمدة الملك باوجود گرفتن وجوه تمغا، اسپان واسباب ایشان را کشیده بعد از تردد بسیار ثلث یاربع بها بآن می رساند وانواع جفا وایذا[٢] بایشان می پسندد. وازان جمله زبدة الامثال فلان بدرگاه معلی آمده عرض کرد که اسباب اورا آن عمدة الملك ومردم او بقرض[٣] متصرف شده، قریب یك سال پسرو کوچ[٤] اورا مقید ومحبوس دارد. ایں معنی ازان عمدة الملك بغایت غریب وبعید می نماید که بطائفه تجار این چین عمل می کرده باشد. باری اگر واقع باشد در مقام تدارك وتلافی در آمده انچه از مشارالیه وهریك از سود اگر ان گرفته باشد بها بروجه لائق که راضی باشند رساند. ومن بعد چنان سلوك نماید که تجار ومترددین بفراغ خاطر آمد وشد نموده راضی وشاکر باشند. هر آئینه پسندیده خواهد نمود. کتب بالامر العالی وخلد نفاذه ولازال مطاعاً.

(٤٢)
منشور تقرر در قندهار

عمدة الملك، ثابت العقیده، کامل الاخلاص، لائق العنایت

١ـ ع : بآن، ندارد
٢ـ ع : اندوه
٣ـ ع : تمرض
٤ـ ع : پسرو کوچ، ندارد

والاحسان فلان به عنایت الهی امتیاز یافته بداند که در خاطر جهان آرای شاهنشاهی چنان قرار یافته که همواره جمعی از بندگان اخلاص نهاد، خدمت گزیں در قندهار وآں نواحی باشند تا موجب رفاهیت عموم ساکنان آں دیار گردد. بنا براں بمجرد رسیدن فرمان مقدس با جمعیت لائق متوجه آں حدود شود وچوں شش ماه بگزرد حقیقت معروض دارد تا بجای او دیگری نامزد شود. چوں آں جا رسد لوازم دوستی ویك جهتی بجای آورده در اتفاق وائتلاف کوشد. دریں باب قدغن لازم داند.

(۴۳)

منشور به یکی از امراء درفراهم کردن بدرقه

عمدة الملك، رکن السلطنة القاهرة، عضد الدولة الباهره، زبدة المخلصین فی الدوران، لائق الاعتبار والاحسان، قدوة خوانین العظام بین الاقران، مبارز الدین فلاں بصنوف الطاف واعطاف بادشاهی عز اختصاص وشرف امتیاز یافته بداند که عصمت آیات، زبدة المستورات، قدوة العفائف والصالحات فلاں که من المهد الی العهد دریں دودمان عالی شان وخاندان رفیع المکان درحریم حمایت وحجره رعایت مخدرات حجرات عصمت وعفت واهل بیت سلطنت وخلافت شرف پرورش وتربیت یافته وحضرت بادشاه فردوس مکانی اورا از روی نوازش به لقب فرزندی وحضرت بادشاه جنت آشیانی به خطاب همشیر گی ملقب وسرفراز فرموده اند واز زبان در افشان ما درمیان امثال واقران بسمت بیگم ممتاز وموسوم گشته. چوں مدت مدید است که از والده عفیفه خود دور ومهجور مانده، دریں ولا بامید

نوید حدیث صحیح "الجنة تحت اقدام الامهات"[1] بداعیه ملاقات والده خود رخصت حاصل نموده همراهی محرمان ومخصوصان خود متوجه ولایت تته شد و[2] انشاء الله تعالی بعد از حصول این امنیت باندك زمانی متوجه ملازمت شود۔

می باید که چون عصمت مآب مشار الیها در رفتن وآمدن بولایت بهکر وسائر محال متعلقه آن عمدة الملك[3] رسد، مراسم اعزاز واحترام مرعی ومسلوك داشته فراخور آن حالات شرائط ضیافت ومراقبت به تقدیم رساند ودقیقه نامرعی نگذارد۔ وجمعی را تعین نماید که از منازل ومراحل مخوفه بدرقه شده مشار الیها را مع همراهان به سلامت بمقام امنیت واصل گرداند۔ واز آنها که به وسیله همراهی آن عصمت مآب بولایت سند روند وآیند در هیچ محل طمع وتوقعی نکنند ومعترض احوال ایشان نگردند که امثال این امر بغایت پسندیده ومستحسن نمی نماید۔ در عهده دانسته از فرموده در نگذرد۔ تحریراً بالامر العالی خلد نفاذه (فی شهر رجب المرجب)۔

(٤٤)

منشور به یکی از امراء در فراهم کردن بدرقه

عمدة الملك، رکن السلطنة القاهرة،[4] عضد الدولة الباهرة، قدوه سلاطین عالی شان، نقاوه خوانین نصرت اقتران، شجاع الدین فلان باصناف ملاطفت وانواع عنایات واصطناعات شرف امتیاز وعز اختصاص یافته بداند که اگرچه صورت دولت خواهی وحسن عقیدت

۱۔ اخرجه النسائی، احمد، ابن ماجه والحاکم
۲۔ ع : که
۳۔ ع : عمدة الخواص الملك
٤۔ ع : و، زیاده دارد

او از السنه وافواه بسمع اشرف رسیده بود، دریں ولا که عمدة الملك، رکن الدولة العلیه، لائق العنایات الجلیله، قابل الاعتبار والاحسان، نظام الدین فلان بعز ملازمت وشرف مجالست[1] مشرف وسرفراز شد، این معنی[2] سمت تجدید وصورت[3] تمهید یافت. وملاحظه حالات آن که حضرت جنت مکانی امر اعظم القدر مارا نامزد آن عمدة الملك فرموده، خاطر بر انتظام احوال ومقاصد آمال او مصروف می باشد و می خواهد که در ظل ظلیل عاطفت مابه مدارج علیا ومراتب قصوی مرتقی وسرفراز گردد.[4] می باید که روز بروز در تزاید مواد دولت منظور داشته طریق دولت خواهی را باقدام اطاعت بجا آورده همواره این سررشته را از دست نه دهد که بمیامن آن نتائج کلیه باوقات او عائد خواهد شد. وچون شرافت پناه، رفعت دستگاه، مکرمت شعار، معالی دثار، نتیجه دودمان ولایت وعرفان، سلاله خاندان افاضت وایقان، المختص بعواطف الملك المستعان شرف الدین حسین مرزا وسیادت پناهی، رفعت دستگاهی، ملتجی اماجد[5] السادات، جامع المیامن والسعادات امیر معز الملك وامیر علی اکبر داعیه آن حدود دارند، چون بآن حدود رسند این معنی شرف خود دانسته در اعزاز و احترام ایشان دقیقه از دقائق نامرعی نگذارند وجمعی کثیر بدرقه ساخته از محال مخوفه بسلامت گذرانیده بمقام امن رسانند ودریں خدمت شائسته بهیچ وجه من الوجوه تقصیر نکنند که هنگام اظهار شکر او هر آئینه عنایت بیچون عائد خواهد شد. واگر عکس آن ظاهر شود موجب رنجش وآزار خاطر انور خواهد بود ونتیجه نیك نخواهد داد. در عهده دانسته دریں باب تخلف نورزند[6].[7]

۱ـ ع : شرف مجالست، ندارد
۲ـ ع : معنی، ندارد
۳ـ ع : صورت، ندارد
۴ـ ع : و، زیاده دارد
۵ـ ع : الاماجد
۶ـ ع : نه نمایند
۷ـ ع : تحریر

(٤٥)

منشور در باب معاونت در فتح یکی از ولایات

عمدة الملك، رکن السطنة القاهرة، عضد الدولة الباهرة، زبدة المخلصین فی الدوران، لائق الاعتبار والاحسان، قدوة خوانین عالی شان، مبارز الدین فلان بالطاف واعطاف بادشاهی عز اختصاص وشرف امتیاز یافته بداند که بنا بر اعمال ذمیمه ونافرمانیها که درین ولا از فلان بظهور آمده ومستوجب عزل وتنبیه بلیغ شده، حکومت وحراست ولایت فلان وفلان را از انتقال مشارالیه بعمدة الملك، رکن السلطنة القاهرة، عضد الدولة الباهرة، زبدة الخوانین العظام فی الزمان، لائق الاعتبار والاحسان، مبارزالدین فلان تفویض فرموده ایم۔ می باید که چون عمدة الملك مشارالیه بآن حدود رسد از روی اخلاص ودولت خواهی که بایں آستان عالی شان دارد طریق موافقت وامداد در مرافقت واتحاد کما ینبغی مسلوك داشته تا زمانی که آن محال خواه بصلح خواه بجنگ بدست آید متفق ومعاون باشد ونوعی سازد که آثار مددگاری ویك جهتی آن عمدة الملك نسبت برکن السلطنة مشارالیه بوضوح رسد، که دران صورت بانواع عنایت وعاطفت امتیاز یافته حکومت ولایت فلان وتوابع بدستور سابق باو مفوض ومسلم خواهد بود۔ یقین داند که اگر درین باب مساهله واهمال ازو واقع شود جزای عمل خود یابد و(جز) پشیمانی نتیجه نخواهد داد۔ در عهده خود دانسته از فرموده درنگذرد وطریق مطاوعت وفرمان برداری، که سبب نجات ورستگاری است، مرعی دارد۔ تحریراً بالامر العالی خلد نفاذه۔

(٤٦)
منشور در باب معاونت در فتح یکی از ولایات

صادق العقیده، کامل الاخلاص، لائق العنایات والاختصاص فلاں بداند که خاطر مقدس متوجه تسخیر ولایت فلاں است که از بی پروائی جاگیردار آں ناحیت آں حدود از تصرف اولیاء دولت بر آمده است۔ وقبل ازیں فرمان جهان مطاع ورود یافته بود که فلاں وفلاں باتفاق آں مستحسن الخدمت تسخیر آں جانموده بتمامی آں حدود را از خس وخاشاك فتنه وفساد پاك سازند۔ ومجدداً فرمان عالم مطیع باسم فلاں نیز صادر شده که دریں خدمت کمال اتفاق مرعی داشته بکومك حاضر شود۔ باید که باتفاق جاگیرداران آں حدود که بنام آنها فرمان عالی شان علاحده صادر شده که ازروی نهایت اتفاق ویك جهتی تا نوروز آئنده آں ولایت را در حوزه تصرف در آورند۔ واگر عیاذاً بالله دراں خدمت بی اتفاقی یا تکاسل نمایند و تا نوروز ایں خدمت بانجام نرسد، جاگیرهای آں مردم بتمام تغیر خواهد شد۔ وبجهت احتیاط ومزید تاکید معتقد فلاں را فرستادیم که روز بروز سوانح آں حدود را روز نامچه کرده بدرگاه معلی می فرستاده باشد۔ حسب الحکم الاقدس در عهده دانسته از فرموده در نگذرد۔ تحریراً بالامر العالی خلد نفاذه۔

(٤٧)
منشور به یکی از امراء افغان در استمالت

عمدة الملك، رکن السلطنة القاهرة لائق العنایة[1] الجلیة فلاں به عنایت والتفات بادشاهی سرفراز وامیدوار بوده بداند که حضرت

۱۔ ع : الجلیلة، زیاده دارد

کارساز و کریم بنده نواز در هر چندگاه جمعی را از اخص بندگان خود بسمت افزونی اعتبار واقتدار برسائر بندگان امتیاز داده امانی وآمال ایشان را از جویبار عنایت ومکرمت سرسبز وبار آور می گرداند، واز فروغ انوار هدایت چراغ دولت وحشمت ارباب شوکت وعظمت را روشن ومنور می سازد۔ چنانچه مشاهده عالمیان شده باشد که باوجود نسبتی که فلاں را درمیان قوم افغانان بود چند سال بچه طریق اورا سلطنت میسر شده بود۔ بعد ازاں نیز فلاں چندگاه آں نسبت را دریافت۔ چوں دولت ازاں سلسله روی برتافته، واکثر از[1] سرداران مردم سور بعضی بدست ایشاں اسیر ومعدوم شدند وبعضی بمقتضای مقدرات الهی دریں ایام پریشان شده رفتند۔ وچندی که ازاں طائفه مانده اگر می خواهند که بر مسند سلطنت آرام گیرند، چوں ارادت حضرت الهی براں جاری نباشد واستحقاق آن امر عالی بآں فرقه نباشد، مقرر است که بسعی واهتمام وبغی وآثام شروع در سر انجام آں مرتبه عالی مقام فائده نمی کند۔ چنانچه[2] بدیده بصیرت عالمیاں مشاهده می کنند که دریں ایام خجسته فرجام حضرت الهی به محض فضل وکمال کرم ابواب مسرت وفیروزی بر جبهه آمال ما مفتوح داشته هر روز عروس فتحی ازخلوت خانه ظفر جلوه می کند وهر ساعت مخدره نصرتی از پرده بهروزی چهره می نماید۔ ومقرراست که یافتن ایں دولت ودریافت ایں موهبت بسعی واهتمام بندگان رفیع مقام وکثرت سپاه واسباب نیست، بلکه محض عنایت الهی است، باوجود کثرت حشم ولشکر وبسیاری اسباب منظور نظر خجسته اثر بر جمعیت لشکر نیست وامید واری بعون عنایت وفضل وموهیت نامتناهی الهی بوده وهست وباقضای آسمانی وتقدیر الهی ستیزه کردن از روش

۱۔ ع : از، ندارد
۲۔ چناں که

اصحاب عقل وطریق ادب وفراست ودرایت نیست۔

اکنون از سرداران قوم افغانان استماع نموده می شود که باصابت رای وتدبیر وسرداری کسی که مانده آن عمدة الملك است واورا بعقل وفراست می دانیم، ومعلوم شده که عاقبت امور را ملحوظ داشته۔ چون بمقتضای مسلمانی وشفقت، که بعموم خلائق است، اعلام بعضی امور لازم است، خواستیم که اورا از نوید[۱] عنایت بی غایت آگاه سازیم وانچه شعار اسلام باشد اعلام کنیم۔ می باید که نظر بر عواقب امور انداخته از عنایات بادشاهی[۲] امید واری تمام[۳] داشته باشد ودران حدود که است بدانچه تواند در دولت خواهی کوشیده تقصیر نکند۔ وهر کس که باو دردولت خواهی متفق باشد بنوید الطاف واعطاف ما امیدوار سازد۔ واگر تواند آمد ودرآمدن مانع نباشد، خود را بملازمت رساند وملاحظه آن نکند که در رعایت امرای افغانان تاملی است۔ شنیده باشد که در زمان سابق بسیاری امرای افغانان در ملازمت حضرت سلیمانی فردوس مکانی از امرای ترك بیشتر رعایت یافته بودند۔ ودر حال اخلاص وخدمت استحقاق وحالت منظور است وهر کس بقدر استعداد از خوان رحمت و احسان بهره می گیرند۔ مقرر است که چون آن عمدة الملك از روی صدق نیت[٤] و کمال اخلاص کمر دولت خواهی برمیان جان بندد، فراخور آن از عنایات بادشاهی ملحوظ خواهد شد واگر دران حدود که حالا هست ولایت خواسته باشد خواهد یافت یا هر جا که لائق باشد عنایت خواهیم فرمود۔ واگر دریں ولا بملازمت نتواند رسید دران طرف بدولت خواهی مشغول باشد وخود را ازیں طائفه سوا سازد۔ وبعد ازان که

۱۔ ع : نوید، ندارد
۲۔ ع : بادشاه
۳۔ ع : تمام، ندارد
٤۔ ع : نیت، ندارد

بتوفیق الهی خاطر عاطر از ضبط وسامان این ولایت جمع شود وعنان یك ران اقبال بولایت پیش معطوف گردد وانشاء الله تعالی آن جا بملازمت مستعد شود که هر آئینه بعنایت لائق ورعایت تام سرفراز خواهد شد ومدعیات ومطلوبات او بحصول خواهد پیوست۔ وتا زمانی که بدولت ملازمت رسد عرائض حاجات وملتمسات خود را بدرگاه معلی عرضه داشت می نموده باشد۔ دریں باب قدغن لازم داند[۱]

(۴۸)
منشور به یکی از امراء لودی در استمالت

عمدة الملك، رکن السلطنة القاهرة، لائق العنایات الجلیه، مستعد الرعایت والاحسان فلاں بعنایت والطاف بادشاهی عز اختصاص وشرف امتیاز یافته بداند که والد او سابقاً از روی دولت خواهی بملازمت آمده در سلك امرای عالی مقدار انتظام یافته، بعنایت ورعایت سرفراز شده بود۔ چوں باغوای کوته اندیشاں از ملازمت جدا شده بعد از فتح سند بدست عساکر ظفر نشان افتاد وحکم برقتل او صادر نشده بود، باوجود که[۲] بی رخصت رفته بود وبعضی امور ناپسندیده از وی بوقوع آمده، در خاطر اشرف آں نبود که اورا ضائع سازند، غایتش چوں خاطر نشان عالمیاں شده بود که او بغی ورزیده تا بملازمت آوردن میر غضب اورا تلف کرده، بداں جهت به میر غضب اعتراض شده بود، گویا که نصیب او ایں بود۔ اکنوں به مسامع علیه رسید که آں عمدة الملك درمیان قوم وابنای جنس خود از اکثری بحسن وجاهت وشجاعت واستعداد قابلیت امتیاز دارد ومستحق عنایت

۱۔ ع : دریں باب قدغن لازم داند، ندارد، وخاطر اشرف متوجه انتظام احوال وحصول امانی وآمال خود داند، درعهده دانسته از مضمون صدر درنگذرد وتخلف ننماید، زیاده دارد۔

۲۔ ع : آنکه

ورعایت است۔ آن نیز به مسامع علیه رسید که متابعت فلان کرده باو همراهی می نماید۔ چه لائق باشد که مثل او جوان اصیل، مسلمان بواسطه امور مصلحت دنیوی اطاعت کافری کرده بایں وضع می گشته باشد۔ اگر بحسب مقدرات الهی چند سال آن نوع شد که مملکت هند از تصرف بندگان آستان عالی شان بیرون آمد، اما عنایات وتائیدات نامتناهی در هر جا وهر مکان وحال قرین احوال فرخنده مآل ماست ودولت از سلسله افغانان رو برتافته، چنانچه از قوم سور اکثر سرداران ایشان معدوم ومقهور شدند ومی شوند انشاء الله تعالی۔ ملاحظه تمام که بگفتن وشنودن لائق باشد که مثل او جوان اصیل متابعت کافری، ظالمی[1] می کرده باشد۔ چون از قدیم جماعت لودی دولت خواه اند، واکثر ایشان رعایتها یافته اند وخدمات کرده اند ونسبت اخلاص لودیان برضمر انور واضح ولائح است، حیف باشد که اوقات خود را بآن طائفه صرف می کرده باشد۔ لائق بل واجب آنست که بعد از اطلاع بر مضمون فرمان عالی شان عنایت نشان از مخالفان دولت گردون منزلت جدا شده، خود را بملازمت رساند واصلاً دغدغه بخاطر راه ندهد که چون بشرف بساط بوسی مستعد شود بنوعی که مناسب حال باشد عنایت وشفقت بظهور خواهدرسید۔ شنیده باشد که از جماعت لودی بعضی که بملازمت آمده اند بچه درجه در باره ایشان عنایت شده۔ انشاء الله العزیز او نیز بنوعی رعایت خواهدیافت که درمیان اقران وامثال امتیاز تمام یابد۔ ونیز هر کس که داعیه خدمت ودولت خواهی داشته باشد از مخالفان جدا شده همراه او بملازمت آید، درباره او عنایت ومرحمت بظهور خواهد رسید۔ من کل الوجوه خاطر جمع دارد وبزودی خود را بملازمت رساند که مدعیات برحسب مطلوب بحصول خواهد پیوست۔ وتا زمانیکه بدولت ملازمت رسد

۱۔ ع: ظالمی، ندارد

عرائض حاجات وملتمسات خود را بدرگاه معلی عرضه داشت می نموده باشد ومترصد اجابت باشد۔ دریں باب قد غن عظیم داند۔

(۴۹)

منشور به یکی از امراء دراستمالت

تابع الاوامر والاحکام، عمدة المشاهیر والحکام فلاں بعنایت بیغایت بادشاهی عز اختصاص وشرف امتیاز یافته بداند که دریں ولا بحسب تقدیر حی قدیر فردوس مکانی جنت آشیانی از دار الفنا به بهشت اعلی رحلت فرمودند ومابدولت واقبال به تخت خلافت نشستیم۔ چوں آں عمدة الاعیان قبل ازیں نسبت بایں جانب در مقام اطاعت وانقیاد ودولت خواهی بوده، الحال می باید که بمراتب بیشتر اطاعت وانقیاد ودولت خواهی بجا آورده مطلقاً اندیشه بخاطر راه ندهد۔ وهم فرزندان ومتعلقان اعتمادی خود را بدرگاه خلافت پناه فرستد که لطف وعنایت ما درباره او بمرتبه اعلی است۔ وانشاء الله تعالی مدعیات وملتمسات او بحصول خواهد پیوست۔ ازو خدمت واطاعت واز ما لطف وشفقت۔ خاطر من جمیع الوجوه جمع داشته در دولت خواهی تقصیر نکند۔ دریں باب قد غن لازم داند۔

(۵۰)

منشور به یکی از امراء در باب معاونت در فتح ولایت پیش

عمدة الخوانین، قدوة السلاطین، اسد المعارك، عضد الممالك، مخلص دولت خواه بلا اشتباه، لائق اللطف، قابل الاحسان، وافر الاعتقاد فلاں باصناف عوارف بادشاهی وانواع عواطف شاهنشاهی عز

اختصاص وشرف امتیاز یافته بداند که چنان بموقف عرض رسید که بعضی از امراء کلان تران افغانان در ولایت پیش در مقام جمعیت لشکر شده ومی شوند. بامداد[1] عنایت جنود[2] بی غایت حضرت فتاح بی منت چنان است که باسهل وجوه دفع ورفع آنها میسر گشته ولایت خوب ومرغوب انشاء الله بحیطه تسخیر وتصرف در آید. چون فرامین مطاعه باسم خوانین وسلاطین وامرای آن حدود شرف صدور یافته که هر گاه اسد المعارك بعزیمت قلع وقمع مخالفان متوجه شود، بتمامی همراهی نموده طریق مطاوعت ومتابعت مسلوك دارند، واز سخن ومصلحت آن عضد الممالك، که محض صلاح دولت قاهره خواهد بود، عدول نورزند. می باید که خاطر اشرف متوجه حصول امانی وآمال خود دانسته هر گاه که وقت وفا کند[3] لشکر جمع ساخته بولایت پیش متوجه گردد، بعنایت[4] الهی فتح میسر شود وبر مخالفان ظفر یافته ولایات بتصرف در آید. خاطر خود را بهمه ابواب جمع داشته بهیچ جهت دغدغه واندیشه بخود راه ندهد وچگونگی حالات وواقعات را روز بروز معروض گرداند. دریں باب قد غن لازم داند.

(۵۱)

منشور به یکی از امراء بعد وصول عرضداشت

عمدة الملك، رکن السطلنة العالیه، مستعد العنایت والاحسان، مسند عالی فلان بوفور عنایت والطاف بادشاهی سرفراز وممتاز بوده بداند که عرضه داشتی که مصحوب زبدة الاقران فلان بدر گاه معلی فرستاده بود، بموقف عرض رسید و کیفیت اخلاص ودولت خواهی او

۱ـ ع : امید بامداد

۲ـ جنود، ندارد

۳ـ یافته

۴ـ بحسن عنایت

وآن که داعیه دارد که بشرف آستان بوسی سرفراز شود، از مضمون آن بوضوح پیوست، پسندیده ومستحسن افتاد وموجب زیادتی عنایت والتفات گشت۔ قبل ازیں نیز چند مرتبه حسن اخلاص وعاقبت اندیشی آن عمدة الملك بموقف عرض رسیده بود وخاطر اشرف متوجه می بود که چون بکمال فراست وصلاح اندیشی از امثال واقران امتیاز تمام دارد، در ظل دولت ایں آستان رفیع منزلت در آمده به عنایت بیغایت الهی وفضل نامتناهی روز بروز ابواب فتوحات غیبی بر چهره دولت وجبهه حشمت مفتوح ومکشوف شده ومی شود۔ واکنون ولایات چنان که معلوم نموده بحیطه تسخیر وتصرف عساکر منصوره در آمده ودولت خواهان از اطراف وجوانب روی اطاعت و عبودیت سرفراز می شوند، ومخالفان مغلوب ومقهور گشته، بهر طرف پریشان وسرگردان می گردند۔ وفلان که باعنایت[۱] جمعی از ملهوفان[۲] واغواء بعضی از مفسدان دریں ولا جمعیت نموده، بداعیه فساد وشرارت واضرار مسلمانان تا بنواحی فلان وآن حدود رفته بود، فرزند، سعادت یار،[۳] برخوردار، نور حدیقه عین، ونور حدقه سید الثقلین، ثمره شجره متعالی فلان باعساکر منصور سرکار پنجاب ازان جانب وفرزند اعز ارشد، ارجمند، سعادت یار، برخوردار، قرة العیون والانوار فلان، طوّل تعالی عمره وضاعف قدره، وعمده خوانین رفیع مقدار فلان بهادر با افواج قاهره ازیں طرف متوجه شده، بعنایت الله تعالی دفع ورفع او نموده اورا گریزان ساخته اند۔ ومقدمه لشکرهای مذکوره بایشان رسیده قریب هزار کس را بقتل رسانیده۔ وفلان با بقیة البغی[٤] که بدر رفته اند خود را بکوه کشیده وفرزندان موسی الیهما با لشکرهای منصوره در پی قلع وقمع اند۔ امید چنان است که بزودی خاطر ازو

۱۔ ع : باعانت
۲۔ ع : متصوفان
۳۔ ع : سعادت مند
٤۔ ع : بقیة السیفی

جمع نمایند، انشاء الله تعالی۔ واکنون خاطر اشرف بران قرار یافته که درین چند روز عزیمت دار السلطنت آگره وآن حدود نموده متوجه شویم۔ می باید که آن عمدة الملك خاطر من كل الوجوه جمع داشته خاطر اشرف متوجه احوال خود داند واز روی امیدواری با جمعیتی که دارد مستعد ملازمت شده در آگره بپایه سریر خلافت مصیر آید، که هر آئینه فراخور آن درباره او عنایت وشفقت خواهد شد ودر جرگه امرای عظام انتظام یافته برعایت وولایت لائق سرفراز خواهد گشت۔ درعهده داند، درین باب قدغن لازم داند۔[۱]

(۵۲)

منشور به یکی از امراء بعد وصول عرضداشت

عمدة الملك، كامل العقيدة والاخلاص، مستعد الرعاية والعناية والاحسان فلان بوفور عنایت والتفات بادشاهی[۲] سرفراز ومباهی بوده بداند که عرضه داشتی که درین ولا بدرگاه معلی فرستاده بود، بموقف عرض رسید وکیفیت اخلاص ودولت خواهی او که، ازروی عقل وفراست وعاقبت اندیشی، شعار ودثار خود ساخته بود، از مضمون آن بوضوح پیوست، بغایت پسندیده ومستحسن افتاد[۳] موجب عنایت وعاطفت بی نهایت گشت۔ می باید که بهمه حال مستوثق ومستمال بوده، خاطر اشرف متوجه انتظام احوال وحصول آمال خود داند ومن كل الوجوه مطمئن گشته بلوازم دولت خواهی وجان سپاری اشتغال نماید، ومترصد حصول رایات نصرت آیات باشد که چون به توفیق الله تعالی قلع وقمع فلان روی نموده، وخاطر اطهر از مهمات این حدود جمع شده، وبعد برشگال درین حدود امری که باعث توقف شود واقع

۱۔ ع : تقصیر ننماید

۲۔ ع : بادشاهی، ندارد

۳۔ ع : و، زیاده دارد

نیست، انشاء الله تعالی چون برشگال بآخر رسد بدولت واقبال بالشکرهای فیروزی مآل بعزیمت تسیخر ولایاتی که درپیش است عنان توجه معطوف خواهیم فرمود۔ وبعد آں که به سعادت عتبه بوسی مشرف شود فراخور عقل ودولت خواهی وحالتی که دارد آں مسند عالی را بمزید عنایت ورعایت بر امثال واقران امتیاز خواهیم بخشید۔ الحال سرکار فلاں را بنوعی که در تصرف اوست باو ارزانی داشتیم۔ در ازدیاد دولت خواهی کوشیده چنال سازد که روز بروز آثار آں بوضوح رسد ودر دفع ورفع مخالفاں دولت قاهره دقیقه از دقائق نامرعی نگذارد۔ وچگونگی حالات وواقعات را پیوسته باحاجات وملتمسات ومدعیات خود عرضه داشت می کرده باشد۔ دریں باب قدغن عظیم داند۔ تحریراً بالامرا العالی، خلد نفاذه ولا زال مطاعاً۔

(۵۳)

منشور به یکی از امراء بعد وصول عرض داشت

(هنگام بغاوت بیرام خاں)

عمدة الملك، رکن السلطنة القاهرة، عضد الدولة الباهرة، زبده مخلصان جاں سپار، قدوه دولت خواهان ذوی الاعتبار، خلاصه خوانین عالی شان مبارز الدین فلاں باصناف الطاف واعطاف بادشاهی عز اختصاص وشرف امتیاز یافته بداند که عرضه داشتی که بتجدید مصحوب قاصدان خود به درگاه جهان پناه فرستاده بود، بموقف عرض رسید، وآں که بجواب فرمان عالی شان که قبل ازیں مشتمل بر احوال واعمال واخراج فلاں وراه نادادن او بطرف فلاں عز اصدار یافته بود، معروض داشته که از زمانی که حلقه عبودیت آں آستان رفیع المکان را در گوش کشیده از صمیم دل بی غل بخود قرار داده که تا حیات داشته

باشد بدوستان آن دولت عظمیٰ از جان وجنان دوست بوده، بدشمنان آن خلافت کبریٰ، که اگر بالفرض والتقدیر دیده او باشد، دشمنی نماید۔ تفصیل از مضمون آن واضح ولائح گردید۔ اگرچه حقیقت اخلاص واعتقاد ودولت خواهی آن عمدة الملك بکرات ومرات بر مرأت ضمیر غیب آیات عکس پذیر گشته ودرباره او توجه بسیار داشتیم، آن معنی علاوه همه آن شده باعث ازدیاد عنایت وموجب افزونی اسباب عاطفت گشت۔ چون دران ایام که فلان را از درگاه معلی اخراج فرموده حسب الاستدعاء اورا فرمان راه حج فرستادیم که اورا بسلامت گذرانیده درهیچ محل مانع نیایند، بخاطر بعض دولت خواهان می رسید که شاید بحال دیگر کند۔ بآن که به یقین دانستیم که اگر او بطریق مکر وغدر متوجه آن حدود شود یا خواهد که خودرا بجانب فلان کشد وبنیاد فتنه وفساد کند، آن عضد الدوله از کمال اخلاص وعقیدت که بایس آستان خلافت مکان دارد، دفع ورفع او بنوعی که لائق دولت قاهره باشد بخود راه خواهدداد۔ جهت زیادتی تاکید واهتمامی که دردفع مکر وغدر اوداشتیم وداریم آن چنان فرمانی به نفاذ پیوسته بود۔ خاطر من کل الوجوه جمع دارد که نسبت دولت خواهی وجان سپاری آن زبده مخلصان کما هوحقه بررای عالم آرای ثابت وروشن ومبرهن گشته۔ وچون حسن عقیدت وصفای طویت اویوماً فیوماً درترقی وتزاید است، توجه خاطر فیض مآثر ما نیز سمت تضاعف وترادف دارد۔ چنان که کیفیت آن را از تقریر مخصوصان ونوکران خود که بدرگاه معلی فرستاده ومی فرستد معلوم نموده باشد وخواهد نمود۔ بتاریخ ۲ شهر حال بعضی از خوانین فیروزی مآل مثل سیادت پناه، نقابت دستگاه، ثمره شجره نبوت وولایت، لائق اضاف رعایت وعنایت، عمده سادات سعادت نشان، قدوه خوانین متعالی مکان، شجاع الدین محمد قاسم خان، وشرافت پناه، عمدة الملك،

رکن السلطنة القاهره، عضد الدولة الباهره، مقرب الحضرة الزاهره، زبدة المخلصين فی الدوران، لائق الاعتبار والاحسان، قدوة الخوانین العظام بین الاقران شمس الدین محمد آتکه خان، وعمدة الملك، رکن السلطنة العلیه، لائق العنایات الجلیه، زبدة الخوانین بین الاقران، مبارز الدین مهدی قاسم خان رابا بعضی از سلاطین وامراء ویکه جوانان بطریق ایلغار برسر او فرستادیم۔ وچون دریں ولا عمدة الملك، رکن السلطنة القاهره، عضد الدولة الباهرة، موتمن الخلافة الزاهره، مقرب الحضرة السلطانی، اعتماد الدولة الخاقانی، قدوه خوانین عالی شان، خلاصه مخلصان متعالی مکان، مبارز الدین محمد منعم بهادر الملقب باعتماد خان بالشکر سرکار کابل به لاهور آمده، حکم فرمودیم که آں عمدة الملك لشکر سرکار پنجاب را نیز بخود همراه ساخته ازاں طرف متوجه شود۔ امید بدرگاه الهی چناں است که باسهل وجوه اورا در میان گرفته اسیر ودستگیر می نمایند۔ می باید که آں قدوه دولت خواهان خاطر اشرف متوجه انتظام احوال وحصول امانی وآمال خود دانسته بهمیں طریقه مرضیه پیوسته بلوازم دولت خواهی ومراسم جاں سپاری اشتغال می نموده باشد ودقیقه نامرعی نگذارد۔ یقین است که اگر فلاں پیش از رسیدن عساکر منصوره گریزاں شده خودرا بآں حدود رساند، در گرفتن واسیر کردن اومردم او حتی الامکان کوشش خواهد نمود۔

دیگر آں که مکتوب حضرت سلطنت منقبت، شاهزاده جواں بخت، نامدار، خسروارجمند سعادت یار المختص بعواطف الملك الاعلی سلطان حسین میرزا که بآں عضد دولت نوشته بود، بدرگاه معلی فرستاده بود، نیز پسندیده افتاد وموجب استحسان گشت۔ چوں ایشاں بملاحظه نسبت اخلاص واختصاص که ازاں مخلص جاں سپار بایں آستان گیتی مدار معلوم کرده اند، ایں چنیں کتابتی فرستاده۔ مناسب چناں است که بنوعی که صلاح دولت قاهره باشد سلوك

نـمـوده، طـریـقه احتیاط را نامرعی نگذارد وابواب رسل ورسائل را گاه گـاه مـفتـوح دارد۔ ودرعهـده دانستـه از فـرموده درنگذرد وچگو نگی حالات وواقعات را همیشه عرضه داشت می نموده باشد۔ تحریر بالامر العالی خلد نفاذه فی شهر ذی قعده سنة ۱۰۰۳[1]

(٥٤)

منشور به یکی از امراء بعد وصول عرض داشت

ایـالـت مـآب، حکومت انتساب، رفعت پناه، شوکت دستگاه، سلطان اعظم، افتخار اعاظم السلاطین والحکام بین الامم، المخصوص بـعـواطف الـمَـلك الاکبر، غیاث الدولة والدنیا والدین سلطان اسکندر، اعلی الله تعالیٰ شانه، بعد از استشعار[2] بوفور عواطف بادشاهانه واستظهار بـضـوفِ عـوارف خسـروا نه معلوم داند که دریں ایام قدوة الاقران ملك خـضـر بـدرگـاه جهـان پناه که ازقبیل بندگان سلاطین ایام وخواقین انام اسـت، آمـده بسـعادت بساط بوسی استسعاد یافت، وبعد از دعای دوام دولـت ابـد پیـونـد کیفیت اعتقاد واخلاص آن حکومت مآب را نسبت بـعتبـه علیه بعرض رسانید، بغایت پسندیده ومستحسن افتاد۔ یك جهتی واخـلاص او نسبـت بـریـں خـانـدان مـوروثی است وهمواره آباء عظام واجـداد کـرام آن حـکـومـت مـآب التجا بدیں خاندان خلافت دودمان سـلـطـنـت نـموده، بانواع عواطف ومراحم سرفراز شده اند۔ بنابران ایں فـرمان همایون برشرائط عنایت روز افزون درقلم آمد۔ می باید که خاطر اشـرف متـوجـه احـوال خجسته مآل خود دانسته پیوسته عرض حالات

۱۔ سـال اصـدار منشور غلط نقل شده، ایں منشور هنگام بغاوت بیرام خان به یکی از امـراء مـغـل درپـنـجـاب صادر شده۔ سال بغاوت بیرام خان ۹۶۷ است ۔ رجوع کـنـیـد اکبر نامه، جلددوم ص ص ۱۷۴۔۱۷۸؛ مآثر الامراء، جلد اول، ص ٦٤٥؛ جلد دوم، ص ص ٥٣١۔٥٣٥؛ جلد سوم، ص ص ٥٠۔٥٢

۲۔ ع : استمال

ورفع مهمات از لوازم شمرد، چون ملك خضر مذکور منظور مرحمت گشته، نیز سفارش[1] می فرمائیم ورعایت این نوع مردم لازم است، از احوال او بواجبی باخبر بوده رعایت ومراقبت او لازم شناسد، درین باب قدغن[2] لازم داند۔

(۵۵)

منشور به یکی از امراء بعد وصول عرضداشت

عمدة الملك، رکن السلطنة القاهره، عضد الدولة الباهره، قدوه مخلصان وفادار مبارز الدین فلان بعنایت والتفات بادشاهی عزامتیاز وشرف افتخار یافته بداند که عرضه داشتی که درین ولا بدرگاه معلی فرستاده بود بموقف عرض مقدس رسید وکیفیت اخلاص ودولت خواهی واهتمام ایشان درباب نگاه داشت قلعه وضبط وربط مهمات سرکار فلان بظهور رسانیده ومی رساند از مضمون آن بوضوح پیوست۔ پسندیده افتاد وموجب زیادتی عنایت وعاطفت گشت۔ می باید که بهمه حال مستمال وامیدوار بوده خاطر اشرف متوجه انتظام احوال خود دانند وبهمین طریقه مرضیه بلوازم دولت خواهی ومراسم یك جهتی قیام واقدام نموده درمحافظت وحراست قلعه وولایت بیشتر از پیشتر اهتمام نماید، وبوجهی که حکم فرموده ایم امراء وسپاهیان را در قلعه در آورد وسعی کند که همه ذخیره درآورد۔ وهر کس که ابا نماید تنبیه بلیغ کند۔ اصول واعیان آن ولایت را وقضات ومشائخ واکابر بلده وپرگنات را مع کوچ بقلعه درآورد وقدغن نماید که آنها نیز بقدر وسع[3] وامکان ذخیره درآورند، وچنان سعی نماید که خاطر ازممر قلعه جمع

۱۔ ع : سپارس

۲۔ ع : وسعت

۳۔ ع : عظیم، زیادة دارد

باشد[1] ودر اعلاء اعلام شریعت ودفع ورفع ظلمت وبدعت ورفاهیت احوال رعیت واشاعت آثار عدالت وزجر وقتل متمردان ومفسدان وتادیب وتنبیه فاسقان وفاجران وسیاست دزدان وبیبا کان کمال اهتمام بجا آورد، دقیقه نامرعی نگذارد، وچنان نماید که آثار آن روز بروز بوضوح که هر آئینه پسندیده خواهد بود. الحمد لله والمنة[2] که دریں دلافتح مانکوٹ روی نمود چنانچه کیفیت را از مضمون فتح نامه معلوم خواهند نمود، ومهمات این حدود بوجه اراده دولت خواهان صورت یافته، انشاء الله عن قریب بسعادت واقبال عساکر فیروزی مآں بعزیمت تسخیر آں ولایت که درپیش است عنان توجه معطوف خواهیم فرمود، تازمانی که بشرف ملازمت رسد چگونگی حالات وواقعات را روز بروز بتفصیل عرضه داشت می نموده باشد. دریں ابواب قدغن لازم داند.

(٥٦)

منشور بنام عبد الرحیم خان خانان بعد وصول عرضداشت

اعتماد الممالك العظمی، اعتضاد الخلافة الکبری، ذو الخصائل الرضیه والشمائل المرضیه، موتمن الدولة العالیة، مورد العنایات السلطانیه، جامع الکمالات الصوریة والمعنویة، زبده امراء عظیم الشان، عمده خوانین رفیع المکان، مبارز الدین خان خانان سپهه سالار بوفور الطاف شاهنشاهی وصنوف اعطاف ظل الهی عز افتخار وشرف اختصاص یافته بداند که بتاریخ شهر فلاں وقتی که بسعادت واقبال مهمات عرصه دل کشای کشمیر حسب دلخواه سرانجام نموده، برسم استعجال جریده متوجه اردوی معلی بودیم واکثر راه طی

١۔ ع : شود
٢۔ ع : المنة لله والحمد

شده، موکب همایون ما از فلان جا گذشتة بود که عرضه داشتی که ارسال داشته بود بموقف عرض مقدس رسید وحقیقت آمدن امارت پناه مرزا جانی بیگ ودیدن آن خلاصه مخلصان حقیقی (و) سائر احوال فرخنده فال بوضوح پیوست۔ همواره از صادر ووارد حسن عقیدت او بمسامع علیه می رسد، علی الخصوص وقتی که حکیم عین الملك آن جا رفته وآمده، پیوسته توجه خاص بجانب او مصروف بوده۔ لیکن بواسطه کم تجربگی وتبه رائی خویش اندك واژ گون همتی بخود راه داده بود۔ الحمد لله که حسن ظن ما که درباره او بود به یقین پیوست وبسیار پسندیده آمد۔ انشاء الله سبحانه بانواع تفقدات اعلی خاقانی شرف اختصاص خواهدیافت۔ ازیں نوید مسرت افزا که مخبر اتمام مهمات مرجوعه آن نقاوه ارباب اختصاص بوده، شادمانیها روی داده وایزد بیچون می داند که خاطر فیض مآثر حضور اورا چه مقدار می خواهد ۔ امید که اورا عن قریب به شادمانی وبه خوبی بینیم۔ باید که چون بر مضمون عنایت مشحون فرمان مطاع اطلاع یابد، از ملازمان عتبه اقبال از امراء ومنصب داران ممالك وغیره که دریں یورش خدمات پسندیده نموده، به نظر مراحم خسروانی مخصوص اند، درتهاناجات گذاشته با مرزا جانی بیگ متوجه ملازمت شود۔ وانچه درباب مناصب آن مردم التماس نموده بود، هر کدام که بسیار خدمت شایسته کرده ودرافزائش اخلاص ما شده، آن را غائبانه ده پانزده منصب اضافه نمایند۔ واگر کسی مستحق ده بست وزیاده ازاں باشد چون بملازمت مشرف خواهد شد ملتمس او بدرجه قبول خواهد شد۔ باید که جمیع مردم علی تفاوت مراتبهم بعنایت خسروانه ممتاز وسرفراز بوده، همیں فرمان را سند خود دانسته درانچه اعتماد الملك مشار الیه مصلحت داند آن را فرموده ما دانسته تخلف را راه ندهنده وهر

کدام را که چند گاه آن جا گذارد نخوت خیلگی را بخود را نداده، آن مهمات را خدمات خود شمرده، دقیقه کاهلی نورذیده سر گرم آن کار باشند- زنهار صد هزار زنهار که کسی کار کرده خود را باضطراب ضائع سازد وبی استصواب اعتضاد الملك مومی الیه اراده آمدن نماید که ضائع شدن خدمات آنها یك طرف وغضب بادشاهی که نمونه قهر الهی است یك طرف است- وخاطر اشرف را بانتظام احوال خود متوجه داند- دریں باب قدغن عظیم داند- کتاب بالامر العالی وخلد نفاذه ولا زال مطاعاً-

(۵۷)

منشور به یکی از امراء بعد وصول عرضداشت

عمدة الملك، رکن الدولة العالیه، لائق اضعاف العنایة والرعایة والاحسان فلاں بعنایت بادشاهی سرفراز ومباهی بوده بداند که عرضه داشتی که دریں ولا بدر گاه معلی فرستاده بود، ایستادگان پایه سریر بعرض اشرف رسانیدند- دریں ولا اخبار از جانب فلاں آمد که فلاں بعد از فوت فلاں بجای او نشسته بود بدست نوکران خود کشته شد، ودیگر دراں سلسله وارثی نماند، وفتح وتسخیر آن ملك برذمه دولت خواهاں فرض شده، بخاطر اشرف رسید که ایں خدمت را فرزند اعز، ارجمند، کامگار، غره ناصیه خلافت واقبال، قره باصره سلطنت واجلال، گوهر رفعت آرای تخت ودیهیم، شاهزاده شاه سلیم طول الله عمره، انشاء الله بانصرام برساند- دریں محل اگر نوعی می باشد[1] که فلاں متمرد را از ولایت خود بدر می کرد- چوں سابقاً که سعید خاں بملازمت آمد

۱- ع: می باشد

پیشکش های فلان را با وکیل آورده بعرض می رسانید که فلان دولت خواهی اختیار می کنند، حالا هم فرمان مقدس مشتمل بر تاکید نام بفلان فرستاده شد که بفلان سخن کند واورا داخل دولت خواهان سازد، شاید که بخت او یاوری کند ودرسلك دولت خواهان درآید۔ والا بعنایت الله تعالیٰ دفع ورفع او باسهل وجهی خواهد شد۔ درچنین وقت که مهم ولایت فلان پیش نهاد خاطر ملکوت ناظر است مثل او چرا بمهم زمین داری معطل باشد۔ درین باب قدغن لازم داند۔

نامه ها

(۵۸)

مکتوب عبد الله خان اوزبیك بنام جلال الدین محمد اکبر بادشاه

همیشه نسیم نصرت وظفر[1] از مهب عنایت حضرت خالق داور برشقه لوای جهان کشای فریدون فر، شهریار سکندرسیر، ماحی مآثر کسری وقیصر، صاحب سریر وافسر، دارای جمشید اثر، نوشیروان خورشید منظر، طراز کسوت فرمان روائی، نگین خاتم کشور کشائی، آفتاب تابان ملك جلالت، ماه درخشان سپهر خلافت، تاج بخش، عالم آرای، خصم بند، کشور کشای، بیت:-

خجسته ز طالع همایون ز[2] بخت فروزنده تاج وفرازنده تخت

بادشاه اعظم، زبده سلاطین العرب والعجم، قضاتوان، قدر قدرت، ستاره حشم، زمیں وقار، زمان سرعت، فلك تمکیں، کیوان رفعت، ناصب رایات فتح وظفر، رافع الویة العدل بین زمرة البشر، ملك ملوك زمان، المتمکن علی مسند العدل والاحسان:

شاه دریا دل جلال الدین اکبر آنکه هست
زخمهاء تیغ تیزش[3] بر دل پیل وپلنگ
هم بجنب مهر قدرش پایه افلاك پست
هم برای خیل جاهش عرصه افلاك تنگ
زر گر گردون برای بزم جودش روز وشب
از زر وسیم مه وخورشید می سازد تبنگ

لازالت رایات دولته مرفوعةً الی قمة السماء وآیات شوکته

۱ـ ع : ظفر، ندارد
۲ـ ع : ز، ندارد
۳ـ ع : تیر وتیغش

مکتوبة علی صفحات الواح الا فلاك، در اهتزاز باد وطائر دولت واقبال از اوج هواء الطاف حضرت آفرید گار برفراز اورنگ فیروزه[١] آن صاحب شکوه با فرهنگ در پرواز، بالنبی وآله وصحبه الممتاز! داعی صداقت اقتران تحیتی چون نسیم گل وشمامه سنبل، که وقت صبح دم آرد صبا از روضه رضوان، با جواهر زواهر دعوات، که خازنان نقود اخلاص وناقدان مخازن اختصاص از خزانه "ذالك فضل الله یوتیه من یشاء[٢]" هدیه مالکان ممالك اقبال وسالکان مسالك دولت بی زوال می کنند، نثار مجلس اشرف اقدس آن خلافت پناهی می گرداند، وانتظام قاعده محبت واتساع عرصه مودت، که متکفل صلاح احوال عالم ومتضمن حصول امور جمهور بنی آدم همان تواند بود بالعشی والاشراق از حضرت فیاض علی الاطلاق، خالق انفس وآفاق در می خواهد، کسوت حال این مقصود بطراز اعزاز "فاستجبناله[٣]" مطرز باد!

بعده مکشوف رای عالم آرای وضمیر سیما سیماء که بصیقل توفیق انجلا یافته واز اشعه لمعات تحیتی تحقیق اضاءت پذیرفته، آنکه اگرچه قواعد تالیف وتودد ارواح به تلاقی اجسام واشباه نشده وروابط تعارف میثاقی بتقابل اشخاص وتناظر اخلاق[٥] موکد نگشته، اما روائح مکارم صفات علیه مشام عقیده انجام این مخلص را مطیب ومعطر دارد بمیامن این مرابطات:

باخم زلف چو چوگان تو پیش از من وتو
سالها بود که دل گوئی محبت می باخت

هر آئینه مناسب چنان بود که پیوسته برسم ادرار وطریق استمرار رسائل مصادقت انجام اقدام می نمود لیکن حق علیم است که از

١ـ ع: فیروزه رنگ
٢ـ قرآن مجید: ٤/٦٢
٣ـ قرآن مجید: ٧٦/٢١
٤ـ ع : تجلی
٥ـ ع : احباء
٦ـ ع : آن

ممر وقوع موانع غریبه ظهور این اراده از حیز قوت به فعل نیامد واعلام آن در عقده تعویق ماند، چنانچه حقیقت حال شاید که مکشوف رای انور شده باشد ـ وگرنه حاشا که رابطه اتحاد ویگانگی که از مطلع بامداد فطرت وخلقت مرکوز عناصر جبلت گشت، بی عذر شرعی وظهور تعذر نفس امری اقتضاء این عمل بیگانگی کند ـ چون یقین است که پیکر یقین واتحاد[1] بر رای از هرچه گمان برند اظهر خواهد بود، ازان ممر از تکرار آن احتراز نمود ـ مامول آنست که آن سلطنت پناه نیز همواره بارسال مکاتبات شریفه ومفاوضات لطیفه موسّس مبانی خصوصیت ووداد ومشیّد بنیان قرابت واتحاد باشند، واساس محبت را بنوعی استحکام دهند که بهیچ نوع[2] خلل نباشد ومابین رسوم یگانگی مرعی بوده، قواعد بیگانگی بالکلیه مندفع شود ـ

ثانیاً بر خاطر آفتاب مآثر که آئینه مخدرات عالم غیب است، مخفی ومستور نماند که چون برادر مرزا شهرخ از مروت تافته وشیوه بی ادبی را شعار خود ساخته وسلاطین تاشقند وحصار را پناه داده، دران زمان که عساکر نصرت مآثر به تسخیر ممالك ولایت ترکستان واستیصال قزاق واحشام دشت قبچاق اشتغال داشتند، بولایت قبة الاسلام بلخ تاخت آورده انواع حرکات ناپسندیده بظهور رسانید بالضرورت تادیب وتنبیه او منظور داشته جهت تسخیر ولایتش رایت[3] اهتمام واجتهاد برافراشت وتسخیر ولایت بدخشان بامداد "والله یوید بنصره من یشاء[4]" واطفاء نائره او بادنی توجهی رونمود[5] ـ مشارالیه فرار برقرار اختیار کرده، بدرگاه معلی توجه فرمود ـ مترصد است که خاطر

---

۱ ـ ع : به یکسر، زیاده دارد

۲ ـ ع : امکان، زیاده دارد

۳ ـ ع : الویه

٤ ـ قرآن مجید: ۱۳/۳

۵ ـ ع : نموده

فیض مآثر ازان جمع دارند وغبار به ضمیر خورشید تنویر راه ندهند که عقد محبت ایں محب[1] بآن حضرت رفیع مرتبت نه بنوعی است که اورا بسر انگشت فریب کسی تواند کشود ونقش مودت بدرجه منقوش نه گردیده که سیلاب حادثه اورا تواند زدود ـ رجاء واثق است که صور ایں معانی بر ضمیر بی عیب، که نقش پذیر عالم غیب است، پرتو اندازد ـ اشعار که درباب کبوتران دیوان بیگی کبوتر باز صادر شده بود، از تقریر دل پذیر حاجی الحرمین الشریفین حاجی میرك مسموع گشت. بمجرد استماع آن قابقهاء کبوتر با[2] کبوتر باز از ولایت فرغانه آورده با دیگر تحف، که اسامی او در تفصیل علحده مرقوم است، مصحوب سیادت مآب، سعادت آیات، افتخار السادات، منبع العز والسعادات نظام الدین میر قریش، که از اعاظم سادات کرام ایں بلاد واز مخصوصان درگاه است، به ملازمت ارسال فرموده تاشرح خصوصیت وصفاء طویت را بمسامع اشرف رسانیده محرك سلاسل اتحاد گردیده آید ـ زیاده طریق اطناب که مفضی باملال است نه پیموده ختم ایں مقال بایں بیت اختصار نمود ـ

شها اساس جهان داریت ممهدباد
ظلال دولت تو تا ابد مخلد باد

(۵۹)

مکتوب جلال الدین محمد اکبر بادشاه
بنام شاه طهماسپ

تا جمشید خورشید هر صباح[3] بر اورنگ فیروزه رنگ سپهر

۱ـ ع : محبان
۲ـ ع : باآن
۳ـ ع : صبح

نشسته منور جبین روی زمین را مانند دل اصحاب یقین منور می گرداند وساکنان شهرستان وجود را از تیرگی شب ظلمت نجات داده، بروشنائی روز بهجت افروز می رساند، تخت خلافت وسرافرازی وسریر عدالت ومخلص نوازی از فر وجود فائض الجود غیرت فزای عرصه عالم پاك ورشك افزای طارم افلاك باد، وفرق همایونش از افسر تائیدات الهی سرفراز ومفتخر، وآوازه خلافت افزودش در اطراف ربع مسکون شائع ومنتشر، وآستان نه آسمان[۱] مقدارش مجمع جنود الطاف ربانی ودرگاه سپهر اساسش مرجع سالکان طریق سلطنت وکامرانی بحق خاتم الانبیاء والاصفیاء[۲] وعترته الازکیاء! بعد از اهداء لوازم محمدت وثناء واتحاف مراسم اخلاص بدان سده والا بعرض نواب فلك جناب، سپهر قباب، اعالی پناهی می رساند که منشور فائض النور ومثال مکرمت امتثال بخاتم عواطف واقبال مزین وبتوقیع مخلص نوازی وملاطفت گستری معنون که مصحوب فلان ارسال یافته بود "فی صحف مکرمة مرفوعة مطهرة[۳]" شرف وصول وسعادت نزول ارزانی داشت. بطلوع[۴] آن آفتاب دولت که از مشرق اقبال برآمد وبظهور آن نهال اجلال که بچمن افضال در برآمد گلزار امانی وآمال تازه شد وازهار حدائق عز وجلال بیحد واندازه گشت، وگل باغ دولت از دوحه سعادت شگفتگی آغاز نهاد وصورت زیبائی مطالب وشاهد مقصود از پرده غیب بی عیب چهره دل ربائی نمود، واز روائح حدائق سطورش فحواء "روح وریحان وجنة نعیم[۵]" روی نمود واز معانی الفاظ وحروفش موداء "حور مقصورات فی الخیام[۶]" چهره کشود. مراد

۱ـ ع : نه سپهر، ندارد

۲ـ ع : الاصفیاء، ندارد

۳ـ قرآن مجید: ۸۰/۱۳ـ۱۴

۴ـ ع : بطول

۵ـ قرآن مجید: ۵۶/۸۹

۶ـ قرآن مجید: ۵۵/۷۲

شریفش ونکات لطیفش بشرائط تعظیم وتبجیل تلقی یافت۔ ریاض عقیدت واخلاص قدیم از فیوض رشحات ارقامش نضارت از سر گرفت، نهال خصوصیت ومحبت دیرینه از زلال مناظرش سرسبز شد۔ هر حرفی ازان دردانه ایست یگانه که جز در قعر بحر "انی اعلم ما لا تعلمون[١]" صدف پرورش نیارد (و) هر نقطه ازان نیریست درافشان که جز از اوج جلال وجاه "السلطان ظل الله" نتابد ۔ سواد کلمات دربارش چون مردمك دیده منور باصره امید وبدائع مضامین غرائب آثارش مانند پرتو آفتاب خضرت بخش حدیقه سعادت جاوید "هذا کتاب احکمت آیاته ثم فصلت من لدن حکیم خبیر[٢]" قطعه:

ایں نار که چشم جاں ازوپرنوراست
منشور سعادت دل مهجور است
فرمان ظفر نشان شاهنشاهی ست
کزیمن عدالتش جهاں معمور است

در ازاء آں موهبت کبری ودر اداء آں عطیه عظمی کلك اندیشه بر صفحه اخلاص چند تواند نگاشت که سزاوار نواب آں آستان باشد۔

جان که عقل کل نبرد پی بکنه آں
ناید کشایشی زخیال کمندما

اشارتی که درباب ارتقاء شان واعتلاء منزلت ومکان عمدة الملك، رکن السلطنه القاهرة، عضد الدولة الباهرة، زبدة المخلصین فی الدوران، لائق الاعتبار والاحسان، قدوه خوانین متعالی مکان، مستحق الرعایة والامتنان، مبارز الدین سلطان محمود الملقب باعتبار خاں

١۔ قرآن مجید: ٢/٣٠
٢۔ قرآن مجید: ١١/١

بتفویض خطاب خانلارخانی[1] وسپه سالاری شده بود، دران باب معروض می دارد که در صغر سن بندگان نواب حضرت جنت آشیانی، رضوان مکانی اعتماد السلطنة القاهرة، اعتماد الخلافة الباهرة، عقده کشای معاقد دین ودولت، سپه آرای معارك فتح ونصرت، افتخار پردلان جان سپار، خلاصه مخلصان وفادار، صاحب الاحتشام، واجب الاحترام خان خانان شجاع الدین محمد منعم بهادر خان بابام را به منصب ارجمند اتالیقی این مخلص سرفراز گردانیده، زمان حل وعقد وعنان قبض وبسط امور دولت، ومکنت فقیر را بید اختیار وحسن اجتهاد آن قدوه خوانین عالی مقدار سپردند ـ چون آن عمده خوانین نامدار درالوس چغتائی از اعاظم اولیاء دولت گردون منزلت بود وآباء عظام واجداد عالی مقام اورا درین دودمان عالی شان حقوق خدمات شائسته وجان سپاریهای بایسته ثابت است، بعد ازان که خان سعید شهید مرحوم مبرور محمد بیرم بهادر خان بدرجه شهادت رسید، خلعت آن منصب والا برقامت استقامت آن واجب الاحترام چست ودرست آمد وبایں خطاب نامی معزز وسامی گشت ـ ودر قانون سلاطین هند مثبت ومرقوم است که یك کس بایں خطاب عالی مشرف می باشد ودائم الاوقات در استعلاء سلطنت بحسن رای خیر اندیش متکفل سر انجام مهام خلافت ومتعهد نظام امور سلطنت بوده از شعور تا سرحد تمییز در دودمانی بایں خطاب گرامی ثانی خیال نکرده ـ واسترضاء خاطر شریف آن اعتضاد الخلافت بر ذمت همت واجب ومتحتم است وبالفعل در احکام وامثله اسم سامی آن اعتماد الخلافت بخطاب خان بابام مرقوم می گردد. امتثالاً للامر العالی وتمهیداً لقواعد المخالصة والمصادقة اگرچه بنا برین بآن رتبه ارجمند ملقب نه شد بتشریفات ومخاطبات دیگر ممتاز می تواندشد. وقبل ازیں هم کسوت

۱ـ ع : خوانسار خوانی

آمال او بطراز اعزاز اعتبار خانی معزز گشته من بعد نیز بعنایات لائقه ورتبه های نامی مشرف خواهد شد. وچون توجه رای عالم آرای جهان کشای بر انجاح مقاصد ومرام او بظهور رسیده وبنظر التفات ملحوظ شده واین معنی معلوم مخلص گردید بیشتر از پیشتر در رفعت شان وعلو مکان او اهتمام خواهد نمود.

امید که این معذرت را، که بصدق وصواب مقرون است، بسمع قبول اصغاء فرمایند وبر عدم امتثال امر عالی محمول نشود. وچون مطمح نظر وقصاری نیت مستدعی بران است که همواره قواعد قصر اخلاص وخیر خواهی مانند ایوان عالی مکان سبع شداد استحکام گیرد ورياض بنيان مصادقت ونیك اندیشی بسان بستان "إرم ذات العماد التی لم یخلق مثلها فی البلاد[۱]" صفت نضارت پذیرد تا بمیامن آن نیت ارجمند فائز آمده صورت محبت ووداد ونسبت خصوصیت بمکانی معمول ومنظور بوده وباعطاف واشفاق مبذول گشته، نسبت بایں مخلص کمال ظهور یابد. متوقع است که مخلص را احیاناً بوصال منشورفائض النور معزز ومشرف ومسرور سازند ورایات عطوفت واعلام ابوت را در میدان اشفاق والطاف مرتفع ساخته همین قاعده‌های مرضیه والطاف نامیه را منظور نظر عالی اثر دارند، از زمره مخلصان صادق الولاء، موفور الصفاء تصور فرموده رياض الطاف وعاطفت را بزلال شفقت ومخلص نوازی طراوت دهند. زیاده ابرام از طریق ادب نیست. جنود ظفر ورود شوکت وکامگاری وعساکر فیروزی مآثر حشمت وبختیاری پیوسته ملازم آن آستان باد ورایات اولیاء دولت آن خلاصه خواقین باعظمت وابهت مظفر ومنصور واعداء مملکت آن نیر آسمان خلاف وحشمت مکسور ومقهور بحق محمد صلی الله علیه وسلم صاحب لواء الحمد فی یوم البعث والنشور.

---

۱. قرآن مجید: ۸۹/۷-۸

(۶۰)

مکتوب شاه طهماسپ بنام جلال الدین محمد اکبر بادشاه

همای همایون فال وطائر مشکین جناح خجسته مآل[۱] اعنی نامه عنبر همامه نگاشته خامه عبهر شمامه منشیان عطاردنشان حضرت سلطنت مرتبت خلافت منقبت، فلك زینت[۲]، ثریا منزلت، فرزند ارجمند عالی مقدار، بادشاه کیوان وقار، گردون اقتدار، شائسته حشمت وشهر یاری، زیبنده اورنگ سلطنت و کامگاری، خسرو صاحب قران، ظفر قرین، خلاصه خاندان اساطیس سلاطیں، معدلت آئین، داور دارای کشور کشای، جمشید خورشید جبین، عالم آرای، نیر جهان افروز اوج عظمت و کامرانی، آفتاب عالم تاب برج عدالت وجهانبانی؛ مثنوی[۳]:

زیبنده تخت بادشاهی منظور عنایت الهی
سلطان سریر عز وتمکیں فرمان فرمای هند تاچیں

المختص بعواطف الملك الاله، شمسا بفلك السلطنة والعدالة والحشمة والاقبال وقطباً لسماء الشوكة والعظمة والنصفة والاجلال، جلال الدین محمد اکبر بادشاه، لازال کواکب اقباله طالعةً علی معارج العز والعلاء ومواکب عزه واجلاله مبسوطةً علی بسیط الغبراء، چون هدهد فرخنده قدم وحمامه فرخ مقدم بر شاخسار دوستان صادق نزول نمود وبرنهال آرزوی محبان موافق فرود آمده جناح نجاح کشود ـ

هدهدی آمد فرو تاج کرامت برسرش
نامه اقبال ودولت بسته بربال وپرش

۱ـ ع : مآل، ندارد
۲ـ ع : رتبت
۳ـ ع : قطعه

نامه چون نامه چین بسته سر کزبوی آن
یافت بوی جان مشام دل چو بکشادم سرش

نامه چون غنچه ناشگفته توی بر توی، مشک بیز وعنبر بوی[1] از گلزار عز وجلال رسید- ودر اطیب اوقات وردیة الفوحات ببوستان جاه وجلال رسید-[2] از رشحات اقلام عطوفت ارقام ریاض محبت موروثی خضرت تازه یافت واز طراوت غمام کلک رافت سلک حدائق خصوصیت قدیمی نضرت بی اندازه پذیرفت. مثنوی:

نگویم نامه کز فردوس باغی　　شب امید را روشن چراغی
بیاضش چورخ خورشید پرنور　　سوادش نور بخش دیده حور
حروفش منتظم چون عقد گوهر　　عروسان سخن را گشته زیور
نموده باوجود مشک ریزی　　بیاض صفحه اش کافور بیزی
سوادش داده از ظلمت نشانی　　درو معنی چو آب زندگانی

از فوحات مضمون محبت مشحونش نسائم مهر ووفا بمشام ارباب ولاء رسیده واز نسمات مکنون مودت مقرونش شمائم صدق وصفا بدماغ جان[3] خلان الوفاء وزید[4]- عبارات لطیفش که مشتمل بر تجدید قواعد دوستی وخلت بود، موجب انشراح صدور شد، واستعارات شریفش که محتوی بر تشئید مبانی یگانگی وخصوصیت بود، باعث انواع ابتهاج وسرور گشت-

قطعه:

مکتوب جانفزای تو آمد بسوی من　　گویا مگر که باد صبا از چمن رسید
یا آسمان بمجمر خورشید عود سوخت　　یا کاروان مشک ز راه ختن رسید

۱- ع : بوی،، ندارد
۲- ع : در اطیب اوقات وردیة الفوحات ببوستان جاه وجلال رسید، ندارد
۳- ع : جان، ندارد
٤- ع : فائض گردید

واز انجا که مقتضی به نسبت ابوت وبنوت واقتضاء قاعدهٔ[1] محبت ومودت است، ملاطفه سامی ومفاوضه نامی آن فرزند ارجمند گرامی را[2] بوظائف تعظیم واکرام وبمراسم تکریم واحترام تلقی نموده در مقابل آن تحفه سلامی که از فوائح آن بساتین مهر ووفا چون ریاض جنان نزهت وطراوت پذیرد وهدیه ثنای که از روائح آن[3] غنچهای مراد وگلهای محبت ووداد شگفتن گیرد، شعر:

سلام یفوح المسك من فوحاته　　　ویاتی شمیم الانس من نسماته

قطعه:

دعائی که چون غنچه مشك بو　　　مشام جهان شد معطر ازو
ثنائی[4] که چون نغمه عندلیب　　　برد از دل بیقرار ان شکیب

بمجلس شریف ومحفل منیف مبلغ ومهدی، متحف ومودی گردانیده. حقا که همگی توجه خاطر محبت کیش وجملگی تعلق ضمیر عطوفت کیش مصروف ومعطوف بر آنست که علاقه خصوصیت وموالات قدیمی ورابطه موالفت ومصادقات صمیمی که فیما بین نواب همایون ما وحضرت اخوت رضوان پناه، سطوت وغفران انتباه[5]، جنت مکان، عیلین آشیان، محمد همایون بادشاه، اسکنه اعلی فرادیس الجنان، ثابت ومحقق بود، نسبت بدان فرزند عالی شان سمت تزاید وتضاعف ومرتبه ازدیاد وترقی پذیرد ویوماً فیوماً اسباب سعادت مندی انتظام وبنیان شدید الارکان پدر وفرزندی استحکام یابد، وچنانچه عهد ومیثاق وارکان محبت ووفاق میان محب صادق الولاء وآن حضرت والا ممهد ومشید بود وحسب موداء حقیقت انتماء "الحب

١- ع : قاعده، ندارد
٢- ع : را، ندارد
٣- ع : آن بساتین مهر ووفاچون ریاض جنان نزهت وطراوت پذیرد وهدیهٔ ثنائی که از روائح آن، ندارد
٤- ع : پیامی
٥- ع : مغفرت دستگاه

یتوراث" بآن سلطان سپهر اعتلاء نیز مانند مبانی "سبعا شدادا[۱]" بنوعی محکم واستوار گردد که آثار آن علی تعاقب الادوار بر صفائح روزگار وصحائف لیل ونهار باقی ماند، ومآثر فیض مواهب آن چون سحاب نیسان بر عموم عالمیان فائض باشد، انشاء الله تعالی.

بعد هذا مرفوع رای جهان آرای که فی الحقیقت مرآت حقائق اشیاء است، آنکه قبل ازین در صحیفه محبت وولا بر صفحه آنها مرقوم شده بود که چون فیما بین این سلسله علیه وآن دودمان رفیع البنیان[۲] خصوصیت ویگانگی بمرتبه اعلی رسیده وحجاب مباینت وبیگانگی بالکلیه مرتفع گردیده، این معنی باعث آن است که منتسبان وامراء عالی شان آن سلسله بلند مکان به نواب همایون ما ومنسوبان وحکام ومتعلقه این جانب بدان حضرت والا جاه، رفیع الشان باز گشت نمایند تا کمال اتحاد وخصوصیت جانبین وغایت وداد وموالفت طرفین ملحوظ اعیان اعتبار ومنظور انظار اولی الابصار گردد - وایالت ونصفت پناه حکومت وجلالت دستگاه، عمدة الحکام الکرام، افتخار اعاظم الامراء الانام (امراء الانام) منجما للایالة والنصفة والاقبال سلطان محمود خان بدین جهات بیك جهتی واخلاص تمام واعتقاد واختصاص مالا کلام بنواب همایون ما اظهار نموده، ومانیز از روی کمال یگانگی وغایت اعتقاد بعطوفت ومهربانی آن نیر برج سلطنت وجهان بانی استدعا از مکارم اخلاق ومحلسن اشفاق آن بادشاه علی الاطلاق فرموده بودیم که ایالت پناه مومی الیه را به رتبه خانسالار خانی وسپه سالاری بلند وممتاز فرمایند - ومنشیان خجسته بیان در طی کتابت عطوفت نشان مرقوم قلم محبت رقم گردانیده اند که حضرت جنت مکانی ایالت ومعدلت پناه، نصفت وجلالت دستگاه، ناظم مناظم مهام

۱- قرآن مجید: ۱۲/۷۸

۲- ع : الشان

سلطنت، كفيل مصالح امور ملك ودولت، شمسا للايالة والعدالة والنصفة والجلالة والاقبال محمد منعم بهادر خان خانان كه از اعاظم اركان دولت قاهره وافاخم اعيان سلطنت باهره آن حشمت وشوكت پناه است وحقوق خدمات بى نهايت دران دولت ابدى الاتصال وسلطنت عديم الانتقال آن ايالت پناه را مثبت است وبدان سبب مراعات خاطر وملاحظه جانب مشار اليه از لوازم (دانسته) بدين لقب سامى ملقب فرمودند۔ ودر قانون سلاطين هند داب وقاعده چنان است كه در كارخانه سلطنت يك كس بدين اسم نامى منسوب مى باشد ۔ بنا برين ايالت پناه، حكومت دستگاه سلطان محمود خان مومى اليه را بدين رتبه عالى ومرتبه عالى مفتحر نه فرمودند ۔ قبل ازين آن حكومت دستگاه سلطان محمود را بلقب اعتبار خانى مشرف گردانيده بودند وتعهد فرموده اند كه توجهات خاطر بادشاهانه وتعلقات ضمير منير خسروانه بارتفاع منزلت ومكان وارتقاء علوا[1] مرتبه شان او مصروف خواهند داشت۔ مترقب ومترصد است كه حسب الموعود مشار اليه را بنوعى مشمول عواطف ومراحم ومنظور انظار اشفاق ومكارم گردانند كه روز برروز پايه قدر ومنزلت او درجه تصاعد وترقى يابد واز ميامن الطاف واعطاف بادشاهانه محسود اكفاء واقران گشته، بر عالميان نهايت يگانگى[2] ودوستى جانبين آشكار وعيان گردد وآثار سفارش نواب همايون ما بابلغ واحسن صورتى درباره مشار اليه بر منصه ظهور جلوه گر باشد، وبهمه وجهى بوفور التفات وعنايات وظهور ملاطفات وتفقدات آن بادشاه والاقدر، عالى مقدار اميد واستظهار داشته، در ميدان نيكو بند گى گوى تفوق ورجحان از اعاظم امراء ذى شان وافاخم حكام رفيع مكان آن دو دمان سلطنت نشان تواند ربود ۔ رجاء واثق

١۔ ع : علو، ندارد
٢۔ ع :يگانگى، ندارد

وامل صادق است که بمقتضی جاذبه محبت اصلی در انعقاد روابط محبت واستحکام قواعد مصادقت کما ینبغی التفات مبذول دارند وپیوسته ریاض محبت موروثی ومودت صمیمی را برشحات زلال عاطفت واشفاق سیراب سازند ـ وهمواره اعلام نصرت واقبال از مواهب تائیدات حضرت ملك متعال بر مفارق مسلمانان سایه گسترباد، بحرمة النون والصاد[١]ـ

(٦١)

مکتوب شاه طهماسپ بنام حمیده بانو بیگم

عالی جناب، عصمت مآب، مخدومه، معصومه، مکرمه، مخدره ومستوره، صالحه، زبیدة الوقت، رابعة الزمان، زبدة العفائف، ادام الله ظلالها، را بعرض دعا که از فرط اخلاص انبعاث یافته باشد، خود را مذکور مجلس عالیه می گرداند وبالتفات خاطر فیاض مستظهر است ـ وبرمرآت ضمیر میز مخفی نخواهد بود که از تاریخی که فیما بین نواب همایون ما وحضرت بادشاه مرحوم عهد محبت ودوستی وعقد اخوت وبرادری اتفاق افتاده[٢]، همواره توجه خاطر عاطر باعتلاء شان آں بادشاه عالی شان گماشته بودند وقصاری همت بلند بر ارتقاء منزلت ومکان آں حضرت من کل الوجوه مصروف داشته تا چنانچه بر عالمیان ظاهر است که از پرتو سلطنت گیتی افروز ومساعدت بخت فیروز چراغ آں دو دمان عالی شان بوسیله ایں اشیاء روشنائی یافته از سرحد خاوران تا اقصاء هندوستان مالك الرقاب عموم سلاطین وفرمان روای جمهور خواقین آں سرزمین گشت ـ وبی تکلف از انجا که مقتضاء سنت اخلاص ویگانگی واقتضاء عزت

١ـ ع : بحرمة النون والصاد، ندارد

٢ـ ع : افتاد

سلطنت است، نسبت بدان عصمت پناه دیگر اندیشها بخاطر خطیر خطور داشت بمقتضاء[1] "الامور مرهونة باوقاتها" هر یك در وقت فرصت از قوت بفعل آید. چون بر حسب تقدیر ملك قدیر، جلت قدرته، که نفاذ هذا المرام بی رابطه ارادت او منتظم ومیسر نیست ونظام کارخانه عالم بی واسطه حکمت ومشیت او ممکن ومتصورنه، بادشاه غفران دستگاه مشار الیه رخت بقا از تنگنای عالم فانی بفسحت سرای جاودانی کشیده، آن جناب (خیال) در سراپرده غیب مستور ومحجوب ماند. وبعد ازان که بعنایت[2] بی غایت الهی چراغ اهل دودمان آن سلسله علیه ودوستان آن خاندان کریمه بنور طلعت آن نقاوه خاندان سلطنت وشهریاری روشنی یافته، اورنگ سلطنت وکامگاری بفر وجود فرزند ارجمند، شهر یار کامگار فلان مشرف شد. بعزة الله تعالیٰ وکفی به شهیداً که از تاریخ که برحسب موداء 'الملك یتوارث' نسبت بدان فرزند سعادت مند قرار یافت، همواره جاذبه عهد محبت مابین وعقد اخوت جانبین همچنان موید وموکد وآن نسبت قویم وآن قاعده مستقیم می بود، وپیوسته مذکور خاطر عاطر آن که یکی از اعیان کارخانه سلطنت را روانه آن صوب صواب انجام فرمائیم که مراسم تعزیت بادشاه مغفرت پناه ولوازم تهنیت ومبارکباد سلطنت وبادشاهی به فرزند کامگار آن عصمت دستگاه قیام نماید. اتفاقاً در خلل این سبب بعضی موانع متعاقب یك دیگر روی نمود که باعث توقیف وتاخیر دران باب شد. وبعد از فراغ آن موانع مذکور امضاء آن نیت فرمودیم وهمدران چند روز کس روانه فرمودیم که سیادت ونقابت نصاب فلان فرستاده ایالت ونصفت پناه، حکومت ومعدلت دستگاه، افتخار اعاظم الامراء والحکام جلالا للنیابة والحکومة والنصفة والاقبال فلان خان

١- ع : ب، ندارد

٢- ع : بجمعیت

وفادار بدرگاه عالم پناه رسید، عرض اخلاص واختصاص خان مشار الیه نموده واز جانب فرزند ارجمند[1] قواعد محبت موروثی تازه کرد ومراسم مخالصت وموافقت به تقدیم رسانید[2]. وچند گاه بدرگاه معلی توقف داشت وهمواره در اعلی مجالس واسنی محافل اشرف اعلی بعز مخالطت نواب همایون استسعاد یافت وبانواع توقیرات وتعظیمات ممتاز وسرفراز بود، تا دریں اوقات تعظیماً لشانکم اورا برتبه عالی سلطانی[3] سرفراز ساخته با وفور تفقدات وانعامات بادشاهانه روانه فرمودیم وخلف السادات والحکام الکرام سید فلاں ولد سیادت ونقابت پناه، اقبال وحکومت دستگاه، اعتماد الدولة العلیه، اعتضاد الحضرة السنیة السلطانیة، جلا الدولة والدین فلاں را، که بحسب ونسب از امراء عظام ومقربان درگاه عرش اشتباه ممتاز است، برسم ایلچی گری فرستادیم که بمراسم تعزیت بادشاه مرحوم وقواعد تهنیت قیام نموده، بنیان محبت ودوستی را بنوعی مستحکم سازد که بعد الیوم دست تصاریف زمان پیرامن ساحت آں نتواں گشت. ترقب که تاسیادت مآب مشار الیه دراں جا باشد به نظر عطوفت ومهربانی متوجه حال او بوده، در مراعات جانب او غایت توجه واهتمام مبذول دارند وزیادت توقف او ننموده بزودی مرخص ساخته روانه ایں صوب گردانند. بزوائد اطناب نرفت. ظل دولت وعصمت بماناد. والدعاء[4]

از آسمان مکرمت قطرات لطف ومرحمت دریغ ندارنا وباعلام اخبار فتوح مجدده خواطر نیاز مندان مستمند را بنوازند. باقی حالات از رقعه که بعالی جناب فلاں مرقوم گشته واضح خواهد شد، مکرراً مصدع نشد. هر روز نیر اقبال از سپهر عزت وجلال فروزاں وهر

١ـ ع : ایشاں، زیاده دارد
٢ـ ع : رساند
٣ـ ع : سلطان، ندارد
٤ـ ع ء تا، ندارد
٥ـ ع : والدعاء، ندارد

شب چراغ دولت در قصر معادت سوزان باد!

(۶۲)

مکتوب اکبر بنام مرزا محمد حکیم هنگام بغاوت شاه ابو المعالی

برادر اعز، ارجمند، ارشد، امجد، سعادت مند، برخوردار، فرمان بردار، منظور انظار، فیض آثار، المختص بعواطف الملك الذی یامر وینهیٰ، ابو المفاخر فلان ابناه الله فی ظل لواذ الدولة الخاقانیة بالعز والعلی باصناف الطاف وعنایات بادشاهی وانواع اعطاف وتفقد لامتناهی عز اختصاص وشرف امتیاز یافته بداند که چون قبائح اعمال وفضائح افعال فلان بکرات ومرات بوضوح پیوسته بواسطه خیالات فاسده خود مستحق قتل وحبس شده بود، بملاحظه منصب سیادت که خود رابآن سعادت عظمیٰ منصوب ومعروف می داشت از خون او درگذشته از برای تادیب وتنبیه اورا چند وقتی مقید ومحبوس داشتیم، وآخر نظر به صلاح حال ومآل او که باوجود آن هم از قید وحبس تنبیه نشده بود واعتماد را نمی شایست، اورا بزیارت حرمین الشریفین فرستادیم، شاید که به برکت آن امکنه متبر که ترك اطواروا وضاع ناپسندیده خود نموده اکتساب اخلاق حمیده نماید۔ او خود بمقتضای فحواء کریمه "ومن یظل الله فلا هادی له[۱]" بصد طرفگی وبد نهادی ازمنه سابقه مراجعت نموده[۲]، بمجرد رسیدن بسرحد گجرات جمعی از لئام انام واوباش ایام که از حدود ممالك محروسه اخراج یافته دران سرحد متفرق وپریشان می گشتند، بخود همراه ساخت وبسان دجال وحرامیان قدم جرأت بر حوالی مملکت گردون بسطت نهاده

۱۔ قرآن مجید: ۱۸۶/۷

۲۔ ع : کرده

می خواست که بطرف فلان گذرد- وبمجرد استماع آن خبر از سپاه ظفر پناه، فیروزی اثر که درشکارگاه در رکاب نصرت انتساب حاضر بودند چند فوج بقلع وقمع اوتعین فرمودیم که اورا تعاقب نماید- بمجرد رسیدن بکنار آب فلان اکثری را از حرامیان ومفسدان که باو پیوسته بودند اسیر ودستگیر کردند وبه معدودی چند ازان مهلکه بدر رفته بجانب کابل شتافت- تصور چنان بود که چون خبث ذات قبیح صفات او بران عزیز برادر ومردم او ظاهر است، اورا مطلقاً راه نخواهد داد، بلك بطریقی که لائق باشد بدست آورده بدرگاه معلی خواهد فرستاد، که باندك فرصتی خبر رسید که به سخن بعضی از کوتاه اندیشان دران سلسله رفیع[1] راه یافته، وپاداش نیکی وبدی افعال باطنی خود بالفعل ظاهر ساخته وجمعی را بقتل رسانیده تا غایت بعضی از فتنه جویان وبدبختان در مقام ازدیاد مواد فتنه وفساد است- از استماع آن خبر نایره حمیت بادشاهی اشتعال پذیرفته، لشکر عظمیٰ از انچه درپایه سریر خلافت مصیر حاضر بودند و از خوانین وسلاطین ولشکریان سرکار فلان که درهمان چند روز فتح ولایت ککر نموده مستعد ومهیا بودند، بکومك ومدد آن عزیز برادر تعین فرمودیم که بعون عنایت ربانی بدفع ورفع او امداد نموده ساحت آن ولایت را از خبث وجود آن مفتن مردود وسایر ناپاکان پاك سازند، وبه تقویت امر وتمشیت مهمات آن برادر حمیده سیر پردازند، که دران اثناء بعرض رسید که بمیامن تائیدات نامتناهی که شامل دولت بی علت شهنشاهی است، وفودی بعدد رسید وآن وفلان معذب ومعاقب گرفتار گردید- این معنی موجب شکر وستائش حضرت مهیمن بسیار بخشایش گشت- امید که تانفخ صور وهنگام نشور اعداء این دودمان رفیع المکان بهمین دستور مغلوب ومقهور گشته، احبای دولت قویم البنیان مظفر ومنصور باشند ومهمات آن حدود بر حسب اراده دولت خواهان نظام وانتظام یابد- ومی باید که

۱- ع : منیع

آن برادر سعادت مند همگی همت بلند وجملگی توجه خاطر ارجمند به تقویت اعمال ستوده مآل وتمنیت امانی وآمال خود مقصور ومحصور شناخته، پیوسته بلوازم یك جهتی ودولت خواهی ومراسم حق گذاری وفرمان برداری اشتغال نماید۔ واگر جهت دفع عوارض امور ورفع غوامض شرور کومك ومدد احتیاج باشد، کیفیت را عرضه داشت نماید که لشکر تعین شده مستعد ومهیا است، بلا توقف فرستاده شود۔ دریں باب اهتمام تمام داشته مساهله واهمال نگذارد وارباب فتنه وفساد را من بعد بگرد خود راه ندهد۔ وچگونگی حالات وواقعات را یوماً فیوماً معروض داشته مقاصد ومدعائی که بوده باشد درج نماید که بشرف اجابت وانجام مقرون خواهد شد۔

(٦٣)

مکتوب بنام یکی از ملوك

عالی جناب، مملکت آیات، نیابت پناه، حکومت دستگاه، ملك وملوك زاده، نامدار، موید، مظفر، منصور، برخوردار، صاعد مصاعد دولت، عارج معارج ملت، سواره کره خاك، هم عنان توسن افلاك، سپه آرای ملك وملت، گردون کیش عالم فیروزی، غره جبین آفرینش، باصره اهل دانش وبینش، شیر شکار، اسفندریار روزگار رزم وپیکار۔

قطعه:

آن که در ملك ایں زمان کار سلیماں می کند
چوں سلیمان از مسلمان دفع دیواں می کند
اندر آن میدان یکدم قتل اعداء کرد ورفت
ایں چین را آسمان صد سال مهمان می کند

اعز الله انصاره واعوانه واعلی فی الخافقین قدره وشانه، فلان را قوافل دعوات استجابت آیات همرکاب کاروان لیل ونهار مبلغ ومرسل می دارد وبر ورود اخبار نجابت ودلاوری وآثار شجاعت وبهادری آن جوان بخت کامگار که ناسخ همه کار رستم واسفندیار است، مواجب شکر پروردگار به تقدیم می رساند وامیدوار است که جنود توفیقات الهی ووفود تائیدات نامتناهی در سفر وحضر همدم وهمعنان باشد، وبحکم "توجه حیث شئت فانك منصور" روی همت همایون بهر جا آورند اقبال تلقی نماید وعزیمت مبارك بهر جانب که مصروف سازند فتح ونصرت بطریق استعجال پیش آید۔

باد یارب دائما در سایۂ ملك وملك

رزم خواه وداد گستر مال بخش وملك گیر

هر آئینه از طریق مرضیه آن حمیده خصال، ستوده افعال چنان سزد که یك لحظه اوقات قدسی ساعتش به شیوه ملاعب وملاهی آلوده نگردد بلکه جامع همت عالی نهمت بر توسیع دائره حکومت وتفبیع (تفسیح) عرصه دولت مقصور ومحصور۔ آن خود چه مراد بود کو جست نیافت۔ روز گار سعادت آثارش از سر تیقظ واحتیاط بضبط مهام وتدبیر نسق مصالح سلطنت واسعاف حوائج جمهور مصروف شود تا آثار مفاخرش طراز تواریخ ملوك رفیع مقدار ودیباچه مآثر حکام گردون اقتدار گردد۔ ومن الله العون والتائید۔ زیاده اطناب موجب ملال خاطر خجسته فال است۔ مصرعه:

عمرت دراز باد برین ختم شد سخن۔

(٦٤)
مکتوب بنام یکی از ملوك

نفائس دعواتی که از نسائم عباراتش شمائم اخلاص واعتقاد

بمشام جان رسد وخوالص تحیاتی که از فوائد اشاراتش[1] روائح اختصاص واعتماد بوضوح پیوندد، منبی از کمال محبت ویگانگی ومبنی برفرط مصادقت ویك رنگی ایثار مجلس رفیع ومحفل بدیع عالی حضرت، گردون بسطت، فلك رفعت، انجم سپاه، فلك پیش گاه، ملك دستگاه، نصفت وعظمت انتباه، نوئین اعظم کامران، سلاله سلاطین وافر الاحسان، خاقان اعدل کامیاب، قا آن اکرم حشمت مآب، ضابطه اقطار الامصار بالقوة الظاهرة، رابطه اطراف الآفاق بالدولة الباهرة، ناصب رایات الفتح والظفر، رافع الویة العدل من زمرة البشر، واضع قوانین العدالة والجلالة، قامع افانین البدعة والضلالة، اردشیر شیر مصاف، نوشیروان عالم عدل وانصاف، غضنفرفر، بهرام رام، منوچهر دارا مقام، الموید بتائیدات (التائیدات) العلیة الجلیة من عند الله الرحیم الرحمان، رشید السلطفة والجلالة والخلافة والنصفة والعطوفة والرافة والحشمة والشوکة والعز والاقبال فلان، خلّد الله تعالیٰ فی مراضیه ملکه وسلطانه وایّد علی صحائف الادوار بره واحسانه، اتحاف واهداء می دارد وبجوامع نیت وهمگی امنیت مستدعی تزاید ارتقاء بمدارج اقبال ومتمنی افزونی اعتلاء بمعارج اجلال بوده ومی باشد "انه علی ما یشاء قدیر"۔

بعد هذا مشهود رای عالم آرای ومکشوف ضمیر خورشید جلا می گرداند که چون اقتضاء قدرت کامله الهی ومقتضاء حکمت شامله نامتناهی ذات فرخنده صفات وعنصر خجسته سمات سلاطین عظمت آئین را، که اساطین بنیان کشورستانی اند، وسیله نظام احوال عالم وانتظام بنی آدم ساخته وآسائش جهان وجهانیان وآرامش عالم وعالمیان را در ضمن انفتاح ابواب محبت وموانست وافتتاح اسباب مودت ومصادقت میانه خواقین گردون سریر وسلاطین باشکوه وتدبیر

۱ـ ع : آستانش

پرداخته، وچون ظهور مواد محبت واخلاص وشمول بواعث مودت واختصاص که این محب را بدان زبده سلاطین پناه ثابت است بوجوه وانواع که برای آفتاب شعاع واضح ومبرهن است۔ چنانچه در سوابق ایام مکرر بارسال رسائل مصادقت فرجام بنیان موالات واساس مواخات را تمهید وتشئید داده بود واز جانب خدام ذوی الاحتشام[1] نیز ابواب تفقد وتودد برروی روزگار محب صداقت آثار مفتوح ومکشوف گشته، بمیامن این مناسبات ومرابطات در باب مواد وثوق رجاء در کمال داشت ووارد معاقدی که در طرفین ووقائعی که در جانبین بسنوح حوادث ونوائب طاری گردد بموافقت ومعاضدت یك دیگر مرتفع شود۔ چون آن شاهزاده عالم وعالمیان بامداد بخت دولت خواه قدم بر فراز اورنگ سروری نهاد، بمزید حشمت وابهت از سلاطین زمان وخواقین دوران امتیاز یافته اند، اعانت وامداد ایشان واسطه افزونی اسباب عقیدت واخلاص مخلصان ومعتقدان گردد۔ انچه بالفعل بوقوع آمده آنست که برادر عزیز فلان از اطاعت جد امجد خود، که شرعاً وعرفاً بر ذمه او لازم ومتحتم است، انحراف جسته باخراج وتاراج وانواع اهانت که هریك از اقبح اعمال است، راضی شده وحقوق الطاف جد جلیل الاوصاف را نسیاً منسیاً انگاشته۔ وبا آنکه از اولاد واحفاد خاندان رفیع الشان تیموری اصغراست، قانون وقاعده که از قدیم الایام در سلاطین ذوی الاحتشام سیما این دودمان عالی مقام منظور ومعمول بوده تغیر داده خطبه وسکه بنام خود کرده وباوجود حضرت برادر کلان این محب که فرمان فرمای تمام سواد اعظم هندوستان اند، باین طور بی ادبی اقدام بنموده۔ وبررای عقده کشای مخفی ومستور نخواهد بود که تادیب وتنبیه خوردان بر کلان در اسالیب سلطنت وقوانین خلافت امری مقرر است وحفظ ضوابط ومراتب، که سلاطین ماضی وضع نموده

۱۔ ع : ذو الاحتشام

ودستور العمل کرده اند، در قواعد مملکت داری قاعده معتبر۔ لاجرم خاطر بر تادیب وتنبیه ونگاه داشت قانون وقاعده قدیم قرار یافته۔ وامیدوار است.که بعنایت الهی وتوجه خاطر آن نقاوه دودمان خلافت تسکین نائره خلاف ونقار باسهل وجوه میسر شود۔ وچون بنیان اخلاص ومحبت را بدان رفیع منزلت بواسطه معمار توفیق ووسیله مهندس تائید بمرتبه ممهّد ومشیّد نساخته که به صرصر حوادث ومنجنیق نوائب احتمال اختلال آن راه توان داد۔ ترصد امداد واعانت از خدام بلند مقام درباب تنبیه مشار الیه بوده وهست۔ یحتمل که درین باره از ملازمان اعانت جسته بارسال رسائل ووسائل اقدام نموده باشد، لیکن بر عقلاء واضح است که رعایت آداب وفا ووفاق وسعادت در انفاق صفاء واتفاق بر وجهی که لائق تواندبود از پیش هر کسی متمشی نمی شود وایضاً نسبت اخلاص ومحبت وتحریك سلسله اختصاص وموافقت فقیر ازوی بمدتهای مدید سبقت گرفته بود، بواسطه آن چشم داشت بسیار است۔ مامول ومسئول از مکارم اوصاف آنکه اگر مومی الیه از خدام ذوی الاحتشام طلب معاونت کند چون اطوار وکردار او از نهج صواب وسداد دور ومهجور است، که اعتماد را نمی شاید، التماس اورا بدرجه قبول مقبول ندارند بلکه مخلص متخصص را، که در طریق محبت وموافقت ومنهاج مستقیم مخالصت وموافقت چون صبح دویم صادق دم ومانند قطب فلك ثابت قدم است، به نظر تفقد وتودد منظور داشته نوعی فرمایند که این اراده از حیّز قوت به فعل آید وابواب این مقصود بامداد ایادی خدام سپهر احتشام کشاید۔ تا زمان ملاقات فائقة السعادات حدائق اخلاص وبساتین اختصاص را از ترشح ینابیع التفات واعتناء سرسبز وسیراب گردانیده، بمهمات لائقه ممنون سازند که شرائط وداد ولوازم اتحاد تقدیم یابد۔ چون عرض مختصر بود بزوائد اطناب نکشود وبردعاء مدعا ختم نمود۔ همواره آفتاب سلطنت از

مشرق خلافت طالع ونیر خلافت بر سپهر سلطنت لامع باد!

(٦٥)

مکتوب بنام یکی از ملوك

معالی حضرت، گردون بسطت، فلك رفعت، بهرام صولت، مشتری سعادت، خورشید منزلت، جمشید مرتبت، عدالت پناه، نصفت دستگاه، واضع قوانین النصفة والعدالة، قامع افانین البدعة والضلالة، فریدون فر، کیخسرو، منوچهر تدبیر، اعظم سلاطین زمان، اکرم خواقین دوران، المنصور بتائیدات (بالتائیدات) النازلة من السماء وبالتوفیقات[1] الواردة علی الاعداء، برهان ملوك الامم، عامر البلاد بآثار الجودوالکرم، ناصب الویة الفتح والظفر، هادم ابنیه الفتنة والضرر، حامی حوزة الاسلام، ماحی آثار الکفر والضلال، قطعه:

خاقان عالی مرتبت بهرام کیوان منزلت

آفتاب اوج عزت خسرو عالی تبار

در حریم ملك ودولت کامیاب و کام بخش

بر فراز تخت شوکت کامران و کامگار

الموفق بالتوفیقات[2] السنیة والتاتیدات البهیة من عند الله المستعان، شمساً بفلك[3] السلطنة والخلافة بدوام دولته وسعادته ـ محب صادق الولاء، خالص الوفاء قواعد اخلاص ومحبت بمعاقد اختصاص ومودت ممهّد وموکّد می دارد ورابطه اعتقاد وصفاء نیت را بضوابط اعتقاد و نقاء طویت موسّس ومشیّد می شمارد، بامناسبات ذاتی ومراسلات که در این مرتبه وضوح ودرجه رسوخ دارد، به تعاقب

١ـ ع : بتوفیقات

٢ـ ع : بتوفیقات

٣ـ ع : للفلك

شهور واعوام وتواتر ليالی وايام پيوسته تضاعف مواد سلطنت وجهان بانی وترادف اسباب خلافت و کشورستانی واستحصال مقاصد ومطالب واستکمال مرام ومآرب آن سلطنت مناب را از حضرت واهب العطايا آمل وسائل بوده ومی باشد- وبحمد الله که آثار آن يوماً فيوماً در اقطار اشتهار وانتشار يافته وانوار آن ساعة فساعة بر مفارق سکنه بلاد تافته خصوصاً از فتح امجد که بعنايت حضرت احد صمد واعانت بخت مويد مزين روزگار سعادت آثار گشته، آن مقدار فرح وسرور روی نمود که شرح شمه ازان تقرير بيان وتحرير بنان متعذر است واميدوار است که امداد جنود توفيقات نامتناهی اوان استقبال باضعاف ماضی وحال بوده، هميشه کوکب فتح ونصرت از آسمان مراد طالع شود وپيوسته نير ظفر وشوکت بر شهر مقصود لامع گردد، بمنه وکرمه ونعمه وافضاله!

بعد هذا مشهود رای عالم آرای ومکشوف ضمير مهر انجلاء می گذراند که چون در خلا وملا جوامع نيت ومنيت بر رفع اساس محبت وموالات وتشئيد مبانی مودت ومواخات مقصود ومحصور بوده ومی باشد، وارادہ ادعيه باطن وظاهر آنست که صيت علاقات وآوازه صداقت جانبين در اطراف جهان بمسامع عالميان رسيده از ميامن آن اقبال در گلشن آمال شگفتن گيرد ومعاندان را از تشاهد آن خار حسرت در سينه ادبار نهفتن پذيرد- واگر باقتضاء روزگار ومقتضاء سپهر دوّار معاقدی در امور سلطنت وخلافت درجانبين روی نمايد، بمعاضدت طرفين ومعاونت فيما بين مرتفع گردد وآثار دل پذير ونتائج ارجمند متفرع گشته، دستور العمل سلاطين نصرت آئين وخواقين معدلت قرين شود، تا انجام خاطر متعلق است که اگر بعنايت الهی در طرفين بساتين دولت وحدائق سلطنت به ثمرات اعقاب واولاد بارور گردد وصلاح حال اشرف اسلاف وسايه موانست مناسبت اخلاف اعراف شده، آثار آن تا انقراض زمان بر صفحات دوران ثبت ومرقوم

ماند۔ بناءً علیه درین ولا معتمد السلطنت، قدیم الخدمت فلان را، که از ملازمان قدیمی ومعتقدان صمیمی است، بملازمت فرستاده شد که حقائق امور واحوال را کماهی معروض گرداند۔ ترقب وترصد از مکارم اخلاق آن که همگی همت والا نهمت بر امضاء این مرام مصروف ومعطوف فرمایند ودر تشئید وتمهید بنیان مصادقت وموافقت چنان ملتفت شوند واساس محبت ومرافقت را بنوعی استحکام دهند که دست صوارف زمان پیرا من ساحت آن نتواند گشت واندیشه نقص وفتور در سویداء دل هیچ آفریده نتواند گشت۔ همواره ریاض وفا ووفاق را از ترشح حیاض صفا واتفاق نامی وناضر داشته بخدمات لائقه منت نهنند که شرائط لازمه اخلاص واعتقاد به تقدیم رساند۔ همواره نسائم فتوحات نامیات از مهب الطاف حضرت واهب العطیات بر روزگار فرخنده آثار در وزیدن باد بحرمة النبی وآله الامجاد۔

(٦٦)

مکتوب بنام یکی از ملوك

عالی جناب، سلطنت مآب، خلافت انتساب، حشمت شعار، ابهت آثار، قدوة السلاطین العظام، زبدة الحکام الکرام بین الانام، المستعین من مواهب الملك العلام، معز السلطنة والرفعة والحشمة والشوکة والابهة والعز والاقبال فلان را شرائف دعوات نامیات وظرائف تحیات وافیات اتحاف واهداء گردانیده مکشوف ضمیر منیر آن که چون فلان اطوار خود را تغیر داده خبط دماغ پیدا کرده باکثر دولت خواهان درگاه عرش اشتباه در مقام عداوت شده بود وبواسطه صفات ذمیمه در دلها مردود واز خاطرها مطرد گشته بود۔ ودولت خواهان این آستان ملائك آشیان بدین جهت مایوس بودند۔ چنانچه بآن خلاصه

سلطنت همه وقت اظهار اتحاد ویك جهتی می کرد وکتابتی که نوشته برحاشیه آں مهر کرده بود۔ وامثال ایں اعمال که تفصیل آں بطول انجامد از مشارالیه بوقوع می آمد۔ بنابراں اورا از نظر کیمیا اثر انداخته رتبه خانی وعلم ونقاره ازو گرفته اند۔ وایں معنی موجب امیدواری دولت خواهاں ویك جهتاں گشته۔ سلطنت مآب، شوکت انتساب فلاں وفلاں که مولانا مذکور نادولتخواهی نموده بود، بعده آنکه فوجهای برسر او رفتند وولایتی که بتصرف او بوده بدولت خواهی سپرده معلوم کردند که در طریق اخلاص راسخ بوده مشارالیه بواسطه غرض خود ایں نوع خاطو نشان کرده بود۔ مجدداً رعایت فرموده بعواطف وعوارف ممتاز ساخته اند۔ وبحمد الله که از هیچ ممر دغدغه تفرقه نیست ومهمات بر حسب اراده نظام وانتظام دارد۔ وچوں آں سلطنت پناه دم صدق وولاء بایں دولت عظمی می زند، لازم نمود که سوانح حالات را اعلام نماید۔ وظیفه محبت وطریقه مودت آں که آں خلافت مآب سوانح حالات ومهمات را اعلام می نموده باشد وعهد وشرطی که بین الجانبین بوقوع پیوسته در تمهید وتشئید آں کوشند که انشاء الله تعالیٰ ازیں جانب امری که موجب نقض عهد خود بود واقع نخواهد شد۔ ونخبة الامراء والسلاطین فلاں چنانچه فرزند ایشاں است ایں جانب نیز کمال شفقت ومهربانی نسبت بحال او مرعی داشته وخواهد داشت وبه فلاں بهر طریق محبت ومودت مسلوك خواهد بود۔ مادام که از جانب ایشاں امری ظاهر نشود ازیں جانب بغیر نیکوئی چیزی بوقوع نخواهد آمد۔ خاطر انور من کل الوجوه جمع داشته همواره دراں مقام باشند که آثار دولت خواهی ایشاں زود ودیر ظاهر شود ونتائج آں بروزگار فرخنده آثار دیده گرداند که هر آئینه درمیان دوست ودشمن سرفراز خواهد بود ۔ چوں مختصر بود زیاده اطناب نرفت۔

عرائض

(٦٧)

عریضه بخدمت بادشاه متضمن بر شفاعت محمد خان فاوقی والی اسیر

تا معمار کارخانه قضا اساس قصر عالم را بقوائم "إن الله يامر بالعدل والاحسان[١]" از شائبه قصور محروس دارد ومدبر قوی قدر طبائع اشراف بنی آدم را بنفاذ فرمان مطاع "يا ايها الذين آمنوا كونوا قوامين بالقسط[٢]" از ارتکاب ظلم وجور مایوس، همواره بناء قصر سلطنت وفضاء سرای خلافت مقر سلاطین نامدار ومستقر حکام ذوی الاقتدار باد! بعد از اداء ماینبغی للعباد من رواتب[٣] الطاعة والانقياد ومايجب على العباد من وظائف العبودية وخلوص الاعتقاد، بر آئینه گیتی نما منطبع می سازد که درین وقت فرمان همایون ومثال سعادت واقبال وفرخنده طغراء امانی وآمال که از دیوان قضا جریان مصحوب جناب افتخار الاشباه والامثال، مقبول الاوصاف والافعال، الممتاز بمزيد التربية بين الاقران فلان نامزد دولت خواهان صادق العقیده فرموده بودنده، بمراسم تبجیل ولوازم توقیر متلقی گردید وبانواع استمالتهاء بادشاهانه واصناف عنایات خسروانه، که از فحاوی عبارات ومطاوی اشاراتش مستفاد بود، مطمئن القلب ومستمال البال گشته مستعد اقدام بانجام مرام ومتوجه انقیاد بمایستفاد من مدلول مضامین الفرامین بود که از جانب عالی جناب محمد خان فاروقی که کابراً عن کابرٍ متصدی ایالت

١- قرآن مجید: ٩٠/١٦

٢- قرآن مجید: ١٣٥/٤

٣- ع: روابط

ولایت برهانپور اسیر است، مکاتبات رسید۔ ملخص مضامین همه مبنی بر ارادت سعادت تثبت باذیال عاطفت والتفات نواب عنایت مآب ومنبی از حسن عقیدت بکمال اشفاق ومکارم اخلاق معتکفان سده سدره جناب بود، چنانچه شمه ازاں از عریضه خان مشارالیه بر مقربان مجلس اعلی لائح خواهد شد۔ چوں میانه ایں دولت خواه وعالی جناب مشارالیه رابطه انسی والفت قدیمی بود، بنا براں دست عجز وافتقار دراں موقف معلی برداشته وزبان عجز وانکسار بشفاعت مشارالیه کشوده، التماس می نماید که اگر به نهجی که شعار جمعی از سلاطین سابقه وخواقین سالفه، که در مقام جهانگیری وصدد گیتی ستانی بوده اند، خصوصاً اجداد مکرمت شعار، معدلت آثار آنحضرت که کتابت کاخ سلطنت برقوم مناقب ومآثر ایشاں محلی است وعصابه تاج خلافت برسوم محامد شان معلی، موداء کریمه "فاعفوا واصفحوا حتی یاتی الله بامره[1]" را نصب العین رای جهاں آرای ساخته، هفوات اضطراری وعثرات بی اختیاری ویرا بمراحم ذاتی ومراسم مکارم جبلی مقابله فرمایند واز سرلطف وعنایتهاء بی پایان خویش نواب کامیاب را اشارت نمایند که دست تصرف از محقر ولایت او بازداشته در صدد ازدیاد عنایت وتضاعف رعایت باشند، هر آئینه اقتداء باجداد واسلاف طیب الاعراق فرموده باشند۔ قطعاً من جنس هذا الامر الجمیل عند الصمد الجلیل انقیاد قلوب واصطیاد نفوس بسی از ولات وحکام اطراف واکناف نموده، امید که ایں معنی بر کمال خلوص ودولت خواهی محمول افتد وصورت ایں ملتمس مزین بحسن قبول گردد وبنوعی دیگر که در خاطر اشرف اعلی مضمر ومرکوز باشد بهر وجه که امر لازم الامضاء نفاذ یابد وجهت قصد ونیت جز اطاعت وامتثال امر دیگر نخواهد بود۔ والامر اعلی۔

١۔ قرآن مجید: ٢/١٠٩

(٦٨)

عریضه در اعتذار

همیشه آفتاب دولت روز افزون حضرت سلطنت شعار، معدلت آثار ماه سپهر جاه وجلال، مهر فلك سعادت واقبال، صاحب مسند خلافت وشهر یاری، وارث[1] اورنگ سلطنت و کامگاری، همای همایون بخت سپهر آستان فریدون فر[2]، خسرو جمشید تخت کیخسرو نشان، بیت:

نظم عالی مطلع دیوان جود
ناظم دین ونظام وملك وشاه بحر وبر

از مطلع سعادت ازلی طالع واز مشرق عنایت لم یزلی لامع باد! داعی دولت خواه دعای، که نور اجابت از آسمان اقبال باستقبال آن شتابد، وثنائی که پرتو نور اشعه آن بروزنه قلب صادقان وفا کیش تابد، تحفه مجلس گردون اساس بادشاهی وهدیه عتبه سپهر مرتبه سلطنت پناهی ساخته، از روی فرط خجالت وتشویر بیان عذر تقصیر خدمت می نماید وبزبان شوق واخلاص این ترانه می سراید، بیت:

چون قدر دولت وصل ترا ندانستم
بداغ هجر که می سوزم این سزای من است

اما حق جل وعلا به حقیقت حال واقف است که اختیار جدائی از موکب همایون مرضی خاطر محزون نبود بلکه بواسطه تلافی وملاحظه خاطر بعضی واجب مرضی، که استرضاء ایشان بحسب شرع ودین از متحتمات مهمات[3] بود، بآن معنی ارتکاب واقدام نمود ـ الحمد

۱ـ شهریاری، وارث، ندارد
۲ـ ع : عظمت ونامداری
۳ـ ع : مهمات، ندارد

لله كه به يمن اقبال نواب كامياب شرف رضا واسترضاء ايشان را دريافت وبدولت نواب بى حضورى ايشان فى الجمله تخفيفى يافت وباتفاق همگنان وسائر اخوان وفرزندان دعاى دولت ابد پيوند، كه برهمگنان واجب است، به تقدير (تقديم) رسانيده. وانشاء الله در اوائل شهر فلان جهت ازدياد فتح وفيروزى خدام سپهر احتشام بختم احاديث بخارى اشتغال خواهد نمود. همين توقع از وفور عنايت بادشاهانه كه داعى نيك انديش وفاكيش خود را از حواشى ضمير آفتاب تاثير محو نسازند كه تازمان سعادت مجالست مجلس همايون بهشت آئين بامثله مطاعه مشتمل بر لطائف عواطف خسروانه سرفراز سازند. وعرض حال كه به تقرير دل پذير بندگى فلان استقصاء واستفسار آن خواهد نمود بسمع رضا اصغاء فرموده غايت اهتمام آن دريغ نه فرمايند . زياده گستاخى حد ادب نيست.

الهى تاجهان را آب ورنگ است
فلك را دور، گيتى را درنگ است
ممتع دارش از ملك وجوانى
زهر چيزش فرون ده زندگانى

(٦٩)

عريضه بخدمت بادشاه

بسوى آستانش گر رسى اى باد گوازما[١]
كه ماگم گشتگان مرديم تشنه در بيابانها

دعائى كه از نيم طلوعش شميم اجابت فائح واز[٢] نسيم ورودش

١ـ ع : ببوسى آستان كعبه اررسى ازما
٢ـ ع : شميم اجابت فائح واز، ندارد

نسیم اجابت لائح باشد، تحفه مجلس خلد آئین وهدیه انجمن سپهر تمکین گردانیده، عنان قلم از صوب تکلفات رسمی وتعلقات عادی مصروف داشته، بوادی عرض شکستگی ونامرادی باز می گردد۔ کامگارا، عالم مدارا، سپهر اقتدارا، اوقات این مخلص بعد از وظائف عبودیت الهی ودعای دوام دولت شاهنشاهی نامتناهی، خلافت پناهی بشکر نعمت بی زوال وقناعت بر رزق مقسم وشکر انه، شرف اشتغال مطالعه علوم، که درپناه معدلت اقبال وسایه عز وجلال آنحضرت میسر گشته، جاریست۔ والحق مردم عجزه[1] فلان به یمن دولت ومعدلت گردون مدار بسی آسوده حال وازسلوك متصدیان محال فلان بسیار شاکر اند، بمرتبه که فوقی متصور نیست، وبیشك آثار فوائد این معنی بروزگار خجسته آثار دولت ابد پیوند عائد واسباب حصول مطالب دینی ودنیوی مضاعف ومتزاید خواهد گشت۔ الحمد لله علی ماهداکم بالعدل والاحسان وانعم علی المومنین فی ظلالکم ببرکات الهدایة والعرفان والصلوة علی محمد وعترته ائمة الحق والایقان۔

(٧٠)

عریضه در جواب فرمان

هدهد نوازش خسروانه که از سباء قبول برطائر جان بیچاره به پروبال احسان پرواز نموده بود، در همایون زمانی سایه عاطفت گسترانیده صفیر این نظم دل پذیر بگوش هوش رسانید که، بیت:

چون رای بادشاه نشاط شکار کرد

اول به لطف صید دل روزگار کرد

وچون سرپنجه شاهین محبت ومخلب عقاب دل بستگی در

١۔ ع : عجزه، ندارد

نگاهداشت این ناز ونیاز تعلق وتصلب تمام داشت، کبوتر دل مانند نیم بسمل در اضطراب آمده گفت، بیت:

سوار چابك ابرو کمان تیر انداز

بر آهوی دل ما چرخ می بر اندازد

اما شهباز بلند پرواز همت دوال امتثال بر طبق انقیاد زده، سمند اهتزاز وشادمانی در میدان نشاط و کامرانی راند ودرشگار گاه[1] دولت وفضای صحرای دل کشای رغبت بهوای صید التفات خاطر شاهانه طوطی بیان وبلبل زبان آواز استبشار بر کشید که، قطعه:

دولت رفته دیرین بسر آمد بازم

شاه من چون بعنایت طلبیدی بازم

منم آن باز که بی شمع جمالت شب[2] وروز

هم چون پروانه دل سوخته پردازم

ومع ذالك امیدوار است که این باز حقیر را که بردست ایلچی سایه سریر اعلی فرستاده شد، برسم محافظت باز بدین فقیر سپرند تا شرف انتظام در سلك قوشچیان درگاه عالم بیابد وهیچ جانور محل شماتت نیابد. قطعه:

بازم از دست اگر رفت نشود شاد رقیب

باشد آن روز که از لطف دهد شه بازم

دارم امید که باز از نظر شاه افتد

همچون اشك آن شد از روی حسد غمازم

١ـ ع : کبوتران

٢ـ ع : شب، ندارد

(٧١)

عریضه در اظهار آرزوی حج وذکر موانع راه

اتـانـی کتـاب زاد مـورده قـدری
کـمـا جـاء وحـی الـلـه فی لیـلة الـقـدر
کـلک او شـاخ نبـاتـی شد که از هندوستان
بهـر نـقـل طـوطـی جـان شکرستـان آمده
طرفه مرغی شد که منقارش چو در دریای قاز
غـوص کـرده عـالـمی پر در ومرجان آمده
کان نهاده سنگ بردل دیدها پر خون چون لعل
هـر کـجـا ابـر کف او گـوهـر افشان آمده

وهـر آئینـه آفتـاب عـالم تاب هر چند در مدارج ارتفاع صعود بیش نـمـایـد عـمـوم افاضه انوارش نسبت باهر نشیب وفراز زیاده آید۔ بیت:

اگـر دیـوار درویـش اسـت کـوتـاه
بـلـنـد اسـت آفتـاب الـحـمـد لـلـه

برحصول مآرب سنیه ومطالب علیه که از فیض فضل "یوتیه من یشاء[١]" روز بـروز مـفـتـوح روز گـار سعادت آثار می گردد، اقامت شکر وسپاس مهیمن مراد بخش واجب می شناسد۔

خوش کرد یاوری فلك از روز داوری۔
فحمداً لله ثم حمداً لله۔

بـعـد، از اشـارت دل پـذیـر کـه خامه لطائف صریر دبیر روشن ضمـیـر دربـاب تـوجـه ایـں فقیر حقیر ارزانی داشته بودند، موجب مواد

١۔ قرآن مجید، ٧٣/٣

استظهار واعتقاد شد۔ حقا که همگی همت متوجه احرام زیارت بیت الله الحرام واحراز دولت آستان منزلت است وجملگی خاطر دربند آنکه هر چند زود تر کشتی شوق بی پایاں درعمان توکل جریان یافته بکعبه نیل وصال، که خلیل اخلاص در حرم اختصاص برفع اساس آن فائز گشته، وصال یابد وسعادت قصوی تلاقی واستیناس بحصول پیوندد۔ وبه حقیقت تیسر اسباب این دولت را واسطه ابقاء ذکر جمیل ووسیله لقاء اجر جزیل می داند وفتح ابواب این امنیت را ذریعه مباهات ومفاخرت وموجب ناموس دنیا وآخرت می شناسد "لتسألنّ یومئذ عن النعیم[1]"۔ اما سبب تلاطم امواج بحار وحوادث روزگار بحکم "وکان ورائهم ملك یاخذ کل سفینة غصباً[2]" بر تصدیق مخاطرات طریق شاهد صدق است، مجدداً مانعی بر راه این آرزو افتاد که چوں سائر آرزوها نداء حرمان در اطراف واکناف ممالك دل وجان روداد، شعر: تجری الریاح بمالا تشتهی السفن، لا محاله، شعر:

کیف الوصول الی سعاد ودونها
قلل الجبال ودونهن حتوف
والرجل حافیة ومالی مرکب
والکف صفر والطریق مخوف

بیت:

نه دوری دلیل صبوری بود — که بسیار دوری ضروری بود

وهر چند دراں باب کوشش رفت وهر گونه سعی بلیغ مبذول افتاد، به هیچ طریق مفید نیامد ومطلقاً بجاء نرسید۔ "وماشاء الله کان ومالم یشا لم یکن"۔ ومع ذلك بمقتضی "الامور مرهونة باوقتها" چوں هر حکمی موقوف اثری وهر کاری مرهون وقتی است، بتصور "لعل الله یحدث بعد ذلك امراً[3]" مترصد اقبال خجسته مآل است که اگر تمادی

١۔ قرآن مجید، ١٠٢/٨
٢۔ قرآن مجید، ١٨/٧٩
٣۔ قرآن مجید، ٦٥/١

امل وتراخی اجل هم عنانی کند وحسن توفیق الهی معاونت نموده طوائف اهل ایمان را امید امن وامان ونوید "یبشّرهم ربهم برحمة منه ورضوان[١]" بخشد وصداء صلاء[٢] "ادخلوها بسلام آمنین[٣]" بسمع جمع پریشان رساند، پای عزیمت در رکاب مسارعت هم عنان فرسان صبا وشمال متوجه این کعبه آمال گردد۔ مطلع:

کزین بهتر نه پندارم مرادی در جهان باشد۔

الهم حقق هذه المنیة۔ درین وقت که مورد صحیفه نیاز عازم احراز آن عطیه کبری شد، صحبت اورا از بضاعت مزجات دعا خالی نگذاشت واگرچه مناسب چنان نمود که درین باب متصدی اطنات گردد اما بواسطه استعجال او مجال آن که در معرض بیان آید نبود۔ مسئول از کمال عواطف بیدریغ آن که بعفو واغماض مقابل گردد۔ والله المستعان وعلیه التکلان۔

(٧٢)

عرضداشت بخدمت بادشاه

عرضه داشت کمترین غلامان بعرض ساکنان[٤] آستان فلک آشیان می رساند که پیوسته بدعای دولت ابد پیوند قطب الاقطاب نبدگان حضرت اشتغان دارد۔ الهی سایه دولت واقبال تا قیام قیامت برسر جمیع دولت خواهان مخلّد وممدودباد۔ ثانیاً بنده وار عرض می دارد که طغرای رفیع منشور دولت ابدی وتوقیع بدیع سرمدی که

١۔ قرآن مجید : ٢١/٩
٢۔ ع : صلاء، ندارد
٣۔ قرآن مجید، ٤٦/١٥
٤۔ ع : ساکنان، ندارد

محرّران سده سنیه ومنتسبان عتبه علیه این کمترین بی مقدار وملتزم زاویه مسکنت وافتقار را باصدار آن ارتفاع بخشیده بودند، دیده ضریر وذره حقیر از انوار ساطعه آن قریر شد ورزگارِ متظلم بنده فقیر دولت خواه اشعه انوار شاد مانی ومطلع شموش واقمار نظرات حمدانی گشت، هر چند دیده فقیر وذره حقیر را اهلیت وقابلیت آن شریف لطیف نبود اما عجب نیست.ــه

عجب نباشد اگر هدهدی ضعیفی را   تفقدی نماید چنان سلیمانی

بعد از موداء "الحمد لله الذی انزل علی عبده الکتاب[۱]" در ازاء اصناف تفقدات کریمانه خسروانه وعواطف بادشاهانه هر چند پیر امن بضاعات مزجاة خود برآمده جز دعاء از صمیم دل خسته بر مجرای زبان شکسته گذارد وتحفه لائق ندید که معروض دارد.ــه

رد مکن چون دست این درویش مسکین بردعا

بعد هذا بموقف جلال عرضه می دارد که فرمان جهان مطاع واجب الاتباع، آفتاب شعاع، بدریة الالتماع چنان پر تو اشاعت برتافته بود که از جواهر واقمشه وامتعه لائقه غلامان و کنیز ان چرکس جنگی بچنگ آورده بهر سبیل تحصیل شرف تقبیل آستان ملك آشیان تعجیل نماید، برحسب اشارت سیادت[۲] دریں فصل هر چند از غائب وحاضر ومقیم ومسافر حضور خصوصاً فرقه تجّار وفرقه سیّاحان براری وسبّاحان بحار تفحص وتجسس بی شمار کرده که درهای ناب وجواهر نایاب خوشاب مناسب آن باب که زینت گوش هوش صرّافان بازار جهان تواند شد، بدست آورد وآن راسرمایه استظهار واعتضاد راس الماس افتخار واعتقاد نموده، سعیاً علی العمام لامشیاً علی الاقدام برامید "عسی ان یبعثك ربك مقاماً محموداً[۳]" متوجه تقبیل سده سدره

۱ـ قرآن مجید: ۱/۱۸
۲ـ ع : است، زیاده دار
۳ـ قرآن مجید: ۷۹/۱۷

مقام شود۔ آں سعادت ملازمت وخدمت انصرام نیافت۔

(۷۳)

عرضداشت بخدمت بادشاه

عرضه داشت بنده درگاه فلاں بنده وار بموقف عرض بندگان حضرت رفیع، اعلی الله لواء نصرته ومعدلته وسلطنة وخلافته الی یوم الدین، می رساند واحوال عجز وانکسار وضراعت وافتقار خود باز می نماید که ایں بنده لایزال بدعا اعتلاء جاه وجلال وارتفاع مدارج عز واقبال بندگان مشتغل می باشد۔ وچون از سر اخلاص وخصوص طبیعت است، امید که گردد باجابت مقرون۔ عرضه می دارد که طالع ایں بنده مساعدت نموده وبخت یاوری کرده وسهام دعا مقرون باخلاص ایں ذره بی مقدار رسیده که بندگان حضرت بدولت واقبال رایات ظفر وفیروزی را بر ساحت قسمت آں دیار خواهند برافراشت وهمیشه دیده مترصد بر شاهراه ایں مطلب اعلی ومقصد اقصی است، شعر:

کی بود آیا که شود بهره ور
دیده از دیدار چو گوش از خبر

امیدوار است که عن قریب بدیں دولت عظمی وسعادت کبری شرف افتخار یابد۔ الهی سایه چتر همایوں بر مفارق ساکنان ربع مسکوں مسبوط وممدود باد، بالنون ولصاد۔

(٧٤)

عرضداشت بخدمت بادشاه

عرضه داشت کمترین مریدان فلاں بموقف عرض بار یافتگان پایه سریر خلافت مصیر می رساند که این کمترین دولت خواه جان سپار و کهترین مریدان حق گذار بشرف آستان بوسی عتبه علیه قدسیه، که منشأ سعادت دینی ودنیوی ومبدأ دولت صوری ومعنوی است، اذعان واعتقاد نموده همواره آرزو وتمنا همان است که احرام حریم سعادت واقبال وحطیم عز واجلال بسته بطواف آں آستان، که کعبه آستان است ومطاف رستگاران، عازم گردد لیکن چون سرحد است وبی حکم اشرف اقدس جسارت بر فوز سعادت عظمی نه نموده، بنده زاده را بدرگاه خلائق پناه فرستاده که از سر خلوص نیت وخصوص طویت مناسك طواف سعادت مطاف را از قبل کمترین بندها بجا آورده۔ وتا او عازم شده "یا لیتنی کنت معهم فافوز فوزاً عظیماً"[١] ورد زبان وذکر لسان است۔

(٧٥)

عرضداشت بخدمت بادشاه

عرضداشت بنده درگاه فلاں بعد از عرض عبودیت ودعا ورواتب محمدت وثنا معرا از رعونت وریا بعرض نواب امیدگاهی،

١ـ قرآں مجید، ١٠٥/٤

اقبال آثاری، لازال ظلاله العالی، می رساند که این بنده علی الدوام در اوقات اجابت آیات ازلیالی وایام جهت اعلاء اعلام دین ودولت واعتلاء رایات فتح ونصرت بفاتحه فائحه اشتغال نموده ومی نماید۔ رجاء بکرم الهی واثق که دعاء فقراء بی ریا بعز اجابت مقرون (گردد)، یرحم الله عبداً قال آمینا۔ بعد هذا معروض می دارد که این بنده دائم الاقات بذکر مناقب شریفه ونشر محامد منیفه باقتناء غراء مرویه "من لم یشکر الناس لم یشکر الله" رطب اللسان وعذب البیان می باشد۔ ملاذا! امید گاها! چون مهم این فقیر عدیم الاستطاعت، قلیل البضاعت به یمن همت آن حضرت حسب المرام میسر گرداند۔ توقع آن که مخلص خود را احیاناً بوصول پروانچه مفتخر ومباهی گردانند۔ ظل اعلی مخلد باد۔

(۷٦)

عرضداشت بخدمت بادشاه

عرضه داشت کمینه بندگان سده عالی وکهنه غلامان عتبه متعالی فلان بر جاده نیکو بندگی وشارع ضراعت وسرافگندگی راسخ دم وثابت قدم است وبه تضرع وزاری از حضرت باری، که بخشنده سعادات جاودانی است وبر آرنده مرادات دوجهانی، استحکام مبانی درلت وکشورستانی وانتظام معاقد ایالت وکامرانی بندگان حضرت خلافت پناهی، قبله گاهی را، که کافل صلاح عامه رعایا وشامل نجاح کافه برایا، بدعوات سحرگاهی، که مبدء فیضان فیوض نامتناهی تواندشد، استدعا نماید۔ شعر:

این دعا دائم که گردد مستجاب

بعده ذره وار بعرض می رساند که از اشاعت آثار جور وبیداد وعمارات ظلم وفساد ازبکان شامت ونکبت افزون ظاهر شود که هنگام زوال واستیصال آن گروه بی شکوه وجماعت وخیم العاقبت، مخذول الخاتمه شده. ومصداق این مقال آن که همگی سوء همت وقصور نهمت را در آزار وضیاع خلائق، که ودائع حضرت خالق اند، مصروف داشته هرجا که می رسند مردم آن جا را بانواع عقوبت وآزار مبتلا ساختند واکثری رابه ناحق کشتند. ودست تطاول وبیداد دراز نموده اموال ومواشی مردم را متصرف شدند. درین ولا بتاریخ شهر فلان صوبه را که قریب بقلات واقع است تاخته سفك دماء ونهب اموال واسرعیال واطفال نمودند. چنانچه نوشته جات ملك شهلك، حاکم قلات، که بمردم بنده درگاه که در فلان اند، نوشته بود، بجنس ارسال داشته. خلائق پناها! خلائق از جور واعتساف این مفسدان حق ناشناس وظالمان ناسپاس در ورطه عجز واضطرار افتاده اند واز آزار خون ریزی ایشان بجان آمده اند. وآن جماعت بدسگال از سوء افعال وشناعت اعمال به تمثال افاغنه یوسف زئی مستوجب قتل واستیصال ومستحق تخریب وزوال گشته اند. انشاء الله تعالیٰ عن قریب بقهر وغضب الهی گرفتار شده مقهور ومنکوب ومطرود می شوند وبر نوعی مستاصل خواهند شد که اثری از آثار آن سیه بختان تبه روز گار بر صفحه لیل ونها رنخواهد ماند. وپیوسته مترصد ومتفحص حقائق اخبار سانحه بوده کسان را باطراف واکناف فرستاد. هر چیزی که می آرند بپایه سریر خلافت مسیر عرضه داشت می کند. الهی نیر خلافت وجمال وآفتاب ابهت واجلال بر بساط ربع مسکون موبّد وبتائیدات الهی مویّد باد. بالنون والصاد.

(۷۷)

عرضداشت بخدمت بادشاه

عرضداشت بنده درگاه فلان بعز عرض ملازمان آستان سعادت پناه می رساند که عالم السر والخفیات آگاه است وآفریننده لوح وقلم گواه که دریں شش هفت ماه ایں روزگار تباه را نگاه داشته اند هیچ هوس منصب انشاء را در دل نداشته بلکه هیچ منصبی، وایں گمنام به زیور فقر خود را آراسته وپیراسته، از جمیع آرزوها وارسته عنقا وار در کوه قاف قناعت نشیمن ساخته بایں مقال یکی از اهل کمال مترنم بود،بیت:

بدست ما چو ازیں حل وعقد چیزی نیست
بعیش ناخوش وخوش گر رضا دهیم رواست

که ناگاه شخصی که از حریم کعبه وصول آمده رسانید که ترا حضرت به پیشگاه حریم قبول می خوانند۔ بنا بر حکم عالی وتائید توفیق لم یزلی گریبان جان ایں ناتوان را گرفته فلك اشتباه مقصد سالکان آگاه رسانید وبشرف رجوع خدمتی مشرف ساخت۔ طوطی ناطقه ایں شکسته بال را غیر از امتثال آں امر ذی بال طاقت ومجال گویائی نماند، ونیز امیدوار بود که بوسیله ایں خدمت شائسته پنج روزه حیات چهره فراغت در آئینه روزگار دیده شود وآیات ایمنی از صفحه خاطر خوانده آید۔ اما بواسطه شماتت حساد وسعایت اهل فساد که از مادر زاد بایں بنده آزاد بی سببی نفاق دارند، در باطن خبث موطن ایشان ظاهراً تا روز تناد خواهدبود، ایں معنی بر چهره بهبود در آئینه

۱- قرآن مجید: ۲/۲۱۶

مقصود صورت نه بست ومضمون "عسیٰ إن تحبوا شیئاً وهو شر لکم[۱]" بظهور پیوست۔ لیکن

چه نقصان گر نگیرد نظم من اندر دل حاسد

که گوهر نازك ودر غایت سختی ست سندانش

الحال پای سریر جلال را بدست ادب گرفته التماس می نماید که از یار واغیار وصغار وکبار ایں دیار در علم ودانش فقیر یا نوشته او گرفت وگیر در ضمیر منیر برسیده باشد حکم شود که در مشافهه سخن وران بی نظیر در ناخوش تحریر آں را تقریر نمایند تا حق بمرکز قرار پذیرد۔

نقدها را بود آیا که عیاری گیرند

تاهمه صومعه داران پی کاری گیرند

والا جسم ایں خاکسار در گرداب نوائب چرخ دوّار از حیات مستعار دامن افشانده وپیکر نحیف ایں بی مقدار در صحراء مصائب ودر عذاب مشقت دثار در کمال حیرت واضطرار مانده وطاقت صبر وشکیبائی مانند وفا در مردم هرجائی مفقود گشت، خالصةً لله برخصت ایں فقیر حکم شود که دیگر تاب اهانت مثل خود بلکه صد درجه انزل واسفل ندارم وهیچ وجه بودنی نسیتم۔ بیت:

من نگویم که ایں کن وآں کن

بنده ام هر چه بایدت آں کن

(۷۸)

عرضداشت بخدمت بادشاه

عرضه داشت اقل مخلصان فلاں که در مناهج اخلاص به

فتراك دولت قاهره اعتصام نموده ومراصد اطاعت را باقدام انقياد پيموده الوف خدمات وافيه وصنوف عبادات صافيه از روى هوادارى ودولت خواهى به سده سنيه بندگان حضرت عالى مرتبت، معالى منزلت، بهرام سطوت، كاؤس دهشت، شاهباز آشيان اوج سعادت، شهسوار ميدان شجاعت وجلادت، صاحب سرير فرزانگى، ناصب لواى مردانگى، واسطه افاضه امن وامان، رابطه آثار عدل واحسان، بيت:

گوهر پاك وى از مدحت ما مستغنى ست
فكر مشاطه چه با حسن خدا داد كند

بسط الله ظلال مراحمه وعواطفه على مفارق اهل الزمان، در سلك عرض منتظم مى گرداند وآناء الصباح واطراف الرواح ازمبدأ الارواح وفاطر الاشباح تضاعف انوار دولت وترادف انوار مكنت آن صاعد ذروه استعلاء، ع : بزبانى كه دل موافق اوست، استدعا مى نمايد. بعد هذا مخلص نوازا! بر ضمير اشراق تنوير مخفى نيست كه از هنگام طلوع تباشير صبح فتح از افق عالى تنق اين ولايت الى هذا الغاية قلعه فلان مع مضافات وبلوكات در حيطه تصرف وحوطه تسلط حاكمان بكر بوده. ظلال حشمت واقبال از وصمت نقصان وزوال مصون باد.

(۷۹)

عرضداشت بخدمت بادشاه

عرضه داشت كمينه بنده دولت خواه وكمينه چاكر بلا اشتباه فلان صنوف صوالح ادعيه، كه از محض خلوص طويت ناشى شده، وصنوف فوائح اثنيه، كه از لفظ نيت درست اعتقاد واختصاص جارى

گشته، شائع وفائح گردد، بمحل عرض رسانیده خلود ایام دولت ابد پیوند را غرر درر دعاء بی ریا مصون از تطارق قاطع ریا به سر انگشت صدق وصفا در سلك ادا می کشد وبحسب اشارت پر بشارت "ادعونی استجب لکم[۱]" مترصد است که آثار میامن آن به تجدد ازمنه بر صفحات اوضاع وحالات همایون بنوعی ظهور یابد که مشاهد قرة عیون کافه احباء گردد۔ والله حقیق التحقیق۔ ثانیاً بعرض رساند که چون امتداد ظلال عظمت وجلال دریا نوال باعث حصول امانی وآمال وسبب تشبت عامه رعایا ورفاهیت کافه برایا است، دعاء ظهور دولت افزون وبقاء سلطنت ابد مقرون برهمه خلق واجب است، خصوصاً جمعی که پرورده نعمت الطاف وسایه مرحمت آن قبله حاجات باشند بر ذمه ایشان فرض عین وعین فرض است۔ بنا بران حرزجان وورد زبان بنده این ابیات فرخنده سمات است، نظم:

خدایا تو این بادشاه درویش دوست
که آسائش خلق در ظل اوست
بسی بر سر خلق پائنده دار
بتوفیق طاعت دلش زنده دار

(۸۰)

عرضداشت بخدمت بادشاه

عرضداشت بنده درگاه خلائق پناه فلان بذروه عرض حضرت مجاوران آستان رفیع الشان می رساند که لایزال بدعای دولت ابدی

۱۔ قرآن مجید : ۶۰/۴۰

الـدهر بندگان حضرت خلافت پناهی، خلّد الله تعالیٰ خلافته وسلطانه، وشاهـزاده عالمیان، سلّمهم الله تعالیٰ، اشتغال دارد و صبح وشام فاتحه مـی خـوانـد ودعـای خیرمـی کند که الهی ظلال عاطفت تاقیام قیامت برسر جمیع ملت مخلّد وموبّد باد، آمیں رب العالمین۔ مصراع[1]:

ایں دعا از من واز خلق جهاں آمین باد

بـعـده ذروه وار بـموقف عرض می رساند که دریں ایام عشرت انجام واوقات فرخنده فرجام نوید جان فزا ومژده دلکشا رسید که از افق عـزت واقبـال کو کب فرخنده فال طلوع نمود واز سپهر رفعت واجلال اختر خـجسته اثـر چهره کشـود۔ باستماع ایں خبر سعادات[2] بـندگی بتقدیم رسانیده ازدرگاه واهب العطیات استدعا[3] می نماید، قطعة[4]:

بـرومـنـد بادایں خجسته مقال | که شدرسته درباغ عز وجلال

جوان بـخـت بـادا وفـربلند | بـمـانـاد بـا طـالـع ارجمند

ولادت مـوفـور السعـادتش بربندگان حضرت مبارك باد وقدوم میمنت لزومش همیشه برکت کناد، بحق الحق واهله۔

دیـگـر بـعـرض می رساند که مثال واجب الامتثال مزیّن بخاتم جـاه وجـلال از اوج عـنایت بادشاهی شرف نفاذ یافته بود بشرف ورود وعـزّ ظهـَور آن مفتخر گردید وسرتفاخر نهاده بشرف مضمون عواطف مشحـونـش مشـرّف ومعزز گشت۔ چوں ایں ذره حقیر بی مقدار را از خـاك مـذلـت بـرداشتـه بـه پـر تـوعـنـایـت بی غایت والتفات بی نهایت مـخـصـوص گـردانیده، بروفق مدعاء مطلوب ارباب حاجت وبرحسب دولتـخـواهی مستحقان کم بضاعت مرقوم کلك حقائق سلك شده بود، ریاض امانی وآمال ایں بنده که ازباد کثافت وناخوشیهای ایں ولایت به

۱۔ ع : مصراع، ندارد
۲۔ ع : تعلیمات
۳۔ ع :مسألت
۴۔ ع : قطعه، ندارد

خزان رسیده بود، سرسبزو شاداب گردید واز سرنو خضارت ونضارت یافت، وابواب فتوح وحضور وبهجتهای غیر محصور بردل حزین انفتاح نمود. قاطبه دعاگو یان پرمسکنت وافتقار وعامه مساکین ذوالعجز والانکسار[۱] مسرور البال گشته، سجدات شکر ایزدی بتقدیم رسانیدند، ودست تضرع وانابت بامید اجابت برداشته[۲]، بدعای اعتلاء مطالب دارین بندگان حضرت ومزید حیات حضرت اشتغال نمودند، عالی پناها! از خوشحالی بندگان[۳] خدا عرض می نماید وباشمه از افتخار ومباهات خود بمسامع علیه بار یافتگان محافل گردون اساس می رساند:

کان نه بحر یست که پایان وکناری دارد

کوکبه خلافت ودبدبه ابهت ازهر فتح ونصرت شارق وطالع باد، بالنبی وآله الامجاد.

(۸۱)

عرضداشت بخدمت بادشاه

عرضه داشت کمترین دولت خواهان فلان بعز عرض حضرت می رساند که نشان واجب الاطاعة والاذعان که به کمترین درگاه اصدار شده بود کمانزل الروح من السماء، شرف ورود ارزانی فرمود، شرائط بندگی ولوازم عبودیت رابجای آورده برفرق نهاده ممتاز گردید. حکم اشرف اقدس نفاد یافته که تاغایت که بسر حد رفته اخباری بدرگاه ارسال نداشته. خلائق پناها! بتاریخ شهر فلان بقصبه

۱ـ ع : انکسار
۲ـ ع : برداشتند
۳ـ ع: بندهای

فلان رسیده همواره جاسوسان را تعین کرده خبری که بیارند عرضه داشت نماید۔ موقوف برین بود که جاسوسی که فرستاده بود بتاریخ فلان رسیده چنان نمود که از سر کار فلان مراجعت نموده می رود۔ به کسی که نامزد گشته اسم اوصحیح مشخص نشده، بنام چند کسی می گویند۔ تابملتان قاصد فرستاده که از مردم اعیان آن جاتحقیق نموده بیاید، آن اخبار بآن تحقیق موقوف، هر گاه که رسد عرضه داشت مرسل دارد۔ بنده نوازا! بنده که بایں امر مامورشده باشد چون اورا۔ امعاف داشته بی پروا وغافل خواهد نشست، انشاء الله من بعد هر چیزی که رو دهد در روز بلکه درساعت بپایه سریر فلك مصیر عرضه داشت نماید۔ ظلال دولت واقبال بر مفارق عالمیان مستدام باد!

(۸۲)

عرضداشت بخدمت بادشاه

عرضه داشت کمترین غلامان فلان بموقف عرض مقیمان آستان رفیع مکان که قبله ارباب وکعبه اصحاب التجا است، می رساند که لطائف بی تناهی ومراحم نامتناهی که درحق کمترین غلامان ارزانی داشته مصحوب فلان تشریف خلعت فاخره[۱]، واسپ لائق سرفراز وممتاز ساخته بود، چه عرضه داشت نماید که از ورود آن سرمفاخرت[۲] ازاوج چرخ می گذرد بلکه[۳] دامن عز وشرف بر فرقدان می گذشت[٤]۔ وازاء ایں عطیه عظمی وسعادت کبری مراسم حمد وسپاس وسجدات

۱۔ ع : خاصه
۲۔ ع : مفارق
۳۔ ع : و
٤۔ ع : می گشت؛ س : می کشد

شکر بی قیاس بجا آورده۔ الحمد لله حمداً دائماً ابداً۔

(۸۳)

عرضداشت بخدمت بادشاه

عرضه داشت کمترین غلامان ومریدان فلان بموقف عرض شرف باریافتگان پایه سریر خلافت مصیر می رساند که منشور نجح آمال وطغرای فوز بر کمال یعنی فرمان عالیشان، سعادت اقتران، لازم الاطاعة والاذعان از مکمن عنایت وذره پروری بنام کمترین مریدان شرف نفاذ یافته بود که باتفاق فلان قلعه سیوی رابدست آورد، بعز طلوع وشرف بلوغ آن سرفراز گردیده، برتارك افتخار ومباهات نهاده بشرف مضامین عواطف قرینش معزز وموقر گشت۔ "الحمد لله الذی انزل علی عبده الکتاب[۱]" وجعله من الذین فازوا[۲] بالسعادة وحسن مآب۔

(۸۴)

عرضداشت بخدمت بادشاه

عرضه داشت کمترین غلامان ومریدان فلان بموقف عرض فائزان بتقبل آستان رفیع المکان می رساند که توقیع رفیع وحکم جهان مطاع عالم مطیع مع[۳] عطیات سامیه وعنایات نامیه مصحوب فلان عز اصدار یافته بود، باعث وفور امتیاز وافتخار این ذره حقیر گردید

۱۔ قرآن مجید: ۱/۱۸
۲۔ ع : فاز
۳۔ ع : مع، ندارد

وموجب کمال سربلندی این خاکسار شد۔ تسلیمات عبودیت وبندگی بتقدیم رسانیده از ادای لوازم شکر وسپاس این نعم عظمی بعجز وقصور معترف گشته[۱] بدین مقال ترنم نمود:

گر بر تن من زبان شود هر موی
یك شکر تو از هزار نتوانم کرد

اعلام سلطنت در امان خلافت ابد الدهر مرتفع باد، بالنون والصاد[۱].

(۸۵)

عرضداشت بخدمت یکی از بیگمات

عرضه داشت بنده کمترین فلاں که رایات دولت خواهی درساحت خدمت گذاری برافراشته وآیات هوا خواهی بر صفحه خلوص همت نگاشته به نواب حضرت علیا، دام ملکها، آں که چناں معلوم شد که زمره اصحاب اغراض از جاده قویم انصاف انحراف واعراض نموده بخلاف راستی که هر گز نبوده و کسی نه شنوده بموقف عرض رسانیده اند وخاطر مبارك ازیں کمینه متغیر گردانیده۔ حقا که هر گز انا مل فکرت رقم این حال بر صفحه خیال این حقیر نکشیده ومثل این صورتی بخاطر فاتر نرسیده، ع:

واندر این معنی گواه من ضمیر پاك تست

زیاده خودرا مرتبه جسارت نمی داند۔ والامر ارفع۔ سراپرده سلطنت وعصمت وسرادق عظمت وعفت تا منقرض زمان برافراشته

۱۔ ع : بالنون والصاد، ندارد

(٨٦)

عرضداشت بخدمت یکی از بیگمات

عرضه داشت بنده دعا گوی فلان بعد از تقدیم خلود ایام سلطنت ودوام اسباب عظمت وعفت آن که حکم شده بود که کیفیت حالات ایں حدود را عرضه داشت نماید، بذروه عرض می رساند که بحمد الله اشجار جوئبار معدلت از امطار رشحات احسان وافاضت طراوت یافته ونهال گلزار از قطرات باران مکرمت نضارت پذیر فته، سکنه ایں ولایت درمهادامن وامان ومتوطنان ایں دیار درظلال عدل واحسان به آسائش می گذرانند۔ زیاده جرأت نمودن ترك ادب است۔ سروعصمت ومتکای عظمت به جنود "تری الملائکة حافین من حول العرش[١]" محاط ومحفوف باد، بالنبی وآله الامجاد.

(٨٧)

عرضداشت بخدمت بلقیس مکانی

به ذروه عرض نواب بلقیس مکانی، حریم مهد علیا، خلّدت ظلال عاطفتها واقبالها واجلالها الی یوم الدین، می رساند که لایزال بدعاء مزید عمر ودولت اشتغال می نماید۔ حضرت حق سبحانه وتعالیٰ سایه دولت واقبال بر مفارق بندها ثابت الاخلاص تا انقراض زمان ممدود وپائنده دارد، بحق الحق واهله.

بعده ذره واربعرض می رساند که منشور نجح آمال وطغراء فوز

١۔ قرآن مجید : ٧٥/٣٩

هر کمال از مکمن عنایت وذره پروری که به طلب فلان شرف نفاذ یافته بود، بعز طلوع وشرف لموع آن معزز وسرفراز گردید وبرتارك افتخار ومباهات نهاده بشرف مضامین عواطف قرنیش مفتخر ومعزّز گشت۔ همان لخطه ازپی تفحصّ وتجسّس آن بی سعادت هر جانوشته ها فرستاده به شقدار وعاملان پرگنات سر کار فلان بتاکید نوشت که درپیروی او کمال سعی ونهایت اهتمام بجا آورند۔ به یمن دولت واقبال امید وار است که عن قریب اسیر ودستگیر گردد۔ واجب بود بعرض رسانید۔

(۸۸)

عریضه بخدمت یکی از بیگمات

بعد از ترك تکلفات رسمی وتصلقات عادی وطی بساط بسیط مدحت وثنا اقتضاء[۱] بر وظیفه که هدیه مرضیه مخلصه بی ریااست، نموده درمعرض عرض می آید۔ عنایت نامه آنحضرت که از کمال شفقت صادر شده بود، رسید وموجب بهجت وسرور گردید۔ حضرت مهیمن متعال، جل شانه، نوال حال وآمال ایشان را زیاده گرداند ودر آنچه رضاء آن درگاه وخوشنودی حضرت رسالت پناه ﷺ است بدان موفّق دارد، بمنّه وکمال کرمه۔ ثانیاً.. ضمیر منیر مهر تنویر می گردارند که درعنایت نامه مندرج بود که از قبل مخدومی، ملاذی فلان برادران کامیاب مستطاب، مدّظله السامی، را تسلّی دهد وخاطر جوئی نماید۔ انقیاد امر نموده حسب المقدور دلاسای ایشان نموده۔ اگر بخت وطالع ایشان مدد خواهد کرد بمقتضاء عقل کار خواهند کرد ودرمقام

۱۔ ع : اقتناء

اخلاص واختصاص خواهند بود. بزوائد اطناب ننمود. ایام عصمت وعفت ابد الدهر مخلّد ومستدام باد!

(۸۹)

عریضه بخدمت یکی از بیگمات

معلّای حضرت ملکه عظمی، اشعه لمعات دولت کبری، نادره ادوار فلکیه، بارقه انوار ملکیه، سریر آرای بار گاه عصمت، زینت افزای تخت گاه عفت، نقاوه ملکات عالم، خلاصه بنات حوا وآدم، زبده حجله شهریاری، زبیده حجره مکرمت وبختیاری ابداً سریر سلطنت ومسند کامگاری وعظمت باد! مخلصه صادقه که درمقام اخلاص مقیم وبرجاده هواداری مستقیم است، دعواتی که رقوم خدمت از خلال سطور آن باهر وحروف محبت از مطاوی آن واضح وظاهر باشد سمت ابلاغ می دهد ونقوش استدعاء دوام جاه وجلال وخلود عزّ واقبال بخامه نیاز بر صفحات روز گار می نگارد، بشرف اجابت ووقوع استجابت مشرّف باد. مترصد ومترقب[۱] که تواتر مخاطبات وترادف مراسلات بنای مودت را موکّد سازند. بز وائد انبساط نمی نماید. بیت:

دیده مشعله داران شبتسان سپهر   روشن از شعشه شمع شبتسان توباد

(۹۰)

عریضه بخدمت یکی از بیگمات

یارب ایں منشور دولت از کجا واصل شده
کانچه مقصود دل وجان است او حاصل شده

۱ـ ع : است، زیاده دارد

نسائم عطوفت ومهربانی وشمائم مرحمت و کامرانی که از چمن اعطاف وانجمن الطاف حضرت رابعه جاده ایقان، صفیه سجاده اتقان، ملکة الملکات، حاویة انواع المیامن والبرکات، دامت ظلال عفتها وابّدت نوال حشمتها، وزیده ودمیده بود نضارت افزای ریاض اتحاد گردید ومشام وداد ازان بتعطر وتفریح رسید۔ فحمداً له ثم حمداً له۔ ازیں جانب دوری صوری بغایت دشوار است ومهاجرت ضروری بی نهایت دل آزار۔ اما اقتضاء چرخ دوّار وفلك کج رفتار همواره همچنان نموده۔ بهر حال از درگاه حضرت ذو الجلال بادعیه اجابت مقال دولت حصول ملازمت مامول است واز بارگاه واهب المن والافضال باثنیه استجابت مآل وصول سعادت مسئول۔ امید که شاهد آن مقصود از برقع غیب چهره کشاید وپیکر ایں مطلوب از پرده لاریب رخ نماید۔ امید واری از عنایت باری، عز اسمه، چنان است که از نظر عنایت محو نفر مایند وپیوسته از نسائم ابلاغ ملاطفات وشمائم ارسال مفاوضات ریاض جان را نضارت افزائی ومشام روان را عطر سائی فرمایند۔ چون مقصود مختصر بود بزوائد زبان اطناب نکشود وبدعا ختم نمود۔ درّی سروری از سپهر برتری طالع ولامع باد بالنون والصاد۔

(۹۱)

عریضه بخدمت یکی از بیگمات

اشعه رایات آسمان فرسای حضرت ملکه عصمت پناه، مالکه عفت دستگاه، دیباچه نظم امور عالمیان، سرمایه امن وامان، منظوره انظار عواطف ازلیه، مخصوصه آثار مواهب ابدیه درمیان طوائف عالمیان تا منقرض زمان ممتد ومخلّد باد! محبه نیکو خواه که طبقات

افلاك وداد واتحاد را بکواکب ثواقب اخلاص واعتقاد مزیّن دارد، ودعوات موفور وتحیات نامحصور مستفاد از مواد اعتقاد ومستخرج از مصادر وداد واتحاد مبلغ می دارد۔ وهمواره از حضرت باعظمت باری، جل ذکره، دوام ایام کامگاری وانتظام مهام نامداری را مستدعی می باشد، بعز استجابت مقرون باد! ملتمس[۱] آن که کیفیت احوال شرف اخبار ارزانی فرمایند تامواد مسرت ازدیاد پذیرد۔ زیاده اطناب نمی رود۔
بیت:

رفعت قصر معالیت چنان باد که مرغ
نتواند که برو سایه کند غیر همای

(۹۲)

عریضه بخدمت یکی از بیگمات

عصمت مآب، عفت آیات، قدوة المخدرات، اسوة المستورات، مهر سپهر مهربانی، چراغ دیده زندگانی، مدار الشفقته، مقر الرحته، دامت عصمتها وعفتها! بعد از عرض ادعیه کامله واثنیه شامله معروض می دارد که شرح صورت[۲] فراق ووصف حرارت افتراق، که از مقوله مالا یطاق است، در حوصله تقریر ودائره تحریر نگنجد۔ تمنای خلوص آنست که تاحین حصول طواف کعبه آمال به تواتر وتوالی ارسال ملاطفات مشفقانه ومراسلات مهربانه، که موجب سرور وسبب مسرت وحبور است، مسرور ومبتهج سازند۔ چون مقصود مختصر بود بزوائد نه رفت۔ والدعاء[۳]۔

۱۔ ع : ازو، زیاده دارد
۲۔ ع : سورة
۳۔ ع : والدعاء، ندارد

(۹۳)

عریضه بخدمت یکی از بیگمات

ای سراپرده دولت زده بر چرخ برین
برده از حسرت تو پرده برخ حور العین

مسند عصمت وسریر عظمت بمیامن صفات مکرمت آیات حضرت بلقیس روز گار، حشمت آثار، مهر سپهر دولت واقبال، سپهر مهر عظمت وجمال، زیب طراز حشمت وابهت[1] وشمع ایوان عصمت وعفت، خلّدت ظلال دولتها ومواد صولتها، تا انقراض ادوار زمان وانقطاع آثار دوران محلیّ باد ورایات شفقت آیاتش بر مفارق سکنه عالم خاك معلیّ، بالنبی وآله واصحابه! مخلصه معتقده شرائف دعوات وردیة النسمات ولطائف تحیات عطریة الفوحات از خلوص ولا وخصوص وفا ایثار مجلس علیا ومحفل عظمی می گرداند وبررای عالم آرای موضح می دارد که اگرچه این فقیر بواسطه حدوث حوادث وطوارق حدثان ظاهر دولت[2] ملازمت، که وسیله حصول اصناف سعادت و کرامت است، دور ومهجور است اماسر از رابطه عهود قدیم وضابطه عقود قویم ممهّد ومو کّد است وپیوسته پیکر وصال در آئینه خیال جلوه گر است وهمواره صورت اتصال از مرآت خیال در نظر- وعلی الدوام ادعیه حصول مراتب دینی ودنیوی ورد زبان است، واثنیه وصول بدرجات صوری ومعنوی حرزجان- امید که بدرجه اجابت واستجابت اقتران یابد- توقع[3] از مکارم اوصاف علیه آن که فراخور اخلاص فقیر بنظر التفات واعتبار منظور وملحوظ دارند وبمقدار اعتقاد

۱- ع : زینت
۲- ع: آن، زیاده دارد
۳- ع : آن که، زیاده دارد

حقیر عنایت ومرحمت را بدرجه ظهور آرند که مواد وثوق ورجاء لایعد ولا یحصی است۔ وگاهی بعنایت نامه نامی معزز وممتاز گردانند که لوازم آں حتی الامکان بظهور رسد۔ آفتاب دولت تابنده وپائنده باد!

(۹٤)

عریضه بخدمت بلقیس مکانی

بموقف حضرت بلقیس مکانی، مهد علیا، خلّدت ظلال عواطفها واقبالها، می رساند که لایزال بدعاء مزید عمر ودولت کامیاب "طوبیٰ لهم وحسن مآب[۱]" نواب بلقیس مکانی وامتداد حیات شاهزادهاء کامگار، عالی مقدار از عمر ودولت برخوردار استقبال می نماید۔ حضرت حق سبحانه وتعالی سایه دولت واقبال بر مفارق بندها تا انقراض زمان ممدود وپائنده دارد، بحق الحق واهله۔ ثانیاً بموقف عرض می رساند که مدت دوسال کامل است که بنده بخدمت ایں حدود سرفراز شده، پاره ازیں در بکر بخدمت مرجوعه قیام نموده وبرخی دررکاب ظفر انتساب در سیاق سیوستان وولایت ته بوده، حتی الامکان در خدمت گاری وجاں سپاری کوشیده، سعادت دارین خود دریں می داند که جان خود را نثار بندگان صاحب وولی نعمت خود نماید۔ وقبل ازیں نیز بنده مدتی بخدمت کابل وبعده در نسق کشمیر در ملازمت بود ومجموع ده دوازده سال است که از غلام زادها دور ومهجور بوده۔ معلوم است که بقاء عمر آدمی چه مقدار است وبرآں (چه) اعتماد۔ التماس از عموم عنایت والطاف آنحضرت بلقیس مکانی نماید کهٔ اگر غلام خود را از خاك برداشته برخصت غلام زادهاء خود

۱۔ قرآن مجید: ۱۳/۲۹

ممتاز گردد، هر آئینه موجب سرفرازی وغلام نوازی خواهد بود. امیدوار است که ملتمس بنده بانجاح مقرون خواهد شد. همواره سرادقات عزت وسراپرده عظمت براوج رفعت بر افراشته باد!

(۹۵)

عریضه بخدمت بلقیس مکانی

وظائف دعوات طیبات وتحیات مبارکات وارادات بجناب عصمت پناه عفت دستگاه، بلقیس زمان، مریم مکان، خدیجه عهد واوان، خلّدت ظلال عواطفها واقبالها واجلالها الی یوم الدین،.. موظّف ومرتّب داشته از حکایت شدائد اشتیاق وشکایت وقائع زمان فراق، که لامحاله بر صفحه صحیفه ضمیر منیر واضح ولائح ومبرهن است، اجتناب می نماید. بیت:

بس است این که تودانی که هر کس کزتو
جدا شود بکجاها رسد سر انجامش

مدتی مدید است که بحکم "الامور مرهونة باوقاتها" منتظر وقت می باشد که چون فرصتی یابد حوادث ایام را کوچه غلطی داده، بیت:

روبدان قبله اقبال کنند بار دگر
واندران کعبه آمال مجاور گردد

اما بمقتضاء فحواء، بیت:

فرشته ایست برین بام لا جورد اندود
که پیش آرزوی طالبان کشد دیوار

صوارف روزگار دامن گیر اختیار گشته موانع "من بینهم سداً ومن خلفهم سداً[1]" فرسنگ[2] فرسنگ حجاب در حجاب می گردد، مصرع: داعیه ما بازمانه راست نیاید۔

بیت:

تجری الریاح بما لا تشتهی السفن

وبی شبه از فضاء قضاء امری تقدیر رفته باشد جز متابعت فرمان درمان نباشد۔ امید به لطائف کرم الهی، عزّ شانه، آن که از مکامن استار غیب لطیفه صنعی ظاهر گردد که در ضمن آن ادراك دولت مشاهده جمال جهان آرای وسعادت مجاورت بهجت افزای بحصول پیوندد۔ "وما ذالك علی الله بعزیز[3]"۔ تصور چنان بود که چون این مهجور را دوسه روزی بر حسب ضرورت مفارقت بحسب صورت واقع شود برقرار معهود وظیفه عنایت والتفات رعایت نموده، ابواب مکاتبات مفتوح دارند واحیاناً تشریف شریف، بیت:

تفقدی که ازاں سلوتی رسد بدلی

تلطفی که ازاں شادماں شود جانی

منت نهاده نسیان عهود مصادقت وموالات مذموم شمارند، چه خاطر پریشان منزویان زاویه کربت غربت بهیچ چیز چنان متعلق ومشغوف نباشد که باستعلام احوال خصوصاً در ایام ظهور حوادث ونوائب۔ بزیادت اطناب اسهاب نمی رود۔ دولت وسایه مرحمت تابنده وپائنده باد، بالنون والصاد۔

۱۔ قرآن مجید: ۹/۳٦

۲۔ ع: فرسنگ، ندارد

۳۔ قرآن مجید: ۲۰/۱٤

(۹۶)

عریضه بخدمت یکی از بیگمات

بحمد الله که آن یار گرامی— مرا از نامه خود ساخت نامی

ملاطفه مرغوب ومفاوضه مطلوب حضرت ملکه عظمی، مظهر آثار ایالت کبری، طراز کسوت دین ودولت، فروغ دیده ملك وملت، بلقیس زمان، زبیده عهد واوان، سروبوستان عصمت وشِهر یاری، ماه آسمان عفت وبختیاری چون طلعت مشتری دلکشا وچون چهره ناهید طرب افزا، بیت:

آمد و گرد غم از سینه بی کینه برفت
وزنسیم کلماتش گل اقبال شگفت

ورود شریفش را وظائف اجلال واکرام ورواتب اعزاز واحترام مرتّب داشته بلب ادب مقبل ساخته- وچون منطوق آن مخزن اسرار ومطلع انوار از اتساق امور دولت وطراز رسوم رفعت مخبر ومنبئ بود، مراسم حمد ولوازم شکر به تقدیم رسانید- زیاده مصدع نشد- بیت:

باده مرصّع از گهر اختران چرخ
چتر سپهر پیکر خورشید سای تو

ایام عصمت وعفت ابد الاهر بماناد[1]!

(۹۷)

عریضه بخدمت یکی از بیگمات

صحیفه شریفه محتوی بر معانی لطیفه که مرقوم حضرت ملکه روزگار، نادره اعصار وادوار، زبیده حجر بختیاری، زبده[1] حجله

۱- ع : ایام عصمت وعفت ابد الدهر بماناد، ندارد

شهریاری، بانوی زمان، بلقیس عهد واوان از روزنه افضال ودریچه اقبال طلوع فرموده[۲] ـ درمورد آن کتاب کریم وخطاب عظیم دقیقه از دقائق تکریم ووظیفه از وظائف تعظیم نامرعی نگذاشت وبردوام اقبال وحصول آمال که از مضمون آن صحیفه جلال ونامه لازم الاجلال استفاده نموده[۳]، مراسم حمد ولوازم شکر باقامت رسانید ـ زیاده اطناب نرفت ـ عصمت وجلال از وصمت وزورل ابد[٤] الاهر مصؤن ومحفوظ باد!

(۹۸)

عریضه بخدمت شاهزاده

نور حدقه بزرگی وجلالت ونور حدیقه سطوت وخلافت، فرزند برخوردار صورت ومعنی شده، درقدم نبدگان حضرت قبله گاهی، خلافت پناهی، اولاً (استرضاء) والد بزرگوار کامل عیار خود، ثانیاً عمر دراز باد، دولتهای وسعادتهای دنیوی واخروی بیابند ـ عجالة الوقت مبارکبادی ولایت فلان بآن نور دیده خلافت کبری می رساند که حضرت حق سبحانه تعالیٰ این مهم را واین دولت را ارزانی داشته روز بروز[٥] ترقیات نصیب گرداند، وایزدکام بخش شهزاده جمشید سریر را این چنین آفریده که این چیست انشاء الله آن مقدار دولتهای دیگر خواهد شد که این درچه حساب است ـ بیت:

باش تا صبح دولتت بدمد

۱ـ ع : زینبده
۲ـ ع : فرمود
۳ـ ع : نمود
٤ـ ع : ابد، ندارد
٥ـ ع : در، زیاده دارد

کیس هنوز از نتائج سحراست

باید که شکر خدا وسایه خدا نموده بدانچه حضرت خلافت پناهی، شاهنشاهی، ظل الهی فرماید وامر کند بعمل آرند۔ زیاده گستاخی نرفت، والدعاء۔

(۹۹)

عریضه بخدمت شاهزاده

نفائس دعائی که شمائم نسائم آن از روضه رضوان وزیده معطر مشام آمال وامانی تواند بود وخوالص ثنائی که فوائح روائح[۱] آن از ریاض جنان دمیده اندوه از مرأت خواطر مخلصان جا ودانی تو اند زدود، اتحاف واهدامی دارد وخود را از جمله محبان صادق الوداد ومخلصان صادق الرجاء فی شمارد۔ هر چند قواعد تآلف ارواح بتواصل اشباه تمهید نگرفته اما استماع آثار عظمت واجلال وشوکت واقبال آن مظهر الطاف ذو الجلال همیشه همیشه مستدعی دواعی اشواق بدریافت ملازمت آن برگزیده خلافت گشته ومی گردد وافزودی اعتلاء لواء حشمت بی گزند افزوده ومی افزاید۔ امید که سهام این دعا بهدف اجابت رسیده، هرروزی دولتی تازه وهر لحظه نصرتی بی اندازه قرین روزگار همایون آثار گردد وسعادت اتصال آن حضور ستوده خصال نصیب روزگار مخلص صادق الاقوام شود، بمنّه ونواله ونعمه وافضاله۔

بعده مکشوف رای عالم آرای ومشهود خورشید سیما، که مرأت غیب نماست، می گرداند که چون برحسب کلمه کریمه

۱۔ ع : روائح، ندارد

"فاصبحتم بنعمته اخواناً[۱]" طلوع صبح وفا (و) وفاق وظلال آفتاب اتفاق[۲] میانه سلاطین آفاق که إساطین بنیان این زراندودی طاق اند، موجب احوال عامه جهانیان گردد وبمیا من این شیوه رضیه وشیمه مرضیه سرپنجه معاضدت وموافقت ایشان بساط تفرق حال وتوزع بال کافه عالمیان قبله آمال...... متوجه گردید وتحریك سلسله موافقت که همواره طالب وراغب آن می بود، لازم دید۔ نبابرین بارسال این صحیفة الاخلاص اقدام نمود وابواب استعداد بمفتاح قلم بلاغت رقم کشود۔ امید وار اری از جلائل اوصاف خداوندگاری آنست که پیوسته ترشح سرچشمه اقلام فیض انجام حدائق مخالصت وموافقت راناضر ونامی دارند ودر التیام این ضابطه واستحکام این رابطه که درطرفین مستلزم فوائد ارجمند ونتائج دل پسند است، توجه خاطر عاطر دریامقاطر مصروف ومبذول شمارند۔ وچون فلان مشارالیه داعیه توطن وتمکن حرمین الشریفین، زادهما الله تعالیٰ شرفاً ومهابةً، دارد که بقیه عمر را دران ارض مقدس ووادی اقدس صرف وظائف وطاعات وعبادات نموده در ضمن ادعیه خلود عمر ودولت واثنیه ثبات ح شمت وشوکت به تقدیم رساند، امید چنان است که اورا مشمول عواطف عوارف خسروانه ساخته مامولش رابحصول موصول گردانند وبوقوع این موهبت پایه قدر ومنزلت اورا به بلندی وارجمندی رسانند۔ واحیاناً بارسال رسل ورسائل وصحف احیاء مآثر مناسبات ومرابطات جانبین نموده بخدمات لائقه منت نهند که لوازم آن کما ینبغی تقدیم یابد۔ پیوسته اسباب سطوت وشهریاری ومواد خلافت وکامگاری از محض توفیقات وتائیدات حضرت باری ساخته وپرداخته باد، بحرمة النبی وآله الامجاد۔

۱۔ قرآن مجید: ۱۰۳/۳

۲۔ ع : اتفاق، ندارد

(۱۰۰)

عریضه بخدمت شاهزاده

عالی جناب، سلطنت مآب، خلافت انتساب، حشمت شعار، ابهت آثار، قدوة السلاطین العظام، زبدة الحکام الکرام بین الانام، المستعین من مواهب الملك العلاّم، معز السلطنة والرفعة والحشمة والشوکه والابهة والعز والاقبال فلان را شرائف دعوات نامیات وظرائف تحیّات وافیات اتحاف واهداء گردانیده مکشوف ضمیر منیر آن که چون فلان اطوار خود را تعیّر داده خبط دماغ پیدا کرده باکثر دولت خوهان درگاه عرش اشتباه در مقام عداوت شده بود، وبواسطه صفات ذمیمه در دلها مردود واز خاطر مطرود گشته بود، ودولت خواهان این آستان ملائك آشیان بدین جهت مایوس بودند، چنانچه وقت اظهار اتحاد ویکجهتی میکرد وکتابتی که نوشته بر حاشیه آن مهر کرده بود- وامثال این اعمال که تفصیل آن بطول می انجامد از مشار الیه بوقوع می آمد- بنا بران اورا از نظر کیمیا اثر انداخته رتبه خانی وعلم ونقّاره از و گرفته اند، واین معنی موجب امیدواری دولت خواهان ویك جهتان گشته- سلطنت مآب، شوکت انتساب فلان وفلان که مولانا مذکور نادولت خواهی نموده بود، بعد آن که فوجهای قاهره برسراو رفتند وولایتی که تبصرف او بوده بدولت خواهی سپرده معلوم کردند که درطریق اخلاص راسخ بوده، مشار الیه بواسطه غرض خود این نوع خاطر نشان کرده بود، مجدداً رعایت فرموده بعواطف وعوارف ممتاز ساخته اند، وبحمد الله که از بیچ ممر دغدغه تفرقه نیست ومهمات برحسب اراده نظام وانتظام دارد- وچوآن سلطنت پناه دم صدق وولا بدین دولت عظمی می زند، لازم نمود که سوانح حالات را اعلام نماید- وظیفه محبت وطریقه مودت آن که خلافت مآب سوانح حالات مهمات را اعلام می نموده

باشند وعهد وشرطی که بین الجانبین بوقوع پیوسته در تمهید وتشدید آن که انشاء الله تعالیٰ ازین جانب امری که موجب نقض عهد خود بود، واقع نه خواهد شد۔ ونتیجة الامراء والسلاطین فلان چنانچه فرزند ایشان است این جانب نیز کمال شفقت ومهربانی نسبت حال او مرعی داشته وخواهد داشت، وبفلان بهر طریق محبت ومودت مسلوك خواهد بود، مادام که از جانب ایشان امری ظاهر نشود، ازین جانب نیز بغیر نیکوئی چیزی بوقوع نخواهد آمد۔ خاطر انور من کل الوجوه مطمئن داشته دران مقام باشند که آثار دولت خواهی ایشان زود ظاهر شود ونتائج آن بروز گار فرخنده آثار دیده ور گرداند که هر آئینه درمیان دوست ودشمن سرفراز خواهد بود۔ چون مختصر بود زیاده اطناب نرفت۔

(۱۰۱)

عریضه بخدمت شاهزاده

لطف تفقد ونوازش که از شاهزاده خورشید شوکت، ناهید بهجت، خلاصه ابناء خواقین، زبده اولاد ملوك وسلاطین، حافظ اقطار زمین، ناصر انصار دین نامزد این محب صادق گشته بود، برمثال نسیم بهاری عطر آمیز وبر منوال نافه تتاری دلآویز رسید۔ منظومات آن مخاطبه روح پرور مانند جمال دلبران طرب افزای ومنثورات آن مکاتبه روح گستر چون حال عاشقان انگشت نمای۔ باقدام اکرام وسیله اقبال[۱] وذریعه احترام را مستقبل ومتلقی گشت۔ وچون صورت استقامت احوال وانتظام دولت واقبال از مغز آن[۲] صحیفه ظاهر وباهر[۳] بود بانواع شکر گذاری واوصاف سپاس داری مقابل گشت۔ الحمد لله حمداً

۱۔ ع : آن، زیاده دارد

۲۔ ع : مغز آن، ندارد

۳۔ ع : باطن

دائماً۔ زیاده اقدام اطناب موجب سآمت وابرام ومثمر غرام است۔ سایه چتر همایون بر مفارق ساکنان ربع مسکون مبسوط وممدود باد، بالنبی وآله الامجاد۔

(۱۰۲)

عریضه بخدمت شاهزاده

قاصد رسید وساخت معطر مشام من
در چین نامه داشت مگر نافه ختن
این نامه نیست بلکه پی تحفه باغبان
چید از چمن بنفشه وپیچید درسمن

نفحه غنچه فضل وکمال که از جوئبار خامه مشك بار وزیده ولمعه کوکب حسن وجمال، که از مطلع نامه بدائع آثار درخشیده، چون نسیم طره طراء وبیاض غره بیضاء دماغ غمزده معتکف زاویه بیت الاحزان ومشام الم رسیده را منور ساخت۔ وچون از فحاوی آن استشمام روائح میعاد قرب وصال نمود، بزبان حال و[1] لسان مقال به زمزمه "انی لاجد ریح یوسف[2]" مترنم گشت۔ قطعه:

صبح دم باد صبا نکهت جانان آورد
خبر یوسف گم گشته بکنعان آورد
کوکب صبح نشان داد ز خورشید رخش
خبر گم شده ظلمت هجران آورد

لله الحمد والمنة علی ذالك.

ملاذا! باوجود کثرت محن فراق وهجوم مشاق اشتیاق اگر نوید دولت دیدار از تویاد رس جان بیقرار نشود، پیداست که از صبوری

۱۔ ع : مرتبه
۲۔ قرآن مجید : ۹۴/۱۲

دل چه آید؟ واگر مژده مشاهده شاهد خیال غم گسار خاطر افکار نشود، معلوم است که از شکیبائی جان چه کشاید؟ بیت:

ولولا جاء خبرا الوصل ماعشت ساعةً

ولو لا مکان الطیف لم اتهجع

چنانچه حاصل این کلام در سلك این منسب فارسی انتظام یافته، بیت:

فراقت می کشد هردم، خیالت زنده می دارد

بقا بادا خیالت را که از وی زندگی دارم

اکنون بهمه حال ملول در گوشه خمول افتاده وچشم امید بر دریچه رحمت ایزدی نهاده، انتظار مشاهده آرزوی وصال فرخنده مآل می برد که قریب از حجله خفا این عروس دلربا بجلوه گاه ظهور روی نماید۔ قطعه:

خوش آں ساعت که در بزم وصالت شادماں باشم

زتاب آتش جاں سوز هجراں در اماں باشم

جمالت را بکام دل به بینم یك شبی وانگه

زجام عشق تا روز قیامت در اماں باشم

امید گاها! در ضمن نامه مندرج بود که عزیمت این جانب در فلاں تاریخ مصمم خواهد شد۔ ملاذا! قبل ازیں خبر رسیده بود که به فلاں جا تشریف آوره اند، خاطر حزین بقرب وصال بغایت مسرور گشته بود وچوں خبر مکتوبی رسید محنت انتظار به تزاید کشید وفی البدیه ایں بیت بخاطر فاتر روی داد، بیت:

وعده عیدی من بود ز تو قرب وصال

ده که ایں وعده وصل تو بعید افتادست

والحال دیده انتظار به راه آں ملاذ الاحباء نهاده خاطر اندوه گیں ودل غمگیں را بایں مطلع تسکین می دهد۔ بیت:

یوسف گم گشته باز آید بکنعال غم مخور

کلبه احزان شود روزی گلستان غم مخور

امیدواری چنان است که بقدوم شریف این گرفتار هجران را (نجات) از قیدتار عنکبوت است۔ بیت:

چنان فر سوده شد جسم من از غم

که گر دم می زنم ریزد از هم

دیگر مجمل احوال مخلصان چنان است که بعد از مفارقت جمعیت خاطر به تفرقه مبدل گشته وشهشوار گردش فلك در صولجان ایلام این مستهام چوں گوی بیچاره کو بکو گردانیده بسوی سفله ودون دوانیده، واستغناء که در حضور شریف حاصل بود، بافتقار متبدل ساخت۔ والدعاء۔

(۱۰۳)

عریضه بخدمت شاهزاده

همواره صورت هر مراد که خسرو سکندر خصال بر صفحه بال نگارد باحسن وجهی در آئینه حصول حاصل باد وپیوسته تیر تدبیر که از خاطر الهام ناظر در کان کمان نهد، بر هدف مقصود واصل، بحرمة سید الانبیاء ﷺ اولاً وآخراً۔ اقل خدام عتبه سپهر احتشام که مرغ بال به پر وبال بقدم استعجال به سرحد کنه اختصاصش هویدا نرسد، عرضه می دارد که نامه خجسته فال نامی وکتاب وحی مثال گرامی، بلکه آئینه جمال کمال "انی اصطفیتك علی الناس برسالاتی وبکلامی[1]" که نگاشته خامه عنبر افشان دبیران عالی شان سده سدره نشان بود، در احسن ایام از افق مرحمت واکرام چوں مهر منیر برین ذره حقیر طالع گردید۔ رایت افتخار باوج سپهر دوار رسید وجمال سعادت واقبال را در آئینه خیال مثال جلوه گردید۔ "الحمد لله الذی انزل علی

۱۔ قرآن مجید : ۱٤٤/۷

عبده الکتاب ولم یجعل له عوجا[1] " وفتح علینا بمفاتیح الکتاب ابواب الرجاء۔

کیفیات واقعات این جائی بمسامع علیه رسید وحالات این دیار به تکرار نواب درگاه سپهر اعتبار شنیده واز عرائض امراء آن جابر ضمیر خورشید نظیر روشن گردیده، مجدداً بعرض آن تصدیع خدام آستان نشان نمی فرماید وابواب جرأت و گستاخی را زیاده بر ان نمی کشاید۔ اما این قدر عرضه می دارد که اخبار بسیار از اردوی ظفر شعار درین چند روز به تکرار رسیده، وتشریف آوردن شاهزاده بلند مقام بنواحی فلان اکثر مردم را خرم کرد ورفتن افغانان مقهور از نواحی فلان ونابودن ایشان در آن حدود به یقین انجامیده۔ زیاده برین شرح احوال مناسب مقام ومقتضاء حال ندید، ازان روی طناب اطناب[2] را برید۔ التماس آن که همت عالی، که عروج باوج مقال است، ازین[3] مخلص قدیم دریغ نه دارند و کیفیت سیئۀ این کمینه را از جواهر اخلاص واعتقاد مشحون پندارند۔ بزوائد اطناب نه نمود۔ نهال دولت وکامرانی در ریاض اقبال جاودانی از جوئبار وداد سرسبز وسیراب باد، بحرمة النبی وآله الا مجاد اجمین۔

(۱۰۴)

عریضه بخدمت شاهزاده

قاصد رسید وکرد معطر مشام من
در چین نامه داشت مگر نافه ختن

۱۔ قرآن مجید : ۱/۱۸

۲۔ ع : اطناب، ندارد

۳۔ ع : ازین، ندارد

همواره مشام جان مخلصان دولت خواه از فوائح روائح انفاس دبیران عطارد اساس معطر باد وپیوسته دیده دعا گویان بی اشتباه به سواد نامه سعادت نشان، دولت اساس منور! بعد از اقامت وظائف عبودیت واخلاص، که دست آویز از پای افتادگان کوی نیاز وانکسار است، وپس از اداء رواتب ادعیه اجابت اختصاص، که انگشت نمای سررشته از دست دادگان کاشانه عجز وافتقار، معروض عتبه علیه، لازال ملاذاً لکافة البریة، می گرداند که همان زمان که نامه فرخنده فال نامی ومثال واجب الا متثال گرامی بایس مخلص رسید، برسبیل استعجال بی توقف واهمال متوجه ملازمت نواب قدسی القاب، کامیاب، ظفر رکاب[1]، شهزاده عالم وعالمیان، نور دیده جهان وجهانیان گردیده مضمون نوازش نامه را باسخنان نصیحت آمیز، که لائق دولت روز افزون حضرت وموافق کافه برایا بود، بعرض رسانید۔ برغبت تمام تلقی نمودند ودر جواب فرمودند که ماهم درین خیال بودیم۔ انچه نواب قدسی القاب ظفر رکاب مدظله العالی فرموده اند محض صدق است وعین صواب وکسی را دران مدخلی نیست۔ درین باب بنا بر بعضی موانع در دار الخلافه دهلی ملازمت نتوانستم کرد وحالا بآگره می فرمایند چگونه ملازمت بکنم۔ غرض که موکب اعلی را استقبال خواهند فرمود۔ بعد از نیل شرف ملازمت بانچه مناسب ولایق حال خود دانند عمل خواهند نمود۔ زیاده جرآت وگستاخی نه نمود۔ نهال سلطنت واقبال از جوئبار معدلت سرسبز وسیراب باد، بحرمة النون والصاد۔

(۱۰۵)

عریضه بخدمت شاهزاده

۱۔ ع : ظفرر کاب، ندارد

صحیفه فرخنده فال ونامه دولت واقبال، که نگاشته اقلام بدائع ارقام دبیران عطارد نظیر عتبه سپهر تصویر ورقم زده خامه مشکین فام منشیان لطائف تحریر سده سدره نظیر می نمود، در احسن ساعات از افق عنایت والتفات چون مهر انور از طارم اخضر برین ذره احقر طالع گردید- از سواد خط مشکینش شب قدر این بی مقدار روشن گردید واز فروغ بیاض بیضاء آستینش صبح سعادت واقبال را بدیده اعتبار دید- در برابر آن مرحمت ورافت ودر مقابله آن مکرمت وعاطفت جز اعتراف به عجز وقصور چاره نه بود- بنا بران قطع طناب اطناب نمود-

بعد هذا معروض درگاه گیتی پناه، عرش اشتباه می گرداند که همواره داعیه این فقیر وهمیشه تمناء این حقیر آنست که بموجب "حب الوطن من الایمان" عمل نموده بوطن مالوف باز گردد وبه سعادت ملازمت خدام عالی مقدار مفتخر- اما چون زمام اختیار بنده بدست دیگر است غیر از صبر وسکون چاره دیگر نیست- امید که غبار موانع واعذار از پیش دیده دور گردد وچهره شاهد این[۱] مطلوب عن قریب بدیده بخت واقبال منظور- زیاده قدم درمیدان جسارت وجرآت ننهاد وچهره گستاخی وبی ادبی رابدست طناب اطناب[۲] که موجب ابرام است، نکشاد- ظلال عواطف ومراحم خسروانی بر مفارق مخلصان از عالی وادنی پاینده باد!-

---

۱- ع : این، ندارد

۲- ع : اطناب، ندارد

مراسلات وصحائف

(۱۰٦)

مراسله بخدمت وزیر

بعالی حضرت، فلك رفعت، عدالت زینت، وزیر کیوان مکنت، برجیس سعادت، دستور بهرام سطوت، قهرمان خورشید زینت، صاحب رای، عطارد فطنت، ملك آرای ماه لطافت، ناظم مصالح جمهور، خلاصه نتائج ایام وشهور، مدبّر امور مملکت، وزیر خجسته طلعت، خان اعظم فلاں محب مخلص متخصص دعوات خالصات وتسلیمات زاکیات تحفه مجلس سامی ومحفل گرامی می گرداند وبالتفات خاطر فیض مناظر منتظر است۔ بعد از تقدیم مراسم تبجیل وتکریم عرضه می دارد که آں حضرت که هم راز را در زمانه غدار آگاه اند وفراست آں حضرت بر اسرار سپهر دوار مطلع، چه ضبط ممالك ورونق اعمال واقامت خراجات وآبادانی ولایت ومعموری خزائن جمله بر رای صائب وزیر خجسته تدبیر باز بسته است، بجز رای صائب وعزم درست آں حضرت حوادث نواحی چگونه معلوم شود وبر احوال فکر اعداء وعزمات خصماء بچه دلیل وقوف افتد؟ معروض می دارد که جهت قطع نائره فساد ضلال وقمع ماده ظلال جملگی حواس ظاهر وباطن بداں مصروفّ است که سوداء مزاج آں مردوداں به باد فنا (دهد) وآتش استکبار در تنور دماغ آں کفره فجار، که بقوت حصار مشیده رفیعه مسجور است، بآب سیوف مصری وهندی فرونشاند۔ اما آں نابکار، بی مقدار، روباه صفت باجمعی از کلاب در مضائق حصار مستحصن (متحصن) اند وهر چند که عساکر چوں هاله گرد قمر واوراق پیرامون شجر در می آیند، از کثرت آتش صاعقه کردار دخول دراں محصن محال است۔ اکنوں محتاج الیه چند تفنگ است زود مرسل دارند۔ امید که کنگره وطاق وپنجره ورواق آں قلعه آسمان اطباق بمقتضی "فجعلنا عالیها سافلها"[۱] با هامون خاك اطباق

۱۔ قرآن مجید : ۷٤/۱۵

خواهد یافت. انچه مقتضیات سداد وقامعات (قمع) ماده افساد اضداد است علی التفصیل والاجمال فلان، که اخص مخلصان است، بسمع شریف خواهد رسانید، اصغاء فرمایند ودر استماع کلامش ودر اهتمام پیامش کمال اهتمام دریغ نفرمایند. چون بیان الطاف آن حضرت ازان افزون است که مذکر اقلام در صفحات دفاتر شهور وایام مسطور گرداند. لاجرم عذر الطاف آن مجمع مکارم اخلاق بمحاسن آن یگانه آفاق محول گشت. بزوائد اطناب نه نمود.

(۱۰۷)

مراسله بخدمت وزیر

عالی حضرت، دستور اعاظم، کارفرمای ارباب السیف والقلم، مشید قواعد معالی، مرجع اعاظم واعالی، آصف قدر قدرت، داور قضا صولت، زین الله تعالی مسند الوزارة بوجود شریفه (بوجوده الشریف) الی یوم القیام، اقل خدام که دائم در تصاریف لیل ونهار در هر زمان ومکان، نیك آثار حال وماضی ومستقبل بر خود لازم وجازم کرده دست امید به حبل الورید اعتصام حضرت باری مستحکم (دارد)، که استدامت ایام دولت وحشمت آن افضل الملوك ویقین متین این بنده مضاعف ومزید فیه شود وبعنف مقرون نه گردد. بمجرد آن که التفات خاطر فیاض از مقدمات افلاس وقهر هر نافر جام سالم وغانم ماند. اگرچه این بنده بخدمتی مشکور قیام ننموده اما در آناء اللیل واطراف النهار بدعا گوئی دوام دولت ابد پیوند ومزید حیات بابرکات قیام نموده ومی نماید. رجاء به موهبت منان آنکه هر بدنهاد وششت پایه وافراد بدفعل سبك سار که سر از مصدر رضاء آن فهرست مجموعه قدر وقضا

پیچیده خارج شود وداخل نه گردد، حضرت فاعل مختار از[۱] جار المجرور را از حرف علت خالی نگرداند ووجود آن اجوف مفعول من یراد وآن مقبل خفیف مدغم پرغم طعمه تمساح رماح وضرغام حسام گردد تا قدم کف نیاز بدرگاه حضرت بی نیاز برداشته که امرونهی جمهور حاضر وغائب بنی نوع انسان بقبضه اقتدار[۱] والا تبار قرار گیرد. ملتمس ومرجو خدام آن که این بنده را در تعداد عمر وبکر وزید وخالد نشمرند ودر سلك بندگان عالی منسلك فرمایند.

دریں ولا استماع افتاد که خاتم انگشت سعادت مند وخنصر دولت ابد پیوند ارزانی فرموده اند، عالمیان متعجب ومستغرب اند. رای عالم آرای آن حضرت که جز چهره سداد نه بیند خاتمی که مفاتیح ابواب ملك وملت ومقالید اندراج دین ودولت است، وبوسیله این نعمت وذریعه ایں موهبت وبواسطه خنصر راحت افزای دشمن زدای، که خواص یدموسی ودم عیسی دارد وسبب استقامت امور مملکت ودفع عوادی عادی وقهر ارباب غی وضلال ورفاهیت حال اصناف برایا وفراغ بال کافه رعایا، عائد فرموده اند، الحمد لله که اسرار فرّایزدی از سائر جهت آن حضرت شارق واز دیوار تن ظاهر ودر تدبیر ملك داری ونوامیس امور بادشاهی ولی عهد اباً عن جد وارث. معروض رای عالی آنکه اگرچه ایں بنده از غایت قلت عقل وخست منزلت وقصور[۲] ادراك ایں چند کلمه گستاخی می نماید وعرضه می دارد، باعث آن که واجب است بر تمام خدام از صغار وکبار که آنچه دانند از اخلاص ودولت خواهی بعرض صاحب رسانند. اگرچه ذات کامل صفات آن حضرت به رزانت[۳] عقل وثبات رای وکمال حلم وسکینت آراسته وبه زینت صبر ووقار متحلی وبسطت حلم اوربی نهایت

۱ـ ع : آن، زیاده دارد

۱ـ ع : مقصود

۲ـ ع : برجاجت

وجانب عفو واغماض بر بندگان ممهد وآثار کم آزاری شائع وذکر آن بر روی روزگار تابان ودر آفاق سائر۔ چه پسندیده ترین سیرت ملوك آنست که در حادثات عقل وحلم را حاکم سازد، لیکن اکابر فرموده اند که هیچ وقت اخلاق خود را از لطفی بی عنف وعنفی بی لطف خالی نگذارد تا کار میان خوف ورجاء باشد۔ مخلصان را نومیدی ونه مفسدان را دلیری۔ بدین جسارت حقارت قدر آن سخنان که تقریر افتاد وقدم از اندازه خود فرانهاده بعفو مامول است۔ عرضه می دارد که احوال این دیار وملاعین نابکار وشمل اشرار از رعب انصار دین محمدی وخوف احرار سرمدی رغباً ورهباً رقم "کلبهم باسط ذراعیه بالوصید[1]" برجبهه پلید[2] وناصیه عنید کشیده در تجهیز جهازات وساخت آلات ضرب مشغول اند۔ اما کحل فاسد در دیده دل کاسد می کشند وآتش یاس وحرمان بدست غدر در خرمن خیال خویش می زنند۔ امید آنکه این خنازیر آدمی هئیت در قعر بحر زخار ملجا وماوی سازند۔ چون خرد خورده دان بر معارج اصناف آن عاجز وقاصر است لاجرم قدم تجاسر در بساط انبساط نانهاده بدوام دولت خواهی اختصار نموده۔

تا آب در گذر بود وباد در مسیر
تاکوه را سکون بود وخاك را قرار
بادا همیشه جاه وجلال تو بر مزید
بادا اساس دولت وعمر تو پائدار
پیوسته باد رای ترا یمن بر یمین
همواره باد عزم ترا یسر بر یسار

۱۔ ع : قرآن مجید : ۱۸/۱۸

۲۔ ع : پلید، ندارد

(۱۰۸)

مراسله بخدمت وزیر

ضاعف الله تعالیٰ اقتداره واعز اعوانه وانصاره وجعل مجده ممجداً. محب نیازمند که از عمال ولایت اخلاص ومباشران شغل اختصاص جناب وزارت پناهی، امارت شعاری است، ظرائف ادعیه برسم پیشکش وزواهر جواهر اثنیه بر سبیل نثار ایثار مجلس رفیع الدرجات، کثیر البرکات می کند. واگرچه ظاهراً دریں ولا بحصول موصول دران موقف همایون سعادت مساعدت نمی فرماید ودولت مرافقت موافقت نمی نماید اما بمقتضاء حقوق مکارم موفور وعواطف نامحصور که در ایام سابق باحوال دولت خواهان لاحق گشته، همواره فضاء آن سده سنیه وعتبه علیه، که همیشه جاء التجاء نیازمندان باد، ایر نیازمند را دل مجروح در سیران ومرغ روح در طیران است.

وان کنت من هذا[1] الف فرسخ

تنسمت ریح الجود من آل برمک

ایزد متعال دولت اکتحال علی اسرع الحال وایمن القال به غبار آن آستان جاه وجلال میسر گرداناد، بمنه وکرمه. پیوسته از ریاض مجاری روائح تهیا اسباب کامرانی وموجب دولت بختیاری چون نکهت ریاض از نسیم می دمد واز مشارق کمال آمال انوار سروری وجهان داری چون برق ابر آذری می درخشد. لله الحمد والمنة که از مکمن غیب سببی، که واسطه امن وامان وماده آرائش وآسائش جهان وجهانیان است، کرامت گشته ارباب دین ودولت واصحاب ملک

۱- ع : فی، زیاده دارد

وملت را از ملهمات[1] تائیدات ربانی ومنهیان سعادات جاودانی نوید "یبشرهم ربهم برحمة[2]" روی نموده فی الحقیقه، بیت:

ایـــام در انتـــظـــار ایـن بـــود

جـویـنـده فـرصتی چنین بـود

امیدواری بعنایت حضرت باری، تقدست اسمائه، آن که چون ذات ملکی صفاتش مظهر لطف نامتناهی الهی ومکنون ضمیر منیرش محض خیر ونیك خواهی است، یك لخطه اوقات وساعاتش بشیوه ملاعب وملاهی چنانچه شیمه سرخوشان شراب دولت ونشاط جاه تواند بود، آلوده نگردد، بلکه همواره جوامع همت وهمگی نهمت او بر توسیع دائره حکومت وفتح عرصه دولت مقصور ومحصور باشد. آن خود چه مراد بود که آن جست ونیافت، وخلعت معاش پسندیده اش بطراز "الولد الرشید یقتدی بوالده الحمید" مطرز گشته روز سعادت آثارش در حواشی بساط سلطنت واسعاف حوائج جمهور مصروف شود. ولا محاله چون خاطر اهالی اطراف وحوالی مملکت، که مملکت باقی عبارت از انست، از میامن عدل ومرحمت به نور امن وحضور زیور بهجت وسرور آراسته گردد، وپیوسته اسباب ومقدمات در غایت کمال ونهایت جمال دور از آسیب عین الکمال آماده ومرتب باشد وحفظ ربانی در همه حال نگهبانی کند. وبعد ذالك آثار مفاخرش طراز تواریخ وزراء رفیع مقدار وذکر خصائل پسندیدهٔ اش دیباچه مآثر امراء گردون اقتدار باشد. ومن الله العون والتائید انه حمید مجید. زیادت موجب تثقیل است. اسباب استحکام مبانی دولت وقوائم امور رفعت روز بروز در ترقی وتنزاید باد، بحق الحق وذویه!

۱ـ ع : ملهمان

۲ـ قرآن مجید : ۲۱/۹

(۱۰۹)

مراسله بخدمت وزیر

ابقاکم الله تعالیٰ فی ظلال العنایة الخاقانیة ولازال شمساً للدولة والعزة والسعادة الابدیة۔ بعد از عرض نیاز به لسان اختصار وایجاز معروض دارد که پرتو اشعه شمسیة الشعاع که از مطلع شفقت ومخلص نوازی طلوع یافته بوده به مبارك ترین وقتی وخوب ترین ساعتی روزنه مآل[1] وکاشانه آمال مخلص نیازمند بجان آرزومند را منور وروشن ساخت ومورد کریمش را بلوازم توقیر وتعظیم ملثوم گردانیده، مصراع:

بوسیدم وبر مردمك دیده نهادم

از ذوق استماع ولذت سماع مضامین شفقت ومرحمت آئین آن قدر بهجت واستبشار ووثوق واستظهار حاصل آمد که زبان خامه بیان از اداء آن قاصر است وقلم تیز زبان از استقصاء آن هائم وحائر۔

جزاك الله خیر الجزاء واوصلك الی مدارج الاعتلاء که مخلص صمیم الاخلاص را یاد فرموده اند۔ ملاذا شمه از تقصیرات عدم ارسال عرائض ضراعت ومسکنت که برسبیل شفقت ومرحمت رقم التفات یافته بود، چون مراسله قطره بدریا غایت بی ادبی است ومخاطبه ذره بخورشید والا نهایت گستاخی۔ ونیز بواسطه کثرت مشاغل

۱۔ ع: منال

ومهمات ورجوع ارباب حاجات که بدان ذات ملکی صفات مفوض است، وامیدوار است که حضرت حق، سبحانه وتعالیٰ، یوماً فیوماً اسباب ترقیات دینی ودنیوی ایشان را در تزاید داشته بر طبق آرزوی مخلصان مستمند مورد ورود الطاف واشفاق شاهنشاهی، خلافت پناهی، قبله گاهی ظل الهی باشند وسده سنیه علی الدوام ملجا وملاذ انام از خاص وعام باشد، اقدام وجرأت بارسال آن کرده مصدع اوقات فائض بابرکات نمی شد وگستاخی نمی نمود۔ لیکن ذکر[1] اخلاق جمیله ونشر اوصاف ایشان مع اداء وظیفه دعاء خیر، که شیوه ارباب محبت واخلاص است، التزام کرده یك نفس از خیال وتصور محاسن ومکارم شیم ذات شریف ذاهل وغافل نیست نخواهد بود۔ ودران باب تقاعدی نرفته ونخواهدرفت۔ درین ولا از فحواء دل کشای نوازش نامه باشارت دل پذیر در افتتاح ابواب مراسلات مسکنت آیات التفات واشفاق فرموده اند، این معنی را وسیله حصول متمنیات وسعادات خود دانسته علی سبیل التوالی والتعاقب بارسال آن مصدع اوقات میمنت آیات خواهد شد۔ حق علیم است که چه مقدار سرور وحضور وخوش حالی وحبور باستماع این اشفاق واعطاف حاصل گشته۔ خدای تعالی خیر دهد وبمطالب دارین که مطمح نظر محاسن اثر باشد فائز گرداند! چون فرزند یکه ولایت است، بوجوه متعدده نسبتهای اخلاص راسخ وثابت است ترقب که در زمره محبان صادق الاخلاص تعداد فرموده توجه وجیه را دریغ نه فرمایند۔ جریان مهام برنهج مرام ولآلی معالی در سلك انتظام منتظم ومنسلك باد!

۱۔ ع : ذاکر

(۱۱۰)

مراسله بخدمت وزیر

دمیده[۱] صبح سعادت ز مطلع اقبال
وزید نکهت لطف از ریاض جاه وجلال

غره صبح سعادت وطره دوحه سیادت، که عبارت از کتاب مشکین نقاب حضرت اقبال پناهی، وزارت وسیادت دستگاهی، وکیل السلطنة القاهره، کفیل الایالة الباهره، راقم آیات الکرامة علی صفائح الایام، ناصب رایات العدل فی بیضة الدین والاسلام، سمی الامام صادق علیه الرضوان، خلدت ظلال اقباله وابدت میامن عزه وجلاله، باشد، دراعز از منه وایمن امکنه صفا بخش خاطر مهجوران وشوق افزای طبیعت مشتاقان گردید. لوائح طمانیت از بیاض قیامش لائح وروائح تفریح خاطر اندوه گیں از نکهت مواد مشکین نهادش فائح بود وجواهر مناقب ولآلی مکارم ومعالی از ممکن سطور ومعدن عبارتش در کمال صفا وغایت رونق وبها جلوه می نمود.

نامه اقبال چوں آورد مرغ نامه بر
دیده غم دیده روشن شد مرا از دیدنش

درویشان بی ریا ومعتکفان زاویه صدق وصفا نفائس ادعیه زاکیه ولطائف اثنیه بهیه در معرض معارضه مقابله داشته به جان وجنان آرزو مند سعادت مجالست ومشتاق لذت موانست می باشند وپیوسته از سرچشمه دیده اشک بار عقود سرشک در راه شوق محبت می باشند شرف مواصلت که اشرف مطالب ومعانی است سریعاً مقدر باد! بعد

۱ـ ع : دمید

ترویج روائح اخلاص وتنقیح مقاصد اختصاص معروض می دارد که برحسب مثال سدره مثال بسته بشرف مجالس بهشت آئین شاهی که هر آئینه متضمن دولت مواصلت ومخالطت سایر مخادیم وحضرات خواهد بود، استسعاد یابد۔ اما بواسطه وقوع بعضی وقائع محروم ماند۔ امیدوار است که در موسم آئنده نسیم مراد از بحار مواهب الهی وزیده سفینه امید مخلصان را از عمان حرمان به ساحل نجات واصل گرداند وآرزومندان نیاز مند را بکام دل برساند۔ همیں توقع که تا زمان نیل تلاقی از مراسم مکارم دریغ ندارند۔ کوکب سعادت از برج دولت طالع ونیر سیادت از اوج حشمت لامع باد بحرمة النبی وآله الامجاد۔

(۱۱۱)

مراسله بخدمت وزیر

ستاره دولت وسیاره اقبال که از سماء مکرمت وسپهر مرحمت حضرت اقبال پناه، معدلت دستگاه، وزارت انتباه، گردوں رقاب، ممالك مدار، مرحمت آثار، مکرمت شعار، زین الله سماء الایالة بنجوم دولته الزاهرة وشید قصر الامارة بمیامن حشمته[۱] الباهرة، درخشیده بود خلوت مهجوران را مستنیر ساخت وبر کلبه تاریك درویشاں پر تو سعادت انداخت۔ کربت غربت را از مطالع کواکب استمالت والتفات خاطر نواب کامیاب لوائح راحت وسرور مشاهده گردید وظلمت کشیده فترت هجرت از طوالع نجوم عنایت ومرحمت خدام سپهر احتشام لوامع جمعیت معاینه دیده:

۱۔ ع : حثمت

نامه لطف تو کرد از همه ممتاز مرا

نزد ارباب وفا ساخت سر افراز مرا

دعائی چو نفس مسیحا سریع الا جابة بازاء نسیم الطافش راجع می دارد وثنائی چون ید بیضاء کثیر الثناء بحذاء اعطافش در معرض عرض می آرد:

این دعا آسائش خلق جهان را شامل است

آنچه در باب توجه فقیر بجانب وطن مانوس مرقوم خامه مشکیں شمامه عنایت فرموده بودند وبر طبق آں فرمان همایوں، لازال نافذاً فی الربع المسکون، اصدار نموده می خواست که حسب فرموده احرام حریم سعادت واقبال بسته خود را به شرف مجالست مجلس جنت اساس اقبال پناهی وسعادت خدمت کثیر البهجت وزارت دستگاهی فایز گرداند۔ اما به سبب حدوث بعضی حوادث از مخافت[1] راه دریا بار وغیر ذالك امتثال آں دولت نصیب نشد۔ امیدواری بفضل الهی چناں است که هر گاه فی الجمله رفاهیتی در اوضاع روز گار روی نماید وشاهد امنیت از نقاب غیب جلوه گر آید علی اسرع الحال تصمیم عزیمت نموده به سعادت صحبت حیات بخش سرفراز شود، "والله علی ماقول شهید"، وبانجاح المسئول رسد۔ مستدعی از مراحم مکارم اخلاق آنست که چوں حضرت حق سبحانه وتعالی در دنیا بخت بلند ومنصب ارجمند کرامت کرده، اداء لشکر نعمائه در قواعد رعیت پروری وقوانین معدلت گستری کمال بلاغت مبذول دارند ودر رعایت مظلومان ورعایت ستم زدگان غایت اهتمام بجای آرند تا در عرصات سلك دولت مندان دوجهاں منسلك گشته به سرور جاوداں فایز گردند۔ هر چند در امثال این معانی خدام ظفر ارتسام را حاجت

۱۔ ع: مخالفت

نصیحت نیست امّا بموداء مرام "وذکر فان الذکری تنفغ المومنین[۱]" اقدام نمود۔ ظلال وزارت وسایه عدالت بر مفارق عالم وعالمیان مستدام باد، بجرمة النبی وآله الا مجاد۔

(۱۱۲)

مراسله بخدمت وزیر

بعد از تبلیغ صنوف دعوات خالصه آیات والوف تحیات صادقة البینات مکشوف ضمیر منیرمهر تنویر می گرداند که مجله نامی وصحیفه گرامی که درین وقت مصحوب قاصدان مرسل داشته بودند در اعز ازمنه و ایمن او ان بشرف مطالعه آن مشرف شد۔ دران مندرج بود که بعد از استماع خبر واقعه رضوان مقامی بعضی از بار یافتگان درگاه فلك اشتباه بعرض بندگان سده علیا رسانیده اند که اهل فرنگ بایك دیگر اتفاق نموده وغرابها را طیار ساخته اند وقصد آن دارند که بر سرتتّه آمده آن ولایت رابه تصرف خود درآرند۔ وچون بندگان حضرت ایشان را اباً عن جد بندگان درگاه دانسته آن ولایت داخل ممالك محروسه خود تصور می فرمایند، نمی خواهند که اهل فرنگ بران ولایت دستی یابند وباعث تفرقه سامان شوند۔ وزارت پناها! حق سجانه وتعالیٰ ظلال عاطفت بندگان حضرت را همواره بر مفارق دولت خواهان ویك جهتان ممدود دارد که باوجود علوشان ورفعت مکان از ادانی واقاصی خبر دارند ونمی خواهند که دست خادع حوادث زمان پیرامون اذیال مسلمانان گردد۔ اما آنچه از استعداد فرنگ وخیالات باطل ایشان قلمی نموده اند، محض کذب وبهتان

۱۔ قرآن مجید : ۵۵/۵۱

وحرف دروغ وافتراء بمسامع علیه باریافتگان درگاه معلی رسانیده اند، چه مدت شصت هفتاد سال است که مردم این سلسله از وطن مالوف ومسکن مانوس ولایت قندهار جدا شده درین ناحیت افتاده۔ درین مدت از رومی وفرنگی وملی بار ونکامره ونومك، که از سیاحان بحار وسیاران دریابار اند، آمد ورفت این معبر دارند۔ درین مدت اکثر جزائر را بحیطه تصرف خود در آورده اند۔ اما به عنایت الهی وبه یمن توجه بندگان اعلی حضرت این بقعه ازان قبیل نیست که دست تطاول این نوع مردم پیرامون این معنی تواند گشت۔ اگر ممکن بودی البته درین شصت هفتاد سال شاید این مدعی بر منصه ظهور جلوه گر آمدی وآثار این غرض بر صفائح دهور منقش گشتی بلکه در هر سال علی سبیل التواتر والتوالی فیطور کپتان فرنگ رسم خدمت مع تحف وپیشکش می آید وتا آمدن فیطور دیگر التزام خدمت می نماید۔ واین طریقه به مضی شهور وایام ومرور سنین واعوام سمت رسوخ یافته غرض که رقبه انقیاد ایشان بربقه اطاعت مقید است واعناق امتثال شان به طوق بندگی مطوّق۔ ایشان را چه حد ویارای آنست که این نوع خیالات محال بخاطر خود راه توانند داد چه قطرات امطاری که مواد قابله این نوع معامله اند از اوج سحاب الکان در تجاویف اصداف اعیان نزول نه کرده، بل جمره آن از سطوح اراضی وهم شان نحو سماء خیال صعود نه نموده۔ وقبل ازین که حکام گجرات بوده اند همواره ابواب رسل ورسائل ایشان مفتوح بود وتا انقضاء مدت حیات ایشان رشته این معنی بکزلك ناملائمی منقطع نشده۔ وبه سمع شریف ملازمان رسیده باشد که بعد مسافت بین این بقعه وولایات قزلباش قریب بپانزده وشانزده روز است وپیش از ارتباط این سلسله بخاندان عالی شان بندگان حضرت خلافت پناهی آمد وشد این طائفه مثل شیخ زاهد وخلیل بیگ ترکمان

می بود- ازان باز که دست اعتصام بحبل المتین حمایت ایشان مشید آمده اغراس[1] روابط این قوم بالکلیة سمت انقلاع پذیرفته-

دیگر آنچه درباب مخالفت وتنازع برادران بعرض باریافتگان درگاه فلك اشتباه رسانیده نیز خلاف واقع است، چه امری که موجب رفاهیت این سلسله است وباعث بر استمرار ورسوخ حکومت این طائفه همین اتحاد برادران الوس است بایك دیگر- بنابر اشتهار این خبر وانتشار این اثر همیشه از تلاطم امواج نوائب زمن وخدشه تراکم حوادث وفتن محفوظ ومصئون مانده اند والا باوجود اعادی آنجا واطراف مثل فرنگ ورومی وقزلباش وغیره چه گونه مرفه الحال وفارغ البال توانستی بود-

دیگر مرتقم بود که بتاریخ شهر فلان ببلده بکر رسیده منتظر بود که چون ایشان مجاور اند وایشان مسافر البته به تهنیت ومبارك باد ایلچی خواهند فرستاد تا آنکه تحقیق شد که ایلچی فرستاده بودند اما فلان مانع شده نگذاشت وبی توزکی جانبین شد- محبان پناها اگرچه ارسال رسل ورسائل بطریق تهنیت ومبارك باد بیان واقع است اما از جانب فلان منعی دریں باب ظهور نیامده، چه در حینی که سیادت مآب سید فلان به پاتر رسیده بود، ازان جانب لشکر کشی بر سرپاتر شد واین قضیه بوقوع انجامید والا اورا چه حد ویارای آن که ایلچی که ازیں جانب تعین شود اورا نگاه دارد- واطاعت وفرمان برداری این جانب بابندگان حضرت بمرتبه ایست که در اثناء مصیبت کبری وواقعه عظمی رضوان پناه سنن سنیه آباء واجداد را مرعی داشته بمقتضاء فحواء غراء "انا وجدنا آباءنا علی امة وانا علی آثارهم مهتدون[2]" ایلچی بدرگاه خلائق پناه فرستاده شد- سیادت مآب سید فلان را به تهنیت ومبارکباد

۱- ع : اغراض
۲- قرآن مجید : ۲۲/۴۳

بشرف قدوم ملازمان تعین نموده آمد- اگر در ارسال سید مشار الیه تاخیری واقع شد، باعث بر تاخیر این معنی آن بود که دریں قضیه هائله اکثر مردم الوس ابناء جنس والوسات واحشام وسوده وجاریجه از کچ ونانکرنی وغیرهم از اطراف وجوانب برسم عزا پرسی آمده بودند واکثر اوقات به خبرداری ایں مردم صرف شد و حاضر الوقت آنچه بود فراخور هر کسی قسمت یافت- شاید که بسمع شریف خدام نیز رسیده باشد وبر همگنان ظاهر است که دریں مرز وبوم که محصولات آن غیر از شالی وماهی چیزی دیگر نمی باشد، خزائن ودفائن ممکن بلکه متصور نیست- خلاصه وزبده ولایت سند بکر وسیوی وو گنجابه وفتحپور است که محصول مزروعات آن جو و گندم ونخود[1] وجواری است که معلوم نموده باشند که حکام آنجا کرة[2] بعد اولی ومرة بعد اخری تعین شده بودند، چه مقدار از خزانه بدرگاه فرستاده باشند که ازیں شالی وماهی بهم تواند رسید- مغفرت پناه میرزا شاه حسین که حکومت او بجمیع بقاع سند بود، در مدت حیات خود آنچه جمع نموده بود بکلها واسرها انتقال بمرحومی سلطان محمود خاں نموده- آن با آنچه مشار الیه جمع نموده بودند مجموع بدرگاه معلی رسید، معلوم نموده باشند که چه چیز بود- منافع ایں گوشه که محصولات آں شالی است وماهی است ازاں قیاس باید نمود- جزوی که بهم رسیده بود برخی ازاں پیشکش حضرت نموده شد ومابقی برادران وفرزندان والوس ترخان وارغون وبکه و کابلی واحشام جاریجه وسوده وغیره به ننگ وناموس تقسیم یافت- و گوشه جنگلی که هست آن حضرت رضوان مقامی در حین حیات خود از صوبها جدا ساخته به فرزندان خود تقسیم نموده بودند واز سپاه نیز بهمیں دستور- دراں حین برادران

۱- ع : نخود، ندارد

۲- ع :واقعه اولی

وفرزندان در صغر سن بوده اند والآن بدولت بندگان حضرت جوان شده اند وهر کدام ایشان قریب به بیست وپنح سال است وجمعیت ولشکر همراه دارند وهمه از دولت حضرت امیدوار اند۔

دیگر قلمی نموده بودند که بعز الله تعالیٰ وبروح پر فتوح حضرت ﷺ که ازین جانب بخون هیچ بنده خدای راضی نباشند۔ اما چون توزکی از فلان باشد ضرورت این چنین قضیه بوقوع انجامید۔ واضح خدام بوده باشد که چنانچه ایشان به سفك دماء خلائق راضی نیستند بفردانیت رب الاعلی که ایں جانب نیز ایذاء وتضئیع هیچ مخلوقی راضی نیست[۱] بلکه همت بران مصروف است که خلائق که[۲] بدائع ودائع حضرت خالق اند، همیشه فارغ بال ومرفه الحال بوده باشند۔ وپیش ازیں که مسند عالی فتح خاں بعنوان حکومت در بکر بودند با آنکه از ابناء جنس نه بودند اما آں مقدار رعایت خاطر این جانب از سرحد وسیم می نمودند که مشاهد ومعائن وضیع وشریف بوده باشد۔ وایشاں نیز از سکنه بکر معلوم نموده باشند۔ وازایں جانب نیز در ارسال رسل ورسائل رما یتعلق بها از حسن معاش دقیقه نامرعی نمی ماند۔ وازاں باز که ملازمان ظل تشریف مبذول داشته اند چوں ابناء جنس بودند وقدردان ایں سلسله وخدمات آباء واجداد که نسبت بدودمان عالی شان بندگان حضرت سمت ظهور یافته بهتر میِ دانند، همواره مطمح نظر آں بود که برسم عزا پرسی، که میان ابناء جنس متعارف وشائع است، ایلچی خواهند فرستاد وآں نیز واقع شد۔ دیگر احسن والیق آں بود که اگر از جانب فلاں امری که خلاف رای جانبین بود ظاهر می شد که بر سرحد بایں جانب ایماء می نمودند تا تاکید در منع او نموده می شد با آں که همیشه ازیں جانب تاکید می رفت که

۱ـ ع : نیستند

۲ـ ع : که، ندارد

برسرحد وسیم پاتر مناقشه ومباحثه نه کنند ومقوی یك دیگر بوده باشند ودر سلوك ومعاش آن طرف کمال اعتناء وغایت اهتمام بجا آورده نوعی نمایند که بی او امری ظهور نیاید۔ هر چند ازین جانب ممانعت اشارت می شد ازان جانب منازعت وقوع می یافت۔ واگر منازعت ایشان به تیقن می پیوست البته از هر صوبه فلاں تعین می شد۔ اما بنا بر اخلاص ویك جهتی این جانب که اباً عن جدٍ نسبت بخاندان بندگان حضرت خلافت پناهی واقع است، خدشه این معنی در خاطر فاتر خطور نموده۔ ودیگر آنچه در باب اطاعت وفرمان برداری بمقتضاء آیه کریمه "اطیعوا الله واطیعوا الرسول واولی الامر منکم[۱]" سمت اندراج یافته بود بوقوع پیوست۔

(۱۱۳)

مراسله بجانب وزیر در جواب

اقل مخلصان فلاں که در مناهج اخلاص بفتراك دولت قاهره اعتصام نموده، مراصد طاعت را باقدام انقیاد پیموده، الوف خدمات وافیه وصنوف عبودیات صافیه از روی هواداری وراه دولت خواهی بسده سنیه وزارت مرتبت متعالی منقبت آنکه:

گوهر پاك وی از مدحت ما مستغنی ست

فکر مشاطه چه باحسن خدا داد کند

بسط الله ظلال مراحمه وعزه واقباله علی مفارق اهل الزمان، در سلك عرض منتظم می گرداند که آناء الصباح واطراف الرواح از مبدا الارواح وفاطر الاشباح تضاعف انوار دولت وترادف آثار مکنت

۱۔ قرآن مجید : ۵۹/۴

آں صاعد ذروه استعلاء، ع: بزبانی که دل موافق اوست، استدعاء می نماید۔ مخاطبه شریفه ومفاوضه لطیفه که نازل ووارد گشته بود در ایمن ساعات واسعد اوقات عز ورود یافت۔ وچوں صحت ذات عدیم المثال وانتظام امور دولت از مطاوی آں واضح ولائح بود، باعث شکر گذاری شد، الحمد لله علی نعمائه۔ بر ضمیر آفتاب اشراق بلکه خاطر خطیر اهالی خراسان وعراق مخفی نیست که از هنگام طلوع تباشیر صبح از افق عالی تنق ایں ولایت الی هذه الغایته قلعه فلاں ومضافات وبلوکات در حوطه تصرف وحیطه تسلط حاکمان فلاں بود ولهدا بندگان حضرت آں قلعه را به مع منتسبات باسرها در جاگیر ایں حقیر عنایت فرموده اند۔ چوں خلاصه ضمیر ایں خیر اندیش وزبده خاطر ایں وفاکیش متوجه است که سرموئی از جاده قویم مطاوعت وسجاده مستقیم اطاعت بندگان حضرت قدم بیروں نه نهد، بنا براں در صدد آں شده که قلعه فلاں بدست آید والا حاصلات آں معلومات است، ع :

پیداست کزیں جرعه چه مستی خیزد۔

اما قدوه زمره "ان الذین فتنوا المومنین والمومنات[۱]" فلاں که بر سبیل استمرار نادو لتخواهی شعار او بوده وهست ونمی خواهد که آں صوبه داخل ممالك محروسه گردد وپیوسته بی آنکه ازیں جانب سرموئی مخالفت از طریق موافقت روی نماید، اهل قلعه را در گاه بیگاه وشام وسحر گه بدراه می کند۔ چنانچه قبل ازیں فرزندی فلاں بعساکر ظفر مآثر رفته بود، عاجزی فلاں به سرحدی رسید که شق داری قبول نموده وخراج وباج باو می رسانید۔ آخر الامر اغواء وطریق سر کشی پیش گرفت۔ ثانی الحال فلاں باجمعی برادراں رفته آں قلعه را محاصره کرد ونزدیك بود که از قلعه برآید۔ در اثناء آں فلاں مع آذوقه به قلعه در آمد وآں برگشته روزگار عزیمت دیدن را فسح نموده بکثرت اعوان

۱۔ قرآن مجید : ۱۰/۸۵

وقوت انصار غرور یافته از سرنکته، ع:

هر جا که زره گر است پیکان گرهست۔

بکلی غافل است۔

انشاء الله تعالیٰ زود باشد که بامداد وفود جنود الهی وبعز دولت بادشاهی فلاں دراں میان نشانه[۱] تیر تقدیر شده وهریك از اعوان وانصار او گرفتار قید وطعمه تیغ صاعقه گردد مثل فلاں که با دو نفر در جنگ پی توقف ودرنگ به قتل رسیده بدار البوار قرار گرفتند وبقیة السیف مع احمال واثقال وبا ذخائر اموال بذل رقیت وعبودیت ملحق ساخته بدرگاه سپهر اشتباه رواں سازد۔

مخلص نوازا اکنوں که بعواطف مقدم شریف زواهر[۲] عنصر لطیف ایشاں بر هماں هیئت آبروی بدبختان ما دولتخواهی به ظهو می رساند:

درختی که تلخ است اورا سرشت

گرش در نشانی به باغ بهشت

ور از جوی خلدش بهنگام آب

به بیخ انگبیں ریزی وشهد ناب

سر انجام گوهر بکار آورد

هماں میوه تلخ بار آورد

وقبل[۳] ازیں بکمال آں که هوا خواه درگاه خلائق پناه است چند مرتبه کتابت که فحواء آں منبئی از تاسیس بنیان وفاق وترصیص ارکان اتفاق بود بجانب او فرستاده آں را کان لم یکن پنداشت۔ وعلاوه[۴] آں فرزند[۵] نا ارجمند خود را در حد فلاں گماشت۔ توقع آں که بار

۱۔ ع: نشان

۲۔ ع: لطائف

۳۔ ع: قبل، ندارد

۴۔ ع: علاوه، ندارد

۵۔ ع: فرزندان

یافتگان مسند ایالت به نصائح ارجمند متعرض او بشوند یا بجزای لائق وسزای موافق منزجر گردانند۔ چون بندگان حضرت زمام اختیار مهام این صوب[۱] را بایشان[۲] سپرده اند بزوائد اطناب نه نمود۔ والدعاء[۳]

(١١٤)

مراسله بخدمت صدر

شرح الله تعالیٰ صدره للطائف وارداته[٤] وشرائف بشاراته وعظم الله تعالیٰ قدر الصداره بصادرات اوامره وواردات اشاراته ! بعد از رفع صوالح ادعیه، که بوی اخلاص آن بمشام جان رسیده وفوائح اثنیه که روی اختصاص آن از نیام جنان کشیده باشد، مشهود ضمیر صدارت پذیر می رود که تشوق و آرزو مندی بملازمت شریف[٥] زیاده ازان است که پیرامون وصف آن تواند گردید، بیت:

که آن بصدنامه شرح نتوان داد

احراز[٦] سعادت لقاء روح افزای، غم زدای عن قریب مشتمل جمیع متمنیات گردد، بمنه وعز کماله۔

۱۔ ع : ع : ولایت

۲۔ ع : ایشان

۳۔ ع : والدعاء، ندارد

٤۔ ع : دارد

٥۔ ع : شریف، ندارد

٦۔ ع : اجراء

(۱۱۵)

مراسله بخدمت صدر

نواب صدارت پناهی، عطوفت ورفعت دستگاهی، ملاذ الانامی فلان محفوظ باشند! ثنائی که چون انفاس عیسوی از فوائح وداد مژده حیات بخشد وهدید دعائی که چون نسیم بهار عنبر بار گلزار جان مخلصان را تازگی دهد، بصوب مجلس شریف ومحفل منیف اتحاف واهداء داشته معروض می دارد که همواره مستدعی ملاقات موفور السعادات می باشد۔ (امید که) عما قریب دولت مواصلت بخوب ترین وجهی واحسن ترین ساعتی دست دهد۔ از التفات نواب صدارت پناهی بعید است که رقم نسیان بر صفحه اخلاص محبان کشیده گاهی بدو کلمه یاد آوری نفرمودند[1] ۔ متوقع آن که بخلاف مامضی اتحاد قدیمی را مرعی داشته تا زمان حضور موفور السرور حدائق مخالصت وبساتین مصادقت برشحات اقلام مشك فام سیراب ساخته تجویز نسیان نفرمایند بزوائد اطناب نرفت۔ ولامراعلی۔

(۱۱٦)

مراسله بخدمت صدر

خرم آن کس که رو بکویت دارد
پیوسته نظر بر گل رویت دارد
بیچاره کسی که در بیابان فراق
سر گردانست وآرزویت دارد

۱ـ ع : نفرموده اند

الوف اجناس ادعیه وصنوف انواع اثنیه که از خلوص طویت وخصوص عقیدت انبعاث یافته، نثار مجلس حضرت عالی جاه، صدارت پناه، عوارف دستگاه، معارف انتباه، ملاذ الاحباء المخلصین، معاذ الضعفاء المضطرین، کهف الانام، ملجأ الخواص والعوام نظام الحق والدولة والصدارة والدین[۱] فلان، لازال ظلاله العالی الی یوم الیقین، گردانیده، پیوسته خواهان طلوع اشراقات نیر جمال وبروز لمعات خورشید اتصال بوده ومی باشد، وبهمه احوال رجا بکرم حضرت الهی واثق است که عن قریب مرة اخری و کرة بعد اولی مشاعر جسمانی بر مثال مدارك نفسانی سعادت اتصال فرخنده مآل ومراصد چشم خون بار چون مقاصد قلوب امیدوار در سلك حصول سمت انتظام پذیرد۔ ثانیاً منقوش مرآت صدارت آیات ضمیر منیر اطهر آن که ازان که حسب التقدیر بجانب ولایت فلان تشریف ارزانی فرموده اند ابواب مراسلات آن حضرت بر وجه تعاقب وتواتر مسدود است۔ وچون ازان نواحی قاصدی بدین صوب می آید خاطر حزین وجان غمگین امیدوار جویان وپرسان نامه نامی ومراسله گرامی می گردد و بعد الحرمان ازین سعادت بر فقدان مطلوب غایت[۲] اسلوب انواع تاسف وتلهف روی می دهد۔ بهمه[۳] حال ما مول آن که تازمان طلوع آفتاب اوان اتصال از افق آمال این مهجور بارسال نامه نامی بر وجه تواتر واتصال سرفراز وممتاز می گردانیده باشند زیرا که، بیت:

هر آن راحت که در دیدار باشد
بمکتوبی همان مقدار باشد

۱۔ ع : والدین، ندارد
۲۔ ع : مکتوب کرامت
۳۔ ع : بهر

زیاده اطناب موجب املال بود ـ ظل رأفتکم الی یوم الموعود[1]!

(۱۱۷)

مراسله بخدمت صدر

وثیقه محبت ووداد ونمیقه مودت واتحاد که از گذارش خامه بدائع نگار صدارت وفصاحت ایثار[2] ونگارش کلك عاطفت وبلاغت نثار خدام افاضت پناه، حقائق دستگاه، مجمع الفواضل والفضائل، حمید الخصائل والشمائل، المتخصص بعواطف الملك المنان، لازالت ایام افاضته وافادته، رقم تعبیر وسمت تحریر یافته بود، درخوب ترین وقتی وبهترین ساعتی از مطلع اشفاق منور آفاق گشت ـ چون مضمون حقائق مشحونش محتوی بر مژده شریف قدوم مسرت لزوم وبشارت استقامت مزاج کثیر الابتهاج بود، بهجتهای تازه وفرحتهای بی اندازه روی نمود وپیوسته تشوق واوام وتعطش وغرام بزلال بزم وصال افاضه فرجام متجاوز الحدود است علی الخصوص دریں ایام بنابر مصداق که؛ بیت:

وعده وصل چو شود نزدیك

آتش شوق تیز تر گردد

بمرتبه رسید که عشری از اعشار آں بر صفحه بیان صورت ابراز واظهار پذیرد،

کیں حدیث است که چوں وصف توبی پایان است ـ

---

۱ ـ ع : ظل رافتکم ممدداً الی یوم الدین

۲ ـ ع : آثار

(۱۱۸)

مراسله بخدمت صدر

صدر الکتاب صحیفه کامگاری وفصل الخطاب منشور بختیاری یعنی تشریف تفقد عالی که عالی جناب، نیابت پناه، امارت شعار، صدارت دستگاهی، مخدومی، ملاذی، بیت:

آن که جهان را شرف از نام اوست

شرح الله صدره للاسلام واعلی فی خلود الصدارة قدره فیما بین الانام، که دولت خواه قدیم را بحکم "سلام قولاً من رب رحیم[۱]" بشرف صدور آن مفتخر وسرفراز فرموده بودند، فی ایمن وقت واکرم ساعت سمت ورود یافته موجب انکشاف جمال مطلوب وانشراح صدور وقلوب گشت. والحمد[۲] لله. بعد از اقامت مراسم انکسار ولوازم ضراعت نیاز وافتقار بر مرآت ضمیر بی عیب که بحکم "یعلم خائنة الاعین وماتخفی الصدور[۳]" جام جهان نمای اسرار غیب است، مخفی ومحجوب نماند که صورت توفق[۴] وتوقف که سابقاً در مهم چند ابواب معهود از پای برگ لمون وسایر اجناس خزانه عامره وقوع یافته بود بی سببی معقول وعذری مسموع نیست، وحقیقت آن که در عتبان (غلیان) فساد ومواد بلیه طاعون اکثری از ارباب صناعت جامه بافی لباس فنا پوشیده بودند وشرذمه قلیلی که خلعت حیات انسان بطر از مهلت "انك من المنظرین[۵]" مطرز بودند بوادی تفرقه وجلاء چون بنات

۱ـ قرآن مجید: ۵۸/۲۶

۲ـ ع: لله، ندارد

۳ـ قرآن مجید: ۱۹/۴۰

۴ـ ع: توقیف

۵ـ قرآن مجید: ۱۵/۷

النعش عنان عزیمت بدست هزیمت داده، معلولی چند در کسوت عروض این علت موسوم ومبتلا گشته چنانچه در نظر تحفظ واز[1] احتیاط مکروه می نمود که از ملابس اعراض وامراض ایشان به قلیل وکثیر[2] چیزی متوجه موقف همایون گردد، بالضرورت قدم در جاده اعراض نهاده، طریق تعویق مسلوك داشت۔ واگر این مانع که علت تعلل شده دران ولا مرتفع[3] بوده باوجود صدور اشارت واجب الاطاعت چگونه شائبه از تاخیر بحواشی ضمیر متطرف گشتی۔ امیدوار است که چون وجه اعتذار ظهوری دارد بسمع رضا اصغاء فرموده بر قصور وتقصیر محمول نیفتد وبحسن قبول واعتبار مقابل گردد که همگی وثوق واستظهار این کمینه وسوانح ملکی ومالی بعموم عنایت ورعایت جناب خداوندیست "انه علیم بذات الصدور[4]"۔ ظل عواطف ومراحم بیکران مبسوط وموید باد، بحق الحق واهله۔

(۱۱۹)

مراسله بخدمت صدر

خطی گشت از مصدر لطف واصل
زمضمون آن شد مرادات حاصل

نامه بی مثال موقّع بتوقیع فضل وکمال وصحیفه بدائع مقال موشّح بارقام عطوفت وافضال، در ساعتی بسعادت مقرون وزمانی فرخنده همایون عز ورود وشرف حلول یافته موجب انشراح صدور

۱۔ ع : از، ندارد
۲۔ ع : کبیر
۳۔ ع : می بود
٤۔ ع : قرآن مجید : ۵/۱۱

نزدیکان ودور وباعث انفراح قلوب مشتاقان مهجور گردید۔ از مضمون خجسته مشحونش نداء بهجت افزای "اذهب عنا الحزن[۱]" بگوش هوش شنید۔ الحمد لله علی تواتر آلائه وتوارد نعمائه۔ تشوق ونیاز بادراك ملازمت خدام واجب الاعزاز بیرون از احاطه تقریر است وتعطش زلال وصال ملازمان ستوده فعال افزون از دائره تحریر۔ امید که عما قریب از میامن فضل "قریب مجیب" لطیفه انگیزد که حجاب قاصد ونامه از میان برخیزد وصدر محفل وصال محل جلوس ذات خجسته خصال گردد۔ اشارتی که درباب بعض امور مرقوم خامه تفقد واحسان گشته بود بواسطه آن رهین منت گردید۔ اراده بود که بزودی طریق آن کعبه اقبال پیماید ودر ظلال مرحمت وامتنان از تاب آفتاب حوادث ونوائب بیاساید اما موانع متنوع چند روزی این آرزو را در عقده توقف گذاشت، قطعه:

زانجا که نهایت جلال تو بود
توقیع صدارت ز کمال تو بود
دل گرچه مدام در خیال تو بود
کی درخور دولت وصال تو بود

رجاء واثق است که آنچه مامول است بزودی از پرده اخفاء وکتمان بدرجه اعلاء واعلان اقتران یابد وپرتو انوار وصال فرخنده مآل بر ساحت آمال شکشته بال تابد۔ زیاده برین اطناب واملال داب ادب نیست۔ ضلال صدارت وافضال بر مفارق اهل کمال مبسوط وموبد باد!

۱۔ قرآن مجید : ۳۵/۳۴

(۱۲۰)

مراسله بجانب مستوفی

مخلص نیازمند که خود را از اعمال (عمال) ولایت اخلاص ومباشران شغل اختصاص می شمارد وپیوسته سواد لیل وبیاض نهار به ذکر مناقب جمیله ونشر مآثر مرضیه آن سر دفتر اکابر روزگار موشح داشته اعداد دعا وخدمت، که در عقد انامل محاسبان اوهام ومستوفیان اقلام نگنجد، رفع می نماید۔ تمادی ایام عهد همایون که تاریخ روزگار سعادت واقبال وعظمت وجلال وفهرست جریده نهمت وکامگاری وعنوان نامه شهرت وجهانداری باد وتوفیر وتکثیر مداخل دولت از فروغ افاضت چون مبلغ حسابات شوق ونیاز مندی دران نصاب است که تیر دبیر، که نظر دیوان "کن فیکون[۱]" وبتکچی "نون والقلم وما یسطرون[۲]" است، هر چند پیرامون منها ومن ذالك جد واجتهاد گردیده از استیفاء مجمل ومفصل آن در نقل وتحویل عاجز اند وصرفی از دفعات آن مفروغ نکردند۔ لاجرم دران باب دخل نمی سازد چه اگر یك بابت از مفردات آن بر صحائف اوراق زوج وفرد روزگار مثبت نه رسیده به حشو برآید۔ باقی حالات این جائی چون نسخه جمع وخرج ومحصول صادرات وواردات عرض آن از حساب فاضل می دارد وحشو بار تصور می کند۔ سایه عالی بر مفارق ادانی واعالی ممدود باد!

۱۔ قرآن مجید : ۱۱۷/۲

۲۔ قرآن مجید : ۱/٦

(۱۲۱)

مراسله بجانب مستوفی

ای کلك تو آغشته بخون دل من
اوراق سیاق تو حل مشکل من
وصل است مرا باقی وهجران فاضل
از باقی اداکن عوض فاضل من

دعا از حیّز حساب بیرون وثنا از درجه تعداد افزون معروض داشته قسم باسرع الحاسبین که کیفیت افراد جن وانس در دفاتر علوم اوثبت است وکیفیت افعال جزء وکل موجودات بر اوراق روز نامچه موجودات دانش او درج که بقای نقود ایام حساب علی الاستمرار بدعا گوئی وثنا جوئی آن حضرت صرف وخرج می شود۔ وچون شرح شوق ملازمت شریف بیش ازان است که در ظروف وحروف گنجد وبامداد قلم استیفای مجمل از افرادآن توان کرد، لهٰذا در تنقیح آن موقوف نموده، شروح را راجح داشته۔ طمع وتوقع چنان است که تا ادراك سعادت خدمت حرف رافت را از صفائح مکرمت حكّ نفرموده همواره ابواب مکاتبات شریفه مفتوح سازند که خاطر بآن تفرقه جمع شود واز صفحه ضمیر منیر منها نفر مایند، چون بدفعات سوانح حالات عرض شد بیش ازان اطناب ننمود وبدعا ختم کرد۔ قطعه:

همیشه تابه بیاض نهار می آرند
مسودات لیالی برای ضبط حساب
حساب عمر وبقای تو باد چندانی
که درمحاسبه عاجز شوند کلك وکتاب

دولت وسعادت الی یوم القرار ممدود باد[۱]۔

(۱۲۲)

مواسله بجانب بعضی از سادات

عالی جناب، سیادت ونقابت انتساب، مکرمت وشفقت قباب، جامع الفضائل والکمالات، حاوی افانین علم الشرعیات، مرکز دائره فضل وکمال، قطب فلک عز واقبال، قدوه آل طه ویٰسین، سلاله اولاد امجاد سید المرسلین، جلال الملة والسیادة والشریعة والدین فلاں، لازال ظلال عاطفته ورافته علی رؤس طالبیه المخلصین الی یوم الیقین، قوافل دعوات متعطشات ورواحل تحیات شائقات هم عنان قافله سالار صنوف اخلاص وهم رکاب بدرقه سلامت گذار حقوق اختصاص مبلغ مرسل داشته علی التواتر والتوالی سعادت ملاقات افاضت آیات آں مجمع الحقائق والکمالات را بدعاء استدعاء می نماید۔ امید که عن قریب به شعشه سطوت آفتاب دولت اتصال خجسته خصال ظلال ظلمت دیجور فراق عمابین مرتفع ومنعدم گردد۔ بعد هذا مکشوف ضمیر فیض تاثیر آں که به براهین نقلیه وحجج عقلیه مبرهن شده که مساعی جمیله خدام شاں در مهم سازی ایں مخلص مصروف ومبذول است۔ خدای تعالیٰ ایشاں را خیر دهاد که امداد[۲] فقیر عدیم الاستطاعت، قلیل البضاعت سعی جمیل دارند که ایں شیوه ایست مرضیه وسنتی ایست سنیه که در شاں هر موجود غیر موجود است، "ذالك فضل الله یوتیه من یشاء[۳]" مع هذا ایں نوع از مقتضاء مرویه صحیبه

۱۔ دولت سعادت الی یوم القیام ممدود باد، ندارد

۲۔ ع ، س : مصروف ومبذول است، خدای تعالیٰ ایشاں را خیر دهاد که درامداد، ندارند

۳۔ قرآن مجید : ۴/۶۲

که "من کان فی حاجة اخیه المسلم کان الله فی حاجته[1]" وسیله عظمی وذریعه کبری جهت انصرام مهام مساعی این امر خیر است۔ بزوائد اطناب نه نمود۔ ایام سیادت ونقابت مستدام باد[2] !

(١٢٣)

مراسله بجانب بعضی از سادات

رسائل خدمات زاکیات اخلاص آیات وصحائف عبودیات طیبات مودت سمات معروض رای غمزدای ومشهود خاطر فیض مآثر سلاله سادات عظام، سلیل النقباء الکرام، جلیل النسب، جمیل الحسب، خدام فرشته احترام وملازمان عالی جناب رفعت وعزت آیات[3]، شوکت وحشمت انتساب[4]، نظام الدولة والدنیا والدین کمالا للحرمة والعظمة والاجلال ضیاء الدین فلان، لازال عزه دائما فی الاقران، می گرداند وهمواره در مدارس شوق وآرز ومندی کتاب یاد ملازمت بابهجت را علی ظهر القلب وطرف اللسان خواند ومی خواهد که این اوراق رسائل آرزو واشتیاق را بزود دریافت سعادت خدمت باز خواند وبحسن مقابله منظور وملحوظ گردد، انشاء الله تعالیٰ العلیم۔ وپیوسته تسلیه خاطر فاتر از نوشته کلك فیض سلك ودانسته دیده انتظار دیده را براه مطالعه آن چون شوق ناظران تجلی ابکار افکار بوجه زیاده از حوصله تحشیه متن عبارت وحاشیه شرح استعاره میداند۔ ع : باشد که بنوری رسد دیدۀ من۔ التماس از التفات مرحمت اقتباس آنکه این

١۔ بخاری، ابواب المظالم والقصاص، باب لا یظلم المسلم المسلم۔

٢۔ ع، س: بزوائد اطناب نه نمود۔ ایام سیادت ونقابت مستدام باد، ندارند

٣۔ ع، س : آیات، ندارند

٤۔ ع، س : شوکت نصاب

کحل الجواهر را علی الدوام در کاغذ پاره باذیال مخلصان حقیقی پیچیده، ارسال می داشته که چشم منتظر ان لباس "وابیضت عیناه من الحزن[1]" بخلعت نور سرور وروشنائی حضور مسرور گردد "وماذلك علی الله بعزیز[2]"۔ ودوسگ تازی که التفات فرموده بودند رسید، در شکر گذاری آن قلادهٔ عبودیت در گردن اخلاص در آورده فروتنی نموده شد، قبول باد، بحرمة النبی وآله الامجاد۔

(۱۲٤)

مراسله بجانب بعضی از سادات

درر لآلی که ازاں درج معانی در سلك بیان کشیده بود، یعنی صحیفه واجب التعظیم ونامه لازم التکریم عالی جناب عالمین کاملین[3] سیدین طاهرین المهدین، رفع الله تعالی منازلها (منازلهما) فی الدارین بحق سید الکونین که بدین مخلص جانی ارسال داشته بودند، در اسعد ساعات وامجد اوقات کالوحی من السماء شرف نزول یافت۔ نه چندان فرحت وبهجت به حصول پیوست که شرح آن بدو زبان قلم توان داد واگر در بیان شمهٔ ازاں شروع نماید[4]۔

شعر:

لم یبق فی الارض قرطاس ولا قلم

وکفی بالله شهیدا۔ ومضمون مبرهن گردید۔ الوف دعوات محبانه وصنوف دعات (دعوات) مخلصانه راجع وعاید می دارد، امید

۱۔ قرآن مجید : ۱۱۷/۲

۲۔ قرآن مجید : ۱/٦۸

۳۔ ع،س : کاملین، ندارند

٤۔ ع : رود

که باجابت مقرب مقرون گردد۔

بحضرتت چه فرستم که آن ترا شاید
بجز نیاز که آن شیوه محبان است

بر ضمیر منیر کیمیا تاثیر روشن وهویدا باد که قبل ازین کیفیت عقیق[1] از عدد وفروخت که مشروح معروض گردانیده بود، دریں ولا اگر رای صواب اندیش مصلحتی داند باز خرید کند۔ ترقب که تا زمان نیل ملاقات مخلص صادق الاعتقاد وواثق الاعتماد را بارسال سلامی سرفراز گردانند۔

کزان طرف نه پذیرد کمال تونقصان
وزیں طرف شرف روزگار ما باشد

ظلال دولت ابد پیوند بر سر مخلصان مستدام باد بحرمة النبی وآله الامجاد۔

(۱۲۵)

مراسله بجانب بعضی از سادات

خطاب وحی اقتباس معجز اساس و کتاب کریم عواطف اقتباس که از آسمان قدس واعتلاء بریں مخلص نزول یافته بود، مورد اجلالش[2] بجاروب مژگان رفته به لسان وجنان "الحمد لله الذی انزل علی عبده الکتاب[3]" گفته، جواهر التفات وعواطف که در ضمن درج بیانی مندرج بود وشاح مفارق مفاخرت ساخته۔ انچه از شکوه روزگار وحوادث

۱۔ ع : عقیق ، ندارد
۲۔ ع، س : اجلال
۳۔ قرآن مجید : ۱/۱۸

چرخ دوار وانقلاب لیل ونهار شمه آن اظهار آورده بودند از عوارض زمان وطوارق حدثان مستغرب نه نموده[1] - هر چند بنده در میدان سخن رانی باوجود کمال آن معانی نشان عالی شان ماسك عنان ادب باید بود، مع ذالك بمتقضاء "ذکر فان الذکری تنفع المومنین[2]" در عرصه عرض می آرد که حضرت رسالت پناه علیه وعلی آله افضل الصلوات واکمل التسلیمات که حد آن خلاصه اسباط است باوجود شان رسالت کشاکش طائفه قریش را با کمال تحمل تلقی نموده وجفا از خویش وبیگانه برده تا وقتیکه قانون دین اسلام بسمت قرار وآرام موسوم آمده- وبعد بحکم حدیث نبوی "انی ترکت فیکم الثقلین کتاب الله وعترتی حتی لن تضلوا بعدها" تفویض امور المسلمین با اهل بیت که آن حضرت نقاوه ایشان است فرموده- پس به ضرورت از جهت قرار اسلام آن جامع ملك وملت را مرتکب صورتی چند باید شد وازین معنی خاطر عاطر را آزرده نباید داشت که عیاذاً بالله اگر مقدار سر سوزنی تاذی وتضرر بساحت حریم خاطر فیض مقاطر رسد بیم است که حدائق زندگانی بصواعق آسمانی مستاصل گردد وبهار اعمار بخزان از نشو ونما معطل ماند:

مبادا خاطرت آزرده از کس

که باشد خاك تیره جای آن کس

استفساری که درباب توطن این دیار ودوری از قوم وتبار باضطرار اختیار فرموده اند بدان شعور وعثور حاصل شد- برضمیر حق پذیر عرضه می دارد:

ما اخترت نای الدار عنکم بسلوة-

۱- ع : نموده

۲- قرآن مجید : ۵۵/۵۱

نــــه دوری دلیــل صبــوری بــود
کــــه بسیـــار دوری ضــروری بــود

بـعـد از اوان شیخوخت خواست حضرت عزت چنیں است که تـرك دار وديـار وقـوم وتبار کـرده در خـطه سند معیل ومدیون واز دائره خدام بحسب ظاهر برون مانده: شعر :

الالیـت شعــری هـل ابیتـن ســاعة
بــواد وحــولــی ازخــر وجــلیــل

هر زمان دل بسر کوی تو مشتاق تر است
سیری از صحبت احباب نه بیند هر گز

امید بکرم واهب النعم وفاتح هر فرح وغم آن که حزن وهم از لـوح ضمیر ایں مستمند بوصال جمال باکمال آن حمید خصال ازالت فـرمـایـد وبر روی دل دردمند ابواب نصرت وفرح ومسرت بکشاید، انه یسـمـع ویجیب والسائل منه لایخیب۔ شرح حالات ایں صورت که در استنظاف[1] آن استفتاح فرمودند ودر اظهار تعلق خاطر مسابقت نمودند، هیهات:

مــــاه شبـی بــایـد وخـوش مهتــابـی
تــابــا تــو بـگـویـم سـخن از هر بــابی

مـجـملاً آن کـه از کثرت طروق نوائب ووفور حدوث مصائب اصـل ایـں گـوشـه هـریك در حـال خـود حیران ودر بادیـه قلق مبهوت وسـر گـردان۔ اولاً فـاعـل مـریـد وواهـب مراد بسیوف جنود جرار جزاءً[2] لاهـل التـمرد وتنبیهاً للعباد رقم "فجعلناها حصیداً کان لم تَغْن بالامس[3]" مـزروعـات شتـوی وبـقـولات ربیـعی ایں طرف کشیده وضیاع اشجار

۱۔ ع : استنفاق
۲۔ ع : جزاء، ندارد
۳۔ قرآن مجید : ۲٤/۱۰

در معرض ضیاع انداخته سر "ویرسل علیها حسبانا من السماء[١]" بر اوراق واثمار آن ظاهر گردید- چنانچه دریں سال مطلقاً بی نفع وعاطل وحقیقت "وبدلناهم بجنتیهم[٢]" بدان صادق وشامل- وآب سربواسطه قلت زراعت صیفی غیر وافی وارباب طلب دیوانی در مهم خود بغایت ساعی وکافی، مگر فضل الهی از مخزن دیوان نامتناهی "وان من شئی الا عندنا خزائنه[٣]" واز مزرعه امید بیچارگان اسرار کمال جسته "انبتت سبع سنابل فی کل سنبلة مأة حبة[٤]" هویدا گرداند وبازماندگان وحشت صحبت دنیوی را بالطاف مشحونّ والطاف گوناگون از چند وچون وهم وهم از هر گزند برهاند:

ناامیدی بر ارباب طریقت کفر است

گر دری بسته ای دل دگری بکشایند

مفصلا آن که حضرت خداوندگاری که شهریار است ووجود شریفش بر اصناف مکارم اخلاق آراسته وذات نفیسش باقسام میامن اعراق پیراسته ودر مقام عبادت وشرع پروری وحید زمان ودر مقام علم وآیات وحکم عدالت فرید اوان، زمانی که متوطنان بیت الاحزان را تشریف نزول ارزانی داشت از دردمندان نظر عنایت دریغ نه داشت وخاصةً صحیفه امیدواری دردمند که از نفس امداد مهمل نگذاشت- بزوائد اطناب نه نموده[٥].

١- قرآن مجید : ٤٠/١٨

٢- قرآن مجید : ١٦/٣٤

٣- قرآن مجید : ٢١/١٥

٤- قرآن مجید : ٢٦١/٢

٥- ع : والدعاء، زیاده دارد

(۱۲٦)

عریضه بخدمت شیخ

عالی جناب، مشیخت مآب، فضیلت جناب، افاضت ایاب، افادت انتساب، حقیقت شعار، مودت دثار، مرکز دائره فضل و کمال، قطب فلك عز واقبال، نظام الحق والحقیقة والدنیا والدین فلان، رفع الله شانه لاعلاء اعلام الشرع المتین، را دعوات شائقه وتحیات رائقه متحف ومهدی داشته دائم الاوقات آرزومند سعادت مواصلت ایشان، که اهم مهمات است، بوده و می باشد۔ امید که این مطلب اعلیٰ ومقصد اقصیٰ عما قریب از عالم غیب ظهور وبروز نماید:

چه خوش باشد که بعد از انتظاری
بنا امیدی رسد امیدواری

شرح تشوق وتعطش بمرتبه است که شمه شرح آن بدستیاری قلم شکسته زبان نتوان باز نمود۔ لاجرم صرف عنان توسن اختیار نحو اختصار اولیٰ وانسب بود۔ بهمه حال از حضرت باری، عزاسمه، رجاء واثق است که حجاب ظلمت شدت فراق را به شعشعه طلعت آفتاب وصال مابین مرتفع گرداند وکشت زار تشنه بادیه افتراق وانتظار را بقطرهٔ زلال اتصال سیراب وشاداب سازد! ودیگر اگر تراکم امواج محنت وهجران از حد حصر متجاوز است اما به تعارض امید فرحت وسرور اقتران بدرجه تساقط است۔ وهمگی استظهار واعتماد چنان است که تا زمان حصول ملاقات متواتر به نامه نامی دل حزین را مسرور سازند۔ فرد:

هر آن راحت که از دیدار باشد
به مکتوبی همان مقدار باشد

زیاده ابرام نه نمود۔ ظل رافتکم ممدود وعاقبتکم محمود!

(۱۲۷)

عریضه بخدمت شیخ

سلام الله علی مولانا شیخ الانام، قطب الایام، محی السنة والطریقة سلطان المحققین[۱]، بهاء الاسلام والمسلمین السلام ورحمة الله وبرکاته! الحمد لله که آفتاب عالمتاب ولایت حضرت ارشاد ملاذی از ظلمات سحاب حادثه عامه ایمن بوده از فلك ولایت وکرامت برمفارق عالمین سیما نیاز مند انی که بقبول خاطر وحسن تصرف شیخ، متعنا الله بطول بقائه، مشرف گشته اند، تابان است۔ دریں ایام تفرقه انواع اخبار موحش می رسد، اماچوں توجه به باطن می نمود ایں خطاب می شنید:

هرگز نمیرد آں که دلش زنده شد به عشق
ثبت است بر جریده عالم دوام ما

چوں از راه ظاهر طریق استفادت ازاں دریای بی ساحل بجهت موانع معلوم مسلوك نمی توانست کرد، خلاصه دل وجان وروح وروان معتکف وملازم آں آستان بوده ومی باشد وباستفاضه مستظهر ومسرور بوده می گفت:

به شرطی دل بکوی او فروشد
که تا جاں برنیاید برنیاید

المامول ان یختص بمزید توجهات الخاطر الفیاض والله یخلد ظلال ارشاده بالنبی وآله۔

۱۔ ع : محققین

(۱۲۸)

عریضه بخدمت شیخ

حقیقت عبادت خضوع وشکشتگی ونیاز که از شهود عظمت حق سبحانه بر دل ظاهر شود- این چنین سعادت موقوف محبت است وظهور محبت بر متابعث سید اولین وآخرین است، علیه من الصلوة افضلها ومن التحیات ایمنها- ومتابعت موقوف بر دانستن طرق متابعت است- پس به ضرورت از ملازمت علماء، که علم را وسیله معاش دنیوی وسبب حصول جاه گردانیده اند، دور باید بود- واز صحبت درویشان که رقص وسماع کنند- وهرچه خلاف شرع باشد بی توقف وتحاشی کنار گیرند وپرهیز کنند- واز شنودن توحید معارف که سبب نقصان عقیده در مذهب اهل بیت وجماعت شود دور باید بود- وتحصیل از برای ظهور معرفت حقیقت که باز بسته به متابعت حضرت محمد ﷺ باید کرد- والسلام والاکرام-

(۱۲۹)

عریضه بخدمت شیخ

عالی جناب، ولایت مآب، هدایت انتساب، سیاح مضمار الحقیقة بازمة التحقیق، غواص بحار الطریقة باعانة التوفیق، جامع الشرائع والحقائق بعلو الهمة، کاشف[۱] السرائر والدقائق بسمو المرتبة، مزین صحائف الدهر باسمه السامی، مولانا وشیخنا نورالحق والحقیقة

۱- ع : کاشف، ندارد

والدنیا والدین فلان، رفع الله تعالیٰ اعلام الدین فی ظلل برکاته مخلداً مجدداً۔ نفحات عطر سای صدق وصفا وفوحات مشك آسای عقیدت ووفا بانکهت ریاض اخلاص آمیخة از فسحت فضای اختصاص انگیخة اتحاف وابلاغ می گرداند وپیوسة اسباب جمعیت باطن حقائق مواطن را از مرصد غیب ومکمن لاریب مسألت می نماید، انه قریب مجیب۔ بعد هذا مرفوع آستان قدس آشیان آنکه درین اوقات که مباعدت صوری ومهاجرت ضروری سبب حرمان از موائد فوائد مجلس گشة، بملاحظه تقویت بدن شرف نزول در موضع فلان دست داد واز یمن توفیقات ایزدی آن معالجه نافع افتاد۔ به عنایت الهی اخبار واحوال جوانب واطراف موافق خیر وصلاح امانی و آمال است ودر هیچ ممر وره گذر خاطر را دغدغه وضمیر منیرا را تفرقه نیست۔ التماس واستدعاء آن است که در اوقات نفیسه نفائس ادعیه را بجانب مخلصان صافی العقیدة مصروف گردانند که هر آئینه نتائج آن بروزگار همگنان جهان وجهانیان خواهد رسید۔ شجره اسلام برشحات جوئبار هدایت بارور وسایه گستر باد، بمحمد وآله الا مجاد۔

(١٣٠)

عریضه بخدمت شیخ

خط شریف دل کشا از حضرتش آمد بمن

الحمد لله الذی قد اذهب عنا الحزن[1]

روائح گلزار التفات وفوائح ازهار اصطناعات، که عبارت است از نتائج قلم حقائق شیم، وکنایت است از مآثر خامه معارف رقم عالی

١۔ قرآن مجید : ٣٥/٣٤

جنـاب، هدایت مآب، ولایت مناب، قدوهٔ عرفاء الکاملین، اسوة الکبراء العـارفیـن، عـارج مـعـارج الـطـریقة، صاعد مصاعد الحقیقة، ادام الله بـرکـات انـفـاسه الشریفة ومیامن هممه العلیة، در اعز ازمنه عطر افزای آمال وامانی وراحت افزای قلوب مخلصان جاودانی گشت۔ بوسلیه ایں موهبت وواسطه ایں مکرمت لوای مباهات ومفاخرت از فرق فرقدین در گـذشـت۔ فـحـمـدا لله ثم حمداً لله۔ شوق ونیاز مندی بدریافت انامل سعادت دلائل امریست بیرون از احاطه وهم وخیال وشی است فزوں از استیفاء[1] فـاضـلان صاحب کمال۔ لاجرم از[2] شـروع دراں باب اجتناب واحتراز اولـیٰ دیـد ودر بسـط آں نـه پیچید۔ التماس از مکارم اخلاص واسـتـدعـا از مـراسـم اشـفـاق آں کـه در مـظان اجابت دعوات مخلص متحقق را فراموش نفرمایند وبادعیه صالحه وخاتمه فاتحه امداد واعانت می فـرمـوده بـاشـنـد، وگاهی برقعه، که موجب اطلاع بر صحت ذات بـابـرکـات واسـتـقـامت مزاج عالی درجات ومجاری حالات وسانحات بـوده بـاشـد، یاد آوری فرمایند که هر آئینه باعث بهجت وسرور موفور خـواهـد گـردیـد۔ ظل هدایت وارشاد بر مفارق اهل اعتقاد الی یوم التناد ممدد باد، بالنون والصاد!

(۱۳۱)

عریضه بخدمت شیخ

نـامـه فـرخ هـمـایـوں فـال کـه در عکس هر حرفی ازاں فرحی مـنـدرج اسـت، در بهـتـرین ساعات وخوب ترین اوقات رسید۔ موجب

۱۔ ع : استقامت
۲۔ ع : از، ندارد

ازدیاد محبت وسبب تضاعف مودت شد۔ بعد هذا آن که ظاهراً وباطناً همگی همت وجملگی نیت مصروف است بر تربیت آن مرید که مراد باشند که حضرت حق سبحانه تعالیٰ تصفیه باطن آن عالی نژاد الی یوم التناد مزید ومراد گرداناد، بفضله وجوده۔ باید که لمحه ولحظه را بی ذکر وفکر حق تعالیٰ نگذارند چنانچه در قرآن مجید وفرقان حمید یاد کرده است "فاذکرونی اذکرکم[۱]":

در دشت گه سپهر خضراء

غافل مشو ای حکیم دانا

ایزد تعالیٰ جمله طالبان را شراب شوق خود چشانیده از خود راهائی وبا خود آشنائی کرامت فرمایند۔

(۱۳۲)

عریضه بخدمت شیخ

بسم الله الرحمن الرحیم، الحمد لله الملك الکریم والصلوة والسلام علی صاحب الخلق العظیم۔ تحیات مشتاقانه وتسلیمات مخلصانه ودعوات محبانه به مشیخت پناهی، مفخر الفضلاء والعلماء ملاذ الصالحین والاتقیاء، مجمع الفضائل العلیة والمناقب السنیة، المتصف بکمال الورع والتعفف فلان، حفظه الله فی الدارین من کل مایوجب التآسف والتلهف، متحف داشة واضح می گرداند که مراسلات شریف ومکاتبات منیف در احسن اوقات واشرف ساعات بوصول پیوست۔ وچون مبشر بسلامتی آن اعزه بود، شکر انه حق سبحانه وتعالیٰ بجا آورده شد۔ امید که همیشه در حفظ الهی وفضل بی متناهی محفوظ ومصئون باشند۔ واحوال این غریب حیران بهرحال

۱۔ ع : قرآن مجید : ۱۵۲/۲

موجب حمد وشکر است۔ تفرقه احوال نه بمرتبه ایست که شمۀ ازان در تحریر آید۔ بنا برین در جواب آن مشیخت مآب اخوی اعزی از جهت اقامت وسفر هیچ نمی توان نوشت، زیر که در مقام تحیر واضطرار افتاده ام وبه هیچ کار اختیار دولت خواهی نمانده است۔ حکایت[1] فکر وتدبیر برطرف است زیرا که قرض بی قیاس بر خود آورده ام وخلاصی ازان به هیچ وجه ظاهر در نظر نمی آید وباز گشتن بغیر ادا کردن دین هم ممکن نیست که قرض داران ایذاء می رسانند۔ وبودن درین دیار دریں سن بغیر فایده دینی ودنیاوی محض عبث وانتقال کردن بجای دیگر بغیر مؤنت سفر دریں ضعف وپیری قریب[2] محال گشته، باوجود آنکه مرضی قرض داران هم نخواهد بود۔ پس چوں حال بریں منوال گشة، فکر وتدبیر چه کار کند وکسی که از فکر وتدبیر گذشته ودر تحریر وتحیر مستغرق شده، بذکر آن چه رای دهد وبکدام راه رهنمای نماید۔ وفی الجمله انچه مقتضای مصلحت است ایں است که چون واقع چنیں باشد شتابی در امری نباید کرد وتوجه به حق سبحانه وتعالیٰ باید نمود ودعای تضرع وابتهال پیش باید گرفت وامداد از اهل صلاح باید نمود تا مسبب الاسباب سببی پیدا کند که موجب خیریت طرفین باشد عاجلا وآجلاً۔ بعد از تکرار استخاره وتوجه الی الله سبحانه وتعالیٰ هر کاری که پیش می آید دران خوب خواهدبود وبآن راضی باشد که خیریت دران خواهد بود۔ مختار حکیم علی الاطلاق بی شبه از اختیارات ما بهتر وخوب تر خواهد بود وانچه مقدر است البته خواهد شد۔ پس به تضجر واضطرار خود را در محنت ومشقت نباید گذاشت ورضا بقضا پیش باید گرفت وسعی در امری باید نمود که موجب مواصلت وموانست ابدی بوده باشد۔ واعتماد ومواصلت این دار غدار نباید نمود که هیچ اعتبار ندارد۔ وفقنا الله

۱۔ ع : شکایت

۲۔ ع : قریب، ندارد

وایاکم لمرضاته والهمنا مایوجب المرافقة فی جناته[۱]، بجاه النبی وآله وصحبه اجمعین۔

(۱۳۳)

عریضه بخدمت شیخ

لوائح فصوص ولایت ولوامع شموس هدایت، اعنی رقم زده کلك فیض آثار ونگاشة خامه بدائع نگار جناب کرامت مآب، دراست ایاب، معارف دثار، حقائق آثار، الذی عجز لسان الواصفین عن وصف ذاتة ونفر فردوس العارف نسائم برکاته، قطب الحق والحقیقة والدنیا والدین فلان، لا زال مصباح الهدایة لامعة بانوار فتوحاته، در اشرف زمان واسعد اوقات واوان چمن ارادت واسترشاد را نضارت بخشید، وحسن ظن واعتقاد را موجب ازدیاد گردید، ومواد استظهار واعتقاد وسرمایه التجا واستمداد را موجب ومورث تضاعف وتزاید گشت۔ ودر مقابله آن ملاطفه شوق انگیز ومفاوضه صحت آمیز مدحاتی که فضای نزهت روضه ایجاد باشمائم عطر سای گلستان اتحاد آمیخته باشد، متحف ومهدی می دارد۔ امیدوار چنان است که در اوقات زاکیات وساعات متبرکات که مفتاح النجاح ومرآت صلاح وفلاح ونهایة الادراك عارفان سرور افراح است، از گوشه خاطر محو نفرمایند۔ رجاء واثق وذوق صادق است که به شرف اجابت مقرون خواهد بود۔ هدایا تحف آن مهبط عز وشرف از نگین سعادت تزئین عقیق که برقم فقرات لازم البرکات آیة الکرسی ثبت یافته ارسال رفته بود، خلعت سندس منزلت خاص که ازروی اعتنا واختصاص فرستاده بودند، از ایصال

۱۔ ع : فی احبابه

خدمت قدوة السالکین وزبدة الناسکین، سالك مسالك الطریقة بمواظبة النوافل والسنن شیخ کمال الدین ابو الحسن، دامت برکاته، رسید وخاطر مسترشدان را بعز قبول نظر رسانیده۔ مامول آنکه از صفائح ضمیر شمسیة اللوائح که مرآت انوار چهره مراد حقیقی است، محو نفرمایند ودر محال اجابت دعوت از خاطر قدسی مآثر نگدارند۔ شجره وجود طالبان برشحات فیض زلال سرسبز وسیراب باد۔

(۱۳٤)

مراسله بخدمت بعضی از علماء

حضرت رفیع وجناب مطیع، مولانا الاعظم الاعلم، ملجأ اعاظم العلماء بین الامم، محی مراسم الفضل والافضال، بانی مبانی المجد والاقبال، شهاب الحق والدین، مقتدای اعاظم، اسوة اکارم[1]، ملك الدهر، قادر زمان؛ شعر :

اعز علوم الرسل جاء رواته
وقام کما قام الخلائق بالامر

نضّر الله ریاض الفضل والافضال بساحة بقاءه واوراق حدائق العلم والکمال بسحاب عطائه! بعد از تبلیغ دعوات صالحات وتصدیر تحیات فائحات می نماید که مواد حسن اعتقاد واساس کمال اخلاص که محیط مرکز فرط مصافات ونقطه دائره صدق واعتقاد است، بنوعی تمهید یافته که امکان بطریق خلل بقواعد آن معانی پای در سرحد تخیل نتواند نهاد، شعر :

۱۔ ع : اسوه اکارم، ندارد

اذا ذهبت روحی فطار مفاصلی
واصبح عظمی فی التراب رمیما
ففی کل جزء من بقیة جوهری
وداد قدیم ظل فیه مقیما

لاجرم رفع این ذریعه را مظهر خوض ادای دعا کرده در آخر شهر فلان از دهلی مرقوم گشته انهاء می رود که درین سفر .. من عذاب السقر انواع حوادث جواذب[1] اشباح وقوابض ارواح فقیران شد که رمزی ازان بر الواح ضمائر ارباب بصائر منقوش نتواند گشت۔ گاهی دل از دوری دیار مانند هزار به فریاد می یابد و گاه جان از رنج تمام ومشقت بی شمار از قالب انفکاك می طلبد، بیت:

خسرو ندیده بود ادب حادثات هیچ
اینک ز حادثات زمانش ادب رسید

وچون قطع دریاهای بی کران وطی بیابانهای بی پایان کرده از شب خون گوران خون خوار ودزدان کفار نیم جانی بدهلی رسید، محمد شاه گمراه با دعا گویان حضرت تذلیل تمام وتحقیر مالا کلام به ظهور رسانید۔ سبب آن که در هندوستان آوازه انهدام خدام فلان از در ودیوار شد واین داستان در سائر جهان سایر گشت۔

القصة فقیر را کمال عقل وفراست وذکاء وکیاست اصحاب موسی علیه السلام معلوم شد که ترجیح قتل بر سفر کردند چنانچه در تفاسیر کتاب بزرگوار از شرح آن اخبار مملواست۔ هرچند فقیر در مقام "وما ابرئ نفسی ان النفس لامارة بالسوء[2]" باین بیت مترنم است۔ بیت:

۱۔ ع : جواذب، ندارد
۲۔ قرآن مجید : ۵۳/۱۲

مائیم که درهیچ حسابی نائیم
بر مشعله ومیان تهی چوں مائیم
آں دم که حساب نقد مرداں طلبند
آں ذره که در حساب نه آید مائیم

اما امید بانتقام ذو الجلال والاکرام ومدد ارواح پیران جام آں که داد شکشته دلاں ازاں غافلاں که از نداء عزیز "یا ایها العزیز ان له ابا شیخاً کبیراً[۱]" غافل بوده ملاحظه روحانی احمد جام نکردند وسبب جمعیت ایں تفرقها شدند۔ شعر:

انا الواثق المظلوم والله ناصری
وثقتی ممن یجور ویظلم

بیت:

حسن اسیر سر زلف نا مسلمانیست
که زیر هر سرموئی هزار بو العجبی است

استظهار فقیر را کمال شفقت آں جناب چنداں وثوق است که سپارش فلاں وفلاں فضولی تمام می داند۔ ابرام از حد گذشت۔ ظل ظلیل بر مفارق عزیز وذلیل تابنده وپاینده باد، والسلام۔

(۱۳۵)

مراسله بخدمت بعضی از علماء در جواب

بمقتفاء قضا دورم از دیار مراد
چنانکه محنت حرماں زجلوه گاه وصال

۱۔ ع: قرآن مجید: ۷۸/۱۲

همیشه بادیه پیمای حیرتم چه کنم
که نیست راه گذر بر مخیم آمال

نسیم انس ووفا وشمیم صدق وصفا که از رشحات خامه عنبر بیز ونفحات انفاس کلك شوق انگیز عالی جناب، معالی مآب، کمالات اکتساب، فضائل دثار، شمع جمع ارباب فطنت وذکاء، دیباچه قانون مهر ووفا، جلیس شفیق وانیس حقیق، لازال مرتقیاً علی مدارج الاقبال وما برح مهدیاً بانوار العلم والحکمة الی مناهج الافضال، چون نکهت عنبر سار فائح وآشکار فی زمان سعید ومکان سدید از ایراد مفخر التجار خواجه فلان سرمایه عیش وشادی ووسیله نجات وآزادی مایوسان بیت هجران[1] ومحبوسان[2] زاویه حرمان گردید۔ بیت:

مرده بودم از تپ هجران طبیب مهربان
گر نکردی نامه لطف تو دردم را دوا

خدا مشاهد حال است که شاهد دل فریب خیال آن جوهر دراك در آئینه ادراك[3] بصورتی انطباع یافته که زمان زمان توجه جمیل جلوه می نماید وهر جلوه دل می فریبد وجان می رباید۔ معانی اشواق را ترجمانی عبارات رائقه تصدی نمی تواند نمود وابواب مفصلات کتاب فراق را بمفتاح بیان نمی تواند کشود۔ واسأل الله نیل وصاله برای العین واطمع آن یرفع نقاب الحجاب من العین!

بعد هذا بر ضمیر فائض السرور مبهم ومستور نماند که جزئیات امور این مهجور بقانون نظم طبعی در سلك انتظام دارد۔ احوال واوضاع روزگار خویش را بکنف شکر وحمد باری تعالیٰ می شمارد۔ ازان زمان که بحکم قضا سر در بادیه جدائی نهاده وببلاء تنهائی رضا داده

۱۔ ع : الحزن
۲۔ ع : محبوسان، ندارد
۳۔ ع : درآئینه ادراك، ندارد

بقدم صدق واجتهاد وجهت قصد خود اقتناء معارف حقیقت واکتساب علوم یقینیه را دانسته وتا توانسته اوقات انچه نباید ونشاید صرف نمود (ننموده) وبدون ضروری شرعی یا عقلی در مخالطت برونی باجنبی از ابناء روزگار نکشوده۔ وبعد از فراغ مسوده شرح تحفه شاهی من اوله الی آخره بنظر جلیل ودقیق در آورده برسم تحفه مسوده کرده وبه بیاض آورده به طریق درس در صحبت یکی از تلامذه شیخ فلاں که بیواسطه یکی از تلامذه ابن حجر است، صحیح بخاری قرآت می شود وبمطالعه تفسیر بیضاوی مشغول است۔ شرح فلاں عن قریب بانظار شریفه مخادیم آں جا خواهد رسید۔ امید که وجود ناقص این شکسته را وسیله اعراض وباعث اعتراض نسازند بلکه تاممکن باشد به نظر اصلاح بران ارقام اندازند، چه من به نقصان غریزی وقلت حیثیت خود معترف بلکه باکثر نقائص متصف۔ هر چند امثال این احوال هم رعونت وخود نمائی است بلکه به حقیقت داخل زیاده گوئی وهرزه درائی، اما چون می داند که ضمیر آں جناب به کماهی حال این فقیر متوجه ومشغول است، اطمئناناً بخاطر کم بتفصیل نعماء ربانی وبسط تائیدات سبحانی که درباره فقیر سمت بروز وظهور یافته، متحدث ومتکلم شد۔ فالحمد لله حمده والصلوة علی محمد رسوله وعبده، صلی الله علیه وآله الاطهار واصحابه الاخیار وسلم۔

(١٣٦)

مراسله بخدمت بعضی از علماء در جواب

جان فرسوده شد براه تو خاک
ومن القلب لا یزول هواک

نتوان دوخت خود برشته وصل
جگری کز فراق گردد خاک

لطائف دعوات وافیات وظرائف تحیات صافیات مشحون به لآلی متألالی اخلاص ومکنون به درر غرر اختصاص تحفه مجلس فرح بخش گردانیده همواره بذکر خیر رطب اللسان وعذب البیان است ومقارن شوق ملاقات فرحت تو آمان۔ ترقب که بر نهجی، که متضمن اصلاح جانبین وحظوظ طرفین باشد، میسر یابد، بمنه وجوده۔ ثانیاً بر ضمیر انور اطهر، شریعت گستر، مخفی ومحجوب نماند که جناب فضیلت شعار، حقیقت اطوار، مخلصان ملاذی، استظهاری آنکه، ع:
وصفش به شرح نه آید راست۔

فلاں که بواسطه طیب اخلاق وتطیب اعراق در خاطر ارباب معروف ومشهور است، بعضی چیز کها از خانه مومی الیه بقضاء الهی، ظهر سلطانه وبهر برهانه، به دزدی رفته ودر پرده حوادث مخفی گشته۔ ظاهراً بعضی ازان مسروقات از فلاں نام برادر شخصی، که ظن قریب الاذعان بوی داشتند وقرائن وامارات عرف وعادت شهادت سرقه بروی ادا می کردند، دران نواحی یافته اند و گماشتهای والی آں ولایت به طریق ودیعت در محل ثالث سپرده که هر گاه صاحش حاضر شود حواله او کنند۔ وبناءً علیه وکیلی که اسم او در وکالت نامه مسطور است، از قبل خود فرستاده۔ مامول آں که دریں باب توجه بلیغ فرموده، نوعی نمایند که انچه در عالم ظهور آمده بوی سپارند ودر افشاء واظهار آنچه مخفی است مساعی مشکوره مبذول فرمایند که اشیاء مسروقه مومی الیه بدست آید، که آں قدر توجهی که بوقوع می آید باعث منت عظیم بر مخلص بلکه جمیع مخلصان ایں دیار خواهد بود۔ ترقب که لوازم محبت واخوت[1] را نصب العین ساخته نوعی متوجه شوند که حق

۱۔ ع: تقویت

بمرکز قرار یابد۔ زیاده بران اطنان واملال واندیشه نرفت وبدعاء اختتام نمود۔ والدعاء۔

(١٣٧)

مراسله بجانب بعضی از قضات

صحیفه التثام مودت که از خدام شریعت رتبت، معالی مکنت، مولانا اعظم، اکرم، مفخر قضات المسلمین[١]، والی ولات الشرع والدین جامع رضیة[٢] الشمائل وزکیة الخصائل، صدر المجالس والمحافل، لازال شمسا لسماء الافاضل والاماثل به جواهر عبارات غراء مرصع داشته بودند در ایمن ازمنه واحسن امکنه بدین محب صافی الاعتقاد سمت وصول پذیرفته نهال تصادق[٣] ووفاق که در جوئبار سطور کاشته بودند به ریاض سلام وتحیت معارض ومقابل می سازد۔

چون جواری التیاع واشواق بیشتر ازان اند که اعماق بحرین تقریر وتحریر[٤] سباحت توانند[٥] کرد، بنا بران ازان قلاب کلام در لجه بیان نه انداخت۔ توفیق التقاء، که تنها مناسب اوست، در اوفق حیات مقدور کرامت باد، بالنبی وآله وصحبه الا مجاد ! داعی بر رقم این مقال آن که بفضل الله المتعال مجموع واردات غیبی بروفق مآل است۔ وسائر سوانح وقت بر حسب مقتضاء است۔ واگر کتب مغفور مبرور قاضی فلاں در صدد بیع وشراء آید نفائس آن سفارش متعلقان شده

١۔ ع : الاسلام
٢۔ ع : نقیة
٣۔ ع : مصادقت
٤۔ ع : وتحریر، ندارد
٥۔ ع : تواند

بدست آرند۔ یقین که بنوعی اعتناء واهتمام دریں باب خواهند فرمود که مزیدی بران متصور نباشد۔

(۱۳۸)

مراسله بجانب بعضی از قضات

بیت[۱]:

قاصد ز تو نامه رسانید
جان را ز غبار غم رهانید
آن نامه نه نامه امانی
آئینه شاهد معانی

نامه نامی وصحیفه گرامی که مرقوم خامه گوهر بار ونقوش کلك سحر آثار خدام شریعت پناه، فضیلت در گاه، دیانت وامانت آثار فلان، زید قدره وفضائله، شده بود در ایمن اوقات واحسن ساعات شرف ورود یافت۔ وچون مخبر بود از سلامتی ذات با برکات آن شریعت پناهی، موجب بهجت گشت۔ اضعافاً مضاعفةً تحیت ودعاء، محمدت وثناء مزین بزیور صدق وصفا ابلاغ داشت وعظیم آرزومند ملاقات آن فضیلت دستگاه بوده ومی باشد، نیل آن علی احسن الحال میسر ومقدور باد۔ ملاذا[۲] از السنه وافواه استماع نموده باشند که چه مقدار پریشانی وسر گردانی بحال این فقیر راه یافته بود۔ دران باب چه نویسد که موجب حزن والم محبان ودوستان خواهد شد۔ الحمد لله والمنة که مصیبت ومحنت دنیا گذرانست۔

۱۔ ع: بیت، ندارد

۲۔ ع: ملاذا، ندارد

(۱۳۹)

مراسله بجانب بعضی از اطباء

بعد از عرض بیماری فراق ورنجوری درد اشتیاق انهای رای شفا نمای، مشکل کشای آن که چون مجموع قویٰ هر یکی به علتی علٰحده مبتلا، باصره بجز محنت دوری[۱] چیزی نمی بیند وسامعه بجز حکایت مهجوری چیزی نمی شنود وذائقه را تلخی فراق بی حلاوت ساخته، ولامسه را بجز خشونت دوران ومشقت مهجوران کاری نمانده۔ مامول که تا اوان حصول دولت وصال بیمار فراق را به تداوی ارسال رسل[۲] معالجه می فرموده باشند۔ والدعاء[۳]۔

(۱۴۰)

مراسله بجانب بعضی از اطباء

مریض عشق که بر بستر فراق افتاده وتن به محنت هجران جان ستان در داده هنوز امیدوار است که عیسی نفسی به بالین او قدم رنجه فرماید ودرد جدائی ومشقت نهانی را به شربت دیدار روح پرور ونسیم انفاس روح گستر مداوا نماید یعنی باوجود استیلاء محنت فراق واشتداد زحمت اشتیاق وبعد مسافت همیشه مترصد لقای سریع الصفاء وآرزومند صحت کثیر الصفات عالی جناب، حکمت آیات، معالی

۱۔ ع : ضروری، زیاده دارد

۲۔ ع : رسل، ندارد

۳۔ ع : والدعاء، ندارد

نصاب،

یاری وچه مهربان یاری
آرام دل وانیس جانی

عیسی نفسی مسیح رائی
درد دل ریش را دوائی

من یشفی اسقامنا بوصاله ویطفئ سورة آلامنا بخیاله، اجلّ الاحبة، احب الاجلة، کمال الفضیلة والملة، لازال کمال عینه محروساً من عین الکمال ونیر فضله[۱] محفوظاً من الغروب والزوال، بوده ومی باشد۔

بی تودمی[۲] شاد بعالم نزدیم
خوردیم بسی خون دل ودم نزدیم

والمرجو من فضل الله ان تقر عینی بوصاله ویسر قبلی من لطائف افضاله بحرمة سیدنا محمد وآله۔

بعد از بسط مقاصد شوق وغرام وتمهید وظائف دعا وسلام برضمیر منیر پوشیده نماند که این مهجور از شرف صحبت دور افتاده سوای الم فرقت آں جناب مکروهی دست نداده وفیاض بی منت ابواب فتوح صوری وفیوض معنوی بر روی این ضعیف کشاده۔ چه بعنایت الله تعالیٰ اوقات باکتساب عربیه وتفسیر مصروف است وخاطر باقتباس علم دینی ومعارف یقینی مشغوف، واسباب معیشت بروجه احسن واوسع مقدور است۔ واکثر اوقات بمطالعه علوم وشرح اشارات ومحاکمات واکثر مقاصد 'شفا' بنظر جلیل ودقیق رسیده و 'مجسطی' باشرح بتفصیل دیده۔ ابقاءً للآثار واحتفاءً علی قلوب اولی الابصار شرح بر 'تحفه شاهی' سواد یافت۔ چند جزء ازاں بر سبیل تعجیل بیاض آورده

۱۔ ع : کمال الفضیلة والملة، لازال کمال عینه محروساً من عین الکمال ونیر فضله، ندارد

۲۔ ع : دل

بخدمت استاد، علامی، کهف الانامی مع 'رساله در ابطال هیولی' مرسول داشته- یقین که چون نظر شریف جلوه نماید بعد از مطالعه پرده خفا از چهره بکشاید، اگر عبور بر هفوتی واطلاع بر عثرتی واقع شود اصلاح دریغ ندارند- وایں شکسته دل را از محبان جانی ودوستان جاودانی شمارند وتا زمان حصول ملاقات کریم السمات ابواب مفاوضات مفتوح فرمایند وبه نوك خامه مشك فام رنگ غم از آئینه سینه مشتاقان مستهام بزدایند- چون جناب محبت آیات، افتخار الاحباب خواجه فلاں، اعلی الله قدره، که از خطه فلاں باز بسمت رفاقت ایں فقیر التئام داشته وهمواره همت معاونت وامداد وحسن تودد واعتقاد ایں جانب گماشته وعلم مصادقت برافراشته دریں وقت عازم آں دیار بودند وبر نقیر وقطمیر احوال خبیر، مکرراً به تفصیل احوال محتاج ندید- کواکب فضل وکمال همیشه از مطلع عز واقبال طالع باد، بالنبی وآله الامجاد-

(١٤١)

مراسله بجانب بعضی از اطباء

بعد از تلخیص رسائل خلوص وتنقیح وسائل خصوص تحیتی چون انفاس قدسیان مجرد از شوب شوائب ریا وخدمتی چون ماده خلعت روحانیان مقید به صورت صدق وصفا معروض موقف افادت ومشهود مجلس افاضت می دارد وپیوسته ارقام اخلاص به ملك اختصاص بر صحیفه خاطر می نگارد، وحس ارادت وکمال مودت واتحاد نسبت به مقیمان[1] درگاه که معصم ارباب شوق ومطلب وملتم

١- ع : مقیمان، ندارد

اصحاب علم وادب است، مفتقر به زیور خط وخال الفاظ وعبارات نیست ومحتاج به مرتبه غنج ودلال شواهد استعارات وتشبیهات نی۔ حقا که حقیقت شوق ومحبت محاط بسته علمیه نمی شود و کیفیت خلت ومودت که هو حقه در حیز تحریر وتفسیر نمی آید، چه احاطه نامتناهی امری است ممتنع وادراك امور وجدانی کیفیتی است متعذر التعبیر؛ بیت:

قلم را آن زبان نبود که راز عشق گوید باز
ورای حد تقریر است وشرح آرزو مندی

فاسأل الله نیل الوصال واعوذ به من ویل الانفصال والله علی صدق ما اقول خبیر وبایجاب ما اسأل منه قدیر۔ اگرچه از راه صورت مسافت بعید[1] حاجز کعبه مقصود گردیده وباین[2] سبب انواع تفرقه واصناف الم بخاطر محزون رسیده اما همیشه مشام جان به روائح افادات علیه که از گلشن معانی می وزد معطر وظلمت آباد طبیعت از فوائح افادات جلیه که از سپهر باطن قدسی مواطن می تابد، منیر بوده زمان زمان نسیم توجه خاطر فیاض طالبان را طراوت افزوده ونفس نفس به رشحات التفات ضمیر آفتاب تاثیر مزرع استعداد مستفیدان را تربیت نموده است۔

لاجرم اکثر اوقات خود را بعد اقامت ما یجب علی العباد ویستحب للعبد من وظائف التعبد ورواتب العبودیة به تدرب[3] مقاصد قدماء وتتبع مآثر علماء مشغول ساخته وخدمات ومعارف دینیه[4] وملازمت علوم یقینیه را مورث هدایت ونجات ومثمر ارتفاع درجات

١۔ ع : بعیده
٢۔ ع : ایں
٣۔ ع : سداد
٤۔ ع : دینیه، ندارد

شناخته است وبه قدر همت قابلیت خود را از (هر) خرمنی خوشه واز هر سفره توشه گرد آورده، وبانچه مقدور فهم قاصر بوده دران طریق سعی واجتهاد سپرده- ازان جمله چون در اثناء مطالعه عبارات 'اشارات' وشرحش و'محاکمات' خار ترددی چند در نسخه دل خلیده بود وغبار شکی چند بر آئینه خاطر رسیده ودر دفع ورفع[1] منوع ومعارضات صاحب 'محاکمات' سخن چند روی داده بود وراه تصرفی چند در تلخیص وتحقیق مقاصد بر روی طبیعت کشاده- اما از قلت قابلیت وعدم اعتماد پر عزیزه خود آن را وقعتی نمی نهاد وبه مقتضاء تامل در موداء "المرء بصیر بعیوب نفسه" توسن طبیعت را در میدان اشتهار جولان نمی داد[2]- به سبب ایں دغدغه خاطر قرار نمی گرفت وازیں تفرقه آشوب باطن تسکین نمی پذیرفت- به خاطر فاتر رسید که ازان جمله انچه در وقت گنجد از سواد به بیاض آورده به نظر کیمیا اثر که حلال هر مشکل وفاروق حق وباطل است معروض می دارد تا اگر آن خودها بر محك اعتبار کامل عیار نمایند به سکه قبول رسانند ودر بازار صیرفیان سخن رائج گردانند والا جمله در خلاص اخلاص بگذرانند وعارض حق صرف را از عرضه تعرض باطل خلاص سازند وعلی کل التقدیرین کمینه باحدی الدولتین فائز گردد- بناءً علیه تمام بساحت تصورات بیاض آورده بنظر کیمیا اثر مبارك مرسول داشت؛ بیت[3]:

وکلت الی المحبوب امری[4] کله

فان شاء احیانی وان شاء اتلفا

بی ادبی و گستاخی را بذیل عفو واغماض مستور داشتن وهمت

١- ع : دریغ

٢- ع : نمی دید

٣- ع : شعر

٤- ع : اجری

بلند بر تربیت جانب مخلصان نیازمند واصلاح حال مستمدان دردمند گماشتن بی شائبه مناسب شمائل قدسیه آن ذات عالی شان وملائم بزرگی ایشان خواهد بود۔ مصرع:

بزرگان خورده برخوردان نگیرند۔

چون امید دست بوسی باقی است امید است که باقی مشافهه عرض داشته شود۔ سلام الله علی من یعتکف ببابکم ویقتدی بجنابکم۔

(۱۴۲)

مراسله بجانب بعضی از بخشیان

صنائع دعوات صافیات که مرقوم خامه اجابت تواندبود ومسطور اوراق استجابت تواند نمود اتحاف واهداء می دارد۔ پیوسته از درگاه منشی "انا انشاناهن انشاء[۱]" مستدعی ترقیم صحائف عمر ودولت آن صاحب فطنت بارقام ثبات وبقا بوده ومی باشد۔ تشوق وآرزو مندی به تقبل انامل سعادت دلائل بنوعی است که منشی مناشیر عقل دور بین از انشاء عشری از معشار[۲] آن عاجز است ودبیر خرد خورده دان از املاء اندکی از بسیار آن قاصر۔ امید[۳] که عما قریب منشور آرزوی ملاقات بتوقیع حصول موقع شود وصحیفه تمنای ملاقات به عنوان حصول معنون گردد، بمنه وکرمه۔ ترصد از عظائم اوصاف وترقب از کرائم اخلاق آن که همواره به ترشح سواد خامه عنبر بیز شعله آتش جدائی را

۱۔ قرآن مجید : ۵۶/۳۵

۲۔ ع : انشاء

۳۔ ع : امید، ندارد

فرونشانند وبه لمعه بیاض نامه ذوق انگیز کلبه تاریك مهجوران را منور گردانند۔ چون عرض مختصر است بزوائد اطناب چه حاجت۔ فضائل وکمالات در تضاعف وترادف باد، بالنون والصاد!

(۱۴۳)

مراسله بجانب بعضی از شعراء

عمرها گشتم براه وصل ومهجورم هنوز
آمدم بسیار نزدیك تو و[1] دورم هنوز

هزار سلسله دعاء وصد هزار قافله ثناء که زیب وزیور گوش وگردن شاهد بیان وعروس زبان توان ساخت نثار بزم خجسته وتحفه محفل شگفته عالی حضرت، عیسی طبیعت، عطارد خصلت، موسس قواعد سخن وری، ممهد مقاصد فصاحت گستری، صیرفی نقود سخن، مخزن اسرار معانی، جوهری عوالی امانی شهوار، خازن خزائن نیك اختری، نقاب دفائن خاقانی وانوری، زبده اصحاب درك وبلاغت، عمده ارباب فهم وفصاحت، مورخ مکارم حسن صورت، دستور فطنت وبصیرت، خوان نکته دانی واهلیت را نمك، چشم دانائی وقابلیت را مردمك اعنی مالك رقاب ملك معانی وبا صدق ادراك شیرین زبانی، خجلت ده روان شعراء متقدمین بگوهر فشانی ومعجز بیانی، وحید الزمانی، فرید الاوانی فلان گردانیده بنوعی از آرزوی صحبت به کیفیت بیتاب و اضطراب است که درجنب آن بی آرامی ماهی به کنار افتاده را صبر وسکون می توان شمرد وهر وجهی کدورت ومحنت مفارقت ومهاجرت هجوم آورده که نسبت بآن غم والم روزگار را

۱- ع : بس

عیش وخوش دلی نام توان برد۔ دلی که مائل ادراك شرف دیدار چو تویاری باشد، بچه چیزش مشغول می توان ساخت وجائیکه راحت دریافت ملاقات مثل تو نادره گفتاری باشد، بکدام حرف وصوت وفسانه وفسون به وادی دیگرش می توان انداخت۔ تشنه بزم را وصول آب حیوان تیزاب است ومشتاق جنت بزم وصالت را دخول بهشت دوزخ عذاب۔ طبیعت طفلی نیست که در مکتب ارتکاب وسبق تزویر تعلیم کم تاثیر از هوای عهد وصال آن معدن کمال باز آید وشوق تو طائری نیست که دانه ازو دور رساند وبجانب آن بال کشاید یا توجه نماید۔ واگرچه بصورت ظاهر چشم بخت از تماشای جمالت منور نگردیده ولذت شربت[1] وصالت بذائقه آرزو وکام هوس نرسیده[2]، اما باطناً کاری بجز افشاندن تخم محبت در زمین دل وکندن نقش ونام مودت تو بر نگین خاطر نداشته، پیوسته روی نیاز بر زمین ودست دعا بر آسمان، عز مواصلت وسعادت ملازمت از درگاه حضرت واهب العطیات، عز شانه، سائل وآمل بوده ومی باشد۔ امید که تیر دعا بر هدف اجابت آمده جفای تپ دوری وبلای شب مهجوری بسر آید ونهال امیدواری سر آید۔ "انه قریب مجیب"۔

درین چند روز مشیخت پناه فلان از حج کعبه وصال آن حضرت رجعت نموده وتقریر نمود که خوش هنگامه گرم ساخته اند وعجب جماعتی[3] فلك بهم رسانیده۔ در خدمت نواب مستطاب، بلند جناب، قمر رکاب، قدوه امراء خواقین آفاق، زبده وعمده سلاطین وملوك عالم باستحقاق، ملاذ وپناه عالمیان، معاذ وامیدگاه جهانیان نواب فلان نادره چند هستند که درین مدت لآلی چنان دریك سلسله

۱۔ ع : شرب

۲۔ ع : رسیده

۳۔ ع،س : وتقریر نمود که خوش هنگامه گرم ساخته اند وعجب جماعتی، ندارند

منعقد ندیده ودست روز گار درهای چنیں در رشته اعتبار نکشیده۔ خواه از جمعی که نهال استعداد ایشاں در پرورش گاه هندوستان نشو ونما یافته، خواه از گروهی که آفتاب تربیت از افق عراق وخراسان بر ساحت احوال ایشاں تافته۔ استماع ایں معنی آتش بیتابی در کانون سینه مشتعل ساخته واضطرابی در دل انداخته که چرا در حاشیه آں مجلس بهشت مثال ومحفل جنت تمثال، که منزل اهل فضل وارباب کمال واهلیت است، نیستم واز نتائج طبائع سلیمه آں طائفه رفیعه بهره ور نمی گردم، ع:

ای فلك صد هزار داد از تو

باری چوں دست مراد ایں نامراد از وصول بدامن ملازمت کوتاه است گاهی بتقریبی وباعثی که دانی یاد ایں سر گشته نموده همت بر اں مصروف داری که چشم امید رخسار شاهد کام در آئینه مراد بیند ومرغ دل در باغ وصال آں معدوم المثال بی دغدغه شاهین تفرقه واندیشه چرخ حادثه بر شاخسار سلامت ودرخت سکون واستقامت نشیند۔ وهر کسی عازم ایں جانب باشد بادوسه کلمه از سلامتی حال منیف ومزاج شریف مخبر وبر التقات واشفاق تو مشعر باشد، یاد وشاد گردانیده باشی۔ وانچه بتاز گی از بحر فکر غواص طبع بساحل نطق آورده باشند ارقام واعلام آں را منت عظیم ولطیفه جسیم درباره من تصور فرمائی ودریں باب طریق اغتفال واهمال نه نمائی که دل از آرزوی درد آں بی قرار است ودیده خاك نشین راه انتظار۔ خدمتی که از دست سعی فقیربر آید و کاری که اهتمام مخلص در اتمام انجام آں تواند که کوشش نماید اشارتی فرمائی تابجان در فیصل آں مساعی جمیله مبذول دارد واز رجوع آں مهم سرباعلی علیین بر آورده خود را به مباهات از خیل خدام در سلك یك رنگان ومنسوبان آں مخدوم بلند مکان شمارد۔ والامر الیکم وروحی لدیکم۔

(١٤٤)

مراسله بجانب بعضی از شعراء

شعر[1]:

صبا صحیفه مشکین یار می آرد
نوازش قلمی زان دیار می آرد

صحیفه شریفه سراسر سرور ووثیقه لطیفه از مطلع تا مقطع بهجت وحضور که نگاشته خامه صنائع طراز ورقم زده کلك بدائع آثار ناظم مناظم فضائل ونادر نوادر شمائل، نظّام عقود جواهر الابیات، صرّاف نقود زواهر الکمالات، دام فضائله ومعالیه، گردیده بود، در بهترین زمانی وشریف ترین هنگامی از مطلع اشفاق منور آفاق گشت وبوسیله این عطوفت وواسطه[2] این مکرمت غلغله بهجت واستبشار مخلصان از ایوان کیوان در گذشت۔ اگرچه حوادث روز گار ونوائب لیل ونهار صحائف اوقات عمر را از تحریر ابیات مواصلت خالی دارد وصفائح ساعات وحالات را از ترقیم اشعار ملاقات غالی نمی سازد لیکن غائبانه انشاء قصائد مدحت وثنا واملاء فرائد منقبت ودعا در غدا وعشا مرتب وموظف محب صادق الولاء است۔ امید که ذات حمیده خصال در حفظ وحمایت ذوالجلال و الافضال بوده عن قریب تالیف ارواح دولت وازدیاد فر وحشمت اشتغال داشته ودارد۔ امید که چون از صمیم دل بندهای با اخلاص است بعز اجابت لاحق باد۔ ثانیاً بنده وار بعرض می رساند که بورود عنایت نامه نامی وملاطفه گرامی که درین

١۔ ع : بیت
٢۔ ع : مراسله

ولا بـه تـواتـر یـاد آوری فرموده اند در اشرف ساعات چوں مژده حیات رسـید واز مضمون بهجت مشحونش معزز وممتاز گردید۔ حق سبحانه وتـعـالیٰ سـایه مرحمت آں حضرت را سالهای بسیار وقرنهاء بی شمار باقی داراد وشرف ملازمت گرامی که بهترین مقاصد ومرادات است بر وجـه احسـن روزی گـردانـاد۔ امید کـه از حـصول قرب جوار مشرف گـردد۔ لیکن از استماع خبر ولایت دکن نهایت متردد ومتالم گردید، نـگـرانـی تـمـام بخاطر رسید که دریں طور وقت ایں نوع تکلیف بعد از تـصـدیـع آں حـضـرت چیزی دیـگـر نیست۔ حق تعالیٰ در انچه بهبود ورفـاهیـت حـضـرت است بعمل آرد۔ بزوائد گستاخی ودراز نفسی نه نمود۔ ایام عمر ودولت بدعاء مخلصان باقی وپائنده باد، بالنون والصاد۔

(۱٤٥)

مراسله بخدمت مرشد

کـرائم تحیات مبارکات وعظائم دعوات طیبات که در معرض اجـابـت رسـد وثـمـره آں عـروج از حـضـیـض ضلالت وغوایت بر اوج هـدایـت شـود بوسیله این فرط گوش نو عروس اهل طلب معانق عروس مـقـصـود گـردد، عـز ابلاغ گردانیده می آید، باشد که جمهور حائران وادی حیرت را بـمـقـصـد رسـانـد۔ بعده آں که چوں طبیعت آرزومند مـقـصـود حـقـیـقـی را ولـع وغرام به تصانیف معتبره مشائخ کبار واولیاء حـقـائـق آثـار متـجاوز از ضبط افهام واوهام است وبنا بر شرف انتساب وانابت که از سلسله علیه قادریه دارد، شوق در جستجوی تفسیر قادریه وسـائر تصانیف حضرت ایشاں از همه بیش از بیش است، بنا براں فلاں را باعث تحمیل[1] اثـقال سفر گشت که از هر جا انچه ازیں جنس نفیس

۱۔ ع : متحمل

خصوصا تفسیر قادریه یابد بهم رسانیده بیارد۔ ترقب که درین امر خیر توجه جمیل دریغ نخواهند داشت۔ بزوائد اطناب تصدیع نرفت۔ توفیق رفیق باد ونتائج میسر بحرمة النبی الابطحی۔

(۱۴۶)

مراسله بخدمت مرشد

شعر:

مژده وصل می دهی بشرك الله ای صبا

صبح سعادت بدم پیك خجسته بیا

ای نفس معطرت مونس جان خوش آمدی

ای قدم مبارکت راحت روح مرحبا

لله الحمد والشکر والمنة که خبر فرخنده اثر تشریف قدوم سعادت لزوم درویشان صفا کیشان آن حضرت، سلهم الله المهیمن المنان، به مقتضاء 'العود احمد' دیگر باره سر ابستان مخلصان را مورد اصناف مسرت وشادمانی ساخته وطلوع نیر حصول از افق قبول به فحواء "طوبی لهم وحسن مآب[1]" پرتو انوار بهجت و کامرانی بر ساحت احوال زوایای هجران انداخته۔ چه گوید که ازیں بشارت خجسته اشارت چه افراح وانشراح روی داده وچه گلهای خوش حالی در گلشن فارغ بالی کشاده۔ امیدواری بمواهب حضرت باری، عزاسمه، چناں است که عن قریب اتفاق ملاقات روحانی باشراق ملاقات لسانی تکمیل گیرد ودیده از مشاهده دیدار فائض الانوار، که غره مصباح ولایت ولمعه چراغ هدایت است، روشنی پذیرد۔ بیت:

۱۔ ع: قرآن مجید: ۲۹/۱۳

جـان ودل بـاشـد بـه جـانـان متصل
رشك دارد چشم و گوش از جان ودل

ملاذنا ومرشدنا دریں ولا مقرب الحضرت السلطانية، اعتماد الدولة الخاقانية فلاں، که همیشه دم ارادت آں آستان قدسی آشیان می زند، بداں صوب باصواب فرستاده وقرار یافته که اول مهمی که سازد ونخستیں امری که پردازد آں باشد که بدرقه شده آں حضرت وجعمی، که در ظل رافت ایشاں متوجه مقصد اند، از محال مخوفه به میامن رساند وانچه امکان خدمتگاری است خود را به شرف تقدیم گرداند۔ اگرچه فی جمیع الاوقات والاحوال به توجه خاطر فیض اشتمال مستظهر است اما دریں ایام که خبر آمدن مخالفان دریں دیار متحقق کرده التماس استعجال قدوم مبارك می رود که مشافهه استدعاء فاتحه نموده باطفاء معاندان پرداخته شود۔ امید که مامول مریدان به درجه قبول مقرون دارند وبه امضاء مسئول معتقدان توجه خاطر فیض مظاهر گمارند وتا زمان سیر ایں سعادت در اوقات زاکیات وساعات نامیات، که محل واردات غیبی عبارت از همان تواند بود، بادعیه ماثورة الاجابة واثنیه مانوسة الاستجابة امداد واعانت می فرموده باشند۔ ظل هدایت وارشاد بر مفارق اهل اعتقاد ممدود باد، بالنون والصاد۔

(۱٤۷)

مراسله بخدمت مرشد

بعد از عرض عبودیت ونیاز بلسان افتقار وایجاز بحضرت مرشدی، قطبی[۱]، ملاذ المسترشدین، کهف المغیثین، ولایت و کرامت پناه، حقائق ومعارف دستگاه، عوارف وذوارف آگاه، لازال ظلال

۱۔ ع : قطب

ارشاده علی راس قاطبة المریدین والمخلصین معروض می گرداند وهمواره بذکر محامد ونشر مناقب رطب اللسان وعذب البیان بوده مستدعی دریافت ملازمت کثیر السعادت می باشد۔ امید که عما قریب این معنی بظهور وبروز آید۔ امید گاها! ولایت پناها! منشور فائض النور ومثال مکرمت اشتمال که مصحوب مشیخت مآب، فضیلت انتساب، شیخ فلان ارسال داشته بود، کصحف مرفوعة مطهرّة شرف وصول سعادت نزول ارزانی داشت۔ وچون مشعربر انواع نوازش مخلصان ومعتقدان بود، سر مفاخرت بذروه سموات سود۔ احوال یمن توجه عالی بروفق دلخواه[1] مخلصان انتظام دارد واز حقیقت جزئیات تصدیع نمی دهد، چراکه ضمیر انور اطهر که جام جهان نما است، عکس پذیر جمیع واردات وصادرات خواهد بود۔ وبحمد الله سبحانه بدانچه میسر است خود را در خدمت هیچ بنده خدا معاف نمی دارد وسعادت دارین می داند وانچه در ماده سفارش مشیخت مآب مومی الیه مرقوم بود، چون توجه عالی درباره ایشان ظهور یافته، فقیر خود مخلص ایشان است هیچ وجه خود را معاف نخواهد داشت وحتی الامکان در امداد ویاری هاسعی خواهد نمود۔ خاطر مقدّس منوّر من کل الوجود از جانب ایشان جمع دارند که بتقصر از خود راضی نخواهد شد۔ زائد گستاخی ودراز نفسی ننمود۔ ظل عالی برمفارق ادنی واعالی مستدام باد، بالنون والصاد۔

(۱۴۸)

مراسله بخدمت والد

حضرت ابوت مآبی، سعادت ایابی، شفقت شعاری، مرحمت آثاری، استظهاری، ملاذی فی کل الامور، مولوی فائض النور کمالاً

۱۔ ع : دولت خواهی

للاسلام والاعزاز، ملاذاً للانام، قبله گاهی، ولی نعمتی را مراسم بندگی وعبودیت اقامت کرده ادعیه خلود ایام حیات وادامت مآثر برکات از فرط اخلاص مزین- حرارت تعطش ونیاز مندی به سعادت دریافت ملازمت، که وسیله درجات دارین وفتوحات کونین است، نه دران نصاب است که شرح شمه ازان در تصاویر خیال واوهام بگنجد- نیل سعادت اتصال، که اهم مآرب است، از حضرت واهب العطیه مسئول امید که تیر دعا بر هدف اجابت آمده باشد- امید که این کمترین مهجور را از حاشیه خاطر خطیر فرونگدارند وبه التفات ضمیر انور که مفتح درجات ومثمر برکات دنیا وآخرت است، مشرف وبهره ور فرمایند- زیاده اطناب شرط ادب نیست-

(۱۴۹)

مراسله بخدمت والد

ضاعف الله تعالی عزکم وشانکم وتضاعف عمرکم ومکانکم! بعد از فاتحه شفاء ازدیاد عمر وبقاء آن حضرت، مربی ارباب عز وغنا ومشفق اصحاب کرب وبلا معروض گرداند که بموجب حدیث نبوی به عیادت آن حضرت ولی نعمت هر چند خواست اما چون اختیار مسدود بود، راه نیافت، چنانچه بآن حضرت واضح ولائح است که به جنایت حساد قریب یك سال است که در زاویه[۱] محنت وندامت کلبه کلفت وملامت به حالت عجیب وصورت غریب در بندی خانه آفت آشیانه مغموم وپریشان ومالوم وحیران افتاده است وتا این زمان از هیچ جانب رائحه مراد به مشام امید نرسید واز هیچ طرف صورت تخلص

۱- ع :مشقت و، زیاده دارد

استماع نه گردیده۔امید که به مقتضاء "من یشفع شفاعة حسنة[۱]" قدم در میدان اعانت گذاشته از ورطه آفات به ساحل نجات رسانند واختر این مقصود مراد از مطلع توجه وامداد خود طالع گردانند "من فرج من مسلم کربة فرج الله تعالیٰ سبعین کربة من کربات یوم القیامة"۔ زیاده چه تصدیع نماید۔ دولت دارین وسعادت کونین مخلد ومستدام باد۔ (بالنون والصاد)۔

(۱۵۰)

مراسله بخدمت والد

گرو صف کنم زبان وصف تو کراست
ور شکر کنم قوت شکر تو کجاست
گر زانکه بر آرم بدعا دست رواست
در دست متاعی که مرا هست دعا ست

بعد از عرض عبودیت وافتقار که سهام اوهام فصحاء شیرین بیان پیرامن تعریف آن نگردد وضراعت وانکسار که بصائر ضمائر بلغاء زیبا بیان بایراد توصیف آن راه نیابد، معروض بحضرت مخدومی، ملاذی، استظهاری، قبله گاهی، ولی نعمتی می گرداند که این فرزند مهجور همواره بذکر محامد شریفه ونشر مناقب منیفه[۲] رطب اللسان وعذب البیان بوده مستدعی ملاقات افاضت آیات می باشد، امید که عما قریب این دولت عظمی وسعادت کبری دست دهد۔ قبله گاهی چون از شرف ملازمت کثیر البهجت عزیمت این حدود نمود، همگی

۱۔ ع : قرآن مجید : ۸۵/٤

۲۔ ع : میگرداند که این فرزند مهجور همواره بذکر محامد شریفه ونشر مناقب منیفه، ندارد

اهتمام چنان داشت که به فلان جا رسیده از اجناس میوه که بهم رسد به ملازمت فرستد. ثانی الحال که به فلان جا رسیده، تحقیق نموده ظاهر شد که امسال به سبب وزیدن باد گرم باقسام میوه آفت رسیده وقبل از رسیدن این فرزند بقیه نمانده بود وچیزی که مانده فلان وفلان بوده که وجود[1] آن قبله گاهی خوردن آن بر خود حرام می داشت. بعزت الله تعالیٰ[2] طبیعتی که به صحبت وافر البهجت واشرف خو گرفته هر گز به تناول آن اقبال نه نمود واگر احیانا دست می داد بتکلف خورده می باشد. چه توان کرد که بعد مسافت مانع ارسال میوه بود. اگر می فرستاد یقین که در راه مضمحل ونابود می گشت. امید گاها شکر ایام مواصلت ومهر بانیهای آن ولی نعمت را بکدام زبان شرح دهد. حقا که زبان قلم از اداء آن عاجز وقاصر است. از گستاخی ودراز نفسی اندیشه نموده مافی الضمیر را معروض نمی دارد وحواله بر وجدان شریف می نماید. مامول از مواهب عام واشفاق تام چنان است که گاه گاهی فرزند مهجور مهموم را برشحات نوازش نامه یاد وشاد فرموده از حاشیه خاطر شریف فراموش نسازند وبرجوع خدمات لائقه منت نهند که حتی المیسور والمقدور در انجاح آن خود را معاف نخواهد داشت. سایه آن قبله گاهی بر مفارق فرزندان مستقر ومستمر باد، بحرمة النبی وآله الامجاد.

(۱۵۱)

مراسله بخدمت والده

نقاوة الملکات، ذات المیامن والسعادات، نتیجه مقدمات الجلال،

۱ـ ع : شریف، زیاده دارد

۲ـ ع : تعالیٰ، ندارد

مقدمه نتائج الکمال، المختص بعصمة الذات باحسن الصفات حضرت والده عزیزه فلانه را شرائف دعوات وردیة النسمات ولطائف تحیات عطریة الفوحات از خلوص ولا وخصوص وفا ایثار مجلس علیا ومحفل عظمی می گرداند وبر رای عالم آرای موضح وموشح می دارد که اگرچه این مهجور بواسطه حدوث حوادث ونزول نوازل از دولت ملازمت که وسیله حصول اصناف سعادت وکرامت است، دور ومهجور است اما سر از[1] رابطه عهود قدیم وضابطه عقود قویم ممهّد وموکد است وپیوسته پیکر وصال در آئینه خیال جلوه گر است وهمواره صورت اتصال از مرآت خیال در نظر، علی الدوام ادعیه حصول مراتب دینی ورد زبان است واثنیه وصول درجات صوری ومعنوی حرز جان۔ امید که بدرجه اجابت واستجابت اقتران یابد۔ توقع از مکارم اوصاف علیه که فراخور اخلاص فقیر را بنظر التفات وعنایات منظور وملحوظ دارند۔ گاه گاهی به عنایت نامه نامی معزز وممتاز گردانند که هر آئینه از مهربانی ایشان دور نخواهد بود۔ ایام عصمت بماناد ۔ بالنون والصاد۔

(۱۵۲)

مراسله بخدمت والده

سایه چتر عرش فرسای وظل مهر سپهر آسای والده معظمه مکرمه، ولایت پناه طوائف عالم وملاذ اولاد آدم باد وملازمان حرم عصمت پناه ومجاوران حریم مآل بفیض الهی وفضل نامتناهی مکرم ومحترم تحفه دعا منبعث از کمال اخلاص وهدیه ثناء منشعب از

۱۔ ع : اساس، زیاده دارد

محض اختصاص مرفوع داشته غایت الامکان متعطش زلال وصال آں ولی نعمتی، قبله گاهی می باشد۔ انشاء الله که هر چند زود تر چهره ایں امید از ممکن الطاف ربانی[١] واعطاف سبحانی روی نماید۔ حضرت عزت شاهد حال است که در جمیع احوال تسلی صدر غلیل وتسکین قلب علیل بدعاء جان درازی آں عصمت پناه است۔ التماس مخلصه[٢] ازاں حضرت آں است که همواره دست اعتقاد واخلاص را ازدامن عفت ایشاں کوتاه و کشیده ندارد وبخدمات لائقه واشارات عالیه ارزانی دارند که بجان وجنان ایستادگی نماید۔ ظل عالیه لایزال باد۔

(١٥٣)

مراسله بخدمت استاد

بعد از عرض وظائف دعا ورفع صحائف محامد وثناء بر ضمیر الهام پذیر حضرت افادت وافاضت پناه، حقائق ومعارف آگاه، خداوندگاری، استظهاری، امیدگاهی ملجأ الانامی، علامی، استادی می گرداند که تعلق ونگرانی خاطر فاتر وشورش وشغب وتعب مفارقت نه بنوعی است که شرح شمه ازاں بدستیاری قلم شکسته زبان بیان تواند نمود۔ بخدای[٣] لم یزل ولا یزال الذی هو عالم السر والخفیات که کیفیت و کمیت نسبت ذاتی ومحبت تعبیر نمودن از قبیل محالات است۔ بعد هذا معروض می دارد که حقا وبعزة الله تعالی[٤]، وکفی به شهیداً، که صبح وشام بدعاء جان درازی عمر وازدیاد دولت خدام

١۔ ع : انشاء الله که هر چند زود تر چهره ایں امید از مکمن الطاف ربانی، ندارد
٢۔ ع : مخلص
٣۔ ع : خدای
٤۔ ع : تعالی، ندارد

علامی مشغول می باشد- امید که تلامیذ حقیقی را از گوشه خاطر دریا مقاطر بالکلیه محو ومنسی نفر مایند که بدان مستظهر است- واگر مهم تلامیذ بطریقی[۱] که وعده فرموده بودند ساخته شود، باشارت عالی باوجود قلت بضاعت خود را بشرف خدمت وافر البهجت رساند- سایه[۲] علامی، فهامی، استادی لایزال[۳] باد - بالنون والصاد-

(۱۵٤)

مراسله بخدمت استاد

مخلص قدیم بر جاده اخلاص مستقیم بعد از عرض وظائف طیبات ولطائف تحیات زاکیات که کافل نجاح مطالب وحاجات گردد وشامل موهبات حضرت واهب العطیات شود، مشهود رای عقده کشای، روح وراحت افزای مخلصان ملاذی، اعتضادی، استظهاری، علامی، فهامی، استادی[٤]، مدظله، می گرداند که لایزال بذکر اخلاق کریمه عذب البیان ورطب اللسان بوده بدعائی که وظیفه ارباب اخلاص ودعا است مشغول می باشد- حضرت حق تعالی ذات کریم الصفات را از جمیع مکروهات محفوظ داشته بر مسند رفعت وعزت متمکن داراد- بعد هذا عرضه می دارد که سیادت ونقابت پناه، فضائل[٥] دستگاه میر فلان که بحلیه فضائل و اخلاق ستوده آراسته اند ودر لطافت ونزاکت فن شاعری ودیگر فنون وحیثیات گوی تفوق ازمیان برده مدتی[٦] ملازمت بندگان حضرت فلان بوده- وچون دواعی[۷] شوق

۱- ع : بنوعی

۲- ع ، س : نصاعت خود را بشرف خدمت وافربهجت رساند سایه، ندارند

۳- ع : لازال

٤- ع،س : استادی، ندارند

۵- ع : فواضل

٦- ع : در' زیاده دارد

۷- ع : داعی

واشتیاق عتبه یوسی درگاه خلائق پناه، ظل الله بغایة الغایة داشت، ترک وطن مالوف ومافیها کرده احرام حرم حریم این مقصد اقصی ومطلب اسنی بسته است۔ چند روزه بواسطه حرارت هوا بالضرورت درین جا توقف وتاخیر لاحق گردید۔ والحال عازم شده چون بملازمت کثیر السعادت فائز گردد امیدواری چنان است که مخصوص اعطاف والطاف فرموده بتوجه واسعاد شامل حال وکافل آمال ممتاز گردانند ودر وقت سعید بسعادت تلثیم درگاه خلائق پناه مشرفش سازند۔ بزوائد گستاخی نمی نماید۔

(۱۵۵)

مراسله بخدمت استاد

وظائف دعوات عقیدت بیان وتحیات مودت نشان مبنی بر کمال اخلاص ومنبئی از عنایت صدق واختصاص خدام ملاذی، استظهاری، اعتضادی، استادی، ملجأ الکرماء والفضلاء "ذالك فضل الله يوتيه من يشاء[۱]" شعر :

اشکر مآثره فلسن مآثراً
لکنهن قلائد الاعناق
والثم اناملـه فلسن اناملاً
لکنهن مفاتح الارزاق

مبلغ ومهدی می گرداند، بعز قبول موصول باد!

بعده معروض می دارد که سیادت وفضائل انتساب میرعراقی که بنجابت حسبی ونسبی وفضائل وحیثیات متصف ومعروف است، در

۱۔ ع : قرآن مجید : ۴/۶۲

لطافت ونزاکت شعر وتاریخ دانی وشاه نامه خوانی به حظی اوفر مخصوص است چنانچه بر ضمیر آگاه، مصدر فیض اله نیز مشاهده ومعاینه خواهد کرد، مدتی در ملازمت شاه عباس بوده ودریں روز گار سعادت وفیروز مندی قرین حال او گشته[1] ، از درگاه ایزدی احرام حریم عز واقبال وطواف مطاف سعادت واجلال یافته وجواهر شوق عتبه بوسی درگاه عالم پناه در خاطرش جا گرفته ترك وطن مالوف ومافیها نموده، امضاء ایں عزیمت قصوی کرده است۔ چوں در حینی که دریں دیار رسید برشگال بود، شدت حرارت هوا استیلاء واشتداد داشته، روزی چند حسب الضرورت بدین جانب اقامت نموده، وتادریں جابوده همیشه بذکر خیر آں ملاذ مشغول بوده وشیوه حسن اعتقاد ورابطه عبودیت ونیازمندی که بدرگاه افاضل پناه حاصل کرده، افتخار ومباهات می نمود۔ مسئول از کرم اخلاق خداوندی آں که چوں بشرف ملازمت الکثیر السعادت استسعاد یابد، از اشفاق عام ولطائف تام که درحق طائفه فضلاء وغرباء دارند، بقسطی[2] شامل مخصوص فرموده در ساعت مسعود بشرف زمین بوس اطهر، اقدس، مزکی، معلی سرفراز وممتاز فرمایند وبه رشحات توجه فیاض وضمیر منیر حدیقه امانی وآمال او را مخضر نمایند۔ چوں شاگرد نوازی وفیض پروری ملحوظ بود وایں اقل تلامذه را التفاتی ومرحمتی بر وجه اتم به تمام تر شرف امتیازی بخشند۔ بناءً علیه اقدام ایں قسم جرأت و گستاخی نماید۔ ظل عاطفت وافاضت بر مفارق مستفیض لایزال باد۔

۱۔ ع : گشت

۲۔ ع : بحظی

(۱۵٦)

مراسله بخدمت استاد

مقام مخالصت ووداد ومرتبه معاقدت واتحاد که نسبت بآن کمال اهل کمال ثابت است برتر ازان است که به نیروی سخن وری پیرامن آن توان گشت وبزور بازوی زبان آوری به نشیمن آن گذشت۔ هر آئینه عنان بیان ازان اطراف مصروف نموده زبان اختصار بدعاء دولت کشود۔ امید گاها چون فضیلت شعاری مولانا فلان جوانی صالح است اگر در امری باعانت ملازمان التجاء نماید وظیفه اشفاق بی دریغ دریغ نخواهند داشت۔ وقبل ازین سوانح حالات وفرستادن رسد به قندهار که باهتمام مخلص وسیادت پناهی بوده یحتمل که رسیده باشد۔ چون آن مردم درین چند روز مراجعت نمایند اخبار آن صوبه مشروحا در معرض عرض خواهد در آمد وحقیقت قندهار وحوالی آن که به تصرف دولت خواهان درگاه خلائق پناه درآمده وبدولت واقبال شاهنشاهی، خلافت پناهی، ظل الهی معمور وآبادان ومتوطنه آن جا مرفه الحال وشادان اند، وامنیت وقراری نهایت شده ووسعت وارزانی غله بمثابه ایست که نسبت بایں جا ارزان تراست۔ وتلمید زاده را مع عرضه داشت درگاه خلائق پناه فلك اشتباه فرستاد۔ امید که در محل صالح به نظر کیمیا اثر گذرانیده نوعی ملتفت شوند که به مناصب عالی متعالی سرفراز شود وشرف امتیاز یابد که دست تمنی ورجاء به دامن شفقت ومرحمت آن مجمع مکارم وسجایا زده بجز ایشان مربی وملاذ ندارد۔ چون غرض عبودیت واخلاص است بمزید اطناب اسهاب نمی رود۔ ابرام از حد گذشت هنگام دعا است۔ الهی مذاق اوقات میمنت از

شربت شهود حقیقی وزلال تحقیقی محظوظ وبهره مند باد، بحرمة النبی وآله الامجاد۔

(۱۵۷)

مراسله بجانب برادر

برادر اعز، ارشد، ارجمند، سعادت یار، برخوردار بعد از اداء سلام مشتاقانه اعلام می رود که بشر به حب جاه ریاست[۱] مجبول است ونفس بی اختیار وشعور به کسب[۲] آن مطلوب مشغول۔ خاصیت جاه غفلت[۳] افزائی والتفات بادشاه باده که کارش هوش ربائی است۔ خلائق را باچنیں کسی[٤] بسیار وچنیں کس را به هوش بودن بسی دشوار۔ اگر گاهی به مدد عقل خود را بجا آرد اما مستی آں باده بحالش نگذارد۔ ودراں مستی کجا[٥] بخاطر آید که فلك[٦] منتقم وغدار است وخالق فلك حاکم عدل شعار با اقتدار۔ جاهش را بقائی نیست وعمرش را وفائی نه۔ دشمنان از قبائح او در خنده[۷] اند ودوستان از فضائح[۸] او شرمنده۔ آشنایاں از ناخوشیها متاثر اند وبیگانگاں از دیوانه وشیها متعجب ومتحیر۔ پس نفس سلیم وعقل مستقیم باید که دراں مستیها خود را بی خود نسازد وبه خود رائیها وخود پرستیها نیندازد وبه حال درماندگان مظلوم پردازد۔ وایں نادان بی سامان را همه ایں حالات برسر گذشته واز هیچ یك از ینها آگاه وبهره مند نگشته۔ فائده که ایں

۱۔ ع : ثروت
۲۔ ع : حسب
۳۔ ع : عظمت
٤۔ ع : کار، ندارد
٥۔ ع : نظر، ندارد
٦۔ ع : فلك، ندارد
۷۔ ع : بند
۸۔ ع : نصائح

ورقها فلك در نوردیده، نه از آه ندامت کشیدن فائده ونه از اشك حسرت افشاندن فائده:

چون توانستم ندانستم چه سود
چون بدانستم توانستم نبود

ایشان راحق سبحانه تعالی این دولت وجاه کرامت نموده[۱] وسعادت تقرب بادشاه عنایت فرموده[۲]، باید که اوقات[۳] خود را به غرور وغفلت نگذارند وبه خسران دنیا وآخرت روا ندانند (نند) وعجزه وزیردستان را به شفقت ودل جوئی بنوازند وکار خاکساران را به مرحمت ونرم گوئی بسازند، بسخن درشت دل درویشان را نرنجایند وبالفاظ ملائم جراحت دار ایشان باشند۔ از فریب نفس وشیطان ایمن نه نشینند وصدمات ملك الموت را از خود دور نه بینند۔ در همه کارها اخلاص وراستی پیشه کنند ودر جزاء عمل بدان شرمساری روز قیامت اندیشه نمایند وهیچ گه از ترس حق غافل نباشند وهیچ وقت از ملازمت وبندگی سایه حق بیکار وعاطل نشوند۔ سخن راست که صلاح دولت بادشاه وسائر رعایا وسپاه دران باشد نترسند وبگویند۔ واگر اجر آن در دنیا نرسد در قیامت از حضرت حق بجویند از بدکرداری ابناء جنس را چها پیش آمده فراموش نکنند وخود را عیاذاً بالله از شراب غرور مست وبی هوش نگردانند وبه جهت مصلحت دنیا بایك دیگر نه ستیزند۔ وچون نفس را مستی رسد در پناه سپر صبر وتحمل گریزند۔ مصلحت بادشاه که موافق امر الهی باشد مصلحت ظاهر بادشاهی نپذیرند وبملائمت وحکمت عرض رسانند وبتوفیق الهی ازان مقام گذرانند، باخوردان طریق شفقت وبه همگنان مدارات

۱۔ ع : فرموده
۲۔ ع : نمودِه
۳۔ ع : اوقات، ندارد

وموافقت وبابندگان تعظیم وحرمت مرعی دارند۔ والسلام علی من اتبع الهدی۔

(۱۵۸)

مراسله بجانب برادر

اخوت مآب، سعادت ایاب، سیادت پناه، نقابت دستگاه، رضی الشمائل، مرضی الخصائل، لازال اسمه مسعوداً فی الدارین امیر مسعود را از[۱] ذرائع بدائع دعوات وروائع تحیات اعلام می رود که جریان احوال به فیض فضل ایزد متعال، جل ذکره، بعافیت مقرون است۔ الحمد لله حمدا لا انتهاء له۔ انسب آنست که همیشه بارسال مکاتبات وابلاغ مراسلات یاد می کرده باشند که 'الکتاب نصف الملاقاة' بیت:

سموم هجر کند روضه محبت خشک
اگر نه واسطه رشحه قلم باشد

بعد هذا آں که اگر ایں فقیر به دنیای دوں گرفتار گشت ودر بحر مذلت غوطه خورده اوقات شریف وانفاس نفیس را ضائع کرده خیری که در آخرت بکار آید حاصل نساخته اگرچه یك ساعت آستاں بوسی را صد برابر عبادت ثقیلن می داند۔ آں برادر[۲] وعزیزان ودوستان آں جائی باید که طریقه مرضیه آباء واجداد از دست نداده واوقات را به زیان ومالا یعنی ولهو ولعب نگذرانند وهمیشه در خلا

۱۔ ع : از، ندارد
۲۔ ع : برادران

وملاء حتی الامکان به عبادت وذکر الله که مقصود از آفرینش بنی آدم است که "ما خلقت الانس والجن الا لیعبدون[۱]" ای "لیعرفون" اشتغال نمایند۔ مثنوی[۲]:

هر آں که غافل از وی[۳] یك زماں است
دراں دم کافر است اما نهاں است
اگر آں غافلی پیوسته بودی
در اسلام بر وی بسته بودی

وموت را در پیش نظر آورده، فرصت را غنیمت دانسته، پنج وقت نماز با جماعت گذارده از گناه کبیره وصغیرة[٤] تائب شوند۔ واگر بیشتر نتوانند آخر شب بیدار باشند واز صحبت فاسقان وظالمان وجاهلان احتراز کرده صحبت صادقان وصالحان وعالماں اختیار نموده، در کسب کمال کوشند چنانچه حضرت قدس الله سره فرموده اند، قطعه[۵]:

علم است حیات جاوداں پی علماء
چشمی بکشا بچشمه سار علماء
آں چشمه که خورد خضر ازاں آب حیات
بود "آتیناه من لدنا علما[٦]"

وقت آخر است هشیار شوید وتوشه آخرت برداشته ساختگی قیامت کنید۔

۱۔ قرآن مجید: ٥٦/٥١
۲۔ ع: مثنوی، ندارد، س: قطعه
۳۔ ع: حق
٤۔ ع: کبیر وصغیر
٥۔ ع: قطعه، ندارد
٦۔ ع: قرآن مجید: ٦٥/١٨

بیت[۱] :

برگ عیش بگور خویش فرست

کس نه برده زپس توپیش فرست

تا بعد موت حسرت وندامت (نخیزد) وپیش خدای تعالی شرمنده نشوید۔

ودر اعمال صالحه سعی بلیغ کرده جوارح[۲] ظاهری وباطنی خود را از نامشروعات باز داشته امر معروف ونهی منکر بجا آورید۔ وشب[۳] وروز در خلوت وصحبت سلوك عادت کرده بعد از نماز فجر تا طلوع آفتاب سخن نگفته دریں ضمن بیاد حق، جل وعلا، (مشغول شوید) وبه وسوسه نفس وشیطان کار نکنید۔ وموت یاران گذشته خود را یاد آورده عبرت گیرید واز اوقات ماضیه ضائع کرده متاسف ومتلهف باشید که دنیا مکار است وشیطان غنیمی است کینه گذار۔ خلاص از مکر اینها مگر به کرم الهی وتوجه پیر دستگیر ومرشد مکمل مسیر شود۔ بیت[٤] :

بی عنایات حق وخاصان حق

گر ملك باشد سیاهش ورق

پس مهما امکن خلاف آنها کرده خود را در گریه وزاری وجزع وفزع داشته کاری کنید که دراں جهان بکار آید۔ خدای تعالیٰ خواهد پرسید که عمر خود را بچه صرف کرده اید۔ شاید که از مکر شیطان سالم مانده ایمان سلامت برید۔ دیگر بر زیردستان ترحم کرده به ناحق نرنجانید وحق جمله رحم را نگاه داشته بر خلق خدای تعالی به

۱۔ ع : بیت، ندارد

۲۔ ع : حواس

۳۔ ع : پشت

٤۔ ع : بیت ،ندارد

شفقت ومنفعت باشید۔ واین صحیفه را در پیش نظر داشته بر آن عمل نمائید تا در زمره صالحان حشر شوید وهمراه پیغامبران، صلوات الله علیهم اجمعین، در بهشت عنبر سرشت در آمده به دیدار حق، سبحانه تعالی، مشرف شوید۔ اللهم احشرنا فی زمرة الصالحین المغفورین، بمنه وجوده۔ آمین یارب العالمین[1]۔

(۱٥۹)

مکتوب بجانب فرزند

اطال الله تعالی فی دوام السعادة اعماره ورفع علی اعلی المراتب مقداره، ایام عمر وزندگانی فرزند ارجمند، سعادت مند، بصارت حدقه آمال وامانی، نضارت حدیقه حیات وزندگانی فرزند فلاں در حصول مراد وشادمانی ووصول مرام وکامرانی تاغایت اعصار ونهایت ادوار مستدام باد وتحف تحیات مشتاقانه وصحف مدحات آرزومندانه تامل نموده اشتیاق به بازیافت ملاقات فوق الحد والغایت تصور نماید۔ در تحصیل کمال واکتساب فضائل، که اعظم وسائل واجل مقاصد طالبان است، غایت اجتهاد بجای آورده، اوقات حیات را که سرمایه سعادت ابدی است، باشتغال لهو وطرب از دست ندهد که بعد از افاتت ندامت سود ندارد واضاعة الفرصة غصة۔ تا اوان ملاقات حالات اعلام نموده به مهمات رجوع نماید۔

۱۔ ع : یارب العالمین، ندارد

(۱٦٠)

مکتوب بجانب فرزند

مدت هجر زحد می گذرد صبر کجا است
که دریں واقعه صعب کند یاری دل
گر بوصلش نرسم در طلبش نیز خوشم
نیست مطلوب جزائم ز طلب گاری دل

فرزند دلبند فلاں، متع الله الکریم بطول العمر والجاه العریض الجلیل ورفعه باکتساب الخلق الجمیل والعلم النافع الجزیل، بداند که خاطر ایں پدر همگی اوقات ظاهراً وباطناً با اوست۔ می باید که در اکتساب معالی[1] وفضائل واقتباس حسن اخلاق وشمائل سرآمد اقران خود باشد وباز جواهر عالم را[2] در راه طلب آں بپاشد۔

می کوش بهر ورق که خوانی
کز دانش تمام دانی
یك دسته گل دماغ پرور
از خرمن صد گیاه بهتر

دریں وقت که مقتضیات تحصیل کمال بحمد الله المتعال بر وجه اتم است وعشائر موانع از اشتغال بالکلیه واسرها زائل، اگر مجدداً مردانه، چابك وفرزانه به مهیا اسباب طالبانه در راه نیاید، یقین است که از گلزار علم و گلشن زند گانی جز خار افسوس وپشیمانی نخواهد چید وروی حصول مرام بدیده هوش نخواهد دید۔

گفتن زمن از تو کار بستن
بی کار نمی توان نشستن

۱۔ ع : معلی
۲۔ ع : را، ندارد

چوں شیر بخود سپه شکن باش
فرزند خصال خویشتن باش

مقصود ایں نصیحت است که اکنوں در میدان تعلم در آمده سعی نماید که ازیں پدر قصبات مراحل کمال بیشتر باشد تا همچو عم خود صدر نشینی دیوان افاضل واماجد یابد۔ الهم وقفه ومتعه بالخیر وحصنه عن الشر والضرر لمصطفی المختار والاصحاب الاخیار[۱]۔

(۱۶۱)

مکتوب بجانب فرزند

فرزند دل بند[۲] بجان پیوند بداند که به یقین تمام وخواهش مالا کلام از حضرت ملك علام دولت مواصلت بانواع مراد واصناف حضور وسعادت وسداد ورشد ورشاد آں فرزند همیشه خواهاں وجویانم امید که باحسن وجوه چنانچه خواسته ومی خواهد میسر باشد، بمنه وکمال کرمه۔ الغرض که خاطر خوش دارد ودر انچه رضاء ایں پدر نیك خواه باشد، که هر آئینه خیریت دارین دراں خواهد بود، ثابت وراسخ باشد وبه تلطفات عرفی ظاهری اکابر نمایاں مقید وبر طریقه حمیده ارباب دین واصحاب یقین، که مطلوب جمیع طالبان است، متوجه باشد۔ یقین است که مطالب[۳] صوری ومعنوی بر وجه دل خواه[٤] حاصل ومتواصل گردد۔ وانچه اشارت شده در اثناء شفقت مجاورت معلوم شود واگر بنابر شفقت بجانب آں فرزند اظهار شفقت

۱۔ ع : الاخیار، ندارد
۲۔ ع : دلبند، ندارد
۳۔ ع : مطلب
٤۔ ع : دولت خواه

ومرحمت وعنایت بیشتر شود[1]، باید که آن فرزند سیرت پسندیده را زیاده بران کند وتواضع وخلق نیکو را سرمایه سعادات وپیرایه عنایات بدایات ونهایات داند. دیگر آن که آن فرزند در آمدن طریق وبر آمدن نباشد که در هرجائی شریف جادارد:

گاه در دل سازد گه در دیده جا
هر دو جای تست ای بدر الدجی

مگر در حرم یا درخانه طهارت که درانجا ملاحظه نماید والادرهمه وقت چون دل وجان از تن ضعیف این ناتوان جدا نباشد. واگر سخن داشته خود بگوید یا بنویسد، از واسطه غیر نگاه دارد حتی[2] از مبالغه که در تحریر وتقریر شده باشد، چیزی بخاطر نرسد. چون فرض اظهار پند دل پسند بود امید که پسند ودل پسند باشد وپند جان دل بند باشد:

خاطرت خورسند باشد دائما
دائما ودائما ودائما

(۱۶۲)

مراسله در گله مندی وشکایت از عدم مراسلت

در ملت مروت رعایت مخلصان که سالها ریاض مودت را به رشحات حسن عقیدت تازه داشته باشند، واجب ولازم است، ودر شرع فتوت ملاحظه خاطر دولت خواهان که دیر باز نهال محبت در چمن اخلاص و گلشن اختصاص کاشته اند، از مواجب ولوازم است.

۱ـ ع : واگر بنا بر شفقت بجانب آن فرزند شفقت وعنایت بیشتر، ندارد
۲ـ ع : حتی، ندارد

حالا مدت مدید وعهد بعید شد که از خدام استظهاری قلم عدم التفات در نام ونشان این ناتوان کشیده اند ونامه مردمی وصحیفه همدمی چون بساط مروت تمام در نور دیده اند. به عواطف پرسش عزیز نمی سازند ونه به لطائف تفقدی بیچگارگان را نوازند. مانع جز کثرت اسباب دولت[1] نخواهد بود. نزد ارباب بصیرت ومذهب اهل همت محظور است که تکاثر اسباب دولت وتوافر اسباب نعمت موجب نسیان وسبب فراموشی از حال مخلصان گردد.

منم کز یاد او پیوسته شادم
اگرچه سالها نیارد بیادم

(۱۶۳)

مراسله در گله مندی وشکایت از عدم مراسلت

بعد از تقدیم حکایت وشکایت نسیان وفراموشی واظهار گله مندی مخلص نانوازی وغمناك سازی[2] تصویر ضمیر منیر، مصادقت تاثیر آن که صحیفه محبت واخلاص که بعد از عمرها وقرنها به ورود آن یاد محبان نموده اند، به مضمون محبت مشحونش اطلاع یافت. شکایتی که در باب نافرستادن صحائف اخلاص نموده مخلص نیز همین منوال شما را مخاطب دارد،

جانان سخن از زبان ما می گوئی

باوجودیکه همیشه در یاد ایشان است ولحظه غافل وذاهل نیست یك مرتبه که بدو کلمه[3] مخلص نوازی کرده پیش دستیها نموده

۱ـ ع : اسباب دولت، ندارد
۲ـ ع : عم گساری
۳ـ مرتبه

گله ها می فرمایند. بلی سپاه گری تقاضاء این مقدمات می کند. همیشه درین فکر بوده که کتابتی پر غوغا مشتمل پر انواع شکوه وکم التفاتی شما نوشته شود وشکوه بنوعی که باید وشاید ودر عالم یاریها ودوستیها سزاوار آید، کرده شود. اما چون پیش روی کرده اند از سر آن گذشتیم واگر ازین طرف هم تقصیری شده باشد آن محبت شعاری بر سر عنایت والتفات[۲] از سر گناه عاصیان در گذرند. والباقی عند التلاقی.

(١٦٤)

مراسله در گله مندی وشکایت از عدم مراسلت

نسیم التفات ویاد آوری وشمیم تذکر ومحبت گذاری که بعد از عمری وروزگاری از مهب حاشیه مکتوب روح بخش مخصوص این مخلص شده بود، در وقتی که این مهجور مشتاق وگرفتار آلام اشتیاق در کنج شکیبائی تشنه زلال وصال بوده واز گلستان وصال به خارستان محنت انفصال بر آمده حواس مشاعر را به ذکر خیر ویاد ایشان قلمی داشته وشکایت فراموشی وحکایت کم لطفی وبی التفاتی ایشان را خود در گفتگوی بوده که آیا سبب آن چه باشد که این همه را از حاشیه خاطر عاطر متحاشی گردانیده نسیاً منسیاً ساخته اند، وچرا تشنگان رشحات یاد آوری را[۳] به رشحه سلامی دستگیری نمی کنند؟ بوزیدن

۱ـ ع، س : مشتمل برانواع شکوه وکم التفاتی شما نوشته شود وشکوه بنوعی که باید وشاید، ندارند

۲ـ ع، س : از سرآن گذشتیم واگر ازین طرف هم تقصیری شده باشد آن محبت شعاری برسرعنایت والتفات، ندارند

۳ـ ع : را، ندارد

آن سلام فرحت انجام مرقوم حاشیه مراسلت فصاحت وبلاغت انجام مشام جان معطر گشت[۱] وعطر سای دماغ جنان شد. محبت شعارا اخلاص ومحبت این مهجور مشتاق که بآن خدام عالی مقام[۲] به صفت استقرار موصوف وسمت استمرار معروف است، مقتضی ملاطفه علحده بود. اگر بمقتضاء دوستی بوقوع نیاید وموافق متوقع چهره نکشاید، از ضعف طالع مخلصان خواهد بود. امید که بخلاف ماسبق رقم نسیان از خاطر فرح اثر زدوده وشیوه دوست نوازی ویار خوش سازی را بر صفحه محبت ثبت فرمایند وتا حصول ملاقات برشحه سلامی ونفحه پیامی التفات نمایند چرا که:

آنها که طبیب درد دلها باشند
درمان به ازین کنند مشتاقان را

(۱٦۵)

صحیفه در تهنیت ملک

ای به فر سلطنت کشور گیتی ستان
ملک را مالک رقاب دور را صاحب قران

الحمد لله والمنة که از پرتو آفتاب عنایت سبحانی غنچه امید[۳] بر گلبن مراد شگفته گردید واز تواتر تقاطر غمام لطف یزدانی درخت بخت بندگان خدمت گار سربه سپهر کبود کشید. از دیوان فضل الهی منشور "انی جاعل فی الارض خلیفة[٤]" به پروانچه "قل اللهم مالک

۱ـ ع : است
۲ـ ع،س : جنان شد، محبت شعارا اخلاص ومحبت این مهجور مشتاق که بآن خدام عالی مقام، ندارد
۳ـ ع : امیدوار
٤ـ قرآن مجید : ۲/۳۰

الملك[۱]" بنام خجسته فرجام آن حضرت شرف نفاذ یافت وپرتو ماهیچه رایت کشور کشای بر ساحت شرق وغرب عالم تافت. تاج موفور الابتهاج خلافت از برکات تارك مبارکش از جمیع سرفرازان بر سرآمد وتخت عالی بخت سلطنت از میامن اقدام میمنت احتشامش در رفعت[۲] از ایوان کیوان بر آمد. رخسار زر از ابیض واحمر از شرافت نام با احترامش زینت وزیب هرچه تمام تر گرفته به سکه رواج مقرون گشت ودرحیات معتبر. هر دیار وکشور از القاب مستطاب آن خسرو تاج ور ارتفاع دیگر یافته از سپهر اخضر در گذشت. طوائف رعایا که بانواع جور ومحن ممتحن بودند، در ظلال احسان آسودند وطبقات برایا که باصناف بلایا ابتلاء می نمودند در مهاد امن وامان غنودند. قطعه[۳]:

آرام یافت در کنف امن وحش وطیر
آسوده گشت در کنف انس انس وجان
از غصه خون گرفت چون مل ظلم را جگر
واز خنده باز مانده چو گل عدل را دهان

وبی شائبه تکلف وغائله تصلف؛ قطعه[٤]:

جای آنست که اهل اسلام
از سر صدق باخلاص تمام
متصل دست دعا بردارند
روی در قبله جاوید آرند
دولت وصلت از روی نیاز
می طلبند از ملك بی نیاز

۱ـ ع: قرآن مجید: ۳/۲٦
۲ـ ع: نعت
۳ـ ع: نظم
٤ـ ع: مثنوی

بنده دیرینه کمینه که در شبهاء دراز از درگاه مالك الملك کارساز التماس روزی چنیں می نمود، به مجرد سماع خبر بهجت اثر احرام آں کعبه آمال بسته بسرعت تمام متوجه شد که به زودی خود را بآستان بوسی رسانیده ذره وار در معرض استفاضه انوار آفتاب دولت پائدار درآید وچهره شکر گذاری بر خاك آستاں خداوند گاری ساید۔ اما چوں به فلاں موضع رسید بواسطه موانع واضطرار روزی چند اراده در توقف ماند۔ امید که دریں زودی موانع مرتفع گردیده بدولت عتبه بوسی استسعاد یابد، بمنه و کرمه۔

(۱٦٦)

صحیفه در تهنیت تسخیر ملك

بحمد الله که مضمون اشارت[۱] "توتی الملك من تشاء[۲]" از منظره دولت ابدی روی نمود وفحواء بشارت "ان الارض یرثها عبادی الصالحون[۳]" بر منصه اقبال سرمدی جلوه فرمود۔ از عون عنایت ربانی ومدد بی غایت سبحانی زمام تصرف مملکت به قبضه اختیار خدام درگاه عالم پناه وخاتم تسخیر اقالیم باصابع اقتدار ملازمان بارگاه مهر اشتباه درآمد:

سریر سلطنت اکنوں کند سر افرازی
که سایه بر سرش افگند خسرو غازی

۱۔ ع : اشارات
۲۔ قرآن مجید : ۲٦/۳
۳۔ قرآن مجید : ۱۰۵/۲۱

(١٦٧)

صحیفه در تهنیت تسخیر ملك

بشـارت تسخیر مملکت که بامداد "والله یوید بنصره من یشاء[١]" دست داده، کـافـه آدمیـان بـلـکـه عـامـه عالمیان را مسرور ومبتشر ومستظهر گـردانیـد. بـحـمـد الله که تاج وهاج سلطنت بگوهر قیمتی "وآتاه الله الملك[٢]" زینـت گرفته وسریر خلافت مصیر (مسیر) به فروغ اختر عالی زینت "والله یوتی ملکه من یشاء[٣]" سمت رفعت پذیرفت.

نظم:

شـکـر خـدا کـه گـوهر اقبال ودرفتح
دریـای دولـت تـو سعـادت نثار کرد
دولـت عـنـان مـلك بدست تو باز داد
اقبـال بـر سـمـنـد مرادت سوار کرد

(١٦٨)

صحیفه در تهنیت تسخیر ملکی که از دست رفته[٤] باز بدست آمد

الـحـمـد الـله که دیگر بار آفتاب جهان تاب دولت و کامگاری

١ـ قرآن مجید : ١٣/٣
٢ـ قرآن مجید : ٢٥١/٢
٣ـ قرآن مجید : ٢٤/٢
٤ـ ع : رفته، ندارد

باوج مطلع فرمان روائی رسید و کوکب عالم افروز مکنت وبختیاری باشراقات عظمت وجهان کشائی از ذروه سلطنت لامع ووساطع شد، تباشیر صبح نجاح از مطلع ابتهاج وارتیاح دمید وفوائح روضه اقبال از گلشن عظمت واجلال بمشام عالمیان رسید۔ بیت:

محتاج بود ملك به شهنشاهیئی چنیں[۱]

آخر مراد ملك روا کرد کردگار

(۱۶۹)

صحیفه در تهنیت فتح

شاها فلك از سپاه تو پر حذر است

از[۲] فتح همیشه لشکرت بهره ور است

تیغت که چوں آئینه بود عکس پذیر

دروی همه صورت ظفر جلوه گر است

للـه الحمد والشکر والمنة که مرتبه دیگر رایت دولت سلطان بحروبر بر فراز مدارج ومعارج "نصر من الله وفتح قریب[۳]" افراخته گردید وچهره شوکت خاقان غضنفر فراغ فروغ کوکبه "انا فتحنا لك فتحا مبیناً[۴]" افروخته دید؛ طائر فرخ فال ظفر وبرتری از هواء فضاء "وینصرك الله نصراً عزیزاً[۵]" بر[۶] فرق فرقد سای بارگاه کشور کشای بال اقبال

۱۔ ع : محتاج ملك بود به شهنشاهی چنیں

۲۔ ع،س : در

۳۔ قرآن مجید : ۱۳/۶۱

۴۔ قرآن مجید : ۱/۴۸

۵۔ قرآن مجید : ۳/۴۸

۶۔ افراخته گردید وچهره شوکت خاقان غضنفر فراغ فروغ ، کوکبه "انا فتحنا لك فتحاً مبیناً" افروخته دید، طائر فرخ فال ظفر وبرتری ازهوای فضای "ینصرك الله نصراً عزیزاً"، ندارد

کشود وشاهباز زریں بال سلطنت وسروری از آشیان عالیشان "وما النصر الا من عند الله[1]" بر پنجه اقتدار آں خسرو کامگار نزول نمود۔ قطعه[2]:

لله الحمد که هر نقش که خاطر می بست
آمد آخر ز پس پرده تقدیر پدید
خار هر کید که بدخواه براه تو نهاد
خنجری گشت که جز در جگر او نخلید

از استماع ایں خبر بهجت اثر کافة سکنه هر بلاد ودیار را گل امید از نسیم فیض خالق جاوید شگفته گشت وعامه متوطنه هر ولایت وناحیت را نهال آرزو از پرتو آفتاب عنایت رازق العباد به ثمرات مراد ثمر[3] شد وغلغله تهنیت مبارك باد از ایوان کیوان در گذشت۔ امیدواری از میامن الطاف حضرت[4] باری، عزاسمه، چنان است که اوان استقبال باضعاف[5] بل آلاف ماضی وحال بوده هر روز کوکب فتح دیگر بر سپهر مقصود در لمعه آید وهر لحظه پیکر نصرت غیر مکرر در نظر سلطان تاجور چهره کشاید، بمنه وکرمه۔

التماس آں که هرچه از مواهب سبحانی شامل حال خجسته فال آں سالك مسلك جهانبانی گردیده، بارسال فتح نامهاء عالی وامثله متعالی ساکنان ایں حدود ودعا گویان وخیر خواهان را مسرور ومفتخر گردانند وپایه قدر ومنزلت را ازورود ایں اشارت وصدور ایں بشارت به ذروه افتخار واستظهار رسانند۔ زیاده بریں تحریر مقتضی بر اطناب واملال بود، لاجرم زبان اختتام بدعاء دولت کشوده۔ همواره ذات عالی

۱۔ ع : قرآن مجید : ۱۲٦/۳
۲۔ ع : قطعه، ندارد
۳۔ ع : مثمر
٤۔ ع : حضرت، ندارد
٥۔ ع : اصناف

قدر به نظر عنایت واهب العطیات[۱] منظور[۲] باد!

(۱۷۰)

صحیفه در تهنیت فتح وظفر بر اعداء

بحمد الله که عساکر فیروزی مآثر بحکم اشارت "الا انّ حزب الله هم الغالبون[۳]" به صرصر قهر گرد استیصال از دیار منازعان دولت قاهره بر آورد وبآتش حسام آبدار در مقاتله اعداء[۴] خاکسار دود انتقام از بسیط زمین باوج سپهر برین رسانیده اند- از شاخسار فتح غنچه مرادی دیگر سرسبزی نماید-

(۱۷۱)

صحیفه در تهنیت منصب امارت[۵]

ای امارت را بذیل اقتدارت اعتصام

وی حکومت را بدور عدل تو زینت تمام

لله الحمد والمنة که آثار الطاف حضرت بادشاه تاجور بمنصب عظیم القدر دیوان اعلی در قبضه اختیار آن سپه آرای معارك فتح وظفر قرار یافت واز اشعه لمعات آفتاب عنایت سلطان بحر وبر

۱- ع : العطایات

۲- ع : متصور

۳- قرآن مجید : ۵/۵۶

٤- ع : این، زیاده دارد

۵- ع : نویسند، زیاده دارد

تکفیل مهام سرکار معلی بر وجنات احوال آن امیر ستوده سیر تافت۔ حقا که از شمائم ایں بشارت فرخنده اشارت دماغ جان مخلصان امیدوار معطر گردید واز نسائم این خبر خجسته اثر ریاض روح وروان متخصصان اخلاص شعار به نضارت وخرمی رسید۔ وچوں بی شائبه تکلف کافه رعایا از تاب آفتاب حوادث در ظلال معدلت ایشان آسوده وفارغ بال خواهند بود وعامه برایا در سایه درخت مکرمت ایشان مرفح وخوش حال خواهند غنود۔ امیدوار است که بر طبق "واما ما ینفع الناس فیمکث فی الارض[۱]" سالهاء فراوان بر مسند عزت وجلال متمکن باشند، وتوفیق اشاعت خیرات وافاضه مبرات رفیق حال ایشان گردد وبادراك متمنیات صوری ومعنوی فائز شوند، بمنه وکرمه۔ امید که نظر عنایت از حال مخلصان دریغ نه فرمایند وشکر انه این مراتب ودرجات، ابواب عواطف پروری بر روی روزگار ایشان کشایند۔ نظم:

آنی که پناه اهل رازت کردند
بیچاره نواز وچاره سازت کردند
مینداز سر بخاکسا ران جهان
شکرانه آں که سر فرازت کردند

(۱۷۲)

صحیفه در تهنیت منصب وزارت

ای بتو مسند ایوان وزارت عالی
ذات والای تو بر جمع اعالی والی

بدین خوش حالی که به عنایت ذو الجلال مسند وزارت

۱۔ ع : قرآن مجید : ۱۳/۱۷

حضرت اعلیٰ خاقانی به وجود آن بانی مبانی کاردانی مزین شده، اگر بر تدبیر دراهم ودینار چرخ پیر را بر طبق عرض نهاده ایثار نماید رواست، وبدیں فارغ بالی که به عاطفت لایزال مضمون "اذا اراد الله بملك خیراً جعل له وزیرا صالحاً" نسبت خلافت سلیمانی وزارت آن آصف ثانی مشهور شده، اگر برجیس سعادت جلیس جهت دفع آسیب عین الکمال زبان به مداومت "ان یکاد[۱]" کشاید.. الحمد لله والمنة که از ترشح قلم عنایت رقم آن مظهر جود وکرم ریاض احوال واعمال ولات اخلاص ناضر ونامی گردید واز اشعه انوار رای مهر سیمای آن معدن[۲] لطف وشیم ساحت اعمال مباشران شغل اختصاص به نور وضیاء رسید۔ رجاء واثق وامل صادق که تا دم آخر عالم وزارت زیور انگشت سعادت باشد ومتکای جلالت مخصوص بذات شریف بود۔ لائق آن می نماید که به شکر انه ایں موهبت اسعاف مامولات کافه برایا را پیش نهاده همت دارند وبه سپاس[۳] ایں مکرمت در انجاح مسئولات عامه رعایا دقیقه فرونگدارند تا بر طبق "اما ما ینفع الناس فیمکث فی الارض[٤]" عاجلاً سالهاء بسیار بر مسند دولت واقبال ایں جهانی متمکن باشند وبر حسب "هل جزاء الاحسان الا الاحسان[٥]" وآجلاً بر درجات اعمال وامانی آن جهان شتابند۔ زیاده بریں در بسط بساط تصدیع نه پیچید وبر دعا ختم نمودن اولی دید۔ ظل ظلیل عاطفت ورافت مستدام باد[٦]۔

۱۔ اشاره بآیت کریمه'ان یکاد الذین کفروا لیزلقونك بابصارهم لما سمعوا الذکر"۔ قرآن مجید : ۵۱/٦۸

۲۔ ع : معدلت

۳۔ ع : سیاس

٤۔ قرآن مجید : ۱۷/۱۳

۵۔ قرآن مجید : ٦۰/۵۵

٦۔ ع : بالنون والصاد، زیاده دارد

(۱۷۳)

صحیفه در تهنیت منصب صدارت

ای ز قدر تو اقتدار صدور۔ عالم ازرای روشنت پرنور صدور[۱] عنایت ذو الجلال درباره صدر نشینان مجامع الفضل والافضال افزون از دائره احصاء است وبدور عاطفت لایزال واضاءت ساحت احوال جالسان مجالس علم و کمال بیرون از احاطه استقصاء۔ واجلّ مواهب واتم مکارم آن که دریں اوقات فرخنده ساعات مسند صدارت دیوان اعلیٰ که ازمهام وشرائف امور لازم الاحترام امت بوجود با جود آن عاقبت محمود زیب وزینت گرفت و مستقر نیابت که از مناصب رفیع القدر ومراتب عظیم الوقع است به شکوه فلك ستوه آن مظهر جود و کرم رونق وبهاپذیرفت وآن عالی همت ترویج وتنسیق ایں منصب مناصب را منظور نظر کیمیا اثر گردانیدند وانتظام مهام ارباب عمائم وتزئین بقاع خیر رابدرجه کمال رسانیدند۔ قلم دوزبان ازشکر گذاری ایں نعمت قاصر است وبنان زیبابیان از سپاس داری ایں موهبت عاجز۔ ع:

چه شکر گویمت ای کارساز بنده نواز

انشاء الله عن قریب جهت تهنیت بملازمت مشرّف شود۔ بزوائد تصدیع اوقات بابرکات لائق ننمود۔ لاجرم بدعای بی ریازبان اختتام کشود۔ ذات شریف بمقاصد دوجهانی فائز باد!

۱۔ ع : صدور، ندارد

(۱۷٤)

صحیفه در تهنیت منصب نقابت

ساحت عتبه سیادت وفضای سده نجابت را به لب استکانت وجبین ضراعت ملثوم وممسوح داشته بر مرآت ضمیر بی عیب که عکس نمای اسرار غیب است، جلوه ظهور می دهد که تفویض منصب بلند مرتبت نقابت که به ذات ملائك صفات اختصاص یافته هر آئینه موجب حصول امانی وآمال منتسبان[۱] دودمان رسالت وجلالت خواهد بود وبه یمن توجه ضمیر آفتاب تاثیر وبه حسن مساعی جمیله آن مخدوم واجب التعظیم والتوقیر (صحت) انتساب هریك از منتسبان مشکوة نبوت ورسالت به منصه ظهور رسیده امتیاز جید از زیف واستثناء سید از[۲] متسید خواهد نمود. چون قانون قدیم است که در امثال این امور سالکان طریق اخلاص وهو اخواهی اقامت مراسم تهنیت وعبودیت می نمایند وقاعده قدیم است که در نظائر این مهام ناهجان مناهج حق گذاری ودولت خواهی زبان باداء لوازم مبارك بادی می کشایند، امضاء آن ضابطه بر ذمه مخلصان امری لازم نمود. لاجرم به تحریر این چند کلمه فرخنده زبان بیان کشود. ظل سیادت ونقابت ممدود ومخلد باد.

۱۔ ع : مقتبسان

۲۔ ع : از، ندارد

۳۔ ع : منصب، ندارد

(۱۷۵)

صحیفه در تهنیت منصب[۱] شیخ الاسلامی

تفویض منصب جلیل المراتب شیخ الاسلامی بر عالیجاهی[۲] که از ترشح ینابیع مکارم اخلاقش ریاض دین مبین نامی وناضر است و از توضح انوار محاسن ادائش صحائف ملت متین منور و گرامی، مبارک ومیمون باد ومبانی شریعت احمدی واساس ملت محمدی به میامن قواعد اجتهاد ومکارم ودعائم انقیاد آن مظهر رشد وارشاد از وصمت قصور وفتور مصون ومامون باد، بحرمة النبی وآله وصحبه. چون عن قریب ایں هواخواه باسائر مخلصان بلا اشتباه جهت تهنیت متوجه ملازمت است، بزوائد باب اطناب نکشود وبدعاء ختم نمود. برکات ذات عالی مدی الایام واللیالی بر مفارق ادانی واعالی پائنده ومستدام باد.

(۱۷۶)

صحیفه در تهنیت منصب احتساب

بعد از اظهار دعاء وثناء که شیوه محبان عقیدت انتما است، متصور خاطر شریعت مآب می گرداند که از استماع نوید تفویض امر احتساب به ذات فقاهت سمات انواع خوش حالی روی نمود ونداء فارغ بالی از هاتف غیبی شنود. الحمد لله و المنة. ظاهر است که چنانچه از وفور دین پروری وظهور شریعت گستری ایشان متصور است

۱ـ ع : منصب، ندارد

۲ـ ع : عالی جناب می باید

طیلسان عالیشان "الآمرون بالمعروف والناهون عن المنکر والحافظون لحدود الله[١]" را بر کتف همت انداخته ترویج دین اسلام ورفع ودفع بدع وآثام را بر وجه اکمل واتم پیش نهاد همت خواهند داشت ودر اعلاء معالم "و من یتق الله بحعل له مخرجاً ویرزقه من حیث لا یحتسب[٢]" کوشیده دقیقه از دقائق اجتهاد نامرعی نخواهند داشت۔ بزوائد اطناب نه نمود۔ وچون مقصود مبار کباد بود بدین چنه کلمه زبان اختصار کشود۔

(١٧٧)

صحیفه در تهنیت ماه مبارك رمضان

آمد مهی چون طلعت شه در مبارکی
بادا قدوم ماه مبارك مبارکت
بر ما مبارك چون تبارك عطاء باد
ایزد چهارمیں کلمه از تبارکت

وصول ماه مبارك رمضان وظهور شهر رمضان "الذی انزل فیه القرآن[٣]" که بر سوابق ایام واوقات ولواحق شهور وساعات مزین ومرتب دارد وادراك اوهام واحاطه افهام در تفصیل تفضیل آن عاجز وقاصر است، بر شهر یاری که برجیس سعادت جلیس جهت دفع آسیب عین الکمال از جاه وجلالش "ان یکاد[٤]" محافطت می نماید، وپیر کیوان

١۔ قرآن مجید : ١١٢/٩
٢۔ قرآن مجید : ٣/٦٨
٣۔ قرآن مجید : ١٨٠/٢
٤۔ اشاره به آیت کریمه "وان یکاد الدین کفر والیزلقونك بابصارهم لما سمعوا الذکر" قرآن مجید : ٥١/٦٨

باوجود نزول در هفتم ایوان به پاسبانی سرادق عظمت واستقلالش سر افتخار بر فلك اطلس می ساید، مبارك ومیمون وفرخنده وهمایون باد۔ چون در اسالیب وقوانیس سابقه قاعده است که در اوقات متبرکه بندگان خدمت گاری شاهان جم اقتدار دعاء مبنی بر تهنیت ومبارکباد عرضه می دارند وبر وصول[1] اجابت واستجابت از میامن برکات ایں ایام میمنت سعادت چشم امید می گمارند۔ بنده نیز اقتداء به سنت سنیۂ اسلاف[2] کرام واعراف لازم الاحترام نمود وگرنه بنده را حد ایں گستاخی نبود۔ بهر حال از کرم خاقان فرخنده فال امیدوار قبول مامول است۔ والامر اعلی۔

(۱۷۸)

صحیفه در تهنیت شب قدر

شب قدر تو مبارك بود وبس میمون
همه طاعت وعبادت باجابت مقرون

میامن طاعات مومنین ومومنات که در شب قدر که اشرف لیالی دهر است، باقامت رسانیدند وبرکات ساعات روز عید که مستدعی افاضت خیرات ومبرات ومستلزم اجابت دعوات، شامل روزگار جناب فلاں، اعلی الله تعالیٰ شانه، باد۔

۱۔ ع : فصول
۲۔ ع : اسلام

(۱۷۹)

صحیفه در تهنیت عید الفطر

تابنده تر باد شاها در عید
وز عارض جاه تو کلفت باد بعید
از طالع سعد ودولت روز افزون
هر روز تو عید باد وعید سعید

از میامن این ایام بابرکات موجبات تزاید عمر ودولت وتضاعف اسباب شوکت وحشمت محصول وموصول باد وآفت عین الکال بدامن جاه وجلالش مرساد، بالنبی وآله- رجاء واثق ووثوق صادق که لب آرزوی بندگان بی مقدار از هبوب نسیم عیدی لطف خاقان جم اقتدار به سان غنچه طری از وزیدن باد سحری شگفته وخندان شود، غنچه دل بی غل مخلصان امیدوار از نسیم ریاح عنایت خاقان جم اطوار مثل گل از تقاطر شبنم بهار متبسم گردد، بمنه وکرمه- رباعی:

یارب که بناء دولتت محکم باد
صیت کرمت همیشه در عالم باد
هر روز تو عید باد وهر عیدی عید
وز عیدی لطف تو دلم خرم باد

(۱۸۰)

صحیفه در تهنیت عید الاضحی

پیوسته رخ بخت تو گلگون بادا
اعداء تو دیده ودلش خون بادا
ای سرور احرار جهان مقدم عید
بر ذات مبارکت همایون بادا

مقدم عید قربان که موسم مرادات فراوان واوان سعادات بی پایان است، بر مفخر اقران، یگانه دوران، شمس الدولة والدنیا والدین فلان مبارك ومیمون باد واولیاء دولت[1] به فرمان خدمت ایشان مسرور ومحبور واعداء رفعت به قربان فرقت مقهور. حق علیم وعلّام است که بایں همه شمائل بی وسائل حضور پرنور آں حضرت اصلاً وقطعاً ذوقی نداشت. آثار دولت ملاقات عن قریب محصل ومیسر گردد، بمنه وجوده.

(۱۸۱)

صحیفه در تهنیت نوروز

رباعی:

ای هر نفس از تو خصم را سوز دگر
مشتاق تو هر طرف دل افروز دگر

۱ـ ع : والدنیا والدین فلاں مبارك ومیمون باد واولیاء دولت، ندارد

با عیش ونشاط گذران این نوروز
وز عمر به بیس هزار نوروز دگر

وصول خورشید فائض الانوار به برج شرف واقتدار وظهور مواکب فیروزی آثار بهار در صحراء وکوهسار بر حضرت بادشاه که از تقاطر غمام لطف عمیمش ریاض مقاصد عالمیان در ریاض مراد شگفته واز پر تو آفتاب خلق کریمش نهال جهانیان در چمن امید نشو ونما پذیرفته، مبارك ومیمون باد- اولیاء دولتش را درخت میوه دولت واقبال مثمر واعداء دولتش را اشجار حیات از صرصر حرمان زوال عریان وبی نور-

رباعی:

تا بهر سال ز تو چهره نماید نوروز
تا شود شام همیشه بدل صبح بدل
روز تو باد چو نوروز وبد اندیش ترا
صبح امید بود تیره تر از شام اجل

(۱۸۲)

صحیفه در تهنیت نکاح

بحمد الله والمنة که خدام امارت[۱] مخدره تتق عصمت وجلال را موجب "فانحکوا[۲]" درسلك تزوج سلك انتظام بخشید وسنت سیئه "تناکحوا[۳]" که واسطة العقد نشاط است، مستتبع مزید ارتیاح

۱- ع : امارت، زیاده دارد
۲- اشاره بآیة کریمه "فانکحوا ماطاب لکم من النساء، الخ" قرآن مجید : ۳/٤
۳- اشاره بحدیث شریف "تناکحوا تناسلوا تکثروا فانی مکاثر بکم الامم یوم القیامة" (فتح القدر، ۳٤۲/۲)

واستراحت ساخت۔ امیدوار است که از تاثیر این قران سعید آثار سعادت بر صفحات حال جهانیان ظهور نماید واز تمهید قواعد جمعیت جانبین عروس آرائی رفاهیت زپس پرده غیب چهره کشاید، بمنه و کرمه۔

(۱۸۳)

صحیفه در تهنیت زفاف

الحمد لله که دست ارادت در گردن مرادات حمائل[۱] شد وفروغ دولت از طلعت سعادت درخشنده وتابان گشت یعنی

بروزی که دولت برومند بود
نظرها سزوار پیوند بود

ماه کامرانی وآفتاب کامیابی در برج معانی اجتماع نمودند وبرجیس عالم افروز باناهید جهان آرای در اوج مکارم قران فرمودند۔

(۱۸۴)

صحیفه درتهنیت ولادت فرزند

روز مولودت مبارك باد عالم را ازانك
روز ایجاد نظام عالم وارکان اوست

الحمد[۲] لله تعالی والشکر لله که از افق اجلال کوکب[۳] اقبال

۱۔ ع : حمائل، ندارد
۲۔ ع : المنّة
۳۔ ع : کواکب

طالع[1] گشت واز چمن سعادت تازه ریحانی بدمید واز دریای جود وسماحت گوهری پدید آمد یعنی خدام ملاذی، استظهاری را، ابد الله دولته، مبارك فرزندی به فال میمون وطالع سعد مولود گشت که از قدوم او عالمی منور شد وچشمهاء عشائر واقربا را به نور لقاء او روشنائی حاصل آمد۔ چون بنده نیازمند را دولت تهنیت به قدم دست نداد، قلم را نائب او گردانید۔ ایزد تعالیٰ وتقدس این در صدف معالی واین گوهر کان لآلی وماه خورشید پیکر وفرزند نیك اختر را در حجر تمتع والد بزرگوار ارزانی دارد وبه کمال پیری برساند، بمنه وکرمه۔

(۱۸۵)

صحیفه در تهنیت اولاد ملوك

بدین بشارت که بر سپهر خلافت خاقان[2] کوکبی مسعود صفت طلوع نمود، اگر سکنه گنبد خضراء زر مهر منیر را بر طبق عرض نهاده به طریق نثار ایثار کنند درخور خواهد بود۔ وبدین نوید که در شبستان سلطنت سلطان صاحب تائید مولودی عاقبت محمود چهره کشود، اگر متوطنه بسیط غبراء حاصل جهان را طفیل مقدم همایونش نمایند لائق خواهد نمود۔ رجاء به فضل الهی وامید به کرم نامتناهی چنان است که این سرو بوستان نامداری در حدیقه تربیت وپرورش شهریاری باقصی مراتب نشو ونما یافته، عالمی در ظل عنایت ومرحمتش آساید واین[3] ماه آسمان بر خورداری ازان خورشید تابان کامگاری استفاضه انوار

۱۔ ع : طالع، ندارد
۲۔ کیخسرو، زیاده دارد
۳۔ ع : آن

کمالات وجلالات نموده، جهانی از ظلمت جور وطغیان (در سایه) شفقت واحسانش گراید:

ازان پر هنر بی هنر چون بُود

زیاده گستاخی نه نمود وبه دعاء بی ریا زبان اختصار کشود۔ رباعی:

الهی تا جهان را آب ورنگ است
فلك را دور، گیتی را درنگ است
ممتع دارش از لطف وجوانی
زهر چیزش فزون ده زندگانی

(۱۸۶)

صحیفه در تهنیت ولادت دختر

"یهب لمن یشاء اناثاً ویهب لمن یشاء الذکور[۱]"۔ چون به سمع ایں حقیر رسید که از سپهر جلالت زیبنده کوکبی بتافت واز صحراء عدم شهشواری در میدان وجود باخت واز شفق افق عصمت سبزه روی نمود، ابواب شادی وشادمانی وفتوح بر دل وروح ایں مجروح کشوده شد۔ الحمد لله والمنة۔ ملاذا نسل دختر از شرائف مواهب است ونقطه پرکار وجود از دختر منتشر می شود۔ "ابو البنات مرزوق" خوانند۔ حق تعالیٰ مقدم اورا بر ذات ملکی صفات ومجموع عشائر مبارك ومیمون گرداند وآں عاقله خاندان سعادت و آں عقیله دودمان سیادت را در حجره ستره خیر وصلاح وپرده عصمت وفلاح وعفاف ونجاح متمتع دارد، بمنه وکرمه۔

۱۔ قرآن مجید: ۴۲/۴۹

(۱۸۷)

صحیفه در تهییت قدوم سلاطین

عرض می دارد که دریں اوقات میمنت آیات رشحات فرحت وسرور وقطرات راحت وحبور از فیضان عنایت بی غایت ملك متعال بر ریاض امانی وآمال ایں بنده کسیر البال وارد شد که لواء نصرت وشوکت ورایت ظفر وحشمت برافراشته ظلال عدالت ونصفت را بر فضاء ایں ناحیت منبسط خواهند ساخت۔ بمجرد استماع این مژده دلکشا ونوید جانفزا انواع اعتضاد واستظهار از تتق غیب واختفاء ظاهر وهویدا گشت، وبعد اداء حمد الهی به لسان حال مترنم ایں مقال شد۔

مثنوی[۱]:

چه پرتو است که اقبال در جهاں افگند
چه غلغل است که دولت در آسماں افگند
چه منت است که بر گردن زمین وزماں
طلوع رایت ورای خدایگاں افگند
غبار موکب شاه است یا نسیم بهشت
که بوی امن واماں در مشام جاں افگند

امیدوار است که علی اسرع الحال حصول ایں عطیه کبری وموهبت عظمی در سلك انتظام یابد۔

۱۔ ع: نظم

(۱۸۸)

صحیفه در تهنیت قدوم امراء

حقا که باستماع مراجعت موکب مبارك وذات متبرك انواع بهجت وحضور در قلب دعا گویان مخلص افزود واصناف ابتهاج ومسرت هواداران مخلص را روی نمود. الحمد لله سبحانه که دعاء نیازمندان مستجاب وسبب ظهور این فتح الباب گشت:

بس فاتحه خواندیم واخلاص دمیدیم
تا بار دگر روی دل آرام تو دیدیم

(۱۸۹)

صحیفه در تهنیت معاودت از حج

قدمت قدوم البدر بیت صعوده
وامرك عال صاعد کصعوده

حقا وکفی بالله شهیداً که چون بشارت معاودت آن خدام از سفر مبارك با حصول مثوبات اخروی "ومن دخله کان آمناً[۱]" واحاطه برکات "جعل الله الکعبة البیت الحرام قیاماً للناس[۲]" استماع افتاد، وظیفه حمد الهی وراتبه شکر بی قیاس نامتناهی بجا آورد:

بدان که مژده وصل تو ناگهان آورد

۱ـ قرآن مجید : ۹۷/۳
۲ـ قرآن مجید : ۹۷/۵

وخوشحالی بسیار وخرمی بی شمار افزود۔ الحمد لله علی ذالك۔ فقیر می خواست که فی الفور به بندگی برسد ورنج غبار ماندگی از اعطاف جلال بیفشاند اما فلان چیز مانع ایں سعادت کبری گشته۔ انشاء الله العزیز عند الفرصة بآں دولت عظمی و کبری معزز ومشرف خواهد شد[۱]۔

(۱۹۰)

صحیفه در تهنیت معاودت

بیا که مژده اقبال جاوداں آمد
که باز از سفر آں مفخر زماں آمد

دریں اوقات میمنت آیات مژده رسید که خدام بدولت وسعادت باحصول مرادات ووصول سعادت به خیر وطالع سعد[۲]:

فتوح سوی یمین وسعود سوی یسار
سپهر زیر رکاب وزمانه پیش عناں

به وطن مالوف ومسکن معروف تشریف فرمودند۔ فی الحال سجده شکر گذاری بتقدیم رسانید وچنداں ارتیاح واسترواح افزود که در حیز عبارت نگنجد۔ نحمد الله علی ذالك۔

۱۔ ع : امید که عن قریب بعد فراغ ایں به تقبیل اقدام کرام معزز ومشرف خواهد شد، زیاده دارد

۲۔ ع : سعید

(۱۹۱)

صحیفه در تهنیت صحت

بر نامه رشك دارم زان رو که نامه ام
پیش از من شکسته بمقصود می رسد

کمترین داعیان بالاخلاص فلان، آن که عادتش دعاء دولت تست، عرضه می دارد که الحمد لله والمنة که صبح صحت از مطلع سعادت وافق عافیت بآن حضرت روی نمود وصیقل قوت طبعی اثر غبار تغیر از مرآت مزاج صافی صفات زدود۔ دعاگویان را ازیں بشارت گل کامرانی در چمن شادمانی شگفته شد ونهال زندگانی در بوستان آمال وامانی سمت برومندی پذیرفت:

شکر خدا که شربت صحت چشیدۀ
بار دگر به مسند دولت رسیدۀ

ملاذا[1] اگرچه ایں کمینه را عارضه سخت دست داده بود وبربستر هلاکت افتاده وامید از حیات مستعار قطع کرده بود[2]، باوجود ایں حالت حق علیم وعلام است که از حضرت واهب العطیات به تضرع وزاری بدعاء صحت ذات عافیت صفات در لیل ونهار استدعاء می نمود وبنده زاده را هر روز به جهت کورنش به دربار عالی می فرستاد۔ از انجا که ضعف طالع است به سعادت بساط بوسی سرخ رو نمی شد۔ از سرحسرت هم چنان بر گشته می آمد۔ اکثر ایام به همیں منوال می گذرانید وخاطر فاتر بایں بیت تسلی می کرد:

۱۔ ع : حکومت پناها، زیاده دارد
۲۔ ع : بود، ندارد

حافظ وظیفه تو دعا گفتن است وبس
در بند آن مباش که نشنید یا شنید

ذره پرور به توجه ایشان بنده را نیز صحت شده اما در خود هنوز آن قوت نمی بیند که از منزل به منزل تواند رفت۔ انشاء الله تعالی عن قریب به تقبیل آستان ملائك آشیان از دریافت آن سعادت محظوظ می گردد۔ والامر اعلی

(١٩٢)

صحیفه در تهنیت صحت

بیمار مباد آن تن نازك هرگز
که امید بسی خلق بدوبسته شده است

علم الله سبحانه که چون بسمع این نیاز مند رسید که عارضه دست بوس عرض شریف مخدومی کرده است عظیم خسته خاطر وشکسته دل گشت وآتش بیقراری در تن وجان این فقیر افتاد وسر بزانوی حسرت نهاد واز حضرت باری به تضرع وزاری صحت آن خدام درلیل ونهار استدعاء نمود۔

بس فاتحه خواندیم واخلاص دمیدیم

درین ولا نیز بشارت رسید که از شفاخانه "واذا مرضت فهو یشفین[١]" شربت شفا نوشیده ولباس صحت پوشیده پشت مبارك بربالش آسائش باز نهاد۔ سرور وحبور بی نهایت دست داد وشکر واهب العطایا باقامت رسانیده این ندا در داد، بحمد الله والمنة۔

١۔ قرآن مجید : ٨٠/٢٦

شعر:

جمال الليالي في بقائك فليدم
بقائك في عز عليهن زائل

امیدوار است که حق جل وعلا این مرض را موجب محو سیئات بل سبب مزید حسنات[1] گرداند. بنده خواست که سر را قدم ساخته بملازمت برسد ووظیفه تهنیت صحت در مشافهه به تقدیم رساند. اما فلان مهم مانع این سعادت گشت، وبدین دعا ختم نمود.

بیت:

بهر وقتم[2] بیاد خاطر آئی
که خود هرگز نمی کردی فراموش

(۱۹۳)

صحیفه در تهنیت خلاص

الحمدلله که صبح مطلع امیدواری متبسم و گلبن مسرت در گلشن فرح آثار دولت واقبال بارور گشت وروضه امانی به فوائح روائح سعادت و کامرانی معطر شده.

بیت:

بخت رمیده ره به سوئی من نهاد باز
بر من در سعادت ودولت کشادباز

۱ـ ع: حسنات، زیاده دارد
۲ـ ع: وقتی

(۱۹۴)

صحیفه در تهنیت منازل

طلوع آفتاب عالمتاب اعنی ذات بابرکات نواب کامیاب، سلمهم الله تعالیٰ، به بیت الشرف که عبارت از منزل اشرف است مبارك وخجسته باد وتباشیر صبح سعادت درو لامع ولوامع نور کرامت از اطراف جوانبش واضح وساطع:

تا جهاں باشد خدایا ایں بنا معمور باد
ساحتش چوں بیت معمور از حوادث دور باد

بحق الحق واهله

(۱۹۵)

صحیفه در تهنیت منازل[1]

حلول حضرت در محل منیع ومقر رفیع است سبب ایشاں بدیں کلمات ترنم وبدیں مقالات تکلم می نماید۔

رباعی:

حریم ایں حرم پاك تست دار اماں
طرب فزا ودل افروز همچو ریاض جناں
ترا همیشه دریں منزل مبارك باد
تن درست، دل پر نشاط وبخت جواں

۱ـ ع: بنا

(۱۹۶)

صحیفه در تهنیت صلح

بحمد الله که مصالحت متضمن مصالح[۱] جمهور انام وموافق مرافق خاص وعام وجود گرفت۔ همت درویشان شجره ایست بغایت مثمر که عاقبة الامور ثمره وداد داد ودعاء پاکیزه دلان سحابیست ممطر که آخر کار اثر رحمت ظاهر گردانید[۲]۔ ازین[۳] مژده دل کشای و نوید راحت افزای:

جان خرم تازه گشت ودل شاد
یارب که همیشه این چنین باد

(۱۹۷)

صحیفه در تهنیت صلح

الحمد لله مواد دولت انتماء "والصلح خیر[٤]" منظور نظر سعادت مآثر شده کثرت بیگانگی به وحدت آشنائی ویگانگی متبدل گردیده وکثافت مخالفت ومنافات به لطافت موافقت ومصادقت انجامیده۔ از لوازم خیر وجمعیت هر چه در خاطر گذرد حصولش معین ومقرر۔

۱۔ ع : بمصالح
۲۔ ع : کرد
۳۔ ع : اندرین
٤۔ قرآن مجید : ٤/۱۲۸

(۱۹۸)

صحیفه در تعزیت

در ماتم شاه از شفق خون بچکید
مه روی بخست وزهره گیسوی برید
شب جامه سیاه کرد در ماتم وصبح
بر زد نفس سرد و گریبان بدرید

دریغ آفتابی که از مطلع دولت واقبال طلوع نموده عالمی از برکات انوار عدل واحسانش از تیرگی ظلم وعدوان می آسودند به مغرب فنا غروب نمود۔ افسوس کامیابی که نهال اجلال او در حدائق افضال نشو ونما یافته جهانی در سایه بلند پایه امتنانش از حرارت نوائب دوران مرفه می غنودند صرصر حادثه آن را قلع نموده وچتر همایون بادشاهی را که عزت شادروان گردون بود، تقدیر آن را نگوسار گردانید ولواء فلك فرسای شاهنشاهی را که نسرین سپهر در ظلال آن می آسود، دست قضا از ثریا به تحت الثری رسانید و آوازه کوس پر خروش سلطانی که صبح وشام نه رواق مینا فام می پیچید یکبارگی فرونشست وفریاد وفغان سپاهی ورعیت که دران مدت کسی نمی شنود بلند گشته بایوان کیوان پیوست۔ اما چه توان کرد وغم این حادثه باکه توان خورد۔

با قضا بر نمی توان آمد
با قدر در نمی توان آویخت

امیدواری به عنایت باری، عزاسمه، چنان است که دراری برج سلطنت کامگاری ونجوم سپهر خلافت ونامداری را درین واقعه هائله صبر جمیل، که موجب اجر جزیل است، کرامت شده به منتهاء دینی

ودنیوی واقصی معارج صوری ومعنوی فائز گردیده، سالهاء بسیار وقرنهاء بی شمار بر وساده شاهی وشهریاری قائم مقام والد ماجد جم حشمت، فریدون صولت خود بوده تمهید بساط عدالت ورعیت پروری نشیند (نشینند) ومبانی نصفت ومعدلت گستری قیام واقدام نماید (نمایند) ـ زیاده گستاخی حد خود ندید ـ مناسب ذکر الوحشة وحشة اختصار اولی دید ـ والا مراعلی ـ

(۱۹۹)

صحیفه در تعزیت

خوش است عمر دریغا که جاودانی نست
پس اعتماد بریں چند روزه فانی نیست
کدام باد بهاری وزید در عالم
که باز در عقبش صرصر خزانی نیست

حکمت کامله الهی وقدرت شامله نامتناهی همواره مقتضی آں بود که تارك مبارك هر مرد احتشامی که بساط بسیط وافسر آراسته گردد آخر الامر اوقات حیاتش انجام پذیرفته به روضه رضوان انتقال نماید وسنت سنیه سبحانی بدیں نمط تعلق گرفته که قدم هر صاحب دولتی که در عرصه دنیا اورنگ با فرهنگ سلطنت را [1] بیاراید عاقبت آفتاب دولتش به عقده کسوف گرفتار آمده مرغ روحش به گلزار جنان پروازنماید ـ کدام آفتاب اقبال نور بخشی نمود [2] که عن قریب از اوج قبول به حضیض افول نرسید ـ وکدام سرو در ریاض حیات خرامش

۱ـ ع : را، ندارد
۲ـ ع : نوربخش نبود

فرموده که زخم ارّه فوات نچشید۔

قطعه[1]:

کدام دوحه اقبال سر کشید به چرخ

که صرصر اجلش عاقبت زبیخ نکند

آری هلاك مجموع بشر به شربت "کل شئی هالك الا وجهه[2]" است وتمامی اهل دنیا را بر ممر "اینما تکونوا یدرککم الموت ولو کنتم فی بروج مشیدة[3]" راهگذر۔

شعر:

الموت کاس کل الناس شاربه

والقبر باب کل الناس داخله

وبالفرض والتقدیر اگر مشاهده صورت بقاء در عالم مقصود بودی خلعت این موهبت وتشریف این مکرمت به قامت با استقامت انبیاء ورسل که هادیان سبل اند خصوصاً ختم الانبیاء که مقصود از ایجاد[4] دنیا ومافیها ذات مطهر اوست، زیبنده ودرخور آمدی:

بیت:

به عالم گر کسی پائنده بودی

ابو القاسم محمد زنده بودی

چون آن حضرت لباس فنا پوشیدند مارا طمع خلود از عقل وفراست نیست۔

قطعه:

اندیشه زمرگ مصطفی باید کرد

شادی وطرب جمله رها باید کرد

۱۔ ع : قطعه، ندارد

۲۔ قرآن مجید : ۸۸/۲۸

۳۔ قرآن مجید : ۷۸/٤

٤۔ ع : ایجاد، ندارد

چون سید هر دو کونین جاوید نماند

ما را طمع خام چرا باید کرد

پس التماس از دراری اوج سلطنت وخلافت آنست که هرچند ایں واقعه صعب ومهیب ودافع الصبر والشکیب (شکیب) می نماید اما بر وفق "بما صبرتم فنعم عقبی الدار[2]" اندوه خاطر را به دواء صبر مداوا فرمایند وسکینه روح به فتوح "ولئن صبرتم لهو خیر للصابرین[3]"۔ امیدوار است که چند انکه آں حضرت در سایه بلند پایه جنت به آب سرچشمه وصال سیراب باشند آں کواکب آسمان خلافت در سریر فلك مصیر (مسیر) جلالت قائم مقام والد ماجد خود بوده به تمهید بسط عدالت ونصفت قیام نمایند وساحت آفاق را از پرتو عدل واحسان واشعه بر وامتنان بیارایند۔ زیاده گستاخی لائق دعاگو ننمود لاجرم زبان بایحاز واختصار کشود۔ والا مرا علی[4]۔

(۲۰۰)

صحیفه در تعزیت

دلا ز گردش گیتی وفا چه می طلبی

دریں سراچه فانی وفا چه می طلبی

تراکه مسکن اصلی سرای آخرت است

دریں اقامت دار فنا چه می طلبی

۱۔ ع : رباعی
۳۔ قرآن مجید : ۲۴/۱۳
٤۔ قرآن مجید : ۱۲۶/۱٦
٤۔ ع : از "بما صبرتم فنعم عقبی الدار" تا، والامرا علی، ندارد

قطعه:

دنیا که اساس دلربائی دارد
او باهمه خلق آشنائی دارد
انصاف بده که خوش سرائیست جهان
افسوس که داغ بی وفائی دارد

بر ضمیر منیر وخاطر خطیر ارباب بینش واصحاب دانش پوشیده نیست بلکه مقرر ومعین است که تیر قضا را بجز به رضا رد نتوان کرد وحکم الهی را جز تسلیم چاره نتوان نمود۔ نزد علماء عالم وعقلاء بنی آدم چوں آفتاب جهاں تاب واضح ولائح است که ایں دنیای بی وفا که منزل گاه آدمیانست سایه است که به زوال اتصال دارد، هر بدری را محاقی وهر وصلی را فراقی در خیال دارد وهر عشرتی را عسرتی وهر حیاتی را مماتی در حساب شمارد۔

زیں تیره خاکداں مطلب رافتی که هست
نوشش قرین نیش وگل او قرین خار

همه کس را سر انجام ایں جام چشیدنی است وسر در نقاب تراب با دیده پر آب کشیدنی۔ اگر در پوشیدن جامه حیات ونوشیدن جرعه ممات میل ومحابا بودی حضرت رسالت وسلطان بارگاه جلالت کاروان سالار "کنت نبیاً وآدم بین الماء والطین[1]" علیه افضل الصلوات واکمل التحیات به خطاب "انك میت وانهم میتون[2]" مخاطب نگشتی۔ کدام آفتاب از مشرق حیات طلوع کرد که به ممات فرو نرفت وکدام ریحان از بوستان عشرت بر دمید که به صرصر نوائب پژمرده نشد۔

۱۔ ع: علماء ایں حدیث را موضوع قرار داده اند، رجوع کنید محموع فتاوی شیخ الاسلام احمد بن تیمیه، جمع وترتیب عبد الرحمن بن محمد وابنه محمد، دار العربیة، بیروت، ۱۳۹۸ھ، ۲/۱٤۷، ۲٤۸

۲۔ قرآن مجید: ۳۰/۳۹

روز هجر انست ای تیغ اجل خوں ریز باش
گر برای کشتن من خواهی آمد تیز باش

دار دنیا محل حوادث است وساحت این جهاں عرصه گاه نوائب۔ فناء هر مخلوقی از قبیل واجبات است وبقاء هر موجودی از ممتنعات۔ لاشك هر ممکن الوجود که سر از دریچه حدوث بیرون آرد سر انجام پائمال فوات خواهد شد وهر محدث بالذات که پای در بقعه امکان نهد عاقبة الامر سر به کتم عدم خواهد برد۔ پس دریں قضایا دست رضا به فتراك "الرضاء بقضاء الله" باید زد وپای امید در رکاب "لئن صبر تم لهو خیر للصابرین[۱]" باید آورد۔ چه بار قدر همه را کشیدنی وشراب اجل چشیدنی است۔

آفریده چه کند گر نکشد بار قضا
که آفرینش همه در بند قدر محبوس اند

(۲۰۱)

صحیفه در تعزیت

دردا که بحر دانش وکان هنر نماند
شاخ درخت عز وشرف تازه تر نماند
ای دل فغاں بر آر که آرام جاں برفت
وی دیده خوں ببار که نور بصر نماند

شکایت روزگار غدار حکایتی است که "یضیق صدری[۲]" نتیجه اوست وحکایت دهر ناسازگار شکایتی است که "ولا ینطلق

۱۔ قرآن مجید : ۱۲۶/۱۶
۲۔ قرآن مجید : ۱۳/۲۶

لسانی[۱] "ثمره اوست- دنیا مکانی است[۲] که گوش هوش عالمیان غیر صداء "کل نفس ذائقة الموت[۳]" هیچ نشنیده وروایتی است که بصر بصیرت عارفاں دراں جز نقش "کل شی هالك الا وجهه[٤]" ندیده- زبان از اظهار وقائع عجیبه دنیای ستم گار گنگ ولال است وکهنه خامه در طی بوادی حوادث غریبه چرخ دوّار عاجز وپائمال-

فریاد که یارای سخن نیست زباں را

بر بست غم وغصه ره نطق وبیاں را

هر چند عارف خبیر[۵] داند که باعث بر تبئین آں مقال چیست واقف روشن ضمیر شناسد که مقصود از تفصیل ایں احوال کیست[٦]- صریحاً ز همگناں منشرح می سازد که چوں خبر واقعه جاں گداز وحادثه غم پرداز حضرت غفراں پناه، ملاذ ومعاذ صنادید فرادیس الجنان به مسامع سکنه ایں دیار خصوصاً مخلصان صداقت شعار[۷] رسید نه چندان سیلاب اندوه وتیر باران الم کوه ستوه غالب گردید که به زور بازوئی صبر وسپر نصیحت وموعظت در معرض تلف شد وروان براں آمد تا اطفاء نائره اش سیلاب دیده خونبار تصور تواں کرد-

قطعه[۸]:

عالمی راجاں ازیں حسرت پریشاں شد دریغ

خانه معمور او یکبار ویراں شد دریغ

۱- قرآن مجید: ۱۳/۲٦

۲- ع،س: غدار حکایتی است که "یضیق صدری" نیتجه اوست وحکایت دهر ناساز گار شکایتی است که "لاینطلق لسانی" ثمره اوست، دنیامکانی است که، ندارند

۳- قرآن مجید: /۵۷

٤- قرآن مجید: ۸۸/۲۸

۵- ع: متلهف، زیاده دارد

٦- ع: وواقف روشن ضمیر شناسد که مقصود از تفصیل ایں اقوال احوال کسیت، ندارد

۷- ع: وقار

۸- ع: بیت

آفتابی بود در برج شرف ناگاه رفت
آفتابی ناگهان در خاك پنهان شد دریغ

اما بر همگنان واضح است که عالم فانی در ارتحال است وهر موجودی در معرض انتقال۔ شاه و گدا، پیر وبرنا، شیخ ومدرس، سید ووزیر ودبیر ومشیر وقائم وقاعد وهابط وصاعد وغنی وفقیر وصغیر و کبیر وخفته وبیدار ومست وهوشیار همه در چنگال این عنا ومعرض این فنا برابر اند۔

دربارگاه حشر چه سلطان چه بی نوا
بر آستان مرگ چه دربان چه بادشاه

لاجرم از اظهار جزع وافراط فزع که به لسان شرع وبیان شارع ممنوع است ومذموم، توسلی به وسائل صبر وثبات، که دلیل قوت عقل و کمال ایمان است، بایدنمود۔ امیدوار است که اولاد واحفاد آن حضرت که شعبه دوحه شریعت ودین پروری وثمره شجره طریقت وحق گذاری اند، از حالت اول مجتنب وبه وساطت ثانی متوسل باشند ودر زمره "انما یوفی الصابرون اجرهم بغیر حساب[۱]" منتظم وملتئم بوده ریاض روح اطهر آن حضرت از تنسم نسیم ادعیه تازه وریان دارند وبر اشاعت آثار واطاعت اطوار آن حضرت که عروه وثقی سلوك وخدا پرستی است، حتی الامکان توجه خاطر فیاض گمارند۔ زیاده قلم را طاقت بیان نبود بنا بران به همیں قدر اختصار نمود۔

آن که دلش به داغ محبت فگار نیست
گر نیك بنگری بهمه روزگار نیست
تدبیر کار غمزدگان شکسته دل
غیر از رضا بخواسته روزگار نیست

۱۔ ع : قرآن مجید : ۱۰/۳۹

(۲۰۲)

صحیفه در تعزیت

ایں حالت مشکل که مبادا کس را
غم سوخت مرا چناں که آتش خس را
یارب چساں نهاں شد آں گوهر پاك
آیا چه شد آں شاخ گل نورس را

دریغ ازاں سرو گلشن کامرانی ویاسمن چمن شادمانی پیش ازاں که جانش به نسیم طراوت بشگفد از صرصر تند باد[۱] اجل در خاشاك افتاده، ونهال عمرش که بر جوئبار روزگار ازاں سرسبز تر نهال نبود قبل ازاں که ثمره معالی بارور گردد از دست برد خزاں رو به عدم کشید. حقا که از استماع ایں واقعه مهلکه، که اشد وقائع ومصائب است، دل غمگین وخاطر حزین را حالتی طاری شده که زبان را یارای بیان وطاقت املاء آں نه. زهی سنگدل کوهی که از سختی ایں واقعه (در) استحکام آں اختلال راه نیافت وعجب سیه روزی که از استماع (ایں) حادثه خاك مذلت بر سر نکرد. اگر چه صبر وشکیبائی در امثال ایں مصائب از قبیل محالات است ومقوله ممتنعات، اما چوں اولاً از ودائع حضرت بیچون است وعاقل باید که به وصول ودیعت با صاحبش اضطراب واضطرار نکند وخود را در اندوه وعنا نینداز د. وچوں ایں جگر گوشه با شمائل آرام چشم جمیع مخلصان امانتی بود از خداوند علی الاطلاق باید که به فقدان آں صبر وشکیبائی را شعار ودثار خود ساخته رضا به قضا در دهیم وامیدوار مثوبه اخروی باشیم. امید که حضرت الله تعالی نعم البدل کرامت فرماید وبر عمر وزندگانی ایشاں وباقی اولاد برخوردار بیفزاید، آمین رب العالمین.

متفرقات

(۲۰۳)

قباله شراء

ایں دکریست در بیان آں که بخرید فلاں ابن فلاں از فلاں ابن فلاں وفروخت ایں بائع هذا بدیں مشتری هذا از انچه نمود[۱] که حق وملك او بوده ودر تصرف مالکانه خود داشته تا زمان ایں مبایعه شرعیه خالیاً عن حق الغیر وعما یمنع جواز البیع ونفاذه، همگی وتمامی سرای واقع در بلده محروسه فلاں محدود به حدود اربعه با جمیع توابع ولواحق ومرافق شرعیه آں ولکل قلیل وکثیر هو فیها او[۲] منها من الحقوق الداخلیة والخارجیة صفقة واحدة[۳] به مبلغ فلاں بیع وشراء شرعی بات وبتات نافذ ولازم مشتمل بر ایجاب وقبول ولقابض شرعی منها در بدلین مذکورین بشرط واقع شد۔ وبائع هذا بجمیع انچه مذکور شد اعتراف معتبر نمود و از دعوی کذب[٤] در اقرار وفساد بیع وغبن فاحش مع التعزیر من المشتری ابراء وتبرا کرد۔ وضمان درك بر موجب شریعت غراء ثابت ومقرر است اگر واقع آید۔ وکان ذالك من المتعاقدین فی حال نفاذ جمیع التصرفات الشرعیة عنها طائعین فی تاریخ شهر فلاں۔

---

۱ ـ ع :هذا بدین مشتری هذا انچه نمود، ندارد
۲ ـ ع : و
۳ ـ ع : خالیا عن حق الغیر وعما یمنع جواز البیع، زیاده دارد
٤ ـ ع : کذب، ندارد

(۲۰٤)

قباله شراء از وکیل

غرض از نوشته آں که بخرید دولت مآب، سعادت ایاب فلاں بن فلاں از مسمی فلاں بن فلاں وفروخت ایں بائع هذا بدیں مشتری در وقتی که ایں بائع هذا وکیل تمام شرعی بود در جمیع امور فروختن انچه دریں صحیفه مذکور خواهد شد وتسلیم بیع وقبض وانچه از توابع ولوازم آں باشد از قبل فلاں بن فلاں، وآں وکالت مذکوره ایں بائع هذا از قبل موکل مذکوره (مذکور) او به طریق که مذکور شد، در دار القضاء بلده محفوظه فلاں در ضمن مرافعه وانکار واستشهاد بر روی خصم[۱] جاهد بگواهی فلاں بن فلاں وفلاں بن فلاں که معدل شده بودند، بشرط ثابت شده بود وحکم قاضی اسلام نافذ الامر والاحکام بلده مذکوره الذی سیوشح ذیل هذا الکتاب بتوقیعه الشریف به ثبوت آں ملحق شده کماهو طریقه شرعاً، انچه نمود ایں بائع که حق وملك وی بوده ودر تحت وتصرف مالکانه خود داشته تا زمان ایں مبایعه شرعیه، خالیاً عن حق الغیر وعما یمنع جواز البیع ونفاذه، همگی وتمامی محدود کذا۔

اگر خواهد ثبوت وکالت در آخر قباله نویسد[۲] پیش از تاریخ به همیں طریق که اولاً مذکور شد۔ اگر خواهد ذکر ثبوت وکالت را پیش از بیع وشراء در صدر قباله نویسد بدین طریق که بعد ازاں که در دار القضاء بلده فلاں در ضمن مرافعه شرعیه ثابت شده بود که فلاں بن فلاں[۳] وکیل عام شرعی کرده فلاں بن فلاں را در جمیع امور بیع که مذکور خواهد شد وقبض ثمن وتسلیم مبیع و وی قبول ایں وکالت کرده

۱۔ ع :حاضر، زیاده دارد

۲۔ ع : نوشته

۳۔ ع : در ضمن مرافعه شرعیه ثابت شده بود که فلاں بن فلاں، ندارد

بـود وحـكـم قاضى اسلام البلدة المذكورة التى سيوشح ذيل هذه السطور بتوقيعه الشريف بگواهى فلان بن فلان۔

(۲۰۵)

قباله نكاح

الحمد لله رافع لواء الشريعة الغرّاء، محى مراسم الملة البيضاء، منزّل قطرات الامطار من خلال الغمام من السماء فسبحان من شرع النكاح للازواج من الرجال والنساء والصلوة على رسوله محمد خاتم الانبياء وعلى آله واصحابه الابرار الاتقياء وسلّم تسليماً كثيراً۔ وبعد فانّ الله تعالى شرع النكاح حصنا من المخادعات الشيطانية وامناً من المحاربات الشهوانية۔ قال عزّ من قائل "وانحكوا الايامىٰ والصالحين من عبادكم واماءكم ان يكونوا فقراء يغنهم الله من فضله والله واسع عليم[۱]" وقال النبى عليه الصلوة والسلام "النكاح من سنتى فمن رغب عن سنتى فليس منّى"۔ واقول قولى هذا واستغفر الله لى ولكم ولجماعة المسلمين انه ملك جواد كريم۔ دعوى كنم بدين حاضر آمده كه وكيل گردانيده مرا مخدّره صالحه زين المستورات، تاج المخدّرات، نتيجة السعادات فلانه بنت الامير الاجلّ فلان ابن امير[۲] مرجوم فلان درحال نفاذ جميع تصرّفات شرعيه بالطوع والرغبة كه نفس اورا بزنى اين حاضر آمده دهم بر كابين مبلغ فلان مهر موجّل موقوف تا انقطاع نكاح باى سبب كان، بالموت او الطلاق، در مبلغ پنج هزار رائج كه هر

۱۔ قرآن مجيد : ۳۲/۲٤

۲۔ ع : امير، ندارد

۳۔ ع : شريعت

دینار از روی وزن یك مثقال ونیم دانگ نقره خالص است[1]، مهر معجّل تا زمان مطالبه اورا دست پیمان گویند وهر چهار شرط شرعی که مشهور متعارف است درمیان مسلمانان۔ شرط اول آں که ناکح حاضر آمده برسر موکله من زن نخواهد ونکاح فضولی را که کسی[2] از برای وی بقول یا بفعل اجازت نکند چنانچه بروی حلال ومباح شود۔ شرط دوم آں که ناکح حاضر آمده از نزدیك موکله من مدت یك سال پیوسته باختیار خود غائب نشود غیبت منقطعه مدت سفر چنانچه دریں مدت نفس ویا نفقه موکله من نرسد۔ دریں صورت مرموکله من وکیله باشد که پای خود را بیك طلاق بائن بکشاید۔ شرط سوم آں که ناکح حاضر آمده[3] مرا بی جرم وخیانت شرعی لت نزند از سر غضب چنانکه اثر ضرب برعضوی از اعضاء ظاهر گردد۔ در تحقیق وجود هر یك ازیں شرائط مذکوره موکله من وکیله باشد که پای خود را بیك طلاق بائن ازیں مجرم شرعی بکشاید، هر وقت که خواهد در مجلس که باشد۔ ومهر تمامی درذمه ناکح لازم باشد، شرط چهارم آں که ناکح حاضر آمده برسر موکله من سرّیت نگیرد ندارد چنانکه رسم سرّیت است، ازهیچ صفت، نی ترکیه ونی هندیه ونی آرمینیه ونی غیر ازینها، واگر بگیرد وبدارد موکله من وکیل باشد ایں سرّیت را بقیمت وقت بفروشد بجهت مهر خود بردارد و وبزیادت ونقصان بریك دیگر رجوع کند۔ بدیں مهر مذکور وبدیں شرائط مذکوره وکیل گردانیده مراموکله مذکوره که نفس اورا بزنی بدیں حاضر آمده بدهم۔

۱۔ ع :خالص است، ندارد
۲۔ ع : که کسی، ندارد
۳۔ ع : موکله، زیاده دارد

(۲۰۶)

قباله نکاح

الحمد لله الذی جعل النکاح سنة للانام وفصلا بین الحلال والحرام والصلوة علی رسوله محمد الی یوم القیام وعلی آله واصحابه مصابیح الظلام وسلم تسلیماً کثیرا کثیراً۔ اما بعد، این سطور مسطور می گردد دربیان آن که شاب اعز اکرم فلان بن فلان بخواست به زنی ودر حباله خود در آورد نفس عفیفه، صالحه، مخدره، زین المستورات وهی المسماة فلانه بنت فلان بنکاح صحیح شرعی به رضاء ولی وی به حضور شهود عدول، مقرون به ایجاب وقبول علی سبیل الشهرة والاعلان به کابین چهل من ابریشم زرد، خام، خشك، جید، باریك نسج، مزرکش، موزون به سنجاب ابریشم هرات النصف منه بیست من موجل تا زمان انقطاع نکاح بای سبب کان، وبر دست پیمان دو هزار روپیه النصف منه یك هزار مبلغ معجل وچهار شرط که مسطور می گردد۔ واین ناکح مذکور بدین منکوحه خود قبول کرد حسن معاشرت واداء حقوق زوجیت کما قال تعالی "فامساك بمعروف اور تسریح باحسان[۱]" تحریراً فی سلخ شیر کدا فی سنة کذا حامداً ومصلیاً۔

(۲۰۷)

قباله نکاح بنده

بخواست فلان مملوك فلان بن فلان مرنفس حره مکلفه فلان

۱۔ قرآن مجید : ۲/۲۲۹

باذن وامر مولی خودوتمام کند۔ ودر تجویز کنیزك نویسد که بخواست فلاں بن فلاں مرنفس فلا نه مملوك فلاں بن فلاں را ووی نفس خود را بدو داد باذن وامر مولی خود وتمام کند۔

(۲۰۸)

قباله خلع

اقرار شرعی کرد طائعاً فلاں بن فلاں که باز فروخته زن خود فلانه بنت فلاں را به یك طلاق بائن بر جمیع مهر یا بقیه مهر او وایں فلانه قبول کرده ازیں فلاں مذکور ایں خلع را بدیں بدل مشافهةً در مجلس خلع مذکور وابراء کرد ایں فلاں مذکور را از جمیع دعاوی وخصومات که بریں فلانة مذکوره داشت وایں فلانه تصدیق کرد ایں فلاں را در جمیع انچه مذکور شد وایں ابراء از وی قبول نمود دریں جلس مذکور هذا۔

(۲۰۹)

قباله اعتاق غلام

ایں ذکر است در بیان آں که اقرار کرد واعتراف معتبر شرعی نمود طائعاً فلاں بن فلاں در حال نفاذ امور وجواز تصرفات خود که آزاد مطلق شرعی می کرده از انچه نمود که حق وملك او بوده ودر تحت تصرف مالکانه خود داشته تا زمان ایں اعتاق، خالیا عن حق الغیر وغیر الحق وعما یمنع جواز الاعتاق ونفاذه، همگی وتمامی یك نفر

غلام هندی، سفید پوست، کشاده ابرو، میانه قد در سن بیست سالگی تخمیناً، فلان نام مشارالیه را اعتاقاً صحیحاً نافذاً لازماً جائزاً منجزاً، خالی از تعلیق وافاضه واشتراط عوض بل مجاناً خالصاً لوجه الله تعالی وطلباً لمرضاته وهرباً من الیم عقابه ورغبةً فیما[1] وعد رسول الله صلی الله علیه وسلم فی قوله "من اعتق رقبة مومنة اعتق الله تعالیٰ بکل عضو منها عضوا منه من النار[2]"۔ این فلان هذا آزاد شد وچون سائر آزادان فروخته وبخشیده نشود ونماند این معتق مذکور را بر وی از جهت بندگی حقی مگر حق ولاء چنانچه در شریعت غراء مقرر است که "الولاء لمن اعتق"۔ واین معتق مشارالیه تصدیق کرد این مذکور را در آنکه مملوك او بود در وقت این اعتاق۔ وکان ذالك فی التاریخ، شهر فلان، سنته فلان۔

(۲۱۰)

وثیقه اعتاق بر بدل

بهمان طریق که در اعتاق بی بدل نوشته شد که تا آنجا که اعتاقاً جائزاً۔ بعده نبوسید این ذکریست دربیان آن که اقرار شرعی کرد فلان بن فلان بدستور سابق۔ بعده بنویسد که بر بدل مبلغ کذا وصفت زر کند ونویسد که این معتق مذکور عتق را بدین بدل قبول نمود وتمامی بدل عتق مذکور را تسلیم این معتق نمود ووی قبض شرعی کرده وبری ساخته این معتق ذمه این معتق مذکور را از تمامی این بدل مذکور براءة قبض واستیفاء۔ ونماند این معتق مذکور را برین معتق هیچ حقی از

۱۔ ع : فیما، ندارد

۲۔ ع : این حدیث در صحیح بخاری (کتاب العتق، باب ای الرقاب افضل) بدین الفاظ وارد شده "ایما رجل اعتق امرءٍ مسلما استنقذ الله بکل عضو منه عضوا منه من النار"

حقوق وایں معتق را از دعوی فساد ایں اعتاق و کذب دریں اقرار بدل عتق مذکور ابراء وتبرا نمود۔ وایں معتق ایں ابراء را ازوی قبول کرد واورا تصدیق کرد دران که مملوك ومرقوق اوبود در وقت ایں اعتاق۔ وکان ذالك فی تاریخ کذا۔

(۲۱۱)

قباله تدبیر

ایں ذکریست دربیان آں که اقرار شرعی کرد طائعاً فلاں بن فلاں که مدبّر ساخته از انچه نمود که بنده ومملوك اوبود ودرتحت تصرف مالکانه خود داشته یوم التدبیر هذا خالیاً عن حق الغیر وعمّا یمنع جواز التدبیر همگی یك نفر غلام هندی کذا واورا آزاد گردانید بعد از وفات خود تدبیراً صحیحاً نافذاً مطلقاً غیر مقیّدٍ۔ پس ایں فلاں هندی مذکور مدبّر مطلق شد، فروخته وبخشیده نشود ومهر ومیراث نگردد واز ملکی به ملکی انتقال نیابد۔ ومادام که ایں مدبّر مذکور در قید[1] حیات باشد از ونفع گیرد همچناں که انتفاع می گیرند موالی از بندگان خود غیر از بیع واشباه آں۔ وچوں ایں مدبّر مذکور وفات یابد وی آزاد باشد وورثه ایں مدبّر مذکور را بروی هیچ سبیلی نباشد مگر سبیل سعایت درانچه بیروں نیاید از ثلث ترکه مدبّر وایں مدبّر تصدیق نموده ایں را در آں که مملوك او بوده هو یوم التدبیر هذا۔ وایں مربر از دعوی فساد ایں تدبیر ابراء نمود۔ وکان ذالك فی التاریخ کذا۔

۱۔ ع: قبض

(۲۱۲)

قباله استیلاء

ایں ذکریست دربیان آں که اقرار شرعی کرد طائعاً فلاں ابن فلاں که جاریه وی که کنیزك است ترکیه، سفید پوست، سیاه چشم، کشاده ابرو، میانه قد، بست ساله تخمیناً فلاں نام ام ولد ویست۔ زائیده این مقر مذکور[۲] برفراش وی پسر دیگر که مسمّی است بمحمد۔ پس ایں کنیزك مذکوره ام ولد وی گشت وایں فرزند ثابت النسبت[۳] است ازوی۔ ایں کنیزك آزاداست بعد از فوت ایں مقر مذکور۔ نیست سبیلی مرورثه مقر را بروی مگر سبیل ولاء۔ کان ذالك فی تاریخ، شهر کذا، سنة کذا۔

(۲۱۳)

وثیقه مکاتب

ایں ذکریست دربیان آں که اقرار شرعی کرد فلاں که مکاتب ساخت ازانچه نمود که حق وملك اوبوده درتحت تصرف مالکانه خود داشته تا زمان ایں کتابت[۳] خالیاً عن حق الغیر وعمّا یمنع جواز الکتابة ونفاذها، همگی[٤] یك نفر غلام هندی کذا وکذا بر مبلغ کذا مکاتبةً

۱۔ ع : مذکور، ندارد
۲۔ ع : االنسب، ندارد
۳۔ ع : کتاب
٤۔ ع : وتمامی، زیاده دارد

صحیحةً جائزةً که این مبلغ کذا را[1] این غلام مذکور بی تاخیر بدین مقر مذکور را ادا نماید بشرط آن که اگر در اداء این مبلغ تاخیر نماید وپنج روز ازین تاریخ بگذرد وتمام این مبلغ را این مکاتب مذکور بدین مقر نرسانیده باشد، این مقر مذکور را ولایت آن باشد که باز گرداند این مکاتب به بندگی وانچه از بدل کتابت گرفته باشد مر این مقر را حلال باشد۔ واگر پیش از انقضاء مدت مذکوره ادا نماید این مکاتب مذکور آن مبلغ را، آزاد باشد چون سائر احرار۔ واگر بدل کتاب منجّم باشد نویسد که کتابةً صحیحةً منجّمةً ده نجم موجّل بده ماه پیوسته اول از غرّه فلان، آخر آن سلخ شهر فلان۔ هر نجمی ازان مبلغ کذا که ادا نماید آن مبلغ گذشتن یك ماه بشرط آن که اگر عاجز[2] شود از اداء این مال برین نجوم یا تاخیر کند نجمی را از محل آن سه روز، مردود باشد در بندگی۔ واگر جمیع این نجوم را ادا نماید بی تاخیر آزاد باشد چون سائر احرار۔ وتمام کند۔

(٢١٤)

قباله وکالت عامه در جمیع اشیاء

وکیل ساخت فلان بن فلان مر فلان بن فلان را به حفظ انچه مر این موکل را باشد از ضیاع وعقار ومستغلات وامتعه وبنده وحیوان وغیر ذالك من صنوف الا موال وبه بیع واستقلال انچه خواهد ازین اشیاء وبه عمارت انچه محتاج به عمارت باشد وبه اجاره انچه خواهد اجاره آن را ومصالحت آن را وتاجیل وحواله ورهن وتجارت در اموال او به جمیع اصناف تجارت وشرکت ومضاربت وسائر عقود شرعیه ودعوی

١۔ ع : راء، ندارد

٢۔ ع : قاصر

وجـواب دعوی و کیل کرد واو را قائم مقام نفس خود گردانید در جمیع انـچـه مـذکـور شـد۔ واگـر خـواهد بخود کند این امور را واگر خواهد کسـی را وکیـل سـازد جـائـزاً فـاضـع لـه وعـلیه من ذالك وکالةً مطلقةً صـحیـحةً عامةً فی الوجوه۔ وقبول کرد این وکیل این وکالت را مشافهةً مواجهةً فی مجلس التوکیل۔

(٢١٥)

قباله وکالت عامه بر وجهی که حالا متعارف است

وکیـل کـرد فلان مر فلان را وکالت مطلقه عامه در جمیع امور از بیـع وشـراء وتسلیـم مبیـع وقبـض مشتـری واداء ثمن ودعوی وجواب دعوی واقامت بینه وتحلیف خصم وحبس واطلاق وقبض مدعا واستیفاء حـقـوق واعیـان وصلح وابراء وقبض بدل وصلح واسقاطات ومعارضات وغیر ذالك مما یجری فیه الوکالة وبتوکیل من یشاء۔ واین وکیل مذکور قبول این وکالت کرد۔ وکان ذالك فی تاریخ کذا۔

(٢١٦)

قباله کفالت

اقـرار کـرد فـلان که فلان را در ذمه پدر ومورث وی فلان مبلغ کـذا دیـن لازم الاداء بـوده تـا زمـان فوت وی وچون او فوت شده از وی

١۔ ع :مذکور، ندارد
٢۔ ع : النسب، ندارد

تـر کـه وافیـه مانده که به دست وتصرف این مقر است، واین مقر ضامن وکـفیـل شد از پدر مذکور خود جمیع این مبلغ مذکور صحیحاً جائزاً۔ وقبول کرد این فلان این ضمانت را مشافهةً در مجلس این ضمانت۔

(۲۱۷)

قباله هبه

ایـن ذکریست در بیان آن که بخشید فلان بن فلان مر فلان بن فـلان را از انچـه حـق ومـلك او بوده ودر تصرف مالکانه خود داشته تا زمـان ایـن هبـه خـالیـاً عـن حـق الـغیر، همگی وتمامی یك منزل سرای مشتمل بر بیوت وحجرات واقع در بلده کذا در محله[1] کذا محدود بدین حـدود شرقی وغربی وجنوبی وشمالی، به جمیع حدود وحقوق از ارض وبـنـاء سـفـل وعلو کل قلیل وکثیر هو فیها او منها هبةً صحیحةً مجوزةً، مـقبـوضةً، فـارغةً خالی از شروط مفسده وشروط عوض بل به طـریق صله وتبـرع۔ وقبـول نـمـود ایـن فلان موهوب[2] لـه ایـن هبـه را ازین واهب در مـجـلـس این هبه وقبض کرد[3] ایـن مـوهـب را باذن وتسلیم این واهب، فـارغـاً عن کل مانع ومنازع واین واهب از دعوی فساد این هبه ابراء نمود۔

۱۔ ع :درمحله، ندارد

۲۔ ع :موهب

۳۔ ع : کرد، ندارد

(۲۱۸)

تمسك وديعت

ایں ذکریست در بیان آں که اقرار شرعی کرد طائعاً فلاں که فلاں ودیعت گذاشته نزد وی اشیاء کذا که محافظت نماید ایں فلاں مودع آں اشیاء به نفس خود یا به کسی که اعتماد داشته باشد بر وی ازاں کسانی که در عیال وی اند وبه اجنبی ندهد۔ ایں فلاں مودع ایں اشیاء را تسلیم وی نمود[1] و وی قبض شرعی کرد وملتزم حفظ ایں شد مشروط آں که هر گاه که ایں مودع ایں اشیاء را ازیں مودع طلب نماید وی رد کند آں را بوی۔

(۲۱۹)

تمسك عاریت زمین

ایں ذکریست در بیان آں که به عاریت داد فلاں به فلاں تمامی قطعه زمین در موضع کذا محدود به حدود کذا عاریة صحیحة شرعیة مدت ده سال پیویسته از غره محرم سنه کذا انچه خواهد از بیوت ومنازل وخود را در انجا سکنی کند وهر کس را خواهد ساکن سازد۔ یا ایں مستعیر دریں زمین جهت خود درخت ونهال نشاند انچه خواهد وانتفاع گیرد بداں درختان ومیوه های آں وایں مستعیر دریں زمین به عاریت گرفت ایں زمین را وقبض کرد۔

۱۔ ع : نمود، ندارد

(۲۲۰)

تمسك وقف مدرسه

ان الحمد لولیه والصلوة والسلام علی نبیه۔ وبعد، این ذکریست در بیان آن که وقف کرد وتصدق نمود فلان بن فلان از خالص املاك واطیب اموال خود را در حال صحت بدن و کمال عقل ونفاذ جمیع تصرفات خود، طائعاً همگی مدرسه مشتمل بر صفها وحجرات وغرفات مجموع پیوسته یك دیگر در بلده کذا در محله کذا محدود به حدود وجمیع توابع ولواحق ومرافق شرعیه آن بر طلبه علوم شرعیه تا مجمع[۱] اهل علم ودین ومسکن طلاب علوم شریفه سید المرسلین صلی الله علیه وسلم باشد۔ وبعد ازان که این واقف مذکوراین بقعه را از ملك خود اقرار نموده بود واین بقعه وقف[۲] لازم گشته بود، خواست این وقف که این خیر او را دوامی باشد، وقف کرد وتصدق نمود بدین مدرسه مذکوره از انچه حق وملك او بوده ودر تحت تصرف مالکانه خود داشته تا زمان این وقف کردن، خالیاً عن حق الغیر وعمایمنع جواز الوقف ولزومه، همگی عقار وضیاع ومستغلات که واقع است در بلده کذا، منها همگی یك منزل سرای مشتمل بر بیوت وابنیه سفلیه وعلویه در محله کذا محدود بدین حدود۔

پس وقف این واقف مذکور بدین مدرسه مذکوره به جمیع این محدودات مذکورات را به جمیع حدود وحقوق ومرافق وابنیه وقبات وحیطان وسوق واسطوانات وابواب واغلاق واحراث وآلات وادوات

۱۔ ع :مجموع
۲۔ ع : واقف

مرکبه در حمام مذکور واشجار قائم در کروم واراضی وریاحین وعرائس وانهار وجداول وشرب به مجاری آن وکل قلیل وکثیر هو فیها ومنها من حقوقها الداخلیة والخارجیة وقفاً صحیحاً وصدقةً جاریةً نافذةً وهبةً موبدةً محرمةً محتویةً لایباع ولایوهب ولایرتهن ولایرهن ولا یمهر ولا یملك بوجه من الوجوه وسبب من الاسباب الی ان یرث الله ومن علیها وهو خیر الوارثین ومالك[1] رقاب الناس اجمعین۔ وجعل الواقف آخر هذا الوقف علی الفقراء المسلمین۔

وشرط کرد این واقف مذکور که متولی این مدرسه وموقوفات مذکوره آن خود باشد علی سبیل العموم والاستقلال مادام حیات خود یتصرف فیها وموقوفاتها ومحصولاتها کیف یشاء واین یشاء یتصرف الی من یشاء ویصرفها عمن یشاء۔ وتعین مصارف وشرائط وتفویض وازدیاد این واعطاء وحرمان وزمام زیاده ونقصان از هر که باشد وهر چه باشد درین امو ربه کف کفایت وقبضه مصلحت خود نهاد چنانچه کسی را بر وی به هیچ نوع ولایت اعتراض باشد۔ وشرط کرد بعد از وی اولاد ذکور وی واولاد اولاد ذکور وی واولاد اولاد اولاد ذکور وی بطناً بعد بطن وقرناً بعد قرن ابداً هر کدام اعلم واصلح واکفی باشد، متولی این موقوفات باسرها وی باشد۔ واگرهمه در علم وصلاح وکفایت باشند، اسن ایشان متولی این وقف باشد[2]۔ واگر از اولاد ذکور واقف در هیچ بطن کسی نماند از اولاد اناث واقف مذکور واز اولاد اولاد اناث وی بطن بعد بطن به همان دستور متولی باشند[3] واگر از نسل وعقب واقف

۱۔ ع :لوجه من الوجوه وسبب من الاسباب الی ان یرث الله الارض ومن علیها وهو خیر الوارثین ومالك، ندارد

۲۔ ع :واگر همه درعلم وصلاح وکفایت باشند، اسنّ ایشان متولی این وقف باشد، ندارد

۳۔ ع : بهمان دستور متولی باشند، ندارد

کسی نماند هر کس که مدرس باشد متولی ایں موقوفات باشد۔ وچون متولی از اولاد واقف باشد حق تولیت عشر گیرد واگر غیر اولاد باشد بقدر عمل اجرت گیرد۔

وشرط[1] کرد واقف مذکور که ایں موقوفات را زیاده از سه سال اجاره به یك ندهند نی به عقد واحد ونی به عقد مختلفه۔ وما دام که عقد اجاره منقضی نگردد عقد اجاره دیگر نکنند۔ وایں موقوفات را به متغلبه وصاحبان جاه وحشمت وکسانی که اخراج وبدل اجاره از دست ایشان متعذر یا متعسر باشد یا توهم ادعاء مالکیت شود باجاره ندهند۔ وشرط واقف مذکور که انچه ازیں موقوفات حاصل شود از غلات وارتفاعات ومحصولات وفوائد آں هر چه باشد ابتداء کنند اورا به عمارت ومرمت ضروریه ایں موقوفات وموقوف[2] علیها، بس به وظائف قوام وکلاء ایں وقف، پس به اداء اخراجات ومئونات دیوانیان، وانچه ازیں فاضل آید صرف کنند بانچه لابد ایں موقوف علیه باشد از حصیر وفرش وروشنائی وغیر ذالك۔ وانچه ازیں وجود فاضل تر آید متولی به مصارفی که مذکور می گردد صرف نماید، به مدرس، طلبه، امام، موذن وعلی هذا۔ انچه از مصارف نموده باشد به شرح نویسد وتعریف زر وغله نماید۔

ایں واقف ایں موقوفات را از دست خود اخراج نمود واقرار کرد از اموال خود وتسلیم کسی که به تولیت آں نصب کرده بود، نمود خالیا عن موانع التسلیم۔ وبعد ازاں که به عدم لزوم متصرف شده بود قاضی اسلام نافذ الامر والاحکام به بلده کذا الذی سیوشح ذیل هذه الوقفية بتوقیعه الشریف، در وقتی که عالم بود به محل اختلاف ومواضع

۱۔ ع: شروط

۲۔ ع: موقوف، ندارد

اختلاف علماء دین در ضمن مرافعه شرعیه بر خصم حاضر حکم شرعی کرد به صحت این وقف وبعده به لزوم آن قضاء هذا وقفاً صحیحاً شرعیاً لازماً نافذاً موبداً مخلداً۔ واستشهاد کرد بر جمیع انچه در وقفیه مسطور شده این واقف مذکور جمعی از ثقات عدول۔ وکان ذالك فی تاریخ[۱] شهر کذا۔

(۲۲۱)

تمسك وقف برنفس خود وبعده بر اولاد خود

وقف کرد وتصدیق نمود فلان از خالص املاك واطیب اموال خود در حال نفاذ تصرفات شرعیه خود همگی یك منزل سرای واقع موضع محدود بجمیع حدود وحقوق ومرافق آن وارض وبنا وسفل وعلو وکل قلیل وکثیر هو فیها اومنها برنفس خود وبعده بر اولاد خود واولاد اولاد خود ماتو الدوا وتناسلوا، بطناً بعد بطن وقرناً بعد قرن، الاقرب فالا قرب۔ وبعد انقراض ایشان بر اقارب این واقف، الاقرب فالاقرب[۲] وآخره علی الفقراء[۳] المسلمین۔ وشرط کرد واقف مذکور که متولی این وقف[٤] خود باشد مادام حیات خود وهر نوع تصرف که خواهد درین وقف کند وهر شرط که خواهد نویسد وبدستور سابق کند۔

۱۔ ع :فی التاریخ
۲۔ ع : فالاقرب، ندارد
۳۔ ع : فقراء
٤۔ ع : واقف

(۲۲۲)

تمسك وقف

این ذکریست دربیان آن که وقف کرد فلان مبلغ موصوف کذا مشار الیه را مذکور بر مسجد محدوده کذا وآخره علی الفقراء[۱] المسلمین۔ وشروط کرد واقف مذکور که متولی این وقف[۲] خود باشد وبعد وی هر کسی که درین مسجد امام باشد متولی این وقف باشد و[۳] مبلغ موصوف را بطریق قرض یا مصارفه یا مقاربه بمردم امین دهند وبه کسی که مفلس باشد ندهند وبی رهن به قرض ندهند، وانچه از ربح حاصل شود بعمارت این مسجد که ضروری باشد وبفرش وروشنائی صرف نمائند وانچه فاضل[۴] آید ثلثان امام وثلثی موذن تصرف نمایند۔ وقاضی اسلام نافذ الامر موضع کذا که عالم بود بمحل خلاف در ضمن مرافعه شرعیه در وقتی که این مبلغ معین ومشار الیه بود حکم شرعی کرد اولاً بصحت این وقف وبعده بلزوم آن۔ فصار هذا وقفاً صحیحاً جائزاً لازماً۔

(۲۲۳)

تمسك اجاره سرای

۱۔ ع :فقراء
۲۔ ع : باشد و، ندارد
۳۔ ع : وقف
۳۔ ع : حاصل

ایں ذکریست در بیان آں که باجاره گرفت فلاں بن فلاں از فلاں بن فلاں وایں فلاں به اجاره داد بوی از انچه نمود که حق وملك او بوده ودر تصرف مالکانه تا زمان ایں اجاره دادن، خالیاً عن حق الغیر وعما یمنع جواز الاجارة[1] ونفاذها، همگی وتمامی یك منزل سرای در بلده کذا حدودها کذا به جمیع[2] حدود وحقوق ولواحق ومرافق آں وکل قلیل وکثیر هو فیها او منها، مدت یك سال کامل هلالی متوالی اول آں غره فلاں سنه فلاں وآخر آں سلخ فلاں به مبلغ کذا وقسط هر ماهه مبلغ کذا، اجارةً صحیحةً جائزةً نافذةً خالی از شروط مفسده وعاری از معانی مبطله۔ وایں مبلغ مذکور مساوی اجرة المثل ایں موجر مذکور بود یوم العقد۔ مقرر آں که مستاجر دریں مدت مذکور دریں موجر اگر خواهد خود سکنی کند واگر خواهد کسی را ساکن سازد وانتفاع گیرد ایں موجر به وجوه منافع معروف۔ واداء اجرت را بهر نوع مقرر سازند نویسد۔ اگر نقد باشد نویسد که ایں مستاجر تمام بدل اجاره را تسلیم ایں آجر نمود و وی قبض کرد وذمه مستاجر ازاں بری است براءت قبض و استیفاء، واگر هر ماه حصه آں ماه را خواهد داد نویسد که بر آں که هر ماه که منقضی شود ایں مستاجر حصه آن را بایں آجر رساند۔ واگر مجموع را بعد از گذشتن تمام مدت خواهد داد بآن طریق نویسد۔ وبعده نویسد که قبض کرد[3] ایں مستاجر تمام ایں موجر را ازیں آجر بی تاخیر فارغاً عن کل مانع ومنازع ومتفرق شدند از مجلس ایں اجاره تفرق الابدان والاقوال وتمام کند۔ وایں نسخه اصل است در جمیع موجرات از هر جنس که باشد۔

۱۔ ع :البیع، زیاده دارد
۲۔ ع : حدودها کذا بجمیع، ندارد
۳۔ ع : قبض کرد، ندارد

(۲۲٤)

تمسك اجاره زمین

بدستور اجاره سرای نویسد الا آن که اگر بدل اجاره غله باشد بیان مکان ایفاء شرط است، پس نویسد که بر آن که این مستاجر بدل اجاره مذکوره را بعد انقضاء مدت مذکور در موضع از ولایت کذا تسلیم این آجر نماید. ونیز نویسد که بر آن که این مستاجر در تمام مدت انتفاع گیرد بدین موجر بر زراعت ودرین مدت هرچه خواهد درین زمین زراعت نماید از غله زمستانی وتابستانی واین موجر به هر کس را که خواهد باجاره وعمارت ومزارعه دهد، وتمام کند.

(۲۲۵)

تمسك استیجار دایه جهت شیر دادن فرزند

به اجاره داد فلان نفس خود را به فلان ووی به اجاره گرفت مدت دو سال پیوسته هلالی اول آن کذا وآخر آن کذا بر آن که شیر دهد این آجره پسر صغیر فلان نام این مستاجر را شیر خود در منزل این مستاجر ومقیم شود در منزل این مستاجر درین مدت از برای ارضاع این پسر مذکور وی وتربیت وحضانت وی رضاعی که دران تقصیری نباشد به مبلغ کذا اجارةً صحیحةً. واین آجرة این صغیر را دید وشناخت ونفس خود را تسلیم کرد بدین مستاجر از برای این عمل. بیان تاجیل وتعجیل اجرت کند. ودر آخر نویسد که اجازت کرد فلان شوهر این آجره

مذکوره عقد این اجاره را وراضی شد بدان واذن کرد اورا به سکنی در منزل این مستاجر از جهت این عمل۔

(۲۲۶)

تمسك چهار پایه به کرایه گرفتن

به کرایه گرفت فلان تاجر از فلان مکاری پنج سر دراز گوش با پنج شتر معین کذا تا بر آنها بار کند، بر هر شتری چندین گندم یا غیر آن از بلده کذا به مبلغ کذا[1] ۔ واین مکاری این چهارپایان بدین فلان مکتری تسلیم نمود وراضی شد این مکتری وتسلیم کرد این مکتری این بار را بدین مکاری ووی قبض کرد وقبول نمود حمل[2] این بارها را بدین چهار پایان از بلده کذا تا بلده کذا وتسلیم کرد آن بدین مکتری دران بلده مذکوره واین مکاری قبض کرده تمام این کرایه را ازین مکتری۔

(۲۲۷)

تمسك اقرار به دین

به دین اقرار کرد واعتراف معتبر شرعی نمود طائعاً مخبراً اسم ونسب خود فلان بن فلان که برویست وذمه وی ثابت ولازم ومی باید داد او را به فلان بن فلان مبلغ کذا دینی لازم وحقی ثابت واجب که عند المطالبه اورا ادا نماید وبعد از گذشتن مدت کذا ادا نماید۔ واین

۱۔ ع :بمبلغ کذا، ندارد، س : تا بلده کذا زیاده دارد
۲۔ ع : حمل، ندارد

مقر از دعوی کذب دریں اقرار ابراء نمود ومقرله آں را قبول نمود وایں مقرله او را دریں اقرار تصدیق کرد۔ اگر خواهد بیان سبب کند که سبب قرض یا ثمن مبیع مقبوض یا غیر آں هر چه باشد۔ تاجیل درست نخواهد بود۔ واگر اجاره معهود باشد نویسد که به اجاره گرفت مقر مذکور نفس مقرله هذا مذکور را از جهت محافظت نمودن شی کذا ازیں تاریخ یا بعد از گذشتن مدت کذا هر روز به مبلغ کذا وایں مقرله نفس خود را به اجاره بدو داد وملتزم حفظ آں شد۔ وایں مقر از دعوی کذب وفساد ایں اجاره ابراء کرد۔ واگر بیان دین رهنی باشد نویسد که به رهن کرد ایں مقرله مذکور به وثیقه دین مذکور بر مقرله مذکور انچه نمود که حق وملك وی بود ودر تصرف مالکانه خود داشته تا زمان ایں رهن کردن فارغاً عن حق الغیر همگی محدود کذا با اشیاء کذا ووصف آں کند۔ واین مقرله به رهن گرفت وقبض شرعی کرد۔ واگر مقر خود نگاه نخواهد داشت تا زمان ایں رهن نویسد که بعد القبض آں را به عاریت بدین مقر داده وحالا بدست وی است به عاریت۔ واگر در ضمن رهن وکالت باشد نویسد که وکیل کرد ایں راهن ایں مرتهن را که هر گاه خواهد یا چوں مدت کذا بگذرد یا چوں ایں مرتهن طلب دین نماید وایں راهن در اداء آں عاجز باشد یا غائب باشد یا عاطل کند، فروشد ایں مرتهن ایں مرهون را به قیمت وقت وتسلیم مبیع وثمن قبض نماید واز ثمن آں استیفاء نماید دین مذکور را۔ واجرة الحفظ را از انچه شده باشد، وبه زیاده ونقصان به یك دیگر رجوع نمایند۔ وایں مقرله قبول ایں وکالت کرد۔ واگر کسی ضامن ایں دین شود نویسد که ضامن وکفیل مطلق دین مذکور شد فلاں بن فلاں که هر گاه ایں مقرله طلب آں نماید وی ادا کند وایں مقرله ایں ضمانت قبول نموده۔ واگر ذو کس به یك وجودی قباله دهند نویسد که اقرار کردند واعتراف شرعی نمودند فلاں وفلاں که بر ایشاں است ودر ذمه ایشاں لازم

وثابت است ومی باید داد ایشان را به طریق یك وجودی ضمانت یك دیگر به فلان بن فلان مبلغ کجا دینی لازم وحقی ثابت که عند المطالبه ادا نمایند وهر یك ازیں مقرین ضامن وکفیل حصه یك دیگر شدند ازیں دین با هر یك دیگر ومقرله قبول ایں ضمانت کرد در مجلس ایں ضمانت وایں مقران از دعوی کذب دریں اقرار وفساد ضمانت ابراء نمودند به تاریخ کذا۔

(۲۲۸)

تمسك رهن

ایں ذکریست در بیان آں که رهن کرد فلاں بن فلاں جمیع سرای خود را که واقع است در موضع کذا وحدود آں را نویسد به جمیع حدود وحقوق آں۔ وایں مرتهن به رهن گرفت آں را به مبلغ کذا که مرتهن را در ذمه ایں راهن بود دیناً لازماً به سبب صحیح، رهنی وارتهانی جائز نافد شرعی۔ وایں مرتهن ایں مرهون را فارغاً قبض شرعی کرد۔ وتمام کند۔ واگر اذن به انتقاع باشد نویسد که اذن کرد ایں راهن ایں مرتهن را که انتفاع گیرد ازیں مرهون به وجوه انتفاع وکان ذالك فی تاریخ کذا۔

(۲۲۹)

تمسك رهن غلام وکنیزك

اقرار کرد فلاں که در ذمه وی حق دارد فلاں مبلغ کذا دینی

لازم وثابت وبه رهن کرد این مقر نزد این مقرله به وثیقه دین مذکور را از انچه نمود که حق وملك او بوده خالیاً عن حق الغیر وعما یمنع جواز البیع والرهن ونفاذه همگی وتمامی یك نفر غلام یا کنیزك هندی، وحلیه ونام وی را نویسد ووی به رهن گرفته وقبض شرعی کرده آن را۔

(۲۳۰)

تمسك صلح وابراء

اقرار شرعی کرد طائعاً فلان که از هر دعوی که داشت بر فلان در محدود کذا که در تصرف فلان بود، صلح صحیح شرعی کرد بر بدل مبلغ کذا واین صلح را بدین بدل قبول کرده وتمام بدل صلح را تسلیم این فلان مصالح نمود و وی قبض شرعی کرده۔ پس نماند این فلان مصالح را برین فلان مصالح علیه درین محدود ونه در بعضی آن ونه در ثمن وقیمت آن به هیچ وجه من الوجوه هیچ دعوی وخصومتی۔ اگر من بعد این فلان بن فلان بن فلان از جهت این محدود دعوی کند آن دعوی باطل ومدعی مبطل خواهد بود۔ واین مصالح از دعوی فساد این صلح ابراء وتبراء نمود۔

(۲۳۱)

تمسك صلح از دعوی بندگی[1]

بعد ازان که دعوی می کرد فلان بر شخصی سفید پوست کذا

۱۔ این تمسك در نسخه علی گڑھ یافته نمی شود

وکذا فلاں نام مجهول النسب که بنده ومملوك ویست وطلب انقیاد وی کرد وایں فلاں منکر بود دعوی ویرا۔ جمعی متوسطان مصلحت دران دیدند که صلح کنند۔ پس صلح کرد این فلاں ازیں دعوی بندگی بایں فلاں به مبلغ کذا ووی قبض شرعی کرد۔ پس نماند بعد ازیں صلح ایں خواجه فلاں را بریں فلاں از جهت بندگی خصومتی ودعوی۔

(۲۳۲)

تمسك ابراء عام

ایں ذکریست در بیان آں که از هر بحث ودعوی وخصومتی که داشت فلاں بر فلاں از مالی وغیر مالی، کلی وجزوی باوی ابراء نمود وتبراء عام تام جائز صحیح شرعی وایں فلاں قبول کرد ایں ابراء وتبرا را قبول شرعی در مجلس ایں ابراء۔ پس باقی نماند بعد ازیں ابراء ایں فلاں را بر فلاں نه دعوی ونه خصومتی در صنوف اموال۔ اگر خواهد تفصیل کند نویسد که نه در عین نه در دین، نه در صامت نه در ناطق، نه در مکیل نه در موزون، نه در عبید نه در مواشی، نه در عقارات نه در منقولات، نه در هیچ چیز که نام مال بر آں اطلاق کنند، لافی القلیل ولافی الکثیر بوجه من الوجوه وسبب من الاسباب۔ ودر آخر نویسد که اگر ایں فلاں بریں فلاں دعوی کند آں دعوی باطل ومدعی مبطل خواهد بود وایں فلاں از دعوی فساد ایں ابراء وتبرا نمود۔

(۲۳۳)

تمسك صلح از دم عمد

ایں ذکریست در بیان آں که دعوی می کرد فلاں بر فلاں که ایں فلاں مدعی علیه پدر مورث وی فلاں را عمداً بغیر حق به آله محدد جارحه به قتل رسانید وبروی قصاص لازم شده واز وی وارث یکی پسر همیں مدعی مانده وازیں مدعی علیه طلب قصاص کرد پس صلح کرد ایں مدعی بدیں فلاں مدعی علیه از دعوی مذکوره بر بدل مبلغ کذا ووی قبول نمود صلحاً صحیحاً قاطعاً للخصومات وقبض کرد ایں مصالح بدل صلح را ازیں فلاں۔

(۲۳٤)

تمسك مضاریت

دفع کرد فلاں به فلاں مبلغ کذا به مضاریت شرعیه تا عمل نماید ایں مضارب بدیں مبلغ، پس بخرد وبفروشد به نقد ونسیه در سفر وحضر وتجارت کند بداں انچه خواهد از انواع تجارات۔ واگر بخواهد به بضاعت و ودیعت واجاره ومضاربت بهر کسی خواهد بدهد واگر خواهد مخلوط سازد مال مضاربت را به مال خود ومال غیر براں که هر چه حاصل شود از ربح میاں ایشاں مناصفه یا به تفاوت باشد وانچه زیاں شود بر صاحب مال باشد۔ وقبض کرد ایں مضارب ایں مبلع را۔

(۲۳۵)

نمیقه شرکت معاوضه

شریك شدند فلاں وفلاں شرکت معاوضه شرعیه درهر قلیل

وکثیر ودر هر صنف از اصناف تجارت براس المال مبلغ کذا که هر کدام مبلغ کذا[١] برابر ساخته بودند در مجلس این شرکت وعقد شرکت بران بسته، واتفاق کردند که این مبلغ در دست هر دو باشد وبدان خرید وفروخت کند[٢] از صنوف اموال بوجوه تجارات در سفر و[٣] حضر تنها وباهم وبرهر عقدی که درشرکت جائز هست، مجاز ومرخّص باشد وتصرف نماید دران وانچه ایزد تعالیٰ روزی کند میان ایشان مناصفه باشد۔

(٢٣٦)

نمیقه[٤] شرکت تقبل

شریك شدند فلان وفلان شرکت تقبل شرعی در عمل خیاطت برین که عمل کنند ومتقبل این عمل شوند از مردم تنها وباهم وانچه درین عمل بدان محتاج باشد، بدان قیام نمایند۔ وهرچه ایزد تعالیٰ روزی کند میان ایشان مناصفه باشد۔ وزیان نیز همین دستور باشد۔

(٢٣٧)

تمسك مزارعت در وقتی که به درمعین

١۔ ع : که هر کدام مبلغ کذا، ندارد
٢۔ ع : وبدانچه بدوفروخت کنند
٣۔ ع : در خطر
٤۔ ع : تمسك

از جانب رب الارض باشد

این ذکریست در بیان آن که دفع کرد فلان به فلان بر سبیل مزارعه کذا در موضع کذا، حدود کذا، مقدار کذا، معین بود میان ایشان مدت یك سال پیوسته هلالی، اول آن غره کذا وآخر آن سلخ کذا مزارعةً صحیحةً شرعیةً تا زراعت کند این مرفوع الیه این تخم را درین مزرعه وبه نفس خود واجراء خود و گاؤ خود ومصالح وادوات خود بدان قیام نماید۔ انچه الله تعالی روزی کند از دانه و گیاه میان ایشان مناصفه باشد یا ثلاثاً[۱] باشد چندین از صاحب ارض وچندین از بزر گر۔ قبض کرد این بزر گر جمیع این زمین وتخم را ازین دهقان بعد ازان که این[۲] مزارع قبول شرعی کرده بود۔

(۲۳۸)

تمسك زراعت

مقصود ازین نوشته آن که اقرار معتبر شرعی نمود بعد از قبول. وی این عقد معامله صحیحاً شرعیةً فلان بن فلان به گرفتن یك قطعه زمین زرعی ربیعی وخریفی به جهت مزارعت خریف یا ربیع از فلان بن فلان به قرار آن که انچه زراعت در قطعه مذکور بکارد حصه چهاردهم ومحصولی وپی تخم حق الارض برای فلان مقرله بدهد ودر اداء حصه مذکور هیچ عذر ودفع نیارد هر گاه که مقرله مذکور بخواهد۔

۱۔ ع :ثلث

۲۔ ع : این، ندارد

(۲۳۹)

سجل وصیت

غرض ازیں نوشته آں که وصیت کرد فلاں بن فلاں در حال قیام عقل وجواز[1] امور خود که بعد از فوت وی ابتداء کنند از متروکات وی به تجهیز وتکفین وی به معروف بی اسراف وتبذیر بلکه بر وجهی که موافق سنت باشد، پس به قضاء دیون وی، پس به اقتضاء دیون وی بر هر که باشد در ودائع وامانات او وتنفیذ وصایای او از ثلث مال وی۔ وهرچه از امور خیر خواهد نویسد وبعده نویسد این موصی مذکور در جمیع امور که مذکور شد ودر سائر امور خود بعد از فوت خود ودر جمیع امور صغار خود وهم فلاں وفلاں و فلاں وصی عام شرعی ساخت فلاں را وقبول کرد ایں فلاں ابن فلاں ایں وصایت را قبولاً صحیحاً مشافهةً۔ ومر ایں موصی را است که تغیر دهد ایں وصیت را ورجوع کند از هر چه ازاں خواهد وتبدیل کند بعضی را به بعضی۔ واگر پیش از تغیر فوت شود ایں وصیت منعقده باشد علی مایموت علیه۔ وانچه از مال وصیت باقی مانده از متروکه وی منقسم باشد میان ورثه وی علی فرائض الله تعالیٰ۔ واگر خواهد بیان ورثه کند ونویسد که اقرار شرعی کرد ایں موصی که آخر وصیتی است که بداں وصیت کرده ورجوع کرد از هر وصیتی که پیش ازیں کرده بود وفسخ وابطال آں نموده وایں وصی را نصب کرده هیچ وصی غیر از وی ندارد واگر وصی دیگر داشته باشد اورا ازاں بروں آورده۔ اگر خواهد کسی را مشرف وصَی سازد چنیں نویسد که ایں موصی مذکور فلاں را مشرف

۱ـ ع :قیام عقل وجواز، ندارد

ساخت بریں وصی مذکور که بی وقوف وعلم او در هیچ ازیں امور مدخل ننماید وانچه بی علم او مدخل نماید باطل مردود باشد۔

(۲٤٠)

سجل اثبات ملکیت

دریں وقت حاضر آمد در محکمه قضا بلده فلاں مخبر اسم ونسب خود فلاں بن فلاں وبا خود حاضر آورد فلاں بن فلاں را که متصرف بود یك راس اسپ جغر سیاه رنگ وبر ران چپ وی داغی بدیں شکل پنج ساله۔ مشارالیه دعوی کرد که ایں حاضر آمده مذکور هذا بریں حاضر آورده بنده مذکور هذا باخود بمحضر من المدعی علیه هذا بین یدی القاضی نافذ الامر بالبلدة المذکورة مدظله فلاں که این اسپ مشار الیه حق وملك من است که مدعی ام وبه دست وتصرف ایں محضر هذا بغیر حق است وبروی واجب است که ایں اسپ را به من تسلیم نماید واز وی طلب شرعی کرد آں را۔ از مدعی علیه هذا جواب دعوی مذکوره پرسیده شد۔ انکار معتبر شرعی نمود مدعاء مدعی هذا را۔ از مدعی هذا[1] موافق دعوی مذکوره وی بینه عادله طلب داشته شد۔ حاضر آورد دریں محکمه هذا دو نفر مرد حر، مکلف، بینا، شنوا، عدلین مقبول الشهادة را وهما فلاں بن فلاں وفلاں بن فلاں بعد الحواب بالانکار من المدعی علیه هذا والاستشهاد من الشاهدین هذین۔ گواهی دادند ایں گواهان هذان دریں محکمه هذه فی وجه المتخاصمین هذین بمحضر الفرس المدعی هریك جدا جدا متفق اللفظ والمعنی عقیب هذه

۱۔ ع :پرسیده شد، انکار معتبر شرعی نمود مدعاء مدعی هذا را، ندارد

الدعوی واستماعها۔ وشهادت هر یك ازیں شاهدین چنیں بود که گواهم و گواهی می دهم که اسپ مشار الیه حق وملك ایں مدعی هذا است ودر دست ایں مدعی علیه بغیر حق است وبر وی واجب است که ایں اسپ مشار الیه را بدیں مدعی هذا گذارد۔ وشرائط شهادت بجا آوردند واشارت کردند عند الحاجة الیها۔ بعد الاستخارة من الله وتعدیل الشاهدین هذین وعجز المدعی علیه هذا عن الدفع والجرح بالتماس مدعی هذا حکم کرد قاضی اسلام مذکور دریں محکمه هذه فی وجه المتخاصمین هذین بمحضر من الفرس المدعی هذا مریں مدعی هذا را بگواهی ایں گواهان هذان حکما محکما وقضاء مبرما وفرمود مدظله ایں مدعی علیه هذا را که ایں اسپ مشار الیه بدیں مدعی هذا بگذارد۔ وکان بتاریخ کذا۔

(٢٤١)

سجل اثبات دین

دریں وقت حاضر آمد دریں محکمه قضا بلده فلاں مسمی فلاں بن فلاں وبا خود حاضر آورد فلاں بن فلاں را ودعوی کر دایں حاضر آمده مذکور بریں حاضر آورده شده مذکور هذا باخود بمحضر من المدعی علیه هذا بین یدی القاضی فلاں که مرا در ذمه ایں محضر هذا مبلغ کذا حق ودینی لازم الاداء است وایں محضر هذا مثل مبلغ مذکور را بمن می باید (داد)۔ واز وی طلب شرعی کرد آں را۔ از مدعی علیه هذا جواب دعوی مذکوره مدعی هذا پرسیده شد پس اگر اقرار کرده باشد نویسد که اقرار معتبر شرعی کرد تمام مدعاء مدعی هذا[1] یا بعد الاستخارة من الله تعالی بالتماس مدعی هذا حکم کرد قاضی

۱۔ ع :جواب دعوی مذکوره مدعی هذا پرسیده شد۔ پس اگر اقرار کرده باشد نویسد که اقرار معتبر شرعی کرد تمام مدعاء مدعی هذا، ندارد۔

مذکور فی وجه المتخاصمین هذین مریں مدعی هذا به ثبوت دین مذکور باقرار ایں مدعی علیه هذا حکماً محکماً وقضاء مبرماً۔ وفرمود ایں مدعی علیه هذا را مثل ایں[2] مبلغ مذکور بریں مدعی هذا تسلیم نماید وکان ذالك فی التاریخ۔

اگر انکار کرده باشد نویسد که انکار معتبر شرعی نموده مدعاء مدعی هذا را۔ از مدعی هذا موافق دعوی بینه عادله طلب داشته شد۔ حاضر آورد دریں محکمه هذه دو نفر مرد حر، مکلف، عدل، مقبول الشهادة را وهما فلان بن فلان وفلان بن فلان۔ بعد الجواب بالانکار من المدعی علیه هذا والاستشهاد من الشاهدین هذین بدیں گواهی دادند ایں گواهان هذان دریں محکمه هذه فی وجه المتخاصمین هذین هریك جداجدا متفق اللفظ والمعنی عقیب هذه الدعوی واستماعها شهادت هریك ازیں شاهدین چنیں بود که گواهم و گواهی می دهم برای خدا که ایں مدعی هذا را در ذمه ایں مدعی علیه مبلغ کذا حق ودین لازم الاداء است وایں مدعی هذا مثل ایں مبلغ مذکور را بدیں مدعی می باید داد۔ وشرائط شهادت بجا آوردند واشارت کردند عند الحاجة الیها۔ بعد الاستخارة من الله تعالیٰ والتعدیل للشاهدین هذین وعجز المدعی علیه هذا عن الدفع والجرح بالتماس ایں مدعی هذا حکم را، حکم کرد قاضی مذکور فی وجه المتخاصمین هذین دریں محکمه هذه مریں مدعی هذا را بریں مدعی علیه به گواهی ایں گواهان هذان حکماً محکماً وقضاء مبرماً۔

اما بدان که ایں دعوی در دین مطلق بود واگر دعوی به سببی باشد، ذکر سبب باید کرد واسباب بسیار است۔ پس اگر دعوی دین به سبب کفالت باشد، بعد ازاں که نوشته شده بین یدی القاضی فلاں

۱۔ ع : مریں مدعی هذا به ثبوت دین مذکور به اقرار ایں مدعی علیه هذا حکما محکما وقضاء مبرما وفرمود ایں مدعی علیه هذا را مثل ایں، ندارد۔

نویسد که مرا در ذمه فلان بن فلان مبلغ کذا حق ودین لازم بوده واین محضر هذا کفیل مطلق شرعی شده بدین دین از برای من ومن قبول این کفالت کرده ام در مجلس کفالت واین محضر را مثل مبلغ مذکور را بمن می باید داد۔ وبه دستور سابق تمام کند۔

واگر به سبب حواله باشد بنویسد که حق ودین لازم به سبب آن که فلان بن فلان مرا حواله کرده باین مبلغ بدین مخضر هذا واین محضر هذا قبول این حواله کرده ومن بدان راضی شده ام وحوالت تمام شده واین محضر مثل مبلغ مذکور به من باید داد۔ وتمام کند۔

اگر دعوی به سبب غصب باشد نویسد که حق ودین لازم به سبب آن که این محضر مثل مبلغ مذکور را از مال من غصب کرده بغیر حق تصرف نموده وتلف کرده بغیر حق و اورا مثل مبلغ مذکور بمن می باید داد وتمام کند[1]۔

وهمچنین در دعوی ثمن بیع مقبوض وبدل اجاره وغیر آن بیان سبب کند در دعوی و گواهی را موافق سازد وتمام کند[2]۔

واگر مدعی علیه را دفعی باشد درین دعاوی به ایفاء یا به ابراء، ذکر دفع کند واگر دفع را پیش از اقامت بینه گفته باشد بعد ازان که نوشته باشد که از مدعی علیه هذا جواب دعوی مذکور مدعی هذا پرسیده شد، ذکر دفع کند۔ واگر بعد از اقامت بینه دفع گفته باشد بعد ازان که در سجل مذکور گواهی گواهان کرده باشد صورت دعوی دفع را نویسد بدین طریق که پس این مدعی علیه هذا بر سبیل دفع گفت که این مدعی مبطل است درین دعوی خود واورا ولایت مذکور

۱۔ ع :و اگر دعوی به سبب غصب باشد نویسد که حق و دین لازم به سبب آن که این محضر مثل مبلغ مذکور را از مال من غصب کرده بغیر حق و تصرف نموده وتلف کرده بغیر حق و اورا مثل مبلغ مذکور بمن می باید داد، و تمام کند، ندارد–

۲۔ ع : سبب کند در دعوی و گواهی را موافق سازد و تمام کند، ندارد–

ایں دعوی نیست بر من به سبب آن که تمام ایں مبلغ دین مذکور را[۱] از من گرفته ومن به وی تسلیم کرده ام وهمچنیں اقرار کرده۔ یا نوسید که ایں مدعی هذا ازیں دعوی بامن ابراء وتبراء عام شرعی نموده ومن قبول کرده ام آن را۔ پس نویسد که از مدعی هذا که مدعی علیه به دعوی الدفع مذکور است، جواب دعوی دفع مذکوره پرسیده شد، انکار معتبر نموده دفع مذکوره بر مدعی هذا مدعی الدفع هذا را۔ از مدعی الدفع هذا[۲] موافق دفع مذکوره او بینه عادله طلب کرده شد۔ حاضر آورد دریں محکمه هذه فلاں وفلاں را بعد الجواب بالانکار من المدعی علیه هذا والاستشهاد من الشاهدین هذین۔ گواهی دادند ایں گواهان هذان دریں محکمه هذه[۳] فی وجه المتخاصمین هذین هر یك جدا جدا متفق اللفظ والمعنی عقیب هذه الدعوی واستماعها شهادت هریك ازیں شاهدین هذین چنیں بود که گواهم و گواهی می دهم که ایں مدعی علیه بالدفع هذا اقرار کرد که ایں مبلغ دین موصوف را ازیں مدعی الدفع هذا که مدعی علیه به اصل دعوی است گرفته وقبض شرعی کرده۔ وشرائط شهادت بجا آوردند واشارت به موضع اشارت کردند عند الحاجة الیها۔ بعد الاستخارة من الله تعالیٰ و التعدیل للشاهدین هذین وعجز المدعی علیه عن الدفع والجرح[٤] بالتماس مدعی الدفع هذا حکم را، حکم کرد قاضی مذکور در محکمه قضا هذه فی وجه المتخاصمین هذیں مریں مدعی الدفع بریں مدعی علیه بالدفع هذا به ثبوت دفع مذکور مدعی الدفع هذا بگواهی ایں گواهان وفرمود مدعی اصل دعوی را به ترك دعوی مذکوره و کان ذالك فی تاریخ کذا۔

۱۔ ع :ایں دعوی نیست بر من به سبب آن که تمام ایں مبلغ دین مذکور را، ندارد

۲۔ ع : را از مدعی الدفع هذا، ندارد

۳۔ فلاں وفلاں را بعد الجواب بالانکار من المدعی علیه هذا والاستشهاد من الشاهدین هذین۔ گواهی دادند ایں گواهان دریں محکمه هذه، ندارد

٤۔ ع: عن الدفع والجرح، ندارد

(٢٤٢)

صورت دعوی به رهن

دعوی می کنم به رهن محضر هذا که من محدود کذا بامتاع کذا، وبیان صفت آں کند، به مبلغ کذا به رهن ایں محضر کرده ام ووی به رهن گرفته وقبضه شرعی کرده آں را والیوم ایں مرهون رهن است در دست ایں محضر بدین مبلغ ومن ایں مبلغ را حاضر ساخته ام وبر وی واجب است که ایں مبلغ را قبض نماید وایں مرهون را تسلیم من نماید وطلب می کنم۔

(٢٤٣)

سجل اثبات حر الاصل

دریں وقت حاضر آمد در محکمه قضا بلده کذا شخصی سبز رنگ، میانه بالا، سیاه چشم، کشاده ابرو، ملتحی درسن سی سالگی تخمیناً و گفت نام من مقبول است وبا خود حاضر آورد مخبر اسم ونسب خود فلاں را ودعوی کر دایں حاضر آمده مذکور هذا بریں حاضر آورده شده مذکور با خود بمحضر من المدعی علیه هذا بین یدی القاضی فلاں که من آزاد وآزاد اصلم، سبب آں که مادر من رقیه بنت فلاں که آزاد اصل بوده ومرا بر فراش آزادی زائیده۔ وایں محضر هذا بغیر حق بنده گرفته وبند گی می فرماید بغیر حق وبر وی واجب

است که دست تملك وتصرف از من کوتاه سازد، وطلب خلاصی خود کرده- وچون مدعی هذا معترف بود که انقیاد وبندگی مدعی علیه هذا کرده[1]، از مدعی علیه هذا جواب دعوی مذکوره مدعی هذا پرسیده شد- انکار معتبر نمود مدعاء[2] مدعی هذا- موافق مدعاء او بینه عادله طلب شد- حاضر آورد دریں محکمه هذه فلاں وفلاں را- بعد الجواب بالانکار من المدعی علیه هذا والاستشهاد من الشاهدین هذین گواهی دادند ایں گواهان هذان و صورت گواهی را موافق دعوی نویسد وچوں به حکم رسد نویسد که حکم کرد قاضی مذکور دریں محکمه هذه فی وجه المتخاصمین هذین مریں مدعی هذا بریں مدعی علیه هذا به ثبوت آزادی وآزاد اصلی ایں مدعی هذا بگواهی ایں گواهان هذان- حکم فرمود ایں مدعی علیه هذا[3] را که دست تصرف وتملك ازیں مدعی هذا کوتاه سازد- وکان ذالك بتاریخ کذا-

(٢٤٤)

سجل اثبات بندگی

دریں وقت حاضر آمد فلاں وباخود حاضر آورد شخصی سیاه چهره بلند بالا، کشاده ابرو کذا وکذا فلاں نام که سر خود بود وبه

١- ع :و چوں مدعی معترف بود که انقیاد وبندگی مدعی علیه هذا کرده، ندارد
٢- ع : مدعاء، ندارد
٣- ع : به ثبوت آزادی وآزاد اصلی ایں مدعی هذا به طریق مسطور به گواهی ایں گواهان هذان- حکم فرمود ایں مدعی علیه هذا را، ندارد

تصرف کسی نبوده، به بندگی وی دعوی کرد این حاضر آمده مذکور هذا بدین حاضر آورده شده مذکور هذا باخود بمحضر من المدعی علیه هذا بین یدی القاضی فلان که این محضر هذا بنده مملوك من است واو را انقیاد واطاعت من می باید کرد وتمرد نماید وانقیاد نمی کند، ومی طلبم از محضر هذا که انقیاد وبندگی من نماید۔ از مدعی علیه مذکور جواب دعوی مذکوره مدعی هذا پرسیده شد۔ انکار معتبر نمود مدعاء مدعی را۔ واز مدعی هذا موافق دعوی مذکوره او بینه عادله طلب شد۔ حاضر آورد فلان وفلان را و گواهی را موافق دعوی نویسد وصورت حکم را چنین نویسد که بعد الاستخارة من الله والتعدیل للشاهدین وعجز المدعی علیه هذا علی اثبات الحریة علی نفسه، حکم کرد قاصی مذکور درین محکمه هذه فی وجه المتخاصمین هذین مرین مدعی هذا را آن که این مدعی علیه هذا مرقوق ومملوك این مدعی هذا است به گواهی گواهان هذان، فرمود اورا که انقیاد واطاعت این مدعی نماید در احکام بندگی۔ وکان تاریخ کذا۔ واگر مدعی علیه را دفع باشد بر حر الاصل بعد ازان که ذکر شهادت کرده باشد، نویسد که این مدعی علیه بر سبیل دفع گفت که مرا انقیاد وبندگی این محضر نمی باید نمود سبب آن که مادر من فلانه بنت فلان آزاد اصل است ومرا بر فراش آزاد زائیده۔ از مدعی که مدعی علیه بالدفع است، جواب دفع مذکور پرسیده شد۔ انکار معتبر نمود دفع مذکور مدعی الدفع هذا را۔ از مدعی الدفع هذا به موافق دفع مذکور بینه عادله طلب داشته شد۔ حاضر آورد درین محکمه هذه فلان وفلان را۔ بعد الجواب بالانکار من المدعی هذا بالدفع والاستشهاد من الشاهدین بدین گواهی دادند این گواهان وصورت گواهی را نویسد موافق دعوی۔ وحکم را چنین نویسد، حکم کرد

قاضی اسلام به ثبوت دفع مذکوره مدعی الدفع هذا ابگواهی این گواهان وفرمود مدعی علیه مدعی دفع دعوی بندگی را به ترك دعوی مذکوره وکان ذالك بتاریخ کذا سنة کذا۔

(۲٤٥)

تمسك در استدعاء بٹائی غله[۱] وغیره

غرض ازیں نوشته آں که اقرار کردند فلاں مقدمان موضع فلاں من اعمال پر گنه فلاں که چوں از نواب نامدار، اقبال آثار التماس کردیم که اگر حاصل ربیع فلاں از قرار بٹائی بازیافت شود سبب رفاهیت رعایا وافزونی زراعت وآبادانی خواهد بود۔ بنا بران نواب نامداری حسب الالتماس به جهت رفاهیت رعایا و کثرت معموری مقرر فرمودند که حاصل ربیع هر دو موضع مذکور از قرار بٹائی بالمناصفه سواء خرچ بازیافت نموده شود۔ وما به بٹائی راضی وشاکر شده شرط کردیم که در محافظت غله غایت سعی بجا آورده، دیانت وامانت نوعی نگاه داریم که خیانت ودزدی واقع نشود ودر سال آئنده زراعت بسیار کرده از جمع کامل اضافه نمائیم۔ وبر شرط مذکور سوگند کلام مجید وسوگند مغلظه وجعفر نامه خوردند که اگر ثانی الحال دزدی وخیانت وتقصیری بظهور آید مجرم وگنه گار باشیم واز عهده جواب بیروں آئیم۔ وایں چند کلمه بر سبیل سند تحریر یافته تا عند الحاجة حجت باشد۔ تحریراً فی التاریخ کذا سنه کذا۔

۱۔ ع :غله، ندارد

(٢٤٦)

تمسك اجاره

مقصود ازیں نوشته آں که چوں فلاں وفلاں مقدمان موضع فلاں[1] من اعمال پرگنه فلاں از وکلاء نواب نامداری، اقبال آثاری التماس نمودند که اراضی موضع مذکور تا غایت ویران افتاده ومزروع نشده است، حواله ایشاں شود از ابتداء فصل خریف فلاں سنه فلاں زراعت کرده مال واجبی آں را از قرار اجاره جواب گویند۔ حسب الالتماس مشار الیهما وکلاء نواب نامداری، اقبال آثاری حاصل زراعت فصل خریف فلاں اراضی مذکور را مبلغ فلاں اجاره نمودند۔ ازاں جمله مبلغ فلاں به مقدمان مذکور بخشیده اند۔ وایشاں نیز ایں اجاره را قبول کردند وبطوع ورغبت معترف شدند که مبلغ فلاں از بابت اجاره اراضی مذکور فصل خریف مذکوره در خریف مذکور به ارباب حوالات سرکار نواب جواب گویند وبلا قصور وانکسار برسانند۔ همبریں جمله معترف شدند وایں چند کلمه بر سبیل سند سپردند تا ثانی الحال حجت باشد۔ تحریر فی التاریخ کذا سنة کذا۔

(٢٤٧)

تمسک در بیان بعضی امور

مقصود ازیں نوشته آں که چوں مردم سپاهی وشاگرد پیشه وغیره

۱۔ ع :مقدمان موضع فلاں، ندارد

بعضی که جاگیر دارند ماهیانه خود را از حاصل جاگیر متصرف اند وجماعه که جاگیر ندارند[1] ماهیانه خود را ماه بماه از فوطه خانه می گیرد (گیرند) ودر دادن وجوه ماهیانه فتوری وقصوری راه نمی یابد۔ ومع هذا[2] بعضها (بعضی) فضولی نموده از مردم قرض می گیرند وبه مقتضاء فساد زمانه در اداء آن عذر واهمال را پیش می گیرند وقدم از جاده قویم حسن معامله بیرون نهاده می خواهند که حقوق وديون مردم را از[3] در تحت خود نگاه دارند۔ چون این معنی باعث تضئیع حقوق الناس است، نواب نامداری بنا بر رفاهیت حال خلائق مقرر فرمودند که در زمان دولت ایشان احدی از اهل دکاکین وتجار وصرافان وسائر متوطنه بلده محفوظه بکر وقصبه فلان وفلان به کسی از ایشان[4] قرض ندهند، وخرید وفروخت ومعامله داد وستد که به آنها نمایند نقد کنند ونسیه را به حالی وقوع ندهند۔ و جماعت صرافان وبزازان وسائر اهل دکاکین کتبه دادند وقبول کردند که به سپاهی وشاگرد پیشه وغیره در ایام دولت نواب قرض ندهند ومعامله به نسیه نکنند۔ واگر ثانی الحال خلاف این مذکوره ازینها ظاهر شود مجرم وگنه گار باشند ومحل سوال وجواب ومورد خطاب وعتاب شده از عهده جواب برآیند۔ تحریراً فی التاریخ کذا سنة گذا۔

(۲٤۸)

کتبه مردم سادات

۱۔ ع : ع، س : ماهیانه خود را از حاصل جاگیر متصرف اند وجماعه که جاگیر ندارند، ندارد۔

۲۔ ع : ومع، ندارد

۳۔ ع : از روی مکابره، زیاده دارد

٤۔ ع، س : به کسی از ایشان، ندارد۔

مقصود ازیں نوشته آں که فلاں وفلاں وفلاں سادات بلده فلاں قبول کردند به بزرگی و کلانتری سید فلاں وفلاں که هر دو کس را بزرگ ونقیب السادات خود دانسته از سخن وصلاح ایشان که مطابق شرع شریف وحساب ومعامله باشد بیرون نروند. وایشان نیز در جمیع امور از قسمت اراضی وغیره دیانت وامانت را مرعی داشته حیل ومداهنت ننمایند. ودر ملازمت نواب تعهد کردند وبر ذمه خود لازم کردند که فرزندان خود را به علوم دینی مشغول ساخته از اعمال وافعال ناشایسته باز دارند ونگذارند. واگر ثانی الحال خلاف ایں مسطور ظاهر شود از عهده برآیند.

(۲٤۹)

کتبه دیگر

مقصود ازیں نوشته آں که چوں بواسطه آں که از مردم فلاں دزدی ظاهر شده بود[۱] ودزداں را در مواضع خود جا داده نواب نامداری او را قید داشته، بعده باز بر سر عنایت وشفقت آمده گناه اورا بخشیده کتبه گرفتند. او نیز قبول کرد واعتراف نمود که من بعد دزدی نکند و روادار دزداں نباشد. واگر کسی دزدی نماید ومر اورا خبر شود، آمده به عرض رساند. واگر ثانی الحال خلاف ایں مذکور ظهور آید ومرتکب دزدی وسائر افعال قبیحه شود یا دزداں را در موضع خود جا دهد، مجرم و گنه گار باشد، وبدانچه شرعاً وعرفاً مستوجب آں بود اجراء کرده شود. همه بریں جمله اعتراف کردند وایں چند کلمه بر سبیل سند سپردند تا ثانی الحال حجت باشد. تحریراً فی التاریخ کذا

۱ـ ع :شده بود، ندارد؛ س : بود، ندارد.

سنة كذا۔

(۲۵۰)

كتبه ديگر

غرض ازیں نوشته آن که اقرار کردند جماعت زمینداران بومیه پرگنه فلان بر آن جمله که بکومك لشکری، که تعلقه فلان تعین شده اند، عند الاشارة جمیعت نموده از سوار وتیر انداز در قلعه مذکور حاضر شده در خدمت دولت خواهی وجان سپاری خود را معاف نداشته تقصیر ننمایند ودر دفع ورفع مفسدان کوشیده حسب الامکان سعی موفور به ظهور رسانند۔ اگر دریں باب امهال وتکاسل نمایند ودر[۱] همان ساعت که خبر بایشان رسد با جمعیت تمام خود را نرسانند مجرم ومخاطب باشند وواجب سیاست خواهند بود[۲]۔ تحریراً فی التاریخ کذا سنة کذا۔

(۲۵۱)

عهد نامه

قال الله تعالیٰ "واوفوا بالعهد ان العهد کان مسئولا[۳]" الحمد لله رب العالمین والصلوة والسلام علی خیر خلقه محمد وآله واصحابه

۱۔ ع :از
۲۔ ع : خواهند بود، ندارد
۳۔ ع :قرآن مجید : ۳٤/۱۷

اجمعین۔ اما بعد، این ذکریست در بیان آن که عهد وشروط به موجبی که مذکور می گردد واسم ومهر در ذیل حاشیه ظاهر می شود، مضمون آن که فلان وفلان عهد کردند وشرط نمودند از صمیم قلب ولسان به حضرت مالك الملك بی زوال وبادشاه عظیم قدیم[1] بر کمال، جل جلاله وعم نواله، وبهترین کائنات وخلاصه موجودات محمد مصطفی، علیه افضل الصلوات واکمل التحیات[2]، که دولت خواهی وخیر اندیشی عالی حضرت، فلك رتبت، الاعلم، الاعدل، الاکرم، العالی الشان، المختص بمواهب العدل والاحسان، بندگان حضرت خلافت پناهی، شاهنشاهی، صاحبقرانی، خلد الله تعالی ملکه وسلطانه ابداً، ونواب نامداری، اقبال آثار، گردون اقتدار، عالم مدار خلاصه اعظم، اعدل روزگار، اصدق الخوانین قولاً ودینا واشجع واکرم الامراء عصراً وزماناً، اعتضاد وملاذ پناه، عالی شان مکرم فلان، ضاعف الله قدره، ودولت خواهان ویك جهتان این دو دمان عظیم الشان بر هیچ وجه من الوجوه بدی ونا دولت خواهی نکنیم وبدی نه اندیشیم قولاً وفعلاً، نه صریح ونه به کنایه، نه بایماء ونه باشارت، وهرگز رو گردان نه شویم وحیله وغدر نکنیم[3] وانچه کمال دولت خواهی ویك جهتی ودوستی باشد همیشه به تقدیم رسانیم وبا دوستان ایشان دوست بوده،

۱۔ ع : عهد کردند وشرط نمودند از صمیم قلب به حضرت مالك الملك بی زوال وبادشاه عظیم قدیم، ندارد

۲۔ ع : علیه الصلوة والسلام

۳۔ ع : وبدی نه اندیشیم قولاً وفعلاً، نه صریح نه بکنایه، نه با یماء نه با شارت وهرگز رو گردان نشویم ومکرو حیله و غدر نکنیم، ندارد

بادشمنان ایشان دشمن باشیم، مشروط بر آنکه ایشان نیز به عهد وقول راسخ بوده تغیر وتبدیل به قواعد آن راه ندهند ودر سدد[1] قصد حیات ما وبی ناموسی ما نباشند واز روی عنایت وشفقت سلوك نموده در اعزاز واکرام ما کوشند. هر گاه چنین کنند مانیز تا حیات داشته باشیم این عهد وشرط را تغیر وتبدیل به قواعد این دوستی ودولت خواهی اصلاً راه ندهیم. واگر خلاف کنیم یا فعل بدی به خاطر گذرانیم خدای تعالی جل جلاله، ورسول او علیه السلام از ما بیزار باشد وبه لعنت خدا و انبیاء وملائکه وجن وانس گرفتار باشیم. مکرراً عهد می کنیم با الله ابدا که درین عهد وشرط دل وزبان مایك است ودرین قسم مکر وحیله وکذبی نیست. واگر صادق نباشیم دران امور نامرد وبی دیانت باشیم واز دائره[2] مردان بلکه انسان خارج بوده از جنس حیوانات باشیم وکلام مجید وفرقان حمید خصم جان ودین وایمان ما باشد.

(۲۵۲)

عهد نامه

اما بعد، این مقدمه ایست در بیان عهد وشرط وعنایت وشفقت وعفو ذلت وتقصیرات ماضی وحال به مضمون آن که چون به واسطه ذلات سابق وتقصیرات[3]، غباری بر ضمیر منیر، خورشید تنویر نشسته

۱ـ ع، س: سبیل
۲ـ ع: صف
۳ـ ع: عهد

بود، ایشان قواعد معذرت واظهار استغفار وانابت زلت را منظور داشته استدعاء عفو را تمهید نموده اند۔ ما نیز تقصیرات وزلات ایشان را کان لم یکن فرض کرده جرأتی که از ایشان واقع شده بود چون به حبل[1] اعتذار متمسك گشته اند، ازان تجاوز نمودیم وتقصیرات ایشان را به زلال عفو اغماض نائره آن را تسکین دادیم واز صفحه خاطر عاطر محو فرمودیم۔ والعفو عند کرام الناس مامول۔

بیت:

طمع زعفو نبرم چرا که فضل کریم
گنه بپرسد وبر عاصیان بخشاید

من بعد ازان حروف مواخذه ومعاینه مصئون ومامون بوده، به میامن عنایت وشفقت روابط محبت ومودت مستظهر ومستوثق باشند۔

(۲۵۳)

عهد نامه

بیت:

بیا که لطف شهنشه ثبات آن دارد
که منحرف بشود از چنین هزار گناه

مقصود ازین مقدمات که بخدای تعالیٰ، جل جلاله وعم نواله ورسول او محمد مصطفیٰ، صلی الله علیه وسلم، عهد کردیم وشرط نمودیم که بعد از تاریخ... به ایالت پناه، سلطنت درگاه، شوکت انتباه، سکندر جاه، صاعد مصاعد السلطنة الباهرة، عارج معارج الایالة الطاهرة، عمده سلاطین زمان، مسند العدل والاحسان، مهر سپهر عالی

۱۔ ع: به حبال

قـدر فـلان، خلد الله تعالی ملکه ابداً، ودولت خواهان او بدی نکنیم وبد نه اندیشیم وبا کسی نفرمائیم که بایشان بدی کند قولاً وفعلاً، نه صریح نـه بـکـنـایـت ونه بایماء ونه اشارت۔ وانچه لائق شان ورتبه ایشان باشد ولایـت وجا گیر واحسان واکرام وتعظیم وتکریم بایشان ودولت خواهان ومـلازمـان ایشـان عـنـایت فرمائیم ونقض عهد نکنیم وقصد جان ومال وعـرض ونـامـوس ایشـان نـکنیم و به هیچ کس نفرمائیم۔ واگر خلاف کـنـیم کلام مجید وفرقان حمید خصم ما باشد۔ مقرر ومشروط آن که ایشـان نیز بـه مضمون آیه کریمه "واوفوا بالعهد ان العهد کان مسئولاً[۱]" وحـدیث صحیح حضرت نبوی علیه السلام "المومنون عند شروطهم" عـمـل نمایند وعهد نامه که نوشته شده وبمهر ایشان رسیده ازان تجاوز نـکـنـنـد وآیه کریمه "ومن نکث فانما ینکث علی نفسه[۲]" اندیشه نمایند ودولـت خـواهی وامداد ودفع دشمن ما بدانچه مقدور داشته باشند خو درا مـعـاف نـدارنـد ودر مـقام غدر ومکر وحیله نباشند وتغیر وتبدیل مطلقاً به قواعد عهدنامه ومضمون صدر نباشند قولاً وفعلاً۔ تحریر کذا سنة کذا۔

(۲۵٤)

مطائبات مضحکه وبعضی مقولات هزل آمیز وطرب انگیز

اربـاب جـنـد وجیش واصـحـاب طرب وعیش ومباشران شغل سـرور ومـعـاشـران بـزم حضور ومتعطشان زلال نشاط وندیمان انجمن

۱۔ قرآن مجید : ۳٤/۱۷

۲۔ قرآن مجید : ۱۰/٤۸

انبساط[۱] وسازندگان مطائبات فرح انگیز[۲] وگویندگان هزلیات ذوق آمیز وصاحبان مضحکات دل پسند ومرتبان اسباب ریش خند وفارسان میدان بلاغت ومبارزان معرکه استهزاء وسخریه ونگّاسان مجلس شور وسین ودم کشان لافگاه زیب وزین بدانند که هرچند اصل ورسم مسخرگی وحقیقت کار مزاح وکلپتره گوئی به مودایٔ "المومن دعب لعب والمنافق عبوس قطوب" جهت تفریح خاطر واستلذاذ باطن وظاهر وپسندیده هر غائب وحاضر است۔ اماچون از حد اعتدال در گذرد موجب غفلت ودل مردگی گردد، متصور است که سر به نقصان واختلال دین ودولت بازنهد۔ نعوذ بالله من شرور انفسنا ومن سیئات اعمالنا۔

بیت:

جد همه ساله جان مردم کاهد
هزل همه روزه رونق دیں ببرد

نعوذ بالله من شرور انفسنا و من سیئات اعمالنا۔

(۲۵۵)

مطائبات

در زمان بهار واوان جولان سپاه ریاحین وازهار که شگوفه چون دست کریمان آغاز زر افشانی کرده جیب وکنار حضّار باغ و بستان را از نقود ابیض واحمر مملو داشت وسحاب نیسانی چون مآثر طباع کریمان درر ریزی نموده، گوش وگردن جوانان گلزار را از درر غرر آبدار مزین ساخته رایت سخاوت می افراشت، باجمعی از دوستان

۱۔ ع :بساط

۲۔ ع : فرح انگیز ندارد

حاتم خصال وبرخی از محبان معن افعال در موضع[۱] دار الخلافة فلان به طریق سیر عبور افتاده۔ هر روز به منزل وهر شب به جای گذرانیده می شد۔ واکثر اوقات در محفل یاران راحی رقیق وصبهاء صافی تر از ضمیر اهل تحقیق به اباریق و کاس معن معین ووافر بود[۲] وفروغ اقداح رنگا رنگ محفل را منور داشته۔ بعد از تصرفات بحار شراب ناب در مزاج احباب به مقتضاء آن که۔ ع

گل نم دیده را آبی تمام است

عرق[۳] سخاوت اصلی در حرکت آمده است هر یك به ایثار واکرام وانعام اقدام می نمود۔ وچون از لوازم ایذاء واضرار دهر غدار است که هر نعمتی را[۴] محنتی وهر محنتی را نعمتی در عقب است وهرشادی را غمی وهر فرحی را المی مستعقب، به حسب اتفاق نزول در موضع فلان واقع گشته۔ به تکلیف بعضی به خانه دونی زبونی، کم کاسه ونکاسه، جلپاسه، نشناسه. نجس العین، باشور وسینی، حماری، خرسی، سطبری، نافرجامی،بی اندامی رسیده شد[۵]، بیت:

گفتم که مگر درین فتوحی باشد
واز طعمه اش راحت روحی باشد
چه جای غذای خوش که از خون جگر
پیوسته عبوقی و صبوحی باشد

درین اثناء چشم بر مطبخ او فتاد که "واد غیر ذی ذرع[۶]" دران ظاهر بوده، کاسهابه درگاه مسجود در سجود می نمود و کفیگر را

۱۔ ع :مواضع
۲۔ ع : رامی ربود
۳۔ ع : عرق، ندارد
٤۔ ع : را، ندارد
٥۔ ع : است
٦۔ اشاره بآیت کریمه "ربنا انی اسکنت من ذریتی بواد غیر ذی زرع" (قرآن مجید : ۳۷/۱٤)

چشمها باز مانده که "وابیضت عیناه من الحزن[۱]" وخوان از بار کشیدن فارغ گشته که "فابین ان یحملنها[۲]" بر کنار نان او که بروتها ظاهر گشت، مکتوب بود که :

روی تو کس ندید هزارت رقیب هست

ومطبخی به آواز الحان می خواند، قطعه[۳]:

نان تو پارسا تر از زن تست
کس نه بیند زخویش وبیگانه
نان خود را بجای زن بنشان
وآن جلب را برون کن از خانه

وخوان سالار دست به دعا آورده که "ربنا انزل علینا مائدة من السماء[٤]" وبر کنار کاسها نوشته که "من شرب منه فلیس منی[۵]" وبر حاشیه صحنها تحریر نموده "ومن لم یطعمه فانه منی[٦]" بنده وآزاد که در خدمت او اند همه با چشم گریان ودیده بریان این نغمه را ورد زبان دارند۔

قطعه:

از بخیلی که هست امساکش
گر ببرند دست ناپاکش
نیست ممکن که یك دو قطره خون
آید از دست مدبرش بیرون

نعوذ بالله من شرر انفسنا ومن سیئات اعمالنا، من یهد الله فلا مضل له ومن یظلله فلا هادی له۔

۱۔ قرآن مجید : ۹٤/۱۲
۲۔ قرآن مجید : ۷۲/۳۳
۳۔ ع : بیت
٤۔ قرآن مجید : ۱۱٤/۵
۵۔ قرآن مجید : ۲٤۹/۲
٦۔ قرآن مجید : ۲٤۹/۲

(۲۵٦)

این منشور به کلپتره گوئی تحریر یافته که زیر فلک شعبده باز در طرفگی نظیر نداشست

فضیلت مآب، مذمت مناب، مقبول قلوب السلاطین، مفرح خواطر[۱] طبقات العاشرین، رافع غم، کاشف الم فلان به توجه خاطر فیض[۲] وترقب ضمیر کیمیا کردار منبسط ومنشرح بوده بداند که مدتی مدید می شود که بآن حدود رفته وبه واقعی معلوم نیست که وضع وحال او چیست. بافواه مسموع می شود که به تفقد والی آن ولایت منصب کلان تری اقران وامثال بدو تفویض یافته وپرتو انوار این تربیت از طاؤس مهر سپهر بر وجنات احوالش تافته. اگرچه بعضی گفته اند که آن مذمت مآب از قبول این امر ابا نموده واز کمال تنفر عدم تجویز آن به کلا وحاشا موکد نموده، اما بعضی[۳] دیگر بخلاف این عرض کرده اند که از رهگذر خوش حالی وفارغ بالی داشته و کلاه مسرت وبشاشت بر هوا افراشته. بهر تقدیر چون عمریست که بواسطه کشت زخارف روی از پرتو انوار معارف تافته وقرع باب اخذ حطام که شیوه لئام عام کالانعام است، نموده بمقتضاء 'من قرع الباب ولجّ ولج' وباقتضاء 'من طلب شیئا وجدّ وجد' به کلید اهتمام ابواب مقصود ومرام بر چهره خود کشوده باشد، واگر نشده ظاهر است که موجب کلال وملال گردیده باشد. وبهر حال بی شائبه قیل وقال بعد از اطلاع بر مضمون بی مثال

۱- ع :قلوب
۲- ع : فیض آثار
۳- ع : بعض، ندارد

متوجه درگاه کیوان اشتمال گردد ودر توجه معاودت معذرت نگوید که مقرر است که مقدمات عذر غیر از کلپتره چیزی نخواهد بود۔ ویقین داند که چون بآستان بوس فائز گردد در ترفیه معاد معیشت وتوفیر مواد عافیت والتقات او اجتهاد مبذول خواهیم داشت۔

(۲۵۷)

خطبات جمعه وعیدین

الحمد لله المنعم المکرم الماجد المنّان، القاهر المفضل الدائم الدیان الحیّ المنزّه عن التغیر بطوارق الحدثان، القیوم المعرا عن العناء والزوال والنقصان، ونشهد ان لا اله الا الله وحده لا شریك له شهادةً موصلةً الی دار الجنان ونشهد انّ محمداً عبده ورسوله سید الثقلین وحبیب الرحمن، ﷺ وعلی آله وصحبه وخلاّنه نعم الخُلاّن، خصوصاً علی الامام، سید اهل العرفان، خلیفة رسول الله فی کل موقف ومکان امیر المومنین ابی بکر الصدیق الصادق الشفیق لاهل الایمان، وعلی الامام قاتل الاقران لاجل الایمان وناشر العدل والاحسان امیر المومنین عمر الفاروق ناصر اهل لایمان، وعلی الامام الذی جمع القران وختمه فی الرکعتین بعون الملك المنّان امیر المومنین عثمان ذی النورین صاحب البصیرة والایقان واشجع الشجعان وافرس الفرسان ومطمع المساکین والجیعان امیر المومنین علی الرضی الوفی اسد الله المستعان۔

(۲۵۸)

خطبه جمعه

الحمد لله الذی جعل طلعة المصطفی مطلع صبح[۱] السعادة ومشرق النور المبین وعطر عبیر اخباره[۲] ونسیم آثاره اسرار الابرار واذکار المسبحین وافاض بحرمته علی امته سجال الکرم وفضّلهم علی سائر الامم وشرّح صدورهم بنور الیقین، اجری من شریعته زلال المعرفة وانبت به حدائق العارفین، طرّز اعلام الفتح والتائید وامدّه بالملائکة المسوّمین وقرّن الیمن بمیمنته والحق بمسیرته وشدّ ظهره بقلب القران حیث قال "سلام علی آل یٰس، اناّ کذالك نجزی المحسنین، انه من عبادنا المومنین[۳]" ونشهد ان لا اله الا الله وحده لاشریك له خالق السموات والارضین ورزّاق المخلوقات اجمعین ونشهد انّ محمداً عبده ورسوله الموصوف فی قوله "وما ارسلناك الاّ رحمةً للعالمین[۴]" صلی الله علی محمدا المصطفی وعلی آله واصحابه اجمعین، خصوصاً علی الامام نصیر المظلومین وناصر دین الحق علی الیقین وخلیفة رسول رب العالمین امیر المومنین ابی بکر الصدیق الصادق صاحب سید المرسلین، وعلی الامام الذی به تمام الاربعین حتی نزل فی شانه "یایها النبی حسبك الله ومن اتبعك من المومنین[۵]" امیر المومنین عمر الفاروق بین المطیعین والمتمر دین وعلی الامام، زین

۱ـ ع :الصبح
۲ـ ع : انباءه
۳ـ قرآن مجید : ۳۷/۱۳۰ـ۱۳۲
۴ـ قرآن مجید : ۲۱/۱۰۷
۵ـ قرآن مجید : ۸/۶۴

الاسلام والمسلمين، ومطعم الفقراء والمساكين، امير المتقين عثمان ذى النورين، جامع حبل الله المتين، وعلى الامام اسد الله الغالب وافضل المجاهدين الذى (هو) امير المهتدين على الرضى الوفى، جامع اخلاق المحسنين۔

(٢٥٩)

خطبه جمعه

الحمد لله۔ الحمد لله نحمده ونستعينه ونومن به ونتوكل عليه ونعوذ بالله من شرور انفسنا ومن سيئات اعمالنا۔ من يهده الله فلا مضل له ومن يضلله فلا هادى له، ونشهد ان لا اله الا الله وحده لا شريك له ونشهد ان محمدا عبده ورسوله۔ ثبتوا قلوبكم بالطاعات وصلوا على رسوله المصطفى صاحب الشفاعات۔ "ان الله وملائكته يصلون على النبى يا ايها الذين آمنوا صلوا عليه وسلموا تسليماً [١]"۔ اللهم صل على محمد وعلى آل محمد بعدد من صلى وصام۔ اللهم صل على محمد وآل محمد بعدد من قعد قام۔ وصل على جميع الانبياء والمرسلين وعلى ملائكتك المقربين وعلى اهل طاعتك اجمعين برحمتك يا ارحم الراحمين۔ اللهم اغفر للمومنين والمومنات والمسلمين والمسلمات، الاحياء منهم و الاموات، انك مجيب الدعوات ورافع الدرجات برحمتك يا ارحم الراحمين۔ اللهم ارحم على السلاطين الماضين الكرام والملوك الهادين العظام الذين قضوا بالحق و كانوا به يعدلون۔ اولئك على هدى من ربهم واولئك همالمفلحون، خصوصاً على الامير الكبير، مروج التاج والسرير، المستريح فى روضة الجنان امير تيمور صاحب قران، والسلطان الاعظم، العالى شان، الواصل الى جوار رحمة الله العزيز المستعان،

١۔ قرآن مجيد : ٥٦/٣٣

سلطان ابوسعيد بهادر خان، والسلطان الغفور المرحوم، الجالس على مسند الرحمة والرضوان، سلطان عمر شيخ بهادر خان، والسلطان العادل الكامل، المشتهر بالعدل والاحسان، سلطان ميران شاه بهادر، والسلطان الفاضل الباذل العالى والخاقان المعظم الذى كان عليا همته ان يجاهد فى سبيل الله ويغازى، ظهير الدين محمد بابر بادشاه الغازى، نور الله مرقده وعطر مشهده۔ اللهم اغفر للملك العالم السعيد، الشهيد، الغازى بامر الرحمن، العارف، الفاضل الذى ليس مثله فى العدل والاحسان، ناصر رايات المجاهدات والمغازى نصير الدين محمد همايون بادشاه الغازى، طيب الله ثراهم وجعل الجنة مثواهم۔ اللهم ابّد دولة الملك المعظم والخاقان الامجد الاكرم، مولى ملوك الترك والهند والعرب والعجم، ناصر بلاد اهل الايمان، ماحى آثار الظلم والطغيان، قدوة الملوك والسلاطين فى الآفاق، الجالس على سرير السطنة والخلافة بالارث والاستحقاق الذى عدل ساعة منه بعمل الثقلين يوازى ابو المظفر جلال الدين محمد اكبر بادشاه الغازى، خلد الله تعالى ملكه وسلطانه وافاض على العالمين بره واحسانه۔

عباد الله، ان الله يامر بالعدل والاحسان وايتاء ذى القربى وينهى عن الفحشاء والمنكر والبغى يعظكم لعلكم تذكرون۔ اذكرو الله العلى العظيم الحى القيوم يذكركم واشكروه يزدكم واستغفروه يغفر لكم۔ ولذكر الله تعالى اعلى واولىٰ واجل واعز واتم واكبر۔

رحمت وغفران رب مستعان — باد بر آباء آن شاه جهان
میر تیمور آں شه والا گهر — بعد ازاں میر انشاه نیکو سیر
بو سعید آں خسرو عالی مقام — بعد ازاں شاه عمر آں فرخنده نام
بابر غازی شه عالم پناه — شاه دیں پرور همایوں بادشاه
بعد ازاں خاقان عالم خسرو عالم پناه — اکبر غازی جلال لدین محمد بادشاه
صدر جنت باد یارب جای شاں — روضه خلد بریں ماوای شاں

اللهم ابّد دولة الملك المعظم والخاقان الا مجد الاكرم مولى ملوك العرب والعجم۔

(۲۶۰)

خطبه جمعه

الحمد لله۔ الحمد لله ذی العظمة والجلال وولی العزة والكمال، مولی البهجة والجمال ومولی النعمة والنوال والشارع للشرائع بالاعظام والاجلال، عالم الغيب والشهادة الكبير المتعال۔ نحمده ونشكره فی كل الاحوال ونشهد ان لا اله الا الله وحده لا شريك له ونشهد ان محمدا عبده ورسوله، صلی الله عليه وعلی آله واصحابه وخلفائه الراشدين الهادين المهديين من بعده، خصوصاً علی اول الصحابة وافضلهم بالتحقيق، الشيخ الشفيق، قاتل الكفرة والزنديق، خليفة رسول الله ومن له خير صديق، امير المومنين ابی بكر الصديق، وعلی اعدلهم واشفقهم، الناطق بالصواب، حنفی المحراب، الذی وافق رايه بالوحی والكتاب امير المومنين عمر بن الخطاب وعلی احلمهم واورعهم، جامع القرآن، معدن الجود والاحسان، منبع الحياء والايمان الذی استحيت منه ملائكة الرحمن امير المومنين عثمان بن عفان وعلی اشجعهم واعلمهم اسد الله الغالب، مظهر العجائب والغرائب، ليث بنی غالب امير المومنين علی ابن ابی طالب وعلی الامامين الهمامين السعيدين الشهدين المقبولين المقتولين المرحومين المغفورين، للمصطفی سبطين وللمرتضی ابنين وللزهراء قرتی عينين، سيدی شباب اهل الجنة فی الجنة ابی محمد الحسن وابی عبد الله الحسين، وعلی المطهرين من القدم الی الراس، عميه المعظمين حمزة والعباس وعلی

الستة الباقية من العشرة المبشرة وعلى من تابعهم من الناس رضوان الله تعالى عليهم اجمعين وسلم تسليماً دائماً ابداً كثيراً كثيراً۔

اوصيكم عباد الله ونفسى العاصية المذنبة اولاً بتقوى الله (و) التعظيم لامر الله والشفقة على خلق الله۔ "وان الله مع الذين اتقوا والذين هم محسنون[١]"، ايها الناس اعلموا ان القيامة يوم الحسرة والندامة ويوم المحاسبة والغرامة "يوم تبيض وجوه وتسود وجوه[٢]" "يوم لاينفع مال ولابنون الامن اتى الله بقلب سليم[٣]"۔ ان احسن الكلام وابلغ النظام كلام الله الملك العزيز العلام۔ "اعوذ بالله من الشيطن الرجيم" "وتوبوا الى الله جميعاً ايها المومنون لعلكم تفلحون[٤]"۔ بارك الله لنا ولكم فى القرآن العظيم ونفعنا وايا كم بالآيات والذكر الحكيم۔ استغفر الله العظيم الغفار لى ولكم ولجماعة المسلمين انه هو الغفور الجواد الكريم البر الروف الرب الرحيم۔

(٢٦١)

خطبه عيد فطر

الله اكبر الله اكبر لااله الا الله والله اكبر الله اكبر ولله الحمد۔ سبحان من نوّر قلوب العارفين بسراج الهداية والعرفان وشرح صدور الصائمين بنور المعرفة والايمان واكرم عباده المومنين بصيام شهر رمضان۔ باز تكبير بگويد۔ سبحان من فتح على الصائمين ابواب الرحمة والرضوان ووعدلهم دخول باب من ابواب الجنان كما اخبرنا نبى

١۔ قرآن مجيد : ١٢٨/١٦
٢۔ قرآن مجيد : ١٠٦/٣
٣۔ قرآن مجيد : ٨٩/٢٦
٤۔ قرآن مجيد : ٣١/٢٤

آخر الزمان ان للجنة باب يقال له الريّان لا يدخل فيها الا الصائمون شهر رمضان۔ باز تکبیر بگوید۔ سبحان من شرّف خلوف فم الصائمين على ريح المسك والزعفران واوجب على نفسه جزاء صيامهم بالكرم والامتنان وبشّرهم بالحور والقصور ونعم الالوان۔ ونشهد ان لا اله الاّ الله وحده لاشريك له الرحيم الرحمان۔ ونشهد انّ محمدا عبده ورسوله، سيد الثقلين وحبيب الرحمان، صلى الله عليه وعلى آله واصحابه وخلاّنه نعم الخلاّن۔ تعریف اصحاب کرام بکند تا آخربیان فطر روزه کند۔ ايها الناس اعلموا ان يومكم هذا يوم عظيم، يوم شريف، يوم جعله الله عيداً للمسلمين ورجاءً للتائبين۔ احسنوا (الى) اليتامى والفقراء والمساكين بما روى عن النبى صلى الله عليه وسلم ادّوا عن كل صغير وكبير نصف صاعٍ من برٍّ اوصاعاً من تمر اوصاعاً من شعير اوصاعاً من زبيب، اعلموا انّ صدقة الفطر واجبة على كل مسلم حرله نصاب الزكوة فاضلاً عن حاجته الاصلية لنفسه وطفله الصغير وخادمه ملكاً۔ تا آخر بخواند۔

(۲٦۲)

خطبه عید اضحی

الحمد لله نحمده ونستعينه ونومن به ونتوكل عليه ونشهد ان لا اله الا الله وحده لاشريك له ونشهد ان محمدا عبده ورسوله۔ ان الله تبارك تعالى امرنا بامر بدا فيه بنفسه وثنى بملائكته القدسية وثلث بالمومنين من جنه وانسه حيث قال "ان الله وملائكته يصلون على النبى يا ايها الذين آمنوا صلوا عليه وسلموا تسليما[۱]" اللهم صل على سيدنا محمد وعلى آل محمد بعدد من قعد وقام، اللهم صل على محمد وآل محمد

۱۔ قرآن مجید : ۵٦/۳۳

ما طاف بالبیت طائف۔ اللهم صل علی محمد وعلی آل محمد ما وقف بعرفات واقف وصل علی جمیع الانبیاء والمرسلین وعلی ملائکتك المقربین وعلی عبادك الصالحین من اهل السماء والارضین برحمتك یا ارحم الراحمین۔

اللهم ارحم علی السلطان (السلاطین) الماضین الکرام وعلی الائمة الهادین العظام الذین قضوا بالحق و کانوا به یعدلون خصوصاً علی الامیر الکبیر، مروج التاج والسریر، المستریح فی روضة الجنان امیر تیمور صاحب قران وعلی السعید الشهید المرحوم المبرور المختص برحمة الله المنان سلطان ابو سعید بهادر خان وعلی السلطان المغفور المبرور المختص برحمة الله الملك الدیان عمر شیخ بهادر خان وعلی السلطان الاعظم العالی شان والجالس علی مسند الرحمة والغفران الذی کان علیا همته ان یجاهد فی سبیل الله ویغازی ظهیر الدین محمد بابر بادشاه الغازی وعلی السلطان الاعظم العالی، الخاقان المکرم العادل الوالی، قبلة الملوك فی المجاهدات والمغازی نصیر الدین محمد همایون بادشاه الغازی، طیب الله ثراهم وجعل الجنة مثواهم۔ اللهم ابّد دولة السلطان الاعظم والخاقان المعظم الاکرم، مولی ملوك الهند والترك والعجم، ظل الله تعالیٰ فی الارضین، کهف الملوك ومرجع الخواقین، صاحب سرادقات الامن والامان، معز السلطنة والخلافة والمغازی ابو الفتح جلال الدین محمد اکبر بادشاه الغازی، خلّد الله ملکه وسلطانه وافاض علی العالمین بره واحسانه۔

عباد الله "ان الله یامر بالعدل والاحسان وایتاء ذی القربی وینهی عن الفحشاء والمنکر والبغی ویعظکم لعلکم تذکرون"۔ اذکروا الله العلی العظیم الجلیل الجبار یذکر کم وادعوه یستجب لکم۔ ولذکر الله تعالی اعز واجل واعلی واکبر۔

۱۔ قرآن مجید : ۱۶/۹۰

(۲۶۳)

در آداب وارکان وشرائط دعا

قال علیه السلام الدعاء مخ العبادة، معنی دعا مغز عبادتها است۔ بدانکه انبیاء ورسل باکمال عصمت ورتبه نبوت از دعا وزاری خالی نبوده اند۔ پس شاید که مومن از دعا واز سوال از حضرت عزت خالی نبود۔ گفته اند هر که چهار چیز را ترك کند از چهار چیز محروم گردد۔ هر که زکوة را ترك کند از افزونی مال محروم گردد، هر که صدقه را ترك کند از تندرستی محروم گردد۔ وهر که نماز را ترك کند از ایمان محروم گردد۔ وهر که دعا را ترك کند از اجابت محروم گردد۔ پیغمبر گفت، صلی الله علیه وسلم، محروم نیست آن که دعای او (به) اجابت نه پیوندد اما محروم کسی است که از دعا کردن محروم ماند وتوفیق بدیس نیابد۔ در خبر آمده است تارك دعا را باری تعالی دشمن دارد زیراکه ترك دعا از امارات استغناء است از مولی۔ اگر مستحق اجابت نباشد، خالی نبود، بهر دعا وتضرع اورا عبادت نویسند که دعا بنفس خود عبادت است۔ قال علیه السلام الدعاء مخ العبادة، معنی دعا کردن بندگی کر دن است۔ خداوند کریم مطلق است وبادشاه برحق، اگر بنده بحضرت است دعا بر آرد، جلّ جلاله شرم دارد که دست نیاز اورا ردّ کند۔ شیخ سعدی فرماید۔

کرم بیبی ولطف خداوند گار
گنه بنده کردست خود شرمسار

بعض از نادانان گویند که چوں خداوند علیم براحوال عباد مطلع است وتقدیر اشیاء در ازل رفته است، از دعا وسوال چه فائده؟ این حدیث اگرچه بظاهر صواب نمای است لیکن خطای عظیم است

ازانکه مخالف نصوص ومخالف سنت انبیاء است۔ من لدن آدم الی یومنا هذا هیچ مقربی از مقربان درگاه اله از دعا خالی نبود چنانکه آدم درمقام توبه گفت "ربناً ظلمنا انفسنا وان لم تغفرلنا وترحمنا لنکونن من الخاسرین[۱]" قال علیه السلام من لم یسأل الله غضب علیه، معنی هرکه از خدای تعالیٰ حاجتی نخواهد حق تعالی بروی بغضب شود، وشاید که داعی بسرعت اجابت شاد نشود وبدان مغرورنگردد۔ وبسا دعا که مومن عاصی بکند درحال بی توقف با جابت مقرون شود۔ واین منت ربوبیت است، چون خواهد که بنده را از درخود براند، درخواست اورا بی درنگ بدودهد استدراجاً له۔ چنانکه فرعون هر جا حتی که خواستی وسوال کردی، درحال باجابت پیوستی۔ ودعاء موسی کلیم اللهؑ را بعد از چهل سال اجابت آمد۔ اکنون بدان که مردعا را شرائط وسنت وآداب (و) اوقات است۔ دعا سه نوع است، دعای رغبت است، دعای رهبت است ودعای حقیقت۔ آنچه دعای رغبت است دران کفهاء دست کشاده ازیك دیگر جدازیر سینه بدارد وایمان خود را شفیع آرد وحاجت خواهد۔ اما چشم سوی آسمان ندارد۔ انچه دعاء حقیقت است باید که انگشتان دست راست پست[۲] کند خفیف وانگشتان سبحه را راست کند وحاجت خواهد، وانچه دعای رهبت[۳] است دستها فروروی دارد۔

ادب[٤] در دعا آنست که باطهارت باشد وغیر حق را دردل نگذارد ودازنگریستن چپ وراست بپرهیزد وباجابت موقن باشد والحاح بکند۔ قال علیه السلام "ان الله یحب الملحین فی الدعاء"۔ بآواز بلند دعا نمی کند که رفع صوت در دعا معصیت

۱۔ قرآن مجید : ۲۳/۷

۲۔ ع : پست، ندارد

۳۔ ع : رهبت، ندارد

٤۔ ع : آداب

است۔ واز آداب نیست که در دعا بگوید بحق فلان وحق انبیاء لانّ لیس لاحد علی الله حق۔ دعا گوئی ترک اختیاراست زیراچه اختیار مولی رابود نه مربنده را۔ ترک اختیار در دعا اینست که بنده مخصوص بکند چیزی معین وباچیزی محال سوال نکند۔ شرائط دیگر سوال اخروی را مقدم دارد چنانکه سلیمان گفت، علیه السلام، "ربّ اغفرلی وهب لی ملکاً لا ینبغی لاحد [۱]"۔ نیکی دنیا وآخرت خواهد چنانکه خدای عزّ وجلّ وکلام مجید خود تعلیم فرموده است "ربنّا آتنا فی الدنیا حسنة وفی الآخرة حسنة [۲]"۔ وهر که بدیں دعا مواظبت بکند خداوند تعالیٰ اورا در دنیا ودر آخرت عافیت دهد۔

شرط سوم۔ باید که دعا باخلاص وزاری باشد۔ شرط چهارم باید که دعای معین بود۔ شرط پنجم افتتاح واختتام دعا بذکر حضرت کبریا باشد۔ اختیار بعض اینست ده بار قبل الدعاء ودوبار بعد از دعا "یارب" گوید۔ شرط ششم حضور دل است۔ شرط هفتم پرهیز از خوردن وآشامیدن حرام است۔ شرط هشتم پیش از دعا وبعد از دعا ده بار بررسول صلی الله علیه وسلم درود گفتن است۔ شرط نهم۔ دعا را اوقات است واوقات دعا اینست۔ وقت سحر وشب وروز آدینه وبعد از نماز های فرض ومیان بانگ نماز واقامت ومیان دو نماز وبعد ختم قرآن وبوقت مقابل شدن در کارزار باکفار وبوقت باریدن باران ودر سجده دعا کردن ووقت مضطر شدن مصیبت وبعد از طعام پیش شستن دستها۔

۱۔ قرآن مجید : ۳۵/۳۸
۲۔ قرآن مجید : ۲۰۱/۲

(۲٦٤)

دعاء برای حفاظت از سلطان جابر

رسول گفت، صلی الله علیه وسلم، من از جبرئیل شنیدم واو از حضرت ربانی شنید که جل جلاله فرمود هیچ دعائی به نزدیك من دوست تر ازیں دعا نیست ""یا حبیب الفقراء، یا انیس الغرباء ویا معین الضعفاء و یادلیل المتحیرین ویا غیاث المستغیثین، یا حی، یاقیوم، یا حنان، یا منان، یا دیان، یا بدیع السموات والارض، یا ذو (ذا) الجلال والاکرام برحمتك یا ارحم الرحمین" هر که ایں دعا را هر روز بوقت بامداد وشبان گاه سه گان بار بخواند هیچ ظالمی وموذی وسلطان جابر بروی دست نیابد۔

(۲٦٥)

بازو بند معظم

هر که برخود بدارد به جمله خصمان ودشمنان ودر حربها مظفر ومنصور باشد واز جمله بلاها ایمن گردد۔

لا اله الا الله الملك الحق المبین۔ لا اله الا الله الحق الیقین۔ لا اله لا الله الملك الحق الیقین۔ لا اله الله سبحانك انی کنت من الظالمین۔ سبحان الله وبحمده، سبحان الله العظیم، احمده واستغفره من کل ذنب واتوب الیه، بحق کهیعص[۱]، حم عسق[۲]، 'صم بکم فهم لایعقلون[۳]۔ وصلی الله علی خیر خلقه محمد وآله اجمعین۔

۱۔ قرآن مجید : ۱/۱۹

۲۔ قرآن مجید : ۱/٤۲

۳۔ قرآن مجید : ۱۷۱/۲

(۲۶۶)

نوع دیگر

لا اله الا الله الملك الحق اليقين۔ لا اله الا الله الحق المبين، ربنا ورب آبائنا الاولين برحمتك يا ارحم الراحمين۔

(۲۶۷)

تعویذ برای زبان بندی

بسم الله، شهد الله، قل هو الله، ماشاء الله، حسبی الله وتعالیٰ الله، صدق الله، 'توکلت علی الحی الذی لایموت' 'ان الله وملائکته یصلون علی النبی یا ایها الذین آمنوا صلوا علیه وسلموا تسلیماً[۱]'۔ والله 'الا اله الا هو الرحمن الرحیم[۲]'۔ 'لا اله الا الله الحی القیوم، لا اله الا الله، محمد رسول الله ولا حول ولا قوة الا بالله العظیم۔ 'سیکفیکهم الله وهو السمیع العلیم[۳]'۔ بستم بحق کهیعص[٤]، بستم بحق حم عسق[٥]، بستم زبان همه بدگویان ودشمان آں صاحب آں دعا از بدی بحق لا اله الا الله۔ مهر کردم بنام محمد رسول الله۔ بستم بحق 'تبارك الذی بیده الملك[٦]'۔ بستم بحق التین، بستم به 'یسین والقرآن الحکیم[۷]'۔ بستم به 'ق و القرآن

۱۔ قران مجید : ۵٦/۳۳
۲۔ قرآن مجید : ۱٦۳/۲
۳۔ قرآن مجید : ۱۳۷/۲
٤۔ قرآن مجید : ۱/۱۹
۵۔ قرآن مجید : ۱/٤۲
٦۔ قرآن مجید : ۱/٦۷
۷۔ قرآن مجید : ۱/۳٦

المجید'[1] ـ بستم بـه 'ن والقلم وما یسطرون'[2] ـ بستم بحق ا ب ت ث ج
ح خ د ذ ر ز س ش ص ض ط ظ ع غ ف ق ك ل م ن و ه لا ی ـ بستم
بحق 'قل هو الله احد، الله الصمد، لم یلد ولم یولد، ولم یکن له کفوا
احد'[3] ـ بستم زبان همه بدگویان صاحب این این تعویذ هذا ـ 'لا تحرك
به لسانك لتعجل به'[4] ـ یا غیاث المستغیثین ـ 'وصم بکم عمی فهم لا
یبصرون'[5] ـ 'ان شر الدواب عند الله الصم البکم الذین لا یعقلون'[6] ـ

(۲٦۸)

دعاء در آمدن بر ملوك

چون کسی خواهد که بر سلطان در آید بگوید : جسی الله ونعم الوکیل ـ اللهم اجعل لی الیه سبیلاً سهلاً واعطف قلبه علی واعزنی من کل سلطان اعطیته سلطاناً من عندك وهو مستعز بعزتك ـ اللهم ذلله کما ذللت فرعون لموسی وسخره کما سخرت الشیاطین لسلیمان واعطفه کما اعطفت محمداً علیه السلام علی امته فانك تفعل ماتشاء وتحکم ماترید ولا معقب لحلمك ولا غالب لمشیتك ـ

۱ـ قرآن مجید : ۱/۵۰

۲ـ قرآن مجید : ۱/٦۸

۳ـ قرآن مجید : ۱/۱۱۲ـ٤

٤ـ قرآن مجید : ۱٦/۷۵

۵ـ قرآن مجید : ۱۷۱/۲

٦ـ قرآن مجید : ۲۲/۸

(۲۶۹)

چون از کسی ترسد این دعا بخواند

اعوذ بالله الذی سخر مافی الارض الاباذنه ان الله بالناس روف رحیم۔

(۲۷۰)

دعا برای دفع شر ملوك

بوقت پیش رفتن بخواند : اللهم لین قلبه علی وادفع عنی شره بفضلك وكرمك بحق كهیعص وبحق حمسق برحمتك یا ارحم الراحمین۔ نوع دیگر : رضیت بالله ربا وبالاسلام دینا وبمحمد علیه السلام نبیاً وبالقرآن اماما وحکماً۔

(۲۷۱)

دعا برای رستن از کید ظالمان

یا من یکفی من احد ولا یکفی منك احد، یا احد من لا احد له، یا سند من لا سند له، انقطع الرجاء الا منك، اکفنی ما انا فیه واعنی علی ما انا فیه وفرجنی ما قد نزل بی بجاه وجهك الکریم وبحرمة محمد علیه السلام۔

(۲۷۲)

دعا برای دفع خوف دشمن

اللهم اردد کیدهم فی نحورهم ونعوذ بك من شرورهم، حسبی الله وکفی، سمع الله لمن وعی، لیس وراء الله منتهی، نعم المولی ونعم النصیر۔

(۲۷۳)

ادعیه برای رستگاری از بعضی امراض

دعای دفع درد سر : ولا تحلقوا رؤسکم حتی یبلغ الهدی محله فمن کان منکم مریضا او علی سفر فعدة من ایام اخر۔ دفع درد نیم سر کهیعص ذکر رحمة ربك عبده زکریا، اذ نادی ربه نداء خفیاً، قال رب انی وهن العظم منی واشتعل الراس شیباً ولم اکن بدعائك رب شقیاً۔ دفع درد چشم : فکشفنا عنك غظائك فبصرك الیوم حدید، یوسف اعرض عن هذا واستغفری لذنبك انك کنت من الخاطئین۔ درد گوش را : کأن فی اذنیه وقراً فبشره بعذاب الیم۔ درد گلورا : واذا بلغت الحلقوم وانتم حینئذ تنظرون۔

(۲۷۴)

نقش برای دفع رفتن ناف

دفع رفتن ناف ایں نقش را نوشته در کمر بندد نیکو شود۔

٦	٨	٧
٧	ح	٣
٢	٩	٤

(۲۷۵)

دعاء برای بازیافت برده گریخته

سوره والضحی چهل ویکبار بخواند وهر بار بر دیوار پس پشت خانه خطی بکشد۔

(۲۷۶)

دعاء برای یافتن گم شده

شش بار بخواند بزودی باز آید۔ وکفی بالله علیماً وکفی بالله وکیلاً وکفی بالله شهیداً۔

(۲۷۷)

دعاء برای حفاظت کالا

ایں دعا بنویسد ودرمیان آں بنهد : اللهم یا حافظ محمد احفظ بضاعتی ومالی یا ذا القوة المتین۔

(۲۷۸)

دعاء برای اسپان

هذا کتاب براءة وامان من الرحمان الرحیم الی المراکب والبرازین

والانعام المسخرین من جمیع العلل والاوجاع والخنامق والخنازیر والریاح ولکل الحشائش ومقمحة العطش ونزول الماء فی الکفین وجمیع الامراض واعیذ لجمیع الافراس من العلل والامراض الذی ذکرت بالله الاحد الصمد لم یلد ولم یولد ولم یکن له کفوا احد۔ "وان یکاد الذین کفروا لیزلقونك بابصارهم لما سمعوا الذکر ویقولون انه لمجنون وما هو الا ذکر للعلمین[۱]"۔ وصلی الله علی خیر خلقه محمد وآله اجمعین۔

(۲۷۹)

دعاء برای دفع دیو وپری وسحر

این دعا بنوسید وبنماید : عقلتم عقلتم عقروس فرفیس حینا۔

(۲۸۰)

اشکال دفع آسیب دیو وپری

بنوسید وبرابر روی مصروع بدارد بزودی به شود۔ نقش معظم اینست۔

۱	۳	او	و
ب	ل	ل	ط
ج	س	ما	ه
لاع	ح	و	مو

۱۔ قرآن مجید : ۵۲-۵۱/۶۸

(۲۸۱)

دفع هارونی اسپ

بقراط حکیم گوید اسپ را زین کنند وبر نشینند وبرانند، چون آغاز هارونی بکند لجامش بر سرش زنند وبرجاش بدارند چنانکه ستوده آید. اگر خواهد که بجاء برود بگذارند تا برود. واگر باز هارونی کند هم چنیں کنند تاسه بار، هارونی دفع شود. وبهر هارونی وراه راست آورون پسر بی فرمان ودختر گستاخ هر صبحگاه دست بر پیشانی او نهند وروی سوی آسمان کنند وایں نام بخوانند فرمان بردار ونیك بخت گردد. ونام اینست 'یاشهید'.

(۲۸۲)

شکل بجهت دفع علت اسپاں

ایں شکل بجهت علت اسپاں مجرب وآزموده است.

امیر المومنین ابوبکر رضی الله عنه

امیر المومنین علی ابن ابی طالب رضی الله عنه

محمد رسول الله
صلی الله
علیه وسلم

امیر المومنین عمر خطاب رضی الله عنه

امیر المومنین عثمان بن عفان رضی الله عنه

(۲۸۳)

کتاب دواء المساکین
درباب جدری

یعنی آبله بچگان که بهندی سیتله می گویند۔ آورده که این علتی است که یك بار البته در اندام آدمی زاده ظاهر می گردد وبیشتر درایام خوردگی۔ واگر در ایام خوردگی ظاهر نگردد تا وقت کهولت در آخر عمر بیرون آید ودوم بار ظاهر نشود۔ بیشتر آبله در هواء تابستان بیرون آید واین از خون فاسد حادث شود۔ وحکیمان ماضی فرموده اند دران سال که آغاز این علت باشد طفلان وکودکان را خون بکشایند تا آبله بیرون نیاید یا کمتر بیرون آید۔باید که از گوشت وشیرینی پرهیز کنند وهواء خانه معتدل باید داشت وتن را بجامه پوشیده دارد وآن را آب سرد می باید داد اندك اندك۔ وآب کشنیز در چشم اندازد۔ وعلاجش اینست که زیره یك درم وکره نیم درم بآب آس کرده بدهد در ابتداء تا زود بیرون آید وتپ بگذارد۔ وبعد از گذاشتن تپ دانه انار اندك اندك خوردن دهد وعدس مقشر ونخود مقشر پیش از ظاهر شدن آبله خوردن دهد تا زود ظاهر گردد۔ وچون در آبله پختگی بسیار آرد وآب در آبله بسیار بود بیمار را بر خاکستر نرم ویا در آرد ارز ویا آرد جو بغلطاند تا تری آبله را جذب کند وخشك گرداند وغذا از آب منگ وبرنج کند وچون برو آرند وتپ برود کچری نرم بدهد۔ وچون تپ برآید دوغ وبرنج بدهد وچون پخته گردد نان جرث با شهد بدهد تا خشك شود۔

(٢٨٤)

نوع دیگر

پیش ازاں کہ علامات ظاهر شود وبچگان را تپ ظاهر شود چون خواهند آبله آن کس را اندك آيد واز هفت هشت دانه زیاده نشود، زود این تعویذ بریں نقش بنویسد و در زیر بالین وی بنهد

الحمد لله شانزده	رب العالمين ده	الرحمن الرحيم سه	مالك يوم الدين سيزده
اياك نعبد ده	واياك نستعين ده	اهدنا الصراط شش	المستقيم هفت
صراط الذين شش	نعمت دوازده	عليهم غير المغضوب چهار	عليهم دو
ولا الضالين يازده	آمين پانزده	بسم الله هفت	الرحمن الرحيم پنچ

(٢٨٥)

افسون کژدم گزیده

پریت اریا سری، گائی تن گوبر کیا تس منه ارنپڑ، بچهو کون کون کالا، پیلا، بهورا اور مٹیالا، اوتری سو اتاروں نا تو دادوں مور نیل کنٹهه کو، کوا هنکارن بهوی جو پانی سنگهاسن بتیسا هنومنت کی چاك، بچهو لپك، کون کون بچهو ارپنڑا کالا، پیلا، بهورا اور مٹیالا، اوتری تو اتاروں نا تو دادوں مور نیل کنٹهه کو، کواهنکاروں، میری بهگت کروگی سکت پهر، هو منتر ایسر مهادیو کی باچا پهری ناهی تو دهوبی کی گند منه پڑے، کواری کنیا کا سنتاپ پایا جاوی، لونا چماری کی هانکیاں پهری، دهنونتر بید کی هانکیاں پهری، نار سنگ بیر (ناتهن ویر) کی هانکیاں پهری، میری بهگت کروگی سکت پهر هو منتر ایسر مها دیو کی باچا۔

(۲۸۶)

افسون دیگر برای کژدم گزیده

کالی گای، کواری ست کنیا، بچیو لکهه اپنی هرهر، بچهون کومانا، تیری ذات هون پهچانا کی (که) کالی، که پیلی، که هریالی که کوهی کا پد کرون، مٹی کابت کرون، ای بچهو تهاں تهاں دهرون، میری بهگت کروگی سکت (پهر)، ایسر مهادیو کی باچا، لونا چماری کا منتر پهری که پیر، کوی کی پانکهه کرما کی تو پرنه دروهی، دروهی ماتا پتا کی، دروهی تخت سلیمان کی، دروهی چاند سورج کی، دروهی زمین آسمان کی، دروهی پاك پانی کی، ایسر مهادیو کی باچا، لونا چماری کا منتر پهری جای سمندر پار پرے۔

(٢٨٧)

ضمیمه

فرمان الغ بیگ بجانب علاء الدین عالم شاه

اصول شجره کیانی وفروع دوحه خسروانی وامراء کبار ووزراء صاحب اختیار وارکان دولت باهره واعیان حضرت زاهره وسکنه عتبه بارگاه وسدنه سده جهان پناه واهالی مراتب ودرجات وامراء تومانات وهزارجات با اعیان مسالك واکابر از نقباء عظام وائمه کرام وحکام بلاد وحفظه عباد وعامه رعایا وکافه برایا فلان ولایت بدانند که چون با ورود جنود فتح ونصرت الهی وتیسر انتظام اسباب دولت وسعادت نامتناهی تحت گاه خراسان که عصرها وقرنها مستقر سریر خلافت موروث ما وقبله اقبال صنادید خسروان فرمان روا بوده، بروجه احسن وطالع ایمن به تحت تصرف وتسخیر مادر آمده، ومنشی دیوان "جعلناکم خلائف فی الارض[۱]" بقلم ثبات وتمکین منشور خلافت جلالت آئین باسم همایون ما موشح ومحلی گردانید وبرحسب "احسن کما احسن الله الیك[۲]" همگی همت عالی نهمت بدان مصروف است که بچشم عقل ودیده بصیرت نظر فرموده سوانح مصالح هر مملکت وواردات مهمات هر ناحیت به رای عقده کشای یکی از حکام صاحب رای مفوض گردانیم تا پرتو درایت بر ساحت کفایت آن انداخته بقدم تیقظ وتحفظ منازل ومراحل عدالت گستری ورعیت پروری فرموده حاجات وملتمسات محتاجان ومستمدان بانجاح واسعاف مقرون سازد

۱ـ قرآن مجید : ١٤/١٠

۲ـ قرآن مجید : ٧٧/٢٧

وقواعد موجبات امن وامان وقوانین مستدعیات عدل واحسان درمیان طبقات امت، که بدائع ودائع فطرت اند، ممهد وجاری گرداند، وپیوسته بوسائط آن ریاض حسنات تازه وفیوض برکات بی اندازه وعامه برایا شادان و کافه ممالك آبادان؛ بتحصیص ولایت هندوستان که بمزید اعتبار واشتهار در تمامت آفاق واقطار از سائر مدائن وامصار آن دیار ممتاز ومستثنی است۔ وچون وقتی که قائد قدرت کامله "وهو الذی یسیر کم فی البر والبحر[1]" حضرت گردون رفعت، صاحب قران، موید مظفر ظفر کشورستان را حسن توفیق ارزانی داشته بود تا اقامت فرض جهاد را وجه همت عالی ساخته، لشکر اسلام باقصی حدود هند کشید وبهر دیار که رسید عساکر فتوحات غیبی باستقبال همایونش استعجال نموده بر وجهی که کیفیت آن به تفصیل تمام بر صفحات صفائح ایام ثبت است، بسی بلاد وقلاع مسخر فرمود ورسوم کفر وضلال از جمیع سواحل دریا وسائر مواضع آن نواحی بر انداخت۔ وبعد از تیسر فراغت، ملك اعظم، افتخار ملوك البر والیم، اعتضاد سادات زمان، کمال الدولة والدین خضر خان که پیش ازان برهنمونی بخت مساعد روی اخلاص بآستانه گردون اشتباه آورده بود وبدولت زمین بوسی استسعاد یافته واقبال آسا ملازم موکب جهان اساس گشته درمیان امثان واقران بلند پایه وسر افراز شد وبه نظر تربیت وعنایت بادشاهانه مخصوص گشته، مناشیر همایون از مقام مرحمت روز افزون جهت ایالت ملك دهلی وتوابع ومضافات ولواحق ومنسوبات بنام او نفاذ یافت۔ وبعد از سپردن ودیعت حیات فرزند آن ستوده صفات ملك مبارك خان وملك محمد خان وملك دریا خان، که ثمرات شجره سادات وسعادت وغره باصره جلالت وایالت بودند، در زمان دولت خاقان سعید جمشید مکنت توفیق حکومت وفرماندهی آن ولایت

۱۔ قرآن مجید : ۲۲/۱۰

یافتند. دریں ولا خلف صدق آں دودمان مبارک، ملک وملک زاده، کریم الاخلاق، طیب الاعراق، والی مملکة الهند بالارث والاستحقاق، زبده دوراں، دارای جهاں آرای، بقیه خسرواں عدوبند، عقده کشای، منظور نظر عنایت ملک مستعان، ظهیر الدولة والدین فلاں که بعز شهامت وصرامت معروف وبفرط کیاست وفراست موصوف است، وآثار نجابت واستحقاق سروری وانوار اصالت واستعداد فرماندهی در جبین احوال وناصیه آمال او واضح ولائح "الولد الحریقتدی بآبائه الغر" در سلك ملازمان درگاه ظفر پناه شرف یافته در صدد احیاء مراسم آباء مغفرت انتماء خود است "انا وجدنا آبائنا علی امة وانا علی آثارهم مهتدون[۱]" ایالت وسلطنت مملکت دهلی با توابع وضمائم آں علی سبیل الاستقلال بدو مفوض فرمودیم وزمام حل وعقد وقبض وبسط ورتق فتق وضبط وربط مراسم ملکی ومالی آنجا را به قبضه اقتدار وحوزه اختیار او باز دادیم. سبیل تمامی اکابر واعالی وجمله متوطنان اصاغر واهالی آنجا بجمیع بلاد ووقصبات وقریٰ وبلوك واحشام صحرا نشینان بر وبحر آں که آں مملکت را اسیورغال ملك اعظم مشار الیه دانسته اورا حاکم وفرماں روای علی الاطلاق ووالی وبادشاه باستحقاق آں محال شناخته مال واجبی وحقوق دیوانی خود را فصل بفصل وسال بسال باو جواب گفته قاصر ومنکسر نگردانند واز سخن وصلاح او بیروں نروند. دریں باب قد غن لازم دانند.

۱ـ قرآن مجید : ۲۲/٤۲

فهرست اعلام واماکن

(الف)

(د)

(ر)

(ز)

(س)

فهرست مصطلحات

(الف)

ك

(گ)

(م)

فهرست کتب